The Hollywood Musical

Other Books by Ethan Mordden

Better Foot Forward: The History of American Musical Theatre
Opera in the Twentieth Century
That Jazz!: An Idiosyncratic Social History of the American Twenties
A Guide to Orchestral Music
The Splendid Art Of Opera
The American Theatre

The Hollywood Musical

by ETHAN MORDDEN

ST. MARTIN'S PRESS
New York

Library of Congress Cataloging in Publication Data

Mordden, Ethan
The Hollywood Musical

Discography: p.
Bibliography: p.
1. Moving-pictures, Musical—History and
criticism.   2. Moving-pictures—United States—
History.   I. Title.
PN1995.9.M86M6   791.43′09′09357   81-8738
ISBN 0-312-38838-1   AACR2

Design by Dennis J. Grastorf

10 9 8 7 6 5 4 3 2

Frontispiece: Ginger Rogers and Fred Astaire in the "They All Laughed" number
in *Shall We Dance.*

To my students in CSSM 190b:

*Vicky, Tom, Stephen, Ethan, Michael,
Liza, David, Carl, Susan, Tommy, Bill,
Donna, Christian, David, and Laurie*

☆ ☆
Table of Contents

☆ ☆
Preface

I OVERTRAINED FOR THIS BOOK. Reviewing classics and tracking down rarities, I filled notebooks with data that would have made this volume unreadably comprehensive. I apologize to *Reckless, Sweetheart of the Campus, Something to Shout About, Two Girls and a Sailor, Look for the Silver Lining, The Kissing Bandit, Show Business, Rhythm on the River*, and the many other films that didn't get into the first draft, and to others that were dropped at the second cut. I apologize also to readers who were hoping to hear of Jean Harlow's musical, of Ruby Keeler's last musical, of Janet Blair's best musical, and other fine notes of the canon. Less is never more; less is less. But it does make for a trimmer read.

This survey is limited to the American film musical: no foreign works are covered unless they had some impact here. All those that did are British, and often take in major American participation, in director (the first two Beatles films), songwriters and biggest international star (*The Slipper and the Rose*), or in financing. But I have tried to make the book comprehensive within its limits, starting with the first sound films and taking the musical up to the present writing, omitting nothing that is generally thought important or that I find amusing.

The reader will note that the book has a greater concentration in the 1930s than in the 1940s, and lightens as it moves forward: fewer films were released in each succeeding decade and also I find those of the 1930s more interesting than those that followed. Style and form were largely set and most of the most essential persons (Fred Astaire, Ginger Rogers, Judy Garland, Eddie Cantor, Alice Faye, Maurice

Chevalier, Jeanette MacDonald) were launched in the 1930s; in fact the five years of sound before the Production Code enforcement of 1934 stand as one of the most exuberant periods in the history of American art. I think the reader will agree, as we traverse the decades, that the period of Al Jolson and Ernst Lubitsch is worth more analysis than that of Betty Grable and Stanley Donen. This is not to belittle the talents of the latter; but they were largely encircled by convention, whereas Jolson, Lubitsch, and their colleagues covered a wide, free territory.

A number of people helped me research this project. First of all, Romano Tozzi, the ranking expert in the field, guided my advance and corrected the numerous misapprehensions I collected early on. George Caudill, Ralph Straughan, Ken Richards, Clint Bocock, and Charles Silver of the Museum of Modern Art generously screened films for me. The photos used here, which originally emanate from the studios involved—Warner Brothers, Metro-Goldwyn-Mayer, Paramount, RKO, United Artists, Twentieth Century-Fox, Columbia, and Universal—came into my hands from a variety of sources, among which should count Jerry Vermilye and Lou Valentino, who advised on procedure, and Ellis Regenbogen, the Columbia lawyer from Columbia Law. Push come to shove, I bought most of them in New York at Jerry Ohlinger's Movie Material Store and Mark Ricci's Memory Shop, pleasantly enough, and a few at Movie Star News, regrettably. Bill Tynes not only screened films on his whiz RCA projector but also helped open my perspective on the awards pages.

The author wishes to acknowledge the support and guidance of Michael Denneny and Paul Dinas and, as always, the wisdom and persistence of his agent Dorothy Pittman. Also, Carol Robinson went over the manuscript with an expert eye and Robert Hoppe painted a stupendous cover. These are all grand collaborators.

The Hollywood Musical

☆ 1 ☆
The Texture of Sound

SILENT FILM enclosed its audience. Live musicians impassioned the adventure; darkness focused it; the absence of color sharpened it. The stories revealed a density of beauty and sensuality that few people could have hoped to encounter in life. The silents served as a consoling dream yet called for great resources of concentration: their "story" was as much expression as action. Miss a single shot and one might miss a major turn in the narrative. The public drew close.

Today's moviegoers cannot get in touch with silent film. It is seldom seen at all, and when it is the film is often projected at the wrong speed in faded prints and with an insufficient musical accompaniment. Worst of all, the extraordinary acting style developed by silent artists comes off as a dead language trying to scream: because it talked in magic. Lacking sound, film could never be natural; and at its best or blandest it seldom tried to be. By 1920, its experimental stage was over; it had largely ceased attempting to duplicate live theatre and was working out its own aesthetic—a fantasy drawing on naturalism. Film looked real, when it wanted to, in ways no stage could, but it behaved overreal, letting the camera's sense of detail, the narrative force of editing, and the intensity of acting define its art. It was a real garden with imaginary toads.

A host of methods for synchronizing sound and film were developed in the early 1900s, but moviemakers were inclined to do without. Reproduction was not faithful, an obtrusive hiss haunted the recording track, and theatres would have to be wired for one of several possible sound processes, not to mention the expense of regearing the industry itself. How would movie personnel function with a microphone hanging over them? Sets were habitually noisy—the camera thrummed, directors coached the team, actors improvised lines, musicians kept them in spirit. Sound would silence the set, make it anxious. But, mainly, there was the artistic problem: where would sound fit into an art already complete without it?

Film was *not* complete. The musical accompaniment was strategic to its suggestive illusion, a kind of middle point that brought the real-life audience together with the romanticized life on the screen. Only urban moviegoers, who had access to the fully coordinated production of lush lobbies, gleaming ushers, auditoriums like pagan cathedrals, and symphony orchestras playing scores especially composed to extrapolate emotionally on each specific film, got as close as film wanted them to get. So sound, as sheer music, would complete film after all— to take that orchestra, tracked in synchronization with the action, to the nation's moviegoers.

Warner Brothers was the studio that initiated the sound era, and in just this way: sound not as dialogue but as music. The four brothers, Harry, Sam, Albert, and Jack, had incorporated in 1923 after a few years of rather informal production and were doing well. Their rise to power coincided exactly with the rise of radio, the all-picture business side by side with the all-sound business. Perhaps the better-established studios were too used to their status quo to note this irony, but with Rin-Tin-Tin the only infallible box-office draw on the Warners roster and without a single foothold in the competition for top-class exhibition halls, the brothers saw a way to better their standing: combine what radio did with what film did.

Radio made music. Radio also talked; but, as Harry Warner observed when brother Sam pointed out that sound film might tackle dialogue, "Who the hell wants to hear actors talk?" Sam secured the exclusive rights to a sound process developed by Bell Telephone, called Vitaphone ("the sound of life"), in which sounds were recorded simultaneously with pictures and played on discs run synchronously with the film. Jack upped the budget on a swords-and-kisses costume piece, *Don Juan*, from $500,000 to $700,000, a desperate act among the stingy Warners. Sam went to New York to hire the New York Philharmonic to play *Don Juan*'s score plus a posh vaudeville to fill out the evening—violinist Mischa Elman, tenor Giovanni Martinelli, sopranos Marion Talley and Anna Case, Efrem Zimbalist and Harold Bauer performing Beethoven's "Kreutzer" violin sonata, and the Metropolitan Opera Chorus. The Warners would almost certainly go bankrupt if their gambit failed, but on paper it was shaping up nice-ly—*big,* anyway, which it would have to be to go over—and they held an extra ace in the star of *Don Juan,* John Barrymore, almost as im-posing an attraction as Rin-Tin-Tin. The double bill of *Don Juan* and "the Vitaphone," as the musical variety show was called, looked like a reasonably sure thing, provided the studio could follow it up with more Vitaphone sound tracks *and* get them out and earning before the Warners silent pictures had closed and the cash flow dried up.

In New York to produce the variety show and *Don Juan's* sound-track of William Axt's music and added sound effects, Sam Warner discovered what the entire film business was shortly to discover: sound was mined with traps. Subway rumblings ruined takes, construction blasting vibrated the recording stylus out of its groove, radio waves slipped onto the track out of thick air—the still, dead world was sud-denly filled with tunes. Even the arc lights made a contribution on the recording wax in the form of a distinct faint sizzle. Sam worked his way around it all, and on August 6, 1926, at a total cost of $3,000,000 (taking in everything from Mary Astor's incredible "come as thou wert" hairdo in *Don Juan* to the purchase of the Piccadilly Theatre in New York and its refurbishing, as the Warner Theatre, with sound ap-paratus), sound became current. The double bill was opened by Will H. Hays, who had been President Harding's Postmaster General but resigned to preside over Hollywood's "self"-censorship in 1922 after several murder and drug addiction scandals threatened to destroy the industry with bluenose boycotts. Hays was never implicated in the oil-land swindles of Teapot Dome and Elk Hills, Harding's Watergate, but he looked like a guilty rabbit, and made a drab guide to the new world of sound, speaking of the "speech-film" in his midwestern twang. But once Hays was gone, the Warners brought their project home, in *Don Juan's* dramatic scoring and, especially, the classical mixed grill. *Don Juan* was the same old love-thriller silent with the novelty of a recorded score in place of a live one, but the Vitaphone had Martinelli singing "Vesti la Giubba" from *Pagliacci* and an all-out effort by the Philharmonic on Wagner's *Tannhäuser* Overture, made vivid by some shy cutting from one section of the orchestra to another. Marion Talley, who sang "Caro Nome" from Verdi's *Rigoletto,* was the project's one fizzle, but then her short career had been entirely cre-ated by PR manipulation and was about to end anyway. She was a star rather than a talent; hiring her was a very Hollywood thing to do. Still, whether or not one cared for *Don Juan, Pagliacci,* or Talley, the advantage of processing films with their own orchestral accompaniment—thus to make the musical complement to "silence" available to every theatre of any size or budget—was obvious.

Another advantage of the symphonic film score was the arrangers' use of the classics. Many people who had no regular exposure to great music heard it in theatres, Hollywood proudly pointed out—but now that Vitaphone was here, why not expand its territory to include popular music as well? There had been one nonclassical segment in the first Vitaphone, a turn by Roy Smeck on an array of instruments from banjo to harmonica, and the second Vitaphone vaudeville, unveiled on October 5, 1926, in tandem with a comedy starring Charlie Chaplin's brother Sydney, *The Better 'Ole*, stressed popular art. The acts included comedians Willie and Eugene Howard, all-around entertainers Elsie Janis and George Jessel, operatic baritone Reinald Werrenrath (in such selections, however, as "The Long, Long Trail"), and, most significantly, Al Jolson, as big a star as all the others put together. No theatre in the world could have afforded the fees necessary to gather all these performers in one live show; it was like vaudeville with nothing but closing acts. If the camera seldom established any great intimacy with its subjects, preferring a straight-on perspective halfway back into nowhere, still the communication of personality is telling, not least when Jolson turns up in his characteristic blackface makeup in a rural setting to send over "The Red, Red Robin," "April Showers," and "Rockabye Your Baby With a Dixie Melody." Unlike the classical Vitaphone, the pop program incorporated talking as part of the fun—Jessel and the two Howards all worked in verbal comedy. Still, music was the point of the show, music of a universally approachable nature. The appeal—and cultural oneupmanship—of opera and concert material would tempt the film musical throughout its heyday,* from Grace Moore and Johann Strauss to Katharine Hepburn's Clara Schumann (Artur Rubinstein played for her) in *Song of Love*. But as early as the second Vitaphone it was clear that sound's first operation would be the institutionalization of popular music in film.

At least, it was clear to the Warner brothers, who thrust Al Jolson into *The Jazz Singer*, a tale of a Jewish cantor's son whose singing style favors American pop over the pious recitative of his people.

---

*The third Vitaphone program might be said to have inaugurated Hollywood's fetish for getting pop and legit music together, for it featured exemplars of both. The theory behind this coupling might be stated as—to paraphrase Katharine Hepburn's famous analysis of Astaire and Rogers—legit gives pop class and pop gives legit sex.

George Jessel had done the part in Samson Raphaelson's play on Broadway in 1925, and when the Warners bought the screen rights for the usual silent adaptation they wanted Jessel to do it all over on film. But with Vitaphone on hand it seemed wise to stress the character's ambivalent ethnic identity by slipping song sequences into the film, letting music define his Jewish-religious and American-entertainer selves. Jessel, signed to a $2,000-a-week contract, now wanted more— a percentage on any Vitaphone records marketed separately. Negotiations collapsed as the studio considered the other two leading black-face performers of the day, Jolson and Eddie Cantor. Jolson was their man.

The Jazz Singer is mawkish melodrama, the protagonist being disinherited by one culture (in the person of his intolerant father) to fall into the other only after expiating his betrayal by singing the traditional Jewish requiem, the Kol Nidre, at his father's deathbed. Moreover, he bears an insistently Oedipal love for his mother. The Mammy icon, a focus of Jolson's art, is the focus of the character's conflict: she represents the old culture, yet accepts her son's assimiliation into the new. How the Warners could have considered anyone but Jolson for the part is incomprehensible—even Jessel, miffed at having blown the chance to reassert himself in his stage role, admitted that Jolson outdid everyone in that sort of thing.

It was *The Jazz Singer* with Jolson, premiered on October 6, 1927, that inflamed interest in the sound film, though it was a silent with a synchronized score and a few "talking" sequences. These were supposed to have been vocal spots exclusively, carrying a total of five songs, but Jolson never did anything according to the book, and while the mike was on and the cameras turning, he threw in his signature boast, "You ain't heard nothin' yet!" and other rave reviews of his own performance. He also tossed off a paragraph of manic filial gush in a scene with his mother, played by Eugenie Besserer in considerable bewilderment, the usual state for performing with Jolson. Cut off from her for years, her son has risen in show business and now returns to present her with a diamond brooch. "That I should live so long to see my baby again!" Besserer cries, according to the title cards. "Diamonds! . . . You didn't do anything wrong, did you Jakie?" He did: Jakie Rabinowitz has become Jack Robin of Broadway. As the talking segment begins, Jolson stresses the Jack in him with a performance of Irving Berlin's "Blue Skies" on the piano, and then tells his mother that he's going to move her out of the slums into a nice neighborhood: "There's the Ginsburgs, the Guttenbergs, and the Goldbergs. Oh, a lot of Bergs. I dunno them all. And I'm gonna buy you a nice, black silk dress, Mama. You'll see—Mrs. Friedman, the butcher's wife, she'll be jealous of you." Besserer tries to keep up with it all, but she looks edgy and her murmured replies sound like cries for help. "Take me out of this movie!" she seems to plead, but history was manning that mike, and nobody moved. When Jolson gives her his special jazz version of "Blue Skies," with a thumping left hand and plenty of scat improvisation, we understand that Jakie was born to become Jack: his mission in pop music is unstoppable.

That was Jolson off the cuff, and it worked because its casual realism was exactly what film had never had before and was now in the process of acquiring. Till this point, film stars had moved through their remote silence as archetypes of desire and ambition, brutality and self-sacrifice. Even the comics often created an opaquely false world of menace but no real danger, a violence without pain. Jolson's Jack/Jakie came from the real world: with words. He was not only the right man for the part; he was the right man for the whole bloody historical transition from (silent) fantasy into (talking) realism. In 1923, D. W. Griffith had talked Jolson into making a film called *Mammy's Boy*, but Jolson felt like a ghost playing to no audience without his songs and braggart's ad libs, and he quit early in production. But *The Jazz Singer* was the true Jolson. The guy was sound in its essence.

The Jazz* Singer, phenomenon though it was, did not do incredible business, because few theatres were equipped to show it. The more resourceful silent houses screened it without the Vitaphone discs but played Jolson records—not necessarily the appropriate ones—during the vocal sequences. It was the second Warners Jolson vehicle, *The Singing Fool* (1928), that really forced sound on the industry. *The Singing Fool* became the classic of the transition, and was almost always the debut item of houses that had converted to sound.

Like *The Jazz Singer* a "part-talkie"—that is, a silent with occasional scenes synchronized for voice—*The Singing Fool* proposed Jolson as a singing waiter and songwriter who rises in vaudeville, falls in a bad marriage, and rises again with the help of a loving woman. Its most effective element besides Jolson was an intolerably adorable three-and-a-half-year-old, Davey Lee, who played Jolson's son. The child, called

---

*"Jazz" was loosely construed in the 1920s; it covered the whole world of American rhythmic pop music: not only Bessie Smith and Coleman Hawkins, but George Gershwin, Ruth Etting, and "Charleston." In the context of the day, *The Jazz Singer* literally means "The Pop Singer."

"Sonny Boy," inspires the film's theme song, which Jolson, now a doting father rather than *The Jazz Singer*'s doting son, sings on Christmas Eve to the toddler in his lap. Later, Sonny Boy dies, prompting a last reprise of his *Leitmotiv*. It sounds corny, but it stood high in the memory of a generation because Jolson's emotional commitment made it authentic. "B-b-b-boy, I tell you it got to me," he reported shortly after the filming. "I was a wreck ... If you cried real tears on the stage, you'd panic 'em. But I cry real ones here, and have to keep on cryin' 'em for retakes till I feel like an April shower." Jolson, then, was among the first actors to spot the difference between the artificial arrangement of stage illusion and the imposed naturalism of the talking-singing cinema. The point is not how many times Jolson had to play a scene, but how easily his abundant honesty fitted the new real fantasy of film. Because the old fantasy was doomed.

Even before *The Singing Fool* came out, Warners had produced the first "all-talking" picture, a crime drama called *The Lights of New York* (1928), and the end of the year brought out a third singing silent, *My Man*, with Fanny Brice. The silence was dying away—*Photoplay* magazine dubbed *My Man* "a three-quarters talkie." "From shop girl to show star," the PR phrased it—"a tender, heart-tugging story of a girl who won the hearts of millions after she lost the love of her man." Warners hedged its multimillion-dollar bet on sound in a message at the bottom of the ads: "If there is not a theatre in your community equipped as yet to show *My Man* as a talking picture—be sure to see it as a silent picture." But surely the purpose of seeing Brice was to hear Brice sing "I'd Rather Be Blue Over You," "I'm an Indian," "Second-Hand Rose," and the title song. Similarly, the high spot of Warners' *Weary River* (1929) was the piano-playing and singing of silent hero Richard Barthelmess as (the ads again) "a down-and-outer whose plaintive music reaches through prison's bars to find love and new life a thousand miles away." Warners' PR drooled over the revelation of Barthelmess' musicianship—"a voice so sensationally fine he could have won stardom on it alone ... now you can HEAR him TALK and play the piano!"

Was sound a passing novelty in film's grammar or its future tense? The Warner boys were doing incredible business, enabling them to buy up theatres and wire them for Vitaphone, and, thus spurred, other studios tried sound. Warner Brothers controlled Vitaphone, but there were other methods of sound recording, the most likely one being sound-on-film (as opposed to Vitaphone's sound-on-separate-discs approach), already adopted by William Fox as Movietone. The continu-

☆ *FROM SILENT FANTASY INTO THE NATURALISM OF SOUND:*
above, Don Juan *(Barrymore on balcony); below,* 42nd Street, *"It Must Be*
June" number. Off with the getups and on with the life.

☆ *ONSTAGE AND BACK-STAGE AT* THE BROADWAY MELODY: *above, King pleads for Page's love; below, "The Wedding of the Painted Doll."*

ing success of even the dumbest talkies finally convinced Hollywood that sound had come to pass and, as cautious studio heads inquired into patent rights and rental of equipment and learned that everything available had been devoured by more impetuous colleagues, a panic spread through the industry. Not knowing where things were headed, everyone just stood there and screamed, "Move!"

Sorting out the business end of the sound conversion was nothing compared to its technical and artistic problems. These may be divided into two parts: the microphone and the camera. The mike was new to Hollywood, even though Lee De Forest, the unsung "father of sound," had been turning out his talking Phonofilm shorts since 1923. The camera, on the other hand, was the oldest thing in film. But besides the mike's own hazards, it so hampered camera movement that a new filming style for sound had to be evolved in 1928, 1929, and 1930.

Consider the problems of the microphone alone. Some film actors had pleasant or at any rate dramatically useful voices. Some did not; they would have to go. Some were foreign, and spoke English with heavy accents; they would have to go—along with the lucrative foreign market, for what non-English-speaking moviegoer would be able to follow a scenario worked out in English dialogue and lyrics? More problems: some voices turned out to be mysteriously phonogenic, others not; who knew why? Actors without stage experience might not get the hang of delivering dialogue. Film actors were used to blurting out their visuals, so to speak, spontaneously scene by scene; now they would be hamstrung by a text. Most agonizing of all, the mike, which could fail to pick up the strongest voice if an actor happened to turn his head, managed not to miss the slightest rustle of costume, grip's cough, or slip of a prop.

Much of this was recalled with loving fun in *Singin' in the Rain* from the vantage point of several decades of survival. But if one realizes that this meant not the progressive retooling of an industry but the dismantling of an art, the nostalgia becomes more urgent. The camera made noise. The mike picked up that noise. So the camera was placed in a soundproof booth, which severely inhibited its freedom. It stood back, frozen and gaping, then laboriously wheeled in for a close-up and held it, dazed. In the end, an art that had depended heavily on the reportorial mobility of the audience's eye now had to depend on the narrative elaboration of dialogue. By the time the soundless camera was developed, movies had lost much of their kinetics, their plasticity. They had become outdoor plays. "It would have been more logical if silent pictures had grown out of talkies," Mary Pickford told the *New York Times Magazine*, "instead of the other way around."

Sounds like a fanatic, doesn't she? You should have been there then. The uninformed modern thinks of silent film as a romp of vamps, cabaret sheiks, flaming youth running wild, slapstick comedians falling down, and *The Birth of a Nation* and *Intolerance*. In fact, the great last years of the silents brought forth works of profound artistry and thematic depth. Even melodrama, in F. W. Murnau's *Sunrise* (1927) and Victor Sjöstrom's *The Wind* (1928), gained from the imagination stimulated in the moving picture—Murnau's lyrical abandon and Sjöstrom's ghastly Texas sandstorm prove that story in itself was less amazing than how story was told, how it looked. True, irony sometimes needed a title card, as when D. W. Griffith announced "War's peace" in *The Birth of a Nation* and then presented a battlefield strewn with dead men. But what film gained in language it lost ten times over in imagery. One cannot take Pickford's statement lightly, especially as she understood talkies well enough to win her one Oscar as best actress for a sound picture, *Coquette*, in 1929.

By that year, silence was officially over. All Hollywood was geared for sound, and the original plan to make music sound's major element was shelved. Sound pictures were talkies, not primarily musicals, and actors who had assumed they would be spared having to sing found to their sorrow that they couldn't even talk. Could they be dubbed—or, as it was first termed, "doubled"? Few were. Warner Oland, who played Jolson's father in *The Jazz Singer*, was dubbed by cantor Josef Rosenblatt in the musical passages to ensure an authoritative Jewish melisma, and Richard Barthelmess, it finally turned out, had neither sung nor played the piano himself in *Weary River*. But generally actors were expected to cut it or get out. It sounds simple. Those with good microphone voices would be graduated into talkies to do what they did in sound. But it wasn't that simple.

Talkies weren't silents with sound. Aside from the static quality of many early talkies and the primitive literacy of the scripts, the sound films shattered silent fantasy, gave up that remote magic that had poeticized their naturalism. With dialogue, film had to be real—this is where Jolson came in: no one, in any part, was more real than he. But some things the silents did just wouldn't work in the new reality. So it was not just a matter of adjusting film to the technology of sound production, but of adjusting subject matter and approach to a public no longer enclosed by myth.

John Gilbert is generally thought to be the mike's classic victim, the "great lover" of silents whose voice was so high that he was laughed off the screen. Actually, he was a victim of style. He first spoke on film in one of the earliest musicals, *The Hollywood Revue of 1929*, playing Romeo to Norma Shearer's Juliet in the Balcony Scene. In a touch of film-within-film, a voice cries "Cut!" and Lionel Barrymore appears as the scene's director to run it all over in twenties jive at the request of the money bosses in the east, fearful of highbrow art. "Julie, baby," Gilbert obligingly intones, "you're the cream in my mocha and java, the berries in my pie." The choice of role for Gilbert's first venture into sound was apt, as it maintains his silent persona as the ecstatic lover of splendid women. The slang parody, because of its vulgarity, also works—it's so far from the persona that it doesn't challenge it.

However, then came Gilbert's first sound feature in his old style, *His Glorious Night* (1929). Now there was something wrong, but it wasn't Gilbert's voice. Attempting to portray ecstasy in banal dialogue, Gilbert reduced his character from archetype to cartoon. "I love you," he cries, crushing Catharine Dale Owen to him, "I love you, I love you, I love you!" The public giggled and jeered. "It was the problem of an image," director King Vidor noted in a recent interview. "You couldn't put this image into words." Gilbert was not able to reclaim his old identity, or a less florid new one, in succeeding films, though his penultimate movie, *Queen Christina* (1933)—made with his old flame Greta Garbo at her insistence, over the veto of MGM executives—proves that his voice, an okay tenor, was not the problem.

Style was the problem—making it over to suit a chaotically reinvented art. Everything was a wild guess in 1928, in musical formats as well as elsewhere, for while the obvious first move was to imitate *The Singing Fool,* one of the most successful films up to that time, no one was certain how to fill out a silent-with-songs, like Jolson's first two entries, with more sound. More songs? Or dances? More characters who sang? More musical depiction of plot or more songs as part of an entertainment scene, like Jolson's nightclub spots? With all these questions, not to mention the new dull-witted sound cameras and the tricky negotiation of the new film naturalism, it is not surprising that the first film musical to resolve the questions of identity, form, and structure was a cartoon short, *Steamboat Willie* (1928). This was Walt Disney's first experiment in sound, featuring Mickey Mouse as a captain conveying a cargo of animals down a river with Minnie Mouse serving as his crew and Pegleg Pete the villain of the piece. The slim storyline, more a situation than a plot, is not fantastic per se, though the world of cartoon is by nature unreal and of course all the persons in the tale are animals. The only thing distinguishing them from the cargo is that Mickey, Minnie, and Pete wear clothing and own property. What makes *Steamboat Willie* so special is its imaginative score. The animation was laid out to the beat of a metronome and the whole thing sings with rhythm. Disney, besides providing Mickey's voice, worked up a doodle-doo of whistles, cowbells, tin pans, and New Year's Eve noise blowers to guide the sound style, also borrowing folk tunes for the orchestral parts. Obviously, Disney's artists had none of the camera-and-mike trouble that dogged the silent-into-talkie producers of the new tightlocked sound stages, and the characters frolic all over the screen, impetuously musical. Minnie cranks a donkey's tail as if playing a music box and the donkey emits a ditty, while Mickey "plays" a cow's udder and turns the teeth of a bull's huge open mouth into a xylophone. The third of Disney's Mickey Mouse shorts to be made but the first to be released, *Steamboat Willie* was the first fully musicalized talkie. It was a sensation.

But on those sound stages and on location, the makers of the first feature musicals were up to their hairlines in technical experiments of such complexity that they had little time to wonder what their formal aesthetics might be. Furthermore, equipment was in short supply; each studio took every piece it could get and worked it around the clock in the race to get out the first sound films—part-talkies like *The Jazz Singer* or all-talkies like *The Lights of New York*—while sound was hot. Naturally, Warners was far in the lead and—for the first time in its history—solvent beyond most companies' wildest dreams. Universal didn't even have a single sound stage functioning in mid-1928, when it was planning its version of *Show Boat*. Universal's chief Carl Laemmle had bought the screen rights to Edna Ferber's novel when it was published in 1926, and naturally had planned it as a silent. But by 1928 such projects were osmotically turning into talkies. In order to make sound tests for *Show Boat,* Universal borrowed one of Fox's mobile sound trucks, and then—realizing what it had in hand—frantically tossed off one talkie feature and a few sound sequences for already completed silents in what may have been as little as nine days. The talkie, *Melody of Love* (1928), is in a way the first full-length, all-sound musical, though essentially it was a war film strung with a few songs. It was of little consequence, and when word got back to Fox, the truck went steaming back home. But Universal finished and released *Melody of Love* before Fox could release *its* first talkie, *In Old Arizona.*

Show Boat is also one of the first musicals, and its sloppy production typifies the confusion with which Hollywood approached the form. It would have done well as a silent; most of Ferber's books have good film potential, as they deal with grandiose characters caught up in sweeping historical transitions—heroes, fighters, lovers, con men. *Show Boat* contrasts the beautiful patience of the natural world with the restless transformations of humankind in the life of Magnolia Hawks Ravenal, a show-boat captain's daughter who is loved and deserted by a gambler. The story and its various adaptations have become so familiar to Americans that few now recall that when Ferber first wrote her book the show boats of the midwest had become extinct and forgotten. Ferber revived them.

Universal wrapped its silent *Show Boat* just when *The Singing Fool* proved that Vitaphone was no fluke, so it was back to the drawing board to whip up a score and some dialogue sequences. Also, Jerome Kern and Oscar Hammerstein's musical version of the novel had come along at the very end of 1927, and its score, with such resonant numbers as "Ol' Man River," "Why Do I Love You?," "Can't Help Lovin' Dat Man," and "Bill," had made a tremendous popular impression. Universal's *Show Boat* was made from the novel rather than the musical; but wasn't there some way of slipping *Show Boat*'s big tunes into the film to keep up with the public's evolving relationship with the property?

It there was, Universal didn't find it. It came up with a two-hour silent with a synchronized score and dialogue scenes, black spirituals, a few dull new numbers ("The Lonesome Road"), such of the Kern–Hammerstein score as could be accommodated—and a two-reel (about twenty minutes) prologue in which Florenz Ziegfeld, producer of the stage *Show Boat*, introduced some of the Broadway principals to perform a *Show Boat* potpourri. Now, if Universal's *Show Boat* was complete in itself, did it need Broadway spliced in here and there? And if it did need Broadway, how was this self-contained prologue to help, having nothing to do with the story? Worse yet, opening the evening with three performers from the stage musical—Helen Morgan, Jules Bledsoe, and Tess Gardella—put the movie actors—Laura La Plante and Joseph Schildkraut as the lovers, Alma Rubens as the tragic Julie—in a certain perspective. After hearing Morgan deliver Julie's "Bill" and "Can't Help Lovin' Dat Man" in richly forlorn renditions that have since passed into legend, how could Rubens' nonsinging Julie capture attention? After hearing Bledsoe put "Ol' Man River" over in his full basso with the choral backup that the song absolutely needs in its dramatic context, did anyone want to hear La Plante sing it to banjo accompaniment? (No one heard her, anyway: La Plante and her banjo were dubbed by others.)

Furthermore, the sound did not record well and Harry Pollard directed with a heavy hand. Laemmle chose Pollard because he had succeeded with Universal's *Uncle Tom's Cabin* a year before, but Stowe and Ferber have only the southern setting in common. *Uncle Tom's Cabin* is pathetic and ridiculous; the novel *Show Boat* is epic with an edge.* About the only thing the film had in its favor was a genuine-looking show boat, built in Sacramento and filmed floating along the Sacramento River to the thrill and wonder of locals in costume.

No doubt Universal's *Show Boat* would have been better if it had been planned as a musical from the start, but it is notable that as a silent with talkie passages and hodgepodge score it was launched as a special event all the same, with dressy opening nights and inflated prices. Even in its first weeks it did not do anything like the business that *The Singing Fool* had done and was *still* doing, seven months into its run. Everywhere, one heard the same report—*Show Boat* was a well-intentioned, slow-moving dud. The non-Kern songs dissolved as one heard them, and the whole film passed away with scarcely a cheer (though it did make Laemmle some money), for even before it opened it had been superseded on February 1, 1929, by the first of the "all talking—all singing—all dancing" films, the first movie musical, MGM's *The Broadway Melody*.

History is made here. The great discovery of sound was its naturalism, a doom if one attempted to dodge it but a treat for audiences if one met it head on. *The Broadway Melody* meets it. A backstager as zippy as *Show Boat* is weighty, it grins with slang and putdowns, sorrows for the pitfalls in show biz and love, and presents a Broadway where heart and nerve count more than talent. Two sisters, tough little Hank (Bessie Love) and tall blond darling Queenie (Anita Page), come to New York from the midwest at the invitation of Hank's old beau, Eddie (Charles King). Eddie falls for Queenie; she resists him for Hank's sake, and takes up with a playboy to fool them. The story is nothing, but the details are extraordinary. If James Gleason's script overdoes the argot (some of it—"A hotel's for mine," says Hank at

---

*The musical, through which most people know Ferber's tale, sentimentalizes it somewhat by reuniting the heroine and her errant husband at the end; in the novel, he never reappears, and we are left with a picture of the heroine as she ages, weathered and dauntless. Ferber believed in strong women. Universal believed in Happy Endings, and used the musical's resolution.

one point—is way outdated for 1929), the cast plays it and everything else for real. There had been silent backstagers, but not till *The Broadway Melody* could one hear the auditions, the rehearsals, the dress runthrough marred by incidents, and the performance, not to mention King's heavy New York accent. Film historian Alexander Walker has caught exactly the film's sense of creating cliché:

> What was to become convention in every backstage musical is present here in pristine simplicity: the imperious impresario, his cohorts of yes-men, the dilettante backers, the star of the show breaking her leg at rehearsal, her replacement wowing the audience by apparently not even singing a note or swinging a limb or doing anything else except simply stand there, and the big-hearted heroine surrendering her own chance of stardom and happiness for the sake of her kid sister.

One cliché *The Broadway Melody* didn't get to: the urgency of Putting on the Show. Gleason and director Harry Beaumont are less interested in the play-within-the-film, also called *The Broadway Melody*, than they are in Hank, Queenie, and Eddie, and once the show opens, partway through the film, we never hear of it again.

The movie is technically primitive, and some of it is inane. The girls' agent, Uncle Jed (Jed Prouty), is one of those "comic" stutterers who tries, tries, tries, and then suddenly lets out a wholly different phrase. The two girls are terrible singers, and their vaudeville act, "The Harmony Babies of Melody Lane," is a tomato-baiting horror that could hardly have scored the success we're told it has. The title song is plugged unmercifully throughout the picture, and after singing it for the girls in their apartment, King cries out, "Let's pull back the table, kids, and go into our dance!" But only Hank dances, plunking on a ukelele, while the other two make razzle noises. It's a little strange.

Still, these are minor flaws. The overall rightness of the realism—the projection of the contradictions of glamor and drudgery in the idea of Broadway—is very taking. King sings the ballad, "You Were Meant For Me," to the sister he prefers, and, as the tune continues under, he says, "Queenie! I wrote it for you. I wrote it . . . *about* you. It's you. Don't you *know what I mean*?" Just as he is about to kiss her, the door bursts open and Hank blunders in, inches away from them; Queenie, revolted at herself for nearly betraying her sister, pretends to have been arguing with Eddie. It's a banal situation made fresh by its spontaneity. For visual attack, the opening aerial shots of Manhattan followed by a montage of workers in a Tin Pan Alley hive cutting jarringly into each other over Cohan's "Give My Regards to Broadway" and a bit of Victor Herbert's "In Old New York" may be the best of many such sequences that were to open backstagers. And the scene in which the girls audition their act for producer Francis Zanfield suggests *cinema verité* in its seemingly unstructured flow. A nasty chorus girl has sabotaged the piano, and the accompanist stops several times in bewilderment. "Say, are you trying to crab our act?" Hank asks him. The pianist says he's innocent. "Well, will you play it then," she replies, "hot or cold?" The piano's tinny ring, Hank's slang and anger, and Queenie's confusion all create just the off-the-cuff naturalism that sound film had to develop in order to make sound work.

Sound also needed performers with the spunk that Hollywood loves about New York. King has it, and he knows how to project ego without losing our sympathy. Page is the gentle sister who has to appear to go bad before the love plot is straightened out, and she brings off the quandary nicely. Bessie Love, however, steals the picture as Hank, cynical, curious, tense, and then tired until she sees that she is the weak corner of the triangle and sends King into her sister's arms.* Alone in her dressing room, she then goes to pieces, sobbing and laughing; this scene alone was so brilliant that Love was nominated for an Oscar. If she was deficient as a singer and only charmingly odd as a dancer, she was quite an actress, and this was an innovation in the American musical. On Broadway, singing, dancing, and comic play exclusively comprised the musical's expedients. Acting was a sometime thing. But Hollywood, where only acting had been established when the musical was suddenly invented in 1929, could offer thespian commitment that Broadway could not match. Love's subtlety is remarkable in the last shot, inside a cab taking her, her new vaudeville partner, and her agent uncle to the station en route to a tour that will separate her from the two people she loves. The uncle pulls off one last idiot stutter joke, the partner giggles, and Love tries a wan smile. She'll recover, she tells us—but not just yet.

The Broadway Melody was MGM's first sound film, and the aural reproduction is faulty, though Nacio Herb Brown and Arthur Freed's score generally comes through. Everything was recorded on the set

---

*Trivium Footnote no. 1: the Duncan Sisters, Vivian and Rosetta, were originally to have played the parts, but couldn't get out of a vaudeville tour. MGM simply waited until they were free and, some months after *The Broadway Melody,* released a virtual remake, the Duncans in *It's a Great Life,* complete with the stuttering Prouty. Lawrence Gray played the King role.

during filming, orchestra and all, and while this created many head-aches for the techies, it makes each scene very immediate. But when producer Irving Thalberg decided to reshoot the film's big number, a color sequence on "The Wedding of the Painted Doll," it was decided to play back the sound portion of the already shot footage, as the num-ber is a dance and the only singing involves an unseen tenor. Why rehire singer and orchestra when the dancers can simply move to the playback? But then: why not use the playback in general, let-ting the singers prerecord the vocal parts and then mouth the lyrics when the camera rolls? All movie-making is illusion to begin with. MGM tried the procedure on its next musicals, and as it proved vastly more efficient than trying to please the mike on the spot, the practice took hold at all studios on most singing and dancing numbers.

The Broadway Melody was a smash. It cost MGM $280,000 and made $4,000,000; it also copped the Oscar as best film. And it proved that, more than any other kind of movie, musicals exploited sound. But some questions had yet to be answered in terms of what a musical was. How many songs, and for what purposes? What settings, stories, characters work best in music? What actors are right for a musical, aside from who can sing and dance? Theatre stars? Newcomers with stage experience? Or film veterans who can get through a tune or move well? And does every musical have to be a backstager, or will the audience accept characters singing in nonperformance contexts, as they do in theatre?

Hollywood answered these questions haphazardly, and while it was doing so it enjoyed the only artistically ingenuous era in its history. As a novice, the film musical was versatile and open, even radical. As an old campaigner, it sought imitations of past success, ever ready for a remake and treating convention as Scripture. In many ways, we're go-ing to start wild and grow tame as the years go on.

☆ 2 ☆
What's a Musical?

IT WAS A matter of course that Hollywood would draw on Broadway's resources when instituting the film musical, for both creative and performing talent. But there was no certain guide as to what parts of a stage musical would carry over into film, and there were misgivings about how national Broadway was. Jolson was weird and Brice had bombed; what if the rest of Broadway were like them? There was also that touchy naturalism, troubled by plot and character songs that burst out anywhere. On Broadway it was the thing. In film, it was an offense; or so Hollywood thought. So it turned to subjects that would provide a casual background for song and dance. The groundbreaking Jolson and Brice part-talkies presented their stars as entertainers. Entertainers perform. Even in *Show Boat* once the Ziegfeldian prologue was over, the songs came out of situations in which people might reasonably sing—on stage, or to pleasure themselves in a solitary moment. *The Broadway Melody* pointed the straightest way: music is auditions, rehearsals, performance. This rule was continually broken but has held out through the years and may be seen fully operative in such very recent films as *A Star is Born* and *The Rose*, wherein the character songs that tell us who the principals are are filmed exclusively in concert settings.

In the first year of regular sound production, 1929, there were backstagers: *Close Harmony* with Nancy Carroll and Buddy Rogers; *Mother's Boy*, an Irish equivalent of *The Jazz Singer*, with Morton Downey; *Footlights and Fools,* with silent star Colleen Moore in an unusual role as a sweet little girl (typical Moore) who turns into a French sophisticate on stage (unforeseen Moore—but she seems to have brought it off). There were nightclub films: *Honky-Tonk* with Sophie Tucker; *Queen of the Night Clubs* with Texas Guinan; *Syncopation*, also with Downey; and the stage hit *Broadway*, filmed by Paul Fejos on an innovative, noiseless, $75,000 camera crane that shot sixty feet into the air in six seconds flat to look down on a spectacular art deco set that connected this underworld melodrama to the expressionism of the German cinema. There were revues as well. None of these proposed song as a vehicle of narrative motion. In some cases, the narrative was just an excuse to get the entertainers on stage in the first place.

Obviously, Hollywood could not go on indefinitely pumping out musicals about the performer caste on and off stage. It had to coordinate musical and dramatic elements into story forms and expand them cinematically. One musical element had been developed as soon as the soundtrack had come into use in 1927: the theme song. Cut into otherwise nontalkie films, the theme tune might become popular on its own and bounce interest back onto the film retroactively, thus creating new sources of revenue in record and sheet-music sales and "extra" audiences attracted more by the song than by the story or stars. *Seventh Heaven* (1927) had "Diane." *Our Dancing Daughters* (1928), the one in which Joan Crawford fixed an era with her Charleston, had "I Loved You Then as I Love You Now." Eventually, producers realized that a title (or nearly) theme song was the best advertisement; *Ramona* (1928) set the trend with the excessively popular "Ramona." As the theme tune was invariably a love song, this posed problems for the less dovey titles. *Varsity* (1928) came through with "My Varsity Girl, I'll Cling to You," and *The Pagan* made a novelty of convention in "The Pagan Love Song," sung by Ramon Novarro in a loincloth as he lolled on the beach strumming a ukelele. But some attempts to ride a theme song on an immobile title were ludicrous, and the practice fell away in 1931 when the public, glutted with film music, found the pointless singing irritating.

The musical didn't need a theme song, but it couldn't hurt, and *The Broadway Melody* honored the practice with its title tune, whose lyrics encapsulate the film's view of Broadway as Tough-luck City where the show must go on. The theme song, then, would provide a nucleus for the musical film score in such disparate approaches as those tried with "42nd Street" (which is heard at the picture's end and sums up the experience), with *Naughty Marietta*'s "Ah! Sweet Mystery of Life" (which as a longtime pop hit creates suspense for the stars' big duet and raptures on the closing reprise), and with *The Wizard of Oz*'s "Over the Rainbow" (which is heard early in the film and never reprised, but which sets a tone for the entire event). Still, even a slam-bang hit theme tune would not put a full score over—so how many songs did a musical need?

These and other questions Hollywood at times answered by looking east to the stage musical even when it wasn't adapting a stage proper-ty. Broadway set a teaching example in the matter of integrating songs into the story, and by the late 1920s had amassed ambitious talents such as George and Ira Gershwin, Richard Rodgers and Lorenz Hart, and Cole Porter, who followed the leadership of Irving Berlin and Je-rome Kern in extrapolating American attitudes out of the possibilities in musical comedy.

But think of the traps. Broadway musicals ran two and a half hours, considerably longer than films were willing to run at this time, and had to balance ratios for plot, comedy, song, and dance. Where would the shorter film musical put all the impedimenta of fun? Too, Broad-way was still wrestling with comedy as an extrusive component, rely-ing on improvisatory star comedians or extraneous and virtually self-contained sketches. And there was the pitfall of physical shape: theatre musicals were put together with an eye on how the whole stage looked from a point somewhere in the middle of the auditorium, with no consideration of the advantages of film—editing, special effects, spectacle, the pan, or the close-up. Too much Broadway in the rec-ipe—especially given the camera's necessarily static role while record-ing techniques were being perfected—and the Hollywood musical might end up as an inert duplicate of the stage.

And this is, at first, what happened. The long history of all-talking, -singing, -dancing adaptations of Broadway originals begins with Warners' *The Desert Song* (1929), and the adaptation was faithful. "With all its original stage enchantment," the ads promised, anticipat-ing critics' misgivings that *The Desert Song* had not been sufficiently turned out for film. Adaptor Harvey Gates and director Roy del Ruth aimed a largely unenlightening camera at the original, shearing off some of the book and the Sigmund Romberg–Oscar Hammerstein score. Desert is handy to Los Angeles, so there was real sand at least. There was also a new cast drawn mainly from film people: John Boles as the hero, a dashing sheik who leads an anti-French revolt while masquerading as the milquetoast of the foreign legion post, comics Louise Fazenda and Johnny Arthur, and Myrna Loy as an Arab vamp. Carlotta King was imported from the east to play the heroine, torn between the sheik's Valentino-like allure and the milquetoast's gallantry; neat that she could get both. However, King made no impression in the part. She sings the hell out of "The Sabre Song," but that comes late in the picture, after Fazenda and Loy have erased her from the screen, and King sat out some months of empty waiting for a second role that was never offered before she gave up and returned to the stage. It's too bad, as long as they were hiring theatre talent, that Warners didn't use the excellent Vivienne Segal, who played the part on Broadway. Hollywood could not ignore Segal's sexy voice and dynamite looks, and she did come west early on, but she was trapped in a series of operettas that were far less successful than *The Desert Song*. Going from *Song of the West* into *Bride of the Regiment* and thence into *Golden Dawn* and *Viennese Nights*, all released in 1930, Segal had little chance to convince producers of her worth—they didn't want talent as much as they wanted success. *Viennese Nights*, conceived for the screen by Romberg and Hammerstein, worked out well, but the first three all came from Broadway, and not especially first-rate Broadway at that (though *Song of the West* was derived from *Rainbow*, Hammerstein's experimentally realistic show with a great Vincent Youmans score, hurt by a disastrous production as well as its ambitious nonconformity). With a *Desert Song* to give her career momentum, Segal might have ended up as valuable a commodity as Jeanette MacDonald did. MacDonald's first films argue a strong case in how to launch a career, for among a few flunks and sillies were Ernst Lubitsch's first two musicals, *The Love Parade* and *Monte Carlo*, which not only show MacDonald at her most winning but argue a case in how to sustain a career after death, as they stand among the most frequently revived films today. Segal missed out flat in imperfect adaptations from Broadway, getting no help from directors who didn't know how a musical worked. *The Desert Song* made too stately a movie, true, but the material itself was first-rate and carried it through. Besides, it was the first of the direct-from-Broadway films and the public was curious.

What's a musical? Not everyone who was making them was sure, and those few who lucked into the better ones had the chance to take them wherever they were going while colleagues just as talented fell by the way. MacDonald might have been thinking something along the lines of "There but for Lubitsch go I" about Segal, for when they appeared together in *The Cat and the Fiddle* in 1934, star MacDonald is said to have greeted supporting player Segal with something like, "Enjoy your part, darling; I've had it cut down so badly you'll be lucky to get three words in a row." The tale must be apocryphal—MacDonald wasn't that kind of person. Still, it airs the feeling of competition and insecurity that dogged the musical in those early years when a performer's future depended heavily on the fumbling of technicians.

Another possibility for the musical was the adaptation not from Broadway but from old films: brighten up a script, shift the decor, and slip in four or five songs, ideally into the mouth of someone entertaining at a party but if necessary letting the characters open up and sing out; a musical's a musical. With so many movies being made—335 talkies in 1929, the last year in which silents were still being produced, bringing the total of Hollywood and New York* studios to about 500 films—it was assumed that nobody saw even most of the good ones, and remakes became a regular occurrence. Studios remade their own films, so there was no royalty to pay to Broadway authors, and there were few complaints about Hollywood's repeating itself. On the contrary, moviegoers appeared to like getting the same stories over and over: there are only so many different tales in any mythology. Thus, in 1930, when MGM was building up Robert Montgomery as William Haines' successor in light comedy, it reached back a mere three years to *Spring Fever*, in which Haines played a shipping clerk who bluffed his way into the country club set and romanced Joan Crawford. *Spring Fever* became a musical called *Love in the Rough*. Montgomery and Dorothy Jordan now had the leads; Jimmy McHugh and Dorothy Fields supplied a few songs, pushing hot diggety in "I'm Doin' That Thing," hedging their bets with the old-fashioned "One More Waltz," and peaking in "Go Home and Tell Your Mother (that she certainly did a wonderful job on you)." *Love in the Rough* had less music than *The Desert Song*, but more cinema.

Least cinematic of all, because of its theatrical origin, was the revue. Later, Hollywood would find ways of wrapping its vaudeville in thin storylines, but the earliest revues mirrored the Broadway style, complete with emcees and curtained stages. They did at least strive for special effects impossible in the theatre. Universal's *King of Jazz* (1930) set Paul Whiteman and his band atop an immense piano with keyboard enough for five pianists; *Paramount on Parade* (1930) stuffed Abe Lyman's band into a shoebox and had Nancy Carroll dancing out

---

*In 1928, the coast studios all opened up and expanded supplementary stages on Long Island to exploit the pool of theatre actors for use in talkies; actors busy in a show could face the cameras on their free afternoons. The major film work was accomplished in Hollywood, with its amenable conditions for climate and location shooting, but some Long Island studios remained active through the mid-1930s.

of a shoe; and in MGM's *The Hollywood Revue of 1929*, Bessie Love emerges from emcee Jack Benny's pocket and chats with him from inside his palm. As the all-star Vitaphone revues had done, each studio revue featured a once-in-a-lifetime cast pulled from the contract file. Fox was underpowered. *The Fox Movietone Follies* (1929), dimly unified by a sort of narration, came up with a cast of little reverberation: Lois Moran, Sue Carol, Dorothy Jordan, Dixie Lee, David Percy, and David Rollins. Compare that list to MGM's in *The Hollywood Revue*: John Gilbert, Norma Shearer, Joan Crawford, Marion Davies, Buster Keaton, Marie Dressler, Laurel and Hardy, and William Haines, plus the three principals of *The Broadway Melody* as well as emcees Benny and Conrad Nagel. "More stars," ran MGM's motto, "than there are in heaven."

These all-star revues demonstrated that there was talent available for musicals (though more than a few of their singers and dancers were actors out of their league and some of the chorus lines were embarrassingly sloppy). But there was no organization, no sense of sifting through effective possibilities. Hollywood quickly defined the musical as any film with four or more songs. But it never attempted to define the *elements* of the musical—its shape and point of view, its characters, its use of singing and dancing. Thus, James Cruze's *The Great Gabbo* (1929) has some seven or eight numbers but isn't a musical— it's a drama about a dour ventriloquist (Erich von Stroheim) and the girl (Betty Compson) he abuses, intercut with ludicrous production numbers. What are those numbers doing there? Well, this ventriloquist works in nightclubs, and nightclubs have production numbers, see? At one point, Cruze attempts to fuse music and plot by sending Compson on stage with a nice man (Don Douglas) who wants to save her from von Stroheim, to sing "(When you're caught in) The Web of Love," an apache dance with a spider motif. But neither Compson nor Douglas can hack it, so Cruze films the number with acrobats and splices in close-ups of Compson and Douglas in the acrobats' costumes earnestly mumbling to each other. Okay, this was a primitive era— Von Stroheim's act with his personable but oddly Teutonic dummy Otto is so stupid that even the extras hired to play the audience can't laugh at it, and Cruze didn't bother to reshoot scenes in which von Stroheim flubbed his lines. But was Hollywood learning from such mistakes, or just making them?

One element that seemed a natural for the musical was color. Technicolor had developed a two-color process even before the Vitaphone years, though its fascination with red and green and erratic hold on blue made for an odd look. Musicals were capricious, so the bizarre color scheme only added to their appeal, and many musicals in 1929 and 1930 came out in color or with color sequences stripped in to embolden the production numbers or to close a film on a merry note. However, color was expensive—Technicolor printing costs ran to four times the fee for black-and-white film, and the firm insisted on running its own cameras and sending out its own crew, who would stand around surveying some artist's lovely set and mutter, "You'll never get that yellow into the camera." Worse yet, the thick film tended to buckle in the projector and was easily scratched. Color became so identified with the musical that when the form ran out of juice in 1930–31, color was given up with relief and not used again till later in the decade, after Technicolor had come up with a more lifelike reproduction.

What's a musical? I'm not making it clear in this chapter because it wasn't clear at the time. Certain films seemed to know; others floundered; still others were hopelessly wrong, comedies or melodramas with two or three theme songs too many. Let's examine the full range of musicals produced in the early years before and during the big slump of 1931–32, when few musicals were released and fewer made money, to decide what the film musical happened to be. Happened: virtually by accident.

☆3☆
The Early
Musicals

An EXTRAORDINARY FILM of 1929, King Vidor's *Hallelujah*, couldn't have been less like a musical, yet showed Hollywood how music may belong to a film so organically that all the worry about how to cue in the songs and dances and what roles should be cast with what types seems trivial and unartistic. *Hallelujah* tells of black life in the south with such zest for the everyday that its melodramatic plot, which takes in several counts of manslaughter and murder, does not detract from the overall honesty. MGM must have thought Vidor out of his mind when he proposed the project, which would almost certainly alienate or altogether fail to reach the entire southern market. A more "appropriate" view of black life would be found in *Hallelujah*'s exact contemporary, Fox's *Hearts in Dixie*: "Hear those hearts beat the cadences of their race," the Fox ads ran, "along the levees and in the cotton fields . . . strummin' banjos . . . chanting [not chantin'?] spirituals . . . All the happy-go-lucky joy of living, laughter, and all-embracing gusto of plantation life"—not to mention the yas-suh comedy of Stepin Fetchit. Vidor, one of Hollywood's most socially enlightened directors, would have none of this in *Hallelujah*, and he finally brought MGM around by offering to contribute his fee to the production fund.

Hallelujah really does sound the cadences of a race. Its music is not so much a "score" as it is a momentary substitution for words when the feeling's too strong for speaking, and it chimes in without ado—in a banjo and kazoo duet at a small wedding party, when three little boys dance just for the fun of it; in work songs; in a hussy's dance to a harmonica to lure innocents to a crap game; in a kind of accidental production number in a waterfront dive where the same dancer inspires customers and waiters to strut; in a preacher's trainlike motion as he lectures on evil in a railroad cap and calls repentance "the last station"; in the hussy's attempt to abandon her lover by humming him to sleep so she can sneak out of the house. Most remarkable was Vidor's view of one night and the following morning with the protagonist's family, who sleep in a row of adjacent beds. The mother (Fanny Belle deKnight) starts a lullaby, rocking the youngest children to sleep by turns before they are placed in bed; the next morning, seeing one bed empty, she guesses (correctly) that tragedy has struck and without preamble rouses the household with a wailing prayer. Tucked into this astonishingly casual musicality are two songs by Irving Berlin, the dive number and the folklike, blues-tainted "Waiting at the End of the Road."

Vidor shot the film as a silent. He had to—the company arrived on location in Tennessee to find that the sound trucks had not arrived. This gave Vidor's camera a wonderful freedom but necessitated a post-shooting synchronization procedure that literally gave the sound editor a nervous breakdown. It was easy to overlay a choral track onto a scene of workers coming home from the fields, but difficult to fit spoken words to mouths or find the right "lead" in a crowd scene wherein a number of people are talking at once. *Hallelujah*'s sound quality is poor even for 1929, so poor that the mounting effect of honesty in action and music must make up for the constant drawback of having to strain to hear the dialogue.

The fault is the microphone's, not the actors', for though Vidor's all-black cast had little or no acting experience, they are believable and moving (and distinct when the sound reproduction falls clear every so often), whether as principals in the central story or as extras in the big religious parade, mass baptism, and revival meeting scenes. The main characters are a decent fellow who gets into trouble (Daniel Haynes) and a weak woman (Nina Mae McKinney) who first cheats him in partnership with a crooked gambler and then, when he has become an evangelist, gets religion, falls for him, lives with him, and leaves him for the gambler. Pursuing them, Haynes causes her death and then hunts the man down in a swamp and kills him. This is *Hallelujah*'s most celebrated scene, short but absorbing for its deadpan approach. The camera follows the hunt curiously, wanting to see for itself. It tracks Haynes, tracks his quarry, cuts back to Haynes. The sound almost dies out, except for a few effects—a twig breaks, a bird cries, water slurps—and the melodrama thus comes off more as reportage than as entertainment. Similarly, *Hallelujah*'s last two scenes of Haynes' punishment on the rockpile and his homecoming resist the temptation to suggest an epic. Life, Vidor seems to say, has no perspective in itself; the objective onlooker must supply it. Vidor's uncanny ability to duplicate existence instead of stylizing it makes *Hallelujah* the forerunner of the Italian neo-realist cinema of the 1940s and 1950s. And he has a better sense of tempo than Visconti and better actors than Rossellini.

When *Hallelujah* was released, critics admired it. Even *Photoplay*, the most influential of the fan magazines and somewhat suspicious of art—the best it could say of Vidor's brilliant *The Crowd* was "an interesting experience"—hailed it as an experiment that works, and critics have continued to cite it as a great event in film history. Lately, voguish white guilt has caused some backtracking doublespeak, and a few opportunists have called the film "patronizing." It isn't. The Berlin songs supplement the folk tunes excellently; Berlin was, after all, the father of "jazz" as American pop song, out of ragtime and blues into Gershwin, so culturally he has more than a little black in him. The story is universal in scope and not, as has been suggested, a depiction of black laziness, criminality, and sensuality. Nor does the ecstatic revival scene, with its freakouts being carried out to recover outside the meeting hall, cast any racial slur. Moderns should remember that, in the 1920s, such white-conceived and white-supported concerns as Aimee Semple McPherson's chain of Four-Square Gospel tabernacles equalled any black efforts in that arena. How is *Hallelujah* patronizing? True, it doesn't show us any white oppressors. But you can't have everything.

Vidor, like Ernst Lubitsch and Rouben Mamoulian, was a standout director who instinctively understood what music could do for film. Most of his colleagues learned as they shot—those who learned. A good apprenticeship was the Broadway adaptation, since this was less a matter of creation than of editing: take what you need and leave out the rest. And there was some adding in; because each studio owned a music publishing house (to market all those theme songs; sheet music pulled in a lot of money in the days when everyone played the piano), producers liked to commission new songs for Broadway adaptations. The original score might be superior, but the new numbers would bring in subsidiary profits from the song sheets and recordings. The practice varied considerably. *The Desert Song* was not sullied, but another Romberg operetta-turned-film, *New Moon* (1930), lost more than half its score and suffered a few interpolated indignities. It could go even harder with modern-dress musical comedy, whose scores were considered shallow compared to operetta's more fulfilled rhapsody. *Little Johnny Jones*, George M. Cohan's 1904 show about an American jockey smeared in a bribe scandal in England, seemed a natural for the screen, with its spunky do-right hero and Yankee Doodle score. But First National's screen version (1929), with Eddie Buzzell as Johnny, updated the sound with such new ditties as "She Was Kicked on the Head by a Butterfly" and "Go Find Somebody to Love," which suffer by comparison with "Give My Regards to Broadway" and "Yankee Doodle Boy," retained from the original.

Other Broadway subjects fared less well. *Queen High* (1930), a tremendous stage hit in 1926 for its comic look at two business partners who settle their feud in a poker game, winner take all (including the loser, as his butler), kept little more than its story and star, Charles Ruggles. (Frank Morgan stepped in as the other partner; a sharp team.) Similarly, Bert Lahr and the plot were about all that remained of *Flying High* (1931), though the film did give Charlotte Greenwood a fine opportunity to test her dryly agile style against Lahr's moist burlesque. They made a great pair, which is more than was said for Grace Moore and Lawrence Tibbett in *New Moon*. "She drew him quietly into her boudoir," the ads moaned. "Tonight she was his, but tomorrow she was to be the wife of another!" Actually, Moore looked as if she would like to draw Tibbett a map back to the Met, whence they both issued. It appears that Moore hadn't yet figured out how to apply her abundant oomph to the screen. Tibbett alone had been a sensation in *The Rogue Song* earlier that year, but Moore and *New Moon* almost finished him in Hollywood.

Audiences took casting more seriously than producers, who were concerned with finding work for stars already on salary rather than with finding the most suitable possibilities for set roles. Producers trusted fame—or tried to create it—more than they trusted the material itself. Sometimes even good casting didn't work; maybe that made them cynical. Jeanette MacDonald and Dennis King made an odd couple in *The Vagabond King* (1930), the Rudolf Friml piece about François Villon and a screen favorite in several versions with and without music, from a one-reel silent (drawn from Justin Huntley McCarthy's E. H. Sothern warhorse, *If I Were King*) to a remake of the operetta in 1956. Paramount did a real job on Friml's version, keeping most of the score and filming it in two-strip Technicolor. Carrying over King's Broadway Villon seemed as wise as following up on Mac-Donald's smashing debut in *The Love Parade* the year before: she makes a svelte heroine, and King is surprisingly sinewy for an operetta baritone, with the pale, flawless face that the silent camera would have made love to. But his hammy stage style took the sound camera by too much force. He was a John Gilbert of operetta, overlover, and MacDonald, possibly bored in a dull part, didn't extend herself. It can't have been fun to play opposite a terminal matinée idol, either. It was director Ludwig Berger who really ruined the film. In the duet "Only a Rose" Berger decorates his close-up of MacDonald with bits of King's profile—*while* MacDonald is singing. She later dubbed the business "Only a Nose."

Rarely, a film version of a Broadway show focused a scattershot original; *Good News* (1930) is an example. The college musical is one thing Hollywood got down fast for its youthful zip, hedonism, and chaste romance. Such entries as Universal's *College Love* (1929), Paramount's *Sweetie* (1929), and First National's *The Forward Pass* (1929) set the style—*College Love* with its Greek parties and dances; *Sweetie* with its definitive *dramatis personae* of sweet coed Nancy Carroll, football hero Stanley Smith, wacky-cute comedienne Helen Kane, and wacky-ridiculous comedian Jack Oakie; and *The Forward Pass* with its culminating Big Game footage. When MGM tackled *Good News*, a 1927 Broadway hit, tradition advised the adaptors to keep the love plot (coed and football hero), the wisecracking secondary couple, the best of the songs ("Lucky in Love," "The Varsity Drag," "The Best Things in Life Are Free"), and to dump just about everything else. It was a good trade. Much of what is lost was fill; the new stuff is the real collegiate hot-cha, from the use of John Held, Jr., sheik and sheba caricatures—the emblem of the age—on the posters to the inclusion of Cliff Edwards (known as "Ukelele Ike") for strumming *ton*. As usual, MGM had some new songs run up by house writers, and they go well with the B. G. DeSylva–Lew Brown–Ray Henderson originals. "Gee, But I'd Like to Make You Happy" has tender bounce, "I Feel Pessimistic" spry introspection, and Nacio Herb Brown and Arthur Freed donated two samples of their art of making the inconsequential sound totally committed: "If You're Not Kissing Me" and "Football." Casting was right, too. Broadway's heroine, Mary Lawlor, and chief comic, Gus Shy, were brought in to do what they did; Shy was paired with Bessie Love, utterly in her element as a clown after her dire Hank in *The Broadway Melody.* Even the chorus was ace. However, the college genre turned out to have no potential for expansion. If *Good News* was the best, it was already rich in cliché, though the form (discounting the college silents) was scarcely a year old.

One of the best of the Broadway adaptations, oddly, was the most faithful to the original, RKO's *Rio Rita* (1929): full score (additions by the original authors), static camera, mixed cast of screen and stage veterans, last third in color. It's horribly primitive—sound troubles on the set were almost insuperable. Bebe Daniels' fan sounded like the crackle of fifty crackers until specially treated, and though in a garden scene every other potted plant seemed to hide a mike, each turn of Daniels' hand meant a gap in her dialogue. Moreover, as *Rio Rita* is a modern western, outdoor shots of mounted rangers were unavoidable, though this meant filming silent and then adding the sound, *Hallelujah*-style. The whole thing was shot in twenty-four days, and while Daniels for one found it impossible to post-dub her part and had to get it down during filming or not at all, the choral singing clearly doesn't match the lip movements and must have been recorded separately. The technique of mating sound arbitrarily to moving mouths was called "wild track" dubbing; a number of these early musicals resorted to it. But when John Boles and his fellow Texas Rangers team up for "The Rangers' Song" and we notice that they don't seem to be singing what we're hearing—not at the second we're hearing it, anyway—we stop enjoying the show and begin to concentrate on technique. Underscoring obscures the dialogue, balance in duets is a problem (especially in regard to Daniels' and Boles' relatively high voices), and at each new sound series the track cuts in with a little explosion. The camera, locked into its soundproof booth, also adds to the rough quality of the film; at one point late in the action, Boles is in hiding around a corner and Daniels leans around to speak to him. As they confer, the camera just sits there, showing us . . . nothing.

Yet the film is a great pleasure even so, and earned a huge success. A shoot-'em-up complete with villain who almost takes Daniels from Boles, *Rio Rita* was originally a Ziegfeld show poised halfway between flowery operetta (sample love song: "If You're In Love, You'll Waltz") and wiggy musical comedy (a comic duo wanders in and out with little or no reference to the action). Ziegfeld staged it sumptuously, and RKO attempted to follow suit, though the color sequence had to be shot at night because the studio's one Technicolor camera was tied up on another film in the daytime. The Harry Tierney–Joseph McCarthy score is cute, and by drafting the stage original's two comedians, Bert Wheeler and Robert Woolsey, RKO filled its two-and-a-half-hour special* with all the intent charm that Broadway musicals have. It has been called stagey, especially for the straight-on angle used in the dance numbers, but Daniels and Boles valiantly sustain a sense of movement in their garden scene, to hell with the microphones, and Wheeler and Woolsey really keep the film hopping. Baby-faced Wheeler is the stooge of the pair, Woolsey the hustler. Their friendship is amorphously friendly-hostile, like those of some silent comic pairs: Woolsey is nominally Wheeler's lawyer yet continually gets him into trouble. Near the end, when Woolsey takes Wheeler's first wife off his hands so he can gambol with Dorothy Lee, the two couples sit on the rail of a ship, the girls on the outside and the men between them. The girls launch a reprise of the song, "Sweetheart, We Need Each Other"—pointlessly, and they seem to know it; they keep looking away at nothing or smiling to themselves—while the men play Laurel-and-Hardy-like "hits" on each other. At length they embrace and fall backwards into the water. The girls do, too. The whole thing is wonderfully stupid, recalling the rhythms of silent comedy (officially dead that same year) when structural symmetry mattered more than sanity.

If the Broadway adaptations pointed to nothing peculiarly cinematic, they gave inexperienced filmmakers a chance to learn their craft while dealing with material of a strong narrative drive. Perhaps this was why the revues seemed so lifeless: they reflected Hollywood's uncertainty about story, vocal range, and character, its fear of flying. A revue was a cinch, Hollywood thought: anything goes. It was hard to miss them—MGM advertised *The Hollywood Revue of 1929* with two billboards of living showgirls, one each in Los Angeles and New York—and revues did boast an eye-catching collage of celebrities. But movies were supposedly killing vaudeville, not adopting it. How hard they worked to make you like them. *The Hollywood Revue* had Marion Davies tap dancing (well, by the way) on a drum, Joan Crawford singing "Gotta Feelin' For You" and kicking into her famous charleston, Laurel and Hardy messing up their magic act (Hardy slips on a banana peel, crashes into a huge cake, and primly observes, "I faw down and go pwop"), and then everybody troops on in slickers at the end in a big production number based on "Singin' in the Rain" (another two-

---

*This timing refers to the original roadshow release, two screenings a day at top prices. Neighborhood houses got a shortened *Rio Rita* and surviving prints run even shorter, with whole numbers missing.

color reel, wisely set in an orange grove so the green looks almost reasonable). Big.

John Murray Anderson's superb revue *King of Jazz* was even bigger, opening with a cartoon on Paul Whiteman among the jungle animals, where jazz is born, going on to "The Song of the Dawn," led by John Boles and featuring some five hundred cowboys galloping out of the ocean onto a beach and into the sky, and perching one number on a gigantic staircase with sixteen bridesmaids supporting the biggest bridal gown in history. The aim was to out-Broadway Broadway, and *King of Jazz* did. But this was the wrong aim: film must out-film *silence,* not imitate another medium.

Paramount on Parade (1930), one of the better revues, was comfortably cinematic, neither stage-bound nor crazed for spectacle. Elsie Janis, a veteran Broadway revuer, supervised the program, but nearly a dozen directors (including Lubitsch) kept it three-dimensional, and an imposing array of stars gave it personality. Its comedy is shaky, but the musical segments are quite good, especially the finale, "Sweeping the Clouds Away," in which Maurice Chevalier and chorus girls dressed in rainbow colors dance up and down peaked roofs and are last viewed high up in the heavens. Everyone gets to do what he or she does best, except Ruth Chatterton (famed in the first sound films for her lustrous speaking voice), who is made to sing as a lonely Parisian tart, and Clara Bow, who sings "I'm True to the Navy Now," walking here and there on a battleship while a squad of sailors works hard to make us think she's dancing with them.

I said enough in the last chapter on the defects of the revue as a form, but let's look at one in detail, Warner Brothers' *The Show of Shows* (1929). This was the most stage-bound of them all, literally performed on one, curtain and all. It's worth investigating because it illuminates Hollywood and would-be Hollywood talent in what the Chinese call interesting times: when the studios were trying to decide who and what was musical material. For some of the cast, *The Show of Shows* was not unlike an audition.

The potpourri opens with a drastic and irrelevant scene at the French guillotine. An aristocrat is beheaded, a revolutionary proclaims "The Show of Shows!" and we are whirled into too much footage of a military march routine in geometric groupings. At length, emcee Frank Fay introduces a double sextet, "What's Become of the Six Original *Florodora* Boys?" sung by the Girls and succeeded by six comedians (including cross-eyed Ben Turpin) who show by their waiter's, iceman's, and other such uniforms that the Boys have fallen on rough days. The staging is awkward, the camera following the dancing as best it can. Fay returns to attempt "She's Only a Bird in a Gilded Cage" but is interrupted, and a big Pirate Number is unveiled, featuring Ted Lewis and his band (in tuxedos) trapped on a pirate ship, where Lewis trucks and warbles, calling himself a "pirate of jazz." Everyone trucks off stage left, including the pirates, who truck clumsily, which is supposed to be funny.

Next—stay with me; I'm driving at something—a top-hat-and-tails man leads the girls in a dull tap routine; all strip to gym togs and do dull exercises. Fay attempts another number, but is interrupted by the next performer, Winnie Lightner, who delivers the ebullient "Pingo Pongo." Lightner is full of pep and the song is strange and fun, the first item so far that works. Fay now attempts to interrupt singer Nick Lucas, fails, and eventually joins Lloyd Hamilton, Beatrice Lillie, and Louise Fazenda in a tedious blending of four "art" poems in quartet style, ending with chic nonsense verse on "Your Mother and Mine," one of those "M is for . . ." numbers but with a wrong letter correspondence and no mention of mother.

At least Fay is gone; his pushy self-belief has been a little wearing. Richard Barthelmess introduces a huge number made up of six (real-life) sister acts, each with an ethnic ditty, twin costumes, and a change of backdrop. The dancing again follows stage patterns, letting the camera serve as a remote eye instead of a frame for composition. Winnie Lightner returns and *The Show of Shows* comes to life again. Her number, set in a bathroom, is "Singin' in the Bathtub," and the hulking, slosh-mouthed Bull Montana joins her at the end for a put-on of *The Broadway Melody*'s "You Were Meant For Me."

Comes next Irene Bordoni, French, suave, and lovely, to sing, to piano accompaniment, in a surprisingly sexy style—surprising not for Bordoni's Broadway but for Hollywood. Now Warners pulls out its biggest star, Rin-Tin-Tin, who introduces (by pulling off the cover of a vaudeville signboard with his teeth) an inscrutably hebetudinous Chinese Number led by Nick Lucas and Myrna Loy. Their song, "Li-Po-Li," deals with some sort of tai-pan who does fearful things. He will, one couplet asserts, "take away all your rice-cakes" and, rather inevitably for this level of songwriting, "take away all your spice cakes." This leads to chorus girls climbing up and down ladders while the orchestra plays the tune over and over. The whole act, in song, dance, and decor, is of a monumentally failed ineffability.

Worse yet, Fay is back, harried by comedian Sid Silvers, who does a comically poor Jolson imitation. At Silvers' second overgone

"Nyaah," Fay says, "What is that, asthma?"—his first (and only) good line of the evening. A Bicycle Number follows, stationary cycles pumped against a moving background. Fay and Silvers return for a round of halitosis jokes—really—capped by "If Your Best Friend Won't Tell You, Why Should I?" Now for a bit of Pirandello: the Black and White Girls dance on a tremendous stairway in dresses half black and half white. Partway through they give up and call Fay on-stage to complain about the length of their dresses.

Fay now takes his big solo spot, the apex of dreary. John Barrymore does a scene from *Richard III*, the comics play a firing squad sketch, and we have reached a grandiose finale based on the song "Lady Luck." The singer, Alexander Gray, is post-dubbed very poorly, his rich baritone coming out constricted and out of sync, and the dancing goes on forever—acrobatics, shimmy, tap, black minstrels, the show-to-end-the-show-of-shows works. At last, the stars (including Rin-Tin-Tin) reprise "Lady Luck," their heads poked through holes cut in canvas, the cheap effect refreshing after so much forced splendor. One hundred thirty minutes of two-strip Technicolor are over.

And what have we? The least pretentious numbers are the best—Bordoni does more with one piano than the feet of the entire Warners backlot can in "Lady Luck," Barthelmess' amused dignity goes down more affably than Fay's practiced shtick, and Lightner's socko fun provides a more natural comedy than the contrived sketches. And note the wide range of possibilities here—Bordoni's sensuality, Barthelmess' self-possession, and Lightner's lampoon dovetail nicely, because they seem really to be what they seem. Most of the theatre people are gaming with what they are, even as they seem to be something else. That's one paradox too many for film to encompass.

Warners disclosed no new useful talent with *The Show of Shows*. Barthelmess, Barrymore, and Rin-Tin-Tin went back to their habitual roles, and Bea Lillie, Ted Lewis, and Frank Fay (the last after several further attempts to found a film career) went back to the stage. Bordoni, in Hollywood to film her stage hit *Paris* (1929), was for all her appeal too special for Hollywood. Lightner, too, though she figured prominently in a number of films in these early years, made no place for herself and ended up in featured bits. She was a little overweight and underpretty for the styles of the age, even for sidekick parts, and her high spirits had an earthy base to them that the musical wasn't ready to utilize.

Warners' choreographers Larry Ceballos and Jack Haskell had not developed anything even vaguely suitable for cinema, and, given *The*

Show of Shows' explicitly theatrical concept, director John Adolfi had no chance to conceptualize a film revue. But what is most wrong about the piece is the material, with its wild gallimaufry of tones—its sophisticated literate comedy side by side with slapstick and vaudeville standup patter; its screwy Lightner spots (which still give pleasure) next to the misfired romance of the Chinese number (instant camp); its creaky exhibition marches and exercises leading up to the final greedy collage of dances traditional and contemporary. *The Show of Shows* is not only a mess; it lacks character. That was true of many of the early musicals. They maintained silent film's narrative tropes but couldn't use the nimble silent camera. They borrowed Broadway's output but marketed it for a public not entirely used to Broadway ware. They hired film actors and Broadway actors arbitrarily, failing to make use of talent at hand and misusing new talent. The studio chiefs, producers, and directors simply did not understand the musical form, either historically (in its stage evolutions) or imaginatively (in what film could do with it). Certain moments in *The Show of Shows* reveal a savvy innocence—an informality cynical about life but romantic about film's role in the culture—that was to survive these difficult early years to guide the musical film in its greatest days.

It happens that some of the least durable first musicals got this informal tone down without much trouble. Conceived for the screen and relatively well written and cast, they weren't filmed well and now seem horribly leaden. DeSylva, Brown, and Henderson brought their distinctive vernacular touch—lowdown in rhythm, piquant in love—to Fox' *Sunny Side Up* (1929), the tale of a Manhattan waif who loves and finally wins a Prince Charming of Southampton. As authors of smash hit Broadway scores (*Flying High* and *Good News* among them) they held a close collaboration, and wrote all of *Sunny Side Up*, screenplay as well as score, pinning its appeal on Janet Gaynor's charm as the heroine. The star of such great silents as *Sunrise* and *Seventh Heaven*, Gaynor revealed a bearable singing voice, and if her constant screen lover Charles Farrell didn't, that did not militate against his taking the indicated part in *Sunny Side Up*. Gaynor carried the show, singing the title song, a champion cheer-up rouser, and what in part-talkie days would have been the film's theme song, "(I'm a dreamer) Aren't We All?" Many would call it the theme song of all Hollywood musicals, but this is to discount the earthy sarcasm that complements the wishfulness. *Sunny Side Up*'s six songs feature with-it complacence more than optimism, for the authors were adept at capturing the slangy, self-boosting world of the lower-middle-class drifter who emphasizes fun over ambition. "If I Had a Talking Picture of You," "You've Got Me Pickin' Petals Off of Daisies," and "You Find the Time, I'll Find the Place" may sound like love ditties, but in tone they slyly mock the sentimentality of "Aren't We All?," and for all their naiveté they are more about making love than being in it.

Gaynor and Farrell still had magic for many moviegoers, and the film did so well that Fox more or less remade it a year later with Gaynor as the heiress and Farrell as the waif in *High Society Blues*. But both these films and DeSylva, Brown, and Henderson's second original, *Just Imagine* (1930), were handed over to a director, David Butler, who had no sense of pace. He can't connect one line to another, lingers over the insufferable contortions of comedian El Brendel, and renders *Sunny Side Up*'s production number, "Turn on the Heat," almost motionless.

At least *Sunny Side Up* had a good score and Gaynor. *Just Imagine*, a look fifty years into the future, has nothing. Suddenly, DeSylva, Brown, and Henderson—or Fox?—got nervous about letting characters express themselves as the musical spirit moved them, so every number has an "excuse"—party entertainment, a club drinking song, even a dream vision. However, the film's structure is like that of the authors' stage musicals, with its two couples, one romantic (John Garrick and Maureen O'Sullivan) and one dizzy (Frank Albertson and Marjorie White), a lead comic (Brendel again), forced gag finishes to each scene, and an "umbrella" for jokes (like *Flying High*'s aviation or *Good News*' anti-intellectual undergraduate life): the future. The opening shot of New York in 1980, with low-flying aircars humming past art deco skyscrapers, is intriguing, but after that the movie looks as if it cost fifty cents. One can't blame *Just Imagine* because many of its pushbutton luxuries, viewed as wild in 1930, are old hat today. But the combination of Brendel as an inhabitant of the past brought back to life and Butler's sleepy camera makes this one of the worst musicals ever made. Brendel had a light Swedish accent, a clown's face, and no sense of humor whatsoever. He joins the two male leads on a trip to Mars, saves them from a hostile Martian, and brings the latter back to earth—which, for reasons not worth going into, resolves the love plot. Let's try a sample of Brendel's art just for the record:

BRENDEL: So this is Mars? We got a place just like this three miles from my hometown.
ALBERTSON: You should be on it.
BRENDEL: [With neither timing nor inflection] You're telling me!

☆ *MASTER DIRECTORS: above, Josef von Sternberg's* Morocco *(Dietrich and Cooper in the "What Am I Bid for My Apples?" number); below, Ernst Lubitsch's* The Merry Widow *(MacDonald in window).*

Other than *Hallelujah*, we have not seen much to build an aesthetic on, but there were works of astonishing quality in this time, all of them from Paramount and some of them as good as anything that followed. They were the work of directors Ernst Lubitsch and Rouben Mamoulian, and suddenly we find no stymied camera, no confusion about format, no fumbling for character. Lubitsch, with his famous "touch" of arch eroticism, and Mamoulian, with his kaleidoscope of images and sounds turned simultaneously, found the personality for a musical cinema.

Influential as they were, their styles flourished only from 1929 to 1932, when Lubitsch produced his first four and Mamoulian his first two musicals. They were too special to create a trend; moreover, the institution of the Legion of Decency by the Catholic Church in late 1933 promised an end to the subjects and characters that Lubitsch especially dealt with. Coming at a time when movie attendance figures had hit a disastrous low, the Legion of Decency's threatened boycott forced Hollywood to revise the Hays Production Code of 1930—more precisely, to enforce it. This didn't stop Lubitsch from completing his series of salacious operettas with *The Merry Widow* in 1934; still, it sounded as if in a vacuum.

Lubitsch's first musical, *The Love Parade* (1929), brought Jeanette MacDonald and Maurice Chevalier together as the queen of Sylvania and her prince consort, who is treated as Sylvania's royal lapdog until he compels his wife to turn over the power to him. In a medium that couldn't decide what sort of stories to tell, much less how to tell them, Lubitsch's exposition plays like lightning: in Paris, Chevalier and a woman are caught in adulterous tryst; Chevalier just has time to fill the audience in on the facts. "She's very jealous," he explains of the woman, and, when a man enters, "Her husband." She shoots herself. The husband takes the gun and shoots Chevalier in the chest at point-blank range. Chevalier feels for the wound. Nothing. A little embarrassed, he shows the husband that he's unhurt. They turn to the woman; she's unhurt. The gun was loaded with blanks. Chevalier drops the gun into a drawer—filled with guns. About to leave, the husband tries to draw his wife's zipper. He fumbles. She impatiently goes to Chevalier, who suavely pulls it to. "Voilà."

The whole film is like that, reducing every event to its center, dressy, unblushing, velvet with bite. Everything in *The Love Parade* is different from everything else so far, and it seems impossible that it inaugurated rather than capped a tradition. Not only Lubitsch's direction, but Ernest Vajda and Guy Bolton's screenplay (from a French piece), Victor Schertzinger and Clifford Grey's score, and the cast are all unexpectedly confident. Chevalier and MacDonald especially were made for sound. His "Paris, Stay the Same," sung when he is recalled to Sylvania because of his wicked life, and "Nobody's Using It Now," when neglected by the queen-oriented court, sound a note of jauntiness and manly grace beyond matters of portrayal: Chevalier *is* a prince; he must dominate; MacDonald will succumb. Her "Dream Lover" promises it, though her "March of the Grenadiers," delivered in full uniform to (and with) troops on parade, suggests a stalwart woman. And she does have the power. But he's the man.

Like *Just Imagine*, *The Love Parade* has a secondary comic couple, his valet (Lupino Lane) and her maid (Lillian Roth), but the comedy is built into the story, not painted onto it. And, as opposed to *Just Imagine*'s cardboard fantasy, *The Love Parade* doesn't only refer to castles, it inhabits them. Lubitsch rides his camera up and down halls, out onto terraces, into the opera house, showing only essentials. MacDonald first meets Chevalier in her office, where she reads a report of his escapades. Nothing need be said—Lubitsch has the orchestra quote a theme heard in the first scene to recall Chavalier at his sport. They love each other from the start, of course, and have dinner while her Cabinet, the servants, and the populace in general watch anxiously outside. At last their queen will marry! We see the new couple through outsiders' eyes, through the window. The pair enter her boudoir and, later, MacDonald sits at a piano to sing a reprise of "Dream Lover." But we only hear her do it: Lubitsch focuses on a group of couples on a patio—each a mirror of Chevalier and MacDonald—on the Cabinet, and on Lane and Roth listening blissfully. The new naturalism of sound can absorb fantasy as long as we in the audience can enter the story ourselves, eavesdropping and peeking.

Lubitsch had less to work with in *Monte Carlo* (1930), though the quality of sound had improved. (Every other line in *The Love Parade* seems pitched at a different volume, and the orchestra and voices, shoved together into one track, dissolve into mush at times.) MacDonald is back but Jack Buchanan's got her, as a count masquerading as a hairdresser. The Richard Whiting–W. Franke Harling–Leo Robin score contains "Beyond the Blue Horizon" but the script is dull and Buchanan, a smarmy British wimp who played opposite Irene Bordoni in her *Paris* film, has a voice like tapioca pudding on a high speed and the most irritating laugh a leading man ever tried to get away with. One scene has made *Monte Carlo* famous, that of MacDonald's flight from an arranged marriage with a pompous old prince. The film opens with the wedding, lingers just long enough to establish that MacDonald isn't going to show up, then cuts to a train standing in a station. A woman gets on—MacDonald, it seems—and from this standing start Lubitsch turns her trip into an experience of space and bulk and motion—the straining on the tracks, the pulse of the iron ride, the adventure hissing and steaming as much in music as in cinema. The chugging and whistling turn into the accompaniment to MacDonald's song as she settles by the window seat of her compartment. The opening wedding had been shot in the rain, but now the sun beams on the heroine: the rules of romance favor beauty. The ostinato of train noises thickens as the voyage roars on and, her scarf flying in the breeze and peasants in the passing fields waving to her, MacDonald soars through "Beyond the Blue Horizon," voice, music and lyrics, and visual expression all expanding in one moment of exhilaration.

Chevalier, a bigger star than MacDonald, drew better projects without her than she did without him, as in Lubitsch's *The Smiling Lieutenant* (1931), based on Oscar Straus' operetta *A Waltz Dream*. Chevalier played "between" Claudette Colbert and Miriam Hopkins, and his endless charm even brings off Clifford Grey's extreme lyric to "Breakfast Table Love" (such as "With every bit of liver I start to quiver"). But Lubitsch reunited the ultimate operetta twosome in *One Hour With You* (1932), a very up-to-date piece about a doctor (Chevalier) madly in love with his wife (MacDonald) but trapped into infidelity with her best friend (Genevieve Tobin). *One Hour With You*, a boudoir comedy that gets around, is less musical than Lubitsch's earlier trio, tossing off some of its lyrics in lightly accented speech, avoiding the heavy character songs that enriched *The Love Parade,* and doing a full-out number only in the title song, performed at a dinner party by dancing couples who glide in and out of each other's arms trying to arrange assignations.

At first, Lubitsch was to produce the film and George Cukor was to direct it. But midway through shooting Lubitsch began to horn in with advice and Cukor departed. It's impossible to tell Lubitsch from Cukor in the finished product; examples of the Touch abound everywhere, as when Charles Ruggles, dressed as Romeo for what he believes to be a costume party, learns that it's a simple black-tie affair. It's the butler's fault—why did he tell Ruggles to don a getup? "Oh, sir," says the butler with a shameless grin, "I did so want to see you in tights."

Lubitsch was already a Hollywood pro when sound came in (*One Hour With You* was a remake of his 1924 comedy, *The Marriage Cir-*

cle). Rouben Mamoulian came in for sound from Broadway, where he had led the so-called art movement into the highly collaborative production that blended acting, motion, sound effects, decor, and lighting as one conceptual organism. Movie historians regularly cite his dynamic orchestration of noises in the opening scene of DuBose and Dorothy Heyward's play *Porgy* (based on Heyward's novel and the source of Gershwin's opera *Porgy and Bess*), a jazz of street workers, snores, brooms, rug beatings, knife sharpenings, and so on in harmonious and competing rhythms as dawn comes up and the black ghetto comes to life. "Inside his brain," wrote critic Tom Milne, "there must be an invisible metronome . . . One is almost tempted to say that every Mamoulian film is a musical." In *Hallelujah*, King Vidor washes his action in an overlay of emotionalism. Mamoulian pumps a heartbeat into his.

Mamoulian learned film at Paramount's Astoria studios watching Herbert Brenon direct Jeanne Eagels in *Jealousy*. He was signed to slide into the business as a "dialogue director," meaning a coach for witless actors. But he picked everything up so fast that in little over a month he was directing *Applause* (1929), a sordid look into the life of a fading burlesque dancer. *The Dance of Life* (1929) upped burlesque's tempo with high-stepping numbers; *Applause* is as shabby onstage as it is off. The famous opening sequence proves Mamoulian's genius for film in its cascade of messages cued into the cheesy street parade of Kitty Darling and her Gaiety Girls. A poster fluttering in the wind announces the procession, a mutt tears at it, a little girl picks him up and more children race up the lane to see the fun. Some fun: as the parade passes, the band music dissolves into a cheap music-hall tune and the camera steals into a burlesque theatre to spot the heavy legs and exhausted gaudy of the Gaiety Girls.

The role of Kitty Darling gave Helen Morgan the challenge of her career. Exploited by her lover and an embarrassment to her convent-reared daughter, Kitty slides from despair to despair, but Mamoulian cuts the tale's potential for easy pathos with his constantly essentializing images, forcing the spectator to apply the same alert eye that the silents required. When Garrett Fort's script brings in a sailor to spark some palliative love interest with Morgan's daughter, Mamoulian hammers sorrow home by cutting from a shot of the daughter drinking a glass of water to one of Morgan drinking poison.

Morgan's two onstage numbers and some incidental use of folk and old pop tunes give Mamoulian's sharp musical steerage few opportunities for song-and-dance narrative, but he has his moments. He entered the annals of technical reform in a scene in which Morgan sings a lullaby and her daughter whispers a prayer, simultaneously. The sound and camera men insisted it couldn't be done on one mike, with one-channel recording. "Why not use two mikes and two channels," Mamoulian recalls asking, "and combine the two tracks in printing?" Unheard of. But Mamoulian was nothing without his sound sense, and he was something. "I threw down my megaphone . . . and ran up to [Adolph] Zukor's office . . . 'Look,' I said, 'Nobody does what I ask' . . . So Zukor came down and told them to do it my way, and by 5:30 we had two takes in the can." Mamoulian knew he had brought it off for sure when he got an effusive welcome from the studio doorman the next morning.

Mamoulian's second musical (if we count *Applause* as his first; many don't) ranks with Lubitsch's *The Love Parade* as one of the two masterpieces of the era. Like the Lubitsch film, *Love Me Tonight* (1932) is a continental fairy tale without sorcery. Its magic charms comprise a superb score and cast and a sense of motion so palpable that one rides right into it on a dream cloud without having to pay the price in prefabricated sentimentality that too many operettas were charging. It's more beautiful than life, yet its appetites are realistic. "Love, Your Spell Is Everywhere," sang Gloria Swanson in her first talkie, *The Trespasser* (1929); that might well be the theme of *Love Me Tonight.* Consider its opening sequences, three songs and some dialogue scenes unfurled in a medley and presenting two different worlds, that of vital Paris and that of a sleepy country chateau where ancient nobles play eons of bridge and an anemic princess waits for a man to kiss her awake. Mamoulian opens in Paris as the day begins, with his hero, a tailor named Maurice, cataloguing the noises of the day in "That's the Song of Paree." En route to his shop, he greets tradesmen and girl friends in the immediately succeeding "How Are You?", the various characters jumping fluently from song to speech though every line is in fact a lyric. In his shop, Maurice finds music latent even in tailoring, and a conversation with a customer grows into another song, "Isn't It Romantic?", which now leaves Maurice to follow different people around the town—the customer reviews the tune, passes it to a taxi driver, who passes it in turn to a musician, who gets off at a train station. Chugging wheels urge the tune on; traveling soldiers toss it to marching troops, who give it to a passing gypsy violinist, who brings out its sensuality at his camp in the forest. We have reached open country, and Mamoulian takes us to the song's last beneficiary, Princess Jeanette, who sings it full out with a new set of lyrics. "Isn't it romantic?" she asks. "Music in the night, a dream that can be heard." We have spent a whole day in minutes, with all its persons and events, and have met our hero and heroine in their respective settings: the artful tailor, engaged by the adventure of living, the languishing princess in her bloodless storybook castle, and love's spell heading her way on the energy of song.

Jeanette and Maurice are, of course, MacDonald and Chevalier, contributing to, yet undercutting, the fantasy by using their real-life first names. They are splendid, and the score, by Richard Rodgers and Lorenz Hart, exactly amalgamates their separate qualities of (his) brisk urbanity and (her) romantic vulnerability. His "Mimi," sung when they meet, is raffish, but it gives away a secret: he loves her. Her "Lover," sung just before they meet while she is out riding, is elegant but comically interrupted by commands to her horse.* One duet, "The Man for Me," written for the film but cut before release, stresses comedy. She is writing to a friend and he dictates some ideas, flattering to himself; she takes the second chorus, deflating his vanity. Their other duet, the title song, stresses romance. Mamoulian splits the screen, and the two separately affirm the inevitable romance in wonderfully wide-spanned tune, insistent in off-the-beat accents.

Chevalier has come to the chateau to collect on debts owed by Jeanette's cousin Charles Ruggles. He impersonates a noble, is unmasked to general horror, yet wins Jeanette anyway. Actually, she has to win him, by riding after his train to halt it by planting herself on the tracks. The chateau scenes provide the bulk of the ninety-minute running time and give Mamoulian plenty of chances to cast his signature shadows and shoot huffy servants from below. This gloomy manse even has three witches in residence in the persons of Jeanette's aunts; it also has early Myrna Loy in one of her best roles, as a man-chasing cousin. When Jeanette faints, Ruggles asks Loy, "Can you go for a doctor?" and she replies, "Certainly, bring him right in."

What did these six films have that their contemporaries did not? Style, sophistication, sex—a continental personality, richer than the all-American product. They also had technique, obviously, with scripts, scores, and visual planning by masters. More than anything,

---

*Trivium footnote no. 2: "Lover," one of Rodgers' loveliest waltzes, has become a standard, but in the film its lyrics are so wedded to the situation that Paramount's publishing house despaired of selling it and didn't bring it out till 1933, with a plain cover and all-purpose "love song" lyrics.

they had a sure sense of themselves, which leads them from a smart premise through congenial development to the right resolution. What did they lack? Dance. Not till Astaire and Rogers would choreography be integrated into narrative, and Lubitsch and Mamoulian preferred doing without to underdoing.*

However, even these films suffered from the general distaste for singing cinema that rose up in 1930. Hollywood had churned out too many shapeless musicals without tempo or grace; the public began to balk, and Hollywood cut back. Warners, the studio that virtually invented the film musical, pulled all the songs out of *Fifty Million Frenchmen* (1931), from a Cole Porter stage hit; Fox's *Oh, For a Man* (1930), a Jeanette MacDonald–Reginald Denny comedy about an opera diva in love with a singing burglar, lost most of the numbers that told who these people were; and Universal's *Reaching for the Moon* (1931), a Douglas Fairbanks vehicle with Bebe Daniels, Bing Crosby, and an Irving Berlin score, lost all but a song or two. (Even the title tune, the theme song so endemic to filmmaking but two years earlier, was thrown out except in underscoring.) Nineteen twenty-eight had produced some sixty musicals, and 1930 more than seventy, but less than fifteen were released in 1932 and only two of them—*One Hour With You* and an Eddie Cantor romp, *The Kid From Spain*—made much of a profit.

Darryl F. Zanuck, Warners' head of production, broke the bottleneck on a hunch. Something had to work—maybe something with a more everyday flavor than the musical had yet tasted. Zanuck decided to pull off another backstager, this one with a New York pulse to it, greasy with sweat and paint—something to do for show biz what *The Love Parade* and *Love Me Tonight* had done for romance, something to fall into its subject and be, rather than indicate, it. This is something special: a $400,000 musical at a time when even cheap ones were a poor gamble, filled with the slick Broadway types that most Americans dislike, and created entirely by Hollywood, not New York, tal-

---

*This is not to count the occcasional waltzing, a ground-zero minimum in operetta. By dancing, I mean out-and-out character choreography. Lupino Lane and Lillian Roth dance in *The Love Parade*, showing some relation to Broadway, where secondary comic couples often broke into relatively meaningless "eccentrics" to put a song over. Still, Lubitsch has them more sparring than dancing, making Roth seem tougher than she is. She climaxes their "Let's Be Common" by throwing Lane out of a second-floor window, right through the glass.

ents. The structure is familiar. A number of people with diverse stories work together to put on a show; at the last minute, the star is knocked *hors de combat* and an unknown goes on for her with terrific success. Zanuck had to keep the project as secret as possible, for in those days a movie could be written, shot, edited, and released in a few months, and trend starters could find themselves scooped by their competitors if they dallied.* On the quiet, he got a screenplay from Rian James and James Seymour, based on a novel by Bradford Ropes; it's hard to imagine the kind of novel that would translate into this particular movie, flimsy in plot and character but rich in atmosphere. The cast is a big one, and Zanuck filled it more with actors than with singers: Warner Baxter as the director, Bebe Daniels as the star, George Brent as her lover, Guy Kibbee as her elderly protector, Ned Sparks as a producer, Dick Powell as a juvenile, Ginger Rogers and Una Merkel as chorus girls, and Ruby Keeler in her film debut as the novice who goes on for Daniels. Lloyd Bacon directed and Busby Berkeley, a three-year veteran of film musicals, choreographed, taking over the camera himself for the musical sequences. All these people somehow caught the alienation and community and enchantment and exhaustion of the New York theatre world. For the first time, a mass-appeal film musical got so close to its subject that it made audiences understand why sound had to happen, how the artful naturalism of cinema worked, after all. This film has the pace and the vernacular. It introduced an aesthetic of dance conceived for the camera. It saved the musical from extinction by setting a new style for it. Right from the start, so you'll know where you stand—even before you see the street signs and hear extras shout "Jones and Barry are doing a show!" and note Bebe Daniels reading a *New Yorker* with Eustace Tilley on its cover—the film tells you it's hot-shot, ace-high, lowdown, dirty, crazy New York show biz by its very title: *42nd Street.*

Nothing like it preceded it. It's tough—not lovable tough, either. Rogers is known as Anytime Annie; she walks into Baxter's auditions faking an English accent, carrying a pug dog, and sporting a monocle. But she's recognized, and Baxter's choreographer calls her out to her face: they dubbed her Anytime, he tells us, because "She only said no

---

*Today it takes four or five years to get a trend going. Except for quickie exploitation films, the average American movie counts some fifteen months from planning to public viewing, and such recent movements as extrasensory horror and the revival of space fiction took half a decade to implant themselves. In the 1930s, one could pull off such a development inside of a year. When six imitative films from as many studios might hit the screens within five months of their mutual predecessor, innovators have to work fast to assert a cultural copyright.

once—and then she didn't hear the question."* A few other chorines razz her, and Rogers hits one of them and says, "It must have been hard on your mother not having any children," as she stalks off. The sass has grit. True, much of it is simply funny, as when the choreographer nudges Baxter, indicating Rogers, Keeler, and Merkel. "How about keeping the three on the left?" he asks. Baxter is wise: "I suppose if I don't, you'll have to." Still, the atmosphere of nonstop putdown is heavy.

As in the real-life theatre, much of this is because the people involved are insecure and so anxious for recognition. The desperation to succeed spills over into their love lives—there are almost as many liaisons as there are principals—and their professional day-to-day life, so everyone snaps at everyone else. Yet the characters are so fully drawn that the authors can express the fellowship of Broadway, the sense of sharing that hides in the snapping, without straining credibility. Bebe Daniels is at her considerable best as the star of *Pretty Lady*, running through a song with aplomb at the piano, alternately trusting and doubting her lover, drunkenly repudiating her sugar daddy, and, at last, after a broken ankle throws her out of the show, confronting Keeler on crutches. Direly, she eyes her replacement. "So you're going to take my place!" Keeler is sympathetic: "I—I'm sorry, Miss Brock." But Daniels isn't there for Keeler's apology:

> You're nervous, aren't you? [A pause while we wait to learn what her mood is.] Well, don't be. The customers out there want to like you. Always remember that, kid. I've learned it from experience. And you've got so much to give them—youth, beauty, freshness. Do you know your lines? And your songs? And your dance routine? Well! You're a cinch!

The toughness and the fellowship combine in the urgency of getting it on, an urgency felt right from the start, when we learn that Baxter is ailing and wants to cap his career with a tremendous hit. *Pretty Lady* must be perfect, as Baxter angrily points out after witnessing a runthrough of a terrible production number built around a tedious ditty and couples waving garlands. "Don't you like this number?" he is asked. "Sure, I like it," Baxter replies. "I liked it in 1905. What do you think we're putting on, a revival?" This is exactly what *42nd Street* is

---

*Historians joyfully lore over this line, but it's a bloody rude thing to say to someone, and if you watch Rogers carefully while he says it, you'll see a nice woman refusing to show it but feeling terribly hurt. (I mean, of course, Rogers as Annie, not Rogers herself. Let's not confuse actor and character yet; we'll get to Judy Garland in good time.) It only lasts a second, but for my money this is one of the most uncomfortable moments in film.

not. Its proletarian outlook, characteristic of the Warners studio, changes its familiar elements. The things people say, who they are in the first place, what they need, and even the subjects of the songs—the familiar has been rendered so real it's strange. *42nd Street* spawned a series of backstage musicals allied with Depression attitudes to the extent that a successful opening night is no longer an event of gathered glamor but of mass employment. "Two hundred people!" Baxter cries, rallying Keeler just before she goes on. "Two hundred jobs!" And he hands down the famous command, half shopgirl's dream and half egalitarian imperative: "You're going out there a youngster, but you've *got* to come back a star!"

Keeler does, which might seem to throw *42nd Street* off its realistic axis. She's certainly pretty, and if her true-life identity as Al Jolson's new bride carried an interest to *42nd Street*'s first audiences not shared by *Pretty Lady*'s, still she does have that freshness Daniels mentions. Her singing, however, is less than passable and her dancing, though excellent in its speed and power, is sometimes ungainly. Worst of all, she appears to have no conception of language. When she has to deliver two sentences in a row, she sometimes glides right over the break between them as if the words were an incantation in an occult tongue. But in the end the uniquely charming Keeler's replacing the meticulously expert Daniels is not a mistake, because the Warners backstagers see Broadway not so much as the pinnacle of show biz as its foundation. Broadway is where you start—Hollywood is where you finish, though this is never mentioned, to avoid wrecking the illusion of the Broadway success as the happy ending. If we were to root for the most *talented* character, then *42nd Street* is a tragedy: Daniels doesn't go on, even if she does apparently end up with lover Brent, which is fine with her. We root, rather, for the most pleasant character, the one with the open, determined rightness. Admittedly, Keeler can't portray this for us. But she doesn't need to: she has it naturally.

So it is the personality, the racy efficiency, of *42nd Street* that makes it different. But more: its musical numbers accord with the overall tone, besides setting up Berkeley's geometric spectacles of a theme multiplied into countless interchangeable variations. He gets four numbers to stage, not counting the garland thing which presumably is dropped in rehearsal, and the quartet builds gradually in size and impact, stopping just this side of epic—that would come a few months later in *Gold Diggers of 1933*. The first of the four, "You're Getting to Be a Habit With Me," staged midway through the film during a dress rehearsal, is simple: Daniels, a bench, four men in sweaters, and a Father Time figure who comes out to sing the final line and truck off with Daniels. Later, the last three numbers come all together on opening night. "Shuffle Off to Buffalo" is presented as it might look on a real stage, featuring one special effect when the end of a train jack-knifes open to show a sleeping car in cross-section. The lyric expresses banal honeymooners' plans, but composer Harry Warren and lyricist Al Dubin fell right in with the general air of naiveté mixed with cynicism, so Merkel and Rogers, chomping on fruit in an upper berth, offer a burlesque second chorus of the song, involving the "well-known traveling man," the farmer's daughter, their shotgun wedding, and a Reno divorce; at one point, Rogers charges into the word "belly" only to change it to "tummy." The vulgarity is so correct for the film that it defines the number better than the prancing of the honeymoon couple (Keeler and Clarence Nordstrum) or the pantomime of a porter falling asleep as he shines shoes.

Berkeley is known not only for his imaginative layouts, but for how his camera picked them up, and the third number, "Young and Healthy," plays around with odd angles, both from overhead and underfoot—literally so at the end, when Berkeley pans around the lip of his three-tiered revolve beneath the girls' legs for a close-up of Powell and a blonde resting supine. Berkeley's great invention was filming dance from a dancing camera, taking part in his own action. "Young and Healthy" is staged as it might be in a theatre, only we see it more variously than a theatre audience could. In the finale, "42nd Street," however, Berkeley steps out of the theatre somewhat. Here again, Warren and Dubin come up with a song as hard-hearted as it is fun-loving, pitched in a minor key to suggest the sinister Tenderloin, "where the underworld can meet the elite." As Berkeley stages it, New York is a ceaseless dance whose drive impels crimes of passion and contemplation, numbers runners and players, shoeshine boys and "little nifties from the Fifties," secrets and headlines. Keeler launches it, tapping on what is revealed to be a limousine taxicab; the dancers take over as the set expands to beyond theatre proportions, and Powell surveys the scene from a second-floor window, bootleg hooch in hand. Now occurs the strongest indication so far of what was to come from Berkeley, as files of dancers line up on a broad stairway carrying dark patterns. When they fill the view, they turn—and vanish behind the patterns, cardboard cutouts of the New York skyline. A center aisle between them dissolves into the projection of a skyscraper, and Berkeley flies up to its summit, where Powell and Keeler grin delightedly. It makes a good finish—but Bacon has one last picture in mind, that of

Baxter watching wearily as ritzy first-nighters leave the theatre. It's strangely downbeat, but then the crescendo of noise and motion in the three closing numbers has given us too much of a lift, perhaps, floated us high on the electricity of entertainment. "The big parade goes on for years," Powell has sung from his eyrie over the town. "It's the rhapsody of laughter and tears." Accordingly, Bacon wraps the film with his director, physically and artistically spent. After the enchantment, exhaustion.

42nd Street is often said to be a remake of an earlier Warners backstager, *On With the Show!* (1929). This could only be said by someone who has not seen them both. *42nd Street* follows *Pretty Lady* from auditions through rehearsals to opening night of the Philadelphia tryout, showing little of the show itself until the final reels, to concentrate on how its characters live outside the theatre. *On With the Show!* (which derives from a different source in the first place) happens entirely in the theatre in which *The Phantom Sweetheart* is playing, on a Broadway-or-bust Saturday night in an unnamed city, and has no equivalent for any of *42nd Street*'s characters. *Pretty Lady* is a weird piece, fun with a bite; *The Phantom Sweetheart* on the other hand is utterly conventional, one of Hollywood's few attempts to duplicate the Broadway style. An updated "plantation show," the tale of a young man who falls in love with a veiled goddess on the eve of his wedding to another, it has the hurdy-gurdy opening chorus, the pointless dance specialties, and the idiotic storyline that American musical comedy was in the process of retiring, while *Pretty Lady*'s numbers are one-of-a-kind oddities. Larry Ceballos' *On With the Show!* choreography is amusing but stupid, and Harry Akst and Grant Clarke's score is too willing to engage the available Broadway clichés (as in "Lift the Juleps to Your Two Lips") whereas *42nd Street*'s Busby Berkeley and Warren–Dubin team distills the sense of Broadway through cinematic conceptions. Furthermore, Robert Lord's *On With the Show!* script is quaint even for 1929, whereas *42nd Street* has dated only in its slang.

Even the two casts, separated by a mere four years, tell how different the two works are: *42nd Street*'s mix of old hands (Baxter, Daniels, Brent) and newcomers (Keeler, Powell, Rogers) shows prudent observation of film's ability to "sell" certain personalities. *Everyone* in this cast plays successfully not just as an actor but as a person. Baxter has the command and the desperation of a famous showman who may be terminally ill. Daniels truly seems the talented star who's tiring of the stage. Brent is the perfect third-rater, Keeler *the* youngster, and so on. Next to them, *On With the Show!*'s gang is a lot of bad news from the

west. Only Ethel Waters comes through—and she plays herself, singing two songs, "Am I Blue?" and "Birmingham Bertha," on the fringe
of the stage while the stagehands ready the next big set behind her.
Arthur Lake, *The Phantom Sweetheart*'s juvenile, can do nothing right
but whine. Joe E. Brown, *The Phantom Sweetheart*'s comedian, isn't,
not this time out. Star Betty Compson, dubbed behind her veil, producer Sam Hardy, hat-check girl Sally O'Neil, usher William
Bakewell, and gold digger Louise Fazenda are hampered by a weak
script and Alan Crosland's weak direction, which says everything
twice in slow motion. O'Neil provides *On With the Show!*'s one discernible link with *42nd Street* in that she goes on in the veil when
Compson refuses to play her last scenes, but the little bit we see O'Neil
do is enough to conclude a performance, not make her a star.

This comparison between 1929 and 1933 shows how far the film
musical had come. Technical defects in sound reproduction and camera movement cut *On With the Show!* into two parts, picturefilm and
soundtrack; we can't make out the words when the chorus sings, and
when Waters finishes "Birmingham Bertha" she ad libs a parting shot
at the audience that doesn't turn up on the audio portion, leaving a
foolish pantomime. *42nd Street* has no such problems. *On With the
Show!* also comes from the two-strip Technicolor days—it was the first
all-color sound feature—and has the patronizing insecurity of that
time when musicals were being milled like product, without imagination. *42nd Street* belongs to a more structured time. It, too, was product, but one manufactured by specialists. *On With the Show!* can't
figure out how to make music without taking it from Broadway; *42nd
Street* loves New York but doesn't trust it, and hears its own sweeter
melodies. In 1929, the musical film is shouting blind. Four years later,
it has been tamed and taught where to look.

Another point: *42nd Street* located the naturalistic style that the
musical needed to complement the airier art of operetta. The latter,
whether Lubitschian satire or the-student-prince-meets-the-goosegirl,
plumes itself on extramusical values and escapism. Modern-dress musical comedy prefers less definitively musical pop tunes and an everyday directness. Operetta will survive into the 1950s (and occasionally
thereafter, in such instances as *The Slipper and the Rose* and *A Little
Night Music*), but the *42nd Street* model will predominate. The model
is flexible. It leans to vernacular guts in the 1930s and to patriotic nostalgia during World War II, and seeks out an odd hybrid realism in
period costume in the late 1940s. With its contradictory elements of
zip and tension, *42nd Street* has created a rich and influential form.

☆ 4 ☆

The First Stars

IF THE MUSICAL as form at first baffled the studios, marketing techniques did not. Eager to amass a pool of talent who through PR manipulation would consolidate an audience for their work on an indefinitely self-renewing schedule, producers cast their first musicals in a kind of flash-forward in time. They knew where they wanted to end up but not where to start.

Counting the part-talkie *The Jazz Singer* as the start, they lucked into something exactly right, for the time being. Al Jolson was the essential stage entertainer, helpless without his spontaneity and intercommunication with a responding public; but this very life force made Jolson's screen debut and the debut of story sound a sensation. Sound exacted its condition of film—fantasy is dead—and Jolson, with his ad libs and lack of polish, was as real as they come. He called himself "the world's greatest entertainer," got his friends to publicize the notion, and it caught on. He wasn't the world's greatest anything, but he fascinated because his image—he was nothing but an image, playing it in every role—was so ambiguous. He is hardly good-looking, yet he does well with women. He prances and minces in an uptempo number, yet he is all man, very believable in his hunger for sex, gambling, and booze. He is irreverent, yet ballads bring out a flood of bathos. Nothing in his parts suggests anything ethnic, yet he continually inserts Jewish jokes and occasionally even an obscure phrase in Yiddish. In a business where almost everyone was a type, Jolson was a riddle.

Everything he does is so unforced, however, that one suffers no frustrating mystery watching his films. Jolson is, typically, a man in one of the "unsettled" professions (a singer, a nightclub owner, a jockey) mixed up in some shady business (murder enters into at least four of his films), who loves either his mother or his little son with a gargantuan trembling heart, and who best expresses himself in singing, especially in blackface. The clichés work because Jolson obviously lays so much importance on them. No one else would have wanted to come out in the overstated black makeup and costume to clutch a straw hat and put so much into "Let Me Sing and I'm Happy" (which cites as utopian lyrical references "Dixie's charms," "mountain fields" and "Mammy's arms") and follow this minutes later with "(I'm everything to my) Mammy," as Jolson did in *Mammy* (1930). He sang in the old vaudeville "sell it!" style that had already fallen out of fashion, replaced by a more evenly leveled belt or the radio croon, and he adds words, scants notes, and sometimes rewrites whole melodies. But he adds to a song's spirit—no, to *his* spirit. All Jolson material was by process of performance transformed into a component of Jolson.

Which returns us to who he was. His incessant blackface routines suggest an ambivalent sense of identity as much as his nervous laughter and momentary escapes into arcane Jewish references. In *Say It With Songs* (1929), Jolson is a radio singer approached by distributors of the Excelsior automobile, who want something special for their radio show. Jolson mockingly suggests a theme song, "Excelsior, I Love You." The businessmen have something else in mind, along the lines of "I'm Going to Smother My Mother With Kisses When I Get Back to My Home in Tennessee." "Let's see," says Jolson. "How would it be if he said, 'I'll Smother My Father in Gedaemfte Rinderbrust* When I Get Back to Odessa'?" *Say It With Songs* finds Jolson in prison, cutting into his time for donning the black, but he played all of *Bigboy* (1930) as a Negro, and made this transracial turn the big moment in his films wherever possible. Why? The blackface tradition, like Jolson's overacted vocals, was outdated by 1930. It grew out of the segregated acting troupes of the 1800s (when whites went on in the outlandish makeup or couldn't have played a decent *Uncle Tom's Cabin*), and fell out of use when black performers such as Bert Williams

---

*Pot Roast. *Say It With Songs*, looking back at *The Singing Fool*'s phenomenal profits, brought little Davey Lee back to life as Jolson's kid, called Little Pal—so was the movie, until just before release. For all Jolson's spoof of the theme song craze, he plugs *Say it With Songs*' theme, "Little Pal," with fanatic abandon. "Doesn't my Daddy thing thway-yull?" lisps little Davey, an ear on the radio and an eye on the invisible millions in the theatres. I'll say: a recording of "Little Pal"—and a double-exposed vision of Daddy Jolson—brings back the child's voice, lost traumatically in an auto accident.

and Ethel Waters broke the color bar on Broadway's main stages. It can't be a coincidence that the best-known of the last bigtime black-face performers were largely Jewish; possibly they were having a joke at the expense of white Christian audiences, doubling their own outcast status in contempt for bigotry mingled with self-abnegation. Nowhere is this double identity more acute than in Jolson. His cantor's son in *The Jazz Singer,* culturally assimilated yet possessive of old-world ties, was an odd character to preside over the launching of a new phase of American film. But possibly the Warner brothers, also Jewish, suffered the same problems of identity. Is Jolson Jakie Rabinowitz or Jack Robin? Throughout his career, he kept the question open, and thus maintained a now vigorous, now tenuous hold on the public: they thought him exciting, yet tired of him at intervals.

When Jolson was at his peak of popularity in Hollywood, in 1928, Warners attempted to follow him up with a chip of what they presumed was the same block, specifically the Lower East Side comic-singing establishment. But Fanny Brice was different from Jolson in style, more continually Jewish in inflection, and less outgoing, though no less giving, in song. Not remotely good-looking, Brice made an unlikely romantic heroine, but in the aforementioned *My Man* she won, lost, and won him (Guinn Williams) back, and in her first all-sound musical *Be Yourself* (1930) she did it again as a nightclub singer who manages a boxer (Robert Armstrong). Boxer strays, Brice sets him up to lose a championship fight (by coaching his opponent to smash Armstrong's proud new nose job), boxer comes back chastened. It was too much like *My Man*, though it did give Brice her first chance to play a character whole, through serious and comic dialogue as well as through her amazing versatility in serious and comic songs. In her opening spot, "When a Woman Loves a Man," she is still in the flirting stage with Armstrong, and plays her number to him from the nightclub floor. In "Cooking Breakfast for the One I Love" she does just that while he reads the paper and she examines the bacon with her google-eyed grin. In her last number, "When a Gal Cares for a Man," a torch-carrying complement to "When a Woman Loves a Man," she gives it all she's got yet underplays, so that we lean into the song rather than have it mashed into us, Jolson-style.

Brice was too special. *Be Yourself* is an apt title, for as Fannie Field, Brice is herself in all but the final "y" in her first name. She was a lot for Hollywood to take, aggressive and only reluctantly vulnerable. She couldn't faint or twinkle like her woman colleagues, and in a business run by men she must have seemed natural in a troublesome way: subversive. "Just another movie," *Photoplay* called it. Anything but. Just another movie in which a heroine of unconventional appeal creates a formidable character—likeable but not to be challenged—who attracts us despite the pedestrian script and supporting cast. *Be Yourself*'s failure, however, is ultimately not one of material. Nor can one blame the director, Thornton Freeland. A capable storyteller, he cuts from a shot of Brice and Armstrong lazing around to the same shot—with Brice replaced by her successor in Armstrong's love life. And he shoots part of Brice's big torch song from Armstrong's table, letting Armstrong and his new girl, cooing at each other, frame Brice, a dim figure in the distance. *Be Yourself*'s obstacle, unfortunately, was Brice. No, the obstacle is Hollywood's narrow world view. How can it make use of the most gifted performers when their very gifts render them too eccentric to adhere to the set, or still setting, code?

Absorbing eastern stage talent was a tricky business; better to ride on already flowing tides of cinema personality, if possible. But such was the level of panic when sound was thrown into production that not all possibilities were scouted. Through wasteful pep, studios tested some stars for sound and singing but not others. Or they successfully piloted a silent star through debuts in first a talkie and then a musical—and suddenly, mysteriously, dropped the whole thing. Ironically, the most successful talkie-singie debut belonged to Bebe Daniels, whose studio, Paramount, had written her off without a test when sound came in. Daniels sold the remainder of her contract to RKO, suggested herself for the title role in *Rio Rita*, and walked off with one of the big critical and popular successes of the year. Daniels' singing voice was not all that superior to those of her colleagues, but it had a wide range that enabled her to switch from high soprano to Broadway belt. She had trained well, somehow getting down not only the rudiments of vocal projection but a detailed understanding of musical theatre styles as well. In *Rio Rita* she is all passion and high notes, as befits the character; in *42nd Street,* she is down to earth, the New York pro at ease on her turf. Janet Gaynor could have sung "You're Getting to Be a Habit With Me," but not with Daniels' confidence, nor could she have brought it off "on stage" dancing and clowning the way Daniels does.

As with Daniels, John Boles' and Walter Pidgeon's careers received adrenalin shots when they revealed viable singing voices. (Boles revealed several—a light baritone, he could sound higher or deeper than himself depending on what sound expert manned which mike.) Daniels' husband, Ben Lyon, also fitted nicely into musicals, though his singing was more game than accurate. There was Something in one's look, in the way one moved, in the way one dealt with comedy or pathos, that added up to a characterological dossier for musicals. Aside from the voice and, sometimes, an ability to pass in dance, actors needed that Something, and if producers didn't know what to call it, they thought they knew what it was. Neglecting to strive for pace, art direction, musical editing, or any of the many factors that film depends on, producers put everything into casting, looking for Something to build a genre on.

Before *42nd Street* articulated the musical's latent qualities of cynicism, human inconsistency, self-belief, and ribald facetiae, the ideal Something ran to a pliant virility in men and a crumply cuteness in women. This is why *The Show of Shows* seems so wrong, with its Frank Fay and Irene Bordoni, and why *Paramount on Parade* seems so right, with its Chevalier and Nancy Carroll. It was not a question of talent. Fay, in the right role, carried whole plays and films on sheer personality, and, in the realm of womanly give, Bordoni was the goods. It was a question of what most Americans wanted to see and also of what producers thought they wanted—not necessarily the same thing. Especially after 1934, when the Joseph Breen office put the Production Code into effect, a lot of the rich character of humankind— the real-life Something—was outlawed on the screen. This meant a smoothing down of some people's interesting edges and an implementation of supposed universal American attitudes that turned people into genres—good-hearted loose women, strong-hearted men, tolerant, passively long-suffering good women, strong but selfish men who go bad; one collection for crime drama, one for backstagers, one for society comedy, and so on.

Even before 1934, however, producers sought a code for painting personality in a limited number of colors—the code was the Something. The status quo for the American male was set by Buddy (nominally Charles) Rogers in his medium-dark, unthreatening handsomeness, easy singing style, and walkaround nonchalance. Rogers was the sort of man who looks comfortable in a bowtie and doesn't take art so seriously that drama utterly subsumes him. Women thought him cute and men liked him. Hollywood tried to coach several would-be Buddy Rogerses, but the model could not be readily copied.

Then try other models; find Something. Hollywood imported eastern talents by the trainload, but the studios weren't always able to fit these diverse people into workable forms. As a musical hero, for instance, Lawrence Tibbett was wonderfully powerful but right only in extravaganza roles; his operatic *confrère* Everett Marshall was a dud in anything, but especially in *Dixiana* (1930) with Bebe Daniels; Stanley Smith looked pallid even in college musicals; Rudy Vallee, hauled in from radio for *The Vagabond Lover* (1929), seemed completely out of his depth; Harry Richman in *Puttin' on the Ritz* (1930) revealed too much of the New York slick; Lawrence Gray had a toneless singing voice and the same last name as Alexander Gray, a grand singer a little short on acting charm. Both Grays turned up in *Spring Is Here* (1930), an adaptation of a Rodgers and Hart show (with all but two of the original songs dropped) that could stand as a textbook case in the pre-*42nd Street* musical: silly, simple middle-class plot, breezy girl– and boyfriends, and dignified theme song (by Harry Warren, Sam Lewis, and Joe Young), "Have a Little Faith in Me." *42nd Street*'s city hustle swept this all away, but until it did, searches for Something led up some odd alleys while refusing to take some highly promising roads. Ethel Merman should have been just what Hollywood needed, and she came along at the right time, turning instant Broadway star in the Gershwins' *Girl Crazy* in 1930 for her *con blasto* vocals, no-fault diction, and all-around gutsy allure. But Merman's early film roles were all supporting parts as scheming molls or screwball friends, and failed to exploit her remarkable instrument. She got onscreen as early as 1930, in the Ed Wynn vehicle *Follow the Leader*, and made a cute short called *Roaming* (1931) as a romantic waif in a medicine show, singing "Shake Well Before Using" and "Hello, My Lover, Goodbye." But Hollywood had no place for a waif with a voice as big as a small country. Merman's stage roles defined her as a brassy dame who cried for men but didn't turn gooey at the sight of them, and her great parts had to be toned down for film to such an extent that Merman was no longer right for them. Except for her Reno Sweeney in *Anything Goes* and her Sally Adams in *Call Me Madam*, all Merman's parts went to others in the film versions—Ann Sothern got *Panama Hattie*, Lucille Ball *DuBarry Was a Lady*, Betty Hutton (replacing Judy Garland) *Annie Get Your Gun*, Rosalind Russell Mama Rose in *Gypsy*. They never gave Merman a chance; as early as 1932, when *Girl Crazy* was filmed, Kitty Kelly was playing what was left of Merman's part, even singing Merman's big tune, "I Got Rhythm."

On the other hand, Paramount tried to mold Lillian Roth, a singer not unlike Merman, into a heroine with suitable Something. It never panned out. In her extremely short French maid's skirt in *The Love Parade*, Roth wears a simper when looking on MacDonald and Chevalier's romance and an assortment of leers when pushing fellow servant

Lupino Lane around—she seems to be two different people. In *Paramount on Parade*, she delivers "Any Time's the Time to Fall in Love" with Buddy Rogers and a chorus, and does achieve an ingenue's melting agreeability, except when the choreography has her (and the girls) bullying Rogers (and the boys). She also sings in a pleasant high register Broadway belters don't normally have access to. So far, Roth is potential. But in *Honey* (1930), as a fun-loving heiress, Roth must look conventionally fetching, which she doesn't, and in *The Vagabond King* she looks rather lost as Huguette, a fun-loving prostitute whose numbers call for a fuller sound than Roth's. Where Merman was left out of the right roles, Roth was cast in the wrong ones.

Marilyn Miller, the epitome of Broadway's idea of ingenue Something, had no casting problems—two of her three film roles were hers from Broadway originals, and the third was more or less suitable. But her famous elfin charm, so lovely from the fifth row across an orchestra pit, dwindled on screen into a crazy grin and, for a dancer, some bizarre ideas on posture. First National's accountants, surveying the take on Miller's three films, must have thought Broadway mad—what was it that Miller was supposed to have? But this trio was hardly the stuff on which a career is built. *Sally* (1929) is a reckless spectacle, *Sunny* (1930) a small musical with almost no music, and *Her Majesty Love* (1931) confusedly European in feeling.

In *Her Majesty Love* Miller plays a waitress at the Berlin Cabaret, courted by playboy heir Ben Lyon. His snobbish relations come between them and Miller has to marry titled roué Leon Errol before Lyon can win her back—before her wedding night, of course. (A twist ending: his family had made him sign an agreement not to wed Lia Toerreck—Miller—but made no mention of the Baroness von Schwarzdorf, which she has just become.) Director William Dieterle does some nice things pictorially, as when Lyon decides to forget his troubles in Venice and the office papers he scatters in the air turn into the pigeons of St. Mark's Square. But an insistently continental gleam in the proceedings leads one to expect the imminent entrance of Lya de Putti or a consort of *Ländler* dancers. Even W. C. Fields, playing Miller's father, has been affected, almost transformed. In a moustache and attempting a German accent (luckily only in his first few lines), Fields does what he can to lift the tempo, horrifying Lyon's relations by juggling their plates at a fancy dinner and repeatedly referring to Miller's obsequious husband as "Bar*on*" in his characteristic vacant growl. And Miller does have one good moment when she shows up at a banquet of the Lyon clan, tells them off, and overturns their laden table. The lesson is one of Hollywood's favorites: the working class has vitality and only democratically minded plutocrats (like Lyon) are interesting. But the one thing that Miller certainly could do—dance—she never does once in the whole film, except for a routine, nonexhibition tango with Lyon.

Something was elusive, yet some had it to spare. Among the men, Maurice Chevalier easily led the ranks in the romantic class, his Gallic flavor coming across in the midst of the typical American strong, shy silence as a natural hot, emphasized in the roles and songs written for him. He seemed to toss off his love plots to conserve energy for singing: head lolling, lips swimming, arms beating out the rhythm. John Gilbert was not so much hot as flaming; Chevalier brought the great lover syndrome into the perspective of sound, setting his own terms for type and defeating the character code Hollywood was trying to institute. If he hadn't been unique, the studios might have pinned their code on him, for his films were immensely successful, even in the post-1929 musical slump. But he was unique, and after he departed the scene in the mid-1930s, the studios got deeply into genre; one can speak of an Alice Faye musical, a Shirley Temple musical, a Danny Kaye musical, or a Doris Day musical and be reasonably clear on a host of set variables from costuming and costars to quality of score and direction. But the musical's first years, predating the studio codes, offer a welcome diversity in their floundering.

Chevalier, in a way, inspired his own genre at Paramount: risqué romantic comedies with strong scores and delectable leading women. He had first tested for MGM, in Paris, when Irving Thalberg and Norma Shearer caught his act at the Casino de Paris, where he sang some of his numbers in a heavily accented but comprehensible English. Negotiations collapsed, but a few weeks later Paramount chief Jesse Lasky screened the test and closed a deal. Chevalier's debut as a singing junkman in *Innocents of Paris* (1929) put him over in second-rate material, and the much better succeeding films placed him to general satisfaction. The protruding lower lip, the commentative eyes and nose, the explosive consonants, the poise under fire, and the dash in courtship were not only different from what all other screen heroes had, but were more correct, artistically, for what the musical—Paramount's musicals, anyway—could use. Lawrence Tibbett invaded a song, John Boles comforted it. Chevalier attended it as if it were a party in his honor. His "That's the Song of Paree" that opens *Love Me Tonight* captures a wonderful bemusement containing both affection and irritation; his "Mimi" is nothing less than a seduction on promise, and it

☆ *STAGE STARS IN HOLLYWOOD: clockwise from above left: the one true Jolson as* The Jazz Singer; *Guinn Williams confronts the perhaps even truer Fanny Brice in* My Man; *Joe E. Brown at the fights (with Winnie Lightner) in* Hold Everything; *Marilyn Miller (with Lawrence Gray) in* Sunny. *Miller alone repeats a stage role she created.*

won't take long; his "The Poor Apache" spoofs the brutal lover yet respects the need his brutality fulfills; his share in "Love Me Tonight," even after he knows he has won MacDonald, is earnestly playful, almost two different versions of the song in one chorus. So what if he often fell flat of a note or revised a high-running melody to fit his limited range? No one else sang half as well or had as much fun in his parts. In *Paramount on Parade* he crashes into the second verse of "All I Want Is Just One Girl" a whole beat behind the orchestra, but his joy is so telling that one must forgive him. Chevalier is so into it that even when he looks right into the camera and addresses the audience—which he does in several pictures—he retains his character.

He had good luck in his directors, writers, and costars, not least in Jeanette MacDonald, in what might be termed her negligée phase because of the views of her getting into and out of bed that thronged her early operettas. A Broadway veteran but not yet a star, MacDonald got only featured billing with Chevalier, but without him, more prominently billed, she found herself in lackluster events such as the shipwreck farce *Let's Go Native* (1930) or Rudolf Friml's operetta *The Lottery Bride* (1930), with characters named Jilda, Nels, Olaf, and Boris, and MacDonald in blond pigtails. Some of her early films had few or no songs at all and drew only on her comic talents—good enough, but this is a fraction of MacDonald. Her beauty was perfect for the times, a svelte redhead look and an endless supply of pouts and smiles. But her voice was her glory, and it never sounded better than in duet with Chevalier, precisely because the two instruments did not match. His was that of a *diseur*, who delivers everything verbally; hers, that of an opera diva, every word a note. He was earthy, she sumptuous—but he was suave as well, and she had It; they met not at the center, but at the edges. In *The Love Parade* they love at first sight, in *One Hour With You* they are married, in *Love Me Tonight* she at first resists him. So in their last picture together—the first in which her name joined his above the title—he has to resist her. This was *The Merry Widow* (1934), Ernst Lubitsch's last completed musical and a fitting third masterpiece to match his *The Love Parade* and Mamoulian's *Love Me Tonight*. Franz Léhar's original was completely revamped with a new plot and lyrics—new not only compared to Adrian Ross' translation, then traditional on English-speaking stages, but offering entirely new ideas on character. The original premise survives: as the widow controls so much of the property in her Ruritanian homeland, she must quickly be married to a native, the womanizing Captain (formerly Count) Danilo. The ensuing romance takes in not only the original's

Paris but Lubitsch's finely extracted middle Europe. The credits set the tone: a magnifying glass hovers over a map of Europe, trying to locate Marshovia. When it does, the film bursts into a synopsis of the love story in a single moment: Chevalier leads marching Marshovian troops in "Girls, Girls, Girls" as village lasses call out his name in a thrill . . . and a glowering carriage passes by with a veiled woman inside, mourning her late husband. Chevalier and MacDonald cross paths at first, at last, again, forever.

Many feel *The Merry Widow* is their best collaboration, but it turns out that Chevalier wanted Grace Moore as the Widow. He had switched over to MGM from Paramount. So had MacDonald, but Chevalier felt a little uncomfortable with her, finding her temperate demeanor something of a down. (For her part, MacDonald later referred to Chevalier as "the fastest derrière pincher in Hollywood.") Moore's life-loving ways would be more fun to work with; moreover, Chevalier resented the implication that he and MacDonald were a team. But Moore, just back in film after a smashing comeback in *One Night of Love*, wanted top billing and that was that. MGM considered Joan Crawford, Lily Pons, and Vivienne Segal among others, but Thalberg pressed MacDonald on Chevalier. With Ernest Vajda and Samson Raphaelson to handle the book and Gus Kahn and Lorenz Hart to write the new lyrics, MGM had one of the spiffiest entries of the decade. Interestingly, the lyricists suppressed the playful and sardonic strains that respectively distinguished them in musical comedy, adapting themselves to Lubitsch's special view of operetta as fleshly romanticism. Remember, MacDonald, like Chevalier, has self-satire; only later, with Nelson Eddy, was she to become the Iron Butterfly, tense with profile and unyielding in duet. Lubitsch brought out the elf in her. In *The Love Parade*, staring down her matchmaking Cabinet, she pulls up her skirt and, as Lubitsch pulls in with a view of her well-turned left leg, announces, "There's only one other leg like that in the whole of Sylvania." She displays her other leg: ". . . And that's it." But to make the vivacious MacDonald believable, operetta must show also the vulnerable MacDonald. All her best roles do. *The Love Parade* had given us "Dream Lover" to complete MacDonald's file; in *The Merry Widow*, her most ravishing moment is "Tonight Will Teach Me to Forget," drawn from a duet, "Sieh dort den kleinen Pavillon," that is sung in the show by two supporting characters. The melody, updated as a fox trot, ripples with arabesques, and MacDonald sings it with winsome resignation, a lonely widow whose marriage was of such little import that we learn virtually nothing about it. "Today only taught me to regret," she sadly admits, letting a violin solo weep for her, and then prepares to close her "book of dreams . . . and forget." But ho! Not long after, to propulsive variations on Léhar, the widow finds a purpose in life. "Get everything ready!" she tells her maid. "We're going to Paris! Tomorrow! Tomorrow morning! As soon as possible." She tosses her head. "There's a limit," she observes, "to every widow."

Less rich environments than these called for less highly embellished persons. Who would play, say, the lovable day-to-day girl that modern-dress musical comedy requires? The odds-on favorite was Nancy Carroll, a fine actress of healthy sweetness who could sing adequately and dance a little better than that—a natural complement to Buddy Rogers. Carroll alone made the insipid, darkly photographed *Honey* (1930) bearable, as a southern girl who rents her house to a vacationing northern family and poses as the live-in maid, with her brother as butler. (This was the film that tried to make an ingenue of Lillian Roth; with Carroll around, Roth hadn't a chance.) A farce that never hits tempo, *Honey* throws in anything to get a laugh, but on its tiny budget there is little to grab. Jobyna Howland plays Roth's snooty mother, Skeets Gallagher Carroll's brother (to court Roth), Stanley Smith Carroll's vis-à-vis, Harry Green a Jewish hanger-on with little charm, ZaSu Pitts a tearful cook, and little Mitzi Green Pitts' bratty daughter. Most of the film takes place in Carroll's house. Suddenly, director Wesley Ruggles takes us to a black jamboree for the film's one production number, "Sing You Sinners," in which Mitzi displays her precocious vocal heft. This is not enough to enliven a dead film. Even Carroll begins to sink after a while, and one ceases to wonder why her career bogged down in mid-decade. Entries like *Honey* murdered her.

In the early 1930s, both MacDonald and Carroll were Paramount girls, demonstrating the considerable character range of the time; and Marlene Dietrich, a third Paramount contractee, blows that range wide. Dietrich's first six American films, five directed by Joseph von Sternberg and one by Rouben Mamoulian, are in no sense musicals, but most of them feature Dietrich in a few songs and are sometimes thought to have influenced musical staging in their erotic approach to the nightclub specialty. It can't be disputed that Dietrich's famous delivery of "Falling in Love Again" in her last German film (also with von Sternberg), *The Blue Angel*, inspired Bob Fosse and Liza Minnelli in her "Mein Herr" number in *Cabaret*, for if Minnelli gambols on her chair with a mania where Dietrich simply toyed with hers, and if Fosse's Groszlike Kit Kat Club is not as unnerving as von Sternberg's more odiously banal Blue Angel, still the two numbers are much alike.

But how influential could the von Sternberg Dietrich be for the American musical, with her mannish outfits and opaque sexuality? In *Morocco* (1930), Dietrich sings the raunchy waltz "What Am I Bid for My Apples?" as a bored Eve, dispensing forbidden fruit to the customers, tasting a man's champagne and his date's lips, taking a flower from her and tossing it to a bored legionnaire (Gary Cooper). They don't stay bored long. Not even Chevalier and MacDonald burned the screen the way Dietrich did—and in *Blonde Venus* (1932), playing a housewife who returns to the nightclub stage to finance her husband's treatments for radiation poisoning, Dietrich begins "Hot Voodoo" to pounding jungle drums in a gorilla suit. The song was the work of studio writers Ralph Rainger and Sam Coslow, but when Dietrich sings "All night long I don't know wight fwom wong," we are hurled far out of the naive idiom in which, just for example, Coslow wrote the words to *Honey*'s "Sing You Sinners."

Dietrich was billed as "the woman all women want to see," if only to learn what stupendously meticulous lighting can do for what was already a once-in-a-lifetime face. The musical sequences in her film were not, in the end, influential; no musical could contain such fatal hedonism. Dietrich is useful here in pointing up the film musical's sensual limitations: it moved from MacDonaldlike fairy princesses with resilient but not unchartable libidos to next-door sweethearts like Nancy Carroll. That left a lot of room, but it was as far as the musical could go. Later, gathering Alice Faye, Betty Grable, Deanna Durbin, and Judy Garland at its center, it would not go even that far.

The men had more latitude, as they did in the culture at the time, especially the comedians, who could take or leave the otherwise obligatory love plot. Jack Oakie actually seemed happier when he didn't get the girl, and Joe E. Brown, a large-mouthed acrobat whose films reveled in athletic settings (he had been a baseball player in a former life) in which Brown would be mistaken for a champion or otherwise lured into getting himself half killed, screamed and yelled more naturally than he kissed. When Brown "stole" Bert Lahr's Broadway part in the adaptation of *Hold Everything* (1930), he drew heavy fire, mainly from Lahr, but in truth this role of a punchy boxer was right up Brown's roller coaster—though giving him Winnie Lightner to play the romance to only underlined Hollywood's confusion as to how best to cast essentially comic personalities.

Eddie Cantor's vehicles institutionalized the comic musical better than those of other comics, not least because Cantor's were among the few musicals to show a steady profit in the slump years. Short and thin, the excitable type, Cantor fell into Chaplin's underdog-outwits-bullies mode, but in verbal patterns. Cantor was something like an uncluttered Jolson, and like him made no attempt to resist the odd Jewish joke when the mood struck him. But where Jolson sublimated his talmudic wail in blackface bathos, Cantor expressed his more discreetly yet more lightheartedly, moaning and cringing when cornered by his enemies in traps we know he's bound to spring out of, singing of how his girl could do a lot better but loves him anyway, and citing instances of his worthlessness, as when in *Roman Scandals* he loses his position as the emperor's food taster: "I'm a failure. I can't even keep a job as a slave." Strongly in Cantor's favor was his collaboration with the independent producer Samuel Goldwyn, for Goldwyn gave Cantor lavish budgets and smart supporting talent. The six Cantor–Goldwyn films make up a kind of series, all featuring Cantor more or less playing himself in some alien setting, eluding menaces, slipping into blackface, and closing in a wild slapstick melee. At intervals, the irrelevant but superb Goldwyn Girls hang around, have a parade, or dance. Cantor's rolling eyes and flibberty hands, clapping at the merest scent of terror or joy, counted among the least irritating of all comedians' mannerisms, and the similarity of one film to another didn't seem to hurt them. In *Whoopee!* (1930) he is Henry Williams, out west for a rest cure; in *Palmy Days* (1931) his Eddie Simpson is plagued by Charlotte Greenwood and hired thugs; in *The Kid From Spain* (1932) Eddie Williams flees a gang of bank robbers south of the border; *Roman Scandals* (1933) puts yet another Eddie, dreaming, in old Rome and wakes him with a blow on the head during a mad chariot race; *Kid Millions* (1934) is Eddie Wilson, Jr., an heir at loose ends in Egypt and back home opening up a mammoth ice-cream parlor in an inserted color sequence dominated by Cantor's extremely green top hat; and *Strike Me Pink* (1936) closed the set with Eddie Pink running an amusement park, getting stuck high up in a Ferris wheel, and eluding gangsters disguised as Keystone Kops.* Throughout, Goldwyn's thriftless approach to moviemaking kept the decor eye-filling, the material top-notch, and the performers worthy of the material. But it was Cantor that made it go with his vivid hysteria and likeable horniness (some of

---

*Cantor took the serviceable format with him when he moved to Twentieth Century-Fox for *Ali Baba Goes to Town* (1937): dream adventure in a dangerous place (ancient Araby), harem girls, blackface number ("Swing Is Here to Sway"), Jewish jokes, references to contemporary politics, and climactic melee (with Cantor on flying carpet).

the lyrics he sang count among the most suggestive of the day). By 1934 he was the highest-paid actor in films, earning $150,000 plus percentage points that took him to $270,000 for a single film.

Whoopee! stands out from the others because it was very closely based on a stage show, a smash Ziegfeld special that might have run as long as Cantor was willing to play it, had the producer, strapped again, not sold the property to Goldwyn, who promptly closed it and readied the cameras. For once, most of the show's cast replayed their Broadway roles; of the leads, only the ingenue, Eleanor Hunt, was new, and even she had been in the show, in the chorus. Ziegfeld himself co-produced with Goldwyn, making *Whoopee!* a historical document as a transcription of the Ziegfeld style—one of the most formative in American theatre. One thing Goldwyn and Ziegfeld had in common was big spending. An expensive film musical cost about $250,000 in 1930, but Goldwyn laid out a million, and it shows, especially in the detailed dance numbers, staged by Busby Berkeley in his first screen assignment. Feeling his way, Berkeley tries out a few of the overhead shots, the symmetrical groupings, and the slow pan of the chorus line, face upon face, that he would perfect a few years later at Warner Brothers. But mainly he had all he could do working out a cinematic replica of the complex rhythmic push he was noted for on Broadway. The Goldwyn Girls were not only dancers, but showgirls who looked fine just standing there beaming. This is where Ziegfeld came in, with his elegant promenade routines that nobody else ever got right.

Good as *Whoopee!* was on stage, some felt the film was better. Goldwyn shot in color, for one thing, and no real-life color show was ever as much fun as two-strip Technicolor. The story was tightened and the score actually improved, Walter Donaldson and Gus Kahn's originals (including "Makin' Whoopee") joined by some new gems including their own ebullient "My Baby Just Cares for Me" and the comic torch song "A Girl Friend of a Boy Friend of Mine" and Nacio Herb Brown and Edward Eliscu's "I'll Still Belong to You." With Betty Grable leading the Goldwyn Girls in a rip-roaring opening number, Ethel Shutta (in her only feature film) launching "Stetson," a hat number with much Berkeleyesque arrangements of the girls' white cowboy hats, and a better-than-average run of choral settings for wedding and Indian scenes, *Whoopee!* is a musical in its fullest sense, its only drawback being the poor quality of the sound, which makes the lyrics of the first number unintelligible even on repeated hearings. However, George Olsen and his band, another holdover from the Broadway

Whoopee!, came through most effectively with some of the most virtu-
oso playing ever recorded. Too many musicals went in for large or-
chestrations which, when fed into the track, came out all highs and
lows, woefully depleted of body. Olsen's smaller group has an insane
immediacy, its rampaging saxophone and savage banjo right in keeping with Cantor's nerve-wracked craziness.

What is most amusing about the star-comic vehicle is the utter seriousness with which the lovers and villains go about the plot business in
the face of the top banana's constant immaterial tricks. They seem not
to "get" him, as if they were frozen senseless during his lines, like the
characters in *Strange Interlude* during the interior monologues. Cantor is locked into *Whoopee!*'s action to a certain degree, as he helps a
young couple (she white and he Indian) when the girl is about to be
married to the local sheriff, and thus gets into trouble with the neighboring he-men. Yet Cantor plays around the story as well as in it, and
sometimes drops all pretense of character, as when the heroine breath-
lessly tells Cantor that she and the Indian are going to elope and en-
train east for their honeymoon. Cantor immediately chimes in—on a
tangent: "Honeymoon! That reminds me. You know, my sister's husband wanted to take her to Florida on their honeymoon, but she's
been to Florida, so she sent a girlfriend. Ha-ha, ha-*ha*!"

Truth to tell, these ad lib-like digressions had been holding the
American musical back artistically for decades. If we don't take Cantor's character seriously—and how can we, when he doesn't?—then
neither we nor the authors take the story seriously. So *Whoopee!* is resolved in nonsense: (1) the Indian turns out to have been a white
foundling raised by Indians, which removes all objections to the marriage, and (2) Cantor decides, for absolutely no reason, to cease resisting his amorous battleaxe nurse Shutta and marry her. Yet, idle as the
story is, Cantor's character does leave an impression: he is the little
guy who tames a boisterous world with subterfuge. If the plot is an
excuse for bits, the bits are choice, as when Cantor, masquerading as a
singing cook, is ordered to prove his identity to a menacing posse. "Go
on," snarls the heavy. "Let's hear ya. Now!" And with scarcely a
breath, Cantor pours himself into "My Baby Just Cares for Me," Olsen's combo pointing up his anxiety with syncopated brass notes
bumped in just after the downbeat of each phrase. Is Cantor really
anxious? The character should be, but this is a big star number, and
Cantor gives it all it needs as fun, not illumination. In the second
chorus, accompanied by a percussively swinging two-piano solo, Cantor elaborates on the theme, asserting, in a Charleston rhythm, "My

baby don't care for Lawrence Tibbetts." Why? "She'd rather have me around to *kibbitz.*" What baby? Surely not Shutta. And who, outside of a few New Yorkers, knew what *kibbitz* meant? No matter. Jolson helped Cantor instill in film the free-and-easy Broadway approach to plot, and it held on.

The personalities useful to the musical were a varied lot. But so were the musical forms themselves—Lubitschian operetta and heavy-handed operetta, collegiates and backstagers, star-comic farces and slightly comic romances all called for different voices, looks, movement. There was room for Chevalier and Cantor and Buddy Rogers, for Nancy Carroll and Jeanette MacDonald. But already, performers of undeniable talent were being found wrong by type or at best of subsidiary possibilities: Fanny Brice, Winnie Lightner, Lillian Roth, Ethel Merman, Bernice Claire, Evelyn Laye, Charlotte Greenwood, Gertrude Lawrence, Ramon Novarro, Rudy Vallee, Alexander Gray, Jack Whiting, Paul Gregory, and Ted Lewis. Whether they had been over-exposed, cast in the wrong parts, defeated by poor writing or direction, or victimized by the public's impatience with musicals in the very early 1930s, it was all the same to producers. Either you clicked or you thudded. And the producers added a corollary to the rule: whoever clicked should be succeeded by more like him or her. No one could follow Chevalier or Cantor or Jolson. But eventually the certain Something was settled on in such contract players as Alice Faye, Betty Grable, Deanna Durbin, Bing Crosby, Dennis Morgan, and Howard Keel—people of popularity and impact but chosen for kinds of go-everywhere, mid-American charm that would cause no offense. No American hero was allowed to do what Chevalier did. He was foreign; they're supposed to be quaint when they're sexy. No American heroine was supposed to express her lighter side with Fanny Brice's daffiness; you can't make love to a lampoon.

The sifting period is over. Art is transformation, and transformation feeds on idiosyncrasy. But the studios will as much as possible consolidate a series of genres around Something as often chosen for its lack of idiosyncrasy as for its talent. Before *42nd Street,* musicals were conceived in chaos, but they were rich in spontaneity. From now on, many of them will come forth with a touch of the assembly line about them.

The Texture of Popular Music

THE CLOSEST CONNECTION between film and stage musicals lay in their songs, as Tin Pan Alley (meaning the community, bylaws, traditions, and economics of the American songwriting industry) supplied composers and lyricists for both mediums. Almost all the major Broadway songwriters worked in Hollywood in the 1930s on at least one project, and in later years a few of Hollywood's regulars moved to Broadway (notably Frank Loesser and Jule Styne). Then, too, the constant filming of stage shows kept the two schools in tune.

But two schools they were, separated by aesthetic imperatives while creating for the same national audience. Some songs "feel" theatre, others feel Hollywood, and still others could belong to either—Harold Arlen and E. Y. Harburg's "It's Only a Paper Moon,"* for instance, which actually fills all the above conditions. It was written for a non-musical play, Ben Hecht and Gene Fowler's *The Great Magoo*, in 1932, but did not find an audience until it was used in the film *Take a Chance* a year later. On first hearing, it has the artless appeal of a movie ballad. But on investigation it shows the sophisticated craftsmanship normally associated with Broadway, especially in Arlen's incisively compressed melody.

Was the Hollywood score simple where the Broadway score was wily? It was in some ways. For one thing, it had fewer numbers, generally four or five to Broadway's twelve or fourteen. For another, Holly-

---

*Billy Rose's name appears on the song's byline, but historians have questioned his contribution.

wood feared contextual plot or character songs, always hoping for hit tunes that transferred effortlessly to radio or recordings. Someone like Irving Berlin should have made the most comfortable transition from Broadway to Hollywood by virtue of his ease in all-purpose pop—yet Berlin's earliest efforts were not his best. Neither *Hallelujah* nor *Mammy* seems to have inspired him; only the title song in *Puttin' on the Ritz* (1929), a backstager featuring the extremely ill-received Harry Richman, suggested the great Berlin who put individual bite into conventional pop structures. Not till he wrote *Top Hat* (1935) for Fred Astaire and Ginger Rogers was Berlin in fettle. *Top Hat*'s five songs float on the film's dressy style with a chic that never loses its roots on earth—exactly the tone that the Astaire–Rogers films purvey. "Cheek to Cheek" is an especially long-lined ballad with a main phrase that strains upward and glides down and a release (the middle section) that screams for motion. "Dance with me!" Astaire begs; and it is this same section that prompts the most athletic moment in the dance that immediately follows. As on Broadway, Berlin is writing for the work, for the people in it. "Isn't This a Lovely Day (to be caught in the rain)?" is as confidently persuasive as Astaire always is when courting Rogers, "The Piccolino" grins and preens because the love plot is running smoothly, and "Top Hat, White Tie, and Tails" might well have served as the theme song of the whole Astaire–Rogers era. Most interesting of all is "No Strings," *Top Hat*'s first number, which trips into song literally in mid-phrase. "No yens, no yearning," Astaire tells Edward Everett Horton about himself, "no strings and no connections," and suddenly he's singing "no ties to my affections . . ."

George and Ira Gershwin, too, failed to make film work for them at first, though their score for *Delicious* (1931), another Gaynor–Farrell romance, did serve to introduce George's *Second Rhapsody,* a kind of sequel to the *Rhapsody in Blue,* meant to accompany Scottish waif Gaynor's walking tour of Manhattan but cut to a few minutes in final editing. Like Berlin, the Gershwins came through in an Astaire–Rogers item, *Shall We Dance?* (1937), extrapolating the moods of boy-meets-girl in "Beginner's Luck" (the meeting), "Let's Call the Whole Thing Off" (mock trouble), "They Can't Take That Away From Me" (real trouble), and "Shall We Dance" (the getting).

Some of Broadway's most adept songwriters never found a place in film. Sigmund Romberg and Rudolf Friml bombed out with their original scores and saw their strongest Broadway efforts reduced to a few numbers in the MacDonald–Eddy adaptations. But one Broadway songwriter found Hollywood so congenial that he gave up songwriting. This was B. G. DeSylva, the "idea" man in DeSylva, Brown, and Henderson, who turned producer at Fox and Paramount, leaving his partners without a foundation.

Of them all, Richard Rodgers and Lorenz Hart must have had the most fun in Hollywood, for they alone carried out experiments that rivaled Broadway at its most audacious. Their first original film score, for *The Hot Heiress* (1931), opens with construction worker Ben Lyon singing, "A girl can love an actor, a lawyer, or contractor, but nobody loves a riveter but his mother." Somebody loves him—heiress Ona Munson, who lives in the building next to his site. As his work proceeds from floor to floor, she moves up from flat to flat to keep him in view, and strikes the democratic chord by singing one chorus of "Like Ordinary People Do" in a takeoff on a ritzy accent. There are only three songs, but each makes its point. In "You're the Cats," she wonders what makes him so irresistible. "You're unconventional, and I'm very glad," she says. "No, I'm American," he answers; "so's my ma and dad."

Rodgers and Hart were unconventional, not at first in their subjects so much as in the odd combination of Hart's savvy wit and Rodgers' even-lined, sentimental tunes. This interior contradiction set them apart from others; perhaps that was why Hollywood let them do such bizarre things—such as composing the *Love Me Tonight* score before the script was written (no wonder: the songs *are* the script). They could be conventional, too. Like many of their colleagues, they appeared in a short to showcase their stuff, and as *Masters of Melody* (1929) sketch out the ideas that gave birth to three hits, letting singers deliver the songs. ("The Girl Friend" is murdered by two of the worst performers ever, who also leave out the no-no word in the line, "Hell, the girl's ideal.") But hits were not on the Rodgers–Hart mind necessarily, and with the invention of their "rhythmic dialogue"—rhymed passages delivered as speech in time to music—they made it difficult for the average ear to follow the shape of their musical sequences. In *Love Me Tonight* they used it sparingly, mainly in a doctor's examination of despondent Jeanette MacDonald; presumably Rouben Mamoulian contributed to this collaboration of speaking, singing, accompaniment, and sound effects, for little operas were his thing. MacDonald is a widow. The doctor asks her, "Were you very happy with your spouse?" "He was the son of a noble house," she replies. "It was the happiness of great peace." Now we see why. To the strains of Mendelssohn's sappy "Spring Song" MacDonald presents a photograph of her late husband. Not only does he look repulsive—he *sounds* it: Mendelssohn goes sour as we look and the tune staggers down into the bassoon like a drunk.

In the same year, 1932, Rodgers and Hart extended the rhythmic dialogue technique in *The Phantom President*, George M. Cohan's talkie debut in a double role as a stodgy candidate and the medicine-show salesman who impersonates him during the campaign. Many critics were reminded of the Gershwin stage musical *Of Thee I Sing* of the year before, because it treated the same general subject similarly, pushing beyond the borders of the AABA pop song form to raise up whole scenes in music. The structure was operatic, but the sound style was musical comedy. This marked a terrific breakthrough for the American musical—as Walt Disney pointed out by implication in his cartoon short *The Three Little Pigs* (1933), which takes the form of a one-act opera: sung throughout. At the same time, Rodgers and Hart also leaped the verge, playing about half of *Hallelujah, I'm a Bum* (1933) in rhythmic dialogue.*

Hallelujah, I'm a Bum is a curious item. It's a Depression tale, set almost entirely among the citizenry of Central Park, hoboes with a home. It's also a Jolson tale, though here he is not protected by his usual shtick, and never even gets a real Number in the Jolson style. It's surprising that he did the film at all, for he liked confrontational entertainment wherein the audience either loves you or hates you—few spectators knew what to make of this tale of a tramp who falls in love with the mayor's girlfriend when she gets amnesia and has to give her up when she comes out of it. Not only is the story unusual, but the treatment keeps promising tunes that it delivers only once, in the ballad "You Are Too Beautiful," which Jolson renders with what is for him astonishingly good taste. Perhaps he felt defeated by the continually blown opportunities to implant the music in the public's lazy ear. The wonderful "I Gotta Get Back to New York" isn't heard even once straight through, and a jazzily lyrical melody, "I'd Do It Again," makes more of an effect when played instrumentally in the opening credits than it does in the action—because it is so well integrated into the action that one hardly notices it. Moreover, the most dramatic scenes, normally the ones set to music in a musical, are played in plain speech. It is the in-between incidentals that are sung. Hart and his co-librettist S. N. Behrman did a splendid job in characterizing Bumper

---

*Actually, Sigmund Romberg and Oscar Hammerstein wrote a film opera as early as 1931 in *Children of Dreams*, the action carried through in song and accompanied dialogue. A quick failure, the movie had little discernible influence.

(Jolson), the irresponsible mayor (Frank Morgan), the girl (Madge Evans), Bumper's black sidekick Acorn (Edgar Connor), the Communist sanitation man Egghead (Harry Langdon), and the smaller parts (Rodgers and Hart each appear in a walk-on), but while the roles are clear, the musical passages aren't, not on first hearing. The authors make a tour de force of a scene in which Bumper finds a purse with a thousand-dollar bill in it ("the aristocratic rag," sneers Egghead, "of a plutocratic hag"), but who would attend this film the two or three times it takes to catch all the rhymes and absorb the volatile flow of melody?

Composer Vincent Youmans had less provocative notions about what comprises a film score; he also had the unpleasant experience of seeing his *Great Day!*, a Joan Crawford vehicle, closed down by MGM after ten days' shooting in 1930. Three of his shows, including *No, No, Nanette* and *Hit the Deck*, became films that year, but his first original score came in 1933, for *Flying Down to Rio*, the film in which Fred Astaire and Ginger Rogers were first teamed up. Youmans was careful. He sat down and wrote four very first-rate examples of pop prototypes. With no established Astaire–Rogers ambience to worry about, Youmans and his lyricists Gus Kahn and Edward Eliscu wrote outside of any characterological reference. "Music Makes Me (do the things I never should do)" is upbeat and syncopated, the sort of thing hundreds of belters might sing with a band (as Rogers does here). The "Carioca" is another of the Latin dances that were trying to sweep the country as of Roosevelt's Good Neighbor Policy. "Orchids in the Moonlight" tells of tango in the minor key, with a major-key middle section of slithering harmonies. And the title song would have been the theme song, done to death, only a few years before.

Youmans was a tricky composer when he wanted to be, and he builds "Flying Down to Rio" out of a single phrase varied with an intent rhythmic drive that makes it a natural for a big dance number. As it happens, however, choreographer Dave Gould made the "Carioca" the big floor number. "Flying Down to Rio," sung by Astaire, accompanies an aerial ballet of girls on planes, the machines themselves doing what "dancing" there is and the girls doing little more than hanging on. There is some movement—wing-walking and a few kicks—and at one point a girl falls off a wing and is caught on a plane below—*very* realistic in effect, though the whole business was filmed on planes suspended a few feet off the ground and the horizon and terrain added through back projections of Rio de Janiero and, yes, Malibu Beach.

Are four songs a musical? Even four as good as these, counting lengthy "Carioca" dancing and Astaire's tap reprise of "Music Makes Me"? Rodgers and Hart's Chevalier–MacDonald operetta *Love Me Tonight* had nine numbers, and this seems a more comfortable proportion, especially because they are more necessary to the action than Youmans' *Flying Down to Rio* quartet. Rodgers and Hart are lithe where Youmans is effusive. Cole Porter, too, was lithe. On the coast he could not employ the horny double meanings of his Broadway lyrics (most of them sorrowful gay *mots* masquerading as carefree hedonism), especially after the Production Code clamped down in 1934. But he could spend freely of his musical eroticism, always looking for the odd note or a chromatic run cut into the heart of a tune to bring out the beast in love. Porter got to Hollywood early, in *The Battle of Paris* (1929), the flop that ruined Gertrude Lawrence's hopes of a career in Hollywood musicals; at least Lawrence did manage to get in on one of Porter's more suggestive lyrics, "They All Fall in Love."

In the late 1930s, Porter wrote his first full-length film scores, and like Gershwin and Rodgers showed how much spryer Tin Pan Alley's eastern office could sound compared to the midcult approach of the western branch. Hollywood teams often wrote songs without knowing much about a film. The Broadway bunch wrote for story. *Born to Dance* (1936) and *Rosalie* (1937) were dancing musicals starring Eleanor Powell, so Porter wrote her highly rhythmic "up" tunes that cull their energy from her stunning tap. *Born to Dance* gives her "Rap-Tap on Wood," a jiver whose melodic kernel repeats itself obsessively as a tap routine might; *Rosalie*'s "I've a Strange New Rhythm in My Heart" locks that strange rhythm into its tune, cross-metered from fox trot to waltz and back again. Broadway people are also attuned to *styles* of pop. *Born to Dance*, with sailors and chorus girls in its cast, calls for modern spunk—"Hey, Babe, Hey" and "Swingin' the Jinx Away." *Rosalie*, a modern-dress operetta about a West Point cadet (Nelson Eddy) in love with the Princess of Romanza (Powell), calls for a savor of middle Europe—"Spring Love Is in the Air," assigned to Ilona Massey, who has more voice than Powell as well as an amusing Graustarkian accent, and who looks neat in the company of balalaikas, gypsy fiddles, and dirndl dancers.

Porter is trying to meet Hollywood on its terms, it seems. *Rosalie* has a title song, which Eddy uses, along with "M'appari" (from *Martha*), to serenade Powell outside her Vassar dormitory, and Porter worked especially hard on it, turning out some half-dozen versions before he hit on the right one. How right is it, though? The melody is jovially antique, almost a satire on banality, and it sounds great on Eddy. But the words suggest Porter's embarrassment—"I date, I suppose"—rather than the character's confident virility. So Porter remains Porter, hating love because he can't find it, yet needing to believe in it because what else is there?* Accordingly, Virginia Bruce delivers "I've Got You Under My Skin" in *Born to Dance* and in *Rosalie* Eddy tries "In the Still of the Night," and a haunting waltz called "Close" (written for *Rosalie* but used only in underscoring) tells of a kiss "so soft, so sweet, so warm." Hollywood, however, is sloppy about style, and fills out Porter's *Rosalie* score with filchings from Sousa, Borodin, and Chaikofsky (the second movement of the "Pathétique" Symphony—which oddly bears a slight resemblance to the first phrase of "I've a Strange New Rhythm in My Heart").

Integrity of style is essential to the Broadway score, incidental in film. As far back as Gilbert and Sullivan and Offenbach, musical comedy has reveled in parody, and ersatz recreations abound, sometimes to set time and place and sometimes for satire's sake. Victor Herbert found ragtime takeoffs and military marches indispensable; Romberg and Friml were always faking locale melodically. Broadway composers introduced this practice into film, as in Irving Berlin's "Waiting at the End of the Road" in *Hallelujah*, Walter Donaldson's Indian pastiche in *Whoopee,* or Romberg's Johann Straussian "You Will Remember Vienna" in *Viennese Nights.* By the late 1930s, the imitations grew prankish, and whoever arranged the dance music in *Born to Dance* developed Eleanor Powell's big turn after "Easy to Love" into a balletlike affair that keeps sounding like certain pensive moments of "The Dance of the Hours" from Ponchielli's *La Gioconda* until at last it bursts into a whirlwind can-can that combines Porter's tune with Ponchielli's orchestration. Hot dog!

Though the Broadway émigrés outclassed the Hollywood regulars, most of these came from the east, too: they simply weren't well-known. Nacio Herb Brown and Arthur Freed were a rare team for their experience logged in west coast theatre circuits, but they helped set the style for Hollywood film songs with as little rarity in them as possible. Brown's harmonies favor the simplistic and Freed's lyrics go for the easy rhyme. Such a tune as "You Were Meant for Me," the love song in *The Broadway Melody*, derives its strength from simple

---

*Porter wrote one of his most honest, even autobiographical songs in "I Know It's Not Meant For Me," for *Rosalie*. It would have been Ray Bolger's solo spot, but was cut from the score during production.

repetition, and the title song has nothing but an emphatic final line ("That's the *Broad*-way *mel*-o-(bum-bum)-*dy!*") to paint it bold. The only interesting item in the whole score is "The Wedding of the Painted Doll," mainly because the melody jitters back and forth from major to minor in a jumpy vocal line suggestive of dancing puppets. Anyway, the "Painted Doll" number is the highlight of *The Broadway Melody* for a number of reasons—the oddball xylophone in its orchestration; the important first use of color in a sound feature; the careful attempt to root the visuals on a literal Broadway stage while doing things that only Hollywood's sound stages could do, with electrified trap doors and spatial relations; and the effete *tenorino* who sings the number. All this collides perfectly in a scene as weird as it is straightforward: it's inventive, yes, but it's also simple.* Moving on through the years, Brown and Freed could be counted on for novelty numbers like Joan Crawford's "Chant of the Jungle" in *Untamed* (1929) or ballads like "You Are My Lucky Star" from *Broadway Melody of 1936*, both as simple as pie. But the latter has a sweet tang, while the former is rotten with drum-drum and "exotic" flatted notes. Sounding *appropriately* simple is not as easy as it sounds.

But simple—let's say direct—was what Hollywood wanted; *direct* sold sheet music and records in the millions. When the *Fox Movietone Follies* opened in mid-1929 in saturation bookings, it swept the nation with three song hits by Con Conrad, Sidney D. Mitchell, and Archie Gottler: "Breakaway," "Walking With Susie," and "That's You, Baby," pushing some 100,000 sheets and discs. Yet these are almost irritatingly puerile numbers. "Breakaway," another of those "new" dance sensations comprising down on the heels and up on the toes, claims "it's got the snappiest syncopation" yet has little syncopation at all. "Walking With Susie" is cliché melody that stutters for novelty. "That's You, Baby" nauseates with its baby-talk flirtation. But, as William Fox might have pointed out, you can't argue with a bank account.

Despite the fortunes that songwriters made for them, the producers treated their tunesmiths as laborers, expecting hits to be turned out like cut cookies, light, medium, well. And there was something just in this: if the ballads, dance numbers, and comedy songs are all interchangeable, then what difference does it make who writes them? The

---

*Brown and Freed liked the "Painted Doll" so much they rewrote it at least twice—in "The Woman in the Shoe" in *Lord Byron of Broadway* (1929) and "Hot Chocolate Soldiers" in *Hollywood Party* (1934).

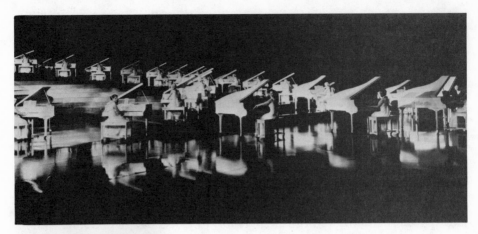

☆ *THE BERKELEY EFFECT: top to bottom:*
"The Words Are in My Heart" from Gold Diggers
of 1935 *(fifty girls, fifty hollow pianos, fifty men in*
black moving the pianos from underneath); Rogers
sings "We're in the Money" in pig latin in Gold
Diggers *of* 1933; *"Lullaby of Broadway" (Powell*
and Shaw, center) in Gold Diggers *of* 1935.

☆ *THE BERKELEY IMITATION: above, Warners'* Ready, Willing and Able *had Keeler and Shaw but lacked the Berkeley zip, except momentarily in the Whiting–Mercer "Too Marvelous for Words" (Keeler with Lee Dixon); below, MGM's* The Great Ziegfeld: *Ray Bolger leads "You Gotta Pull Strings."*

producers respected fame and thus approached the great Broadway creators with respect, at least in person (and Cole Porter's elegance, backed by an independent fortune, really did impress them). But the producers did not especially respect the work that had prompted the fame, and never thought of a given work as being particularly right for a given team—as for example, on Broadway, Kern and Hammerstein would be right for a Marilyn Miller show or the Gershwins for Fred and Adele Astaire. Nor did Hollywood promote its songwriters in the ads. "Who writes the words and music to all the girly shows?" Dick Powell sings in *Dames*, and tells us: "No one cares and no one knows." For sure—the *Dames* credits don't even bother to spell out the six songwriters' first names.

Richard A. Whiting, a composer who worked with too many different librettists for even the cognoscenti to get his name straight, had versatility—perhaps too much: his autograph is not as easy to pin down as Porter's, Gershwin's, Kern's. His oeuvre as a whole, from 1929 to his death in 1938, has no stylistic distinction, yet individual scores and tunes do. *Monte Carlo*, which Whiting wrote with co-composer W. Franke Harling and lyricist Leo Robin, could have been expanded for Broadway, with its prudent observation of character—trivial ("She'll Love Me and Like It") for MacDonald's odious fiancé, irreverent ("Trimmin' the Women") and sincere ("Give Me a Moment Please") for her vis-á-vis Jack Buchanan, and of course the famous train sequence would be nothing, despite Lubitsch's flying camera, without the driving rhythm of "Beyond the Blue Horizon." Whiting wrote equally well for the salacious Chevalier and the circumspect Buddy Rogers, the lush MacDonald and the squirty Nancy Carroll and the even squirtier Shirley Temple (only once, but it was a long one: "On the Good Ship Lollipop").

Composer Ralph Rainger, who worked mainly at Paramount with Leo Robin, was less story-oriented than Whiting, but like him Rainger disproves the simplicity rule maintained by too many of his colleagues. He, too, worked on a Chevalier film, *A Bedtime Story* (1933), in which Chevalier adopts a foundling whom he calls Monsieur Baby, played winningly by six-month-old Ronald Leroy Overacker, billed as Baby Leroy. Who was stalwart enough to resist Baby Leroy's delightedly arching his back whenever someone picked him up or clutching the edge of his crib in wonder and worry? A popular publicity still showed Baby sucking his bottle in Chevalier's arms, wearing a little copy of Chevalier's boater; this was perhaps the last straw. Still, nobody upstages Chevalier,* and Rainger defended the star with four songs in the official Chevalieresque style. When Chevalier sings, the world watches, but he must sing *his* songs.

Hollywood scores were not only simple, but also failed to engage their stories with context songs. Never, *never* did Hollywood get over its horror of characters singing for purposes of plot—somewhere, there has to be a band, or a microphone, or an audience, or even just a guitar, to reassure the public that of course real-life people don't sing. There were countless exceptions, such as the Astaire–Rogers or Mac-Donald–Eddy series. If you're in love, you'll waltz. But the horror does explain the proliferation of theatre, nightclub, and radio settings.

And this led to a lack of context. Pop songwriters, which is what most of the Hollywood regulars were, suffered institutional pressures to make every song a hit. To do this, they had to express what most people feel but are too inarticulate to say: to generalize. The subjects are banal but the lyrics set up a vernacular poetry and the music enhances the communication. The right mating of words, music, and image—no matter how overworked that image may be—is what gives pop music its stimulation, and explains why so many film scores could be written without the authors' knowing much about the character who would sing them. In film musicals there is always someone who wants, finds, loses, and reclaims romance; there is always a spot for a new dance sensation; there are bands to sing with, a football team to cheer up, a newlyweds' kitchen to cook breakfast in, a magic moon to address; if not, we can fit one in. With no plot songs to write, who needs to know the details of a plot?

Thus, a prolific team such as Harry Revel and Mack Gordon could turn out upwards of a hundred love songs, script unseen. How to make each sound different? Composer Revel bore the brunt of the work, distilling a sense of everyday American sensitivity in his melodies while Gordon plucked his titles out of the colloquial ozone. The Revel–Gordon songs sound like cuttings from conversations: "Never in a Million Years," "It's Swell of You," "Love Thy Neighbor," "May I?," "Stay as Sweet as You Are," "You Say the Sweetest Things." The team appears briefly in *Sitting Pretty*, one of the nine movies that Ginger Rogers made for release in 1933, with Jack Haley and Jack Oakie as

---

*Not long after, W. C. Fields attempted to block Baby Leroy's scene-stealing by feeding him alcohol. "The boy's no trouper," he then said. "Anyone who can't hold his liquor shouldn't drink on the job."

songwriters, Rogers as their fervent supporter, and some very gentle burlesque of the film colony, including one of Thelma Todd's best parts as man-eating star Gloria Duvall. Here, Revel and Gordon test themselves by writing three uptempo love songs, but Revel's harmonically defined vocal lines, which always seem to be pursuing a chord, and Gordon's right-on titles bring them home. "You're Such a Comfort to Me" is a list of clichés ("like a port in a storm," "like honey to a bee"), yet Revel finds something odd to do in the release, and the song works. "Good Morning Glory" suggests the treat of waking up to thoughts of one's boy- or girlfriend. "Did You Ever See a Dream Walking?", the film's hit, pushes simplicity to the brink of emptiness, yet these craftsmen make it sound fresh. Again, it is more directness than simplicity.

Revel was the craftsman, espcially good in leading the main strain of his tunes into an expansive release. If Gordon held to the surface of things, Revel found the idiosyncratic edge in the universal. In an Alice Faye–Don Ameche picture, *You Can't Have Everything* (1937), Gordon lectures the impatient among us in his lyrics to the title song, another of those messages that purport to equalize inequity yet basically support the status quo: "Don't envy neighbors and the fortunes that they get." Revel makes it swing in a long-lined rising phrase that hops at its crest, and then he pulls off a nifty syncopation in the release. "The Loveliness of You" works even better, for here Gordon's ear for natural dialogue glides along with Revel's tricky melodic phraseology in a perfect fit. Speaking of "cheek to cheeking," the singer admits he is not articulate in love talk—"But, unaccustomed as I am to public speaking," his girl's beauty will inspire his tongue. Thus the song contains a self-fulfilling prophecy: she *is* beautiful, so he *can* sing.

Without question, the standout of all the Hollywood songwriters was composer Harry Warren, who worked with a number of lyricists for a number of studios after a few years on Broadway writing revues or very loosely structured book musicals. His was just the background for Hollywood, and Warren, teamed with Al Dubin on the four songs in *42nd Street*, fit right. They worked right through the series of Warners backstagers with Busby Berkeley dance numbers, sometimes being called in to bolster other men's scores when Berkeley found these lacking in big-number potential. Dubin was irreplaceable for the way his lyrics prompted pictures from Berkeley; Warren was irreplaceable because his tunes were so strong. Of all the Hollywood teams, Warren and Dubin caught the most basic images in the most unusual patterns. Few others extrapolated the mixed buoyancy and bitterness of the Depression years as well as they did in two songs from *Gold Diggers of 1933*, the opening "We're in the Money," square-cut and kicky in the major key, and the closing "Remember My Forgotten Man," angular and drooping in the minor.

One can see why Berkeley depended so much on the Warren–Dubin numbers, and why they probably would not have fared as well on Broadway as in film: their songs don't fit a context, but rather invent one. A song like "Lullaby of Broadway" from *Gold Diggers of 1935* is not in the "Broadway Melody" line of smiles and tears in the old show town. This song is more specific, almost a day in the life: activity ("the hip hooray and ballyhoo"), sound ("the rumble of a subway train"), people ("the daffydils who entertain"), and place ("Angelo's and Maxie's"). And while it opens with a jazzy, stepping strain, it does indeed work up to a lullaby. Musicians delight to point out that this most artless of tunes is constructed harmonically on a generous plan: where most pop songs assert a home key, leave it in the release, and return to it for the close, the first half of this song, the Broadway jazz, actually sets up a modulation *into* the home key, which is not established till the second, lullaby, half.

Warren and Dubin could write to order, as in *Go Into Your Dance* (1935), a Jolson film. This was probably Jolson's most autobiographical role, that of an irresponsible Broadway star mixed up with the underworld and in love with Ruby Keeler. Jolson's career had been on the decline for some time and Warners hoped to attract crowds for him by pairing him with his wife, Keeler. Good thinking. But Jolson didn't like to admit that he needed help from anyone, and not only did he refuse to do another film with Keeler, he also hogs the screen in *Go Into Your Dance*. Of the seven songs Warren and Dubin wrote for the film, Jolson takes five of them (plus "Cielito Lindo"), gives one to Helen Morgan as an actress in love with Jolson, and allots another to Keeler and the chorus girls in a nightclub scene but talks through most of it while trying to make time with one of the girls. It's just as well. Morgan's "The Little Things You Used to Do" is so perfect for her that she really takes the stage with it, and Keeler was no singer. She taps like a zealot in "She's a Latin from Manhattan," wherein Jolson unmasks the would-be *flamenca* as "Senorita Donahue," and she makes a lovely entrance down a stairway between rows of men in tails to Jolson's salute in "About a Quarter to Nine." To complete the survey, Warren and Dubin hand over the inevitable "Mammy, I'll Sing

About You" and the cheer-up rouser, "Go Into Your Dance." What's amazing is that the authors tailored the score for Jolson (and Morgan) without betraying their own style.

Is it because they didn't have a style—they and all Hollywood? AS-CAP* ranks Warren seventh in the list of the biggest-selling songwriters, and the specialists parse him for days, yet he is unknown outside the business. Why? Possibly it is because of that tricky simplicity, which kept film scores focused on the center of human universals, away from the peculiar, individual edges that produced, for example, Porter's tortured, Hart's puzzled, Berlin's incurious, or Ira Gershwin's chaste love lyrics on Broadway. Hollywood most certainly did have a style, too tight a one. When Warren and Dubin wrote a love song— and they were the best in the industry—it loved love, period. If you have love, you're cheery; if you've lost it, you're blue. Thus even Warren and Dubin were held back, not from writing great songs, but from testing themselves with the challenge of art. To study Warren's setting of Dubin is to delight in the confidence of an astonishing spontaneity. "About a Quarter to Nine," which simply suggests a man's looking forward to a date, uses a minor key in the verse (the introduction, so to speak) for expectation, blows it open in the main theme, takes a swinging strut in the major, revs up in the marchlike release, and sails straight home. The verbal idea produces the sound, dynamite. But the idea is old and Dubin's lyric thinly spread; only Warren makes it go. This is pop music at its heart, so universal in appeal that it lacks the penetration of individuality. And this universalism is what Hollywood based its dynamic on: a paper moon.

---

*The American Society of Composers, Authors, and Publishers, the major union of the Tin Pan Alley giants.

☆ 6 ☆

The Allure of Genre

AMERICAN FILM is unique in the arts in that it went freelance only after its first fifty years. Until then, except for the films of a few rugged individualists in the early silent days and such self-capitalized auteurs as D. W. Griffith and Douglas Fairbanks, movies were produced not by freely collaborating individuals but in factories—the studios—where executive pressures hampered individuality. The oppression was not consistent. Many distinctive talents were given latitude—directors King Vidor, F. W. Murnau, and Victor Sjöstrom, for instance. Even the stubbornly improvident (but brilliant) Erich von Stroheim got several chances to create till his gamey eroticism made him outlaw. Moreover, even assembly-line production encouraged qualities of diverse character—innocence (*Sunny Side Up*), sophistication (*Love Me Tonight*), aggressiveness (*Puttin' on the Ritz*), earthiness (*42nd Street*), anarchy (*Hallelujah, I'm a Bum*), and ironic downfall (*Applause*).

Still, as flop musicals and—therefore—flop personalities were weeded out in the first years, the studios realized that the musical worked best within certain emotional categories. Each studio defined the categories differently, however, and originality somehow thrived in this environment, as long as it took some form that either created or maintained a profit-making genre of musical. Thus, Jeanette MacDonald moved comfortably into operetta, which already existed; Fred Astaire just as comfortably invented the art deco society-put-on dance musical.

The smash success of *42nd Street* prompted its studio, Warner Brothers, to institute a series of backstagers in which cynical show people find something to believe in: their jobs. Warners favored stories about the working class, about boxing, racing, organized crime, and organized societal brutality, and naturally the studio brought the musical into line as well. The Warners outlook was less political than socio-cultural—Warners writers pointed out inequities in the system without urging partisan solutions. It was the Depression studio, saturated with the feelings of the time and anything but escapist, and it is notable that one of Hollywood's most bitter arraignments of economic injustice was heard in a Warners musical—the "Remember My Forgotten Man" number in *Gold Diggers of 1933*.

If Warners had an opposite, it was Paramount, where escapist fare was an old tradition, not an antidote to the Depression. Paramount was the place where the deftest designers experimented, where Lubitsch, Mamoulian, and von Sternberg worked, continentally droll and extreme. Warners' musicals were bold and their characters raw. Paramount's were witty and prankish. MGM had the biggest stars, but Paramount colored in a broader spectrum, taking in Mae West and Nancy Carroll, Bing Crosby and Maurice Chevalier.

MGM was the gala studio, where more money meant polish. Its workers, from expert to laborer, were well paid and never rushed; this allowed for high gloss in every A-budget feature. Even the B pictures were better produced than some studios' A films. Paramount couldn't have afforded the outlay that MGM spent on its many operettas, and Warners wouldn't have wanted to. And when MGM produced modern-dress musical comedy, it avoided the rooming houses and back alleys of the Warners backstagers, instead haunting the country mansions and flashy nightclubs of the privileged.

William Fox lost control of his studio in 1929, but it hung on in financial chaos until Darryl F. Zanuck, who left Warners in 1933 to form Twentieth Century Pictures, merged with Fox in the middle of the decade. Zanuck was the man whose brainstorm had produced *42nd Street* and revived the moribund musical film, but Twentieth Century-Fox turned out the most formula-oriented musicals, centering on series built around Alice Faye, Shirley Temple, and skater Sonja Henie. Faye's films had a plot—the same one—and were loosely constructed to allow room for vaudeville by dancers and comics. Temple's films were tighter, and Henie's consisted largely of ice. There was little of the proletarian self-belief that marked Warners' output, little of Paramount's verve or MGM's sheen. Fox, more than the others, honored genre above all.

The other major studios released fewer musicals. RKO concentrated on Astaire and Rogers, Universal's thirties releases peaked in its horror cycle turned out by James Whale, Tod Browning, and Karl Freund, and Columbia wasn't interested in musicals. There are exceptions, but it is true that procedures for mass production supplanted the helter-skelter of the early years—and the public apparently preferred to settle down with something steady. Some of these series stand among the most lasting contributions to American art. In the Astaire–Rogers films, Astaire's offhand manipulation of elegance from a nonsocial viewpoint—his films seem aware of an American class system but Astaire functions outside it—tells us something about the American social outlook. And the Warners backstagers are not only aware of the system but are clearly fighting it from the outside pushing in. The Astaire–Rogers films are backstagers too, in a way, though they deal mainly with the offstage love life of two characters rather than the efforts of a whole cast to get a show on. But the difference points up the two series' very different outlooks. Astaire and Rogers never mention the Depression; they're too busy dancing. The Warners characters are obsessed with the Depression: that's why they dance.

In late 1932, before *42nd Street* had come out, Warners was already working on the second *42nd Street*, *Gold Diggers of 1933*, a remake of *The Gold Diggers of Broadway* which in turn had been a remake of *The Gold Diggers* (1923), a silent with Hope Hampton and Louise Fazenda. All are based on Avery Hopwood's play of 1919, telling of a stuffy aristocrat who attempts to break up his nephew's engagement to a chorus girl. The girl's best friend poses as the woman in the case, the uncle falls for her himself, and all ends well in a double marriage. Hopwood specialized in sentimental stories painted with coy ribaldry, but *Gold Diggers of 1933* took its tone from *42nd Street.* The screenwriters, Erwin Gelsey and James Seymour, liked Hopwood's ersatz erotica as little as they liked his sentimentality, and while they honor true romance they otherwise stick to the blunt realities of hard times on the mean streets. This has to be one of the most honest musicals Hollywood ever produced.

Mervyn LeRoy directed, shooting on an outlay of $300,000 in forty-five days with a team that typifies the Warners thirties backstager: Warren and Dubin writing the songs, Busby Berkeley staging the numbers, and a cast including Joan Blondell, Aline MacMahon, Ruby Keeler, and Ginger Rogers as chorus girls; Dick Powell as the young Boston blueblood involved with Keeler; Warren William as his guardian (brother this time around) who first takes Blondell for the "gold digger" and finally for his wife; fat, ludicrous Guy Kibbee as a Boston lawyer; and deadpan, pop-eyed, buzz-saw-voiced Ned Sparks as a producer. All of them are at their sharpest; they spit out angry jokes and deliver more feeling lines with a hint of the same anger, all the world of money, love, and ambition snapped out in the black and white of success or unemployment.

The film opens in a lavish burst of optimism that dissolves as we watch. Rogers, Blondell, and Keeler lead the Berkeley girls in "We're in the Money" in costumes made of coins, flanked by piles of coins, against a backdrop of huge coins, and waving a line of coins in precise oscillation, all smiles. Rogers gets off one chorus in pig Latin and Berkeley pulls in so close on her that one can almost lick her teeth. But we're not in the money and the movie knows it. The producer has not paid his bills and the number fades out unfinished as the sheriff and his men clomp in to cart away the scenery and costumes, the girls' coins included. "You can at least leave me carfare!" Rogers wails as some oaf yanks off her gilt. The girls' vitality revs up again when Powell decides to back Sparks' show. He's not only rich; he's a songwriter. "I'll cancel my contract with Warren and Dubin!" says Sparks. The show is on, with a part for everyone. MacMahon, the wisecracker of the group, will be the comedienne. "It'll be the funniest thing you ever did," Sparks tells her. MacMahon replies, "Didja ever see me ride a pony?"

As the film proceeds, the show opens and loses our interest—except insofar as it provides the film's three big numbers—and we instead follow the love plots as the girls and Powell conspire to win his brother's approval for his and Keeler's engagement. Then Powell and Keeler lose our interest: Blondell and William dominate the film as they toy with and then genuinely find each other. In the general glow even MacMahon and Kibbee end up as a couple, and we wonder what happened to the gold diggers we were promised. The worst we see is MacMahon stealing milk ("That's all right," she observes grimly; "The farmer stole it from a cow") and Rogers making a play for Kibbee. We do see Blondell and MacMahon tricking the two Bostonians into buying them expensive hats, but this is treated as fair revenge for the two men's snobbishness. Anyone who would stand between Powell and Keeler in a backstager is The Enemy.

The pushing earnestness about The Show that drove *42nd Street* does not dominate *Gold Diggers of 1933*, then, but when it's felt it's wild. Blondell is literally hysterical with relief on the phone as she tells her friends that they all have jobs, and we get another of those last-minute opening-night substitutions when Sparks' aging juvenile comes down with lumbago, and tunesmith Powell is implored to go on for him. Powell refuses—he's still incognito and fears that someone will recognize him if he appears on stage—and MacMahon hammers at him impressively on his obligation to "the kids" who need the work. This changes his mind, of course, and as he is hustled off into costume, MacMahon keys us into Hollywood's admiration for Broadway grit: "He's got nerve. He's regular. He belongs in the show business." Because he shares.

All we see of the show, *Forgotten Melody*, are three numbers that bear no relation to each other*: a risqué scherzo, a romantic idyll, and a stunning Marxist tableau of common-man disillusionment. Just as the numbers in *42nd Street* progressively grew beyond the boundaries of a theatre stage, in *Gold Diggers of 1933* Berkeley disbands any attempt to formulate a theatre style for more than a few minutes at the beginnings and ends of numbers. Hollywood has been criticized for this unreal view of theatre production, but Berkeley and his disciples do not pretend to be filming theatre: they give us the cinematic equivalent of what theatre does. The same imagination and energy ignite both forms, but each employs them differently; with film one must step through the looking glass, not just gaze into it. "I edit in the camera," Berkeley said. His camera doesn't follow his choreography but rather initiates it in overhead holds, fast tracking shots, slow pans. Other directors might use four cameras at once on a dance number, to choose later from the different views. Berkeley used one camera. The way he used it, one is all you need.

"Pettin' in the Park," the first of *Gold Diggers of 1933*'s three big ones, is a "story" number, following flirtations through the four seasons. It starts small, on stage, with a sleek vocal from summer petters Keeler and Powell and Keeler's energetic tap, but soon opens up into an expanse of sound-stage park with lounging couples, policemen, and a sinister baby. (One of Berkeley's most famous quirky bits, the kid was played by a midget, Billy Barty.) As the seasons change, so do the activities, from fall rollerskating to snowball throwing to summer

---

The Broadway Melody established the rule in backstagers that The Show be a revue rather than a story musical. That way, no one has to work around a plot, set characters, or context songs; in a revue, anything—from solo specialty to big number—goes. Every rule has its exceptions, however, and *On With the Show!*'s onstager, *The Phantom Sweetheart*, has so much in the way of story that if Warners had only filled in the missing scenes it might literally have been staged.

swimming in an art deco pool. Rain sends the girls scurrying into a pavilion, where they undress in silhouette. The baby, grinning in a slicker, pulls up a shade and peeks. The petting, meanwhile, goes on, the boys in raincoats and the girls in armor-plated bathing suits. For the finish, the baby hands Powell a can opener and he sets about "opening" Keeler.

"The Shadow Waltz" takes one onto a more delicate plane. "In the shadows let me come and sing to you," the song begins, and that's about all that occurs. In darkness, girls costumed in stiff, layered white skirts billow around Keeler (in an unconvincing blond wig), all playing white violins. For the climax, Berkeley ascends on his boom to shoot the violins, glowing in neon outline and grouped to form one huge violin, bow and all. Reaching back a few years, Warren rescues the "hesitation waltz," pushed out of fashion by jazz; it sounds an odd note amid the realistic bite of the rest of the film.

The realism runs especially heavy in the finale, "Remember My Forgotten Man." Even now, five decades later, this sequence has terrific impact. It was probably inspired by the desperate march on Washington by the "bonus army" of World War I veterans, tired of waiting for promised benefits in the worst of times, and by Franklin Roosevelt's reference on a radio address to "the forgotten man at the bottom of the economic pyramid," both events of spring 1932. The scene sneaks up on us, for the love plots are still being resolved backstage as assistants knock on dressing-room doors calling for all hands in the "Forgotten Man" number, and Blondell misses her cue. We are still in the theatre, looking straight-on at the stage; at last in place, Blondell lights a bum's cigarette, leans against a lamppost, and launches the number, which passes to a black woman (Etta Moten) and takes in a vignette of a cop hassling the bum till Blondell points out his medal of honor, all this still on stage. Now Berkeley pulls out of physical reality to collect a collage of war and postwar, from heroism on the field to breadlines curling around the block. At the end, Berkeley returns to the stage, showing files of soldiers marching along metalwork ramps and a civilian population arranged along steps that run from wing to wing, with Blondell in the center, all raising their arms in supplication. Commentators have questioned the number's inclusion while praising its power—but it seems that *Forgotten Melody* is supposed to be the kind of show that might contain such a number, despite the frothy atmosphere of "Pettin' in the Park" and "The Shadow Waltz." When Powell first describes the number to Sparks, the producer is thrilled: "That's just what this show's about—the Depression—men marching—marching in the rain—doughnuts and crullers—men marching—jobs—jobs . . . a blue song—no, not a blue song, but a wailing—a wailing . . . the big parade—the big parade of tears. . . ."

Like *42nd Street*, *Gold Diggers of 1933* thrilled the public and helped ensure a future for backstagers with naturalistic bite, and as Warners had signed Berkeley to a seven-year contract, he continued to complement the tough-talking scripts with his expressionistic whimsey. The third Warners backstager of 1933, *Footlight Parade*, confirmed Berkeley's fondness for matching patterns, fluently metamorphic sets, and panning shots of girl upon girl. With Lloyd Bacon as director and James Seymour working with Manuel Seff on the screenplay, the *42nd Street* style remains sound. James Cagney, in one of his few musical roles, gives it distinction as a Broadway showman thrown out of work by talkies who recovers by producing short stage shows to accompany the films. And what shows! *Footlight Parade*'s first hour concerns the rehearsals and the love plot, involving Cagney and Blondell as his neglected secretary, and each of the last three reels presents a Berkeley special as Cagney's troupe scrambles from theatre to theatre putting on their "prologues." Warren and Dubin again came through: with "Honeymoon Hotel," a story sequence that brings back the fascinatingly unpleasant Billy Barty as a tot who harasses Powell and Keeler, and with "Shanghai Lil," in which an American serviceman seeks and finds his Oriental sweetheart. Cagney himself ends up in the number by accident, shoved onstage in his first-night duds by a soused actor. As before, Berkeley abandons the theatre environment immediately, putting Cagney and company—including an endearingly out-of-place Keeler as Shanghai Lil—through changes of costume and decor for a grand finale of marching troups. *Footlight Parade*'s biggest number is the centerpiece of the trio, "By a Waterfall." This time, the idea came before the song: hundreds of girls frisking in an aquacade. Warren and Dubin were on vacation when Berkeley planned the number, and he introduced a new sound to the series, that of Sammy Fain and Irving Kahal. With the girls diving, splashing, floating, and sliding, with pools, fountains, and spills, and with hydraulic lifts and pumps sending 20,000 gallons of water a minute over the falls, the number represents Berkeley's most extended variation on nothing.

After three Broadway backstagers in a row, Warners felt something new was indicated, so the next in the series, *Wonder Bar* (1934), moved to a Paris nightclub. Old hands Lloyd Bacon, Berkeley, Warren and Dubin, Dick Powell, Guy Kibbee, Hugh Herbert, and Ruth Donnelly held their form, but new recruits Al Jolson, Delores Del Rio, Kay Francis, and Ricardo Cortez supply a change in tone. *Wonder Bar* is a *Grand Hotel* set in Jolson's club, where jealousy prompts Del Rio to stab Cortez. Despite the Production Code, Jolson disposes of the corpse so Del Rio can pair off with Powell. Warren and Dubin provided a haunting theme song with a continental flavor (Powell sings it straight American, however) and of course provisioned Jolson's blackface spot, "Goin' to Heaven on a Mule." Berkeley is at his best in "Don't Say Goodnight," which grows out of Del Rio and Cortez's pas de deux into a staggering geometry of whiteclad dancers and columns (which turn into trees), set off by a Cinderella bit involving a woman's lost slipper. At the height of it all, eight mirrors enclose a circle of dancers, the reflections turning a hundred people into a thousand, the whole shot from an overhead angle so the mirrors can't pick up the camera. The "mule" number has been attacked as racist for its picture of a black heaven out of *The Green Pastures*, with an instant fried-chicken machine and a celestial Cotton Club (plus, for Jolson's sake, a Yiddish newspaper), but the brief shot of Jolson and mule trekking across a thin arched bridge to the fortress of heaven is stupendous.

By this time, the name Berkeley had become a byword of imagistic spectacle, using people as objects and objects as people. Some few doubters noted similarities between his exhibitions and those thrown by dictators in Germany and Italy and called the Berkeley numbers a naive American fascism, with their anonymous multitudes and lockstep precision routines. But no fascist would have raised such pointlessly fanciful parades as Berkeley's. One mother made a stir with a magazine article entitled "I Don't Want My Daughter Growing Up to Be a Human Harp," after seeing the big number in *Fashions of 1934*— in which, indeed, the front of the harp frames were hung with Berkeley girls. But the article was taken as part of the fun rather than as serious dissent, and Berkeley's kaleidoscopes became part of the era's autograph, their fantasy a science-fiction of beauty and their exaggeration a quaint comix.

However. A sameness was creeping into the series. *Dames* was *Gold Diggers of 1934* in all but name—Dick Powell again a songwriter, Keeler again his girl, Blondell and Kibbee as the hustling chorus girl and her mark. Other men were writing the scores, but Berkeley needed the story guides that sparked him in "Shuffle off to Buffalo" and "Pettin' in the Park," and Dubin and Warren were socked in to do the songs for the three big numbers, "I Only Have Eyes for You," "The Girl at the Ironing Board," and the title song. The first is the usual variations on a theme—that Powell sees Keeler everywhere—which lead from girls in Keeler masks to girls forming a Keeler jigsaw puzzle. "The Girl at the Ironing Board," however, is a production number largely using one person: Blondell dances with laundry animated puppet-style. "Dames" is choice Berkeley, girls in black and white bent through a prism of patterns and pictures on the question, "What do you go for? Go see a show for?" At the climax, they fly high to dazzle in close-up. (The scene was shot with the girls starting at camera level and gently being lowered on a wire; the film was then speeded up and run backwards.)

So the numbers stayed inventive; but the plots and characters were tired. *Gold Diggers of 1935*, with Powell again and an amateur charity show and some ridiculous plutocrats for novelty, marked Berkeley's debut as sole director of a film. We finally get our first hardcore gold digger in Glenda Farrell, a stenographer who has snuffbox expert Hugh Herbert sign a love lyric so she can blackmail him with the threat of a breach-of-promise suit. We also get a look at the gold digger's night world in "Lullaby of Broadway," Berkeley's most sensational number. It opens with the face of Wini Shaw singing the tune, a dot approaching from the distance. As her face tilts upside down and she smokes a cigarette, Manhattan shows through her skull. Morning. A lone cop dwarfed by the buildings, coffee in the pot, newspapers in bales, crowds rushing the subway, fancy-dress people staggering home from their parties—and the city is seen at a tilt: alienation, dizziness, drunkenness. We focus on Shaw, a Broadway baby. She hits the sack and after a full day's sleep is up and at 'em. We cut to a huge, empty nightclub with a tiered dance floor. As one Latin couple in white dance, Powell and Shaw watch at a table. Now an entire dancing corps in gray and black stamp in, and the music pulls out under the assault of the tapping. The number treats size and coldness and hysteria as the modes of the city, catching them with a rightness that smashes Hollywood's emotional categories and codes for starry Something. "Come and dance!" the men beg Shaw, their refrain and her answers set right into the melody. She joins them and Powell joins her, but suddenly, with a scream, she plunges off a balcony to her death. As a men's chorus quietly restates the song, the dream runs backwards, the Manhattan skyline dissolving back into Shaw's face and the face slipping back into darkness.

Where did Berkeley get his ideas? Warren and Dubin provided the springboard, but no one knew when the leap into a picture plan might land. With salaries at rock bottom (Powell was getting less than $200 a week at the time of *42nd Street*) and working hours virtually unlimited, Berkeley could rehearse his people for weeks on one number till it was perfect, and then shoot—sometimes in one take. To the executives who pressed him for details in advance, Harry Warren later recalled, Berkeley would give "long-winded explanations in doubletalk . . . He was the bane of the production chiefs. They would come onto his sets and see a hundred girls sitting around doing their knitting while he thought up his ideas."

"Lullaby of Broadway" marked the apex of the Warners backstage series; few of the numbers and none of the films as wholes rivaled what had preceded them. But a uniquely American style had been set in the film musical, one that owed little to the Broadway model. "Lullaby of Broadway" for instance, is pure film and pure Hollywood: visually, in its real-life montage; physically, in its cavernous nightclub; musically, in its seedy populist jive; and ideologically, in its horrified fascination with New York night life. Berkeley went on to such events as *Bright Lights* (1935), a Broadway backstager with Joe E. Brown; *In Caliente* (1935), a nightclubber set in Mexico; *Stage Struck*, more or less the *Gold Diggers of 1936* with Powell, Blondell, Warren William, and a Harold Arlen–E. Y. Harburg score; and *Gold Diggers of 1937*, with Powell and Blondell and one of Berkeley's best numbers, "All's Fair in Love and War," in which whiteclad sexist troops do battle, having made peace in huge rocking chairs.

The Warners backstager was created for the Depression and couldn't outlast it, but when fresh it had tremendous impact. Every studio had to put on its own *42nd Street* in 1933. MGM typically hued its entry, *Dancing Lady*, in starry glow, casting Clark Gable as the showman and Joan Crawford as the chorus girl whose determination to dance takes her from burlesque to a triumphant Broadway debut. This was a David O. Selznick production, and it shows the good taste of the well-meaning Hollywood honcho rather than the guts of a Warners man. We have no trouble believing the Gable–Crawford romance (complicated by Franchot Tone as a playboy who wants to buy Crawford). But New York naturalism is hard to fake and Selznick, who didn't understand or like the musical as a form, seems to have tried to soften the Warners genre. The result is a hybrid at war with itself. Like *42nd Street*, *Dancing Lady* shows us a real New York—we take the A train uptown with Crawford, riding through a tunnel to the bright land of Broadway. Like *42nd Street*, *Dancing Lady* has the ironman director with the hidden heart (Gable even looks like Warner Baxter). But MGM's director Robert Z. Leonard hasn't Lloyd Bacon's sense of pace, and we don't feel Crawford's drive to succeed as strongly as we feel Blondell's drive to stay off the breadline. Unwilling to trust the public to enjoy nonstop seedy Broadway, MGM gazes admiringly on Tone's country mansion and penthouse.

The support is fine—Winnie Lightner as Crawford's roommate, May Robson as Tone's eccentric grandmother, the Three Stooges as backstage help, Fred Astaire in his film debut as Crawford's partner in Gable's show, Nelson Eddy, Robert Benchley, and Gloria Foy as the girl who is callously thrown out of, back into, and out of the lead to make way for, replace, and make definitive way for Crawford. Berkeley made the big number obligatory, and *Dancing Lady* places it near the film's end, just before Crawford dismisses Tone and embraces Gable. As several teams supplied the score, the big number is a patchwork, starting with the lavish "Hi ho! The Gang's All Here," moving to a Bavarian locale for a ripoff of Arthur Schwartz and Howard Dietz' "I Love Louisa" in the stage revue *The Band Wagon,** and then showing an antique minuet, which Eddy interrupts to sing a Rodgers–Hart song, "That's the Rhythm of the Day," a strange item written more for beat than melody. Everyone takes to the beat, the costumes magically turning current and a horse-drawn cab becoming a lush open limousine. As in Berkeley, some of this is stage-possible and some cinematic, as when Crawford and Astaire are transported from "Hi ho" to Bavaria on a flying disc.

Dancing Lady was a huge hit, thanks to its polish. Other imitations of *42nd Street*, however, retained the grime: cheaper. United Artists' *Broadway Thru a Keyhole*, also in 1933, uses Walter Winchell's voice for authentic report, and claims that its story is based on an idea of Winchell's, though it seems drawn from the personal lives of Al Jolson and Ruby Keeler. There is no attempt to duplicate Berkeley's spectacle, but the casting goes for color and diversity in the Warners manner, with Constance Cummings as the shy chorine, Paul Kelly as the gangster who loves her, Russ Colombo as her true love, and Blossom Seeley, Texas Guinan, Eddie Foy, Jr., Gregory Ratoff, and Abe Lyman and his band for Broadway smarts. The dialogue is not as sharp as it needs to be and only Cummings can act. Guinan in particular is

---

*Trivium Footnote no. 3: the beer-and-blondes number is announced as "Let's Go Bavarian" in the film itself but the opening credits call it "In Bavaria."

embarrassing as Tex Kaley, sporting her "Hello, sucker!" and "Give that little girl a great big hand." At one point, she says she weighs 138 pounds. "Stripped?" she is asked. "I don't know," she replies. "The drugstore was pretty crowded." I don't get it. Seeley comes off no better, though she accords with the Warners realism in a last-minute pep talk to Cummings. She begins almost bitterly on a "Why should the show go on?" theme: you work and hope and a day later you're forgotten. The speech seems genuine, but then Cummings' call comes and Seeley is a thrilled comic going for the boff. "The show must go on!" she exults.

Not all the Warnerslike backstagers subscribed to the Warners belief that guts makes a star. Universal's *Moonlight and Pretzels* (1933 again) teaches a youngster that she has no business Going Out There if she lacks training and talent: grit isn't everything. *Moonlight and Pretzels* is the most theatrical of this group, Bobby Connolly's dance numbers more comfortable when aping the stage than aping Berkeley, and Monte Brice and Sig Herzig's script working hard for backstage sassiness. They thought of one thing Warners didn't: the effeminate choreographer, played by Brice himself in beret and gummy grin. But something is very wrong with *Moonlight and Pretzels*—several things, actually; they take turns. One number will be fine, another ghastly. A character will play realistically here, get mannered there. Director Karl Freund had served as cameraman in such classic silents as Murnau's *The Last Laugh* and Lang's *Metropolis* and had directed a superb piece of horror in *The Mummy* a year before *Moonlight and Pretzels*, but his sense of the grotesque does not suit this material, especially in the appalling staging of the title song (another "I Love Louisa" beer garden spinoff) as a pretext for pointless comic violence. It's a big scene, and ruins the film. The plot is acceptable, taking an unknown songwriter (Roger Pryor) to glory as a Broadway producer despite problems of love (with smalltown girl Mary Brian), of temperament (star Lillian Miles), and of money (his backers, including Leo Carillo as Nick, a Greek Gambler, keep selling or sporting away their interest). But the score, by Jay Gorney and E. Y. Harburg, runs limp. Herman Hupfeld, a specialist in crazy novelty songs, bolstered it with "I Gotta Get Up and Go to Work" and "Are You Makin' Any Money?", both presented straight-on in stage style with a few dull overhead shots of girls glumly spinning on a turntable for "I Gotta Get Up" and with Lillian Miles alone before the curtain for "Are You Makin' Any Money?", relying on a repellent grabby-fingers gesture to put it over.

Freund and Connolly get cinematically ambitious only twice, but these scenes save the film. We see Pryor compose "Ah, But Is It Love?" at the piano, speaking admiringly of Beethoven's and Liszt's staying power; the schmaltzy melody is supposed to represent a cross between pop and legit. Miles hates it. She wants jive. Pryor gives her both, and the camera cuts over to a model of the proposed set, which then comes alive with the number. For a finale, Harburg and Gorney offer an uplifting antidote to their "Brother, Can You Spare a Dime?", written the year before for a stage revue: "Dusty Shoes" looks forward to the end of the Troubles with the election of FDR. Something of a commercial for the New Deal, the song begins as Alexander Gray sings it to his fellow tramps around a campfire, and then goes into a review of the twenties boom and crash in newsreel footage as well as a staged production number, culminating in the kind of pageant Harburg loved, everyone jubilant in an implied share-the-wealth apotheosis—Gray, for example, now beams in a business suit, his jutting chin clean shaven and his eyes sighting a braver world.

Where *Moonlight and Pretzels* really defies the mold is in its treatment of ingenue Mary Brian. This is the Ruby Keeler role, pure girl amid the gold diggers, and Brian has the Keeler style, more charm than talent. We have to like Keeler to believe in her, because people with her limited gifts don't become theatre stars (including Keeler, who had to come to Hollywood to make it big). Her distinction in tap is not enough to offset her amateur singing and line delivery; so we are pleasantly surprised when *Moonlight and Pretzels'* Brian, thrust into the star part by her rich *protégeur*, is rejected even by Pryor. "You and I can't make stars," he tells the backer, his hand waving at the audience where life watches art and knows what's real. "The people out there do." Kern and Hammerstein made a point of rebutting the youngster-to-star device in their stage show *Music in the Air*, wherein the youngster is fired at the dress rehearsal and replaced by a pro. Hollywood dutifully kept this in for the film version of *Music in the Air* (1934), and with *Moonlight and Pretzels* it somewhat mitigates the fantasy that camp collectors delight in in these thirties backstagers.

The camp element in all these films is, of course, applied externally by certain of today's moviegoers. Warners' writers used the word "swell" because people used it then, not to raise giggles, and Zanuck made Keeler *42nd Street*'s youngster because she had the sweetness the role calls for. The slang has dated, the Berkeley look has become a cliché, and few people today remember what it was like to live through an apparently bottomless depth of hunger and despair and to have to look for symbolic redemption in art. So this whole backstage series has lost its edge, granted. But to sit through these films today braying like donkeys has more to do with the currently gathering vogue for solipsistic smugness than with anything in the films themselves. Otherwise, how can a form that struck off a universal response fifty years ago have lost all its persuasive potency? It is outmoded—but not inarticulate.

Less interesting but undeniably popular were the films with a radio setting. The public was very used to radio, and enjoyed *seeing* it, for once, in action. Hollywood loathed radio, for it gave the citizenry something (free) to do besides pack the cinemas; but it gave exposure to film singing stars. It has been suggested that studio executives enjoyed picturing the blunders and flukes that supposedly plagued radio, but in fact the radio films tended to look much more benignly upon the airwaves than the backstagers did upon show biz. Paramount ran an annual radio series in the late middle 1930s, known as *The Big Broadcasts.* The original *Big Broadcast* (1932) built itself around an irresponsible radio singer (Bing Crosby, in his first lead) who loses job and girl but is bailed out by heir Stuart Erwin to preside over a "big broadcast" on a national hookup. This served roughly as the form for the later entries: trouble at station, trouble resolved, and a glorious vaudeville finale. Crosby was on hand for *The Big Broadcast of 1936* (1935), this time in a one-song spot; Jack Oakie led the plot scenes as a bankrupt station owner. *The Big Broadcast of 1937* (1936) went all out with Jack Benny, Burns and Allen, Martha Raye, Larry Adler, Benny Goodman and his Orchestra, and Leopold Stokowski and *his*; and *The Big Broadcast of 1938* (1937) offered two ocean liners, W. C. Fields twice (as twin brothers), and Bob Hope and Shirley Ross singing "Thanks for the Memory."

Story-oriented radio musicals had no big broadcast but more consistency. Mike fright was a favorite ruse for pushing plot, as was poking fun at commercials and announcers' oleaginous delivery. Oddly, many of the actors used in these satires were also prominent in radio, which must have put something of a punk on the satire. Dick Powell made his film debut in a featured role playing an asinine radio star in *Blessed Event* (1932), as enthusiastic in his hymn to Shapiro's Shoes as in "How Can You Say No (when all the world is saying yes)?" But he was a sympathetic hero in *Twenty Million Sweethearts* (1934) as a waiter tapped for stardom by agent Pat O'Brien and coached through his nervousness by Ginger Rogers. The film's theme song, Warren and Dubin's "I'll String Along With You," is heard much too often, and Rogers doesn't sing enough, but the lack of pretension is winning. *Wake Up and Live* (1937) was more high powered, tying its tale of a mike-spooked singer around the alleged real-life feud between Walter Winchell and bandleader Ben Bernie and peppering the results with assorted specialty singers, dancers, and comics—"I don't know whether to marry you tomorrow or go to the dentist," barks Ned Sparks to Patsy Kelly, and she replies, "It's a date!" As the singer, Jack Haley creates a sensation when he unknowingly sings baritone velvet into a mike plugged into a radio show. Haley's breathy tenor was dubbed by Buddy Clark, who really does sound terrific, and as Rogers did for Powell in *Twenty Million Sweethearts*, Alice Faye helps Haley assert himself as fame threatens to unnerve him. But *Wake Up and Live* makes a bigger impression for the most basic of reasons: a solid score. Harry Revel and Mack Gordon say the same old things, but with *such* grand ease; Faye's "There's a Lull in My Life" has become one of the classic love ballads, an "Un bel dì" of the swing era in that singers' reputations are made or shredded in it.

Then there was the college musical, made entirely of quartets, student bands, and devout dancers. The film musical pursued youth and candor, and academe promised a great deal of it: students have no grandeur, no bitterness, and, in the Hollywood version, they spend so little time in classes that there's plenty of time for flirting, proms, and football. Then, too, there are fine opportunities for dizzy deans, nutty professors, perhaps a college widow. Paramount's *College Swing* (1938) has more staff in it than students. Betty Grable (the *New York Times* said "She shags through the entire action"), Ben Blue, Florence George, and John Payne were still young enough to matriculate at a median age of about thirty-two, but Martha Raye (as "Professor of Applied Romance"), Bob Hope, Burns and Allen, Jackie Coogan, and Edward Everett Horton got top billing as the academics.

Of all the college musicals, Twentieth Century-Fox's *Pigskin Parade* (1936) may be the most typical, though it's hard to single out one film when they are all so alike. Here, the big game pits a small Texas school against Yale through some mistake; Jack Haley is the ineffective coach, Patsy Kelly his wife who accidentally incapacitates the star player with a bar bell, Stuart Erwin the new star plucked from the watermelon patches of Arkansas, Judy Garland his sister Sairy who has renamed herself Murine ("I got it off'n a bottle"), Anthony (later Tony) Martin the campus bandleader, and Betty Grable, Johnny Downs, Dixie Dunbar, and the Yacht Club Boys fill in as students.

Never was a campus so innocent, though the Yacht Club Boys in "Down With Everything" call themselves the "Anti-super-boopa-doopa-commu-bolsha radicals," turn a grind into a maniac, and send him off to heave a brick through a bank window. Otherwise, all is an American fairyland where an obscure Texas college that builds its football hopes on wimpy Erwin can actually beat Yale, and where everybody majors in romance. Launching the verse to "You're Slightly Terrific," Martin informs us that movies teach greater truths than any college can, and near the end Garland presents the movies' greatest truth at halftime of the big game in "It's Love I'm After (I don't want to be a millionaire)."

Garland, fourteen years old, out on loan from MGM (which didn't know what to do with her), and billed ninth, is wonderful, raw exuberance. She looks dowdy till she acclimatizes herself to undergraduate life, and then suddenly blossoms. No: explodes. The train ready to leave Texas for New Haven and the scene packed with wellwishers, everybody screams for a song. Garland momentarily unveils the trembly insecurity that would survive her in legend. "I've got a song," she says. "Can I sing it?" "Would it make you happy, honey?" she is asked; she knows she's in and beams, "Oh, it sure would!" and belts out "The Texas Tornado," her ease and power spreading the voice out in sound waves thick enough to see. *Pigskin Parade* didn't break any house records, but it told MGM what to do with Judy Garland.

Unlike the backstage, radio, and college musicals, operetta had little comedy, few leads, and a lot of pretension. As genres go, this was the tricky one: expensive, temperamental, and too quaintly non-American. So few costume operettas succeeded in the first sound years that the form had been almost discontinued, but Columbia reorganized the movement with *One Night of Love* (1934), Grace Moore's comeback as an American girl who goes to Europe to learn her craft and falls in love with her impresario (Tullio Carminati). Moore had learned from her earlier film failures, setting a new personal style for operetta on Broadway in *The DuBarry*, an engagement that she apparently promoted specifically so that Hollywood could rediscover her. Columbia's standing in the industry placed it somewhere between the major studios and the quickie garages of Gower Gulch (known as Poverty Row), and *One Night of Love* is a small piece in modern dress. All it has is Grace Moore singing opera: all it needed. Moore was an exciting soprano who communicated not through acting but through musical intensity; here, in "Sempre Libera" from *La Traviata*, the Habañera from *Carmen*, "None But the Lonely Heart," the title song, and others such, Moore is slim and confident; her phrasing caresses and her high notes blaze. The opera selections are not in English, the *Traviata* excerpt is horribly scrappy, and a rehearsal of the sextet from *Lucia di Lammermoor* is covered by dialogue. But Moore makes all the points, especially in "Ciribiribin," an Italian pop song sung in a tavern to a rapt gathering who join in for the last chorus while Moore flies high on an extravagant obbligato.

One Night of Love's huge profits heartened Hollywood to try operetta all over again, each studio sending to New York for legit singers. MGM, with its ample contract pool, already had the goods on hand in Jeanette MacDonald and Nelson Eddy. The pairing seemed unlikely: MacDonald, the boudoir dazzler of the Chevalier films opposite Eddy, the nonactor whose movie experience consisted of singing spots in three films? Allan Jones was suggested—but he was under contract to the Shuberts and couldn't cut free. So it was MacDonald and Eddy. MGM was hoping to launch not just a film but a whole series, and the sense of a team in the making was essential to the scheme, so the little-known Eddy shared billing with the famed MacDonald, his stolidity side by side with her vivacity. Eddy was the singing tree, immobile, and MacDonald the ornate kite trapped in its branches. Either one alone was a still picture; together they told a story.

MGM gave them a smart vehicle, Victor Herbert's 1910 stage hit, *Naughty Marietta*. Twenty-five years old, its score—"The Italian Street Song," "I'm Falling in Love With Someone," " 'Neath the Southern Moon," "Tramp, Tramp, Tramp," and "Ah! Sweet Mystery of Life"—still treated those who thrill to operetta, and its tale of a French noblewoman and a backwoods soldier of fortune in old New Orleans was still serviceable. The original *Naughty Marietta* had two opera-trained stars, Emma Trentini and Orville Harold (Eddy had sung opera and MacDonald was eventually to do so), and the music sounds it, with lots of coloratura embellishment for her in "The Italian Street Song" (the one with "Zing! Zing! Zi-zi-zi-zi-zing-zing! Boom! Boom! Ay!") and an all-out lyrical bazooka for him in "I'm Falling in Love With Someone"—the words say "Aw, shucks" but the notes carol lustily. Possibly the two stars had some inkling of how well the experiment would turn out; they're so glad to be in on it that they're already singing an overture before the story has begun.

We quickly learn that MGM has determined not to make another continental operetta in the Lubitsch style. His *Merry Widow* in 1934 had done acceptable business only in the metropolitan centers. *Naughty Marietta* in 1935, directed by W. S. Van Dyke II, would be national, something everyone can cotton to right off. Jeanette is popular, highborn, generous, and creative. She helps an old musician tap out a mystically romantic tune on the piano, inspired by the bells that rang out at the end of the title credits. "It's like the music of the spheres," MacDonald coos. "The melody of the universe, everything." Moments later, she is editing the tune—"Let's give it rhythm and move it up a tone." Presto! "Ah! Sweet Mystery of Life" is in gestation. It's not the heroine we love in Lubitsch, but a flash of the old MacDonald brightens the scene in which her unwanted suitor and his sisters present her with her proposed trousseau—all black. "Has there been a death in your family?" MacDonald snaps.

Nelson is popular, low-born, generous, and stalwart. Fleeing the diplomatic marriage disguised as a casquette girl, MacDonald and the other casquettes are captured by pirates; Nelson and his men rescue them. Immediately, the two stars bicker, but seriously: romantically. There is none of the self-spoof Lubitsch found in such plots, and it turns out that the public preferred the new MacDonald. They didn't want spoof. They wanted romance—spectacle, adventure, crinolines and uniforms, broad comedy from the comedians, as little as possible from the stars, and *lots* of voice.

MGM provided it all, reinventing the operetta genre all over again. Spectacle: the scene in which MacDonald departs France is a grand one, with a real harbor, a real ship, and a huge chorus with a fun tune, and then a hymn as the boat pulls out. Adventure: the pirates are really menacing (one of them coldbloodedly shoots the duenna who attempts to protect the girls) and Eddy's cohort intervenes when they are on the verge of raping their prisoners. The villain, MacDonald's French fiancé (Douglas Dumbrille), is nasty and haughty. MacDonald's outfits before she changes her identity and after she is unmasked are lavish. The comedians (Frank Morgan and Elsa Lanchester) don't intrude on the love plot and the lovers don't intrude on the comedy, contenting themselves with getting on each other's nerves in coy ways. (Eddy calls MacDonald "Bright Eyes." Try to imagine Chevalier doing that.) And the score pays full measure in vocal splendor. Eddy is in spectacular voice for "The Owl and the Bobcat," pumping tone out in exposed high lines as if it were the easiest thing in the world.

For him, it was; certainly it was easier than acting. Eddy's baritone boasted a phenomenal upper register that took him well into tenor territory, and he sang so grandly so casually that his numbers alone put his characters over. It's unfair to belabor the joke about his wooden acting, but he never did get the hang of reading lines, and it robs his roles of the panache they need. His inflection is not wrong so much as weak. MacDonald has to carry their dialogue, playing both their parts. She projects her insulted dignity and, by a kind of reflection, his braggadocio. That was their secret.

More about this team later. Let's consider other Broadway adaptations in these years of stabilizing genre-ism, especially in light of what the post-*42nd Street* Hollywood thought too sophisticated to use. The 1930s bring us into extremes of type, Warners' backstage guts or MGM's operetta glister. But Broadway always finds vitality in a combination of the two—*Of Thee I Sing*, for instance, with its taut political satire heightened by Gershwin's operatic structures. There was no *Of Thee I Sing* film, needless to say. *Naughty Marietta*, on the other hand, was an MGM cinch, once the two leads were cast, with sensible, "One Take" Van Dyke in charge and Herbert Stothart, himself a veteran of Broadway operetta (he collaborated with Rudolf Friml in composing the *Rose-Marie* score) shaving off outdated or unwanted numbers and rearranging others. Half the original Victor Herbert–Rida Johnson Young score remains in some form, beefed up by two interpolations from other Herbert works, and not a note is out of place. But Paramount brought *Anything Goes* to the screen in 1936 with its sharp comedy dulled, its characters prettied, and its Cole Porter score trimmed to "You're the Top," "I Get a Kick Out of You," and the minor "There'll Always Be a Lady Fair." Yet *Anything Goes*, a shipboard farce involving a nightclub singer, a stowaway, an heiress, and a mild-mannered public enemy no. 13, should have been right for the screen as it was. Letting Bing Crosby and Ida Lupino play the roles originated by William Gaxton and Bettina Hall was good thinking, as Crosby was more amiable and Lupino more exciting than their predecessors, and at least Ethel Merman was held over from Broadway, though setting her in a revolving swing for "I Get a Kick Out of You" was somebody's very strange anticipation of high-tech camp.

Hollywood did better with operettas like *Naughty Marietta* because operetta flattered the sentimentality that Hollywood liked to flatter—musical comedy too often degraded it. A piece like Kern and Hammerstein's *Sweet Adeline* lay right up Hollywood's alley, with its 1890s nostalgia, backstage whoop-de-do, and Cinderella romance of a beer garden owner's daughter who becomes a toast of Broadway in *The*

Belle of Hoboken. One thing *Sweet Adeline* had that Hollywood couldn't use: Helen Morgan as the heroine. When the show opened in 1929, Morgan was on the brink of a breakdown from assorted ills; by 1934, when Warners made the film, she was a little grainy for heroine parts. Irene Dunne took over the role and she seems out of place. She has a trained soprano, finesse in phrasing, and of course acts rings around her material. But that's the problem—she reads her more importunately melodramatic lines with a flip of emphasis that questions their validity. "Is this for real?" she almost says; *does* say it—watch her eyes. Her colleagues alone must have tried her actress' patience. Wini Shaw as her rival, sappy Donald Woods as her composer boyfriend, wooden Louis Calhern as *his* rival, Ned Sparks as a producer, and dithering Hugh Herbert as a backer are strictly flimsy. What holds *Sweet Adeline* together is Mervyn LeRoy's direction. He keeps everything sweet and dear, as the authors planned, but obviously sympathizes with Dunne. He takes in a touch of Berkeley, small-scaled, in "Lonely Feet" (one of those "through the mirror" numbers), and gets off a Pirandello at the end, when the camera pulls back from what we have thought is the last scene of *Sweet Adeline* but what turns out to be the last scene of *The Belle of Hoboken*. The suggestion that operetta romance is true romance may be hard to take, but it is not debatable that, in the Broadway adaptation, Hollywood felt most comfortable with Broadway's beauty rather than Broadway's sharp perceptions.

Universal attempted to combine the two, and redeem its mistaken part-talkie *Show Boat*, in a 1936 remake. This is by far the best of the three *Show Boat* films, though it emphasizes the sentimentality of the Kern–Hammerstein epic (love lasts a lifetime) rather than its salient idea (human strivings fall away to nothing; the natural world outlasts us all). The casting is superb: Dunne as the heroine, Allan Jones as her gambler love, Helen Morgan as Julie, Charles Winninger as Captain Andy, Helen Westley as his sour wife, Paul Robeson and Hattie McDaniel as family retainers, Queenie Smith and Sammy White as show boaters. Except for Westley and Smith, all had played their roles on stage in the original or revivals—and note that Morgan in the role of an outcast of mixed blood and (we eventually infer) sordid lifestyle is perfectly acceptable. As with *Moonlight and Pretzels*, the director was best known for horror, but James Whale did a fine job in balancing the show's lighter moments with the sorrow and survival that the story mainly features. The film is a quite faithful adaptation—Hammerstein wrote the screenplay himself—so the performers' experiential ease with their characters makes it rich in personal depth. Dunne ages artfully, from frisky teenager to a woman abandoned by her husband to a grande dame of the theatre now coaching her daughter for Broadway. Morgan is at her best, much more attractive than she had been in *Applause* in a similar role, and the chance to see a classic portrayal of Broadway history is no small windfall. Robeson was no actor—McDaniel utterly outclasses him—but his part mainly calls for an easy presence and a rolling basso for "Ol' Man River," and these he has. Jones is useful and the others exactly right, Winninger's jovial Andy well mated with Westley's humorless Parthy.

Show Boat is an atypical operetta in the opportunities it gives strong actors, but all operettas need strong voices; here, too, Universal did the show proud. All the major singers have trained instruments except Morgan, and what she didn't have in technique she doesn't need. Her little voice seldom carried far in a Broadway house, but here on microphone she can reach millions yet retain the intimacy performers like her rely on absolutely. Robeson, who had no problems with volume, nevertheless sang "Ol' Man River" live for the camera, without a playback, bringing it home not as a concert piece but to express it in character as Joe, a lazy and likeable deckhand. Conductor Victor Baravelle keeps the song moving—few conductors do—and at the close, backed by men's chorus, Robeson at last opens up and lets the tune soar.

Because Kern and Hammerstein worked so closely with Whale and producer Carl Laemmle, Jr., where the film *Show Boat* isn't faithful to the original it surpasses it. The authors wrote three new numbers, "Gallivantin' Around," an onstage ditty for Captain Andy's floating theatre; a new love song for Dunne and Jones, "I Have the Room Above"; and a comic duet for McDaniel and Robeson, "I Still Suits Me." All are excellent, though Dunne performs "Gallivantin' Around" in blackface, rolling her eyes and contorting her lips in one of the most objectionable racist jokes in film history. (She also shuffles, rather amusingly, in "Can't Help Lovin' Dat Man.") Though it's seldom thought of as one, *Show Boat* is a backstager, using the changing styles of American pop theatre to play cultural transformation against natural stasis. As the years pass, we get melodrama and minstrel variety, nightclub standup solos, antique story waltzes, and at last modern jive. It was somebody's grand idea to cap all this by letting Dunne's daughter reprise "Gallivantin' Around," updating it with hot Harlem dancing, but the number was cut from the release print—as was "Why Do I Love You?", one of the show's hit tunes—in an effort to clean up the ending. *Show Boat*'s resolution has always been a problem, as Hammerstein never found the way to tie up his theme and his love story contiguously. In the end as we now see it, Jones meets Dunne, after years of separation, in the theatre where their daughter is making her debut. Dunne seems surprised to see Jones, but not much moved. (Their daughter, still on stage with her big moment shattered by the real life going on in the balcony, looks stunned.) In desperation, Whale has the couple sing "You Are Love" again and calls it a wrap. It's a terrible letdown for an epic, but up to that point, Universal really has put itself out nobly—the arrival of the show boat, the drive of the Mississippi in flood and at peace, the midway of the Chicago World's Fair, and the sense of time and space that the story turns on has been experienced as never on stage.

Meanwhile, Hollywood hit on an almost wholly unexploited new form, the musical biography. Pick a subject involved in the music or entertainment world, and there was an instant musical: composers write songs for lavish sopranos, who sing them and the world weeps; impresarios mount spectacular shows and have colorful fetishes; performers hide a wounded heart behind the clown's twinkle. And, as studio chiefs prudently noted, such films are edifying and informative. Also great: *The Great Ziegfeld*, *The Great Waltz*, *The Great Victor Herbert*. Twentieth Century-Fox virtually made *The Great Fanny Brice*, calling it *Rose of Washington Square* (1939), and settling out of court with both Brice and Nicky Arnstein for not having said May I?

The credits for MGM's *The Great Ziegfeld* (1936) warn that the film was "suggested by romances and events" in Ziegfeld's life, *very* suggested. The film had a set format: a medley of guest stars, impersonated or in the flesh; specialty numbers of no relevance to plot or characters; little or no attempt to recreate the style of the artists involved; and the "suggested" approach to truth. There are exceptions, but most of these biographies, it turns out, are neither edifying nor informative: they are stories, like all other Hollywood films. They need romance, thrills, rise through fall to recovery or rise and fall mitigated by dream vision. *The Great Ziegfeld* takes the latter approach, both the rise and the fall stemming from Ziegfeld's extravagant showmanship, which could not survive the Depression (the man himself had died as recently as 1932) and the dream vision describing a *Follies* to end all *Follies*. William Anthony McGuire, who knew Ziegfeld well, wrote an episodic script, but the sequences are tied together in that new characters are introduced while characters about to fade out of the chronicle are still prominent. Thus, midway in the segment devoted to Ziegfeld's business and romantic involvement with Anna Held,

Ziegfeld presents Held with a diamond bracelet. She shows it to the chorus girls, and one, a cold blond gold digger, is unimpressed—by other women's jewels. The blonde wants diamonds the easy way. "I'll work," she says. "But I won't suffer" (warning us that of course she will). Seconds later, a dancing stagehand begs Ziegfeld for a chance to perform. Both blonde and stagehand become important later on, when Held has divorced Ziegfeld and falls out of the story. So the very long film never runs out of steam though the story has no suspense—Ziegfeld rises early and stays high till the last few scenes.

MGM went all out on this one and had a huge success, establishing not only a genre but a blue-chip profit history for it. *The Great Ziegfeld* runs three hours, cost two million, earned four, won an Oscar for best picture, and remains a treat, largely for its cast. As Ziegfeld, William Powell embodies the character: spendthrift, unscrupulous, imaginative, impetuous, with superb taste in women and women's clothes. And women find him irresistible. Frank Morgan is his usual excellent self as Ziegfeld's rival and friend, Virginia Bruce as the blonde suffers nicely, Ray Bolger does a fine turn as the stagehand, and Eddie Cantor, Will Rogers, and the muscleman Sandow are authentically duplicated. Best of all is Fanny Brice as herself.* Her sequence is frustratingly brief and director Robert Z. Leonard cuts into her songs with annoying dialogue, but it's the utter Brice as she really was. A kind of *verité* vaudeville sketch in her dressing room in a burlesque house, where she mistakes Ziegfeld for a peddler pushing a mink coat, is the funniest three minutes in film.

As Anna Held, the Austrian Luise Rainer has the second-biggest part. Hers is a controversial performance. She got an Oscar for it, so somebody must have liked her, but modern commentators regularly assault her, especially for the famous Telephone Scene, wherein she realizes she has lost Ziegfeld forever. I think Rainer is pretty special, a gorgeous woman with perhaps too ready a projection of doomed vulnerability. Her accent is right, her figure is right (Held popularized the tiny waist), her pleasantly erratic soprano is right. Her first scene with Powell, in her dressing room in London after a performance, defines the two opposing temperaments that will provision the film's emotional material. Rainer does all the work: she plays the neurotic. Powell is uninvolved, a man who loves woman; Rainer is a one-man doll. Her

---

*Trivium Footnote no. 4: MGM hoped to have Marilyn Miller in it as well, but Miller asked for too much money; Rosina Lawrence impersonates her in a walk-on bit.

inability to hold him substitutes for the lack of dramatic hurdles in his rise to fame as Broadway's spectacular showman.

Naturally, the film is spectacular. There is a balloon number, "You Gotta Pull Strings." There is a tails-spangles-and-ruffles number, "You Never Looked So Beautiful Before," with a few of Ziegfeld's signature walking showgirls. Biggest of all the numbers is Irving Berlin's "A Pretty Girl Is Like a Melody," originally heard in the 1919 *Follies*. This, at least, is historically appropriate and the set designer John Harkrider worked for Ziegfeld, though in this Berkeley age the "stage" is beyond the facilities of any theatre that Ziegfeld used. It begins simply, with Dennis Morgan (dubbed by Allan Jones) alone before a curtain. As he finishes the first chorus, the camera pulls back, the curtain rises, and the stage revolves to show an expanse of winding stairway loaded with dancers, singers, and showgirls. We travel the stairs through changes of decor and sound style to the top of what is now seen to be a gigantic wedding cake with Virginia Bruce grinning at the top.

The ice broken, the spring began to bubble. MGM's *The Great Waltz* (1938), on the rise of Johann Strauss, drew great tunes, what with his concert waltzes, marches, polkas, and operettas providing the score with new lyrics by Hammerstein. The project apparently meant the realization of L. B. Mayer's lifetime dream, and he carefully brought in an unusual number of foreign talents. Fernand Gravet is Strauss, Luise Rainer his wife, and Milizia Korjus the opera diva who almost wrecks their marriage. Gravet is the most direct of the three, intensely caught up in his success as musician and lover, forelock wet and tossing as he scrapes his violin. Rainer embellishes her Anna Held: now she is patient and sensible rather than capricious, though she still sobs hysterically. But even Rainer is not as odd as Korjus, as a lavish diva whose appetite for men and high notes is equally insatiable. With her Mae West looks, lopsided smile, and heavy accent, Korjus was already bucking Americans' sense of the feasible, and when, at their first meeting, Strauss catches his foot in her dress and observes, "I seem to be caught," she whispers, "So soon?" That sort of part.

But Julien Duvivier's direction and Dmitri Tiomkin's musical arrangements are amazing, their collaboration surpassing what Mamoulian and Lubitsch did in urging the pictures on with a musical drive. *The Great Schmaltz*, detractors have dubbed it, but the insult comprehends Duvivier and Tiomkin's achievement—Strauss' tunes have never resounded with such *Schwung*. Even Korjus' incessant bizarre coloratura begins to thrill; this music, the movie tells us, is the spirit behind which all Vienna unites, bourgeois and artists, aristocrats and revolutionaries. It must sound more than charming, more than heady. It must sound obsessively self-absorbed; and it does. The film's highlight shows Gravet and Korjus composing "The Tales of the Vienna Woods" out of a carriage horse's clip-clop waltz rhythm, piping shepherds, birdsong, and a coach horn while a back projection affixes real woods, moistly shining at dawn, to the MGM sound stage. To seal the triumph, Duvivier immediately transports us to a bandstand where Gravet plays and Korjus sings the new piece. Carried away, they waltz around the bandstand in the moonlight, strings running wild and Korjus riding a roller coaster of scales, stalked by one of the most astounding tracking shots ever seen. Duvivier also captures the most eliciting close-ups, making the most of Gravet's wildness, Rainer's pathos, and Korjus' cynicism. The entire movie is a study in techniques none of the various stage *Great Waltz*es could encompass, and its success, along with that of *The Great Ziegfeld*, guaranteed the rise of the musical biography. There were setbacks, such as Paramount's *The Great Victor Herbert* (1939), one of the first attempts to film the life of an American composer. But this wasn't a biography so much as a medley of Herbert hits swirling around a fetid love plot (Mary Martin and Allan Jones).

In this time of consolidation of form, the most gifted directors struggled for freedom. Josef von Sternberg, with his hagiographic approach to the Paramount Dietrich classics, should do wonders for Grace Moore, Columbia thought, and brought the two together for *The King Steps Out* (1936). But this adaptation of a Fritz Kreisler operetta was a disaster. Dietrich in the hands of less exquisite directors was reportedly heard to murmur, "Jo, Jo, where are you?" Moore found him less flattering. "Von Sternberg began," she wrote in her memoirs, "by modestly declaring he was the greatest director in Hollywood. 'I know,' declaimed the Great One, 'exactly what to do with the music . . . I know what to do with you.' " This meant, among other things, having Moore milk a cow during one of her numbers. The quarrels were heated, and despite Sternbergian flashes, the film has no supporters, including von Sternberg; who disowned it and fervently hoped that once closed it would never be seen again.

Rouben Mamoulian had better luck and managed to work outside the genre structure altogether. *The Gay Desperado* (1936), like his *Applause*, is not even precisely a musical. Of its principals, only Nino Martini sings, and the score is a potpourri taking in "The World Is

Mine Tonight" and Spanish folk and pop as well as "Celeste Aida." It's a delightfully ridiculous satire, though it never quite tops out on its premise. Martini, active again in Hollywood as part of the post-*One Night of Love* opera wave, is mainly around to admire Ida Lupino. The bulk of the fun in Wallace Smith's script belongs to a band of Mexican bandits headed by Leo Carillo, who wants to observe procedures laid down by the American underworld as reported—created?—by gangster movies. *The Gay Desperado*, then, is a burlesque of crime *and* of crime films; it is about itself, a funhouse mirror turned inward, as when Mamoulian opens with a typical Chicagoan take-'em-for-a-ride slaughter and then pulls back to show a rapt audience of Mexican filmgoers: film-within-film. Everyone in Mamoulian's world is clued into crime, commits it (not well) or suffers it (with equanimity or impatience). Martini, under Carillo's wing, meets Lupino when he stops her car for his first holdup. She's one of the impatient ones. "Something told me," she says, "this was amateur night."

The Mexican landscape provided Mamoulian with choice compositions, huge cacti guarding desert roads, hacienda walls on which to cast the famous Mamoulian shadows, the moonlit campfire. But his next film, Paramount's *High, Wide and Handsome* (1937), tells a more substantial tale in less consistently exotic scenery. Here, too, is a musical that resists genre. Oscar Hammerstein's screenplay recounts the historical discovery of oil in Pennsylvania just before the Civil War, and follows the farmers' attempt to develop their find despite vicious sabotage from the railroad money bosses. Randolph Scott is the idealistic hero, Irene Dunne the snake-oil salesman's daughter who marries him, Dorothy Lamour the openly sensual woman that small-minded townspeople call "marked," Alan Hale and Akim Tamiroff the railroad magnates, and Elizabeth Patterson Scott's tetchy grandmother; all could have played their roles in a songless melodrama, with thrust jaw from the hero, quiet wisdom from his wife, and sneers from the villains. But Mamoulian rises above traditions of format. Scott is Scott, true. But Dunne is unusual. Whether resenting her husband's preoccupation with his oil battles, or defending Lamour from a mob of the righteous, or coaching her in beer-hall singer's protocol, Dunne reinvents her type. She is more genuine than in *Sweet Adeline* and more interesting than in *Show Boat.* The Dunne–Scott romance and the oil-railroad war form the film's two plot lines, but Dunne implies a third line, that of a gifted woman whose society prizes her wifely gifts and no others. Because she sings the Kern score's big numbers, she dominates the film's emotional poetry, and we constantly see her in performing situations—medicine show, circus, and beer hall. Scott opposes her working, especially as a performer, but we need her on stage to define the film's sentimentality and energy, to reconcile Mamoulian's components of love story and western.

High, Wide and Handsome has been attacked for this collaboration of populist melodrama and nostalgic musical, but because Mamoulian finds the flint in romance and the suave comedy in villainy, he brings it off. His railroad tycoons, thoroughly evil, are no cardboard heavies—some viewers find them almost pleasant—and the use of Lamour as a turncoat who sides with the farmers, against them, and back with them keeps matters humanly ambivalent. Melodrama is all blacks and whites; *High, Wide and Handsome* is grays. Consider the visual environments alone. Mamoulian films the medicine show for shabby, provides splendid vistas of forest and valley (Chino, California, in fact), and shoots a Scott–Dunne orchard as falsely candy as any set ever built. These are extreme stylizations of settings, not accidents. Mamoulian wants his action plot as real as possible so the violence will be believable, but wants the love plot as fanciful as possible to make up for the violence and give us something to root for besides democratic self-reliance.

There is plenty of this. Scott and his comrades speak of their pipeline project as a means to "keep the poor man warm and light up every shack in the country." Dunne, being apolitical, calls the scheme "daffy." But one gets involved. When the railroaders try to smash the farmers with prohibitive rates, Scott calls it "a few men stealing what belongs to all men," and one of the fat cat villains calls *that* a reasonable definition of business. Mamoulian shoots his face tilted back in raucous laughter—not to type evil but to wonder about its insensitivity. Mamoulian keeps things open, wondering. In a western, the essential American good-versus-evil melodrama, the villain must die, or the evil never stops coming at you. But here, once Mamoulian brings out Dunne's circus friends—acrobats, sideshow freaks, and animals—to protect the pipeline (the elephants give it the feel of a Tarzan finale), the villains just shrug and give up. They're not in a western: they're in business. Yet, note that Mamoulian's sense of fantasy is as vital as his naturalism—elephants defending an oil conduit in the Pennsylvania hills! Hammerstein and Kern may have been the era's chieftains of schmaltz, but Mamoulian blends a rich mixture.

Coming out of the silent dream, talkies added new myths to those long established and reorganized Hollywood battles of good and evil.

Yet good is still good, evil the same evil. Under *High, Wide and Handsome*'s visual overlay is a simple story of the salt of the earth inheriting the earth the only way it can be done: by fighting for it. This simplicity, old as film, still had the power in Hollywood, and the film business continued to see its purpose as ratifier of basic truths and instiller of the American virtues, though each studio held different ones to be self-evident. Some films attacked the defects in American democracy; these were not musicals. Still, the musical had a moral system. Its paradigms have already become repetitive—paradigms that suggest the musical's purpose as entertainment based on messages of American self-esteem.

There is, for instance, the egalitarian self-congratulation of *The Hot Heiress, Sunny Side Up, High Society Blues, Love in the Rough*, and *Love Me Tonight*, in each of which a commoner mates with a noble. The men are almost always the commoners: Hollywood sees egalitarianism not as a doctrine of humanist fairness but as a stunt of unstoppable virile initiative. You can't keep a good man down, whether Ben Lyon's construction worker or Robert Montgomery's golfer. *Love Me Tonight*'s castle reverberates with cries of "The son of a gun is nothing but a tailor!"; only dusty aristos would see Maurice Chevalier as "nothing but" his profession. The independent man has something more than a job: good instincts. Or call it charm. In *Happiness Ahead* (1934), one of Warners' tiny musicals, window washer Dick Powell wins blueblooded Josephine Hutchinson without extending himself much. True, he does kiss her—by mistake—on New Year's Eve in a Chinese nightclub where the checks are tallied by abacus. But it is not so much Powell's force of personality as the insuperable male's ease with himself that conquers Hutchinson. Love doesn't disqualify status and money—male self-sufficiency does.

Corollary to democratic (male) self-congratulation is a more universalized paradigm, begot by the work ethic on the Depression fixation with employment. This may be stated as "everybody has the right to succeed if he or she is cute and lucky": the Keeler syndrome. Talent is less important than spunk, or perhaps talent *is* spunk. Get up and *do* it, and they'll cheer; all the world's a Gong Show. But charm conquers.

A third paradigm is an equalizer: little guys outsmart bullies. Eddie Cantor taught in sound what Chaplin had taught in silence: it's how you feel that counts, mainly how you feel about yourself. The little Texas college that beats Yale in *Pigskin Parade* believes in itself; so, more seriously, do the farmer-prospectors who fight the railroad mo-

nopoly in *High, Wide and Handsome*. All these types of self-esteem—
sex appeal, backstage spunk, and a convinced sense of cause—are really one type, related to such other varieties as Astaire's elegance and
Temple's optimism. All stem from a belief in oneself, whether one is
one of a kind (like Ziegfeld) or one out of many (like Keeler's youngster).

One other paradigm is that of community; in the musical, friends
are terrifically loyal and strangers often supportive. By far, the musical's favorite pattern for teamwork was the threesome. Three sailors
on leave, three gold diggers hunting marriage—these trios turn up in
all arts, but the screen musical featured them with outlandish frequen-
cy. It became a genre, an easy win with its built-in variety of persons,
one tender, one peppy, one silly. In 1929, *The Gold Diggers of Broadway* chalked the slate with Nancy Welford, Ann Pennington, and
Winnie Lightner, replaced in the remake, *Gold Diggers of 1933*, by
Ruby Keeler, Joan Blondell, and Aline MacMahon. The threesome
was already a cliché by mid-decade in *Born to Dance*, with James
Stewart, Buddy Ebsen, and Sid Silvers as sailors and Eleanor Powell,
Frances Langford, and Una Merkel as their girls: a main team, a cute
team, a funny team. The threesome didn't even need exactly rationed
opposites, as *Sally, Irene, and Mary* (1938) proved. The property had
been a stage musical and then a silent, in 1925, with Constance Bennett, Joan Crawford, and Sally O'Neil, and the possibilities in the title
so haunted Twentieth Century-Fox that it bought the rights from
MGM with no intention of using the original plot. In the new version,
Sally (Alice Faye), Irene (Joan Davis), and Mary (Marjorie Weaver)
are manicurists who break into show business on a renovated boat.
Faye sings the ballad "This Is Where I Came In" in close-up, lips
trembling, and romances Tony Martin. Davis performs the big apple
in "Who Stole the Jam?" Jimmy Durante clowns. Louise Hovick
(June Havoc) menaces Faye. Fred Allen hangs out. For catastasis, the
boat snaps its moorings during a performance . . . the usual. The film
has nothing in it but fun and the promise that if they hadn't stuck together, the girls might not have made it.

It was genre-oriented studio thinking that made the threesome a
regular event, and canny but never bold casting kept the trope alive till
the studios collapsed in the early 1950s. If it had bored moviegoers, it
wouldn't have lasted: it didn't bore moviegoers. It was the novel that
failed, not the familiar, and these post-*42nd Street* years are loaded
with a sense of series, of resilient repetition. Hollywood at last had defined the presiding elements of the film musical. Dance, musical style,

comedy, and personality were established components, serving various genres in certain proportion. Genre means stagnation—yet the artists seldom complained, for format gave them an identity. Astaire and Rogers didn't lose their vitality playing the same roles in nine RKO films. They flourished. Mae West dined out on formula; MacDonald and Eddy and Abbott and Costello soared on convention. Regard the series format as a sonnet, with fixed rhythm and rhyme: it is a challenge, a frame for concentration.

☆ 7 ☆
The Dance Musical

DANCE WAS SUDDEN, strange, and necessary in 1929. In the scramble to shoot and release musicals, Broadway choreographers were brought in for the kicklines and hoofing that added nothing to character or action. Dance was extra. Only the overhead camera shot, introduced by Maria Gambarelli in *The Cocoanuts* in 1929, distinguished dancing as a function of film.

Anyway, who would film dance in Hollywood? The choreographer? The cameraman? The director? Too often, directors who knew nothing of dance took charge, filming a number from several angles simultaneously and letting an editor paste it together with absurd reaction shots from bystanders. Obviously, dance would work best when an inventive director pulled the motion into his overall conception, or when a smart choreographer took over the camera for the numbers. Two examples: at the end of *The Merry Widow*, Ernst Lubitsch fills the screen with couples waltzing down halls to fill a ballroom in layered swirls of black and white. As the music builds, Lubitsch sharpens the sense of climax by intercutting shots angled from above, shot after shot to tighten the whirl, coil it like a whip. For once, we understand why everyone in Viennese operetta thinks the waltz is so sexy.

The other exemplar is Berkeley. We have already dealt with his trick photography, his expressionism, fantasy, and narrative geometries. But what makes him most influential historically is his discovery that the motion of the camera was as much a part of the dance as the dancers were. Take "Shuffle Off to Buffalo," the opening number in *42nd Street*'s *Pretty Lady*. This is a plot number, opening in the station and taking off for Niagara Falls. Berkeley begins straight on, curtain

☆ 109

up and the line kicking on to a rousing strain more Broadway than Broadway itself. Keeler plows onstage—a superb split-second as she cases the house—greets a friend, and dashes on board with her mate as the number begins and the dancing starts—but does it? There is very little dancing in "Shuffle Off to Buffalo," yet so much happens in it that only on repeated viewings does one realize that the camera is doing almost all the work. By the time Berkeley filmed the title number in *Dames*, he hardly needed dancers at all except for some rudimentary tap. Beautiful girls, yes; acrobats, even. Not dancers.

Besides editing and composition, style was discovered, the personal styles of Fred Astaire and Eleanor Powell that outmoded generalized choreography. Dancers had no great public outside of New York in the early sound years—as Marilyn Miller proved—but they started coming west after Astaire did, in 1933. An oft-quoted and almost certainly apocryphal report on his screen test discredits his looks, acting, and voice, and closes, "Can dance a little." Powell, however, seemed a natural. She made her debut in Fox's *George White's 1935 Scandals*, an Alice Faye backstager, but wasn't noticed till her second film, *Broadway Melody of 1936* (1935), for MGM. Noticed? She was seized. MGM made her "the Broadway Melody Girl" in the 1938 and 1940 editions and starred her in two spectaculars, *Born to Dance* (1936) and *Rosalie* (1937). The picture of Powell, thighs bared in black net tights and back bent to forty-five degrees, dancing all over a battleship in the former or hopping on a set of oversized drums in the latter, makes one of the era's great memories. In the end, her musicals were Powell films rather than dance films: she didn't spread dance all over the screen. *She* danced; the other characters sang, joked, and ran the plot. Powell, too, sang, joked, and plotted, but by focusing on *her* dances as the special things in her films, she eliminated the need for dance as expression of person or story. She didn't even have partners. Ray Bolger appears in *Rosalie* in a supporting role, but scarcely dances at all, and while George Murphy, Buddy Ebsen, and Astaire did dance with Powell, she didn't get all that much out of a duet.

This didn't hurt her career, as she was personally engaging and, frankly, the greatest woman dancer in Hollywood's history. *Born to Dance*'s battleship finale, "Swinging the Jinx Away," has been attacked for its too-much production, but it still supplies thrills today, and *Rosalie*'s "I've a Strange New Rhythm in My Heart" discloses a subtle Powell, gliding ornately from room to room of her Vassar dorm as she admits to loving Nelson Eddy. "So you're a princess!" he more or less cries later, when her royalty is revealed. "And I'm a fool." It's a foolish movie, with some peasant ballet that can't hope to compete—but tries to—with Powell.

It was Astaire who created the dance musical, collaborating with first-rate directors, scenarists, composers, and lyricists—and Ginger Rogers—at RKO throughout the 1930s. Alone, he is the statusless dandy, she the shopgirl princess; together, they catholicize class, over-throwing the received wisdom on caste as family and fortune for a new understanding of caste as charm. He gave her class? She has it already, or they could not have taken the ballroom so effortlessly; *she* gave *his* class a shot of energy. She gave him sex? He had it; or what on earth were they dancing about?

They fell into step by chance, as two supporting players still in search of The Break. She had made a swank feature film debut in *Young Man of Manhattan* (1930) as Puff Randoph, uttering the catchphrase "Cigarette me, big boy" and singing "I've Got It (but it don't do me no good)," but was getting nowhere in eighteen films at various studios. Her "Shuffle Off to Buffalo" duet with Una Merkel in *42nd Street* was her best sixty seconds on film till then, an essential Rogers as yet unrevealed: relaxed, a little sloppy but clean, and con-vinced—for the time being—that romance is the bunk. In mid-1933, they were each a brand X, he walking Joan Crawford through *Danc-ing Lady* and she getting dubbed (by Etta Moten) in *Professional Sweetheart*, a radio burlesque. Suddenly, they were cast in the "aerial musical picture" *Flying Down to Rio* (1933), RKO's attempt to create genre competition with Warners' Berkeley backstagers: South Ameri-can tropicana, noble Brazilian beauty loves handsome American band-leader, a woman vocalist and man accordionist-singer for laughs, an aviation motif. It sounds lively.

Messy, too. But this wasn't an Astaire–Rogers film. They were billed fourth and fifth under Delores Del Rio, Gene Raymond, and Raoul Roullien, and make a pair only nominally. We know, from hindsight, that Astaire is recklessly debonair and Rogers wistfully frosty and that they have only to meet to get it on. They don't here. They dance together, but not conclusively. They joke around, but don't get under each other's skin. They don't even meet: they already know each other when the film begins, which cuts them off from the classic Astaire–Rogers "meeting" scene—his ripping her skirt in *The Gay Divorcee*, his ruining her sleep in *Top Hat*, his getting her in trou-ble with a cop in *Swing Time*, his pretending to be a Russian ballerino in *Shall We Dance*. Not only are they not a duo in *Flying Down to Rio*; they aren't yet themselves. Rogers is more relaxed than we're used to in the later films, less serious about herself but, conversely, lacking her self-spoof. Where are her extremes? Astaire is very second man here, making sardonic huhs about Raymond's scrapes instead of getting into his own. But Astaire, Rogers, and *Flying Down to Rio* are at their best in the big number, the "Carioca."

The origin of a dance craze because of its distinctive head-to-head formation (which must be retained even when a couple goes into a turn), the "Carioca" is florid with South American riffs and doodles, and like just about every other dance lyric, gives the slimmest instructions: "Two heads together, they say, are better than one." Choreographer Dave Gould goes crazy, laying out three separate versions of the number, with Astaire and Rogers (who overdo the head touch and bonk their skulls), then Brazilians, then a black group, then all three casts simultaneously, with Astaire and Rogers on a stage made of seven interlocking, revolving white pianos.

The couple's second film together, *The Gay Divorcee* (1934), sets up the format that was to pull RKO out of its financial troubles and set Astaire and Rogers among the biggest draws in film. *Flying Down to Rio*'s many outdoor scenes were traded in for a distinct sound-stage look emphasizing art deco sets for plot and the huge white Bakelite floor for dancing; Astaire and Rogers were promoted to lead status with eccentric comics in support; the plot kicks into action when he accosts her and she resists; and the courtship is celebrated in a big number and extrapolated in intimate duet. *The Gay Divorcee*'s big one is "The Continental," possibly the longest single number in American film at a little over seventeen minutes; the duet is "Night and Day," a sinuous line riding a dangerously subtle beat. "The Continental" prides itself on its seductive powers, but it is the quiet dance for two on a hotel parquet overlooking the ocean that at last presents the sensual Astaire and Rogers as we know them. "Please don't ask me to stay," she tells him. "All right," he says, adding as she turns to leave, "Don't go." She turns back, smiling. "I've so many things to say to you," he adds, rolling into the importunate song. They continue the tease in the dance that follows, entirely set to the "Night and Day" tune with only a change in meter from fox trot to waltz for emotional expansion. The motion starts as she tries to leave again—he heads her off, pulls her into his arms, and she is suddenly his partner, gliding to his lead yet continuing to resist. He has to force her around, and at one point she repulses him with a slap on the chin, sending him off-balance across the floor. This is momentary, however. The first of their great duets suggests what all the others will confirm, that each is irresistible to the other, as she realizes when the music tapers off and he deposits her on a lush couch. She looks dazed, as if she had just lost her virginity. He looks smug. He gives her class *and* sex.

The Gay Divorcee, the foundation of the Astaire–Rogers style in film, derives from a show that Astaire had done on Broadway in 1932. Called *Gay Divorce*,* it was old-fashioned three-act bedroom farce with an English accent and was written to help Astaire weather the retirement of his sister Adele, who—many thought—carried the team. The show was cut down and cleaned, leaving Astaire and his vis-à-vis, their respective confidants, the hired correspondent in the heroine's divorce case, and in small parts a waiter, a bathing beauty, and the husband. Everyone is reduced to being obstacles for Astaire and Rogers so we can enjoy seeing them surmount them. Also reduced was Cole Porter's Broadway score; only "Night and Day" survives of songs that were either too sophisticated (the confidante's "Mister and Missus Fitch") or trivial (the waiter's "What Will Become of Our England?") for the movie. Some of the Broadway cast came in along with Astaire, though Erik Rhodes' correspondent became sillier than he had been and Eric Blore's silly waiter is cut to bones. A little Blore goes a mile, and with Edward Everett Horton as Astaire's lawyer friend, the comedy minces and dawdles obscenely. Director Mark Sandrich seems to have let Blore and Horton direct their own scenes, and the two—along with their moues and quadruple takes—unfortunately carried over into the whole Astaire–Rogers series.

What is most striking about *Gay Divorce*'s adaptation into *The Gay Divorcee* is how a conventional farce-with-songs became a dance musical, Hollywood's first. The major difference is the difference between an Astaire who has been dancing with his sister all his life and an Astaire who has become a romantic lead. *Gay Divorce* kept reverting to tradition whenever Astaire was not on stage with Claire Luce but *The Gay Divorcee*'s five-song score stresses the dancing lover and dancing in general. "Don't Let It Bother You," the opener, offers showgirls executing a can-can with their fingers; Astaire reprises it dancing for his dinner in the same club. "A Needle in a Haystack" has Astaire literally dancing all over his room: dancing is what he is, so he dances wherever he happens to be—something new in film. "Let's K-nock K-neez" pulls even Horton into the picture with Betty Grable and the

---

*Note the change of title in prudish Hollywood: there's nothing jolly about divorce, but once it has occurred, an ex-wife might as well frolic. By the same principle, death is no joke but everyone appreciates a merry widow.

chorus line; he looks ridiculous but he is dancing. The "Night and Day" duet derives from Astaire's Broadway staging, but "The Continental" is new—the very idea of pulling in spectacular numbers of dancers to gaze down and up at them is not available to Broadway.

It was available to Busby Berkeley, of course, and he might easily have staged something like "The Continental." But in Berkeley's films dancing is not an essential of character. Warner Baxter, Joan Blondell, Dick Powell, and such don't crave to express themselves in dance, and Ruby Keeler could, one believes, do without it. Even Rogers in her two Berkeley films was strictly a chorus dancer, part of the parade in "Young and Healthy" and mainly singing in "We're in the Money." But "The Continental" climaxes the budding Astaire–Rogers affair. It nearly dwarfs them, with its files of black-and-white costumed dancers, several different vocalists, intercut plot scenes, slow pans, long shots, mediums, and close-ups. But Astaire and Rogers start and end it. Locked in Rogers' hotel room by Rhodes, they look down on the dance floor as the music starts and Rogers takes the first chorus. They can't resist the "dangerous rhythm" and dance in the room until Astaire mounts a cutout silhouette of themselves—dancing, of course—on a record turntable. Rhodes fooled, they prance down and join the fun. They *are* The Continental: all the other dancers are mere patterns, smiling and joyless. Sandrich keeps the film moving by bringing in Blore to waddle to the beat as he squires a tray and catching Rhodes on the balcony, singing a chorus to his own accordion accompaniment. Still the dance spreads, as Rhodes discovers the ruse, but the unstoppable Astaire and Rogers claim the number at the close.

The dance musical, then, doesn't just have a lot of dance—it uses dance as an element of narration and character. Anyway, there isn't that much dancing in these Astaire–Rogers films. Their duets, usually three to a picture, last only two or three minutes each. With Astaire's solos (Rogers has few) this yields something like twelve minutes' total dancing in 110-minute films. But the emotional intensity of these numbers builds them big proportionately, anticipating and recalling them during the plot scenes rallies the public, and what a wonderful couple they make. Even when they are shunted into the secondary spots in their third film, *Roberta* (1935), they dominate. Irene Dunne and Randolph Scott are the apparent heroine and hero, she a Russian émigrée dress designer and he an American football hero, with the Paris fashion world the film's gummy setting (hideous clothes) and all the big Kern ballads going to Dunne. Dunne is no dancer and Scott's just a lump, and *The Gay Divorcee* has set a tempo for dance, so every time

Astaire and Rogers appear the film forgets the clothes and the balalai-kas and does what we want it to. Astaire's dance band, the Wabash Indianians, extend gloved figures to form an organ keyboard; Astaire plays them. Astaire and Rogers make "I'll Be Hard to Handle" a challenge dance that looks improbably spontaneous. Neither one could do what Dunne does for "Smoke Gets in Your Eyes," but they can dance it into the air, and do, literally: at a climactic, rising line in the melody, they swing themselves high onto a stairway. And whom does *Roberta* fade out on? Astaire and Rogers, in a last gleeful runthrough of "I Won't Dance."

Who exactly choreographed these films? A dance director laid out the ensemble numbers, but Astaire did his own choreography, improvising with pianist Hal Borne and Hermes Pan, who came on the lot as Dave Gould's assistant in *Flying Down to Rio*. For the duets, Pan learned Rogers' part, and then taught it to her. Astaire was a perfectionist, and a three-minute routine took weeks of creation and rehearsal before it was ready to shoot—and then it went up in whole takes until they had a clean one. Nor did Astaire vanish when the editing took place. (He also dubbed in the taps with Pan to keep the sound bright.) These were Astaire's films more than anybody's, which is why he's so admired by film and dance historians as well as by dancers of all kinds. The Astaire–Rogers musical, as form, was synthesized by a number of people—the topnotch songwriters who wrote to fit, the scenarists, the designer Carroll Clark, producer Pandro S. Berman, and supporting comics like Alice Brady, Helen Broderick, and, hell, even Horton and Blore, whose screwball dithering adds another level of fantasy to an already highly textured romance. (Everyone in these films is at least a little crazy; the fun of it is that Astaire knows this and Rogers, each time, has to learn it.) But Astaire created himself and initiated Rogers into his art, and these two acts are central to the formation of Hollywood's dance musical.

Rogers has been unfairly treated by commentators. Because Astaire planned the dances, they say he made her look good. Because women's fashions have changed more than men's have, they reprove her flamboyant ball gowns—that feathered job in *Top Hat*'s "Cheek to Cheek" and the buglebeads in *Follow the Fleet* that cracked Astaire on the jaw in the printed take of "Let's Face the Music and Dance." Because Astaire went on singing and dancing and she almost entirely gave musicals up, they suggest that she can't have been "serious" about style.

This is scummy putdown. Rogers' clothes in these films are smashing in any age, from her tomboy slacks to her backless gowns—and

☆ *THE ELEMENTS OF ASTAIRE AND ROGERS: above left, the screwball cohorts (Horton and Brady in* The Gay Divorcee*); right, the duet (*Shall We Dance*); below, Astaire's specialty solo) "Bojangles of Harlem" in* Swing Time*); opposite above, he's wry and she's wary (*Swing Time*); below, the big number ("The Continental" in* The Gay Divorcee*).*

the "Cheek to Cheek" feathers, which Rogers wore over virtually everybody's objection, were a national sensation. As for serious, no one put out harder than Rogers did when working with Astaire; if she hadn't been willing to work she wouldn't have made ten films with him. It is a commonplace to call Rogers Astaire's most effective partner, but I think she was also the best dancer he ever worked with, given his style. Eleanor Powell was technically more proficient, Cyd Charisse more graceful, Rita Hayworth just about the most stunning event in the history of Hollywood's woman dancers. But not even counting personal chemistry, Rogers still did what an equal partner must do with Astaire better than the others did. The quirky hopping turns, the look of surprise when some cranky maneuver is floated off like a soap bubble, the rigidity bent to suppleness and back again, the hand motions, the jests, the grins, the conviction—Rogers isn't just capable: she's *of* it. That's why it works so well.

By the time they made *Top Hat* (1935), it couldn't have worked better. This was the first property conceived entirely for them, with an original screenplay, a great Irving Berlin score, and the usual shenanigans from Broderick, Rhodes, Horton, and Blore. Huge profits assured RKO of the wisdom of the format—in the following year, 1936, Astaire and Rogers placed third in the exhibitors' list of top draws (after Shirley Temple and Clark Gable). *Top Hat* has more of the team's Famous Moments than their other films: Astaire crashing into a tap in a pompous, deadly silent London men's club; Astaire dancing on sand in his hotel room to caress Rogers to sleep in a room below; Astaire, pursuing Rogers, driving the hansom cab in which she hoped to elude him, tapping on the roof to tell her what's what; the two of them dancing "Isn't This a Lovely Day (to be caught in the rain)?" in a gazebo; Astaire shooting down a line of white-tie rivals with his cane in the title song; the startling crane shot that lifts "Cheek to Cheek" just as the music bursts out with a thrill; the view of the famous feet as they step onto the Bakelite Venetian piazza for a brief whirl in "The Piccolino."

The Astaire–Rogers milieu needed a change of air. In *Follow the Fleet* (1936), the pair go proletarian as a sailor and a dance-hall hostess. This time, she does not dislike him on sight: they're old friends, and Rogers has to chase a somewhat reticent Astaire. There is no deluxe Europe, no gala farceurs, no Horton or Blore. It's all shipboard and kitchen in San Francisco. Randolph Scott is back, paired with Harriet Hilliard (later Nelson) as Rogers' ugly duckling sister. Everyone who sees the film dumps on Hilliard, but worse people have played such parts, and she at least gives Lucille Ball something to do as a dance-haller drafted to coach Hilliard in lovemanship. Are there any rules to meeting a sailor? "Yes . . . and no," says Ball. "Yes before . . . and no after."

As in *Roberta*, the Scott romance is the main one, and Astaire is made to contrast with Scott, who is a cinch with girls, a champion rule-obeying sailor, and nonmusical, while Astaire can take or leave them, gets into navy trouble, and not only dances but plays the piano and leads a band. It's a little wearing seeing our stars sharing the terrain with people who don't belong in a dance musical,* and, despite the change of setting, *Follow the Fleet* has a distinct sense of cliché, though the big ballroom duet, "Let's Face the Music and Dance," is Astaire's most ambitious effort in this mode, a tiny one-act dance drama about two losing gamblers who flirt with suicide, then each other.

Berlin wrote the *Follow the Fleet* score, and Jerome Kern and Dorothy Fields wrote *Swing Time* (1936), the masterpiece of the series. With old Broadway hands on the set, there's none of the Hollywood fear of characters singing out wherever they are—another feature of the dance musical: *use* the music. Only two of *Swing Time*'s six numbers are performing spots, "The Waltz in Swing Time" and "Bojangles of Harlem." The others erupt out of the action. Thus, Rogers teaches dance and Astaire pretends he needs a lesson,† takes a few spills, and they're into "Pick Yourself Up," a song about trying, trying again followed by a glorious, breathless exhibition of hot pop stepping capped by the comic duo's attempt to do the same thing. Rogers had been fired for telling Astaire off, and her sidekick Helen Broderick had been fired for insulting Astaire's sidekick Victor Moore. Blore is so impressed with Astaire and Rogers' dancing that he reinstates her, so Moore grabs Broderick to dance her back into her job too. Their parody offers fake ballet, the demolishing of some of the dance-floor furnishings, and an absurd pose for the finish. "You're *still* fired," snaps Blore.

---

*It might be argued that Scott doesn't belong in any kind of musical, but the Hollywood form is more flexible—less fully musical—than the Broadway form, and nonsingers have no problem fitting in between the numbers. It's hard to picture Scott or James Stewart or Clint Eastwood or Jean Harlow in a stage musical, but in Hollywood they waited out the numbers, talked through them, had them dubbed, or depended on mike and mixing techniques.

†Eric Blore runs the dance studio. He offers Astaire a choice of "tap, ballroom, and aesthetic dancing," and Astaire asks for "a little of each"—the neatest description of his style ever observed.

Swing Time reclaims the opulence of the earlier pictures yet keeps one hand in *Follow the Fleet*'s empty decorative till. The Depression is sensed, if not mentioned, and the setting is a rather plain New York, the opulence confined to nightclubs. Director George Stevens even shows us Rogers washing her hair during a love song, "The Way You Look Tonight." So we learn that the glamor of Astaire and Rogers inheres not in fancy duds or continental places but in the offhand manner in which they assert the poetry of musical comedy. What else is the dance musical if not a reordering of the priorities in the musical to stress line, rhythm, image, over other elements? This is why there were so few dance musicals in the 1930s—Eleanor Powell had rhythm, but no image, and Berkeley worked almost exclusively in image. Astaire and Rogers pull the whole style together in a lovely and disturbing number, the most extraordinary seven minutes in the whole series, "Never Gonna Dance."

Never Gonna Dance was the film's title till just before release, and though *Swing Time* says it better—its buoyancy conveys the image most completely—the "Never Gonna Dance" scene proves how deeply feelings run in these movies. It's late in the film, and the couple has reached a parting stage, each to marry another. They're alone on a dance floor dominated by a double stairway, he in tails, she in white, and as she sadly starts up the stairs, he breaks into song. Kern shaped it in rondo form, and Fields filled it with bold puns and references to famous people that sound almost like dada in the context of a pop song. "To Groucho Marx I'll give my cravat," he swears, and "To Harpo goes my shiny silk hat," passing from a sauntering, blue refrain into heartfelt and then rhapsodic strains and back to his blue promise: "Only gonna love you! Never gonna dance." She has come back to join him on the floor, and the dance begins in a walk, their arms waving in despair. The music recalls "The Way You Look Tonight," then changes into something jazzy. He gestures at her: "*Why* must we part?" The "Never Gonna Dance" music pushes in, then cedes to "The Waltz in Swing Time," each shift in melody tightening the vise. They climb separate stairs, meeting at the top in the abandon of utter helplessness, the "Never Gonna Dance" strain full out with a gigantic piano descant as they almost beat each other in their turns. Suddenly, she propels herself out of the scene and he bows alone. It is nothing less than a retrospective of the whole film, and took forty-eight takes to can; somewhere around take number twenty-five, Rogers' feet began to bleed.

Swing Time ends, of course, with the pair in each other's arms, singing "A Fine Romance" and "The Waltz in Swing Time" in counter-point high over snow-covered Manhattan, but the sorrow of "Never Gonna Dance" makes a bigger impression than the happy ending, be-cause it's so different. Actually, all Astaire's dances are different. *The Gay Divorcee*'s "Night and Day" is ballroom seduction, *Roberta*'s "I'll Be Hard to Handle" contains spoken comedy, *Top Hat*'s "Cheek to Cheek" is trick ballroom, *Follow the Fleet*'s "Let Yourself Go" is jit-terbug and "I'm Putting All My Eggs in One Basket" is vaudeville butterfeet put-on, *Swing Time*'s "Bojangles of Harlem" is blackface with trick photography, and *Shall We Dance* (1937) features a ma-chine-age rhythm dance in a ship's engine room, ballet burlesqued and ballet for true, a walking number, and a roller-skating duet. *Shall We Dance* is the terpsichorean equivalent of Hollywood's legit-pop musi-cal crisis. Astaire is a ballet dancer, Rogers a musical-comedy dancer, and the climactic number hopes to contrast and blend the two. It doesn't work. The whole film suffers from dualism, for the ballet busi-ness uses an actress (Ketti Gallian) in the plot and a dancer (Harriet Hoctor) in the big number. Very confusing. Otherwise, *Shall We Dance* would have been top. Perhaps RKO had evolved the dance mu-sical so well that it no longer worried about the quality of dancing as long as it had an integrated musical, with its special ability to collect all sorts of *objets trouvés* into a sort of theme. In *Shall We Dance*, the theme is recognition of romance, knowing the love of your life at first sight, seeing him/her through disguises, and so on. The film is full of thematic jags—Astaire puts on a false front when he meets Rogers, the pair are falsely believed to be married, they fake a quarrel in "Let's Call the Whole Thing Off" (the one with "You say either and I say eyether"), they fake a romance and really do marry to bust the rumor with a divorce, and we even see iconographic representations of Rog-ers—in a flip-picture book of her dancing (which director Mark Sand-rich then turns into the real thing), in a plastic dummy in a PR stunt, and in the big number, in which, denied the real Rogers, Astaire dances with a stage full of girls in Rogers masks.

As a style, Astaire and Rogers never grew tired despite their consis-tency—same places, same people, same (or nearly) love plot. Every one of their nine RKO films was a success, and the elated beauty of their personality that impelled the public to clap at the screen after their numbers never lost its appeal, but neither of the two stars liked their interdependence. Rogers demanded more money, more publicity (to equal Astaire's), and the chance to make diverse nonmusicals on her own. And their last film for RKO, *The Story of Vernon and Irene*

Castle (1939), turns another change in style, being a bio in which the romance is concluded early and the adventure of making it as newfangled ballroom dancers finds them stranded in Paris and domestic in the United States. And Astaire actually dies at the end. Still, the split was due: the history was already made now, nine times.

Nowadays, many delight to tell of an Astaire–Rogers feud and fondly point out that in their reunion film, *The Barkleys of Broadway* (1949), Astaire tells Rogers: "It took a lot of patience to put you where you are . . . I pulled things out of you! I molded you! Like Svengali did Trilby!" But Astaire needed Rogers more than she needed him, for while she was eager to try anything, his character and talent needed the precisely appropriate partner. Sure, Astaire alone is genius enough. But the public longed to watch him find ultimate completion in a partnership. He himself set this up in the affecting honesty with which he played the love plots and the sensuality that came out in his duets with Rogers. In *Roberta*'s "I Won't Dance," she tells him, "When you dance you're charming and you're gentle," and he is—on the condition that she totally surrenders. This is why they come to blows in "Night and Day": *The Gay Divorcee* only established the seduction. The following films affirmed it.

So Rogers made a flurry of films between those with Astaire, but he (who, remember, spent far more time than she did preparing each one) made only one non-Rogers musical, *A Damsel in Distress* (1937). Fine entertainment, it has its troubles—and lost money.

The plan seems right. The source and co-author is P. G. Wodehouse, the setting London and a country palace. The people are English eccentrics, two American wisecrackers, and a lonely princess locked in a chateau. (It sounds like *Love Me Tonight*, but the atmosphere is entirely different from the Parisian Chevalier–MacDonald idyll. That was operetta with shadows; this is musical comedy in a mist.) Astaire is an American musical-comedy star bedeviled by PR about his love conquests; George Burns and Gracie Allen play the comics, Constance Collier the heroine's dragonlike aunt, Reginald Gardiner a scoundrelly butler (with, however, an irresistible craving to sing Italian opera, to Collier's horror); there are also bandleader Ray Noble as an impeccable noble dope who breaks into swing when he gets near a piano, little Harry Watson as a scrappy page, and a fest of madrigal singers. In other words, very Wodehouse, cut with some American pep. The same old team served brilliantly as always: producer Berman, director Stevens, designer Clark, with a Gershwin score. Fine; but who shall dance with Astaire? RKO considered Ruby

Keeler (too American), Jessie Mathews (too giddy), and at last settled on Joan Fontaine, who could neither sing nor dance. The splendid dance musical suddenly pulled back to the old days when a musical was just a film with some songs and things. *A Damsel in Distress* ingeniously works around Fontaine, giving Astaire, Burns, and Allen a comic dance with whisk brooms in a country inn where they kick each other, get kicked by suits of armor, and kick the armor back; and letting Allen sing "Stiff Upper Lip" outside a funhouse, into which the three then proceed for wild visual-cum-musical effects. The madrigal takeoff, "The Jolly Tar and the Milkmaid," is wonderful: Astaire has sneaked into Totleigh Castle with the singers, and must perform with them to evade detection. It's Wodehouse country weekend snafu made vital. Moreover, Stevens films "A Foggy Day" through a handsome fog as Fontaine, high up in the castle, watches Astaire strolling through the park.

But sooner or later the lovers have to duet, and the agreeably laid-back "Things Are Looking Up" is it. Astaire sings it and they do dance, but we clearly see him extending himself to make his partner look good. At one point, she actually sits down while he glides over her, trying to get a little poetry going. To do her justice, Fontaine is fine doing what she does well. This just isn't her part.

Obviously, Astaire was going to have to find a suitable partner after Rogers: someone who danced. On a larger scale, the musical, dance or otherwise, was going to have to consolidate and replenish the form that made it artistic and peculiarly American—a form that hit its prime in these Astaire–Rogers films because it found character and style through song and dance. It was more musical than the Warners backstager, more fluid and natural than the costume operettas, more integrated than the star vehicles. The dance musical exercised highly evolved musical instincts that most people supposedly can't respond to, and made a fortune. It liked and respected its audience, and taught a self-esteem at once egalitarian (Fred as Mr. Yank) and elite (Fred dances), casual (Fred's self-spoof) and special (Fred's tails), everyday (Ginger) and unique (Ginger). Now, can Hollywood develop this aesthetic with different stars and staff? Or will the integration of musical parts simply disperse as Astaire and Rogers did?

☆ 8 ☆
Opera Versus Croonbelt

THE SOUND FILM'S first purpose was to transmit music, preferably respectable music. But sound turned out to be mainly talking, and the music, to suit the stories, was popular. Still, studio executives longed to find a place for opera—meaning "real" music. William Fox hoped to do well, as well as good, when he brought Irish tenor John McCormack to the screen in *Song O' My Heart* (1930), partly filmed in Ireland on little more than McCormack's charm and art. The film was a public service, for its slight sentimental storyline is a peg on which to hang McCormack's repertory, thus bringing his recital to a national public. Fox even ran ads asking that public to help choose the songs for the film, from such as "When Irish Eyes Are Smiling" and "My Wild Irish Rose." Like the first Vitaphone vaudeville, this was fine musicianship. Like the second Vitaphone, it was popular material, of universal appeal. Immediately successful, *Song O' My Heart* proved film's commercial potential for the real-music voice. McCormack couldn't act and the proceedings were kept dramatically subdued in order not to overextend him, but nobody complained, for *Song O' My Heart* acted like what it was: a chance to hear great singing set off by some romantic and some comic characters. Why didn't Fox just film McCormack in recital? That wouldn't have been a movie; people like a story.

Most opera singers, used to filling huge theatres, tended to a huge dullness or a huge excitement; neither one, we remember from the early musicals, was good for film. But Grace Moore's comeback in *One Night Of Love* reopened the case for the legit singer, and in they came. Baritone Lawrence Tibbett returned for *Metropolitan* (1935) and *Un-*

der Your Spell (1936); tenor James Melton, soprano Lily Pons, and mezzo Gladys Swarthout all followed up debuts with second, third, or fourth films. Now secure about form, Hollywood fit the singers into the framework more gracefully. The studios tried lavish costume operettas or inexpensive modern-dress stories—Mamoulian, always the odd man in, united the two approaches in *The Gay Desperado.*

The modern-dress opera-singer films lacked purpose. Even when Warners put Busby Berkeley in charge of the dances in Melton's debut, *Stars Over Broadway* (1935), the result lacked flash. Melton performs legit and pop ("Carry Me Back to the Lone Prairie") and some Warren–Dubin, and the story—agent Pat O'Brien discovers and manipulates hotel porter Melton, aiming him at a pop radio market until Melton hits the skids and O'Brien gives up and sends him off to Italy—is serviceable. But when Berkeley smelled a production number in "September in the Rain" and planned his usual fiesta in a forest of dancing trees, Warners waxed stingy, and the song had to wait till its reprise in *Melody for Two* (1937), Melton's third and last film, to make its effect.

Melton himself made little effect, but then all of the opera singers had something wrong somewhere. Swarthout's problem was her acting. She wasn't incompetent; she was . . . an opera singer doing film. Paramount's *Rose of the Rancho* (1935), with John Boles, plenty of guitars and mantillas, and a Ralph Rainger–Leo Robin score, is Swarthout's best, with big duet, "Thunder Over the Prairie"; big rouser, "Got a Gal in Californ-i-a"; "If I Should Lose You" for Boles; waltz flirtation title tune ("I could call you a flame or a flower . . ."); and Swarthout's gala set piece, "Where Is My Love?" with swirling strings, flamenco stompings, sneaky waltz theme ("Some night in summer by the moon, my love will come riding"), the usual rhetoric from the chorus ("Why does he hesitate? Why does he linger?"), and a high note on the significant word ("Where is my *love?*").

Pons had less voice than Swarthout but more va-va-voom; she also had a Jerome Kern–Dorothy Fields score to back up the operatic stuff in RKO's *I Dream Too Much* (1935). Detractors have dubbed it *I Scream Too Much*, fans call it *I Cream Just Right*, and Pons does draw heavily on her top register. Henry Fonda, Osgood Perkins, and Eric Blore fill out the cast, but the film is all Pons. She starts at the piano with "Caro Nome," cheers up a child at a fairground with a men's chorus in "The Jockey on the Carrousel," tries swing in "I Got Love" and bares her exquisitely impertinent naval in *Lakmé*'s Bell Song. A drawback was Pons' heavy French accent, impenetrable in the highflying "Jockey," wherein the choristers have to step in with solo lines so we can follow the lyrics. But what American pop singer could bring off such a number, with its volatile tempo and harmony geared to suggest the abandon of a carousel ride? A sad tale of figurines, a jockey who loves and dies for a dancer, the song lies well beyond the reach of the actors who inhabited the average musical and makes a splendid impression.

The "opera" musical, then, had its advantages. Grace Moore's five Columbia films offer an instance, for while Moore is no actress—she smiles a lot and seems unaware that she's wearing the weirdest clothes in film history—she sure was a singer, and carried her films with vivacious renderings of opera and pop. *One Night of Love* led to *Love Me Forever* (1935); the aforementioned von Sternberg opus *The King Steps Out*; *When You're in Love* (1937), with Cary Grant; and *I'll Take Romance* (1937). The last is typical, small in budget, with Moore as a diva courted by opera company manager Melvyn Douglas. As actor, Douglas is expert, leaving Moore looking foolish until she rehearses or performs opera or accompanies herself on the piano in the title song, a gentle waltz, as Douglas looks on. The opera includes bits of *La Traviata*, *Martha*, *Manon*, and *Madama Butterfly*, the pop "She'll Be Comin' Round the Mountain," and French music hall; Helen Westley plays Moore's tough mother, Margaret Hamilton does a maid, Stuart Irwin is Douglas' sidekick, and the two leads take turns having each other kidnapped. That's the film.

The constant emphasis on pop is no stunt, though it goes a mite haywire when Moore blats her way through "Minnie the Moocher" in *When You're in Love.* It is an attempt to make up for the often scrappy singing of the regular musical-comedy types. Anyone can sing pop, but not everyone has the musicality that penetrates the material to deliver all it has in emotional conception. Fred Astaire had it, and songwriters were crazed to hear Astaire perform their work, though his was neither a golden nor a trained voice. But most of Astaire's colleagues were not great interpreters—which is where the opera people came in, with their cowboy songs and "Shortnin' Bread." They worked pop as well as Astaire, and with a lot more voice, and the drive for musicality became contagious. Kirsten Flagstad, Helen Jepson, Charles Kullman, Lauritz Melchior, Leopold Stokowski, José Iturbi, and others were drummed into the corps; the call went out to ballet people such as George Balanchine; and Jascha Heifitz even undertook a speaking role (as himself, giving a concert to save a slum-area music school) in Samuel Goldwyn's *They Shall Have Music*

(1939). The title reads like a fetish. The odd thing is that Hollywood had already built up a company of extraordinary musical talents, widely enjoyed but uncelebrated. Because they sang pop.

The American singing style had changed remarkably in the decade or so that preceded the implementation of sound in cinema. The parlor ballads, waltzes, and novelty songs largely written and performed by the white Protestant middle class had ceded to black saloon piano and its derivations, the startlingly everyday feeling of the Irish George M. Cohan and the Jewish Irving Berlin and Jerome Kern, who touched base with black ragtime to create an American idiom. New singers appeared to sing the new songs. A more conversational approach to lyrics subdued the "lay 'em in the aisles" bombast. Baritones and belters elbowed aside the clammy tenors and sopranos. Upstart minorities in vaudeville imposed odd jargon and inflections on the midcult. Imaginative "scat" variations on the tune or lyrics made each performance fresh and personal. Bold instrumentalists helped layer the new styles with their explosive accompaniments. And, finally, the rise of radio in the 1920s promoted the new song styles as vaudeville, cabaret, and Broadway could not, sending Fanny Brice and Nick Lucas and Ethel Waters to all corners of the nation.

These three typify the new wave, Brice with her heavy Jewish slant on comedy and—in a wholly different voice—unutterable doomed grandeur in torch songs; Lucas (the "Singing Troubador") with his light presentation, so suitable over a strummed guitar; Waters with her black savvy and sexy repertory. Each got into a few films, and others carried on after them, but the studios never saw these singing talents as exponents of a native art, and continued to look for that touch of opera to "redeem" pop. Yet American art history was made in pop, not in opera. Pop liberated the underdog races, and let women show their guts and men be capricious and tender.

Take Sophie Tucker. In her first film, *Honky Tonk*, in 1930, she delivers "Some of These Days (you're gonna miss me, honey)" in a robust woman's basso, warning a lover of her impending departure and sounding rather pleased about it, and hits a combination of speech, recitative, and all-out singing in her motto tune, "I'm the Last of the Red-Hot Mamas." Tucker's was a sturdy voice, one that puts over rather than dandles a song, but she knew how to build a number, letting it dance out like a lariat to pull it taut at the climax. This she does in "Feathering a Nest (for a little bluebird)," a man's song that she sings without bothering to change the pronouns. This would have been unthinkable for Brice, who acted her songs; Tucker just delivers them.

She even asks her nightclub audience to join in, easing down one aggressive *espontanea* with a "Lovely, darling! Lovely, dear! Lovely!" as Tucker prepares to take over and push home to a big-bang finale. The girl's slender amateur's soprano contrasts vividly with Tucker's husky professionalism: Tucker represents the new mixed culture, up from the tanktown music halls to take the nation, music with an ethnic face, whereas the girl is the old pure culture, a slice of white bread far from her box. An unknown Marilyn Miller or Nancy Carroll might have played the part.

If pop music let women express initiative, it let men relax. Woman belted, men crooned. The word "croon" has been so overused it has no meaning anymore; let's reclaim its definition. The microphone invented crooning. No longer having to send a song into the ozone the hard way, men singers took to using the barest veneer of voice on the radio, giving everything a mellow and intimate air. Many men were crooners, but because Bing Crosby was the best known, his singing style is called crooning. Wrong. Crosby's amazing inventiveness led him into all sorts of riffs and embellishments way beyond crooning. True, his voice rang mellow and he aimed at the intimate. But his rhythmic dexterity, his sly phrasing, his athletic leaps up and down the scale, and his sudden strange distillations of emotional give were not in the crooner's vocabulary. And his immense popularity changed the course of American singing.

Crosby hastened the emergence of the easy-style singer. The dramatic baritone survived in Nelson Eddy and Howard Keel, but they were strictly operetta. Modern-dress musicals needed a more vernacular sound. The tenor who bleated story ballads passed away, though film continued to feature tenors with a lively style, such as Dick Powell—here was another gifted stylist, much underrated now that pop tenors are practically extinct. If the monitors of the Production Code counted any musicians, surely they should have complained about Powell, for beneath the clear-cut look and the paper-route smile lurked a hot lad with a ready kiss. In *42nd Street*, he jumps on stage from the wings to launch "Young and Healthy" with boyish verve, and the lyrics do sound innocent (as in "I'm full of vitamin A"). Powell, however, doesn't. As the number proceeds, he invests the tune with a leer, slipping in a wicked m-m-m just before one line and exploding in a satyr's whinny after "vitamin A." Crosby recorded the song with Guy Lombardo; here is a telling comparison, not between the new and the old but between two types of new. Where Powell is eager, overeager, a little crazed, Crosby is just energetic. Both sound amused at their hunger, but where Powell would like to satisfy it pronto, Crosby enjoys the waiting, with a little scat variation chorus to toy with the tune. (Lombardo and his Royal Canadians assist in setting the tone with an extremely precise arrangement whose only gambol is a pouting guitar solo.) Compared to the old-style tenor who insipidly sings "The Wedding of the Painted Doll" in *The Broadway Melody*, Powell and Crosby are new brooms sweeping into the future.

They made it look too easy to be important, however, and the studios kept on sifting through the legit ranks, trying to find repute and profits in a workable genre. It was MGM that made the breakthrough, not with one star, but a pair. Chevalier and MacDonald, together for the last time in as late as 1934, gave way to MacDonald and Ramon Novarro (in *The Cat and the Fiddle* later that same year), and then to Novarro and Evelyn Laye (in *The Night Is Young* the next year). Neither pairing worked. At last MGM found the solution, as we know: MacDonald and Eddy in *Naughty Marietta*.

Their eight pictures together, from 1935 to 1942, are not as consistent as the Astaire–Rogers series, and not unique. When the King and Queen of Carioca made films without each other, they made different kinds of films, but MacDonald made operettas without Eddy and vice versa, operettas that they might easily have made together. Yet MacDonald and Eddy were, in their way, a true team, mixing the chemistry that permits one to accept disguised princesses, dream melodies, and beautiful doom. Operetta was dying on Broadway by the 1930s, but through mostly careful planning MGM concocted a recipe to produce excellent films of lasting appeal: efficient directors to keep the juice flowing (W. S. Van Dyke II and Robert Z. Leonard), simple stories focused on the central romance rather than plot business, lavish decor, resonant titles from Broadway's past, strong scores of diverse origin excellently conducted (by Herbert Stothart), and lots of singing by the two leads with little help from others. These were less fully equipped vehicles than the RKO dance musical, where assorted folderol helped the principals establish their special world view. Take Astaire and Rogers out of their movies and something would remain: much of the "Carioca," "The Continental," "The Piccolino"; all of "Orchids in the Moonlight," "Yesterdays," "Smoke Gets in Your Eyes," "Get Thee Behind Me, Satan," Eric Blore in a hundred tizzies, Edward Everett Horton in a thousand double-takes, Delores Del Rio, Ralph Bellamy, Edna May Oliver, and so on. But take MacDonald and Eddy out of their films and you'd leave nothing behind except an occasional heavy who gives the love plot suspense.

☆ *MACDONALD AND HER MEN: above, she's worried with Ruggles in* One Hour With You; *she's startled with Chevalier in* The Merry Widow *(they're locked in jail by royal order: love or rot!); below, she's pensive in* The Cat and the Fiddle *but Novarro's sporty under an umbrella.*

☆ *Above, in* The Firefly, *she's radiant with Jones in a backlot Breughel; she's at war with Eddy in* Sweethearts; *below, she's pathetic with Barrymore in* Maytime. *Who wouldn't be?*

Rose Marie (1936), which followed *Naughty Marietta*, brings in Allan Jones in the opening opera sequence, and James Stewart has a small but important role as MacDonald's outlaw brother, but this is perhaps MacDonald and Eddy's most resonant team effort (if only because "Indian Love Call" is so basic to the camp lampoon). The pair spend much of the action alone together in the wilderness—she is trying to save Stewart from Mountie Eddy and he is tracking him. The antagonistic nature of their respective interests is what makes *Rose Marie* fundamental to an understanding of the MacDonald–Eddy pact. Where Astaire and Rogers fuss a bit and then slip into love, and where Chevalier and MacDonald had only a plot jag to smooth down, MacDonald and Eddy clear the whole social system to get together. She is the aristocrat, he the insurgent (*Naughty Marietta*, *New Moon*, *Bittersweet*); she the star, he the nobody (*Maytime*); she the frontier maid, he the desperado (*The Girl of the Golden West*). Only in *Sweethearts* are they equals, and in *Rose Marie* they are divided by the law code her brother has broken.

Little of the Friml–Stothart–Harbach–Hammerstein stage *Rose-Marie* survived; MGM's plan was to affirm the personalities unveiled in *Naughty Marietta*: the raving coloratura and the arrogant scout who meet on the high notes. Thus, *Rose Marie*'s early scenes revolve around a temperamental MacDonald, the middle scenes bring in Eddy's oppositional steadiness, and the final scenes attempt to conciliate them. We open on a performance of Gounod's *Roméo et Juliette*; curtain down, MacDonald curses out the orchestra and berates Jones for "holding every high A longer than I did": Rose Marie is proud. Wangling some influential help for her brother—Rose Marie is loyal and loves chastely—she entertains the Canadian prime minister with "Pardon Me, Madame." The singing inspires people all over her hotel to join in, even the switchboard operators: Rose Marie has The Gift. And she is gracious, tossing flowers to her admirers in the street. But she learns that Stewart has escaped from prison and killed a Mountie. Rose Marie runs off—cancel her dates!—to the rescue.

Enter Eddy and his Mounties. In the tradition of movie "half-breeds," Rose Marie's Indian guide has robbed her, and she winds up in a frontier saloon singing for supper. Here is a main chance to trade off pop and legit, as MacDonald stands a honky-tonk belter (Gilda Gray) in a challenge sing on "Dinah" and "Some of These Days." MacDonald flounders, and Eddy sympathizes. "One thing about Belle," he says. "If she ever got lumbago, she'd never sing a note." He looks dandy in his uniform, though he is as stiff on location as on a sound stage. Lake Tahoe provides a stirring setting for an Indian-festival big number, "Totem Tom-Tom," very barbaric with an immense opening long shot and precise closer views of a huge drum (rolled in, played, danced on, and revolved), wild animal costumes, grand totem poles, lake, and mountains.

But we're here for a love duet—if this were RKO, Astaire and Rogers would have danced by now—and MGM attempts to bring the stars together with song and charm. Eddy serenades MacDonald with the title song in a canoe, admitting that he sings it to other women, inserting the appropriate name. "But it didn't work with Maude. Nothing worked with Maude." The line is a dud—neither MacDonald nor Eddy can play corn.

Only a Martian, in 1936, could not have known that "Indian Love Call" is the centerpiece of *Rose Marie*, a mantra of operetta in general and these two in particular. When MacDonald discovers an echo and sings "Three Blind Mice" with herself (Rose Marie has wit), we moderns brace ourselves for the notorious close-up shots. She'll stare grimly at his mouth, right? They'll fight for right of profile, right? Actually, Van Dyke directs straightforwardly, letting out the rope of operetta by inches. First, MacDonald has to shiver in the wild and have mishaps and finally accept Eddy's help. *Now.* She hears distant singing—the Indian love call of Romeo-and-Juliet ghosts! Eddy tells the legend: when a lover gives the call, they answer. Still Van Dyke holds back, giving Eddy the song for a verse and chorus. No Indian echoes, no MacDonald. They separate for sleep. Only later does Van Dyke give in, in a reprise, and this is the one, with MacDonald very into the mime, looking tender, looking away, closing her eyes, and Eddy staring at her transfixed. When they kiss, we hear the Indian spirits' echo.

With *Naughty Marietta* and *Rose Marie* behind them, MacDonald and Eddy set the scene for the standout operetta series, a reference known to millions who have never seen them in action. This is a questionable credit. And it seems that MacDonald had no desire to spend all her career singing love calls with anybody, and she called to MGM's attention a script by Robert Hopkins about a nightclub owner and an opera singer in old San Francisco. MacDonald wanted to play the singer opposite Clark Gable; Gable couldn't see it. But with the script rewritten by Anita Loos and a strong feeling of drama with songs rather than operetta minus one voice, the project showed great possibilities, with lots of Barbary Coast goodtime, a smashing earthquake finale, and a part that screamed for Gable. *San Francisco* (1936) ended up as one of the year's big films and its lengthy earthquake sequence rivals any recent disaster film for verisimilitude and terror. Where does it stand as operetta? MacDonald handles most of the music—everything from *Faust* and *La Traviata* to ancient music hall and "Nearer My God to Thee"—and makes a nifty couple with Gable. "If there's anything I admire," he tells her when she repulses his first advance, "it's a woman you can trust out of town." (A bit later, he tells his mirror, "Goodnight, sucker!") Marietta's reticence and Rose Marie's strength are portable. And it's fun to hear the odd number in what would most likely have been a straight tough guy–demure gal epic. The fetish for setting pop and legit side by side inspires two versions of the title song: MacDonald sings it and swings it. Her highflying descant in "The Battle Hymn of the Republic," a big choral finale as the San Franciscans march back into their wrecked town, is a little much, but Van Dyke makes the moment so exhilarating that only a creep would complain. It may well be that operetta helped to reassimilate vocal music into dramatic film after the antimusical reaction of 1930–31. Any movie might contain a song or two, but if a MacDonald could bring presence to melodrama, the sky was the limit.

MGM was eager to get the next operetta going, and MacDonald rejoined Eddy for *Maytime* (1937), from a Sigmund Romberg show so successful that two productions ran simultaneously on Broadway in 1917. Irving Thalberg felt the time was right to try Technicolor in its more natural three-color process,* but his sudden death halted shooting. L. B. Mayer took over, starting from scratch in black-and-white with a complete change of script, score, staff, and supporting cast. The result has been called the best of the MacDonald–Eddy films, though Romberg would have recognized little more than the title, one melody, and his name in the credits. John Barrymore, so wet that he had to read his lines off huge cue cards and seems ever about to topple over, comes between the stars like a beached ham, but with a rich score taking in a large snatch of Act One of Meyerbeer's *Les Huguenots* (a rare item at the time), Delibes' "Les Filles de Cadiz," special material for Eddy, and a fake opera, *Tsaritsa*, culled from Chaikofsky's Fifth Symphony, the story hardly matters. The spectacular decor is a relief after *Rose Marie*'s endless trees, the theme—love matters more than ca-

---

*Trivium Footnote no. 5: The first three-strip Technicolor musical was *The Dancing Pirate* (1936), a fast failure remembered only by Rodgers–Hart buffs for a superb ballad, "Are You My Love?" Yes, the pirate danced.

reer—consistent with the stars' personae, and the big ball sequence tremendously lavish.

But is *Maytime* a masterpiece? Possibly the best of the MacDonald–Eddy series is *The Firefly* (1937), mainly because Eddy isn't in it. Its male lead is an Eddy role—that of the gallant Napoleonic spy who trails enemy spy MacDonald, loves her, yet must destroy her—but this script called for more comic agility than Eddy had, and Allan Jones stepped in, gentle in comedy, a Zorro in war. As with *Maytime*, the original Broadway libretto was tossed out, but its best songs (by Rudolf Friml and Otto Harbach) were retained and a wonderful new one added, "The Donkey Serenade."

MacDonald had been a dancer on Broadway before she came to Hollywood, and *The Firefly* introduces choreography into the opera musical, with the Albertina Rasch girls twirling during the title credits followed by marching soldiers. This is wartime, France against Spain. MacDonald gets off on an odd foot for a costume operetta, saying, "I can't imagine any man as exciting as service to my country," but the songs are all about love: "When a Maid Comes Knocking at Your Heart," "Love Is Like a Firefly," "The Magic of a Woman's Kiss," "Sympathy," Jones' serenade, "Giannina Mia," MacDonald's "He Who Loves and Runs Away" (performed with a *Tosca* cane), which starts out as a tango and ends as a military march sung by the male chorus while MacDonald throws off coloratura decoration in a Napoleon hat. "The Donkey Serenade" is the gem, set to a clopping beat and accompanied by guitar and a reed pipe as Jones rides along with MacDonald's carriage trying to thrill her. She doesn't thrill easy, but the song's infectious rhythm captures her duenna, the driver, and his boy, who merrily bob to the beat. Friml adapted it from a swinging fox trot, "Chansonette," and it became so popular that revivals of the stage *Firefly* have had to include it, though no one can find a good place for a coach and donkey in a show about an Italian waif taken up by the country club set who becomes an opera singer.

Democratic revolution is touched on in a number of these films, but *The Firefly* gives us a full-scale rebellion when Napoleon's puppet Joseph Bonaparte is plopped onto the Spanish throne and a mob is forced to welcome him to Madrid. A fetid cripple spits, the army shoots at hostile children, and revolt breaks out. Operetta as musical concept and dramatic faerie dissolves into war chronicle—a daring foray out of format, but it is not sustained. In fact, the film falls into inadvertent burlesque that makes "Indian Love Call" look like Edith

Evans and Ralph Richardson reading Magna Charta. We move to the French encampment, where gypsies are entertaining, led by that arch-gypsy, Jeanette MacDonald, who vocalizes a snippet of Rimsky-Korsakof's *Capriccio Espagnol.* "Bring that girl to headquarters," sniffs a French general; how fresh. MacDonald is unmasked and condemned to death. From her prison, she sees Jones wounded and, as the cannons boom, slips into a fraught reprise of "Giannina Mia." After more war montage, a freed people exult and MacDonald finds Jones in a makeshift hospital. A last cut gives us the two plugging "The Donkey Serenade" and "Giannina Mia."

The habit of assigning all song to the two leads is beginning to exhaust our concentration. Is nothing but the love plot worthy of musical elaboration? In expanding the pictorial canvas to include imperialist oppression, MGM had a grand opportunity to expand operetta, too, with choral numbers of populist resistance, with freedom-fighter sidekicks and royalist plotters. MGM didn't take it; and Mayer read *The Firefly*'s relatively low grosses as a sign that Jones lacked Eddy's appeal as MacDonald's partner. Nor did Eddy's film with Eleanor Powell, *Rosalie,* break box-office records. So it was Jeanette and Nelson again in *The Girl of the Golden West* (1938), from David Belasco's play about the tomboy caught between a rogue and a sheriff. There's music in this tale—Puccini made a fine opera of it—but Sigmund Romberg and Gus Kahn's score, original for the film, doesn't dig. Nor was the pair all that well served in a modern-dress backstager in Technicolor, *Sweethearts* (1938). The critics shrugged and the fans reveled, though few supported Eddy's western with a pick-up score, *Let Freedom Ring* (1939), or MacDonald's *Broadway Serenade* (1939), the latter distinguished mainly by a fluffy hat even more spectacular than the one MacDonald wore in *San Francisco.* A better idea was *Balalaika* (1939), which Eddy made with Ilona Massey, a beautiful and gifted actress who got few chances to make her mark. Here she shines as a conspirator in Russia in 1914. Too many writers failed to fulfill the script's premise, an interesting idea for operetta (Cossack loves Bolshevik), and Massey's tense precision shows up Eddy's heavy hand as MacDonald, heavy in an elfin way, never did. But an unforgettable junction of plot and score finds Eddy, a noble disguised as a penniless baritone, singing "The Volga Boatman's Song" for Massey's radical group, disguised as a music school. They test Eddy's cover: is he really a baritone? *Is* he? Does Lenin have a beard? As his voice pours out, the astonished spies/musicians become entranced as musicians, singing and playing along, adding in descants and harmonies, and Massey is stunned. The camera follows Eddy as he moves from man to man, daring them not to succumb; then it closes in on her, capping the scene in her wonder. This is great filming, but for some reason the revolutionary story doesn't pan out and all ends patly in émigré Paris.

Mayer thrust MacDonald and Eddy into a remake of *New Moon* (1940) to retrieve their old glory in *Marietta* costumes and Romberg tunes. This version is more faithful to the original than the Grace Moore–Lawrence Tibbett *New Moon* had been, and the two stars rally us with a potpourri of the hits under the credits; but we have been here before. In the 1940s, Hollywood was to find new ways of bringing Real Music to the people, and MacDonald and Eddy were eased out. *Bitter Sweet* (1940), from Noël Coward's operetta, was a flop *Maytime*, and two solo vehicles—*Smilin' Through* (1941) for MacDonald and *The Chocolate Soldier* (1941) for Eddy—did no better, though the latter gave Eddy his best role as an actor who impersonates a Russian seducer to test his wife (Risë Stevens). Worst of all was *I Married an Angel* (1942), a risqué fantasy that Rodgers and Hart had conceived for the screen some years before and finally turned into a dance musical on Broadway for Vera Zorina. MacDonald and Eddy were wrong for the roles and the score, and they knew it, but Mayer couldn't get Zorina, so in they went. That finished them: came then revue bits and solo outings—Eddy's *The Phantom of the Opera* (1943), with Susanna Foster, *Knickerbocker Holiday* (1944), with Constance Dowling, and *Northwest Outpost* (1947), a Republic western with Ilona Massey; MacDonald's *Cairo* (1942), with Robert Young, *Three Daring Daughters* (1948), with José Iturbi, and *The Sun Comes Up* (1949), with Lassie; the rest was silence. Sadly, MacDonald was passed over for the lead in the film version of *The King and I*, potentially an outstanding meeting of great person and great part.

Operetta's emphasis on fine nonpop music is to be commended, and some of this repertory—MacDonald's "Les Filles de Cadiz" or Grace Moore's *Butterfly* scenes—has not often been bettered anywhere. But operetta seldom used its music as well as the less pretentious musicals did—though pop, on the other hand, suffered guilt for enjoying itself so easily. As early as *The Jazz Singer*, the protagonist endures hideous torment for his love of lowdown performance, and the theme haunted the studios. In *Naughty But Nice* (1939), Dick Powell finished off his Warners contract as a music professor who visits New York to promote his symphony and tangles with Tin Pan Alley. The film manages to respect, need, love, suspect, and ridicule serious music all at once:

Powell wears glasses and has maiden aunts who play violin, 'cello, and harp trios, so he must dance jitterbug; Alley hacks pore through the classics swiping tunes; Ann Sheridan sings a "darky" number (another Alley fetish) called "Corn Pickin'," and Wagner and Mozart vie with Warren–Mercer songs for the ear's pleasure.

Could Hollywood ever accommodate the two styles instead of contrasting them? It did in the 1940s, which is why it no longer needed— or could even bear—MacDonald and Eddy. As an omen, MGM made a short with adolescent contractees Deanna Durbin and Judy Garland in which pop and legit singing stand side by side as allies in the battle for art. Called *Every Sunday* (1936) and based on the screen test that the two girls had just made together, the one-reeler presents "Judy" and "Edna" (Durbin's given name) as boosters of open-air concerts suffering poor attendance. The solution: the girls join the concerts, Durbin singing Arditi's fancy waltz "Il Bacio" for the refined crowd and Garland doing "(Dance to the sweet music of) Americana" for the common folk. No! The point is that everyone enjoys both styles, and the concerts are saved as a huge crowd enjoys the pair sharing an encore of "Americana," Durbin on coloratura.

Ironically, Durbin and Garland went separate ways thereafter, the former to Universal, where Joe Pasternak made her queen of the light classics in modern-dress little miss fix-it comedies.* So Judy sang low and Durbin sang high after all. It's just as well, for mainstream America had already taken its turn into the swing that would eventually lead it to rock, which is as far from legit as music can go (or was, until the Beatles introduced classical technique into the rock sound in such songs as "She's Leaving Home," "Julia," and "Eleanor Rigby"). In the 1940s, the Hollywood musical moved, so to speak, to the left. Or, rather, it created a new center, leaving casquette girls, Mounties, and the whole bittersweet maytime corn dance out on a limb. Early in *New Moon*, MacDonald tells Eddy, "You're very romantic, aren't you?" "Aren't *you*, Madam?" he replies, and she says, "Yes—within reason."

---

*Legend tells that Durbin was let go by accident; Mayer said "Drop the fat one"—meaning Garland—and an underling thought he meant Durbin. But Christopher Finch claims that the MGM music department made the decision, prudently, because two precocious teenagers were too much of a good sing—and perhaps because Garland's pop was going to prove more handy than Durbin's opera.

☆ 9 ☆
The Comedy Musical

Hollywood was expert in comedy in the 1920s; sound smashed all that to pieces. The amoral chaos of Mack Sennett's Keystone Kops, Buster Keaton's unflappable grace under implausible pressures, and Charlie Chaplin's outcast transforming thought into deed against hopeless odds—these and other rules for behavior depended on the same surrealistic naturalism that supported John Gilbert's great loving and Douglas Fairbanks' all-American gallantry. Sound made new plans for comedy, made it verbal and realistic, demoting almost all the experts to has-beens. Harold Lloyd made the transition, as did Chaplin (after his boycott failed to take), but only Stan Laurel and Oliver Hardy stepped out of silence into sound unscathed.

They stepped into a few musicals, too, but made no attempt to assimilate song and dance into comedy or vice versa. They appear in *The Rogue Song*, Lawrence Tibbett's big Russian operetta, as members of Tibbett's bandit gang, but their bits—a shaving routine and an adventure in a cave—have nothing to do with the story. They take more of a part in *Babes in Toyland* (1934), from the 1903 Victor Herbert spectacle, but don't sing in it, an odd way to run a musical. RKO had planned a *Babes* in 1930 as a vehicle for Bert Wheeler and Robert Woolsey, no-fail box office champs since *Rio Rita*, with Irene Dunne, Ned Sparks, Dorothy Lee, Edna May Oliver, and "2,000 others." But this was cancelled and the Laurel–Hardy *Babes*, for MGM, lacks the musical all-aroundness that RKO's blueprint implies, with Dunne's voice, Sparks' gravelly weirdness, Lee's darling charm, and Oliver's fussy pomp. Laurel and Hardy's *Babes* consists entirely of dark settings, infantile horror, and nonentities in every part but the stars'. Moreover, their idea of fun—fighting, panicking, blundering, and crying—adds nothing to the material itself.

It would have been interesting to see what Chaplin or Keaton would have done in an all-out musical. But at least Hollywood could draw from Broadway, vaudeville, and burlesque, where our national comic styles had been evolved over decades of improvisation. All of this transferred easily to the screen. There were standup duos who played games irrelevant to the story (like Wheeler and Woolsey), singles who played the protagonist of their films (like Joe E. Brown), comics who played with the protagonist (like Joe E. Brown's various woman partners), comics who supported (like Horton and Blore in the Astaire-Rogers series), or comics who did specialties (like the Three Stooges, who perform their violent trio in a moment of *Dancing Lady*), some of them singing and dancing and some not. Eddie Cantor was the most complete performer of all, and his vehicles founded the comedy film musical, though they were derived from the stage—*Whoopee!*, direct from Broadway, more or less established Cantor's format. But Cantor's films were too expensive to imitate; only Goldwyn would have poured so much into an idea that could be just as funny without lavish decor, imposing scores, or Goldwyn Girls.

By the mid–1930s, the comedy musical had collapsed. Brown's films suffered poor scores, Cantor was working radio, Bert Lahr and Ed Wynn had not found a place for themselves in film, and other suitable comedians had not tried to. There were to be later attempts, such as the Crosby–Hope *Road* pictures and Goldwyn's Danny Kaye series. But the essentially comic musical—one that exploited comedy through music—remained rare, perhaps because the average musical already had comedy. Some musicals had it organically in the action, or in good lines—the Berkeley backstagers, for instance. Some musicals had it plunked in by improvisational specialists—Fox's Ritz Brothers, say, who would enliven anything with their stupid accents and insulting female impersonations. Because they worked as a unit the Ritzes never individualized themselves like the Marx Brothers, nor were they particularly funny, but they were useful in support of stars who did not play comedy, such as Alice Faye or Sonja Henie. The Warners backstagers are about survival, so their characters joke about working. The RKO dance musicals are about courtship, so their characters joke about love. The Fox musicals aren't really about anything, and had nothing to joke about; enter the Ritz Brothers.

Similarly subsidiary but often the best things in many films were George Burns and Gracie Allen. Both could dance passably and Allen could get through a song, but their speciality was a set of variations on one theme: Allen is daffy and Burns can't believe his ears. Years later, pioneering the TV sitcom, he listened wryly for her crazy comebacks, but in the 1930s he was still playing takes—on a desert island in *We're Not Dressing* or among the English country set in *A Damsel in Distress.* Touring Totleigh Castle, Burns asks the guide, of the present lord, "Does he herd sheep?" Allen corrects him: "One says, 'Does he *hear* sheep' or '*Has* he heard sheep?' "

Most original of the comic stars was Mae West, who kept Paramount afloat during the Depression till mounting resistance to her libertarian ease hunted her from the screen. She was truly subversive; here was one gold digger who meant it, a woman who made no pretense of fearing sex. One of the last of Broadway's actor-managers, her own author and director, West also sang, but she never made a musical. Yet she does truly use the two or three songs that crop up in each film, extending her persona into them, and thought enough of them to hire Xavier Cugat and Duke Ellington and their bands for several of her pictures.

West was one of the country's great humorists. The plots of her films suggest a vanity stunt—1890s-era outfits, pallid competition from the other women, and every man in sight ravening for West's outdated hourglass figure. But she seems to regard the whole thing as a put-on, sociological satire disguised as melodrama in a general air of slang, lawbreaking, and sentimentality. West indulges in the first two and looks on with pleasure while others uphold the third, though she is capable of it herself. But she's no one's fool. She saunters into her first film, *Night After Night* (1932), in a speakeasy. "Who's there?" cries the bouncer at the door. And West's voice comes back, "The fairy princess, ya mug." Or in *She Done Him Wrong* (1933), Salvation Army captain Cary Grant begs her to conform to the Hollywood all-truth of monogamous constancy. "Haven't you ever met a man who could make you happy?" he asks her. "Sure," she tells him. "Lots of times." Or in *I'm No Angel* (1933), a date tells her he's a politician and she replies, "I don't like work, either." These films would have made wonderful musicals. The scene in *Goin' To Town* (1935) in which West attempts to crash society by singing opera—Saint-Saëns' *Samson et Dalila*, naturally—plays a marvelous joke on Hollywood's legit fetish; imagine a whole evening of such spoof.

On the other hand, it takes a sharp talent to set a spoof to music. The films of the Marx Brothers flirt with the notion of going musical, but the brothers' anarchy forbids it. The musical, no matter how loosely structured, has order of a sort; the Marxes are perfect disorder. Because they worked up from vaudeville into the Broadway musical complete with love plot and dances, they figured out how to demolish

☆ *THE COMIC MUSICAL: opposite above, the Goldwyn Girls deliver "Bend Down, Sister" in a Cantor vehicle,* Palmy Days *(note fake city through windows); below, final shot of* The Cocoanuts, *the Marx Brothers in their essence—Groucho and Chico assaulting pomposity, Harpo after love, and Zeppo standing there. Margaret Dumont looks on, right; above, Garland parries Brice's Baby Snooks in* Everybody Sing, *not precisely a comedy—but anything with Brice in it was not precisely anything else.*

musical comedy conventions: join them. You want music? Chico plays piano, Harpo, obviously, the harp. (And their playing is characterological: Chico is devilish and Harpo loves beauty.) You want a love song? They have Zeppo, the fourth and youngest of the team and no comedian—he is regularly booed in theatres today when his name comes up in the credits—to sing one. Or Chico will, accent and all. Groucho will attempt a comic song, but if he thinks of something cute to say, he'll stop the band and say it. Thus, the boys raid convention with their pandemonium.

Still, their first films, replicas of their stage hits *The Cocoanuts* and *Animal Crackers* in 1929 and 1930 respectively, cut virtually all the music. Touches of musical here and there seem bizarre; Mae West sings for the fun of it, but the Marx films actually have plot numbers. Like West, the brothers started at Paramount, a studio more director-oriented than the others and therefore less tightly organized for genre. The fourth Marx film, *Horse Feathers* (1932), suggests what a Marx musical might have been like: Groucho, as incoming president of Huxley College, sings "(Whatever it is) I'm Against It" in front of a line of bearded deans. Tailored to Groucho's character by Bert Kalmar and Harry Ruby, the song is a mixture of Gilbertian patter and rhythmic quickstep, with the half-dead deans joining the zaniness with kicks and wiggles like a hypnotized minstrel lineup. Most zany of all is one dean, three-quarters dead, who irritably occupies his chair, immobile, throughout the number. The film also contains a charm song, "Everyone Says I Love You," which Chico sings to the "college widow," Thelma Todd, as part of his piano number. Whenever she looks too charmed, he insults her.

It is *Duck Soup* (1933), the Marxes' last Paramount picture and one of the masterpieces of American film, that most shows the form a comedy musical might take: the few numbers do not undercut but add to the free-for-all as grotesque burlesques of musical comedy styles. A tale of espionage and war in a central European Graustark called Freedonia, *Duck Soup* plunks the Marxes and their florid blueblood stooge Margaret Dumont—in their usual identities—amid diplomats in morning coats, embassy teas, and peasants. The villian (Louis Calhern) is named Trentino, his Mata Hari (Raquel Torres) is Vera Marcal, and Freedonia's enemy Sylvania bears the name of the country that MacDonald ruled in Paramount's *The Love Parade* four years before. But the boys are the boys—Groucho is Rufus T. Firefly, Freedonia's president—and Margaret Dumont is Gloria Teasdale, though she holds merry widow status in Freedonia as the country's main financial hope. Kalmar and Ruby wrote it, score and all; Leo McCarey, a master in comedy, directed, and the thing zooms by so fast that one's first impression is of a heavily plotted musical fantasy. Repeated viewings reveal little plot and only two numbers. It seems fully constructed because each event leads directly to the next—unheard of in Marxian comedy—and its two numbers are *very* number. The first, "His Excellency Is Due," seems to have fallen out of an ancient operetta. It opens the movie, at Groucho's inauguration party; one person is lacking—Groucho, of course. Almost without provocation—certainly no one wants him to sing—Zeppo breaks into something about the clock on the wall striking ten. Dumont and the chorus take this up, and we cut to Groucho in bed. An alarm goes off, he slides down a firehouse pole, and presto! joins the party at the end of a line of flunkies who sing "Hail, Freedonia" over and over. Groucho leans and peers. "Expecting someone?" he asks. Spotted and welcomed, he goes into a patter song, promising to run Freedonia unreasonably, selfishly, tyrannically. The guests take it all in without an opinion, offering deadpan Gilbert-and-Sullivan repetitions of his lines and just standing there while Groucho goes into a screwy dance.

The second number, "The Country's Going to War," is epic, a lampoon of production numbers made up of noncontiguous elements—black spiritual, hillbilly, swing—each with its own performers, costumes, and choreography. And while the Marxes are in the middle of it all, dancing, waving their arms, crawling around, and playing banjos, they are more at the number than in it. They show much greater commitment in the famous *Il Trovatore*-wrecking finale of *A Night At the Opera* (1935), but by then they had moved to MGM and Irving Thalberg was trying to fit them into an "acceptable" musical structure, so lovers Kitty Carlisle and Allan Jones interrupt the mania with inappositely tuneful moodle. *At the Circus* (1939) goes even further, with a Harold Arlen–E. Y. Harburg score in miniature—a love song based on "Three Blind Mice," "Two Blind Loves"; the heroine's center-ring solo, "Step Up"; and a comic novelty for Groucho, "Lydia, the Tattooed Lady," which Bobby Connolly staged in musical-comedy fashion with a prancing chorus, Chico accompanying on the piano, and Harpo almost civilized. This is fun, but it doesn't need the Marxes. Worse yet was *The Big Store* (1941), which features one of the most disliked examples of populist ecumenism, "The Tenement Symphony," sung by Tony Martin; and the unkindest cut of all was *Love Happy* (1949), a conventional backstager with Groucho hardly in it at all and Chico and Harpo horribly tamed.

The screwball comedy never assimilated music, either, though its salient perception—that wit, charm, and nonconformity make an

American romantic elite—might have inspired an intriguing score. RKO's *Joy of Living* (1938), in which madcap Douglas Fairbanks, Jr., teaches Irene Dunne to be wacky, does qualify, but its four Kern–Fields songs have nothing to do with the screwball whirlwind. Indeed, it's stately even for Kern.

There is another possible screwball musical, the Astaire–Rogers *Carefree* (1938). With only three songs (by Berlin) plus one nonvocal dance, a broad range of comic styles from verbal to stunt to slapstick and a cast typical of a Hepburn–Grant romp (Ralph Bellamy as the dull boyfriend, Clarence Kolb as the dull judge, Luella Gear as the funny aunt; when Kolb invites her onto the dance floor she snaps back, "I don't dance at your age"), *Carefree* was no dance musical. The eighth Astaire–Rogers pairing, it was meant to relaunch them after a hiatus of over a year. Thus its novel style. It allowed them their first onscreen kiss and gave Rogers the grander part as a woman who falls in love with psychiatrist Astaire,* goes on a rampage on narcotics, and has to be hypnotized into hating Astaire—only now *he* loves her and has to hypnotize her back. Rogers' binge is great fun, taking in the smashing of a huge pane of glass and peaking in one of Hollywood's most cherished kinds of lark: a scene in which a radio star ruins a show on the air, insulting the sponsor's product and sabotaging the entertainment. Rogers is at her best here, pokey, watery-eyed, and bowing at the orchestra each time it plays radio's habitual ta-da! chord. The film is a screwball feast. But is it a musical?

What's a musical? By the late 1930s, Hollywood had an answer: seventy-five to one hundred minutes of love plot crossed with some instance of personal or communal achievement, using four or five songs and possibly a dance or two, keeping the whole as often as possible in a modern and comic frame; the music is easy to pick up, the lyrics are simple, and the lead personalities are essentially innocent and giving, even valiant, though such minor flaws as sloth or cowardice are okay if they are redeemed by some life-changing act in the final reel. Operetta stretched the definition somewhat, and obviously such early films as *Be Yourself*, *The Smiling Lieutenant*, and *Her Majesty Love* would not have suited the style. But then the performers who inspired those films were no longer active and the performers who replaced them were very different in tone. Not yet ten years old, the musical has already evolved beyond recognition.

---

*It has been said that Astaire always plays dancers, but this was his second role as something else; in *Roberta* he was a bandleader.

☆ *ADAPTATIONS FROM BROADWAY:* The Gay Divorcee *(Grable, Horton),* Sweet Adeline *(Sparks, Calhern, Dunne, Woods),* The Firefly *(MacDonald). Porter, Kern, and Friml upgrade the Hollywood tone, though Porter's songs all but vanished and* The Firefly *got a new story.* Sweet Adeline *came off nicely, but Woods is a pill.*

☆ 10 ☆

The Stars of the Late 1930s

YOU CAN SEE the change in the people. From the manic Al Jolson and the ebullient Maurice Chevalier we come to the nonchalant Bing Crosby. The various women of the first sound years—Bebe Daniels, Bessie Love, Vivienne Segal, Lilyan Tashman, Dorothy Jordan, Irene Bordoni, and others who could play comedy as well as a love plot, or whose glamor transcended musical comedy frippery—cede to more consistently pretty and pleasant singer-dancers like Alice Faye.

A very few of the old guard were still around. Jeanette MacDonald was now the first lady of operetta, and Jolson hung in there, unreconstructed, in *The Singing Kid* (1936) and *Rose of Washington Square* (1939) and, in the 1940s, was to play himself in *Rhapsody in Blue* and dub his voice in *The Jolson Story*. But their generation had largely dispersed. Ramon Novarro, so big in silent days, should have gone nicely into musicals with his sweet tenor, but somehow or other he didn't fare well, and by 1937 he was attempting a comeback, in *The Sheik Steps Out,* at Republic, not unlike a professional wrestler's making a comeback as the seventh Village Person. Nancy Carroll's last musicals, *After the Dance* (1935) and *That Certain Age* (1938), were obscure addenda. Janet Gaynor gave up on musicals in mid-decade. Lillian Roth vanished as of *Take a Chance* in 1933. Charles King was long departed, Walter Pidgeon was no longer singing, and John Boles, who was, couldn't get a decent role.

Even Chevalier was gone. Plans to follow up *The Merry Widow* at MGM with *The Chocolate Soldier* fell through—it has been said that he requested MacDonald and she said no—and he moved on to Twentieth Century, Darryl Zanuck's new studio which was shortly to merge with Fox. With Merle Oberon and Ann Sothern, Chevalier made *Folies Bergère* (1935), singing all seven songs and playing two roles, a baron and an entertainer hired to impersonate the baron; we get Chevalier in bowtie and boater and Chevalier in tails, Chevalier on stage and Chevalier in the boardroom. It's a wonderful, seldom-seen romp—Roy del Ruth directed in homage to Lubitsch, Dave Gould choreographed in homage to Berkeley, and in one number they have Chevalier and Sothern dancing on a monster version of Chevalier's straw hat. But this was Chevalier's last Hollywood film for two decades. His passing, as much as anything, marks the end of what might be called the First Era of Hollywood musicals.

One might date the Second Era from the emergence of Alice Faye as a top draw in 1937, for Faye, who remained one of the biggest stars till she retired in 1945, set a style that held right up to the collapse of the studio musical in the 1950s. The standard assessment of the style— that Betty Grable precisely replaced Faye and that Marilyn Monroe and Doris Day split the persona's paradoxical halves of sensual woman and tender girl—is a canard: Faye was irreplaceable. She is the nice woman who tries to look tough, a superb singer, a good dancer, and so rich a personality that her success depends not on playing a role but on letting a role play itself while she entertains. The Faye palette dabs anger, pouting, tears; it paints sweet frocks and bad sequins and favors period (usually the wrong one for the film) costumes. She came to Fox in 1934 to replace Lilian Harvey in a backstager, *George White's Scandals*, at the suggestion of Rudy Vallee, back in Hollywood for a second try. The numbers set Faye off nicely. "Nasty Man" shows her lithe and leggy with a pride of showgirls shaking behind her; Vallee sings "Hold My Hand" to a subdued Faye, easily won by the right man but only by him; and the ridiculous "My Dog Loves Your Dog" gives us a pert Faye walking the dog. Fox had the idea of building her up as a Harlow, with bleached platinum hair and pencilled eyebrows, and in her second film, the nonmusical *Now I'll Tell* (1934), she played the third person in Spencer Tracy and Helen Twelvetrees' marriage, sang the lacerating "Fooling With the Other Woman's Man" in a harlot's black satin and feathers—"Headache, headache, nerves you can't control," she cries, "conscience, conscience tugging at your soul!"—and dies in a car crash, Fox's usual method of disposing of homewreckers.

The true Faye, we quickly discover, wants her own home at first hand. In *She Learned About Sailors* (1934), Faye learns only that they—sailor Lew Ayres, anyway—want to get married as much as she does. Yet Faye puts forth such ripe jazz in her flirty-girl production numbers that while her parts become maidenly and the Harlow look fades, her songs remain knowing. So *George White's 1935 Scandals* offers a tintype of "Nasty Man" in Faye's "Oh, I Didn't Know (you'd get that way)," which like its predecessor only pretends to complain about the male's libidinous attack. The lyrics are coy but the music is eager and Faye irresistible. The more she sings, the more she likes it, and after an exuberant dance, she has lost all inhibition; when she hits the line, "My heart is full of joy, oh you naughty boy," she can scarcely go on, and just holds the note on "boy" while the orchestra fills in the tune. This is one of Faye's great qualities, her ability to express the human appetite without making it look smutty. The Production Code encircled the scripts, but it couldn't flatten the spirit.

Faye's spirit was very late thirties, seeing an end to the Depression but having to work to get there. She plays women with talent and initiative who use show biz to pull themselves out of poverty. Faye *was* that part, a New Yorker who moved through Broadway, radio, records, and film, yet somehow never learned to pronounce a final *r*. Faye was always Faye, dressed for the 1930s in films that take place in the nineteenth century and never aging in stories that cover decades. She heads the eternal threesome (completed by Frances Langford and Patsy Kelly) in Paramount's *Every Night at Eight* (1935), trying to land George Raft and singing jobs for her trio and looking into the heart of the rich on a yacht weekend to draw back in disapproval. In *King of Burlesque* (1936), she expresses the age's optimism in "I'm Shooting High," relaxation in "I Love to Ride the Horses (on a Merry-Go-Round)," and informality in courtship in "Whose Baby Are You?" This was another putting-on-the-show musical, and with Warner Baxter as the director (as he had been in *42nd Street*), it seemed twice-told. But the urgency of hard times had blown away. In 1933, "We're in the Money" is irony; *King of Burlesque* plays "I've Got My Fingers Crossed" straight.

By the time Fox and Twentieth Century merged, Faye was ready to star. Even when playing third fiddle to Dick Powell and Madeleine Carroll in *On the Avenue* (1937), it is her contributions to the score that make the film, along with the singing Powell, the fancy sets, the jaunty choreography, the Irving Berlin score, and even the Ritz Brothers, drag and all. Faye, the Ritzes, and chorus open the film with "He Ain't Got Rhythm," telling of a scientist who commits the ultimate sin: he has no music. "He attracted some attention," Faye explains, "when he found the fourth dimension." But he ain't got rhythm; as so often before, Berlin encapsulates a sensual ideology that no one had thought to broach before. It's preposterous—but it's plausible. People don't like intellectuals who can't do what everyone does.

Faye got rhythm. Powell sings "I've Got My Love to Keep Me Warm," but Faye joins him at the end, sashaying onstage in a fluffy white gown embellished with roses to truck to the music beyond all reason. Someone has to keep the energy driving. The musical was getting fat: *On the Avenue* permits Powell to walk out on his own show because Carroll, his love and nemesis, bought a controlling interest— and now no Aline MacMahon lectures him on his obligations to his fellow performers. Only one person remains of the hard luck days: Faye. Berkeley got rural at MGM, Keeler retired, and Powell and Blondell stopped singing. We came out of the tunnel with Faye, watching her strive and win. In *You Can't Have Everything* (1937) she starts out ordering a spaghetti dinner she can't pay for and ends as the author of a Broadway show. In *You're a Sweetheart* (1937), she involves waiter George Murphy in a questionable scheme to keep a show running and ends redeemed, prancing with Murphy in yet another hit.

But she still can't get her mouth around a final *r.* "Drive__! Drive__!" she cries in *In Old Chicago* (1938) when Tyrone Power carries her off in a cab. And "Get out of he__e!" she screams later, when he bursts into her apartment. One of Faye's many costume films, *In Old Chicago* was Fox's reply to MGM's *San Francisco,* with a comparable cast—a woman who sings (MacDonald; Faye), an amoral man (Gable; Power) and a good man (Spencer Tracy; Don Ameche), closing in an exultant disaster finale. But Faye sings no opera; folk, vaudeville, and a rousing Gordon–Revel title tune do for her. Directed by Henry King, *In Old Chicago* was a whopping hit, but not exactly a musical. For the quintessential Faye epic, also directed by King and, like *Chicago*, nominated for a Best Picture Oscar, we turn to *Alexander's Ragtime Band* (1938).

"An American cavalcade!" the ads crowed: from ragtime as a horrid novelty in a San Francisco dive to swing triumphant at Carnegie Hall some twenty-five years later. Faye is caught between Power and Ameche, with Jack Haley as Power's drummer and Ethel Merman as the singer Power hires when Faye marries Ameche. The score is the big thing, a compendium of twenty-one Berlin songs plus the new "Now It Can Be Told" and "My Walking Stick," and if the principals never age, the music does, passing through time from the antique "Ragtime Violin" and "Everybody's Doin' It" to the contemporary "Heat Wave." Appropriately, the title song launches the tale when

Power and his band, auditioning at a club, can't find their music and sight-read the sheets that Faye left lying around. It's tricky stuff, and their first attempts are grotesque. "Swing into it," Power urges, on violin, as Faye indignantly rushes into the picture to take the vocal. And the ragtime band is born.

Comparable to Faye is Bing Crosby. Now recalled primarily as a singer, he, like Faye, was in his time primarily a movie actor: a character who sang. They projected something universally admirable, something the public came to the theatre to recognize and share. It was Faye's moxie; it was Crosby's cool. Two qualities handy in tough times. But where Faye held us through her persistence, Crosby took us along through his extreme lack of it. She is a mover, he an adapter.

With his wingy ears and careless attitude toward his employers, Crosby looked an odd risk for films—he lost a big number to John Boles in *King of Jazz* by getting arrested for drunk driving. But Paramount signed him in 1932 and inaugurated a series of musicals without set format. There is no consistent world view, no musical constants, no regulars. The results are very variable. But they comprise a remarkable document of the American style in pop art, veering without warning from good nature to suspicion and aggressiveness, aware of economic and social relations yet hoping not to face up to them. The Crosby films surprise with their range. If *College Humor* (1933) pictures the usual hurdy-gurdy campus of big games and love-or-die first dates, with Crosby overparted as a drama professor, Richard Arlen a football hero, Mary Carlisle the coed in love with both, and everything happening in no order, suddenly *Going Hollywood* (1933), an MGM loan-out with Marion Davies, presents a more confident Crosby well cast as a film recruit. The hit boosted Davies' flagging and Crosby's as yet unplaced careers, as well as exposing Crosby to MGM's expert manufacturers of film and Davies' famous on-the-set lunch parties.

Crosby was growing. Back at Paramount for *We're Not Dressing* (1934), he played a sailor on heiress Carole Lombard's yacht. She's interested but he's arrogant—i.e., not subservient—which makes things dicey when yacht goes down and Lombard and guests are unable to cope with desert island. Crosby, the free American, copes fine, especially with an unusually serious role that implies a moral judgment on the exploiting class. But Burns and Allen lighten the scene and a charming Revel–Gordon score spells peace on earth. Crosby's soft-colored song style not only made him popular but also helped gentle the hard edges in some of his films—hard and shocking in *We're Not*

Dressing when he and Lombard get into a slapping sequence that looks uncomfortably real.

Crosby's love plot with plutocrat Lombard is significant; a lot of Hollywood's Cinderello trope devolved onto him. In *Here Is My Heart* (1934) he romances a princess (Kitty Carlisle) in Monte Carlo, in *Rhythm on the Range* (1936) an heiress (Frances Farmer) on the loose out west, in *Paris Honeymoon* (1939) a divorced heiress (Shirley Ross)—but lo, he trades her for a peasant (Franciska Gaal). In a costume picture he can commit murder (by accident) and move through the old south with a Reputation, in *Mississippi* (1935), but three Rodgers–Hart ballads define him as a feeling, not an acting, man. Then, in *Double or Nothing* (1937), he begins to take charge. To prove that humankind is honest and bright, a late millionaire has arranged for wallets containing hundred-dollar bills to be found, a cool million to be given to the first stranger to (1) return the wallet and (2) double his or her $5,000 reward. A forgotten classic, the film couples the wish for easy money with a lesson in how to earn it, and presents an intriguing group of wallet finders: Crosby, a penniless singer; William Frawley, a petty hustler; Martha Raye, an ex-stripper who can't control the urge to answer her old calling; and Andy Devine, a bum. The dead man's brother, executor of the will, inherits everything if the quartet fails, and he and his crummy family serve as temptors.

Double or Nothing is rich in music and dance, but some of Crosby's films are scarcely musicals—*Sing, You Sinners* (1938), for example. Yet this film is about music in a way. A widowed mother (Elizabeth Patterson) with three sons (Crosby, Fred MacMurray, and thirteen-year-old Donald O'Connor) had them trained as musicians and expects them to follow through whether they want to or not. They don't. But there they are entertaining in a tavern, O'Connor on accordion, MacMurray on clarinet, and Crosby on guitar, all singing "A Pocketful of Dreams," MacMurray a little stiff but in there. Crosby, as a ne'er-do-well who finds his vocation racing horses, plays a drunk scene, tangles with gangsters, and lets his family down so badly that one dinner scene finds them leaving the table one by one till Crosby is alone staring aghast at the untouched food.

Yet his laziness is his charm: who wouldn't want to be as free a floater as he is? Out dating MacMurray's girl, he sings "Don't Let That Moon Get Away" from his table, and at one point forgets his lyrics, pauses, and recovers the line with a smile. Whether this was staged or an accident of film, it feels so everyday that director Wesley Ruggles let it ride. This is a rare light moment, however. *Sing, You Sinners* deals with struggling more than singing, and when Crosby reluctantly leaves home to find work, his heartbroken mother says, "It'll bring out the fight I know he's got in him." We, too, begin to realize that there's fight in Crosby, and the big blow-up between the family and the gangsters seems to have been filmed without the use of stuntmen. Patterson, too, gives fight, beaning one of the crooks with a chair. At the fadeout, the boys are a singing trio again, like it or not. *We* like it.

It is proof of Crosby's power as an actor that he could get by on a few songs; Faye tended to lose a lot of her personal ethos without a score to put over. But then Faye's style was rhythm and torch; Crosby healed. "Sing a Song of Sunbeams," from *East Side of Heaven* (1939), is classic Crosby, nudging the written melody with vocal bubbles so that it dances about the ear. "People all are softies for a grin," runs Johnny Burke's lyric. "You give out—they're gonna give in."

They gave in most overwhelmingly to a little girl who sings of simple pleasures, dances with Bill Robinson or Buddy Ebsen, chides dad and dollies, defrosts curmudgeons, brings couples together, conquers Depression blues in cities or on the farm with common sense and bottomless idealism, and says, "Oh, my goodness." Those who couldn't see it or who tired of the unchanging format of her films raged powerless at the enthusiasm she generated, but in the late 1930s Shirley Temple became the top-box office star.

In the world.

Doubters persist, but so do her films. There is no legend attached to her, none of the offstage misfortunes common to child stars, and neither her early marriage, early dissolved, nor her political ambitions affected the image of the do-good tyke who was either astonishingly talented or a fluke. She was both—to be able to use one's talent so professionally so young must be fluke. One either likes or hates all her films (the taste cannot be acquired) and as a whole they do not stand up as well as little Shirley herself does. She ran through a not undistinguished aggregate of costars in her prime—Claire Trevor, Gary Cooper, Carole Lombard, Lionel Barrymore, Alice Faye, Frank Morgan, Helen Westley, Robert Young, Victor McLaglen, Jean Hersholt, Randolph Scott, George Murphy, and Jimmy Durante—and John Ford directed her in *Wee Willie Winkie* (1937). But her musicals were whipped out with little ado; they look primitive.

Extraordinarily bright and coached by a no-nonsense mother, Temple got her start in shorts on a minor lot, mainly in Baby Burlesks, kids in diapers and tops spoofing the adult genres. Grotesque. Bits in features at the big lots led to an important spot in the finale of Fox's revue *Stand Up and Cheer* (1934). Temple came on in a high-waisted polka-dot dress to sing "Baby, Take a Bow" with James Dunn, immediately set a fashion for high-waisted polka-dot dresses, and signed with Fox. The studio strategy for launching a personality often jumped off on a crucial loan-out to some other studio at an early stage; the second studio loads the gun and the home studio then fires it, having saved the cost of the first big film. Temple's loan-out, to Paramount, was *Little Miss Marker* (1934), from Damon Runyon's tale of a homeless moppet placed with a bookie. The part is perfect Temple, and Adolphe Menjou as the bookie, Sorrowful Jones, is excellent; with his lank hair, droopy moustache, and flat, wet eyes he looks like a wounded cartoon seal. The script gets a lot of mileage out of Runyonesque lingo, but when Temple delivers lines like "Nix on that" or "Aw, lay off me" when faced with oatmeal, the joke fails: hood jive is not in her catalogue. Worse yet, the film is edited as sloppily as anything that ever crawled out of Gower Gulch. But *Little Miss Marker* was a hit, and Fox reclaimed its prize with a raise of from $150 to $1,250 a week and a careful expansion of her *Stand Up and Cheer* number in *Baby, Take a Bow* (1934), again with Dunn as her gangster father attempting to go straight. Temple is instrumental in the reform, and in keeping Fox in the black. *Bright Eyes* (1934), with Dunn yet again, with her first star billing, with "On the Good Ship Lollipop," and with Jane Withers as a brat who plagues Temple, made back its $190,000 production cost three weeks after it was released. Temple was six years old.

Some enthusiasts prefer *Bright Eyes* over other Temple films for the amusing byplay between the heroine and Withers, who cuts down the sugar content. But sugar was what folks wanted. In *The Little Colonel* (1935), Confederate kid Temple melts Lionel Barrymore to the extent that anyone could, and hits the acme of innocent bliss dancing with Bill "Bojangles" Robinson. Those who dislike hokum probably dislike the Temple–Robinson duets more than anything, but these numbers contributed significantly to the morale of American race relations, especially because they promoted a crossover of racial styles in dance. Temple was a natural tapper, but Robinson taught her to truck; their bald cahoots glows like nobody's business.

As with dancing, so with acting: experts polished her, but she had the basics already. She approached roles as games to be played, learning everyone's lines, and drove Barrymore crazy with her prompting; Menjou called her "an Ethel Barrymore at four." By 1935, her contract nabbed her $4,000 a week, and she was still a bargain, dancing atop a white piano while John Boles played and sang the title song to and about her ("You little bundle of joy") in *Curly Top,* a remake of Mary Pickford's *Daddy Long Legs* or an adaptation of Jean Webster's novel, depending on whether you watch or read. In this one Temple had an older sister, Rochelle Hudson, for Boles to romance while protecting orphan Temple, and the dream of being cared for by a rich benefactor must have been some sugar-plum vision for *Curly Top*'s audiences: kids could be Temple, teenagers Hudson. Boles worked so well with Temple that they teamed up again in a Civil War film, *The Littlest Rebel* (1935), with Robinson back in for "Polly Wolly Doodle" and Temple donning blackface and a miniature Mammy outfit that must be seen three or four times before it sinks in. The horror; the horror. Father Boles, captured up north while visiting Temple's dying mother, must be bailed out by Temple's personal appeal to President Lincoln, which she brings off with a merry gravity.

Temple's mothers tend to die if she had them at all; producer Zanuck must have liked her best as an orphan with a strong crush on daddy. In *Captain January* (1936) this was grizzled old Guy Kibbee (with Buddy Ebsen in for Robinson), from whom do-gooders tear Temple ("Cap! Cap! I don't want to go!" is one of her most famous lines) in a scene pathetic even by Temple standards. In *Poor Little Rich Girl* (1936), another Pickford remake, she has a father but *seems* an orphan. She has to get lost, fall in with two vaudevillians, become a radio star, and sing commercials for a soap company to get daddy's attention. At this point the Temple films drift into a backstager framework, using the stage or radio to excuse Temple's numbers, and with Alice Faye and Jack Haley as the vaudevillians and a Revel–Gordon score, we are assured of some real singing and dancing. (Not all of Temple's films are full musicals.) Temple has a lengthy solo with a squad of dolls, suitably entitled "Oh, My Goodness," each verse in a different style to match the different dolls (from German through Russian and Japanese to some American hi-de-ho) and sings "When I'm With You" in her father's lap, with its somewhat extreme line, "Marry me and let me be your wife." Faye has her spots, and joins Haley and Temple in uniform for the tap finale, "I Love a Military Man." Best of all is "You've Got to Eat Your Spinach, Baby," which Faye first addresses to Haley and which the two then turn on Temple, who has been sent "by the kids of the nation" to expostulate in recitative against the vegetable. They are stern, and she gives in.

She has to; everyone is bigger than she is. Crosby, the ideal American man, Faye the ideal woman, and Temple the ideal kid promoted a standard for endurance under stress: the music in them made survival look easy. And they survived at length. Crosby's career is one of the longest, Faye retired at her option when she was on top, and Temple made twenty-seven feature films, sixteen as the central figure, till her popularity began to wane as of *The Blue Bird* (1940), Fox's attempt to duplicate *The Wizard of Oz*. Drawn from Maurice Maeterlinck's symbolic play, *The Blue Bird* was dull and strange, despite the use of Technicolor a barren adventure. Its high cost made it Temple's first flop, and though she was to make films throughout the 1940s, her age had caught up with her already. She was twelve years old.

One didn't have to be an American role model to gather a genre around one, even at Fox, where the Norwegian skating champ Sonja Henie became a star contemporaneously with Faye and Temple. An Olympic winner in 1928, 1932, and 1936, she produced an ice revue in Hollywood, and the story goes that Zanuck showed up one night, throwing Henie's cohort into a thrill. What should they do? they asked her. And she reportedly replied, "Sell him a ticket." Zanuck bought Henie. What, though, did she bring to Hollywood? As a skater in the Olympics, she had dramatic dash, lent personality to the sport. But as an actress, she was just a skater; she took personality out of film. What to do with her? Obviously, she's the heroine. Give her Don Ameche as a romantic foil, a Cinderella tale for a plot—she's an innkeeper's daughter who enters the Olympics—and lots of comedy from Ned Sparks and the Ritz Brothers and eccentric bits from dancer Dixie Dunbar and Borrah Minnevitch and his Harmonica Rascals. And what have we? *One in a Million* (1936) made Fox two million and ratified Operation Henie. For her second film, *Thin Ice* (1937), Fox built a huge outdoor rink, devised special paint to hide the cooling pipes in the ice, and got everybody into overcoats. *Thin Ice*, too, was a Cinderella tale—Henie loves Tyrone Power, a prince. And so on.

Some said the best thing in the eleven Henie films (nine for Fox) was Henie, pert, wise, and fresh. Others liked the extraneous bits. Presumably everyone liked the big ice ballet—on, say, an Alice in Wonderland theme, as in *My Lucky Star* (1938). The pert and fresh was no act, for Henie couldn't. Neither was the wise: here was one of the most acute horsetraders in the business. She demanded $75,000 a film from Zanuck, and this was *very* renegotiated after the second film to include percentage points; in 1939, Henie made over $400,000. The films are alike, but so are Faye's and Temple's. Henie, however, was no singer, and as an ice film seemed to have to be a musical, hers had holes in their centers.

It may be that the forms that the stars created were more important as stories than the stars were as people: lazybones finds his reason to work in a need to help others; city girl makes it in show biz; tyke challenged by doom is saved by nice big people. These seem to be choice titles in our mythology. And all three stories find their essence in music: lazybones eases into a tune; city girl shakes her thing; tyke sings of nice and dances with big. Yet the stars themselves used music only when convenient, losing the momentum for musical narration established by the dance musical. Look at Henie: they had to make a musical *around* her. Even Warner Brothers, the pioneers of sound, could film the Rodgers and Hart Broadway dance musical *On Your Toes* in 1939, throwing out all music and dance except the "Slaughter on Tenth Avenue" ballet.

Was the musical losing its formal identity? One way to recapture it was to deemphasize dance and operatic vocalism to concentrate on story-telling songs. The major pieces to do this in the late 1930s were Hollywood's first genuine musical fantasies.

☆ 11 ☆

Fantasy and the Story Musical

ONE OF THE MOST fully musical films of the 1930s was a cartoon, Walt Disney's *Snow White and the Seven Dwarfs* (1937). Quaint and magical in the first place, the tale was exempt from the old worry about undercutting naturalism with song and dance, and Frank Churchill and Larry Morey's score—simple tunes, simple lyrics—hasn't a note or word that doesn't feed story or character.* Much has been said of this pioneer work, an eighty-three-minute, $1,500,000 folly that became a fast classic. The highly collective creative structure of the Disney studio, the film's inventive juxtaposition of the comic and the grotesque, the subtle illustrative detail in the backgrounds, and the difficulty in animating Snow White and the Prince, the film's two straights, have often been dealt with. But the score is taken for granted. No wonder: it suits the story so well it serves rather than grabs the senses. What other musical of the late 1930s is as individualized as this one? Sure, it has the directness, the Hollywood hit-trope simplicity in the ballads "Some Day My Prince Will Come" and "One Song." But setting to music such situations as housecleaning, washing for dinner for perhaps the first time in years, and marching home from a day in the jewel mine was novel, and "Whistle While You Work," "Bluddle-Uddle-Um-Dum," and "Heigh-ho" stand out as plot movers, bursting

---

*Disney was so particular about having a plot score that the songwriters created some three dozen numbers before he was satisfied with the eight they used. Disney did approve a ninth, an abysmal theme song, but this was only published and is not heard in the film.

with details of action. For once, a musical film doesn't stand there and sing—it keeps on moving through the songs.

Some critics felt that Disney had betrayed the impishness of the Mickey Mouse shorts. J. C. Furnas speaks of *Snow White*'s "greeting-card simper." But many of Disney's shorts dealt in sentimental fantasy, so this was no betrayal. The low-rental economics of short subjects forced him to stick with features, and his second, *Pinocchio* (1940), is his masterpiece, not despite but through the sentimentality. Like *Snow White* European in look and solemn about its good-versus-evil, *Pinocchio* is unlike *Snow White* in its theme, one already basic to Hollywood musicals: believe in yourself and you'll make it. Like the youngsters who earn stardom in a night, like the kids who put on a show Right Here in This Barn, like the radio singer who conquers mike fright, like the tanktown college team that beats Yale, ad infinitum, Pinocchio is another protagonist who comes through a crisis of self-belief through courage. Pinocchio's crisis is an odd one: he isn't a real boy, but an animated puppet—that's one Frank Sinatra and Alice Faye never had to face. *Snow White* is a fairy tale, *Pinocchio* more a parable. A lonely old woodcutter carves a wooden boy who is brought to life by a virginal goddess with admonishments on the straight and narrow. She assigns the boy a cricket as a conscience, and occasionally materializes when the errant puppet needs help, but the big one—rescuing his father from the inside of a whale—he must pull off himself. This he does, and the fairy turns his wood to flesh.

Yes, it's cute beyond recall, with its cat and goldfish pets and array of cuckoo clocks and music boxes. But the film has menace, for it treats some of childhood's most profound traumas (devotees of Oedipal castration motifs have a field day), and one scene in which bad little boys are transformed into donkeys and carted away is notorious for sending whimpering tykes up the aisle at every screening. Furthermore, *Pinocchio* offers one of Disney's most imaginative musical numbers in Pinocchio's debut in a puppet theatre, "I've Got No Strings," and made technical history in the dazzling opening multiplane panning shot of a sleeping village (to "When You Wish Upon a Star"), so costly that even the ambitious Disney never tried it again. *Snow White* won huzzahs for novelty, but *Pinocchio* is the one with the art in it, the experiment perfected. Anyone who finds it only "sentimental"—and doesn't see why its sentiment makes it so moving—is a jerk.

Between *Snow White* and *Pinocchio*, MGM stepped into the picture with the first live-action feature musical to use neverland magic, *The Wizard of Oz* (1939). This, too, fully integrates its score into its narrative: a story musical. Like the dance musicals, it lets the music express what prose can't, and spreads the poetry around, letting any character dance or sing as necessary. The story musical is not new. The Lubitsch and Mamoulian operettas worked this way, as did the early Broadway adaptations. But in an age dominated by one-size-fits-all love and rhythm tunes, it reaffirmed the validity of plot and character songs. Most important, though it was a typical product of the studio assembly line, with all the front-office censorship and spendthrift collaboration* that implies, it stands as one of the most original and distinctive documents of American art. It is unlike all others, yet holds the key to their form and meaning. It stands midway between the eccentric 1930s and the normalized 1940s—it still has the quirks, but now they're polished quirks. Few musicals have been so carefully put together, yet few unfold so spontaneously. More than any Berkeley backstager or Astaire–Rogers romance, *The Wizard of Oz* is the essential Hollywood musical.

It seemed a white elephant at first, complex to plan, expensive to capitalize, and involving a traditionally risky genre, fantasy. The source, L. Frank Baum's *The Wonderful Wizard of Oz*, made in 1900 a first stab at a native fairy tale, one without princesses, family curses, and the rest of the middle-European elfin cupboard. (Horse-sense lies behind the tale, for while traveling through Oz to get brains, a heart, and courage respectively, a scarecrow, tin woodman, and "cowardly" lion all display those very gifts.) Still, Baum's plan takes in a great deal of out-of-the-world magic. Besides working out all the special effects (including a tornado; the smoky materialization, flight, and melting of a wicked witch; and an attack by winged monkeys), finding enough midgets to accommodate the Munchkin scene, wrestling with the improved but still capricious color film technique, and devising costume and makeup for a human scarecrow, tin man, and lion, there was an artistic problem: what tone does an all-American fairy tale take?

The opening and closing sequences, set in Kansas and filmed in sepia, were easily styled, the dull prairie farm creating its own tone. But once Dorothy has reached Oz, with its witches and creatures and weird places, it's anybody's guess. Baum himself had produced a stage

---

*Eleven writers worked on the script alone. For the record: Herman Mankiewicz started it with a synopsis, Noel Langley composed the basic script, Florence Ryerson and Edgar Allan Woolf added some great bits, E. Y. Harburg edited the above, and Jack Mintz, Sid Silvers, John Lee Mahin, Ogden Nash, Herbert Fields, and Samuel Hoffenstein were also hired in a writing capacity.

musical of the tale in 1902 and several Oz silents, but these were no help—the musical in particular lost much of its native flavor, turning Ruritanian rather than magical and assuming the standard poses in its score. So producer Mervyn LeRoy, director Victor Fleming, and their many assistants and specialists pushed in and invented a new tone, one balanced so delicately between magical horror and everyday charm that only on several viewings does one realize how American the MGM Oz is, with its screwball aunt Glinda, busybody spinster witch, Brooklyn clown lion, and midwestern horsetrader wizard. It shouldn't work—it sounds like a college musical with a tornado. But it works precisely because the magical characters are first introduced to us in the Kansas scenes: Dorothy's grotesque pals are farmhands, the witch is the local bully, the wizard a carnival humbug. When we get to the magic, we know how to take it, as distillations of familiar archetypes. Oz is magical—but it's *our* magic.

The original casting plan projected a different sort of film, with Shirley Temple as Dorothy, W. C. Fields as the Wizard, and Gale Sondergaard as the bad witch. Fields might have worked, but Temple would have been too local and Sondergaard too glamorous for the balance of the familiar and the strange; their extremes would have pulled the film apart. With Judy Garland, Frank Morgan, and Margaret Hamilton in these roles the acting tone was secure. Filling out the event with Ray Bolger as the scarecrow, Jack Haley as the tin man (replacing Buddy Ebsen, felled by makeup poisoning), Bert Lahr as the lion, and Billie Burke as Glinda, MGM had an Oz to stimulate the American imagination.

The single most important factor in the film's success, however, is none of the above. Harold Arlen and E. Y. Harburg's songs do what few film scores have been able to so far: set a style that works for one picture and will never work for anything else. No New Dance Sensation or I Love You would do here: Dorothy sings of a happier place to live in than Kansas (thus setting up the Oz dream and giving the film, Judy Garland's career, and the gay subculture a theme song in "Over the Rainbow"); scarecrow, tin man, and lion sing of their special needs; Emerald City dwellers catalogue the wonders of a specific paradise; and a healthy swatch of action is carried forward in an operatic sequence for Dorothy's first ten minutes in Oz. Arlen and Harburg made one miscalculation, actually including a dance sensation for the hideous forest when the witch's offensive magic attacks Dorothy and her chums, "The Jitterbug." It's a wonderful piece in swing style, and was staged to be the film's big number, with the whole forest in rhyth-

☆ *FANTASY: above, Munchkinland in* The Wizard of Oz *(Burke, Garland); below, black folklore in* Cabin in the Sky *(Waters, Anderson, Bubbles, Horne).*

mic eruption. But the number doesn't fit; it's *too* American, too local to pass in Oz, though Harburg was careful to write the actors' solo lines in character. Thinking that "The Jitterbug" slowed the narrative and might date the film, MGM cut it, though revival houses occasionally screen prints that contain it—*must* viewing for aficionados.

MGM spent twenty-one weeks and $2,777,000 (five weeks and $80,000 on "The Jitterbug" alone) on *The Wizard of Oz*, so it was a white elephant after all—at first. The average big musical tied up two million and two months of studio time at most, and the outsized *Wizard* project lost money on its first release. It was a popular film, though the pretentious critics savaged it. "It has dwarfs, music, Technicolor, freak characters, and Judy Garland," wrote Otis Ferguson in *The New Republic.* "It can't be expected to have a sense of humor as well." This, in the face of Lahr's superb lion, is garbage. Other writers likened *The Wizard* to *Snow White*, but this, too, is wrong. *Snow White* is Brothers Grimm melded with a little off-the-wall vaudeville. It is carefully European. *The Wizard* is more like *Pinocchio*, with its recognizable archons of good and evil battling around a recognizably next-door adolescent protagonist. Jiminy Cricket, like Lahr's lion, roots the fancy in the plain.

This mixture of imagination and folk myth is what makes *The Wizard of Oz* special and what through rerelease and television viewings has made it a classic, one of the few American films that most Americans have seen. It bears little relation to other musicals, as I say—its tornado and broom rides, spectacular color (the Yellow Brick Road and Emerald City glow in shades that will never be seen again), distinctive song subjects, and fantasy set it utterly apart. Yet it is the most basic of musicals in its egalitarian gung-ho that teaches: to fulfill ambition, apply ambition. The wondrous ruby slippers that Dorothy wins when she inadvertently kills the Wicked Witch of the East are like a badge of confidence, and once she learns how to use them, she can, like her friends, get what she wants, a return trip from Oz. Dorothy could have gone home all along: because she always had self-esteem. The shoes did not protect the Witch: because witches have no self-esteem. And the Witch of the West can't obtain the shoes: because evil cannot steal self-esteem.

One of the last musicals* of the decade, *The Wizard of Oz* made the

---

*Many don't consider *The Wizard of Oz* a musical, though it has seven numbers and various bits, more music in all than any of the Astaire–Rogers RKOs or the Berkeley backstagers. Perhaps doubters can't place it because they are conditioned by most complete statement of the theme that the Hollywood musical had been aiming at from the beginning. Looking back, one spots few musicals that didn't strike the note in some way, and the exceptions all fall in the earliest years before the musical had solidified its format—the Lubitsch boudoir was too sultry for the preaching of Horatio Alger, and an experiment like *Hallelujah, I'm a Bum* too nonconformist to preach. But one reads the message pushing up everywhere, in backstagers, in Astaire–Rogers, in Faye and Temple Cinderella tales; and of course by the late 1930s Lubitsch's operetta, *Hallelujah, I'm a Bum*, and everything like them—disorderly art—was suppressed. The coming decades lost a lot of flavor in adhering to the code for form, character, and theme. The code has been attacked as escapism; it is anything but. A true pop-art escapism would advise the disheartened to float or hide. The Hollywood musical urges each person to assert him- or herself, to take a place of choice. Escapism? Say rather moral rearmament. And just in time for war.

---

genre and *The Wizard* resists typing. Also, the deletion of "The Jitterbug" and the "Renovation" scene of welcome when Dorothy and friends return to the Emerald City denudes the film's final third of music.

The Texture
of Swing

WORLD WAR II affected the musical as it did other types of film, in stories with a service background, in patriotic demonstration, in historical and nostalgic investigations of the American experience. The revue came back into style, with studios again throwing as many contract stars as possible into the arena. This time the vaudevilles were excused by threads of plot. Paramount's *Star-Spangled Rhythm* (1942) has studio guard Victor Moore and switchboard girl Betty Hutton attempting to fool Moore's sailor son Eddie Bracken into thinking that Moore runs the studio. After a lot of running around and yelling (mostly by Hutton), the story ends and a variety show begins with, among others, Paulette Goddard, Mary Martin, Dick Powell, and Alan Ladd, Bing Crosby closing the film with the Arlen–Mercer hymn, "Old Glory," set against Mount Rushmore and featuring oral reports on what America means to a New Hampshire farmer, a Brooklynite, and so on. Most distinctive was United Artists' *Stage Door Canteen* (1943), set on Broadway with the likes of Katharine Cornell, Helen Hayes, Ed Wynn, Ray Bolger, Harpo Marx, Ethel Waters, Ethel Merman, Gypsy Rose Lee, Judith Anderson, the Lunts, Katharine Hepburn, and others, all made ridiculous by a script that resists no temptation to cliché or bad taste. James Agee singled out Gracie Fields' singing of the Lord's Prayer as his favorite bit, and thought the film "a gold mine for those who are willing to go to it in the wrong spirit."

Terrible films—but don't you know there's a war on? MGM threw *Thousands Cheer* (1943) around Gene Kelly's resentment at being drafted and his love for Kathryn Grayson, this one also culminating in a big show, too affably hosted by Mickey Rooney; and Fox based *Four Jills in a Jeep* (1944) around the USO tour of Kay Francis, Carole Landis, Martha Raye, and Mitzi Mayfair, with more big show: Betty Grable, Alice Faye, and Carmen Miranda, introduced by George Jessel as "that Brazilian flying fortress," singing "I Yi Yi Yi Yi (I like you very much)." Warners' *Thank Your Lucky Stars* was the odd one for its gag of having the lot regulars perform out of habit. Errol Flynn and Bette Davis sing, Alexis Smith dances, John Garfield attempts "Blues in the Night" (an embarrassment). This sort of thing never works, but with Dinah Shore for ballads and Hattie McDaniel superb in a black number, "Ice Cold Katie (won't you marry that soldier?)," *Thank Your Lucky Stars* came out okay. MGM's *Ziegfeld Follies* (1946), launched in 1944 but so big it took two years to finish, is the best remembered of them all, but it's a great rainbow candybox of horrors. Judy Garland, in her first out-and-out taste of camp, is horrendous in "A Great Lady Has an Interview," written for Greer Garson. Fanny Brice, Keenan Wynn, and Victor Moore in comedy routines are not funny, and Fred Astaire and Gene Kelly in their only film duet, the Gershwins' "The Babbitt and the Bromide," are hoke.

The musicals with a war setting ran little better, tending to favor the uniforms-on-leave structure that had been done to death in the 1930s. But the old tales are gold tales: *Anchors Aweigh* was one of the biggest hits of 1945. How often have we had it before: sailors Gene Kelly and Frank Sinatra—the make-out champ and the wallflower—chase girls, serve as role models for kids, and help Kathryn Grayson impress José Iturbi; so-so score peaks in "I Fall in Love Too Easily" and "What Makes the Sunset," which any character in any film could sing as reasonably as Sinatra does here; Grayson sings "Jealousy"; Iturbi conducts and plays "The Donkey Serenade." It's the usual Joe Pasternak special, lifted by one sequence in which Kelly charms some kids with a tale of a kingdom where a cheerless king has outlawed singing and dancing. Director George Sidney shows the tale in mixed live action and animation, Kelly right up there with Tom and Jerry, teaching the king of joys of music—of being open and uninhibited and therefore influential—and in "The Worry Song" warns him, "Don't expect to get much help if you don't help yourself." It's beginning to sound a little militant.

Kelly's parable is a motto for the whole era of the big band and swing. Music in the early 1930s was generally an autotelic ritual, its own means and end. Increasingly in the middle and late 1930s but especially in the 1940s, music serves; it makes friends, expresses feelings, uplifts, and enlightens. Film scores are obsessed with the benefits of music: Alice Faye tells us "Music Is Magic," Kathryn Grayson orders "Let There Be Music," Judy Garland cries "Everybody Sing (everybody start—you can't go wrong with a song in your heart)." Running through these years is a new awareness of pop music, very nearly a cult of swing. One distinguishes styles. Good-neighbor excursions like *Down Argentine Way* (1940), *That Night in Rio* (1941), and *Weekend in Havana* (1941) pulled in Latin American rhythm and orchestration (not to mention Carmen Miranda),* all sorts of films featured noted bandleaders and their groups, and the still useful Broadway adaptation kept the sophistication and pastiche of the best songwriters, though here the studios proved more cavalier than ever. Hugh Martin and Ralph Blane's *Best Foot Forward* (1943) came west in a respectable facsimile, but Cole Porter's songs for *DuBarry Was a Lady* (1943) and *Something for the Boys* (1944) vanished almost completely. When something inventive came along, like Kurt Weill's *Lady in the Dark*, with its operatic dream sequences, its careful design, and legend-making star turn by Gertrude Lawrence, Paramount paid $283,000 for the rights—a new record—and released it in 1944 having slashed the score (including its theme song, "My Ship"), fudged the design, and handed the star part to Ginger Rogers with little part left in which to star.

Perhaps music was the strongest element in the 1940s film musical, as the stories were mostly old hat and the performers too clean cut after that thirties mob. One even begins to miss Jolson. If he typifies the roughhouse early 1930s, Frank Sinatra typifies the 1940s, with his infinitely engaging vocal quality, smooth delivery, and casual self-portrayal. He appears as himself in *Higher and Higher* (1943) from a Rodgers–Hart show (one of their songs survived the adaptation), and does not quite take part in the plot, about some servants' attempt to pass a maid (Michele Morgan) off as an heiress. Yet without Sinatra, *Higher and Higher* would be half a film, for his many song spots were the action: music is magic. No Crosby film had such a full score, and Sinatra's first starring role, in the backstager *Step Lively* (1944), made it clear how strategic was a great singer to the forties musical. *Step Lively* comes from the stage farce *Room Service*, which had provided the Marx Brothers with their first bad film; here, a pleasant Jule Styne–Sammy Cahn score saves the day, aided by a nice second-line

---

*Economics inspired the south-of-the-border series, as the war closed down European distribution and the studios opened up this alternative market.

cast: George Murphy as a slippery producer, Gloria de Haven as his girl, Anne Jeffreys as a haughty star, and Adolphe Menjou and Walter Slezak as, respectively, canny and foolish hoteliers. Like the Warners backstagers *Step Lively* follows the personal lives of show people to conclude with a show. But aside from a few magical effects in the "Ask the Madam (the Madam knows)" number, Tim Whelan directs for straight and simple. We're still supposed to care whether or not Murphy gets his show on, but we care more about how confidently Sinatra spins out his ballads. Let there be music.

Let there be films about music, about what it means to those who make it. Warners exploited its flair for underworld atmosphere in *Blues in the Night* (1941), on the life of a jazz band. Music is not preached; director Anatole Litvak and author Robert Rossen let an Arlen–Mercer score do the talking. Nor is music a panacea, as it is for Temple and Faye: ecstasy and despair are implicit in the dark photography and in Don Siegel's adventurous montage sequences that synopsize travel and rehearsals in blinding flashes. The actors—Richard Whorf, Betty Field, Lloyd Nolan, Priscilla Lane, Jack Carson, Elia Kazan, and Howard da Silva—hardly make a standard musical line-up, and where other films utilized Jimmy Dorsey or Artie Shaw, *Blues in the Night* used the Jimmy Lunceford and Will Osborne bands, perfect for the freaky, down-and-out look of the piece.

Certainly, the main effect of swing in film was no low-key blues but the exuberance of concert, the rhythmic drive, novelty patter, and improvisational fun. Betty Hutton belting out "Arthur Murray Taught Me Dancing in a Hurry" in *The Fleet's In* (1942) occupies the dead center of Hollywood swing. But swing had an important side effect in its use of black talent, for it brought it into the public eye as film had not yet done. In *On With the Show!* Ethel Waters' part consisted entirely of two numbers so peripheral to the plot that southern theatres could snip them and render the film all-white. But now black singers and dancers were being drawn more into the focus; they had to be, for swing was in many ways a black art. Much of its argot, its rhyme schemes, its rhythm patterns (such as the left-hand "boogie" runs), and dance lore had evolved from black styles, and it seems not only amusing but essential that Harry Warren and Mack Gordon's "Chattanooga Choo-Choo," the strongest number in the Henie vehicle *Sun Valley Serenade* (1941), is played by Glenn Miller but sung and danced by Dorothy Dandridge and the Nicholas Brothers.

Nor were all-black musicals as economically risky as when King Vidor made *Hallelujah*. Songwriters, choreographers, and arrangers knew how much they owed to black music, and began to pay off the debt, so the public's new sense of music as a force in the culture was enriched by their sense of blackness as a force in music—*everybody* sing. In *Birth of the Blues* (1941), Bing Crosby, Mary Martin, and bandleader Jack Teagarden promote the new fairness in Johnny Mercer's "The Waiter and the Porter and the Upstairs Maid," lyrically, musically, and conceptually one of the supreme products of race-relating swing. In the film itself, Crosby forms a white band, but in the song he tells how "stuffy and arty" party guests sent him into the kitchen for some real party with the servants. On dishpan and glasses, "you should have heard the music that the combination made"—and the suggestion that black music has more spontaneity and penetration than white-bread mainline pop is persuasive. At one point, Eddie Anderson (Jack Benny's "Rochester") gives Martin a lesson in how to put over an old standard in black style by conjuring up orchestral vamps and licks out of the soundtrack, and even coaches a black doorman in racial identity by referring to Crosby's band's sound as "our music." The doorman is bewildered: "*Our* music?" "Listen, brother," Anderson tells him, "you ain't no Eskimo." And while it is true that Crosby and his crew make the sound without the help of a single black player, by far the most imposing sequence in *Birth of the Blues* is a black number, a mourning scene for Ruby Elzy (who sang "My Man's Gone Now" in the original production of *Porgy and Bess*) and chorus. Herein we learn yet another of music's purposes: healing. Anderson, injured in a brawl with gangsters, lies in a coma, but Elzy's rhapsody pulls him through.

The swing era peaked just as the United States entered World War II, so its ecumenical outlook coincided with a time of intense national unity. *Birth of the Blues* senses this, hinting at the racial integration of American music in a closing montage over the title song, a retrospective of jazz greats that places W. C. Handy and Fats Waller alongside Paul Whiteman and George Gershwin. The new sound shatters social taboo while it shatters artistic conservatism. Crosby, Martin, and Teagarden in their "Waiter" trio retire the old status-quo pop genres— "We hate 'em; we spurn 'em." Rhythm is the thing now: the rhythms of soul. "And we know who to go to when we want to learn 'em," the song concludes: "The waiter and the porter and the upstairs maid!"

☆ 13 ☆
Wartime People

THE EARLY 1940s saw the heyday of Judy Garland, Mickey Rooney, and Betty Grable: putting on the show. These were amateur benefits, nightclubs, and vaudeville; another America was revealed in these years, remote from the *42nd Street* fleshpots, rural and pure. Garland and Rooney interlocked turns in MGM's *Andy Hardy* series (Garland to Rooney, shyly, in *Love Finds Andy Hardy* (1938): "I . . . sing, you know) with the *Babes* series: *Babes in Arms* (1939), *Strike Up the Band* (1940), and *Babes on Broadway* (1941), good clean fun. Busby Berkeley directed, somewhat down-scale, though he found things to do, as in *Strike Up the Band*'s symphony orchestra of animated fruit and the effervescent "Do the La Conga," shot from a dizzying round of angles. Berkeley at Warners had been dry and cynical; suddenly, he was sentimental for MGM. In *Ziegfeld Girl* (1941), one of the classic threesome sagas, Garland, Hedy Lamarr, and Lana Turner played girls tapped for stardom. But, Paul Kelly warns in an opening-night pep talk in the dressing room, "The Follies is life." The good will make it, the beautiful will bow out for love, and the materialist will fail. Garland is good; she doesn't want to break up her cheesy act with her father Charles Winninger when Ziegfeld calls. Lamarr is beautiful; she marries a musician. Turner is materialistic; she gets spoiled, wrecks her boyfriend James Stewart, and MGM kills her off on a superb stairway, a showgirl to the end. MGM also flogs in a few shots from *The Great Ziegfeld* to cut corners in spectacle.

The most typical of MGM's wartime musicals, *For Me and My Gal* (1942), had Garland and Berkeley but no Rooney. Instead, Gene Kelly was brought in fresh from his Broadway success as the heel-hero of

☆ 165

☆ *HEROES OF SELF-BELIEF:*
Temple (in Little Miss Broadway*) loves*
everyone, Cagney (Yankee Doodle Dandy)
loves fame, Kelly (It's Always Fair
Weather) *loves himself.*

Pal Joey. A film of that sordid, sexy show would have been unworkable in the 1940s, but Kelly brought a little of the hustler to his roles at MGM. More tender than Astaire in a song (yet on less voice) and more aggressive in a dance, Kelly swaggers and grabs. He grins too much; he gets off on the wrong foot. Garland, in *For Me and My Gal*, is not impressed with his "Hello, springtime," and their budding romance and vaudeville act collapses when he deliberately smashes his hand in a trunk to dodge the draft so they can play the Palace—just when she learns that her brother has been killed in action. "You'll never make the bigtime," she tells Kelly, "because you're smalltime in your heart." (It sounds silly, but Garland brings it off.) So Kelly must prove himself in combat; does; happy ending to a last chorus of the title tune.

One couldn't see Astaire or Rooney in the part; their gallantry was unquestioned. But Kelly is a standout for his egoistic intensity, particularly in *Cover Girl* (1944), one of the gems of the era. Columbia had Rita Hayworth under contract, so Columbia was making musicals, even this expensive one, lavish with fashion and Technicolor (though one of the chorus boys spoils a final moment of the title number with the wrong hand motion). Archetypally beautiful and a first-race dancer, Hayworth was a novel goddess, *amiably* gorgeous, the opposite of Dietrich or West. She couldn't sing—all her numbers were dubbed—but she was basic to the wartime musical, suddenly irreplaceable after years of toiling in ghastly programmers on Poverty Row. Some of her fascination was bound up in the "pin-up" syndrome, but her grace in dance with Astaire or Kelly is something else. In *Cover Girl*, directed by Charles Vidor, Hayworth is the star of Kelly's dingy Brooklyn nightclub, rushed by a fashion magazine and the glamor world. Can Kelly hold her—or should he let her go on to fame? His challenged ego erupts on a deserted street at night as he dances with himself in double-exposure, angry and destructive. The Jerome Kern–Ira Gershwin score is gentle and rowdy by turns, but here Kelly gives the picture an element of power wild for expression, for a business to run and a woman to control. (By comparison, Rooney's women are girls who flirt or have crushes and his business is putting on shows in barns or leading a high-school band on to a big broadcast.) Yet Kelly fit as well with Garland as Rooney did—better, for she had the strength to match his. Though we see her die in childbirth in *Little Nellie Kelly* (1940), a dire act redeemed when she promptly continues the film as her daughter, Garland was not to turn woman till she met up with Kelly in *For Me and My Gal* two years later. Then, when she is back with Rooney in *Girl Crazy* (1943), their eighth film together, a western *Babes*, we see her in perspective. Her "Bidin' My Time" and "Embraceable You" carry more weight than her ballads have previously, and suddenly her torchy "I Cried for You" in *Babes in Arms* seems overdrawn for a schoolgirl in a pet over losing Rooney and the lead in his show to Baby Rosalie (June Preisser)—the right delivery for the song but the wrong song for the character. Kelly tempered her, and *Girl Crazy* was the last of the Garland–Rooney films. We didn't need a little Judy anymore.

Betty Grable was a big Judy, the happy Judy that Garland herself seldom projected. Like Hayworth a pin-up and no great singer, Grable had to leave Hollywood for Broadway in the late 1930s to ignite interest. Fox's Zanuck, a specialist in woman-hero musicals, signed her to replace Alice Faye in *Down Argentine Way* (1940): Grable is an heiress, Don Ameche an Argentinian horse breeder, Charlotte Greenwood Grable's mother, Carmen Miranda a lady in a tutti-frutti hat and banana-boat wedgies. Grable shared the Faye roles with Faye and took over when she retired, romancing John Payne, Victor Mature, Robert Young, Dick Haymes, and Dan Dailey. Typical Fox entries, these films reckoned in glitzy settings, all-purpose song and dance rather than character songs, and handsome leading men who were not necessarily singers or dancers. (Dailey, alone in the list, was both.) Zanuck thought the story musical too much bother, but the public was happy—Grable made the top-ten list from 1942 to 1951, number one in 1943. The year is crucial: Grable was essentially the nation's wartime mascot, and Grable knew it. "I'm strictly an enlisted man's girl," she explained, "just like this has got to be an enlisted man's war." Like Faye, Grable was a working-class Cinderella.

Garland, Rooney, Kelly, Hayworth, and Grable do not comprise a vastly different personality squad than we had in the late 1930s for it was not the performers who had changed so much as the forms. Many of the biggest thirties stars were still around. But those who thrived in less ambitious musicals were most comfortable—Crosby, for instance, who could take his three or four easy-street songs into any character, including a priest, which he played in *Going My Way* (1944), winning an Oscar opposite Barry Fitzgerald as the crotchety old pastor Crosby has been assigned to replace. Astaire, who worked best in a story musical where motion is woven into plot, had some trouble.

After the stability of the RKO years, Astaire found himself with neither partner nor studio so he tried MGM to team up with Eleanor Powell for *Broadway Melody of 1940*. It must have seemed like a dream duet on paper, the two greatest dancers side by each for the first time. And their dances are spectacular. They never coalesce as people, but it's a fine film, with a Cole Porter score and a pleasantly familiar backstage tale of two dancers (Astaire and George Murphy) who want the same Broadway part opposite the same starry dancing lady (Powell). We know that Powell's producers will inadvertently hire Murphy when it's Astaire they want, that Murphy's head will swell, that Murphy will date Powell while she and we both want Astaire there. The script manages to act as if it were going over this material afresh, and, when Murphy gets drunk on opening night and Astaire gallantly fills in for him without letting anyone know, we fall in and enjoy the surprise when Murphy pulls the stunt again the second night—deliberately, this time: he is giving up the part to Astaire. Eleven years after the original *Broadway Melody*, Hollywood's Broadway remains a community in which you support your buddies while pursuing glory: Murphy has sinned, and must compensate with a self-sacrifice. As the heel, Murphy is awfully good, and even holds his own with Astaire and Powell at the finale when they resolve their triangle onstage before the public with some friendly stepping.

But what of the dance musical itself? *Broadway Melody of 1940* has lots of dancing, but none of the musicoemotional exuberance that gave us the "Night and Day" and "Cheek to Cheek" numbers. Astaire and Murphy's act routine, "Please Don't Monkey With Broadway," one of Porter's most witless lyrics, tells us nothing about them; Powell's "I Am the Captain" is just another nautical prance. We're in better shape when Astaire plays "I've Got My Eyes on You" and then dances it as an untold valentine for Powell while she watches unseen. Still, it's a bit of a letdown, and Astaire's second release in 1940, *Second Chorus* for Paramount, is a disaster, with Paulette Goddard not to dance with and Astaire and Burgess Meredith unlikely as trumpet-playing college students. Luckily, Astaire moved to Columbia and found an ideal partner in Rita Hayworth.

The format of the dance musical, however, remained elusive; as we shall see, it was losing its dance orientation to a new strategy favoring stronger stories and preferring singers to dancers. (*Cover Girl* was probably the last of the oldtime dance musicals—and note that the flag had passed to Kelly by then.) As proof, the first of Astaire's two films with Hayworth, *You'll Never Get Rich* (1941), was a lifeless look at a drafted choreographer's courtship of a captain's sweetheart. Astaire is convincing in the army setting (you can take him anywhere) but, for the first time, not fun. He hasn't lost his touch—this is the one in which he does the "Bugle Call Rag" (in the guardhouse; he spends a lot of the film there). But the story is drab and silly. It doesn't *deserve* dancing. Hayworth and Astaire were better served in *You Were Never Lovelier* (1942), when director William A. Seiter shot them on a moonlit terrace where Astaire welcomes Hayworth into his element as the essential American hero, the man who incites romance in women. The script tells us that Argentinian heiress Hayworth is cold. Her father Adolphe Menjou hires Astaire to spark a flame, he does, it catches, and Menjou finds an unwanted American suitor on his hands. Cole Porter had helped *You'll Never Get Rich* to fail with a tuneful but irrelevant score; for *You Were Never Lovelier*, Kern–Mercer songs more successfully stress heart, "I'm Old Fashioned," "Dearly Beloved," and the title tune tempering the flame to a glow.

Between the two Hayworth films Astaire made *Holiday Inn* (1942) with Bing Crosby. Something interesting could come of an amalgam of Astaire's tense tap and Crosby's mellow vocals, and for once Astaire is something of a cad and loses out in the love plot; Crosby schemes and sulks. So *Holiday Inn* was different, a little lackluster in its leading women (Marjorie Reynolds and Virginia Dale) but rich in songs— fourteen, all by Irving Berlin and including "White Christmas," the biggest song hit ever written for a film. The story, about two vaudevillians who break up the act and chase the same girl, is no great shake, and it has to stretch to fit nine holiday songs, but Mark Sandrich directed with flair, Astaire thought of yet another weird dance—with firecrackers—and the film was Astaire's biggest hit since he left RKO. Now we want to see Astaire in something special, a sense of aesthetic renewal—something to rival the opulence and imagination of the RKO wonders, something to take a chance, even if it flops. And we get it: *Yolanda and the Thief* (1945), one of the most hotly contested musicals in the canon. Some call it a flawed masterpiece, some a dreary bomb.

It definitely took a chance. A Technicolor fantasy set in a South American land where con men Astaire and Frank Morgan plot to cheat heiress Lucille Bremer, *Yolanda* was produced by the Arthur Freed unit at MGM, known for a certain enthusiasm in letting each property find its own style of musical. Freed, who came to MGM as lyricist (of *The Broadway Melody*, for starters), himself collaborated with Harry Warren on *Yolanda*'s score, not a great one. Nor is Irving Brecher's script all it should be, veering between romance and satire too separately. Bremer is a little stiff, Mildred Natwick as her screwball aunt doesn't come off (one good line, to a servant: "Do my fingernails and bring them to my room"), Astaire's con man gets few chances to flash charm, and the story drags. It was a terrific setback in the careers of all concerned. But visually and choreographically *Yolanda and the Thief* enchants. Director Vincente Minnelli turns his camera on the deliberately artificial land of Patria, as if playing a fantasy within fantasy, and Eugene Loring staged a gorgeous nightmare ballet of Daliesque expressionism. A second big number, "Coffee Time," worked into a street carnival, admirably complements the dream by pushing outward the bounds of realism, which street fairs often do, anyway. Loring hailed from ballet, and had an unfailing eye for the patterns of things—groups still and in motion, doubles and triples, silhouettes, sheets, hats, rocks, trees, and dancers ever gliding toward or away from them. The surrealism of these two numbers aligns with the plot in that the heroine has a guardian angel. Astaire pretends to be one, but she really has one (Leon Ames), interceding on her and then Astaire's behalf in the name of love. In the film's last moment, Ames leaves a photograph with the couple, of them and their children, taken five years in the future.

Nearing fifty and tiring of The Life, Astaire decided to retire and went out with a sure thing: *Blue Skies* (1946), with Crosby and another Berlin score. Most of the songs were oldies like "Always" and "Heat Wave," and there was an air of encore about the whole thing after *Holiday Inn*. In the earlier film Crosby ran a hotel; here he runs nightclubs. Before, Crosby and Astaire were old show biz pals who love the same girl; same game here. And Crosby sings "White Christmas" again. But after the stately *Yolanda*, *Blue Skies* was dynamite, with Astaire and Crosby pranking through ancient shtick in "A Couple of Song and Dance Men," Astaire leaping off a precipice in "Heat Wave," Crosby smoothly digging into "How Deep Is the Ocean (how blue is the sky)?", and Astaire pulling off the novelty of his life in "Puttin' on the Ritz" through trick photography that presents an entire stage of Astaires, each dancing a solo. Paramount dropped three million dollars into the adventure for spectacular numbers and spent perhaps two dollars on supporting talent. Joan Caulfield and Olga San Juan are only acceptable, the fag so-called comedy of Billy de Wolfe is almost as regrettable as the work of El Brendel, and the other parts consist mainly of lines like "Five minutes, Mr. Adams." *Blue Skies* was all Astaire and Crosby, a kind of party in honor of America's coming through the war with its ambition and relaxation intact: with Astaire and Crosby as they were. If they hadn't changed, then we hadn't. Astaire as *Blue Skies'* Jed Potter remains Astaire; the character's name, like Pete Peters, Jerry Travers, Robert Davis, Tony Hunter, and all the halfhearted aliases Astaire played under, is like a printless ticket into life. Only when he danced did he defeat the illusion of putting the everyday into a style. Similarly, Crosby in his many duplications was artlessly restating the obvious—that charm, a sense of humor, a nice feeling about oneself, and stupendous musicianship will send one right to the top.

An odd note: the early 1940s are as well remembered for secondary comic performers as for stars—Carmen Miranda, Eve Arden, Martha Raye (who was for a while mistyped as a romantic heroine), Betty Hutton (who was graduated to heroine parts but played them the way she played her second-banana roles: loud and busy). The comic musical had settled down as comedy plus irrelevant music, as in the Abbott and Costello vehicles. This duo, extremely popular in the war years, revived a failing Universal with *Buck Privates* (1941), filmed for $180,000 in twenty days and quickly grossing millions. The Andrews Sisters were Universal contractees, so they sang at intervals, but this was no musical. Nor was *Ride 'Em Cowboy* (1942), though prime black talent was pasted in, including Ella Fitzgerald for "A-Tisket, A-Tasket." Even *Rio Rita* (1942), on loan at MGM, turned into an Abbott-and-Costello joke fest, though Pandro S. Berman produced and Kathryn Grayson and John Carroll were hired, presumably to sing.

In Paramount's *Road* series with Crosby, Bob Hope, and Dorothy Lamour, the comedy musical almost happened. These films baffle some, but they do stand as a rare case of Hollywood's admitting that personality is the art. The *Road* pictures depend on Hope as Hope—cowardly but devious—and Crosby as Crosby—disloyal but lovable—and a dangerous exotic place with Lamour as local beauty. Constant ad libs and asides to the audience shatter any sense of story. In *Road to Morocco* a camel announces, "This is the screwiest picture I was ever in," and for a reprise of "Moonlight Becomes You" the three stars lip sync to each other's voices, Hope pushing out his ears to look like Crosby when he gets Crosby's voice. Paramount originally offered the series to Jack Oakie and Fred MacMurray, but *Road* spunk calls for the zany on-and-off camaraderie that only Crosby and Hope could put together. *Road to Singapore* (1940) led off, to critics' quibbles; Roads to *Zanzibar* (1941), *Morocco* (1942), and *Utopia* (1946)—actually goldrushing Alaska—led at length to *Rio* (1947), the most musical of all. What with Crosby's big ballads, the Crosby–Hope patter duets, Lamour's spot, and native specialties, the *Road* pictures kept trying musical flight, but *Road to Rio* even pulled in the Andrews Sisters, the

Carioca Boys, and a puppet troupe and let Hope attempt the worst Carmen Miranda imitation in history. By then, critics were grudgingly raving, not unlike icing a cake that has already been eaten.

What of the Hollywood opera lobby? Swing had largely dispersed it—this is the time when the universally popular MacDonald and Eddy evaporated. But Joe Pasternak, who launched Deanna Durbin at Universal, had moved to MGM to oversee the film careers of Kathryn Grayson, Lauritz Melchior, and José Iturbi. In a sense, Pasternak's *Anchors Aweigh* is the most typical mid-1940s musical. It has everything: classical, pop, uniforms, kids, aggressiveness, shyness, coldness, warmth, California, and a cartoon. But it lacked swing, and that was the salient of the day, so perhaps Fox's *The Gang's All Here* (1943) takes the prize. With Berkeley directing, music by Harry Warren, and Alice Faye in the lead, this was thirties musical reconstructing itself, though Faye sings "No Love, No Nothing" in her traditional trembly close-up and Berkeley took a last chance to build his numbers geometrically around a theme, multiplying Carmen Miranda's bananas in a shot so rich in taboo that it was supposedly banned in Brazil. Benny Goodman's band and such numbers as "Paducah" and "Minnie's in the Money," however, emphasized the whimsey of swing. More than that, while *Anchors Aweigh* is a story musical, *The Gang's All Here* stressed the personality musical, made of incidental capers and star persona. Hollywood was running loose these years; loose fun defines it.

☆ 14 ☆

Americana

$\mathbf{B}$ESIDES STAGING all-star revues and stressing the morale of swing, the musical's war effort comprised recalling an older and less embattled America, even a fantastic-folkloric one. The easiest approach was through biography—oldtime composers, oldtime tunes and costumes. Don Ameche played Stephen Foster in *Swanee River* (1940); Alice Faye played *Lillian Russell* (1940) with an enacted Diamond Jim Brady, Tony Pastor, Grover Cleveland, and Gilbert and Sullivan, and the real Weber and Fields; Bing Crosby played Dan Emmett in *Dixie* (1943), minstrel blackface and all; Ann Sheridan, utterly miscast, played vaudevillian Nora Bayes in *Shine On, Harvest Moon* (1944), the title song shot in Technicolor. Suddenly, after the war, bios came faster and bigger. Nineteen forty-five was a bonanza, with *The Dolly Sisters*, *Incendiary Blonde* (Betty Hutton as Texas Guinan), Robert Alda as George Gershwin in *Rhapsody in Blue*, and Columbia's contribution to classical uplift, *A Song to Remember*, the life of Chopin.

No one held these films accountable to fact; as with *The Great Ziegfeld*, they were primarily excursions into nostalgia. But Warners' *Yankee Doodle Dandy* (1942) was reliable as chronicle, with James Cagney a great George M. Cohan, a load of great Cohan songs staged in style, and perhaps the only instance in all the Hollywood bio film wherein a scene from a stage musical is brought off *exactly* as it was—the "Off the Record" number from *I'd Rather Be Right*, Rodgers and Hart's spoof of Franklin Roosevelt. *Yankee Doodle Dandy* succumbed to the usual You Are There approach in showing Cagney alone at a piano on a darkened stage, slowly picking out the notes to what will become

"Over There," but its patriotism felt more sensibly invigorating than that in other films.

Cliché and ludicrous misrepresentation, however, were the norm. *A Song to Remember* cast Cornel Wilde as a fullback Chopin (he got an Oscar nomination, perhaps for being such a good sport) and Paul Muni in the worst performance of the decade as Chopin's teacher. It contains a textbook of classic camp lines, such as the warning to delicate Chopin that "to make this tour is literally and actually suicide." *The Jolson Story* (1946) at least used Jolson's voice (dubbing Larry Parks), and MGM's *Song of Love*, directed by Clarence Brown, successfully investigated the musician's intensity about music. Paul Henreid is Schumann, Katharine Hepburn Clara, Robert Walker Brahms—don't laugh; wait—and when Brahms first plays one of his pieces for Clara, she impulsively kisses him and he says, "Thank you." Audiences scream. But that is what these people are like. Moreover, Brown poured a great deal of first-rate music into the film, and, contrary to rumor, Hepburn's pantomime piano playing looks flawlessly authentic.

The pop bios especially got unforgivably bad. Cary Grant as Cole Porter wanders through Warners' *Night and Day* (1946) in a daze that seems to ask "Am I this year's Cornel Wilde?" and Robert Walker as Jerome Kern in MGM's *Till the Clouds Roll By* (1947) has nothing to do but appear between the countless numbers making and losing friends for unclear reasons. There is one good moment, when Walker and Van Heflin play through "Ka-lu-a" at the keyboard planning its orchestration and the instruments they invoke peal out on the soundtrack. But MGM hit the apex of grotesque in *Words and Music* (1948), an extremely popular and utterly worthless version of the career of Rodgers and Hart. It's a version, all right, with a pallid Rodgers (Tom Drake), an irritating Hart (Mickey Rooney), and no hint that anyone at MGM had the slightest understanding of the subjects' style. Frank Sinatra's "Ol' Man River" at the climax of *Till the Clouds Roll By* is very, very wrong, and the Cary Grant–Alexis Smith romance in *Night and Day* is unacceptably ersatz, but *Words and Music* is foul and stupid from Perry Como's lazy debauch of "Mountain Greenery" to Gene Kelly's uncomfortable spoken tribute to Hart.

The historical story musicals were much more worthwhile. Deanna Durbin went forty-niner in *Can't Help Singing* (1944), her first outing in color, with a Kern score; Kern also worked on *Centennial Summer* (1946), set in 1876 and perhaps the only musical of the decade to cast seven lead roles with nonsingers: Jeanne Crain, the ever-popular Cornel Wilde, William Eythe, Linda Darnell, Constance Bennett, Walter Brennan, and Dorothy Gish. Yet Kern wrote a strong score, characterful in melody (Louanne Hogan sings most of it, dubbing Crain) and smart in pastiche (patriotic hymn, railroad song, and black specialty, "Cinderella Sue"), though its big tune, "All Through the Day," is an everyone song, sung to a lantern-slide show by the whole cast. Better recalled than these two is Rodgers and Hammerstein's *State Fair* (1945), timeless rural midwest where *Centennial Summer* was old Philadelphia. Parents Charles Winninger and Fay Bainter take his prize pig and her mincemeat to the fair along with their kids Dick Haymes and Jeanne Crain (her mouth always full of Louanne Hogan; a great team there), who pair off with slickers Vivian Blaine and Dana Andrews. With *Oklahoma!* under their belts and *Carousel* in the works, the authors integrated their songs to a fare-thee-well, vocal sections slipping in and out of dialogue as if singing were the most casual thing in the world and the story musical the only way to go.

Most ambitious was Fox's *Where Do We Go From Here?* (1945), a fantasy about where we came from. Fred MacMurray, classified 4-F, uncorks a genie in a lamp and wishes . . . to join the army. The genie accidentally places him among Washington's troops at Valley Forge, and MacMurray hops from age into age, each time caught between gentle Joan Leslie and tricky June Haver. What makes the film special is its score, by Kurt Weill and Ira Gershwin, witty and bizarre. Hollywood regularly slashed Weill's Broadway scores (as did G. W. Pabst in his film of *Die Dreigroschenoper*), but Fox released *Where Do We Go From Here?* with, among other artistic advancements, a twelve-minute opera for the Columbus sequence.

Another fantasy, *Cabin in the Sky* (1943), was the second all-black film since *Hallelujah* to be released by a major studio, but swing had so accustomed the public to black performers that another all-black musical came out the same year, *Stormy Weather.* This purported to be the saga of Bill Robinson, but it comes off as a backstager hung loose to provide lots of room for specialties. Many of the greats got into it (Lena Horne, Cab Calloway, Fats Waller) and black standards—"Ain't Misbehavin'," "Diga-Diga-Doo," "I Can't Give You Anything but Love, Baby," and the title song—provide the score. But the film fears being too black, and controls the ad libs even as it encourages them, though Waller managed to slip in, "I've been ballin' all my life and I'll *be* ballin' as long as I live."

Cabin in the Sky is an artier effort, based on a much-admired show with a Vernon Duke–John Latouche score and a fanciful tale about a good woman who saves a weak man while angels of heaven and hell fight for his soul. Here was another chance for segregated talent to step forward—Ethel Waters, Lena Horne, Eddie Anderson, Rex Ingram, Butterfly McQueen, Duke Ellington and band—but in essentially black art, if written and staged by whites. As the heroine, Waters takes the screen and holds it; the prize number consists of Waters just standing there, handkerchief in hand, singing "Takin' a Chance on Love." Horne, as the bad woman, enjoys her only worthy part in her Hollywood career; MGM didn't know what to do with a black woman who wouldn't play a maid. (Even Waters served Jeanette MacDonald in *Cairo* two years earlier.) Everyone in the film seems touched with something extraordinary, and though MGM felt it necessary to make friends for the piece with a little swing that the folk tale doesn't need, it is to be credited with having done it at all.*

Cabin in the Sky's director, Vincente Minnelli, has entered the buff's hall of fame for his flagrant sense of color (useful now that MGM was turning out most of its big musicals in Technicolor), and he had the luck to work with Garland (whom he married), Kelly, and Astaire. He has been identified with a "golden age" of post-Depression MGM musicals, mainly by people who think *Yolanda and the Thief* superb, *Ziegfeld Follies* bearable, and Judy Garland the hooly blisful martir of solemn art-myth. Some of his films are mediocre or terrible, including the two most overrated musicals in history, *The Band Wagon* and *An American in Paris*. But one of Minnelli's films counts among the four or five greatest: *Meet Me in St. Louis* (1944). As folkloric as a nonethnic, nonregional realistic white domestic comedy could be, *Meet Me in St. Louis* was the most nostalgic of the forties costume musicals, as it looked back to a time (1903–04) when cities were suburbs and families stuck together; it made that old, cleaner, immobile America infinitely appealing. Like most of Arthur Freed's productions, this was a story musical, strong in character songs—but this one believes in itself almost devoutly. Minnelli cuts the sentiment with comedy, informality, and adolescent trauma, however, and the result is so well-rounded that we accept its scale as life-size and fall in, rooting for the love plot, doting on the parents, impatiently awaiting the impending world's fair

---

*It has been suggested that all-black musicals comprised an easy way out: racially integrated musicals would have made a more impressive breakthrough. This is so, but clearly the country wasn't ready for that. Hollywood itself wasn't. *Cabin in the Sky*'s cast reportedly had to take their lunches in L. B. Mayer's private dining room to avoid challenging the color bar in the MGM commissary.

and, like the Smith family, viewing a threatened move to New York as high tragedy.

An excellent script (by seven writers) from Sally Benson's *New Yorker* stories, a charming Hugh Martin–Ralph Blane score (including "The Boy Next Door" and "The Trolley Song"), and a fine cast are the film's most immediate benison. The Smiths are routine: father Leon Ames is stern but likeable, mother Mary Astor is wise, older daughters Lucille Bremer and Judy Garland are flirts, younger daughters Joan Carroll and Margaret O'Brien are cutups, son Henry Daniels, Jr., is one big smile, grandpa Henry Davenport is foxy, maid Marjorie Main is testy; even Tom Drake, the boy next door, is just another preppy heartthrob. The Smiths' street, the 5100 block of Kensington Avenue, is so ordinary that MGM could recycle it for countless period films thereafter. But routine is what this film is driving at: a safe place to be. Indeed, most MGM musicals from *The Wizard of Oz* on are obsessed with finding a safe place. Back in the dinosaur days of 1929, Paramount's backstager *Glorifying the American Girl* understood form so little that it gave its heroine no reason for succeeding as a Ziegfeld girl, let her love plot fall apart pointlessly, and gave her a selfish and exploitive mother. A closing shot of the heroine staring into the auditorium in confusion at the height of a big number on Ziegfeld's Broadway tells us there is no safe place, for she has got there and it isn't. Conversely, the formally confident Jolson film *Hallelujah, I'm a Bum* a few years later dared propose a complex naturalism in its Central Park setting, taking for granted mixed-race friendship, political radicalism, and sexual appetites, showing the mayor of New York handing his girlfriend a thousand-dollar bill, letting the love plot end unhappily for the protagonist, and condoning the workless ethic of the Park idlers' lives. Most distinctive is a moment in which the bums suddenly crouch on the ground as mounted police ride by, photographed and scored for real terror.

Now, by 1944, musicals could not make such "mistakes" in plotting and personality, MGM musicals least of all. No MGM forties musical showed an exploitive mother, or looked at police power from the angle of the culturally disinherited, or failed to follow through with romance. A forties musical could be dull, but it had to be nice, had to locate the safe place. Too much nice dulls *The Harvey Girls* (1945), another of Freed's costumers with Garland, set in the old west and directed by George Sidney. *The Harvey Girls* has a sort of family (the Harvey House waitresses, who live in a dormitory supervised by a matron), a more raffish street and boy-next-door (John Hodiak; his pencil moustache tells us he's sly), and a bigger number than anything in *Meet Me in St. Louis*, "On the Atchison, Topeka and the Santa Fe." To emphasize the nice by contrast, *The Harvey Girls* also has a tough saloon girl (Angela Lansbury) to love Hodiak, hate Garland, and—because it's MGM; forget the contrast—bring them together at the end. But *St. Louis* has a secret weapon: Margaret O'Brien.

The kid makes the film. Her portrayal, uncannily detailed, gives the story needed energy at several points—in a wonderfully sloppy cakewalk during a party, in a wrenching Hallowe'en sequence, in her climactic rampage among snowmen after "Have Yourself a Merry Little Christmas," when father Ames realizes that his family will lose too much by pulling up their roots. And at the start, when a ketchup-making scene clouds the atmosphere in sampler gush, Minnelli cuts in the macabre of the truly innocent as O'Brien rides home with the iceman:

TOOTIE (feeling her doll's forehead): Poor Margaretta. Never seen her look so pale.
MR. NEELY: Sun'll do her good.
TOOTIE: I expect she won't live through the night. She has four fatal diseases.
MR. NEELY: And it only takes one.
TOOTIE (beaming): But she's going to have a beautiful funeral. In a cigar box my poppa gave me, wrapped in silver paper.
MR. NEELY: That's the way to go, if you have to go.
TOOTIE: Oh, she *has* to go!

☆ 15 ☆
The Inertia of Genre

WITH JUDY GARLAND, Gene Kelly, and Frank Sinatra on the lot and the Freed unit strong in creative imagination (from Roger Edens, Kay Thompson, Stanley Donen, Betty Comden, and Adolph Green), MGM by 1945 was putting out the best musicals. Warner Brothers, the former prophets of sound, maintained little more than a series of backstagers built around Doris Day, unveiled in a supporting part in *Romance on the High Seas* (1948)—"It's Magic," she sang, often; it wasn't; *she* was, but Warners wasted her in the hideous *My Dream Is Yours* (1949) with Jack Carson and the contemptible *It's a Great Feeling* (1949) with Carson, Dennis Morgan, and a studio menagerie. Gary Cooper says "Yup"; Joan Crawford slaps a face; Jane Wyman faints; and Danny Kaye (not a Warners contractee, but what the hey) imitates a train.

Kaye dominates the late 1940s as Eddie Cantor did the early 1930s. Like Cantor, Kaye signed with Goldwyn and got The Treatment—opulent production, Goldwyn Girls, the works. His films were immensely successful, giving Kaye all the room he needed to be hysterical, fearful, and ridiculous, yet somehow to win out—like Cantor. In *Up in Arms* (1944), from the same source as Cantor's *Whoopee!*, he was a drafted hypochondriac; in *Wonder Man* (1945) he was twins, a tough gangster and his bookworm brother (the gangster was shot early in the story and spent much of the film as a ghost, but let's move right along); and in *The Kid From Brooklyn* (1946) he was a reluctant boxer. These were comedy musicals, for the scores were tailored to Kaye's gifts for mouthy paradiddle, allowing him to spoof jive, opera, movie conventions, or Russian folk song. *Up in Arms* seems the strongest today, for if the war motif dates it, it gives Dinah Shore bright chances in the ballad "Now I Know" and in "Tess' Torch Song," white swing blues fresh off the stalk.

The Broadway adaptations did not stand out much. In fact, when Bing Crosby made *A Connecticut Yankee in King Arthur's Court* (1949), the wonderful Rodgers–Hart version was not consulted, and Crosby ended up with an insipid original score. The same year, MGM made *On the Town*, following the story closely but dropping almost all the songs. Okay; but the music is by Leonard Bernstein. Famed for its location shooting, *On the Town* has less of New York than it thinks it does, as when a shot of the three sailor heroes at Rockefeller Center is so badly faked that one can see the background through the men's bodies. At least it was a dance musical, with Gene Kelly in the lead and co-directing with Stanley Donen; the whole cast leans danceward, for Sinatra and Jules Munshin can get away with anything short of a *plié*, as can Betty Garrett, while Ann Miller and Vera-Ellen are dancers in the first place. Note the threesome plan still vital after all these years—Kelly and Vera-Ellen are the heavy lovers with dream pas de deux, Sinatra and Garrett the perky lovers at first antagonistic in a taxi number (Garrett drives it), "Come Up to My Place," and Munshin and Miller the oddballs. (She's an anthropologist who craves prehistoric man. Munshin will do.)

Kelly's influence as the maximum leader of the post-RKO dance musical was felt all over the MGM lot—in *Good News* (1947), for instance, a remake of the 1930 college romp. There is no Kelly or Vera-Ellen to express the romance in motion, but the exuberance of academe is felt in parades, struts, wiggles, and two big numbers, "Pass That Peace Pipe" and "The Varsity Drag," and the cast is very right: Peter Lawford as the football hero, June Allyson as the sweet coed, Pat Marshall as a gold-digging flirt, Joan McCracken and Ray McDonald as the comic duo. Kay Thompson's late swing vocal arrangements pull the 1920s into the 1940s, and the score is well integrated into the whole in MGM story-musical style, with lyrics to the show's original songs changed to suit specific situations, even to suit the performers. In "An Easier Way," an Edens–Comden–Green ditty deleted from the release print, Marshall and Allyson compare methods of attracting men. Marshall plots to win "chinchilla" and "a villa." Allyson retorts, "I'll take vanilla." It's as much Allyson speaking as the character.

The opera musical was dying, though MGM slipped Lauritz Melchior into *Two Sisters from Boston*, a period piece about a Met hopeful

☆ *POSTWAR PEOPLE: opposite above, Warners had Day, rambunctious in* Calamity Jane; *below, Goldwyn had Kaye, unusually sober in* Hans Christian Andersen *(with Joey Walsh); right, MGM had Sinatra and Durante, insecure in* It Happened in Brooklyn; *and, below, Allyson and Lawford leading student bodies in "The Varsity Drag" in the* Good News *remake.*

(Kathryn Grayson) who works as "High-C Susie" in Jimmy Durante's Bowery cabaret. Very Bowery; says Durante, "Starting next week this place is goin' to be run formal—no one gets in here without a shirt." Grayson's sister June Allyson and proper folks come down to New York, Grayson has to impress them by showing up onstage at the opera, and the plot is on. The film works because—unlike the MacDonald–Eddy series—it isn't solemn about opera: when Grayson makes her debut in the chorus of something MGM calls *My Country* (cribbed from Liszt), she keeps pushing forward to sneak in solo cadenzas, infuriating Melchior and bewildering the rest of the cast but delighting us. And Durante is at his best, working in corny material so ingeniously that an ancient running gag about a piano stool that an assistant keeps lowering on him is a scream. "I don't know what I'd do without you," snarls Durante, "but I'd rather." And of course there's the usual MGM "be yourself" motto—the Bowery can appreciate a high C as well as an operagoer can. Maybe more.

Other established sententia held their ground. *Mother Wore Tights* (1948) let showfolk Betty Grable and Dan Dailey teach their daughter not to be ashamed of their profession. (The film did puncture one cliché in that it opens as a threesome, Grable and two friends off to get a job on stage. But when showman William Frawley asks to see their legs, the other two scatter and are never seen again.) *Up in Central Park* (1948) let Deanna Durbin and Dick Haymes conquer corrupt pols in New York with a Romberg score from Broadway. *Three Little Girls in Blue* (1946) proved that gold diggers (June Haver, Vivian Blaine, and Vera-Ellen) are really sweet kids looking for love (George Montgomery, Frank Latimore, Charles Smith); for depth, Celeste Holm turns up as Latimore's sister for a comedy spot, "Always the Lady," that plays waltz time against march time and ends in French. *It Happened in Brooklyn* (1947) taught the rule of self-confidence to Frank Sinatra, Peter Lawford, Kathryn Grayson, and Jimmy Durante, everyone helping everyone else in the community of the shy or defeated. Grayson hits a height of the bizarre at one point when she says, more or less, "I think I'll sing *Lakmé*," and suddenly does—the Bell Song—fully staged in costume. Durante delivers the film's keynote address while rallying Sinatra, a mellow balladeer in an era of hot swing:

DURANTE: What made Crosby the singer of the age?
SINATRA: His voice?
DURANTE: It helped. But what really did it was his *heart.*

The MGM Freed unit led the field, especially in costume pictures. *Easter Parade* (1948) brought Astaire back (replacing an injured Kelly), with Garland, Lawford, Miller, and a great Berlin score. Garland, already going to pieces in life, still had it on screen (and off, at times; when Berlin tried coaching her during a recording session, she said, "Listen, buster. You write 'em. I sing 'em"). Alleged comedy from Jules Munshin as a waiter proud of his salad is unbearable, but there are so many numbers that there's little action, which is exactly how an empty-silly musical like *Easter Parade* should run. And, wonder of wonders, MGM actually reunited Astaire with Rogers (replacing Garland) for *The Barkleys of Broadway* (1949)—though a comparison of this garish backstager with their RKO classics dampens one's belief in progress. Back in costumeland, MGM found something for Esther Williams to do besides swim in *Take Me Out to the Ball Game*, directed by a now shockingly neglected Busby Berkeley with Kelly, Sinatra, and Munshin recalling the great old Tinker to Evers to Chance double-play infield of the Chicago Cubs in "O'Brien to Ryan to Goldberg." But the studio blew a great opportunity in its musical remake of *The Shop Around the Corner*, Lubitsch's 1939 comedy with Margaret Sullavan and James Stewart as the bickering shopclerks who don't know they're lonely-hearts pen pals. As *In the Good Old Summertime* (1949) with Garland and Van Johnson, under Robert Z. Leonard's direction, Lubitsch's precise charm dribbled and wobbled. The score is zilch, the support poor, and a scene with a drooling baby clears the house. Not till Bock and Harnick's stage show *She Loves Me* did the tale come off as a musical.

But *In the Good Old Summertime* made money while ambitious MGM musicals lost fortunes—Rouben Mamoulian's *Summer Holiday* (1948) for example, in the red to the tune of $1,500,000. Based on O'Neill's *Ah, Wilderness!*, it shattered the ersatz peace of MGM's own *Andy Hardy* series with O'Neill's sharp eye for the details of Growing Up in Smalltown. Here, too, was a safe place, but Mamoulian captures its profound idealism; he shows us what kind of Americans make a place safe. Mickey Rooney as *Summer Holiday*'s protagonist remained Andy Hardy, but around him Mamoulian spins a wonderful tour: through the Miller home in the opening, "Our Home Town," passed from one member of the family to another (as "Isn't It Romantic?" was in *Love Me Tonight*), in a Fourth of July picnic, in young lovers bursting into dance across a green lawn, in the local saloon where Rooney's hard-hearted pickup turns shades of red as Rooney gets progressively more drunk and nervous, and in a last long crane shot of the

Miller porch and street as Rooney cheerfully wanders out into the next commonplace event. Everything in the film is commonplace but, viewed with love and wisdom, seems rare. Mamoulian was hampered by Warren and Blane's dull score, which comes to life only in "The Stanley Steamer"—yet even this appeared to be a reprise of *Meet Me in St. Louis'* "Trolley Song." MGM cut four numbers just before release, though as these were character songs they leave a gap.

An unflawed MGM musical did not fare well, either—Vincente Minnelli's *The Pirate* (1948), now a cult favorite for its blend of dance- and story-musical forms. *The Pirate* lost more money than *Summer Holiday*, even with Garland and Kelly, Cole Porter songs, gorgeous costumes, superb use of Technicolor, and a fine script by Albert Hackett and Frances Goodrich drawn from S. N. Behrman's comedy for the Lunts. In the adaptation, enlivened for youth, an innocent girl in a Caribbean village dreams of loving a brutal pirate, and a vagabond actor who loves her impersonates the pirate; unbeknownst to everyone, the real pirate has been living in retirement as mayor of the village, and is now engaged to the girl. The possibilities for music are uncountable. Porter gave nothing to the villain, Walter Slezak as the former dread Macoco, but set off Garland's dream in the dynamic "Mack the Black" and Kelly's vanity in "Niña" (in which he cascades all over town looking the girls over and suavely rolls a lighted cigarette into his mouth while he kisses one), and celebrates the union of actor and dreamer—for are they not the same?—in "Be a Clown." The dancing is more ambitious, with a savage pirate dance for Garland's vision of her Macoco, and hits a height of style when Kelly goes into a bolero during "Niña" and ends posing before his own poster.

The Pirate tells its tale with wit. Garland has an oft-quoted putdown when Kelly-as-Macoco takes over the town and demands Garland be brought to him. Secretly thrilled, she puts on a doleful face as a shocked citizenry weep for her sacrifice. One girl, overcome, offers to go in Garland's place. Garland peers at her, the prima donna being hustled by a walk-on, and says, "He asked for *me*." Even better is Kelly's advice to Slezak, who, attempting to empty a room, screams and rants to no effect. When Kelly quietly says, "Get out," everyone scrams. "You should try underplaying sometime," Kelly tells Slezak. "Very effective."

Garland's dream motif dominates the film. She thinks Kelly is a pirate; he turns out to be a clever acrobat looking for love. She says of Slezak, "He doesn't drink. He doesn't smoke. He's regular in his church duties." And he's the pirate. At one point, as if she were back in Oz, she cries, "I want to go home!" She does eventually get out of the dream—not by going home, but by leaving it. Garland has grown up. Her Mañuela and Kelly's Serafin make one of the great musical teams, and Minnelli sets them off like jewels in a dream that does at length come true. Yet the film bombed.

A fluke? Or was the story musical losing its hold on the public? The late 1940s saw a time of troubles for Hollywood, from writers and directors eager to treat serious social topics, from federal investigations of moviemakers' politics, and, mainly, from falling grosses. The arrival of television and the courts' demand that the studios dissolve their producing-exhibiting monopolies further eroded Hollywood's economic foundation. More than any other type of film, the musical depended on the studio system: an assembled unit of specialists in musical procedures from arranging to editing. The studios had kept the musical from getting too lively but they kept it alive. If they go down, the musical could easily go down with them.

☆ 16 ☆

The Energy Peters Out

T HE STUDIO EMPIRES crumbled in the 1950s, but in the first half of the decade they maintained an active schedule for musicals. MGM stayed top in story and dance, Warners fostered a horrendous series of backstagers with Doris Day, Gene Nelson, Gordon MacRae, and Virginia Mayo, Fox played out the end of its brassy Grable vehicles, and RKO made what is probably the worst backstager since *Glorifying the American Girl* in *Two Tickets to Broadway* (1951), with Tony Martin, Janet Leigh, Ann Miller, Gloria de Haven, the old vaudeville team of Smith and Dale, and a Styne–Robin score. It looks as if it were filmed in someone's living room. Astonishingly, the director was Busby Berkeley. Not a good sign.

The bio did good business, though with Ziegfeld, Gershwin, Porter, Kern, Chopin, Schumann, Texas Guinan, Jolson, and such already done, some of the subjects had to be fetched from afar. Fred Astaire and Red Skelton played Bert Kalmar and Harry Ruby in *Three Little Words* (1950). *Who?* But it turned out that Kalmar and Ruby wrote quite a few songs worth hearing, if not in MGM's strictly fifties arrangements. Mario Lanza was a natural for *The Great Caruso* (1951) and a subdued Danny Kaye played *Hans Christian Andersen* (1952); the Danes fumed at the liberties taken, though the ballet sequences with Jeanmaire were impressive. Eddie Cantor, Glenn Miller, Eddie Foy, and Eva Tanguay were done, well enough, but Kathryn Grayson was hopelessly ill-equipped to play the young Grace Moore teetering between vaudeville and the Met in *So This Is Love* (1953). This was one of Hollywood's last chances to roll out the old "shall I sing it sweet or hot?" rug, but Grayson doesn't sing either the way Moore did. MGM tried another star-studded retrospective of real tunes and fake life in *Deep in My Heart* (1954) with José Ferrer as Sigmund Romberg. This was quite a potpourri, with songs familiar and obscure and Helen Traubel trying her Brünnhilde mouth on ragtime and "Stout-Hearted Men." Her "You Will Remember Vienna," at least, was very winning.

Doris Day appeared in the two best bios of the time, *I'll See You in My Dreams* (1951) and *Love Me or Leave Me* (1955). The latter, centered on Ruth Etting's on-off romance with a racketeer (James Cagney), revived some great songs and was very high-powered CinemaScope entertainment, but the former, one of the most unpretentious musicals ever made, is a neglected gem. The alleged life of lyricist Gus Kahn (Danny Thomas), it derives its rise-fall-rise plot from simple things like marriage, family, and moderate success. The famous flit in and out, but not portentously; this is really a film about a man, his loving, butinsky wife, and his realization, after some tribulation, that she is the greatest thing that happened to him. No scene stands out for description, no big number may be cited. Yet one comes out of it feeling very nicely served.

Hollywood filmed some classic Broadway these days, in faithful renderings. Ethel Merman recreated her ambassador Sally Adams in *Call Me Madam* (1953), Marilyn Monroe took over Carol Channing's Lorelei Lee in *Gentlemen Prefer Blondes* (1953), Gene Kelly, Cyd Charisse, and Van Johnson made a very sound-stage-looking *Brigadoon* (1954), though most of the action occurs outdoors, and Otto Preminger made *Carmen Jones* (1954) with virtually two casts, one seen (Dorothy Dandridge, Harry Belafonte, Diahann Carroll, Joe Adams) and one heard (Marilyn Horne, LeVern Hutcherson, Bernice Peterson, Marvin Hayes), with Pearl Bailey and Olga James switch-hitting. In the vogue for outdrawing television with spectacle, MGM made *Kiss Me, Kate* (1953) in 3-D—the only musical so filmed—but this was so successful a transplant that it needed no visual ruckus. With Cole Porter's best score and a dynamite book by Sam and Bella Spewack set during the Baltimore tryout of a musical version of *The Taming of the Shrew, Kiss Me, Kate* couldn't wait to be a film: a backstager, rich in decor, dance, and comedy. MGM bowdlerized the book but otherwise honored the original. Even the casting worked. Howard Keel outdid himself—for once the swagger really told—and Kathryn Grayson was almost competent. It was the dancing that kept the screen hot—Ann Miller, Tommy Rall, Carol Haney, Bobby Van, and Bob Fosse. With few numbers dropped (and "From

This Moment On," written for but not used in another Porter show, added), the film argued for a more respectful adaptational process, and with *Call Me Madam* and *Brigadoon* might be said to have inaugurated a new era in Hollywood's relationship with Broadway. Adaptations can be too faithful, however. United Artists filmed the Phil Silvers television spoof *Top Banana* (1954) literally on its Broadway stage, complete with audience reaction shots and drab curtain calls. If nothing else, the *Top Banana* film serves as a document of early fifties musical comedy, with its set-changing numbers "in one," blackout lines, and superficial song cues. But it is nothing else.

MGM readied another Broadway hit, *Annie Get Your Gun*, as its big one for 1950 with Judy Garland in Merman's role as Annie Oakley. For her leading man the studio tested and passed up John Raitt, who would have been terrific, and found Howard Keel, who worked out fine. But Garland was uncomfortable with her role, and she wasn't happy with the director, Busby Berkeley. Perhaps both were pulling the story back into the *Babes* world that Garland had outgrown in *The Pirate*. Her recording of the *Annie* songs, extant today, is halfhearted, and the early footage was terrible. Production was closed till George Sidney replaced Berkeley . . . and Betty Hutton replaced Garland. Now the film worked, with Indian festivals and wild-west rodeo the stage show could barely simulate. But something's missing. The film just isn't fun.

At least the original screen musicals couldn't let one down by failing to keep a Broadway piece buoyant. Walt Disney's fairy-tale cartoons had become less adventurous than *Snow White* and *Pinocchio*, but their scores still sought to engage the narrative. *Cinderella* (1950) and *Peter Pan* (1953) had a lot of story music, and while *Alice in Wonderland* (1951) completely fudged Lewis Carroll's tone, it exploited his zany characters in "I'm Late," "The Caucus Race," "The Walrus and the Carpenter," "The Un-Birthday Song," " 'Twas Brillig," and the nonvocal "March of the Cards."

With Fred Astaire and Gene Kelly on the roster, MGM exercised the controlling interest in dance, though the scores were never as fine as those for the RKO Astaire–Rogers set. Dance in the 1950s was less a meeting of hearts and more a nonallusive celebration, often of the self. Astaire once danced solo to show us his loneliness; Kelly danced to show what a neat guy he is. Kelly made *Summer Stock* (1950) with Garland, recovered from her *Annie* mess, in a revival of the show-in-a-barn theme, featuring a "Get Happy" number shot some time after the main production with Garland in a cut-off tuxedo looking considerably lighter than in the rest of the film. Astaire made *Royal Wedding* (1951) with Jane Powell in a revival of an even older trope, Fred as brother of his dancing partner (Powell romanced Peter Lawford). Still, Astaire found something new in dance, defying gravity in "You're All the World to Me" by gliding all over a room, walls and ceiling included. (The room set was fitted into a huge metal package, the furnishings tied down, and the package revolved as Astaire moved.)

Kelly and Astaire each starred in classic entries, but while Kelly's *Singin' in the Rain* (1952) offers endless delight, I can't see why *The Band Wagon* (1953), Astaire notwithstanding, is so admired. A backstager without the slightest taste of the theatre, it was fashioned by Minnelli, Comden, and Green, all stage veterans who should know better, using Schwartz and Dietz standards. The score is great and "The Girl Hunt Ballet," a Mickey Spillane takeoff for Astaire and Cyd Charisse, amusing. But the story is tired, the attempted burlesque of "serious" musicals rude, Oscar Levant atrocious, and Jack Buchanan as uncharming as when he marred *Monte Carlo* back in 1930.

Singin' in the Rain is a surprise backstager: backstage in Hollywood. Set during the first moments of the silent-to-sound time, when a hit musical seemed like a world wonder, the film tells of good versus evil in what appears to be nonstop singing and dancing, from throwaway bits and plot specialties through a time-passage montage of early musicals to a gala set-piece spectacle. All the material is old—old history, mostly old score (Brown–Freed songs culled from MGM's backlist), old gags, old sentimental therapy—yet the picture is fresh. Comden and Green put wit and joy into this one; they seem to know more about old Hollywood than about their own Broadway. Perhaps the important difference lies in the direction, by Stanley Donen and Kelly. This film *looks* like something, from the cooled-down pastel blue of the night scenes to the sunny hillside where Kelly and Debbie Reynolds close the tale with a kiss.

One remembers a huge film, but a second viewing reveals a few principals and a few bit parts except in the one big number. Kelly is a movie star, Donald O'Connor his sidekick, Reynolds an unknown hopeful, and Jean Hagen, Kelly's costar with an ugly voice and wicked soul. Sound comes in and poses its challenge: how does a sound film act? And what to do with Hagen's silly voice? Answer: make a musical and dub Hagen with Reynolds. But how long should Reynolds have to cover the throat of the nasty Hagen? In romance, in plot, in diversions, the film never slackens, keeps unraveling story; and it has a song for everything. An elocution teacher's tongue twister erupts into "Moses

☆ *THE POSTWAR DANCE MUSICAL: above,* Brigadoon *(Charisse, Kelly); below,* Seven Brides for Seven Brothers *(Mattox, Platt, Powell, Tamblyn, D'Amboise, Richards, Rall in "Goin' Co'tin' ").*

☆ *Above,* The Pirate *(Kelly, Garland in "Be a Clown"); below,* Royal Wedding *(Astaire). All from MGM, last archon of studio craftmanship.*

(supposes his toeses are roses)." A walk home from his girl's place when love has struck causes Kelly to prance through the title song, story musical at its best because the singing and dancing is about what's happening. Kelly's plan for "Broadway Rhythm" in the projected film becomes a saga of new-guy-in-town who "gotta dance," getting famous, tasting love, hitting the top. And "Make 'Em Laugh" reviews the old silent comedy. The song itself is insignificant and copies Cole Porter's "Be a Clown" in scan and lyrics. But as O'Connor performs it, it really jumps with pratfalls, attacks, and miscellaneous geeking. The song's purpose is to define a tempo for comedy—O'Connor, repeating the chorus while he runs off a medley of slapstick tropes, doesn't even bother to get all the words out. He is too busy calling up a time when movies did things rather than spoke: he is battered by plywood boards, does a business with a fake door, flirts and fights with a featureless dummy, walks a circle prone on the floor, and then gives an exhibition of the gag, emended by the whammo, exploded by the double-whammo. This routine builds to a climax so corny I almost can't bring myself to cite it—the old "crashing through a paper wall that you thought was solid" bit. But the audience roars. Here is comedy at its most elemental, so the vapid song actually helps the scene. The music puts a face on the comedy, gives it eyes.

So there were still great musicals to make. But there were fewer great performers who specialized in musicals. Except for Kelly and Astaire, the company had altered drastically. Another classic MGM story-dance musical, *Seven Brides for Seven Brothers* (1954), could star Howard Keel and Jane Powell and feature as his six brothers and their six kidnapped brides people of no major oomph. Imagine what the cast might have been like in the 1930s, when, say, Alice Faye's support drew from a talent pool including Ethel Merman, Jack Haley, Bebe Daniels, George Raft, Patsy Kelly, Joan Davis, June Havoc, Lyda Roberti, Jack Oakie, Charles Winninger, and Helen Westley. Alternatively, consider the daffiness, fantasy, cynicism, and satire that Merman, Haley, and the others worked in, and one sees Keel and Powell in perspective. Keel's work in this era took in such events as *Pagan Love Song* (1950) with Esther Williams, the savorless remakes of *Show Boat* (1951) and *Rose Marie* (1954), and a *Kismet* (1955) that drained the sensuality from one of Broadway's steamiest musicals. Powell, last in the Durbin–Grayson line of trained sopranos, starred in *Nancy Goes to Rio* (1950)—"Whee! Musical spree" the ads trilled—and *Rich, Young and Pretty* (1951), two films of such little content that even camp mavens pass them by, despite the presence of parish favorites Carmen

Miranda in the former and Danielle Darrieux and Fernando Lamas in the latter. Both Keel and Powell worked at MGM, the world's capital of musicals by then, yet all these films lack the shirty self-spoof of a *Pigskin Parade* or a *Wake Up and Live*.

Seven Brides suffers this especially. It's wonderful entertainment, even funny in spots, but it takes itself awfully seriously for a musical that ain't, *au fond*, serious. Choreographed by Michael Kidd, *Seven Brides* has some great dance numbers—the "Barn Raising," "Goin' Co'tin'," and "Lonesome Polecat"—and obviously the brothers, who handle them, had to be dancers rather than all-around performers. Still, where's pizzazz? When Warner Brothers remade *The Jazz Singer* in 1953, they could better their original with a full soundtrack, a multi-camera attack, and color. But Danny Thomas can't show us the compulsion of performance that Jolson had to—does not, as Jolson did in *The Singing Fool*, need to break into a razzle-dazzle quickstep while singing "I'm Sitting on Top of the World." Yet that compulsion is what *The Jazz Singer* is based on and what many of the early musicals had, song and dance going off like firecrackers.

In the early 1950s, performers were being controlled by their vehicles. Or, when they cut loose, they overpowered a public conditioned for safe places and tepid comedy. Frank Sinatra, freed from his MGM shy persona, emerged as a gambling, woman-chasing, blues-blown singer in *Meet Danny Wilson* (1952). This is the Sinatra most people know, casual, underplaying, sharing his jokes with the audience as well as with the other characters, and director Joseph Pevney underlines the new natural Sinatra in a dark underworld setting. *Meet Danny Wilson* even touches on *verité* in Sinatra's occasional rudeness or hostility when performing; at one point he calls himself "the King." Is this *Meet Frank Sinatra*? Wilson sings Sinatra's songs: "She's Funny That Way," "That Old Black Magic," "All of Me," "How Deep Is the Ocean?"—a lot realer than the poor-left-out-me ballads he was assigned in his MGM roles.

Also exceptional was *Calamity Jane* (1953), one of Doris Day's few good roles—the rare one, in her early Warners series, in which she doesn't play an actress. This story musical is set in Dakota Territory, where tomboy Day and Wild Bill Hickock (Howard Keel) spar, embrace, spar, and embrace. Unlike *Seven Brides for Seven Brothers*, *Calamity Jane* offers no scenic outdoors (no color, even) and no dancing. It concentrates on narrative, allowing for an unusually full score by Sammy Fain and Paul Francis Webster. "Secret Love," the hit ballad, is dull and dully photographed, but the opening number is a knockout, taking us from Day's ride aboard "The Deadwood Stage" into town, where she introduces a few of the local characters in "A Very Good Friend of Mine," the two songs tied together by a musical refrain, to the words "Whip crack-away" in the first and "Set 'em up, Joe" in the second. Typically, neither *Meet Danny Wilson*'s *film noir* nor *Calamity Jane*'s musical comedy made much of an impression: they were not what Sinatra's and Day's publics wanted from their favorites.

On the other hand, Judy Garland got the vehicle of her career in *A Star Is Born* (1954). Director George Cukor and author Moss Hart must have studied William Wellman's 1937 version with Janet Gaynor and Fredric March, for many of the earlier film's verbal and visual details remain. But in making Esther Blodgett a singer they and songwriters Harold Arlen and Ira Gershwin reinvented the character's impetuosity and frankness. Ironically, Garland had to switch over from MGM, weary of her erratic behavior, to Warners for the role that all those MGM story musicals had been working up to. The film is not a musical so much as a drama with plenty of numbers for Garland, and because her most intense acting always came out in her singing, the performance is a revelation. All the weight problems, comeback concerts, and tabloid snitching notwithstanding, if Garland had not made *A Star Is Born* it is likely she would not have become the legend she did; her first big musical, *The Wizard of Oz*, and her last big one, this one, structure the myth of an innocence so likeable that, grown old and cynical, it still begs for and receives the public's indulgence. Never was Garland so lost as she is at first here, an unknown in a town comprised exclusively of the famous, never so winning as when she gets the parts and the attention, never so alone as when the actor who helped her succeed and whom she helped in more personal ways finally sinks alcoholically into nothing. "It's the true Judy," the fans whisper, awed at the life-art. Hardly. It is an electrifying performance that expands Garland as no MGM role had done.

An immense improvement on the Wellman *A Star Is Born*—Garland wipes Gaynor away and James Mason in March's role is really superb—the musical is apparently a mutilated version of itself. Without Cukor's assistance, Warners added the windy if enjoyable "Born in a Trunk" number, an autobiographical showcase that takes the heroine from vaudeville to bigtown cabaret and Hollywood through a string of old standards. But the completed film now ran three hours. It was a big one, in color and CinemaScope, but not so big that exhibitors would be glad to lose one showing's take a day. "They didn't cut the picture," Garland later reported. "Harry [Warner] gummed it to pieces." Pieces is the word, insiders tell—Cukor's careful development of the Garland–Mason bond is shredded to the point that the audience cannot care about its decline as they should.

Some buffs date the decline of the Hollywood musical from this moment on, marking *A Star Is Born* as the last of a kind: the last big Garland musical, the last original score by golden-age oldtimers, the last of the big remakes when the new version might actually supersede the old. One could as well mark the moment from *There's No Business Like Show Business* (1954) for its gala cast (Ethel Merman, Marilyn Monroe, Mitzi Gaynor, Dan Dailey, Donald O'Connor, Johnnie Ray), gala score (Berlin old and new), and backstager traditions, three elements that faded in the late 1950s. Perhaps the farewell was most succinctly made in *It's Always Fair Weather* (1955), in which Gene Kelly, Dan Dailey, and Michael Kidd, inseparable buddies in the service, meet again ten years later and hate each other, their mutual alienation rendered the more immediate by a masking process that cut the screen into three separate disgusted close-ups. Not to put too fine a point on it, the threesome had dissolved.

☆ 17 ☆

Economics of
a Stereo Era

Big CAME IN in the late 1950s. True, 3-D was retired, but CinemaScope and it variations (VistaVision, Cinerama, Camera 65, and such) held on in larger theatres. (The neighborhood houses made do with reduced prints, which could play hell with composition.) There were few of the technical difficulties that terrorized film when sound came in, few impositions on art—Hitchcock, John Sturges, and others exploited the wide screen like veterans of big—and even some gains for the musical in the expanded use of location shooting. Fred Zinneman shot *Oklahoma!* (1955) in the Todd-AO process in Arizona (Oklahoma looked too modern), showing the corn "risin' clear up to the sky," the "wavin' wheat," and the scurrying chicks and ducks that the score mentions. The film followed the original virtually line by line, cut two songs that no one likes, retained the original orchestrator and conductor, and let Agnes de Mille rework her history-making choreography, so *Oklahoma!* was one of the most exact renderings from Broadway in Hollywood's history.

It was big, but only as big as it needed to be. "It's a pastoral opera now," de Mille noted, citing "the fine skies in the desert" and the animals. "It's different. But I find it very beautiful to look at." It was well cast, too, with Gordon MacRae, Shirley Jones, Gloria Grahame, Gene Nelson, Rod Steiger, and Charlotte Greenwood (as Aunt Eller, written for her in the first place), and James Mitchell and Bambi Linn dancing the dream ballet. If Hollywood was losing its touch in originals, could it concentrate on filming Broadway classics?

But Joseph Mankiewicz's *Guys and Dolls* (1955) suggested that Hollywood looked upon Broadway originals as settings for stars. Frank

194 ☆

Loesser's songs were kept or replaced by Loesser himself, and Michael Kidd restaged his dances, crucial in the show's distillation of the Damon Runyon Tenderloin of gamblers and broads. But producer Samuel Goldwyn planned to hire Gene Kelly, Grace Kelly, and Betty Grable for roles only the first could have played. He ended with Marlon Brando, Jean Simmons, and Vivian Blaine, who made an odd mélange with Frank Sinatra, supposed to be a tense finagler and not half trying. Blaine, who had played her part on Broadway and had logged Hollywood experience in the 1940s, is the worst of the lot, overworking the lines and gestures. Add to this sets that are half real and half stagey and Mankiewicz's labored pace and you have a perfect Broadway show playing the screen like spilled milk.

The problem was that pop music, which as "jazz" and swing had furnished Hollywood with an appropriate sound style and an inextinguishable source of stories in backstagers, had lost its national constituency. In the 1930s and 1940s, most Americans listened to the same music. But the rise of rock and roll in the 1950s splintered the listening audience; and, unfortunately, the studios couldn't figure out how to use the new sound in story films. It was 1929 all over again: which performers to hire, what stories to tell of them, how does a song work, what's a musical? Early tries at rock film, in *Shake, Rattle and Rock* and *Rock Around the Clock*, both in 1956, were loose and silly and, worst of all, square. Wiseass adolescents circulated the rumor that grownups deliberately made them rotten as part of the well-known fiendish conspiracy to silence the new music. Actually, the early rock films did good business. They were cheap to make, as rock had no "production" in this golden age: the musicians stood there and played and sang. These movies look terrible now, with generation-gap plots plus obtruding musical bits—a band plays for a prom—or "big show" tales. And then came Elvis.

Presley's first role, in *Love Me Tender* (1956), was a featured part in a southern post-Civil War romance. Thinking older brother Richard Egan dead in battle, Presley has married Egan's sweetheart Debra Paget. The film was no musical, though Presley does his stuff in four songs, getting rather modern-sounding screams from the Confederate girls standing by. Launched in a hit—Presley made it one—he became a star and made thirty story musicals for various studios from 1957 to 1970. He plays the same fellow in each, with variations—a convict in *Jailhouse Rock* (1957), a quasi-delinquent analyzed by Hope Lange, tempted by Tuesday Weld, and reformed by Millie Perkins in *Wild in the Country* (1961), a boxer in *Kid Galahad* (1962), twins in *Kissin'*

☆ *CLASSIC NUMBERS: above, "Tiptoe Through the Tulips" from the first threesome classic,* The Gold Diggers of Broadway; *below, "You Gotta Have a Gimmick" from* Gypsy *(Wood on trunk); right above, Rooney and Garland in "Do the La Conga" from* Strike Up the Band, *one of Berkeley's most dancey numbers (though the camera still adds much to the motion).*

☆ *Above, Garland's "The Boy Next Store,"* Meet Me in St. Louis; *below, Gingold and Chevalier in* Gigi's *"I Remember It Well."*

Cousins (1964), an heir who trades places with a water-ski instructor in *Clambake* (1967), a hip doctor in love with nun Mary Tyler Moore in *Change of Habit* (1970). Who is he? A country boy, quiet, unselfish, tolerant, not smart but intuitive. Presley couldn't act, but that renders the illusion all the more telling—he *must* be the character because he wouldn't know how to fake it. His was probably the nicest persona in film history, and critics savaged him. "Is it a sausage?" asked *Time*. "It is certainly smooth and damp-looking . . . Is it a Walt Disney gold-fish? . . . Is it a corpse? The face just hangs there, limp and white with its little drop-seat mouth . . . A peculiar sound emerges. A rusty fog-horn? A voice? Words occasionally can be made out: 'Goan . . . git . . . luhv.' " But this was the most successful series of films ever made. To dismiss Presley is New York solipsism.

The films themselves are atrocious. The scores are dull, the support-ing casts often amateurish, the productions hasty, and the helter-skel-ter decor makes Alice Faye's vehicles look like an expert's seminar in the history of costume. *Frankie and Johnny* (1966), with a showboat setting, is typical, with supremely ungifted youngsters (Donna Doug-las, Sue Ane Langdon, Anthony Eisley), defeated veterans (Audrey Christie, Harry Morgan, Jerome Cowan), unintelligible plot, a load of songs, extras apparently hired on a come-as-you-are basis, and abso-lutely no sense of style—a title-song production number imitates boffo staging without suggesting it; and later, when the number is reprised, the original footage is simply run over again.

But Elvis has charm. He's at his best when fighting for the dispos-sessed, as in *Follow That Dream* (1962), a pleasant argument for popu-list anarchism. "How many times I got to tell you?" his father Arthur O'Connell says. "The government don't run out of money. *People* run out of money. The government's loaded." Presley takes on both a fed-eral welfare agency and gangsters, politely, naively, but with admira-ble efficiency. The film manages to suggest not only that authoritarian interference is harmful, but that authoritarians are crummy people who use their power vindictively. The better Presley films are actually rather beguiling, and have only one drawback: by the time he made them, Presley had ceased to sing rock.

Ironic that the very centerpiece of rock-as-rebellion, the popularizer of take-no-prisoners rockabilly sensuality, should have crossed over to midcult white fifties "rhythm," but that's probably why Presley's movies work so well as story musicals. No one knew, then, how to make real rock work for story contexts in film, which is why the major rock mediums are still the concert and the record album. Rock opera?

It's more a rock song cycle, not readily stageable. But then Presley's rock and roll really died (temporarily) when Buddy Holly did and the folkies moved in. Not till the Beatles remixed ragtime, twenties pop, Schubertian *Lied*, and a host of other styles with American rock did the sound open up elastically. Then, we'll shortly see, there were possibilities for rock musicals.

Obviously, Hollywood was going to stick to the Broadway sound with the old regulars as much as possible. Danny Kaye made his best film in *The Court Jester* (1956), a lampoon of the Ivanhoe sort; wiseass kids not clued into the antirock conspiracy went around quoting its "Get it?" "Got it!" "Good" and its dire message, "The pellet with the poison's in the vessel with the pestle." (Don't ask; you had to be there.) Sinatra, Crosby, Grace Kelly, and Louis Armstrong graced *High Society* (1956), *The Philadelphia Story* with a Cole Porter score and all its wit flattened; Porter really went Hollywood in the hit tune, "True Love," a simple-minded waltz he would never have thrust upon Broadway. Gene Kelly squired Mitzi Gaynor, Kay Kendall, and Taina Elg, his club act, in *Les Girls* (1957), better Porter and a *Rashomon*-shaped narrative: three versions of the same past. Astaire was at his best in *Funny Face* (1956), made of old Gershwin songs (and with the title, but nothing else, of an old Gershwin show) and an Americans-in-Paris plot that for location work, zest, and freshness is far superior to *An American in Paris* (1951), a film whose reputation seems to be based entirely on Gene Kelly's intriguing ballet set against a palette of painters' styles. *Funny Face* has no big number, but it has Audrey Hepburn, ravishing in "How Long Has This Been Goin' On?" as a bookworm twirling rhapsodically in a model's chic hat.

The prize of the era is *Gigi* (1958), the capstone of MGM's so-called golden age and one Arthur Freed film that actually exceeds its reputation. Hepburn had played the part (without music) on Broadway, that of a young French girl raised to be a courtesan who chucks the whole thing for love. Leslie Caron, so winning in *An American in Paris*, *Lili* (1953), *The Glass Slipper* (1955), and *Daddy Long Legs* (1955), at last lucked into a champion: Minnelli at his most imaginative, a Loewe–Lerner score, Hermione Gingold and Isabel Jeans as Gigi's mentors, Louis Jourdan as her friend, then protégeur, then suitor, and, best of all, the return of Maurice Chevalier as Jourdan's uncle. A greedy location schedule devoured Paris, including Maxim's, which closed for four days so Minnelli could film an extraordinary sequence wherein *le tout Paris* gossips in song—Loewe, master of pastiche, set it as a cancan—as Jourdan upholds his playboy status with a lavish rendezvous.

Gigi was Freed's last original musical, and the line begun in *The Wizard of Oz* and continued through *Meet Me in St. Louis, On the Town*, and *Singin' in the Rain* came to an end in one of the ritziest films ever—a three-million-dollar production, and it looks it. Here is a musical that uses decor, color, motion, even the juxtaposition of true locale and sound stage, for tone. At Maxim's, in the Bois de Boulogne, in the pages of a Parisian *Tatler*, all over the city as Jourdan berates and surrenders to his love in the title song, or on the beach on holiday, where Minnelli cuts from young love frolicking on the sand with a donkey to Gingold and Chevalier, who style a reminiscence of their old liaison against a painted sky, Minnelli makes a *movie*, as Lubitsch and Mamoulian did when almost no one else knew what a musical was, and as few knew now that musicals were turning into Broadway souvenirs. Even Mamoulian, in *Silk Stockings* (1957), made no history, though with Astaire and Cyd Charisse in an adaptation of the Porter hit. True, this last of Porter's stage scores is dull where *Gigi* sparkles; true also that *Silk Stockings* has nothing to compete with Chevalier, aged, a little pastured, and absolutely in character until the movie can't resist giving him an encore specialty and out comes the old straw boater for "I'm Glad I'm Not Young Anymore." But the Mamoulian film, except for Charisse's frosty commissar (which Garbo brought off so much more incisively in *Ninotchka*), is the same old thing, right down to Peter Lorre's trepak.

If Hollywood had to overstress the Broadway adaptation, at least let it respect the original while turning it out for film. *Pal Joey* (1957) cleaned up John O'Hara's tale, gave Frank Sinatra a spate of songs from other Rodgers–Hart shows, and miscast Rita Hayworth and Kim Novak; *The Pajama Game* (1957), on the contrary, preserved the original score and cast (Doris Day in for Janis Paige). *Damn Yankees* (1958), the tale of a middle-aged baseball fan who sells his soul to the devil to be Tab Hunter and win the pennant for the Washington Senators, was too faithful. Co-directors George Abbott and Stanley Donen threw a camera on a Broadway cast overplaying with Broadway timing and Broadway pauses (for laughs? coughs? latecomers?). What on stage looked game and stylish here looks like a metal-booted cartoon, though Bob Fosse's dances come off well, even "Two Lost Souls," in which Hunter partners Gwen Verdon. She looks better with Fosse in the "Who's Got the Pain?" duet, but the same problem that dogged the Verdons of 1929 and 1930 kept her from making it in film: too expert, too special, too New York (born, however, in Culver City). The cartoon approach could work only on a cartoon—*Li'l Abner* (1959), filmed virtually on stage with one major cast change (Leslie Parrish for Edie Adams), one change of ballad ("Otherwise" for "Love in a Home"), and Michael Kidd's freaky Al Capp plastique intact, is in its bold color the Sunday funnies come to life.

Hollywood in the late 1950s caught up on the Rodgers–Hammerstein classics whose long runs prohibited hasty transformation, and here big began to come into play—had to, with all that reputation to deal with. *The King and I* (1956), with Deborah Kerr and Yul Brynner, upheld the *Oklahoma!* treatment: make it film but keep all its parts in place. A grand event, even if Marni Nixon had to dub Kerr. But *Carousel* (1956) didn't work out well, mostly through ho-hum casting. Sinatra, hired for the lead, ducked out just before shooting—a smart move, as he's completely wrong for the part. But his replacement, Gordon MacRae, was correct, no more. John Raitt, who created the role, would have been perfect; not till *The Pajama Game* did Hollywood give him a tumble. *South Pacific* (1958) was the first really overdone musical, turgidly directed by Joshua Logan and photographed through blurry filters with Rossano Brazzi (dubbed by Giorgio Tozzi), Mitzi Gaynor, John Kerr (dubbed by Bill Lee), and, from the stage, Ray Walston and Juanita Hall (dubbed, for some reason, by Muriel Smith). Not only was the whole score retained, but "My Girl Back Home," dropped from the original, was put back in; Logan treated the property as if it were Scripture. Big, I tell you. The *New York Post* called it "a three-hour ruin of a magnificent musical."

Potentially the biggest event would be *Porgy and Bess* (1959), Gershwin's opera of black life in a Charleston ghetto, originally staged by Rouben Mamoulian with extravagant pictorial intensity in 1935. There were several big considerations here—the filming of a too long underrated American masterpiece, the eliciting stylization of the black idiom in music and dance, and the first American attempt at filming a major opera. Goldwyn controlled the film rights and hired Mamoulian to direct, but after disagreements Goldwyn replaced him with Otto Preminger. Much more of the score than one had hoped to hear was there, and the casting was good—Sidney Poitier, Dorothy Dandridge, Brock Peters, Diahann Carroll, Pearl Bailey, and Sammy Davis, Jr., brilliant as Sportin' Life. But Gershwin's line calls for extremely vital singing, the one thing dubbing can't deliver; and this film was *plenty* dubbed. Opera movies never work. That kind of big—the full-out mutuality of singer-public vocal communication—film cannot raise.

Movies, like popular music an art form that in America never pretended to be anything but a business, had banked nothing against posterity. Except for the rare re-release of a major film, Hollywood's output was product, to amass profits and be forgot. But when television proved unbeatable, the studios joined it, producing series and—most important—selling off the dead backlist for airplay. Television became a museum of film. A wicked museum: with commericals and cutting for time slots. Still, the home screen served to introduce a new generation to films they might otherwise not have seen. Musicals suffered cutting the worst, for since their songs were often subsidiary to plot motion, music and dance were the first things to go when footage was snipped. But it is ironic that while contemporary Hollywood was falling back on the big Broadway transmission, *Million Dollar Movie* was airing Astaire and Rogers, MGM story musicals, and Depression backstagers—all great examples of Hollywood as creator. The film musical, it appears, was here to stay, no matter what Hollywood was doing to it lately.

☆ 18 ☆
The Big Broadway Roadshow

SAPPY AS MOST of them were, Elvis Presley's films were Hollywood's main body of original work in the musical in the 1960s, and among the few that didn't go epic. There were others, but *Let's Make Love* (1960), in which Yves Montand courted Marilyn Monroe with blasé *laissez-faire*, or *Get Yourself a College Girl* (1964), with Chad Everett, Mary Ann Mobley, Nancy Sinatra, and a few rock acts, are not worth more than a mention, and the last of the Crosby–Hope–Lamour vehicles, *The Road to Hong Kong* (1962)—the only *Road* picture with a definite article in its title—was more of the same fun we had had six times before.

The Disney Studio, churning out its family fare, tried its first live-action musical, but *Babes in Toyland* (1961) showed none of Disney's imaginative mythopoeia. This filming of the old Herbert operetta had far more of the score (souped-up, however) than the Laurel–Hardy edition, but the special effects were greasy, the magic heartless, and Ray Bolger as the villain, Annette Funicello and Tommy Sands as the lovers, and nearly everyone else but Ed Wynn as the toymaker were wrong, wrong, wrong. Disney's *Mary Poppins* (1963) was a vast improvement. It lacked the tartness of Pamela Travers' stories, but the magic was true, especially in blends of animation and live action. A runaway hit for its broad appeal, *Mary Poppins* heartened those who felt Julie Andrews was swindled when Jack Warner cast Audrey Hepburn in *My Fair Lady*, and also gave nice opportunities to Dick Van Dyke, Ed Wynn, Glynis Johns, Elsa Lanchester, and Jane Darwell (Ma Joad in John Ford's *The Grapes of Wrath*) as a strange bird woman. Maybe *Mary Poppins* wasn't strange enough, though Travers restrained Disney from bringing Andrews and Van Dyke together romantically and made him honor her downbeat ending: Mary Poppins leaves the Banks family, as she arrived, by flying umbrella. Richard M. and Robert B. Sherman's score is childish, but it does provision a full-scale 140-minute story musical; and, true, if you've got to write songs about the medicine going down and the concept of supercalifragilisticexpialidocious (-*dozisch* in the German dubbing), it's hard to sound sophisticated.

Talk about childish, American-International, the Republic of the 1960s, made a series of story musicals with a surfing theme, starring Frankie Avalon and Annette Funicello supported by oldtimers (Robert Cummings, Buddy Hackett, Buster Keaton, Don Rickles), menaced by a burlesque motorcycle gang led by Eric von Zipper (Harvey Lembeck), and backed up by choruses of California blonds in swimming togs. These films inhabit an amazing innocence; was this the 1960s? In *Beach Party* (1963), Avalon and Funicello arrive for a week at a beach house, but she has secretly invited the whole gang down, to protect her virginity. For plot complications, Funicello takes up with anthropologist Cummings, studying teenage tribalism; for comedy, there is beatnik lampoon and Lembeck's clumsiness. For music, astonishingly, the style is early fifties midcult without a hint of rock. The two leads sing "Beach Party Tonight" at the start, as sweet as two Yodels in cellophane; "Surfin' " provides party entertainment; Funicello gives herself love advice in double-exposure in "Treat Him Nicely," and so on. It's so wholesome that a harmless kiss between Avalon and Luciana Paluzzi in *Muscle Beach Party* (1964) has Funicello calling Paluzzi a nymphomaniac and Paluzzi calling Funicello a professional maiden. Even Rickles, supreme in put-down assaults, is tame.

For musical sophistication, fine star turns, and something bright in story, one had little option but to see the latest Broadway adaptation, bigger and bigger as the decade wore on. Some perpetuate grand performances, such as Judy Holliday's in *Bells Are Ringing* (1960); Robert Preston's in *The Music Man* (1962), delightfully reproduced in toto by the original director, Morton da Costa; or Rex Harrison's and Stanley Holloway's in *My Fair Lady* (1964), though Jack Warner first wanted Cary Grant and James Cagney. In the end, Hepburn was the only major alteration; George Cukor even filmed the show (at a cost of $17,000,000) using Cecil Beaton's costumes and Oliver Smith's sets virtually direct from Broadway. Warner's *Gypsy* pulled the biggest switch of all in replacing Ethel Merman's Mama Rose—one of Broadway's legendary portrayals—with that of Rosalind Russell in a score very dependent on Merman's trumpet. But Russell brings it off, songs and all, talking and whispering through "Small World," forcing "Some People" to work through force of personality, letting warmth ride her through "You'll Never Get Away From Me," and revving up for a wonderfully pushy "Everything's Coming Up Roses" after spilling out her hurt, bitterness, and fury on the last word of the first line: "You'll . . . be . . . *swell!*" A considerable portion of Russell's singing was dubbed by Lisa Kirk, so this analysis feels a little foolish; nonetheless Russell plays a spectacular Rose. The film as a whole has been hated and praised. Mervyn LeRoy's direction is so-so, but the original material comes through, including the brilliant orchestrations, complete with overture. Nothing in the tough story is softened or cosied, and the show's claustrophobic atmosphere of overpopulated rented room and cramped backstage is respected. LeRoy realized that the film needn't look big because it has a big character.

But big paid off, most notably in *The Sound of Music* (1965), one of the two or three most thoroughly viewed films of all time; those attracted by a Cinderella story containing nuns, kids, Nazis, and Julie Andrews were literally overwhelmed (there's a lot of all four) and had to sit through the picture two or three times before they could settle down and go on with life. The Rodgers–Hammerstein show, a vehicle for Mary Martin on Broadway, had been freshened, lightened, and opened wide with a youthful heroine, with "I Have Confidence in Me" to replace the sardonic "No Way to Stop It" and "How Can Love Survive?", with a new premise for "The Lonely Goatherd" incorporating the Baird Marionettes, and with thrilling Austrian topography (the stage show, for all its Franz and Brigitta, could have taken place in the West Bronx), one shot of Andrews whirling alone in the green hills as the camera swoops down and the title song whips in having passed into the nation's memory.

In fact, *The Sound of Music* is neither all that great nor all that horrible. It's not sticky-sweet, despite the kids, for the Nazis have real menace—they didn't in the show—and even the nuns aren't as nice as non-Catholics always think nuns must be. Andrews is fine in a dull part, Christopher Plummer opposite her is a bore, the score is variable, Robert Wise's direction is excellent for this sort of thing, and so on down the line: okay. *The Sound of Music* is less important for what it was than for what it inspired in the industry. Producers determined to clean up ordered more *Sounds of Music*; but there is no menu for art, even pop art, and instead of Broadway-into-film hits, Hollywood produced the biggest squad of bombs in film history. Producers panicked;

☆ *BIG BROADWAY: above,* Camelot, *with real magic and sweaty chivalry; below, the title number in* Mame, *Onna White's stage choreography moved outside (Lucille Ball, center).*

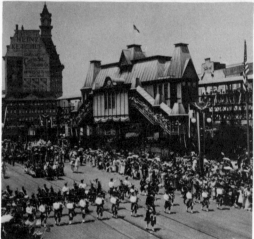

☆ *Above, Streisand recreates Brice's Baby Snooks in* Funny Girl *(in a scene deleted from the release print); center, the notorious parade in* Hello, Dolly!, *irrelevant to the film however thrilling in its detail work (the station is all there, but the building at left is painted flat); below, Chakiris in* West Side Story.

why isn't it working? Do like *The Sound of Music*: big Broadway property, big stars, big score, big money, big hit. The recipe seemed right, but in movie houses all over the country these *immense* cakes were falling, and with *such* a noise. Why did no one take notice of Richard Lester's spry, tight *A Funny Thing Happened on the Way to the Forum* (1966), the one Broadway transplant that found more in less? Too much of Stephen Sondheim's score was dropped, but the piece became a true comedy musical in that only songs that indulged the farce could pass. Applying the fast-cut wacky style he had developed for the first two Beatles films, Lester let Zero Mostel, Phil Silvers, Jack Gilford, and Michael Hordern do their stuff against a sarcastically naturalistic ancient Rome of brutality, oppression, and buzzing flies. The camera runs as screwball as the plot to catch the rhythm of farce, as when hero Michael Crawford, letting go with a love song, hits on a tree and a lute plops down, or when "Everybody Ought to Have a Maid" creates a mosaic of film fun—quick turns, strange sets, close and far views (of the four comics, at one point, forming a kickline way atop an aqueduct), overhead Berkeley spoofs, funny poses, and other craziness.

Mostel, for one, thought the film too busy. "The great thing about the piece on stage," he said, "was that it was one set, sixteen characters, three houses, and you did it very simply. You go to the movie and there's horses, zebras, peacocks shitting all over the place, your father's moustache, orphans, winos, donkeys with hard-ons . . ." Lester almost alone among directors observed a sharp style in filming Broadway. But Lester is a satirist, and in Hollywood a big investment is a solemn event. Prototypal, then, was *Camelot* (1967), grimly festive, a big show with big stars and score in the first place. Jack Warner envisioned a faithful rendering with the epic made manifest—real castle, jousts, and round table, Excalibur resplendent, the sweat of the Middle Ages and the poetry of chivalry. Alan Jay Lerner adapted his Broadway libretto, finding the spots for twelve of his and Frederick Loewe's songs (including "Then You May Take Me to the Fair," dropped from the show early in its run). So far, so good, if you enjoy the original's ham-handed reduction of T. H. White's highly textured burlesque-romantic pageant of political-psychological self-hatred. The casting followed the new trend favoring personalities not always musically talented or, if musical, not right for their parts. In *Can-Can* (1960), calling in Frank Sinatra, Louis Jourdan, Shirley MacLaine, and Maurice Chevalier necessitated a ruthless overhauling of the original for the fit, and no attempt was made to reconcile Chevalier's and Jourdan's Gallic suavity with Sinatra's and MacLaine's flat American informality. In *West Side Story* (1961), Jerome Robbins' choreography called for dancers for the bulk of the cast, and they cut striking figures against real New York streets. But of the leads, Natalie Wood can neither act nor sing, Richard Beymer seems like something scraped out of a pie, and only Rita Moreno can do what her role calls for. She and the dancing carry the film, in fact. Yet *West Side Story*, if not *Can-Can*, intended to film the stage show with utmost fidelity.

As did *Camelot*. And much of it does look right, in the callous gung-ho of the jousting tournament or in castle eyries by the hearth. But Richard Harris as Arthur, ranting his songs and lines, makes a tricky part impossible and Franco Nero as Lancelot had to be dubbed (by Gene Merlino) in a role expressly designed for the Broadway baritone. The man who sings "C'est Moi," "If Ever I Would Leave You," and "I Loved You Once in Silence" is supposed to know why those songs are there; Nero clearly doesn't. Granted that the naturalism of film acting is vastly better than the mechanical caricatures that Broadway musicals depend so much on (as in Carol Channing, Ethel Merman before and after *Gypsy*, everyone in Gower Champion's *42nd Street* staging, and even Richard Burton in the grungy 1980 *Camelot* revival), aren't there any real actors who really sing? Vanessa Redgrave, as Guinevere, almost is one, for she learned how to weave her thread of voice into something adroitly musical. It's all mike, but it works. Logan pulls an occasional film trick, as in a montage of adulterous rendezvous that creeps in on "If Ever I Would Leave You," but all directors of musicals have at some point to come to terms with the performance of character songs; how can they do so with nonsinging actors or with revamped properties whose scores no longer suit the actors singing them?

Not all the big films were antimusical or antistyle. A Hollywood original, *Thoroughly Modern Millie* (1967) had the right idea in putting Julie Andrews and Mary Tyler Moore into a mystery plot with a twenties setting, with Beatrice Lillie as the villain (she sells girls into slavery), John Gavin and James Fox as stalwart and comic boyfriends, and Carol Channing for a Broadway turn. But the period was flubbed, Lillie given no chance to *do,* and a "Jewish Wedding Song" shoved into the action at what must have been gunpoint. Another good idea, on paper, was the building of a musical around Rex Harrison, based on Hugh Lofting's Dr. Doolittle character, with crazy animals (like the two-headed pushmi-pullyu and a giant lunar moth), circus joys, and Anthony Newley to carry the ballads. But Leslie Bricusse's dead score (a prize of the soundtrack album to anyone who can explain why "Talk to the Animals" won the Oscar as Best Song) and a sluggish determination to wow with size and color sent the picture to the deep six in short order. An even faster flop was *Star!* (1968), a bio with Julie Andrews carefully indicating the elements of zaniness, hysteria, pathos, and selfishness in the character of Gertrude Lawrence and never being anything but a weird Julie Andrews. The woman has supreme talent; this wasn't her part. Nor was the damn thing about anything, despite its strict adherence to the rules: rise-and-fall career, emotional turmoil behind the façade of success, old standards, famous people. *Star!*'s director Robert Wise had become a specialist in the $15,000,000 musical, and at least he did try to recreate something of old theatre styles (and Daniel Massey made an impeccable Noël Coward), though he blew the big number from *Lady in the Dark* out of sync with Kurt Weill's percussive manner. Wise, Logan, and their colleagues were in the process of murdering the film musical by their failure to make decent movies. Not all of these blockblusters went bust, but an investment of $15,000,000, tied up for a minimum of two years, is supposed to return two or three times that amount, not break even or yield pin money.

The blockbuster syndrome might have collapsed by the late 1960s if some of the big musicals hadn't done so well. *Oliver!* and *Funny Girl* in 1968 proved that there were more *Sounds of Music* to be heard after all, and *Funny Girl* promised fresh gala for the form in the successful launching of Barbra Streisand in cinema. Director William Wyler wrapped the newcomer in a prize package, shooting her from the air as she sped out to Omar Sharif's departing ocean liner by tugboat while singing "Don't Rain on My Parade", adding in a roller-skating number that Streisand hilariously ruins and a ballet takeoff (trimmed to seconds in release) to explain Brice as comic and closing, shockingly, with Streisand singing "My Man" in close-up, Brice as person. Francis Ford Coppola might have done better with *Finian's Rainbow* that year had he similarly found film in it. Coppola played it straight, so this classic satire on capitalist-consumerism and racism, daring on Broadway in 1947, seemed commonplace in 1968. The cast, at least, was fine: Astaire as Finian, Tommy Steele as his leprechaun nemesis, Petula Clark and Don Francks as the lovers, and Keenan Wynn as a southern senator. Now that Coppola has become Coppola, film buffs screen *Finian's Rainbow* to place it in the canon, and to be sure it is craftsman's work, "Old Devil Moon" especially—few love scenes in musicals have felt so hot. But the film just doesn't fizz, perhaps because much of the original's charm lay in Michael Kidd's choreography. The film has very little dancing, even from Astaire and Steele.

Kidd, however, pumped a great deal of dancing into *Hello, Dolly!* (1969), directed by Gene Kelly and the first of the huge disappointments that finally closed the era of blockbuster musicals. A meticulous reconstruction of little old New York's Fourteenth Street for a parade sequence was cited as the dead center of overproduction and Streisand, in the name role, was jeered. But the film was at least partly a victim of the escalating expectations that the blockbuster syndrome aroused: *West Side Story* is the greatest, *The Sound of Music* more tremendous, *Camelot* shatters the world; what's left? Kelly did mount a spectacle, true, and Streisand's Dolly is made of ill-assimilated parts of Jewish wiseguy, crypto-glamor girl, and Mae West. Still, other than in the parade the movie fills its space, and Streisand is so gifted that she's still superb. Isn't the character supposed to be chaotic, flamboyant, and a mixture of identities in the first place?

"She's too young for Dolly!" they screamed. In her big number she *returns* to the night life after an absence. When was she last there, at age three? Actually, Kelly is at pains, in a dandy opening, to establish that Streisand is not unknown in town. A still of New York in the '90s comes alive in a period strut as Streisand, face unseen, passes out business cards. The chorus takes up a "Call on Dolly" refrain, the camera pulls around her feathered hat to show us who, and the first song begins. She may be young, but a station porter and ticket man know her well—so she *has* been around. As her train steams up to Yonkers, the credits come on and tempo is set: a farce with time for detail. Sure enough, every song is a Number. When "Dancing"—on Broadway a quintet—becomes an epic with tennis players, bicycles, a park setting with character vignettes and Dolly's waltz with a sanitation man, one has to admit that the proportions are majestic. But everyone in it is good and it's a real musical, unlike so many of its fellows: the story needs the music, the performers know what singing and dancing is for, and everyone gets a chance to utilize his or her talent. The kids are delightful, Walter Matthau elegant, and Louis Armstrong unlooked-for benison. What's wrong with *Hello, Dolly!*? Nothing. The press was gunning for Streisand and big musicals, and the public for such events was limited. In the event, it didn't do that badly.

Paint Your Wagon and *Sweet Charity*, the same year, did very badly; the clink of the money they dropped rings yet. *Paint Your Wagon*, the first all-talking, no-singing, no-dancing musical, directed by Joshua Logan, has Lee Marvin, Clint Eastwood, Jean Seberg, little story, weak comedy, and lots of songs with no lead to sing them. Based on a Loewe–Lerner western with a grand score and three splendid Agnes de Mille ballets, *Paint Your Wagon* became a film embarrassed to be a musical. When Seberg, holding Marvin at bay with a pistol, likens him to her father, "born under a . . . wanderin' star," an allusion to one of the songs, she blushes at the musical-comedy silliness. No; you have to believe in it or not do it. Or: when Harve Presnell's baritone rips into "They Call the Wind Maria," a drugged audience stirs in confusion—what's *he* doing here? *Sweet Charity*, directed by Bob Fosse and starring Shirley MacLaine in Gwen Verdon's role, had no problem of identity—on the contrary, its musical portions are stunning. But the stage show was a slick piece of goods that borrowed the plot but none of the spirit of Fellini's *Nights of Cabiria*, and Fosse carried over the faults in the original. Who besides a New Yorker or a Woody Allen fan wants to see a musical about crummy New Yorkers using each other? *Sweet Charity*'s first bookings did such poor business that the film virtually went into release in revival houses.

This was not the end. Big Broadway musicals continued to roll out in the 1970s, though they were fewer and no longer hoped to equal *The Sound of Music*. Luckily, something new had come along in the meanwhile: rock film.

☆ 19 ☆
The Texture of Rock

$\mathbf{B}$ YE BYE BIRDIE (1963) was the first film to use rock effectively. The Broadway original parodied rock and roll to tease its sweet middle American setting, which erupts in comically innocuous confusion on the appearance of the Presleyesque Conrad Birdie (cf. Conway Twitty) as a PR stunt before he enters the army. Here was rock viewed from the outside with mild contempt, but it was a second start now that the real Presley was doing truly innocuous musicals antithetical to rock's spirit, and the continuation was provided by two Beatles movies, *A Hard Day's Night* (1964) and *Help!* (1965), directed by Richard Lester in the jumpy style that was to work so well in *A Funny Thing.*

A Hard Day's Night follows the Beatles at work and play with irrelevant song breaks and a zany script. (When the quartet amusingly subverts the efficiency of a television station, manager Victor Spinetti foresees his demotion with a sigh: "The news in Welsh for life.") Most writers prefer *A Hard Day's Night* to *Help!* for the absurd atmosphere of *cinema verité*—it's so disorganized that it must be real—but the better-knitted *Help!* boasts a storyline of inspired lunacy involving the sacred ring of the eastern deity Kaili, which Ringo wears. Cultists engaged in human sacrifice need the ring, fail to steal it, and then decide to sacrifice Ringo. The bulk of the action comprises the quartet's flight from the fanatics, with assistance from Scotland Yard, the army, and Spinetti again as a mad scientist ("M.I.T. was after me, you know—wanted me to rule the world for them"). The songs offer puns on the action ("I Need You" sung over shots of military preparations) or heedless of it, as the action is heedless of itself, but the title song effectively expands a wild closing melee. The nuttiness is all-pervasive and irresistible: a Yard detective does a poor imitation of Ringo (George: "Not a bit like Cagney"), a man-eating tiger named Roger responds docilely (in homage to *Bringing Up Baby*) to the finale of Beethoven's Ninth, the story never does end, and the closing credits unroll to Rossini.

Lester had found a successful format for rock, if one that could hardly become common property. An easy way out for others was the concert film—no story, no casting, just a visual record of a rock event, sometimes with a documentary frame of interview or news footage. In 1970, *Woodstock* and *Gimme Shelter* recorded two crucial happenings in the quickly gathered and dispersed rock nation, bigger as history than as music. *Woodstock* captures itself with tactless ease, but *Gimme Shelter*, Albert and David Maysles' film of the Rolling Stones' free show at Altamont, is meant to exculpate the Stones—Mick Jagger, especially—from any responsibility in the several deaths that occurred at the concert, one not only on camera but run through in slow motion and stop-action. Those who feared rock's Dionysian incitement found *Woodstock* palliative, *Gimme Shelter* disquieting. But then rock, unlike twenties jazz, swing, opera, Broadway, theme song, and Hollywood's other musical approaches, admits of interior contradictions that defy all attempts to manipulate it for genre. Rock is larger than story, more riotous than dance, and it carries its character wherever it goes. *What* character? *Woodstock* preached community and transcendence; *Gimme Shelter* might have been set in hell. When Presley was young, rock and roll was already complex in derivation but chartable: controllable. By the late 1960s rock had been so reconstructed as to be pluralistic, ungraspably independent. From group to group, person to person, the art varied instrumentation, performance practice, verbal structure, and world view. It varied from film to film as well. *200 Motels* (1971), composed by Frank Zappa, takes in electric rave-up, atonal symphony (played by London's Royal Philharmonic Orchestra), country put-on, chorale, piano blues, and song titles like "Magic Fingers" and "Dew on the Newts We Got," and parades a freak of incoherent hallucinations concerning the Fifth Dimension's concert tour. *Tommy* (1975), Ken Russell's realization of the Who's song cycle, comprehends post-sixties rock's elastic use of pastiche and the intimacy of *Lied* and *chanson* in a linear narrative about a pinball-playing messiah that touches on adultery, sadism, homosexual rape, and apocalyptic show-biz mysticism, all magnified into Russell's characteristic nightmare realism. *Lady Sings the Blues* (1972) deals in black song in a straight bio (of Billie Holliday). Three completely different movies: yet all are rock films.

So what's a rock musical? Any number of things—with the catch that most rock and roll, heavy metal, and acid, three of rock's most basic styles, do not express character or plot very well and thus resist dramatic motion. Rock is, somewhat, autotelic, intense but narrow, too complete in itself to adapt to the needs of a larger form that would have to contain it. Rock inevitably carries certain cultural associations in its very sound, whatever its lyrics say. In the heyday of the Hollywood musical, in the 1930s, 1940s, and early 1950s, we took for granted that musical characters were sexually monogamous, patriotic, and like "most people" in their perceptions, whereas singers of rock are wired into a subculture that is sexually promiscuous, anarchic, and countercultural. "Sex, drugs, rock and roll!" runs a cheer heard in *The Rose*. True, the fifties sound epitomized by Buddy Holly is sweet and quaint by comparison to new wave groups, and much of rock fits within a folkie blues frame that can encompass almost any cultural outlook. Rock is tricky: because it's so rich. It isn't even definable anymore, so without trying to define it let's consider the four forms that most rock film observes. First there's the story musical, with the songs worked into the action; in *Tommy*, they attempt to carry it entirely. A second type separates story and score, letting the songs comment on the action from outside. *American Graffiti* (1973) is the most famous example, but notice that it merely spliced together old recordings and tracked them over the action, much as a car radio might underscore a conversation; this is hardly a musical. More open use of music is heard in the other two types of rock film, the concert and the bio.

Nineteen seventy-eight is a good year to compare these four forms; it was a big year for rock musicals. The notable concert film, *The Last Waltz*, is the biggest disappointment, though the concert itself proved to be one of the most glorious occasions in American popular music. The Band celebrated its retirement at San Francisco's Winterland with a vaudeville of the great in every rock class from blues to cabaret narrative, culminating in a reunion with Bob Dylan, for whom the Band formerly played backup. Dylan and the Band are steeped in legend together, especially for the "Basement tapes," so popular as a bootleg item that they came out on a commercial label as an afterthought, and the Winterland concert also offered such outstanding numbers as Dr. John's "Saturday Night (If I don't do it, somebody else will)," Joni Mitchell's "Coyote," and the whole gang (Eric Clapton, Muddy Waters, Ronnie Hawkins) together again for the first time on Dylan's "I Shall Be Released." Instead of filming the event whole and letting the music speak for itself—it tells volumes about what rock is—Martin Scorsese captured it clumsily in segments interrupted by superficial interviews with the Band and doesn't even include the single most electrifying moment, Dylan's entrance.

The commentary approach worked well for *FM*, as this picture of an embattled radio station trying to retain its selfhood in a commerce whose name is conformity ran loose enough to permit just about any rock selection the audience might care to hear. Radio's subject matter *is* rock, so let it roll, any way at all; the participation of Linda Ronstadt alone gives the silly story presence. But perhaps *FM*'s main purpose was to provide a two-record soundtrack album, which through *Saturday Night Fever* the year before had become the record industry's hotcake.

Three story musicals, *Grease*, *The Wiz*, and *Sgt. Pepper's Lonely Hearts Club Band*, flooded stores with two-disc albums in 1978, but only *Grease* repeated *Saturday Night Fever*'s success—a joke had it that *Sgt. Pepper*, with its cover of bas-relief cardboard, was shipped platinum and returned double-platinum. If there's a remainder bin for cinema, *Sgt. Pepper* should fill it. An opera made of Beatles songs (mainly from *Sgt. Pepper* and *Abbey Road*) placed end to end, the film told how Peter Frampton and the Bee Gees, from Heartland, U.S.A., conquer corporate villainy and bring music *back to the people!* A number of actors played parts suggested by the songs—George Burns as ("Being for the Benefit of") Mr. Kite, Dianne Steinberg as Lucy ("in the Sky with Diamonds"), Steve Martin as Maxwell (of the silver hammer)—and a host of the famous turned up, unbilled, in the finale. A big deal and a terrible film, especially in the stars' nowhere performance of the songs. The arrangements are careful copies of the originals (produced by George Martin, the Beatles' producer), but the closeness exposes the stylistic gap. In "With a Little Help From My Friends," Frampton is effete where Ringo was charmingly neutral; Sandy Farina, on hand for what romance comic books call "kiss panels," makes "Here Comes the Sun" sound like a Vegas lounge act; and Aerosmith (playing villains) in "Come Together" completely miss the original's slinky grotesque. Most objectionable of all was the film's false naiveté, its picture of rock as a weapon against The Corporation. The pop music world is the big oil of American art, after all; how far can you characterize as innocence the sound of a business run by billion-dollar grubbers?

The Wiz, drawn from Charlie Smalls and William F. Brown's black version of Baum's book, did better business than *Sgt. Pepper*, but its terrific expense did not pay off. Word of mouth reported that the film was failing because Diana Ross was too old to play Dorothy (whose age was upped to twenty-four), the choreography was confusingly filmed, and the whole thing, like *Hello, Dolly!*, was too big. All wrong. Ross is fine, if insistently doelike, the dancing is fine, a raw Motown party, and the story calls for spectacle in the first place. What killed *The Wiz* was too many songs and Sidney Lumet's sluggish pacing. The cast, particularly Nipsey Russell as the tin man, works hard and knows what to do, but in the grindingly slow motion one comes to resent everyone's sense of detail and wishes they'd stop acting and make the scene. It could have been a nifty film, for, while respecting the stage show's free use of blackness as style for fantasy, it went a step further and turned Oz into a dream vision of New York City. Tony Walton's design makes the Munchkins' playground graffiti come to life; fits the scarecrow's cornfield between burned-out tenements; turns the poppy field into a drug-and-sex tenderloin; places the Emerald City in midtown, obsessed with fashion; and Dorothy can't get a cab. The plot perspective is upended: the original book, the Garland film, and *The Wiz* on Broadway featured a little girl who wants to get home, but the new film gives us an older Dorothy who needs to get out in the world. All the versions advise on the wisdom of achieving self-confidence, proving that rock, for all its contrary ideology, can work for the old-line musical—most beautifully at the end when Lena Horne as Glinda breaks into a gospel rocker and the joint finally starts jumping.

The hugely successful *Grease* was also a Broadway adaptation, this from Jim Jacobs and Warren Casey's spoof of fifties high-school mores. In contrast to *Sgt. Pepper*'s Beatles diversity and *The Wiz*'s rhythm and blues, *Grease* hearkens back to primitive rock and roll, some numbers deliberately recalling certain oldies. "Mooning" and "Beauty School Drop-Out" revive the triplet bass of the stroll, "Magic Changes" reconstructs the elementary chord patterns of one's first guitar lessons, "Born to Hand-Jive" resurrects rock's version of the dance sensation, and so on. The show was still running when the film came out, but there could be no sense of the work's competing with itself, because the film threw away the spoof and turned romantic. The show *Grease* opened with a performance of Rydell High's Alma Mater, immediately reprised by the kids with their own nasty lyrics; the film opens with a shot of John Travolta and Olivia Newton-John kissing on a wave-smoothed beach. Where was this? California, of course—the show took place in something like Detroit. The best number, "There Are Worse Things I Could Do," was sung in the show by Adrienne Barbeau as a proud smash at the nice-nice heroine. In the film, Stockard Channing played it as a sentimentalized torch song directed, from a distance, at her boyfriend Jeff Conaway. *When* was this?—early middle Alice Faye, without Faye's morality of ambition. The film had incredible impact; kids returned to it so often they performed Travolta's hand motions in "Summer Nights" right along with the number on screen. But did they buy all this heartfelt love stuff? At least the romanticism was easier to take than the comedy, largely assigned to oldtimers who couldn't ruin the illusion of growing up taut and tanned near the surf. Frankie Avalon and Edd Byrnes returned from the 1960s (note wrong decade) to do what they did; but Sid Caesar, Eve Arden, and Dody Goodman disgraced their reputations and, as the local hash waitress, the once formidable Joan Blondell acted and sounded like hamburger helper. Only one thing the movie *Grease* had of value: a new theme song that set mood and viewpoint. Written by Barry Gibb and sung by Frankie Valli over cartoon credits, "Grease" the song revived the old "love thyself" message—"We start believing now that we can be who we are"—while the film was too busy making money to contain any message at all.

Of these rock films of 1978, only the bio, *The Buddy Holly Story*, came through well, and that mainly because the star, Gary Busey, carefully revived classic Holly in precise recreation of the sound. (Busey moves around more than Holly did and makes the act outrightly sensual, but it's hard to go back to the straight days after all we've seen.) The storyline takes in the usual simplifications and distortions: Holly's minister denounces his music in church, his parents tell him to give it up, his band the Crickets is reduced by one, Holly plays on tour with a string orchestra; all false. But it's thrilling to hear "That'll Be the Day," "Peggy Sue," and "True Love Ways" virtually as they were first heard.

The question of where rock fits into film was not yet answered. Has it replaced other styles as the correct sound for the American musical? Is it suffering the general incompetence that afflicts the musical today? Or is it wrong for the American musical? Does it carry connotations that militate against the form of the threesome, the go-getters, the romancers, the egalitarian conquerors? What if rock not only connotes but actively deals in the nonideological revolution of the violent energy level that never subsides? Sex, drugs, rock and roll: how do you fit a

☆ *A TOUCH OF ROCK: Above,* Frankie and Johnny *(note sloppy decor), vastly lacking in beat; below,* Jesus Christ Superstar—*note careful blend of ancient and modern in decor.*

story to that? An intriguing possibility was unveiled in a British release of 1979, *Quadrophenia*, in the commentary form—rock soundtrack enhancing an otherwise nonmusical narrative. The track is based
on the Who's 1973 album, like their *Tommy* a cycle that didn't pan
out except musically. Something seemed to be happening *between* the
songs, and the film, directed by Franc Rodam to find the compulsion
and/or exuberance in British teenage riots of the 1960s, filled in without drawing anything away from the music. On the contrary, the
songs feed the film. The Who do not appear, except momentarily on a
television screen. Rather, Rodam follows the fortunes of a young proletarian Mod in his home, club, and love lives, battles with the Rock-
ers, and climactic suicide. What happens to Jimmy? Rodam asks;
what happens to rock? ask the Who. If it can find itself a niche in films
as absorbing as this one, rock needn't worry.

On the other hand, how many films can be made about joyful bed-
lam? How silly and unworldly the earlier musicals were compared to
these—but what ideals they proposed. Heavy rock of the Who's sort is
bold realism and terrific art but in the end it is negative art and cannot
sustain a musical, which is not a realistic form. Rock tragedy—now
you're talking. But how many tragedies do people want to see? They
can see *Grease*, you say? *Grease* isn't a tragedy? Right. But *Grease* isn't
rock, either. It's a doo-wop sitcom with kiss panels.

☆ *20* ☆
Interesting Times

ONCE, the Hollywood studios were where films were planned, written, shot, and edited, and studio theatres played everything made. By 1970, the studios were mainly financiers and distributors and had no "where." It's all freelance now, but while the philistine totalitarianism of the money bosses survives, the craftsmanship is gone. The lack of industry organization does at least permit unusual subject matter—*The Little Prince* (1974), say, based on a dear little French fantasy about an extraterrestrial child's metaphysical adventures. But the lack of organization has dispersed the experts who knew how musicals were made, and in such a world even Stanley Donen, trained at MGM in the gala years, could not bring *The Little Prince* off.

Amid the confusion, straight adaptations of Broadway successes promised to be no-fail properties. *Fiddler on the Roof* (1971) and *1776* (1972), opened up but not changed, worked well, the latter with most of its Broadway cast. *Man of la Mancha* (1972), on the other hand, suffered lack of voice in its cast—Peter O'Toole, Sophia Loren, and James Coco—and *Mame* (1974) gave the decade's choice oomph role to Lucille Ball, suddenly turned grande dame, painfully dry in the songs, and not even clearly seen through a mass of Ponce de Leon filters.

Typical of the post-studio confusion was the film of Stephen Sondheim's *A Little Night Music*, drawn from Ingmar Bergman's *Smiles of a Summer Night* and written to coordinate with a production concept too stageworthy to transfer to the screen. Still, director Harold Prince tried a transfer, opening in an antique theatre with the stage dressed as the Broadway one had been, then pulling back into a real world outside. Sondheim replaced the expressly theatrical "The Glamorous Life" with a new song to cover the same ground in cinematic procedure, the elegant but antinaturalistic Brahmsian quintet chorus was dropped, and Elizabeth Taylor and Diana Rigg joined some of the stage leads to promote the project with celebrity glister. Yet the completed movie had trouble finding a distributor and was released like a convict, in sullen spot appearances in a few cities.

If the 1970s had been the 1930s, Barbra Streisand would have made twenty musicals and every one would have been worth seeing. But filmmaking is slow now and musicals are risky; Streisand made three, worth seeing mainly for her. *On a Clear Day You Can See Forever* (1970), from the Lane–Lerner show, cast Streisand as a modern girl who relives a former life in Regency England under hypnosis, and let director Vincente Minnelli exploit his eye for decor in the preincarnation scenes, but a sleepwalking Yves Montand so taxed the action that the picture was slashed into chaos, losing some of Minnelli's best work and leaving—because he shares the romance with Streisand—mainly Montand. Disaster.

Funny Lady (1973), *Funny Girl*'s sequel, also had problems. Supporting characters fall in and out of the scene precipitously, "Let's Hear It for Me" looks and sounds like a copy of "Don't Rain on My Parade" with a plane instead of a boat, and Streisand's last scenes, played in a grotesque double-bun hairdo, appear to promise a third installment, *Funny Crone*. The film won a following if only because Streisand is the greatest thing to happen to the musical in some time; and James Caan's easy style as Billy Rose didn't hurt.

Both *On a Clear Day* and *Funny Lady* drew on the Broadway sound, even in *Funny Lady*'s new songs (by John Kander and Fred Ebb), but *A Star is Born* (1976) is contemporary. The two lead roles now depict rising and falling rock singers. Like Garland in her version, Streisand had to carry the score singlehanded, for Kris Kristofferson's noteless voice and lazy diction are as unpleasant as the famous Scavullo photograph of the two clutched in nude embrace that served as the film's logo and aptly sums up its *vanitas vanitatum* air. "A Bore Is Starred" crowed the *Village Voice*. No way; Streisand is top. But the film is a putrid mess and a vanity production from first to last. The one thing that makes it go is the score. These are good songs, mostly by Paul Williams, Kenny Ascher, and Rupert Holmes (Streisand collaborated on two of them), but the kind that throw around a lot of cynical verbal ideas without finishing a thought, or the kind that float on love lines. They don't fit the story as well as Garland's did hers, but then there's little story to fit here and the best of them, "Queen Bee," "Woman in the Moon," and "I Believe in Love," are Streisand vehicles to the nth, perhaps defining the actress's personal aggressiveness more than the character's.

This might alternatively have been the decade of Julie Andrews musicals, but *Darling Lili* (1970), in which she played a spy for the Germans in World War I opposite American air ace Rock Hudson, finished her off. It might have been a Liza Minnelli decade, except like Streisand and Andrews she made more nonmusicals than musicals, and has also fallen victim to the ignorance of contemporary moviemakers, most notably in *New York, New York* (1977), Martin Scorsese's big-band romance with Robert de Niro as a saxophonist (Georgie Auld dubbed his axe) and the look of the 1940s constantly outfitted in attitudes of the 1970s. Look, if you want to do an oldie, do it; what is this "commentative museum" approach supposed to express other than contempt for the old forms?: in which case, why revive them? Even worse than *New York, New York* was Peter Bogdanovich's *At Long Last Love* (1975), an assault on screwball comedy using a load of Cole Porter songs. Bogdanovich doesn't seem to know anything about Porter's style, musicals in general, or screwball comedy, and a good supporting cast (Eileen Brennan, Madeline Kahn, John Hillerman, and Mildred Natwick) look like amateurs and a poor star (Cybill Shepherd) gives the most atrocious performance in musical history. She's supposed to charm; why is she angry and pushy? Only Burt Reynolds has any idea about screwball comedy and musical delivery—and he's the one who should be most at sea.

This was, then, the decade in which people who didn't belong kept turning up in musicals and people who did belong were betrayed by their material and staff. An antique approach pervades—old songs in *Funny Lady*, *Darling Lili*, *At Long Last Love*, and *New York, New York*; old genre in Stanley Donen's *Movie Movie* (1978), consisting of a boxing movie, a trailer ("War at its best!"), and a backstager, all neatly spoofed (though one notes that the would-be Berkeleyesque finale of *Baxter's Beauties* is cheap and dull). Charles Jarrott's *Lost Horizon* (1973), a remake of Frank Capra's spectacle, subverted the old with the new in undercutting the wonder of Shangri-la with the highly seventies sound of Bert Bacharach and Hal David. The film is misconceived from its first moments, when a view of ice-capped mountains under the credits suffers Bacharach's suburban jive ("There's a lost horizon . . .") instead of something suggestive of fantasy. Worse yet, our first sight of Shangri-la—an oasis of peace and long-lasting youth in the middle of the Himalayas—is filmed like a motorcade's arrival at a Holiday Inn. Except the Holiday Inn's pool would be bigger. Bad enough that Hollywood's original work was weak; could it not even keep its past whole?

Of all the failed revivals, a British effort most nearly made it, Alan Parker's *Bugsy Malone* (1976), a revival of the Warners Prohibition-era gangster romance with a period-flavored score by Paul Williams. Parker's script lacks the snappy attack of the Warners writers, but his camera tells a story well and the production has the right look. But Parker cast all the parts with kids, and their limp, in some cases abysmally invertebrate performances (except those of Jodie Foster, Martin Lev, and "Humpty" Albin Jenkins) and the inevitable dubbing in the numbers destroy the film. Moreover, rather than bloody the children in their constant shoot-outs, Parker hits them with whipped cream (though they do die, until an apocalyptic finale sprays everyone with candy death and all sing and dance pointlessly). Still, there are some fine things here. The small band heard on the track is dynamite. The club numbers, "Fat Sam's Grand Slam" and "My Name Is Tallulah," are filmed well, and "Tomorrow" ("a resting place for bums, a trap set in the slums"), a black's commentary on the status quo, is one of the best four minutes of song and dance produced in the 1970s. A scene of Broadway auditions, paced by a constant heartless "Next," is funny, as are the ancient acts—but why, when a singer attempts "Brother, Can You Spare a Dime?", not written till 1932, does someone sneer, "That old chestnut"? A surer grasp of pop history, and the decade's most successful samples of retrenching, were found in two MGM collections of old footage, *That's Entertainment!* and *That's Entertainment! II*, in 1974 and 1976.

Interesting attempts to stay young enlivened several Broadway adaptations which reinvented the originals without ruining them. David Green's *Godspell* (1973) spilled its Gospel parables all over Manhattan: kids bathe in Bethesda Fountain and throw away worldly things to become hippie clowns who tour the town while the camera catches them on a rooftop pool, the Bulova Accutron sign, Lincoln Center, or the top of the World Trade towers, then under construction. The stage *Godspell* was static and episodic, the film *Godspell* busy and episodic; that still leaves one less than overwhelmed. Norman Jewison's *Jesus Christ Superstar* (1973) similarly moved a theatrical event outside, in this case to the Holy Land, relating the ancient myth to modern jive by juxtaposing early Christian and contemporary design.

Ken Russell's *The Boy Friend* (1971) did more for its source, and to it. Sandy Wilson's thin twenties charmer remains, but now we see it on two extra levels, from below in the backstage lives of a provincial British troupe playing it to a sparse matinée public, and from above in the dreams of a Berkeley-minded director, called Max de Thrill, who reviews the stage numbers as he would film them. Many felt that Russell had trashed Wilson and noted a lack of regard for his characters, but one must admit that the movie is vastly entertaining and its Berkeley spoofs stylish. Are they vicious? Russell portrays the chorus girls as sly and talentless, the boys as big, dirty dwarfs, and everyone as a ham directing his part at de Thrill in hopes of being discovered. One person retains innocence in all this—Twiggy, the fashion model who came out of retirement at something like twenty-one to play the heroine, a backstage gopher thrust into the star's part after the usual accident. Twiggy is the first genuine Ruby Keeler we have had since Keeler, not an imposing talent but a champ in charm, and when Glenda Jackson as the injured star clumps backstage on her crutches for confrontation as Bebe Daniels had done in *42nd Street*, we realize that Russell has moved the Warners backstager forward in time to prove that the old community is broken. It's everyone for himself now.

No wonder the old forms no longer work: moviemakers don't believe in their morale anymore. The heroine of Bob Fosse's *Cabaret* (1972) gets by living entirely in lies. *Cabaret* derives, like *Godspell, Jesus Christ Superstar*, and *The Boy Friend*, from the stage, but more radically, with fewer songs and more character than the original. Its grungily splashy Kit Kat Club contrasting with a plain, almost sepia-toned Berlin rooming house; its acidly commentative numbers cutting vertically into the narrative; its palpable sense of history running wild caught in an elated number, an ironic number, an alienated number, all made it a sensation, and it stands as one of the best musicals of the era. Yet it is not exactly a musical.

On stage, directed by Ronald Field, *Cabaret* was two musicals intertwined, one a tale of foreigners and natives in pre-Nazi Berlin and the other a series of cabaret turns explicating the tale. Fosse realigned the story with Christopher Isherwood's original telling and stripped it of music, limiting all the numbers to the onstage scenes and a Nazi youth's beer-garden performance of "Tomorrow Belongs to Me," which turns into a spontaneous Nazi rally in one of Fosse's best ideas. No question that his camera narrates and describes insightfully, but because only one of the story characters (Liza Minnelli) works in the cabaret, we don't get to know them through their songs—which is what, at base, a musical does best. Minnelli we know, from her frenzy in "Mein Herr," materialism in "The Money Song," momentary honesty in "Maybe This Time," and final passive accommodation of evil in the tumultuous title song. But her friend, writer Michael York, their mutual lover Helmut Griem, York's pupil Marisa Berenson, and the other people have no numbers, in what might be called the Randolph Scott effect: they hear the music but have none themselves. This makes them a little remote, almost imperceptibly at first but increasingly on the repeated viewings that classics like *Cabaret* tend to get.

In all, this was a troubled time, one of talent and creativity but of a depleted or misunderstood form. If 1929–1933 was the experimental era, the rest of the 1930s the time in which genre was defined, the 1940s and 1950s an age of story musicals, and the 1960s one of big Broadway, what were the 1970s? There was a little of everything; it's hard to generalize. Perhaps the 1970s are best thought of as the decade which loved *The Rocky Horror Picture Show* (1975) and *The Slipper and the Rose* (1976), the two most unlike musicals ever made. *Rocky* derives from a British show, a spoof of monster movies painted with kinky isms and assorted punk boogie. *Slipper* is Cinderella, with fairy godmother, wicked stepmother, and the whole Perrault peruke. Both films are story musicals, *Rocky*'s score tending to rock and the Sherman brothers' *Slipper* songs upholding the simplistic sweetness of tradition. But where *Slipper* was lavish family fare, the low-budget ($1,000,000) *Rocky* plays midnight shows to costumed kids who smoke dope, throw things at the screen, call out set responses to lines, and, at the more hip centers, stage their own *Rocky Horror* in the aisles synchronously with the action on screen. In *Slipper*, a lovely waltz theme characterizes the ball, dancers pair off, the audience coos in pleasure, and Cinderella and the Prince later sing lyrics to the theme ("He Danced With Me/She Danced With Me"), wistful and winning. As *Rocky* begins, Barry Bostwick and Susan Sarandon get a flat while driving through a storm in a forest. Bostwick must go for help. "Try the castle!" the kids scream, squirting each other with water pistols.*

Yet both films teach the advantages of personal liberation; one could argue that most art does, except tragedy. Cinderella has to get out from under her stepmother's rule; Bostwick and Sarandon discov-

---

*The ritual responses are witless, but one trembles to think what these kids might be doing if they didn't have their weekly *Rocky* habit to busy them. Outsiders can view the proceedings without risk in a segment of *Fame*.

er sexual openness. Perhaps *Rocky*, written by Richard O'Brien, really teaches nothing but the joy of spoof. It's very seventies: nihilist, exhibitionistic, and contemptuous of outsiders. When it is finished, nothing is left; even the straitlaced narrator is drawn into the proceedings during a dance number called "The Time Warp," which has the gentleman first holding up a ludicrously precise footmap of the steps and then, repeating the words, jumping around on a table with his hands on his hips. *The Slipper and the Rose* ends with Cinderella in the Prince's arms, but *The Rocky Horror Picture Show*, in a way, doesn't finish, though the story is somewhat wrapped away in a few pointless murders and the return of some characters to their planet. One could go on endlessly comparing the two, but it is in casting that they seem most apart. *Slipper* draws on front-line talent, with Gemma Craven a wonderfully taut heroine, Richard Chamberlain possibly the only Hamlet who played the Prince in a Cinderella musical, and Edith Evans and Michael Hordern as the royal ancients. It's creamy and condign. *Rocky*, on the other hand, puts forth unknowns and director Jim Sharman shows them at their worst; one presumes he's supposed to, given the campy nature of the material. Tim Curry in the central role of the transsexualizing Dr. Frank N. Furter, who makes the Rocky monster, manages to suggest that he's crossed five or six rather than a mere two genders, Meat Loaf in a small part (he gets eaten) is if possible more unappetizing than usual, and author O'Brien as Curry's henchthing is a pictorial history of sinister. It's the pits, all of it, and glad to be.

Slipper was extra traditional, *Rocky* extra novel, and maybe the 1970s was the era that didn't know what it wanted. As many big Broadway musicals flopped as succeeded, neither contemporary nor traditional music could necessarily save a film, old formulas both bubbled and fizzled, and even the biggest stars could suffer enormous popular failures. What were the 1970s, then? Who can say? The success of *The Muppet Movie* (1979) suggests incoming innocence, but don't those little Muppet fans grow into *Rocky* freaks? Or will the Muppets' whimsy bless them with a thirst for faerie that can only be slaked by *The Slipper and the Rose*?

☆ 21 ☆
Rest in Peace

NO MATTER HOW the musical's confused present develops, it is undebatable that the form has been running down since the 1950s. We know the reasons—inflation has made the middle-budget musical unworkable; rock doesn't work well for most stories; the current generation of moviemakers doesn't know how to make a musical; and the intense naturalism of contemporary American film makes anything but a backstager unthinkably quaint.

Yet they keep coming, often in the old genres. Nineteen seventy-nine and 1980 saw at least one entry in most of the established categories of musical. There was a bio, for instance, *Coal Miner's Daughter*, with Sissy Spacek ably recreating Loretta Lynn's singing style to affirm the nation's growing interest in country music. There was a comedy musical, *The Blues Brothers*, about the reformation of a band but directed by John Landis as a demolition derby with allusions to music-making. The stars, John Belushi and Dan Aykroyd, had exhausted their bop spoof on television's *Saturday Night Live*; unlike the Marx Brothers, they haven't worked up characters tasty enough to fill a screen—even Landis' crashing cars lose the weight of shock and surprise after a while. Worse yet, Belushi and Aykroyd are totally upstaged by the musical help, especially Aretha Franklin, who tears the screen apart in "Think" as the proprietor of a soul-food café. The comedy musical always had more comic action than comic (or other) music, but *The Blues Brothers* isn't rich in comedy.

Many had hoped that Bob Fosse would second *Cabaret* with something special, and in *All That Jazz* he reinstated the dance musical. Unlike those of Astaire, Powell, and Kelly, this one avoided story songs, concentrating on dance and at that giving more to ensembles than to principals. Astaire, Powell, and Kelly distilled themselves in dance; Fosse distills show biz. So *All That Jazz* is special, a piece about the performing industries and the people who inhabit and exploit them, set as a narrative about the last days of . . . well, Bob Fosse. The autobiographical correspondence is uncanny. Fosse's stage shows, films, collaborators, acquaintances, and enemies are not merely depicted; some of them play themselves. We see Fosse's tintype, Joe Gideon (Roy Scheider), planning and rehearsing a musical called *N.Y./L.A.* (i.e., *Chicago*) that stars Scheider's ex-wife Leland Palmer (i.e., Fosse's ex-wife Gwen Verdon), using a model of *Chicago*'s set, referring to a conductor named Stan (played by *Chicago*'s conductor Stanley Lebowsky), reading the script with, among others, Mary McCarty (who was in *Chicago*), suffering heart failure (as Fosse did during *Chicago*'s rehearsals), possibly being replaced by somebody called Lucas Sergeant (as Fosse nearly was by Gower Champion), who is seen planning lighting design on a model of the set for *I Do, I Do* (which Champion directed); and so on, from the film's start to finish.

For some reason, a great many people objected to this, though Fellini is praised for his autobiographical renderings. Fosse's use of Giuseppe Rotunno, Fellini's cinematographer, inspired sympathetic commentary that *All That Jazz* is Fosse's *8½*, his attempt to order in art what has happened to him in life. It is certainly one of the most provocative and imaginative musicals ever made and, to the surprise of the Hollywood smart money, became a hit. It could not have been produced in the age of the studios, for it has no genre, no star Something, no safe place (the protagonist doesn't even dance)—not with its frank sexuality, open-heart surgery, and surges of contempt and horror for the hypocrisy of show biz. In a kind of television eulogy before the fact, Ben Vereen calls Scheider "the *numero uno* game player." *The Girl Most Likely*, "Who's Got the Pain?", *Sweet Charity*, *Cabaret*, *Lenny*, the snake number in *The Little Prince*, *Chicago*: all a game. That's why Fosse is the best, he seems to say: he was the most insincere, more so than raving television hosts, idiot television critics who review themselves, producers who bury their star director at the crucial point, or a fellow director too eager to inherit Fosse's project and who, in a startling Felliniesque pre-death wake, chews out a resentful farewell. Yet it must be worth the game, for Fosse captures the exuberance of the musical no less than Astaire, Powell, and Kelly did. Or, rather, he drags the camera around to show what lies behind "The Continental," "Swingin' the Jinx Away," and "Broadway Rhythm," from the opening cattle-call auditions to a special birthday tribute in top hats by Scheider's girlfriend (Ann Reinking) and daughter (Erzsebet Foldi) in his living room. The death, though heralded by a luscious angel and a last grand dance number, is flat fact; but the life has been full. Most viewers felt lifted.

The backstager was still with us in Alan Parker's *Fame*, observing the new *Chorus Line* vogue for digging into the offstage lives of performers with more intense revelation than *42nd Street* or *Moonlight and Pretzels* did. Of course, nowadays the characters have more to reveal: *Fame* takes in child molestation, porno film, gay shame, abortion (which earlier backstagers couldn't show), and even failure (which earlier musicals didn't believe in). The failure belongs to a minor character, an actor who departs high school in the flush of Hollywood promises and turns up years later waiting table in a hamburger joint. *Fame*'s central figures may suffer, but we're sure they'll make it, and perhaps *Fame* might better have been called *Talent*, since we see the drive of the gifted more than the urgency of coming celebrity. (The title song, however, emphasizes making it—"Baby, remember my name.")

Christopher Gore originally named his script *Hot Lunch*, which is way off. It tells mainly of eight kids at New York's High School of Performing Arts, from auditions to graduation, and tells its story well. A hostilely illiterate black dancer (Gene Anthony Ray), a lively black actress-singer (Irene Cara), a Puerto Rican comic (Barry Miller), a shy actress (Maureen Teefy), a shy actor (Paul McCrane), a blue-book dancer (Antonia Franceschi), a lazy dancer (Laura Dean), and a musician (Lee Curreri) who seems the only one without a major problem engage us deeply because Parker makes their lives as interesting as anything they might do on a stage—and can they do! The hot lunch refers to a number improvised in the cafeteria out of musicians' idle riffs and dancers' exercises; audience and cast at once, the whole crowd gradually joins in, and while Parker centers on Curreri at the piano and Cara next to him singing the lyrics, the camera roves, pulling all the practice, relaxation, and fulfillment of performance into the scene to show us not the desperation but the fun of using one's talent. It's not an obsession, it's what you always do. So why call it *Fame*?

The narrative is inevitably episodic and its pieces don't always tally. The comic's story overpowers the others, for Parker seems to think it's the most interesting; so do we. Franceschi and Dean are made too minor; we want more. And there are sensational or formalistic touches that humiliate the otherwise brilliant naturalism, as when an obvious creep lures Cara into a "screen test" that is immediately revealed to be a porn loop. She sobs, but goes along with it—ridiculous; no one's that dumb. Ray's vulnerability under the hostility is indicated but neither defined nor developed. And Curreri's cab-driver father parks outside the school to play an amplified tape of his son's music, causing a traffic jam so the kids can dance around and on top of the cars. This is an unreal excuse for a number; obviously, in going in for realism Parker can't make a story musical (as he did in *Bugsy Malone*) and thus has to reach a little for his numbers. But we don't buy it. Far more successful is the finale, graduation ceremonies set to Walt Whitman's "I Sing the Body Electric" and involving the whole class—dancers, singers, chorus, and orchestra. Thrilling in itself, the scene complements the cafeteria number narratively: "Hot Lunch Jam" is raw and spontaneous (the amateurs) while the graduation is polished (the ready professionals). When the movie cuts out suddenly at the commencement's climax, one senses the audience's unwillingness to leave. They want the rest, want to learn, now, about the fame. The real High School of Performing Arts thought the script too raunchy to approve and denied Parker permission to film there (the unoccupied Haaren High on Tenth Avenue stood in; some of Performing Arts' teachers appear as themselves, very effectively), but it would be hard to conceive of better PR for the school than this, or a film with more claim on a sequel. What *does* happen next?

Broadway adaptations were as uncommon as story musicals these days; Milos Forman combined both in *Hair*. Unlike recent big Broadway films, *Hair* avoided the box-office but nonmusical stars and the slavish reproduction, using only the stage show's score and spirit. It seemed odd to film one of the keynote works of the 1960s for 1979, but Forman had wanted to do *Hair* since its premiere in 1967 and the project had been on and off for years. At one point Forman visited Gerome Ragni and James Rado, the show's librettists and stars, to discuss it, but the two called in a tarot reader and he advised against it.

The show *Hair* is about as stupid as that story suggests it might be; what carried it was Galt MacDermot's inventive music and Tom O'Horgan's staging. Forman had Michael Weller (author of another prototypal event in the sixties *Zeitgeist, Moonchildren*) write a script to contain the score, handed the dancing over to Twyla Tharp, cast John Savage, Treat Williams, Annie Golden, Don Dacus, Dorsey Wright, Beverly D'Angelo, and Cheryl Barnes for character rather than celebrity, and filmed a splendid picaresque of coming into and then fleeing the 1960s. Forman's Central Park hums with the high color of the freewilling outcast, his middle-class party is sedate, his church a vision of redemptive beauty, his army post a pandemonium of uptight. Savage is the protagonist, heading from middle America to service in Vietnam, but on the way he passes through the hippie kingdom and his life is changed. He never even makes it to Vietnam, for Williams, the hippie ringleader and Savage's social and cultural opposite, takes Savage's place in the barracks while Savage enjoys a final rendezvous with D'Angelo; Williams is dragged off to war in Savage's place, and dies in combat. End of the 1960s.

Rather than invent another Oz, Forman combines his visual attack with MacDermot's music to present a veristic magic, and the first sight of the Park, with the movie theatre virtually flying in a circle around the singer introducing "(the age of) Aquarius," counts as one of the most intoxicating shots in film. Unfortunately, the expensive production was not popular: most adult moviegoers had no intention of celebrating a time they disliked and could not forgive. Those who let bygones be were put off by Forman's sharp re-creation of the destructiveness and selfishness of the time, not to mention the unapologetic sexual promiscuity. Treat Williams' Berger was too familiar a figure, with his self-righteous freeloading and trashing and stealing. Paradoxically, amid all the emotional violence, and in a time of war in which he is supposedly to take part, Savage finds a safe place: it is Berger who dies.

In 1979–1980, then, the genres proved resilient, still functioning, if sparsely. There was no original story musical and no opera musical, and this in itself points up the two most crucial problems in the form today: the music that called for extraordinary personal communication—that elated a narrative to its utmost and burst the limitations of naturalism and fantasy alike—is the least important element in the contemporary musical. The earthiness that kept *The Wizard of Oz* close to home and the romance that floated Astaire and Rogers over the Bakelite are lost arts in American pop music. Rock's special gift is to merge the earthy and the romantic, but this worked well only for surreal farce like that in *Help!*. True, *Hair* floated—but when *The Wiz* needed to, it couldn't. Rock is heavy.

Yet it was a rock film that afforded a most astonishing musical experience, Mark Rydell's *The Rose* (1979). Written by Bill Kerby and Bo Goldman with a score picked up from here and there, the film tells of the last few days of a singer not unlike Janis Joplin. It's not a bio, but some of Joplin is there in the heroine's love for/fear of her southern hometown, voice-shredding vocal style, pronounced sexuality and alcoholism, and death by drug overdose. Mary Rose Foster suffers a messy celebrity, bullied by her manager (Alan Bates), sleepwalking or rampaging through an exhausting, endless schedule, and unable to work things out with the nice, strong, simple man (Frederic Forrest) who might be able to make her happy, burning out of control onstage as in life. Yet the mania that destroys her is what makes her so vital in concert. We begin to feel that you can't have one without the other, or you'd have to be Bing Crosby or Alice Faye, and the kind of music they sang so well is no longer our kind. Rock demands more of a performer: it is the opera of pop, which is why we need Jeanette MacDonald and Deanna Durbin even less than we do a Crosby or Faye today. Throughout the story we see Rose making impossible mistakes, and she doesn't seem to lack perspective so much as flourish, like a trapeze daredevil, without it. She must live on the edge or she couldn't take her music so deep and digging.

The Rose was a huge hit, but critics complained that Rydell and the authors had left holes in the tale, and that Bette Midler, in her film debut, was simply swishing around in her stage persona of the silly, dirty female queen. The first charge is fair. We never do find out about Rose's problem with her parents, why she so badly needs to conquer in her hometown that she insists on singing in the local bar where she got her start despite the customers' contemptuous behavior and her boyfriend's obvious distaste, why she lets everyone push her around. The film appears to think that it has told us, and if this is a tragedy, we have to know. Otherwise, it might be a cheap quickie with an implied rise and grisly fall with no reason for either. *The Rose* was years in the making and looks all it should; moreover, it *is* a tragedy in that Rose, a hero of great impact in her culture, does identify the force that destroys her: she is utterly alone. But what flaw made her alone? Why does rock cost its artists so much—where are they all going? *The Rose* could have told us.

The second charge, that Rose is pure Midler, is unfounded. Much of the score calls for a mean, wailing blues rock that Midler had to master for the film, and the ad libs in the concert scenes paint the character, not the actress. Midler live plays flaky self-spoof in the seventies manner. The Rose is vulnerable and rebellious, with the unpointed hysteria of the 1960s. More to the issue, Midler manages to act around the gaps in the script, making Rose uniquely complete as a principal in a musical; where else have we had a portrayal of this breadth and nuance? Of the film's nine numbers, she carries eight of them alone (the ninth is a drag act at a Manhattan club, where "Barbra," "Carol,"

"Diana," "Judy," and others salute Rose with one of her songs), a feat rivaled only by Garland in *A Star Is Born*; and Midler gets more out of her music because it's more sharply oriented to the character. "Whose Side Are You On? (Are you with me, or am I all alone?)" sets Rose's inability to believe she's worth belief; "Midnight in Memphis" cites the restlessness in being solitary; "Sold My Soul to Rock and Roll" makes the connection between rock and sex; "Love Me With a Feeling" and "When a Man Loves a Woman" show the two sides of romance, the fleshly and the spiritual; "Stay With Me" follows what seems to be the last of many desertions.

It is. Her boyfriend gone in disgust, Rose kills the pain with heroin and phones her parents in sight of the high school football field where she had sex with the whole team one night in her senior year. As she spaces out in the phone booth, a younger team finishes its practice and the field lights go out like a shutter clicking over a corpse. Delivered to her fans by helicopter, Rose barely holds on for "Stay With Me," then attempts "Let Me Call You Sweetheart" *a cappella* but breaks off to ask, in one of the great exit lines in film, "Where you goin'? Where's everybody goin'?" And dies.

Midler has not been given her due for *The Rose*. This is a spectacular performance, one of the few in recent musicals inextricably wired into its musical component. The character structures the rock; the rock defines the character. Few of the great acting-singing parts we have crossed paths with here have been so exclusively portrayed; as with Jolson in *The Jazz Singer*, Garland in *A Star is Born*, and Streisand in *Funny Girl*, without Midler there could have been no *Rose*—indeed, it was originally drafted as the tale of a male singer, precisely because it would have been much easier to cast that way. Given that Midler has made the final breakthrough for rock as a successful medium for the musical, is it too much to ask that she now consider doing as much to revive the great Broadway sound that went quiet when the blockbusters crapped out? Hollywood was once the land where musical talents of many kinds came to find their ultimate place in the American pop mythology—as lovers, loungers, fighters, or crazies—because they were basic to an American vision or so necessary to expand it, from Broadway, vaudeville, radio, and wherever else there is. Yes, Hollywood failed to place such people as Fanny Brice in the parables, but the culture has opened up considerably since then. (Would a Streisand or Midler have made it in film in 1930? Doubtful.) One of the reasons why it has is the participation of such people as Eddie Cantor, Fred Astaire, Mae West, the Marx Brothers, and Deanna

Durbin, none of them standard-cut role models in the received virtues. Yet all worked their altars. Midler and *The Rose* are, in a sense, the latest event in a history of transformation through stasis: Jolson, in steady helpings, broke the ground for West, while Astaire readied a stage for Kelly, while Chevalier's finesse necessitated the clumsiness of Crosby, and then Garland grew up to connect the aggressiveness of Eleanor Powell with the innocence of Alice Faye, and then Streisand claimed Brice's unplayed cards, dealing in Midler, while Minnelli took over for Garland by right of genes. Nobody changed character from role to role: that's stasis. But each role-player enlarges possibilities in the game. Hollywood has lost its tenacity in maintaining the generations, but—who knows?—smash adaptations of *A Chorus Line* and *Annie* could reinvent the film musical all over.

I refuse to end on an up note. Midler and *The Rose* are exceptional; a tour of the state of the art is better taken in the two would-be whizzes of 1980, *Can't Stop the Music* and *Xanadu*. These are the films that the 1980s deserve, though moviegoers rejected both. The two used old genre—putting on the show—and *Xanadu* even used old face, Gene Kelly's. He didn't dance much; who can blame him: to *that* noise? Olivia Newton-John has two expressions. She used the miffed one in *Grease*, so in *Xanadu* she shows the impish one, as a muse who flies off the wall (so to speak) to inspire Michael Beck as she apparently inspired Kelly decades before. The "show" Kelly and Beck want to put on is a disco-jazz club, and, mission accomplished, tutelary Newton-John vanishes in a special effect to leave a mortal copy of herself behind to console Beck (as Ava Gardner did for Robert Walker in *One Touch of Venus*). Disco is impossible in film, even one as foolish as *Xanadu*, because disco is entirely narcissistic. It's made for dancing, partying, and exhibitionism, not for watching or listening, not above the age of eleven. So how can one bring off a disco musical?

Can't Stop the Music tried hard to. The first gay musical, its "show" comprised the assembling and launching of a singing group. To make a disco musical, you must not only employ disco, but think disco in all elements of production. The script must be as stupid as the lyrics. (As in "YMCA": "You can do whatever you feel." Whatever you feel *like doing? Whomever* you feel?) The disco sound is combined with the disco "look," which results in a two-hour jeans commercial. The singing stars will be *the* disco group, the Village People, and other lead roles will be filled by those who are to acting what the Village People are to music: Bruce Jenner, Valerie Perrine, and Steve Guttenberg. Because disco aesthetics are set by the gay regime, a certain tone is observed: in the Village People's Christopher Street fantasy costumes, in Village locations, in at least one bared-torso shot from every male principal, and in a production number to "YMCA" for the stars and a horde of teenage brutes that, according to rumor, caused two fatal seizures, three heart attacks, and nineteen cases of aggravated drooling among Hollywood notables at an industry preview. But because gay is still a Secret, cover procedures are observed: the Village People will be assigned girlfriends in the "Magic Night" sequence, Nancy Walker—as opposed to, say, Franklin Pangborn—will direct, and Valerie Perrine will have breasts. The score is a cinch, as the Village People come with their own cockamamie concert written by a Frenchman named Jacques Morali, and for miscellany places are found for a roller-skating number, for veteran pros encouraged to make asses of themselves (June Havoc as Guttenberg's mother did; Russell Nype as a blue-chip lawyer provided the film's sole moments of show biz expertise), and for I-Love-New-York comedy (when Jenner is mugged by what he took to be a lovable granny). Critic Stephen Harvey got this film's number in describing its audience as "those eight-year-old boys whose favorite movies, when they grow up, will be *Auntie Mame* and *All About Eve*" and in predicting that "by the year 2100, it's probably going to be hailed as the *Gang's All Here* of the Eighties." In other words, folks, what you have here is camp that doesn't even bother to *be* before it *turns. Can't Stop the Music* and *Xanadu* are the fast-food trays of the Hollywood musical: little lies in bags.

That's where it stands. Not with *The Rose* and its sense of continuity in art, but in the cynicism of the opportunists of trend. Sure, the musical survives in revival and even on television—where negatives haven't deteriorated and where fade-resistant Technicolor prints were struck—but the form is mainly one of old energies now. Like Fanny Brice's "Rose of Washington Square," the musical "ain't got no future, but oy! what a past." Nice thing to have, a past. Nice to consider who you were, in times when it isn't easy to be what you are.

A Selective Discography

THE STUDIOS' INSISTENCE on turning out musicals with every tune a potential hit makes for engaging home-listening, though one would be hard put to reconstruct plot line or characterization from the love, dance, and comedy songs as the action is often carried out *between* the numbers. Also, there is a major problem in the late discovery of the soundtrack album. Not till the 1950s were relatively complete recordings standard practice; earlier, recording-studio-cut hit tunes filled the gap, not necessarily made by the people who sang in the film. Even if they were, it's not the real thing. Luckily, enterprising individuals have taken it upon themselves to issue private (or "underground"; or "pirate") recordings of old musicals. These can be hard to track down, however. Those interested should apply to the nearest serious record store, the kind that stocks imported recordings or elite cabaret artists. Somewhere near Mabel Mercer and Charles Trenet you might find the undergrounds.

Let's take it all chronologically. For the very first sound years, two excellent collections recommend themselves. *Stars of the Silver Screen* (RCA LPV-538) compiles sixteen ten-inch 78 discs by such as George Jessel, Lupe Velez, Maurice Chevalier ("Louise"), Bebe Daniels, and Dennis King. Miles Kreuger's liner notes provide historical perspective and the stars take the ear in a tour of the first musicals, variable in quality but always fascinating. Charles King in "Broadway Melody" is subdued compared to what he does with it on screen, Gloria Swanson full of voice in a tune from *The Trespasser*, the Duncan Sisters astonishing in a jazz obbligato on "I'm Following You" from *It's a Great Life*, Fanny Brice irreplaceable in "Cooking Breakfast for the One I

Love" from *Be Yourself*, Everett Marshall thrilling in a "darky" number from *Dixiana* with some of the strangest lyrics ever heard, and Jeanette MacDonald the living end in "Dream Lover," the big ballad from *The Love Parade*, written as a "hesitation waltz." MacDonald sails right over the hesitation marks, keeping the phrasing symmetrical and winning all hearts. *Legends of the Musical Stage* (Take Two 104) is even more enticing. Though its notes don't say so, these are all sounds off the track, and thus bear a sharper witness than Victor's commercial cuts. *Sally* (Marilyn Miller and Alexander Gray), Ethel Merman's short *Ireno, Puttin' on the Ritz* (Harry Richman), and *Honky Tonk* (Sophie Tucker) are among those present, the Tucker cuts alone worth any five MGM albums of the 1940s.

Maurice Chevalier and Jeanette MacDonald may be heard to advantage on, respectively, an import (WRC SH 156) and an American bargain release (VIC 1515). The Chevalier is a treasure, fourteen selections from his first eight Hollywood films (except *The Smiling Lieutenant*), half of them in French. These are studio-made, but Chevalier was one performer who could give as much in the recording booth as on the sound stage. MacDonald is less outgoing here than she had been on screen, as most of the selections were taped when she was past her prime. Still, it's a fine souvenir, and students of Hollywood's poplegit fetish, so suitable for the academic monograph, will want to contrast MacDonald's sedate and sassy verses of "San Francisco."

The spirit of the Warners backstager has been preserved on two United Artists releases, *The Golden Age of the Hollywood Musical* (LA 215-H) and *Hooray for Hollywood* (LA 361-H), drawn from the soundtracks. Most of these cuts represent big Berkeley numbers, and without the visuals one has not that much more than one tune repeated over and over. Still, consider the titles: "I Only Have Eyes For You," "Remember My Forgotten Man," "42nd Street," and "Lullaby of Broadway," among others, on the first; and "You're Getting to Be a Habit With Me," "The Lady in Red" (from *In Caliente*; terrific), "Dames," and "All's Fair in Love and War" on the second. Not to hear Dick Powell, Ruby Keeler, Wini Shaw, and the rest in this material is never to have heard it—and nothing touches Frances Langford's voice-cracked "Hooray for Hollywood" from *Hollywood Hotel*.

From the private Box Office label come two-disc compilations on Porter, Rodgers and Hart, and Kern. The Porter set contains soundtracks of *Rosalie*, *You'll Never Get Rich*, and *Something to Shout About* among other tidbits (the best being Gertrude Lawrence in two cuts from her 1929 disaster *The Battle of Paris*). The Rodgers and

Hart set is the best: *The Hot Heiress, Love Me Tonight, The Phantom President, Mississippi*, and *Hallelujah, I'm a Bum* (including the "Sleeping Beauty" footage, cut from release prints) under one cover. The Kern has a lot of Irene Dunne—*Roberta, High, Wide and Handsome, Sweet Adeline*, and *Joy of Living*, plus *Music in the Air*. These are the Broadway masters; what of the Hollywood specialists in simplicity? As of this writing, Box Office has just released albums on Richard Whiting and Ralph Rainger, and there is sure delight in an import, *The Great British Dance Bands Play the Music of Nacio Herb Brown* (SH 267), taking the Brown–Freed collaboration from *The Broadway Melody* to *Babes in Arms*. Dance bands can be annoyingly persistent about holding to a beat and the vocalists are vapid, but Brown's transparent chording and direct melody benefit from this approach. "Singin' in the Rain" is especially well done.

In the late 1930s, both Alice Faye and Shirley Temple have their collections. Columbia CL 3068 features Faye's studio recordings; Silver Screen 100/3 carries her—on soundtracks—from *Now I'll Tell* to *Hello, Frisco, Hello*, virtually the whole career. One may invest in both albums without doubling a single title. Temple has had several retrospectives, the best being Fox 3006, one disc's worth of her best stuff hot off the track.

For separate thirties titles, one applies to the pirates. One company that evades identification by issuing each record under a different label has provided some great double features: *The Broadway Melody* with the Tibbett–Moore *New Moon, Whoopee!* with *Puttin' on the Ritz, The Love Parade* and the Lubitsch *Merry Widow*, and *Everybody Sing* with *Pigskin Parade*. The sound is erratic, *Whoopee!* is missing "A Girl Friend of a Boy Friend of Mine" (to be heard on Take Two 104, cited above), and *New Moon* is billed as *Parisian Belle*, but it's the goods, all right, complete with portions of dialogue and the blips and pops of the Vitaphone days. *Whoopee!* in particular is unmatched for punk whimsey. After hearing it you may want to dive back into the 1930s and never come out. It's been done.

Pelican 2019 presents *The Rogue Song*, Tibbett's debut sensation, a lost film (the sound discs survived the negative and prints) and a rather dull score, though Tibbett is wild and bright. Operetta fans may also collect MacDonald and Eddy in *Naughty Marietta* on Hollywood Soundstage 413, to my mind the best of their scores. The 1936 *Show Boat* comes and goes; I have it on Xeno 251. Perhaps the choice operetta disc of the decade is that to *The Great Waltz* (Sountrak 109), though without Duvivier's omnipotent camera one takes but half an art. Musical comedy fans will prefer Alice Faye, in modern dress no matter what the setting, in *Wake Up and Live* (HS 403), a fine Revel–Gordon score; buffs of the comedy musical will thrill to an Eddie Cantor double feature on CIF 3007, *Kid Millions* and *Roman Scandals*; and Garland fans will cream twice over for *Babes in Arms* coupled with *Babes on Broadway* (Curtain Calls 100/6–7), despite odious cover art. And of course there's Jolson, at his best in two Warren–Dubin scores, *Wonder Bar* and *Go Into Your Dance.* With Helen Morgan and Dick Powell also in evidence, however, you learn to treasure singers who can deliver a tune as the composer set it down.

What about Astaire and Rogers? This part is tricky. Their scores are so popular that the undergrounds go out of and come back into print at some pace. British EMI (EMTC 101) issued a disc of *The Gay Divorcee* and *Swing Time*, and the tautologically named Scarce Rarities Productions (SR 5505) put out *Follow the Fleet* and *A Damsel in Distress*, but these have both vanished and no doubt have been replaced by others. Keep alert—four or five Berlin, Kern, or Gershwin songs performed by these two, twice over (as each film fits on one side) is no mean bargain.

Nineteen thirty-nine brings us to the first commercial soundtrack issue, MGM's of *The Wizard of Oz*, actually published decades after the premiere. In 1939, the only Oz album was Decca's set of four ten-inch 78s made in the studio with Garland and the Ken Darby Singers. MGM's LP (E 3464) includes a great deal of dialogue and omits "The Merry Old Land of Oz"; the Decca set, lately on MCA-521, omits "If I Were King of the Forest" but lo, includes "The Jitterbug." It's listener's choice. The MGM, taken off the reel, is authentic and presents more of Lahr's classic turn as the lion, but one should hear "The Jitterbug." Ideally, get both, and supplement them with the tiny chorus that connects the poppy field sequence to the Emerald City entrance, called "Optimistic Voices," on a Bette Midler recital (Atlantic SD 7270), which also contains Midler's nicely updated "Lullaby of Broadway."

The 1940s. With Decca's discovery of the Broadway original cast album, made with the stars and orchestra and in the performing style of the debut production, Hollywood began to see the light, though at first it continued to make studio albums—one or two stars and a pickup orchestra in "radio" arrangements: Deanna Durbin in *Can't Help Singing*, Nelson Eddy and Risë Stevens in *The Chocolate Soldier*, Garland in *Meet Me in St. Louis* and *The Harvey Girls*, and Crosby and Astaire in no less than twelve tunes from *Holiday Inn*. Toward the end of the decade MGM began to release soundtrack albums but cut the selections to fit the ten-inch disc; the pirate LP remains one's best bet. Sountrak 111 pulls up whole swatches of *Good News*, dances and all, and *The Gang's All Here* (CIF 3003) proves a heyday of swing. The disheartened will need to play Carmen Miranda's "The Lady in the Tutti-Frutti Hat" from the latter for cheer-up purposes, whereas the giddy will come down to earth to Alice Faye's "No Love, No Nothing." CIF also backs the Rodgers–Hammerstein *State Fair* with the Kern–Hammerstein *Centennial Summer*, a veritable Louanne Hogan festival, Hogan being Jeanne Crain's voice in both. Dance buffs should investigate Silver Screen 100/24: *Cover Girl* and *You Were Never Lovelier*, a Nan Wynn sampler, Wynn being Hayworth's voice. Kids, the stars are out tonight. Forbidden material awaits in *Cut!* on DRG (ORTF 1), outtakes from 1938 to 1971 but centering on the 1940s and Judy Garland, in deleted songs from such as *Ziegfeld Girl*, *The Harvey Girls*, and *The Pirate*.

By the 1950s, the commercial soundtrack LP became standard equipment, and at this point we cease to depend on underground productions. A personal selection: in the bio, *Love Me or Leave Me* (Columbia CL 710) holds twelve cuts, all by Doris Day and all worth hearing; Day's background as a band vocalist connects with Ruth Etting's, though Day attempts no imitation. (Those in search of the real Etting should try Columbia ML 5050 or Take Two 203.) *Star!*, shorn of its dumb script, makes pleasant listening and revives quite a few forgotten beauties. (Surprise hit: " 'N' Everything," sung by Garrett Lewis.) In the Broadway adaptation, *The Boy Friend* (MGM 1SE-32 ST) is fun, especially when Twiggy takes two old Brown–Freed hits, "You Are My Lucky Star" and "All I Do Is Dream of You." *A Little Night Music* (Columbia 35333) is a must for Sondheim's following, with one new song and some new lyrics for old ones.

In the original, *Gigi* remains a standout on MGM E 3641, though the wonderful Maxim's "Gossip Chorus" is not included; students of the Broadway-Hollywood interchange might check out the cast album of the more recent stage version (RCA ABL 1-0404), with four new Loewe–Lerner songs. No Chevalier, but plenty of chances for Ph.D. dissertations with endless footnoting. *Bugsy Malone* (RSO RS-1-3501) grows on you, as does *The Slipper and the Rose* (MCA 2097), particularly its chromatic waltz tune, "He Danced With Me." In rock, you can move from the basics through MOR to post-Beatles pastiche by sampling, respectively, *The Buddy Holly Story* (Epic 35412), the Streisand *A Star Is Born* (Columbia 34403), and *200 Motels* (United Artists

S-9956). And while I have reservations about *The Last Waltz* as film, the concert itself (Warner Brothers 3146) is a glorious Baedeker through the great rock past. Perhaps the last note is to be heard in *The Rose* (Atlantic SD 16010), in the final cut when, after two hours of voice-grating blues, Midler eases one down with Amanda McBroom's transcendent title song, a folkish ballad accompanied simply on piano. The song is heard over the credits, but no one leaves the theatre. On the contrary, one listens in amazement.

In the mid–1970s, MGM re-released most of its prize soundtracks on two-disc albums. Best bets are *The Pirate/Pagan Love Song/Hit the Deck* (2-SES-43ST), *Seven Brides for Seven Brothers/Rose Marie* (2-SES-41ST), *Singin' in the Rain/Easter Parade* (2-SES-40ST), with a Jane Powell sale-quake on 2-SES-53ST: *Royal Wedding/Nancy Goes to Rio/Rich, Young and Pretty*. "It's thrilling," MGM's *Rich, Young and Pretty* ads explained, "when Vic Damone sings love songs to Jane!" By a stroke of luck, contract commitments kept Damone off the album, so it's largely Jane; one Powell fan I know suffered a nervous breakdown trying to decide which title to play first. So you see how it is.

The Disney people have smartly kept all their major tracks in print, by separate title in various children's editions or in compilations. The best of the latter is *The Magical Music of Walt Disney* (Ovation-5000), a four-disc set moving from *Steamboat Willie* to *Pete's Dragon*, a live-action fantasy of 1977. Cleverly arranged medleys from the soundtracks give eloquent digests of *Snow White, Pinocchio, Dumbo, Bambi, Cinderella, Peter Pan, Lady and the Tramp, Sleeping Beauty*, and *Mary Poppins*. One complaint: the last side is mainly given over to Muzak used in the two theme parks, which reminds us that democracy will never work.

☆ ☆
A Selective
Bibliography

TAKING THE general histories first, I'm sorry to say that they aren't an impressive lot. Douglas McVay's *The Musical Film* (New York: A. S. Barnes, 1967), limited in size by its series format, is superficial (of the 150 Hollywood musicals released in 1929, 1930, and 1931, McVay mentions two, in passing) and ruined by weird opinions. (McVay spends twenty pages on the Garland *A Star Is Born*, "the greatest picture of *any* kind I have ever seen"; I'll take vanilla.) Lee Edward Stern's *The Movie Musical* (New York: Pyramid, 1974), similarly concise, ranges more widely, holds sensible opinions, and is nicely illustrated. But the lack of original analysis and the failure to engage rock are drawbacks. John Kobal's *Gotta Sing, Gotta Dance: A Pictorial History of Film Musicals* (New York: Hamlyn, 1970) is the lavish entry, without color, however, and garishly designed. Kobal relies heavily on the reminiscences of people like Ben Lyon, Joan Blondell, Ann Sheridan, and Vincente Minnelli, which is just as well because Kobal's part of the writing is loaded with errors.

Illustrated studies of individual actors' careers have become popular. Pyramid's small-format, paperbound life-and-work series, well illustrated, offers among others studies by Lee Edward Stern of Jeanette MacDonald, with the same virtues as his history cited above; by Patrick McGilligan of Ginger Rogers, nicely detailed and fair rather than effusive; by Barbara Bauer of Bing Crosby; by James Juneau, refreshingly level-headed, of Judy Garland; by Jeanine Basinger of Shirley Temple and Gene Kelly, both cliché bound; and by George Morris of Doris Day, with a good report on Day's early Warners musicals. Citadel Press has specialized in large-format books opening with a biographical essay, and then taking each film through a cast-and-credits list, plot summary, and contemporary critics' blurbs, the whole profusely illustrated. I think there's something wrong here—why reprint the idiot comments of journalists when the author, presumably an expert, can tell us so much more about each film? Those I haven't daunted might look into volumes on Maurice Chevalier by Gene Ringgold and DeWitt Bodeen; MacDonald and Eddy by Philip Castanza, who gushes; Shirley Temple by Robert Windeler; and Elvis Presley by Steven Zmijewsky and Boris Zmijewsky. There are many others, though other subjects made fewer musicals. In Citadel's format but more carefully designed and with more complete data and notes is W. Franklyn Moshier's *The Alice Faye Book* (Harrisburg: Stackpole Books, 1974). Faye and her films are basic to the musical, both historically and today on television, and serious students should put some time in here. A good start: turn to page 98 for a still of what Moshier captions as the "distinctive Faye pose." Try striking this pose yourself, if possible in one of Faye's costumes. How do you feel?

Volumes on Fred Astaire and Judy Garland each cover their subjects much better than anything Citadel has published, both verbally and pictorially. Stanley Green and Burt Goldblatt's *Starring Fred Astaire* (New York: Dodd, Mead, 1973) boasts much commentary on the making of the films and the experience of seeing them; with Astaire, most creative of stars, one must have more than data, and this book supplies it. Christopher Finch's *Rainbow: The Story of Judy Garland* (New York: Grosset and Dunlap, 1975) is a biography rather than a career study, but Finch's analysis is so acute and Will Hopkins' design so stylish that one must call it *the* book on a musical star's work. There have been Garland biographies trashy and earnest (a few are both), but only Finch has caught her and the legend; and his pictures, from the cover's frame enlargement* of Dorothy entranced by the magic to the last view of Garland in concert, exhausted by it, are a book in themselves.

Buffs of auteur theory prefer studies of directors, but few of the voguish ones worked in the musical and the pickings are lean. Try

---

*Frame enlargements are photographs made using the film itself as a negative, as opposed to stills, which are snapshots posed on the set. Stills supply perhaps 99.9 percent of all movie illustrations, yet obviously they are not authentic records of what one actually sees in the theatres. You can tell a frame enlargement from a still in that the actors in a frame frequently look a little awkward or off-center and the focus is sometimes a little awry.

Tom Milne's *Mamoulian* (Bloomington: Indiana University Press, 1970), which records *Applause*'s opening sequence and *Love Me Tonight*'s finale in frames eloquently depictive of the director's mobile eye. A terrible event is Hugh Fordin's *The World of Entertainment!* (Garden City: Doubleday, 1975), a lengthy chronicle of the Freed unit that records release dates, production grosses, telegrams, and so on, and doesn't say word one about the films themselves. A terrific event, in Citadel's bio-and-films format but comparable to Finch in design, is Tony Thomas and Jim Terry's *The Busby Berkeley Book* (Greenwich, Conn.: The New York Graphic Society, 1973), rich in analysis, reminiscence, and rare photos, including frame series of "Shuffle Off to Buffalo," "Lullaby of Broadway," and "All's Fair in Love and War."

Walt Disney instances a special case, as his studio prudently controls the use of illustrative material; but a Disney study without pictures lacks resonance. Leonard Maltin's *The Disney Films* (New York: Popular Library, sec. ed., 1975) emphasizes the features over the shorts, telling much, but the black-and-white reproduction isn't too nifty. Richard Schickel's biography, *The Disney Version* (New York: Simon and Schuster, 1968), is favored by the cognoscenti, but Schickel's resentment of Disney's wealth and power nags through the text like a soapbox nut's exhortation. Horrors! the genius turned out to be a capitalist. The Disney people withheld permission from Schickel's publisher to use Disney art; I'm with them. On the other hand, the studio put a trove of sketches, storyboards, outlines, and other art at Christopher Finch's disposal for a smashing coffee-table issue, *The Art of Walt Disney* (New York: Abrams, 1973). The studio holds the copyright on the book.

Now, a miscellany. Alexander Walker treats the first sound years with wit in *The Shattered Silents* (New York: Morrow, 1978), and Miles Kreuger has collected all pertinent material that appeared in those years in *Photoplay*, the most adult of the movie magazines, in *The Movie Musical From Vitaphone to 42nd Street* (New York: Dover, 1975): articles, photos, and brief reviews. Alec Wilder's *American Popular Song* (New York: Oxford University Press, 1972) offers somewhat technical analysis of "The Great Innovators" in the first half of the century, and deals with Hollywood specialists like Harry Warren and Richard Whiting as well as the big Broadway names, almost all of whom composed for the screen as well. Publishers are increasingly putting out shooting scripts, including those of a few musicals, but these may be so edited on the set that they serve more as a record of what was planned than of what was filmed. I followed *Gold Diggers of*

1933 (Madison: University of Wisconsin Press, 1980) along with the film and found virtually every other line altered and whole sections missing (some were dropped, others filmed but cut before release). Wisconsin's series is well produced, with juicy frame enlargements and introductory notes; they have also put out *The Jazz Singer* and have promised *42nd Street*, *Footlight Parade*, and *Yankee Doodle Dandy*. For general reference, try Tom Vallance's *The American Musical* (New York: Barnes, 1970), with alphabetical capsule notes on actors, directors, choreographers, and songwriters, as well as a few abstracts on such topics as ballet and "ghosting," and an index by film title so you can work backwards to check a work's credits.

Two books deal with the planning and filming of one production, Aljean Harmetz' *The Making of the Wizard of Oz* (New York: Knopf, 1977) and Doug McClelland's *Down the Yellow Brick Road* (New York: Pyramid, 1976), which affirms my belief that this film is the A-prime Hollywood musical. McClelland's paperback has more pictures but Harmetz has the advantage of Knopf's bibliophile elegance and some stunning color frames. Moreover, she has researched the subject with completeness and affection. Harmetz is heartily recommended—to anyone, film buff or not.

I have saved the best for last: Arlene Croce's *The Fred Astaire and Ginger Rogers Book* (New York: Dutton, 1972). Croce, dance critic for *The New Yorker*, is a brilliant stylist, a perceptive analyst, and grand company. Film by film, she takes one through the nine RKO classics and *The Barkleys of Broadway* with appreciations of every detail of production, an excellent choice of illustrations, and, for dessert, tiny flip-page preservations of a moment each from "Let Yourself Go" and "The Waltz in Swing Time." Croce went to a lot of trouble. When she wants to show something and a still won't do, she has the appropriate frame enlarged: Rogers' *Swing Time* shampoo or "Eric Blore in consternation." Charm and wisdom, unbeatable.

☆ ☆
The
Ethan Mordden
Hall of Fame
and Disrepute

BEST FILMS

The Love Parade
Whoopee!
Love Me Tonight
42nd Street
Gold Diggers of 1933
The Merry Widow [1934]
Top Hat
Swing Time
Show Boat [1936]
The Great Waltz [1938]
The Wizard of Oz
Pinocchio
Meet Me in St. Louis
Singin' in the Rain
Gigi
Cabaret

WORST FILMS

Glorifying the American Girl
Just Imagine
Honey
Variety Girl

☆ 243

Two Tickets to Broadway
Frankie and Johnny
Never Steal Anything Small
Lost Horizon
Paint Your Wagon
At Long Last Love
Sgt. Pepper's Lonely Hearts Club Band

BEST PERFORMANCES

Bessie Love in *The Broadway Melody*
Eddie Cantor in *Whoopee!*
Maurice Chevalier in *One Hour With You* and *The Love Parade*
Jeanette MacDonald in *Love Me Tonight* and *Naughty Marietta*
Helen Morgan in *Show Boat* [1936]
Bert Lahr in *The Wizard of Oz*
Judy Garland in *The Wizard of Oz* and *A Star Is Born* [1954]
Ethel Waters in *Cabin in the Sky*
James Cagney in *Yankee Doodle Dandy*
Margaret O'Brien in *Meet Me in St. Louis*
Jimmy Durante in *It Happened in Brooklyn*
Rita Moreno in *West Side Story*
Zero Mostel in *A Funny Thing Happened on the Way to the Forum*
Rosalind Russell in *Gypsy*
Barbra Streisand in *Funny Girl*
Walter Matthau in *Hello, Dolly!*
Nipsey Russell in *The Wiz*
Gary Busey in *The Buddy Holly Story*
Bette Midler in *The Rose*

WORST PERFORMANCES

The complete works of El Brendel
Jack Buchanan in *Monte Carlo*
Josephine Hutchinson in *Happiness Ahead*
Kathryn Grayson in *So This Is Love*
Lana Turner in *The Merry Widow* [1952]
Oscar Levant in *The Band Wagon*
Pamela Tiffin in *State Fair* [1962]
Natalie Wood in *Gypsy*
Cybill Shepherd in *At Long Last Love*
John Cassisi in *Bugsy Malone*
Peter Frampton and the Bee Gees in *Sgt. Pepper's Lonely Hearts Club Band*

MOST BIZARRE PERFORMANCES

Lillian Roth in *The Love Parade*
Marilyn Miller in *Her Majesty Love*
Baby Leroy in *A Bedtime Story*
Joan Crawford in *Dancing Lady*
Burgess Meredith in *Second Chorus*
Ray Bolger in *Babes in Toyland* [1961]
Carol Channing in *Thoroughly Modern Millie*
Julie Andrews in *Star!*
Lucille Ball in *Mame*
Everyone else in *Sgt. Pepper's Lonely Hearts Club Band*

MOST UNDERRATED PERFORMANCES

Joan Blondell in *Gold Diggers of 1933*
Aline MacMahon in *Gold Diggers of 1933*
Harriet Hilliard in *Follow the Fleet*
Luise Rainer in *The Great Ziegfeld*
Ann Miller in *Easter Parade*
Doris Day in *Calamity Jane*
Barbra Streisand in *Hello, Dolly!*
Lee Marvin in *Paint Your Wagon*
Twiggy in *The Boy Friend*
Burt Reynolds in *At Long Last Love*

BEST DIRECTORS

Rouben Mamoulian for *Applause, Love Me Tonight, The Gay Desperado*, and
　　Summer Holiday
Ernst Lubitsch for *The Love Parade, Monte Carlo*, and *The Merry Widow*
Lloyd Bacon for *42nd Street*
Busby Berkeley for *Gold Diggers of 1935*
Julien Duvivier for *The Great Waltz*
Vincente Minnelli for *Meet Me in St. Louis, The Pirate*, and *Gigi*
Richard Lester for *A Funny Thing Happened on the Way to the Forum*
Ken Russell for *The Boy Friend*
Bob Fosse for *Cabaret* and *All That Jazz*
Milos Forman for *Hair*
Alan Parker for *Fame*

BEST ORIGINAL FILM SCORES

The Love Parade
Love Me Tonight
Hallelujah, I'm a Bum
Top Hat
Swing Time
Shall We Dance
The Wizard of Oz

BEST MUSICAL NUMBERS

"The Wedding of the Painted Doll" in *The Broadway Melody*
"Stetson" in *Whoopee!*
"Beyond the Blue Horizon" in *Monte Carlo*
"Sweeping the Clouds Away" in *Paramount on Parade*
"Isn't it Romantic?" in *Love Me Tonight*
"Shuffle Off to Buffalo" in *42nd Street*
"Remember My Forgotten Man" in *Gold Diggers of 1933*
"Don't Say Goodnight" in *Wonder Bar*
"Dames" in *Dames*
"Night and Day" in *The Gay Divorcee*
"Cheek to Cheek" in *Top Hat*
"Lullaby of Broadway" in *Gold Diggers of 1935*
"The Waltz in Swing Time" in *Swing Time*
"Bojangles of Harlem" in *Swing Time*
"Never Gonna Dance" in *Swing Time*
"All's Fair in Love and War" in *Gold Diggers of 1937*
"The Yam" in *Carefree*
"Can't Help Lovin' Dat Man" in *Show Boat* [1936]
"A Pretty Girl Is Like a Melody" in *The Great Ziegfeld*
"I'm in Love With Vienna" in *The Great Waltz*
"Your Broadway and My Broadway" in *Broadway Melody of 1938*
"Takin' a Chance on Love" in *Cabin in the Sky*
"Under the Bamboo Tree" in *Meet Me in St. Louis*
"The Trolley Song" in *Meet Me in St. Louis*
"Singin' in the Rain" in *Singin' in the Rain*
"Broadway Rhythm" in *Singin' in the Rain*
"The Barn Raising" in *Seven Brides for Seven Brothers*
"Don't Rain on My Parade" in *Funny Girl*
"There's Gotta Be Something Better Than This" in *Sweet Charity*
"Wilkommen" in *Cabaret*

"Tomorrow" in *Bugsy Malone*
"Aquarius" in *Hair*
"Hot Lunch Jam" in *Fame*
Special citation: "The Jitterbug" [deleted from *The Wizard of Oz*]

MOST TANTALIZING LOST FILM:
The Gold Diggers of Broadway

MOST DISTINGUISHED CAST ASSEMBLED FOR ONE FILM:
Show Boat [1936]

LEAST DISTINGUISHED CAST ASSEMBLED FOR ONE FILM:
Show Boat [1951]

BEST NEGLECTED FILM:
Folies Bergère

WORST CELEBRATED FILM:
The Band Wagon

MOST ORIGINAL PREMISE:
Fantasia

LEAST ORIGINAL PREMISE:
Alexander's Ragtime Band

MOST AUTHENTIC BIO:
Yankee Doodle Dandy

LEAST AUTHENTIC BIO:
Look for the Silver Lining

BEST KNOWN HOLLYWOOD ORIGINAL:
The Wizard of Oz

MOST OBSCURE HOLLYWOOD ORIGINAL:
Oh Sailor, Behave!

MOST OBSCURE ADAPTATION FROM BROADWAY:
The Five O'Clock Girl (completed through a rough cut but never released)

LEAST FAITHFUL ADAPTATION FROM BROADWAY:
Sally, Irene and Mary [1938]

MOST ORIGINAL CONCEPTION FOR GENRE:
the RKO dance musical
> **honorable mention:**
> the Warners Berkeley backstager

MOST DARING STUDIO:
Paramount

MOST STRIKING USE OF COLOR:
The Wizard of Oz
> **honorable mention:**
> *Whoopee!*

BEST ARGUMENT FROM THE LEFT:
Gold Diggers of 1935

BEST ARGUMENT FROM THE RIGHT:
The Wizard of Oz

BEST ANARCHIST ARGUMENT:
Hallelujah, I'm a Bum

TAJ MAHAL AWARD FOR MOST IMPRESSIVE DESIGN:
The Wizard of Oz

BURGER QUEEN AWARD FOR LEAST IMPRESSIVE DESIGN:
Honey

OUTSTANDING TRAINED SINGER:
Lawrence Tibbett

OUTSTANDING UNTRAINED SINGER:
Maurice Chevalier

MOST STRIKING ORCHESTRATION AND/OR PLAYING:
Whoopee!

OUTSTANDING COMPOSER:
Harry Warren

OUTSTANDING LYRICIST:
E. Y. Harburg

BEVERLY SILLS AWARD FOR OUTSTANDING CONTRIBUTION
   TO SERIOUS MUSIC:
MGM, for capturing the musician's intensity in *Song of Love*

BEST EDITING:
All That Jazz

WORST EDITING:
Little Miss Marker [1934]

MOST WONDERFUL WOMAN:
Rita Hayworth

MOST WONDERFUL MAN:
Fred Astaire

MOST WONDERFUL KID:
Shirley Temple
         honorable mention:
         Mitzi Green

MOST BIZARRE PERSON:
Carmen Miranda
         honorable mention:
         Milizia Korjus

DULLEST PERSON:
Gordon MacRae
         honorable mention:
         Susanna Foster

MOST IMPRESSIVE TEAM:
Astaire and Rogers
         honorable mention:
         Garland and Kelly

LEAST IMPRESSIVE TEAM:
Gaynor and Farrell

ONE-TIMER AWARD:
Ethel Shutta in *Whoopee!*
         honorable mention:
         Kirsten Flagstad in *The Big Broadcast of 1938*

SURVIVOR AWARD:
Maurice Chevalier
> **honorable mention:**
> Charlotte Greenwood
> **second honorable mention:**
> Pert Kelton

ROD STEIGER AWARD FOR MOST OVERACTED ROLE:
Rod Steiger in *Oklahoma!*

RUBY KEELER AWARD FOR LEAST OVERACTED ROLE:
Yves Montand in *On a Clear Day You Can See Forever*

OUTSTANDING TROUPER AWARD FOR UNBILLED APPEAR-
ANCE:
Glenda Jackson in *The Boy Friend*
> **honorable mention:**
> Jack Benny in *Gypsy*

MOST PRECISE CHOOSER OF ROLES:
Lena Horne

LEAST PRECISE CHOOSER OF ROLES:
June Haver

GALE STORM AWARD FOR LEAST WELL EXPLOITED PERSON-
ALITY:
Fanny Brice
> **honorable mention:**
> Vivienne Segal

VIRGINIA KATHERINE McMATH AWARD FOR MOST VERSA-
TILE PERFORMER:
Jeanette MacDonald
> **honorable mention:**
> Ann Sothern

FERNANDO LAMAS AWARD FOR BEST MALE SINGER BORN IN
ARGENTINA WHO APPEARED IN FOUR JILLS AND A JEEP:
Dick Haymes

Index

Critical Issues
in Contemporary
Culture

Critical Issues in Contemporary Culture

CHRISTOPHER GOULD

University of North Carolina at Wilmington

ELE BYINGTON

University of North Carolina at Wilmington

Allyn and Bacon

Boston ✦ *London* ✦ *Toronto* ✦ *Sydney* ✦ *Tokyo* ✦ *Singapore*

Vice President: Eben W. Ludlow
Editorial Assistant: Elizabeth Egan
Marketing Manager: Lisa Kimball
Production Administrator: Susan Brown
Editorial-Production Service: Matrix Productions Inc.
Cover Administrator: Linda Knowles
Cover Designer: Susan Paradise
Composition Buyer: Linda Cox
Manufacturing Buyer: Suzanne Lareau

Library of Congress Cataloging-in-Publication Data

Critical issues in contemporary culture / [edited by] Christopher
    Gould, Ele Byington.
      p. cm.
    ISBN 0-02-345402-4
    1. Readers—Civilization, Modern.   2. Civilization, Modern—
Problems, exercises, etc.   3. English language—Rhetoric.
4. College readers.   I. Gould, Christopher
II. Byington, Ele.
PE1127.H4C75   1996
306—dc20   96-16416
                                         CIP

Printed in the United States of America

10 9 8 7 6 5 4 3 2 1   01 00 99 98 97 96

Contents

7   Education, Social Class, and Ethnicity: Achieving Excellence and Equity   369

8   Identity and Polarization   432

9   Telling Stories, Revealing Cultures   493

Preface

———————◆———————

Critical Issues in Contemporary Culture is a collection of readings aimed at stimulating critical inquiry by inviting students to examine contemporary issues relating to gender, social class, and ethnicity. Designed to complicate students' understanding of "mainstream culture" as well as to highlight the diversity of contemporary America, this book contains selections by authors who critically examine convention and tradition.

With so many multicultural reading anthologies currently on the market, we have designed *Critical Issues* to provide several distinctive features:

1. The emphasis is on issues. As one reviewer remarked of the text: "It makes the multicultural and multidisciplinary viewpoints implicit in a thorough examination of issues."
2. Topics should appeal to a broad range of students, nontraditional as well as traditional, and are addressed in a wide variety of texts—autobiographical, literary, academic, journalistic, and argumentative.
3. At the end of most reading selections are activities that lead students from informal holistic response to more detailed analysis. Writing suggestions at the end of each chapter encourage students to synthesize sources and make other kinds of connections among the readings.
4. The instructional apparatus allows teachers to adapt the book to their individual aims.

Though chapters need not be assigned sequentially, we recommend beginning with Chapter 1, which examines some of the problems and confusion that surround *culture* and *literacy* as terms of discussion. Since *Critical Issues* is intended to suit the needs of first-year students, each of the chapters following Chapter 1 introduces approaches to reading and writing analytically—reading strategies and reading journals (Chapter 2), group inquiry (Chapter 3), creating a synthesis of ideas (Chapter 4), rhetorical analysis (Chapters 5 and 6), Peter Elbow's "Believing Game" (Chapter 7), and reading texts complicated by abstractions (Chapter 8). Chapter 9 completes the text with a focus on the power of stories to reveal our cultures to each other—stories that are a blend of fiction, nonfiction, newspaper account, and even one created by a research project.

We wish to thank the following individuals for their helpful, constructive responses to earlier drafts of our book: James C. McDonald, University of Southwestern Louisiana; Marjorie Roemer, University of Cincinnati; Susan Simons, Community College of Denver; Dana Thomsen, Johnson and Wales University; K. J. Walters, Lehman College of CUNY; and Linda Woodson, The University of Texas at San Antonio.

C. G.
E. B.

1

Culture and Literacy: Entering the Conversation

◆

One of the most gratifying and challenging opportunities you face as a college student is the invitation to participate actively, as a reader and writer, in new *discourse communities.* The educated adults who comprise these communities abide by formal, though often unwritten, rules and customs about sharing information and ideas. The challenge of participating in their conversations is not just a matter of gathering facts and understanding concepts; it is also a process of looking at familiar objects and routines through different, at times unfamiliar, lenses. Reading selections in this chapter, and throughout *Critical Issues in Contemporary Culture,* are intended to engage this process. Many of the readings in this book examine issues and artifacts from the standpoint of persons outside *mainstream culture*—the primarily white, Anglo-Saxon, middle-class community whose values and opinions, until recently, defined what most people regarded as American. Other selections are by authors who, though members of that community, try to shed its biases and preconceptions.

Culture, a crucial term in this book, is one of the most complex words in English. Tracing its history, Professor Raymond Williams has shown that centuries ago the term was used only to describe the cultivation of plant or animal life—a meaning retained in such words as *agriculture, horticulture,* and *viticulture.* Gradually, however, *culture* became associated with the cultivation of intellect, taste, artistic talent, and etiquette. (Today, a "cultured" person is assumed to be educated, sophisticated, and polite.) As a result, *culture* became synonymous with *civilization,* describing both a state of learning and refinement and a process of historical development. Until the 1800s, most English-speaking people considered that process to be uniform and inevitable, culminating in the adoption of customs, tastes, and attitudes similar to

1

those of the more privileged classes in Europe. However, an important change took place in the nineteenth century, when people began "to speak of 'cultures' in the plural: the specific and variable cultures of different nations and periods, [as well as] the specific and variable cultures of social and economic groups with a nation."* Thus, *culture* came to mean the way of life exemplified by one group of people during a specific period in history. Today, the ingredients of a culture are understood to include its moral values, etiquette, customs and rituals, gender roles, and a number of other factors that insiders take for granted.

This more inclusive definition of culture discourages judgments of relative worth: no one culture, so defined, can be called better or worse than any other. However, discussions of culture are complicated by still another definition of the word. When people talk about "cultural events" or the "cultural resources" of a city or region, they typically refer to museum collections and artistic performances that reflect the tastes of a privileged class, an *elite*.

Restricting the boundaries of culture to the customs, artifacts, and tastes of an elite may not seem remarkable, but as a way of thinking it has had historical consequences. For example, public revenues have been allocated under the presumption that opera and oil painting are more worthy of government support than other more popular forms of art and entertainment. Persons outside or on the fringes of the cultural elite—even such prominent figures as Andrew Jackson and Harry Truman—have been belittled as "uncultured."

The first reading selection in this chapter, "High Culture/Low Culture" by Herbert Gans, contrasts two very different "taste cultures" in American society. Gans considers some of the practical consequences of unequal funding for endeavors that reflect the preferences of these two cultures.

Literacy is another complex term with a similarly fluid definition. While any colonial American able to write his or her name was deemed literate, more rigorous criteria define literacy at the end of the twentieth century. Today, it is widely assumed that literacy entails a specific set of mental proficiencies: decoding symbolic representations of spoken language (translating letters of the alphabet into sounds, words, and ideas) as well as casting ideas and information into a symbolic code (putting them into written language in such a way that readers can understand them). Although individuals or groups may use language in other complicated ways, they are often (and incorrectly) labeled illiterate unless they also possess this specific set of mental proficiencies and can exercise them with ease.

---

*Raymond Williams, "Culture," *Keywords: A Vocabulary of Culture and Society,* rev. ed. (New York: Oxford University Press, 1983), p. 89.

Clearly, culture and literacy intersect. A culture is delineated, at least in part, by how it defines and uses literacy. And since some cultures have more power than others, certain definitions and uses of literacy have been privileged. Furthermore, literacy is a primary means by which culture is perpetuated or reproduced (through stories, performances, sacred texts, literature, textbooks). Consequently, scholars, politicians, religious leaders, and other citizens are concerned not only about the technical skills that define literacy, but also about which texts (oral and written) should be preserved. The ongoing debate over *cultural literacy*, addressed in reading selections by E. D. Hirsch, Jr., Alan Purves, and John Ogbu, is an example of that concern.

Following Ogbu's essay are three readings that examine the practical consequences of literacy and literacy education for specific individuals and ethnic communities outside the cultural mainstream of the United States.

Herbert Gans

High Culture/Low Culture

◆

Born in Germany in 1927, sociologist Herbert Gans emigrated to the United States in 1940 and currently teaches at Columbia University. In the following selection from his book, Popular Culture and High Culture: An Analysis and Evaluation of Taste, *Gans describes the tastes of a cultural elite, then contrasts them with those of a very different social group. Throughout his book, Gans demonstrates that American society encompasses a variety of "taste cultures," each of which is as worthy as any other. He goes on to advocate public support for cultural events reflecting the tastes of persons often excluded from the mass media—for example, the poor and the aged.*

High Culture

1   This culture differs from all other taste cultures in that it is dominated by creators and critics and that many of its users accept the standards and perspectives of creators. It is the culture of "serious" writers, artists, and the like, and its public therefore includes a significant proportion of creators. Its users are of two kinds: (1) the creator-oriented users who, although not creators themselves, look at culture from a creator perspective; and (2) the user-oriented, who participate in high culture but are, like the users of other cultures, more interested in the creator's product than in his or her methods and in the problems associated with being a creator. Even so, the creators and both kinds of users are similar in one way: they are almost all highly educated people of upper and upper-middle class status, employed mainly in academic and professional occupations.

2   The culture itself is in some ways more of an aggregate than the other taste cultures. For example, it contains both classic and contemporary items which are formally and substantively diverse but are part of high culture because they are used by the same public. Thus, the culture includes simple lyrical medieval songs and complex formalistic modern music; "primitive" art and abstract expressionism; *Beowulf* and *Finnegans Wake*. (Other taste cultures also use the classics, but to a much lesser extent, and they concentrate on those which are more congruent with contemporary items.) In addition, high culture changes more quickly than other cultures; in this century alone, its art has consisted of

expressionism, impressionism, abstraction, conceptual art, and many other styles. Indeed, the major unchanging features of the culture are its domination by creators and the elite social position of its users.

Even so, there are some stable elements in the culture that set it off from other cultures. Perhaps most important, high culture pays explicit attention to the construction of cultural products, such as the relationships between form, substance, method, and overt content and covert symbolism, among others, although the relative emphasis that high culture places on these varies over time. In recent decades, innovation and experimentation in form have particularly dominated high culture art and music and, to a lesser extent, its fiction and architecture, just as methodology has dominated the social sciences. The culture's standards for substance are less variable; they almost always place high value on the careful communication of mood and feeling, on introspection rather than action, and on subtlety, so that much of the culture's content can be perceived and understood on several levels. High culture fiction emphasizes character development over plot, and the exploration of basic philosophical, psychological, and social issues, with heroes and heroines of novels and plays often modeled on the creators themselves. Thus, much high culture fiction deals with individual alienation, and the conflict between individual and society, reflecting the marginal role of the creator in contemporary society.

High culture's nonfiction is basically literary; in the past it relied on novelists for its analyses of social reality, and on critics who content-analyzed novels for what they reported about society. Today, the culture relies more on essayists for its nonfiction, leading at least one critic to argue that the serious novel has lost its major function. Social scientists who live up to the culture's writing standards are also read, but as I suggested earlier, high culture is often hostile to the social sciences, partly because of their proclivity to jargon (although the equally technical language of literary criticism is rarely condemned for this reason) and partly because they refuse to accept literary observations and autobiographical impressions as evidence.

Since the culture serves a small public that prides itself on exclusiveness, its products are not intended for distribution by the mass media. Its art takes the form of originals distributed through galleries; its books are published by subsidized presses or commercial publishers willing to take a financial loss for prestige reasons; its journals are the so-called little magazines; its theater is now concentrated largely in Europe, New York's Off-Broadway, and occasional repertory companies. High culture has still not entirely accepted the electronic media, but its movies are often foreign and are shared with upper-middle culture, and what little high-culture television exists is also shared with this culture and is shown on public television. . . .

Low Culture

6 This is the culture of the older lower-middle class, but mainly of the skilled and semiskilled factory and service workers, and of the semi-skilled white collar workers, the people who obtained nonacademic high school educations and often dropped out after the tenth grade. Low culture was America's dominant taste culture until the 1950s, when it was replaced by lower-middle culture. Its public, though still large, has been shrinking steadily, partly because of longer school attendance even among blue collar workers, but also because of the exposure to television and other lower-middle mass media on the part of young working-class people who have broken out of the isolation of urban ethnic and rural enclaves.

7 Low culture publics are still likely to reject "culture," and even with some degree of hostility. They find culture not only dull but also effeminate, immoral, and sacrilegious—which is why Spiro Agnew's caricature of upper-middle college students as "effete snobs" attracted so much attention—and they often support church, police, and governmental efforts to censor erotic materials. At the same time, their preference for action and melodrama . . . explains their reluctance to support censorship of violence. . . .

8 Low culture is provided through the mass media, but despite the size of this public, it must share much of its content with lower-middle culture. Often it does so by reinterpreting lower-middle-class content to fit working-class values. For example, in a working-class population that I studied, people watching a detective serial questioned the integrity of the policeman-hero and identified instead with the working-class characters who helped him catch the criminal. They also protested or made fun of the lower-middle-class heroes and values they saw depicted in other programs and commercials.

9 Exclusively, low culture content exists as well, but since this public lacks the purchasing power to attract major national advertisers, its media can survive economically only by producing content of low technical quality for a very large audience. Moreover, partly because of poor schooling, low culture publics do not read much. As a result, they are served by a handful of tabloid dailies and weeklies, some with the highest newsstand sales among newspapers, which report sensational and violent activities—or invented activities—by celebrities and ordinary people.

10 Most Hollywood films were once made for the low culture public, until it gravitated to television. Although it shares this medium with lower-middle culture publics, initially network programming catered extensively to low culture, for example, by providing Westerns, the comic action of Lucille Ball and Red Skelton, the acrobatic vaudeville of the Ed Sullivan Show, and situation comedies like "Beverly Hillbillies"

(which described how working-class people of rural origin outwit the more sophisticated and powerful urban middle class), and the music of Lawrence Welk. Some of these programs are disappearing from the network schedule as the low culture public shrinks in size and purchasing power, but the reruns survive on independent television stations, which are now perhaps the prime transmitters for low culture. This public is also served by independent radio stations which feature rock and country music and brief newscasts that use sound effects to imitate the attention-getting headline of the tabloid newspaper.

Low culture art reflects the sexual segregation of its public. The 11 men often choose pinup pictures (of more overtly erotic and sexually aggressive-looking women than those featured in the upper-middle culture *Playboy*), which they hang in factories and garage workshops. The women like religious art and secular representational pictures with vivid colors. Home furnishings reflect the same aesthetic: they must be solid looking and "colorful." While high- and upper-middle culture publics value starkness and simplicity, low-culture publics prefer ornateness—either in traditional, almost rococo, forms, or in the lavish contemporary style once described as "Hollywood modern."

◆ Discussion Questions*

1. Herbert Gans identifies artists and academic scholars with high culture. Since Gans himself is a university professor, does this presumed affiliation with high culture affect his objectivity and authority? If so, can you point to instances of bias in Gans's writing?

2. How do you suppose a "typical" representative of each of the two cultures would respond to this portrayal of his or her tastes?

3. Gans cites *The Beverly Hillbillies* as a television comedy that exemplifies low culture in its depiction of "working-class people . . .[who] outwit the more sophisticated and powerful." A more recent comedy, *Roseanne*, also depicts tension between social classes. What are some of the similarities and differences between these two programs and their treatment of class conflict? Do you think Gans would classify *Roseanne* as low culture?

---

*Chapters 2–9 will feature questions that elicit an immediate personal response to each reading, progress to a closer look at the arrangement of important ideas, then lead finally to a critical view of specific details. Before presenting this sequenced process of response, however, we want to introduce freewritten journal responses (in Chapter 2) and processes of group inquiry (in Chapter 3). Consequently, the reading selections in this chapter are followed only by a few discussion questions, such as those appearing on this page.

E. D. Hirsch, Jr.

Literacy and Cultural Literacy

———————◆———————

Historically, the high culture described by Herbert Gans in the preceding selection has been privileged—held to be superior by those with power and influence. Consequently, many people equate culture with high culture— an attitude promoted by the poet Matthew Arnold (1822–1888), who defined culture as "the best that has been thought and said." The consequences of such thinking have been felt during the past 150 years as technology and the promise of universal education have raised hopes of a uniform national culture. David Hawkins, a professor of philosophy, explains the process in these terms:

> *It is not just coincidence that the growth of public schooling has taken place over the same time period as the latter phase of the industrial revolution, the period marked by the growing impact of the sciences on technology. This period of the industrial revolution also saw a vast growth of population, and of energy consumption. A few wealthy countries gained and then lost control of the rest. Extremes of poverty in the poorest countries coincided with large pockets of economic despair even in the richest. The early educational reformers could not anticipate all this, of course. But they sensed that the older parochialisms were threatened, that the life-circuit of any citizen would traverse an ever widening territory of concern, and that it must be matched by the spread of education. What had been a culture of an elite minority must somehow evolve to become that of the majority.... The ambition of the reformers was valid and their efforts have shaped us all.**

As Hawkins suggests, educational reforms have not always been shaped by conscious political motives. Nevertheless, any effort to impose an elite culture as a majority culture has political ramifications: some people stand to gain more than others.

Historical facts about culture and schooling provide a context in which to consider recent criticisms of public education. Among these criticisms is the complaint that schools have not managed to instill the knowledge and values of a particular culture as though it were or ought to be made

---

*David Hawkins, "The Roots of Literacy," in Stephen R. Graukerd, ed., *Literacy: An Overview by Fourteen Experts* (New York: Hill, 1991), p. 12.

the national culture. This line of thinking appears in the writing of E. D. Hirsch, Jr., a professor of English who argues that education is not likely to improve until Americans agree upon a core of knowledge shared by all citizens. In principle, Hirsch rejects cultural hierarchies, insisting that any such core must be pluralistic, accommodating various ethnic groups and social classes.

In the following passage from his book Cultural Literacy: What Every American Needs to Know, *Hirsch argues for a national school curriculum based on a core cultural knowledge. The passage is followed by a page from Hirsch's "Preliminary List" of items that might belong in such a core.*

In the mid 1980s American business leaders have become alarmed 1 by the lack of communication skills in the young people they employ. Recently, top executives of some large U.S. companies, including CBS and Exxon, met to discuss the fact that their younger middle-level executives could no longer communicate their ideas effectively in speech or writing. This group of companies has made a grant to the American Academy of Arts and Sciences to analyze the causes of this growing problem. They want to know why, despite breathtaking advances in the technology of communication, the effectiveness of business communication has been slipping, to the detriment of our competitiveness in the world. The figures from NAEP surveys and the scores on the verbal SAT are solid evidence that literacy has been declining in this country just when our need for effective literacy has been sharply rising.

I now want to juxtapose some evidence for another kind of educational decline, one that is related to the drop in literacy. During the period 1970–1985, the amount of shared knowledge that we have been able to take for granted in communicating with our fellow citizens has also been declining. More and more of our young people don't know things we used to assume they knew. 2

A side effect of the diminution in shared information has been a 3 noticeable increase in the number of articles in such publications as *Newsweek* and the *Wall Street Journal* about the surprising ignorance of the young. My son John, who recently taught Latin in high school and eighth grade, often told me of experiences which indicate that these articles are not exaggerated. In one of his classes he mentioned to his students that Latin, the language they were studying, is a dead language that is no longer spoken. After his pupils had struggled for several weeks with Latin grammar and vocabulary, this news was hard for some of them to accept. One girl raised her hand to challenge my son's claim. "What do they speak in Latin America?" she demanded.

At least she had heard of Latin America. Another day my son 4 asked his Latin class if they knew the name of an epic poem by Homer. One pupil shot up his hand and eagerly said, "The Alamo!" Was it just a slip for *The Iliad?* No, he didn't know what the Alamo was, either. To judge from other stories about information gaps in the young, many American schoolchildren are less well informed than this pupil. The following, by Benjamin J. Stein, is an excerpt from one of the most evocative recent accounts of youthful ignorance.

I spend a lot of time with teen agers. Besides employing three of them part-time, I frequently conduct focus groups at Los Angeles area high schools to learn about teen agers' attitudes towards movies or television shows or nuclear arms or politicians. . . .

I have not yet found one single student in Los Angeles, in either college or high school, who could tell me the years when World War II was fought. Nor have I found one who could tell me the years when World War I was fought. Nor have I found one who knew when the American Civil War was fought. . . .

A few have known how many U.S. senators California has, but none has known how many Nevada or Oregon has. ("Really? Even though they're so small?"). . . . Only two could tell me where Chicago is, even in the vaguest terms. (My particular favorite geography lesson was the junior at the University of California at Los Angeles who thought that Toronto must be in Italy. My second-favorite geography lesson is the junior at USC, a pre-law student, who thought that Washington, D.C. was in Washington State.). . . .

Only two could even approximately identify Thomas Jefferson. Only one could place the date of the Declaration of Independence. None could name even one of the first ten amendments to the Constitution or connect them with the Bill of Rights. . . .

On and on it went. On and on it goes. I have mixed up episodes of ignorance of facts with ignorance of concepts because it seems to me that there is a connection. . . . The kids I saw (and there may be lots of others who are different) are not mentally prepared to continue the society because they basically do not understand the society well enough to value it.

5   My son assures me that his pupils are not ignorant. They know a great deal. Like every other human group they share a tremendous amount of knowledge among themselves, much of it learned in school. The trouble is that, from the standpoint of their literacy and their ability to communicate with others in our culture, what they know is ephemeral and narrowly confined to their own generation. Many young people strikingly lack the information that writers of American books and newspapers have traditionally taken for granted among their readers from all generations. For reasons explained in this book, our children's lack of intergenerational information is a serious problem for the nation. The decline of literacy and the decline of shared knowledge are closely related, interdependent facts. . . .

The lack of wide-ranging background information among young 6
men and women now in their twenties and thirties is an important
cause of the illiteracy that large corporations are finding in their middle-
level executives. In former days, when business people wrote and
spoke to one another, they could be confident that they and their colleagues had studied many similar things in school. They could talk to
one another with an efficiency similar to that of native Bostonians who
speak to each other in the streets of Cambridge. But today's high school
graduates do not reliably share much common information, even when
they graduate from the same school. . . .

My father used to write business letters that alluded to Shakes- 7
peare. These allusions were effective for conveying complex messages
to his associates, because, in his day, business people could make such
allusions with every expectation of being understood. For instance, in
my father's commodity business, the timing of sales and purchases
was all-important, and he would sometimes write or say to his colleagues, "There is a tide," without further elaboration. Those four
words carried not only a lot of complex information, but also the persuasive force of a proverb. In addition to the basic practical meaning,
"Act now!" what came across was a lot of implicit reasons why immediate action was important.

For some of my younger readers who may not recognize the allu- 8
sion, the passage from *Julius Caesar* is:

There is a tide in the affairs of men
Which taken at the flood leads on to fortune;
Omitted, all the voyage of their life
Is bound in shallows and in miseries.
On such a full sea are we now afloat,
And we must take the current when it serves,
Or lose our ventures.

To say "There is a tide" is better than saying "Buy (or sell) now and
you'll cover expenses for the whole year, but if you fail to act right
away, you may regret it the rest of your life." That would be twenty-
seven words instead of four, and while the bare message of the longer
statement would be conveyed, the persuasive force wouldn't. Think of
the demands of such a business communication. To persuade somebody that your recommendation is wise and well-founded, you have to
give lots of reasons and cite known examples and authorities. My father accomplished that and more in four words, which made quoting
Shakespeare as effective as any efficiency consultant could wish. The
moral of this tale is not that reading Shakespeare will help one rise in
the business world. My point is a broader one. The fact that middle-

level executives no longer share literate background knowledge is a chief cause of their inability to communicate effectively.

The Nature and Use of Cultural Literacy

9   The documented decline in shared knowledge carries implications that go far beyond the shortcomings of executives and extend to larger questions of educational policy and social justice in our country. Mina Shaughnessy was a great English teacher who devoted her professional life to helping disadvantaged students become literate. At the 1980 conference dedicated to her memory, one of the speakers who followed me to the podium was the Harvard historian and sociologist Orlando Patterson. To my delight he departed from his prepared talk to mention mine. He seconded my argument that shared information is a necessary background to true literacy. Then he extended and deepened the ideas I had presented. Here is what Professor Patterson said, as recorded in the *Proceedings* of the conference.

> Industrialized civilization [imposes] a growing cultural and structural complexity which requires persons to have a broad grasp of what Professor Hirsch has called cultural literacy: a deep understanding of mainstream culture, which no longer has much to do with white Anglo-Saxon Protestants, but with the imperatives of industrial civilization. It is the need for cultural literacy, a profound conception of the whole civilization, which is often neglected in talk about literacy.

Patterson continued by drawing a connection between background information and the ability to hold positions of responsibility and power. He was particularly concerned with the importance for blacks and other minorities of possessing this information, which is essential for improving their social and economic status.

> The people who run society at the macro-level must be literate in this culture. For this reason, it is dangerous to overemphasize the problems of basic literacy or the relevancy of literacy to specific tasks, and more constructive to emphasize that blacks will be condemned in perpetuity to oversimplified, low-level tasks and will never gain their rightful place in controlling the levers of power unless they also acquire literacy in this wider cultural sense.

Although Patterson focused his remarks on the importance of cultural literacy for minorities, his observations hold for every culturally illiterate person in our nation. Indeed, as he observed, cultural literacy is not the property of any group or class.

> To assume that this wider culture is static is an error; in fact it is not. It's not a WASP culture; it doesn't belong to any group. It is essentially

and constantly changing, and it is open. What is needed is recognition that the accurate metaphor or model for this wider literacy is not domination, but dialectic; each group participates and contributes, transforms and is transformed, as much as any other group.... The English language no longer belongs to any single group or nation. The same goes for any other area of the wider culture.

As Professor Patterson suggested, being taught to decode elementary reading materials and specific, job-related texts cannot constitute true literacy. Such basic training does not make a person literate with respect to newspapers or other writings addressed to a general public. Moreover, a directly practical drawback of such narrow training is that it does not prepare anyone for technological change. Narrow vocational training in one state of a technology will not enable a person to read manuals that explain new developments in the same technology. In modern life we need general knowledge that enables us to deal with new ideas, events, and challenges. In today's world, general cultural literacy is more useful than what Professor Patterson terms "literacy to a specific task," because general literate information is the basis for many changing tasks.

Cultural literacy is even more important in the social sphere. The aim of universal literacy has never been a socially neutral mission in our country. Our traditional social goals were unforgettably renewed for us by Martin Luther King, Jr., in his "I Have a Dream" speech. King envisioned a country where the children of former slaves sit down at the table of equality with the children of former slave owners, where men and women deal with each other as equals and judge each other on their characters and achievements rather than their origins. Like Thomas Jefferson, he had a dream of a society founded not on race or class but on personal merit.

In the present day, that dream depends on mature literacy. No modern society can hope to become a just society without a high level of universal literacy. Putting aside for the moment the practical arguments about the economic uses of literacy, we can contemplate the even more basic principle that underlies our national system of education in the first place—that people in a democracy can be entrusted to decide all important matters for themselves because they can deliberate and communicate with one another. Universal literacy is inseparable from democracy and is the canvas for Martin Luther King's picture as well as for Thomas Jefferson's.

Both of these leaders understood that just having the right to vote is meaningless if a citizen is disenfranchised by illiteracy or semiliteracy. Illiterate and semiliterate Americans are condemned not only to poverty, but also to the powerlessness of incomprehension. Knowing that they do not understand the issues, and feeling prey to manipulative oversimplifications, they do not trust the system of which they are supposed to be the masters. They do not feel themselves to be active participants in our republic, and they often do not turn out to vote. The civic importance of cultural literacy lies in the fact that true enfranchisement depends upon knowledge, knowledge upon literacy, and literacy upon cultural literacy.

14   To be truly literate, citizens must be able to grasp the meaning of any piece of writing addressed to the general reader. All citizens should be able, for instance, to read newspapers of substance, about which Jefferson made the following famous remark:

> Were it left to me to decide whether we should have a government without newspapers, or newspapers without a government, I should not hesitate a moment to prefer the latter. But I should mean that every man should receive those papers and be capable of reading them.

Jefferson's last comment is often omitted when the passage is quoted, but it's the crucial one.

15   Books and newspapers assume a "common reader," that is, a person who knows the things known by other literate persons in the culture. Obviously, such assumptions are never identical from writer to writer, but they show a remarkable consistency. Those who write for a mass public are always making judgments about what their readers can be assumed to know, and the judgments are closely similar. Any reader who doesn't possess the knowledge assumed in a piece he or she reads will in fact be illiterate with respect to that particular piece of writing.

16   Here, for instance, is a rather typical excerpt from the *Washington Post* of December 29, 1983.

> A federal appeals panel today upheld an order barring foreclosure on a Missouri farm, saying that U.S. Agriculture Secretary John R. Block has reneged on his responsibilities to some debt ridden farmers. The appeals panel directed the USDA to create a system of processing loan deferments and of publicizing them as it said Congress had intended. The panel said that it is the responsibility of the agriculture secretary to carry out this intent "not as a private banker, but as a public broker."

17   Imagine that item being read by people who are well trained in phonics, word recognition, and other decoding skills but are culturally illiterate. They might know words like *foreclosure*, but they would not understand what the piece means. Who gave the order that the federal panel upheld? What is a federal appeals panel? Where is Missouri, and what about Missouri is relevant to the issue? Why are many farmers debt ridden? What is the USDA? What is a public broker? Even if culturally illiterate readers bothered to look up individual words, they

would have little idea of the reality being referred to. The explicit words are just surface pointers to textual meaning in reading and writing. The comprehending reader must bring to the text appropriate background information that includes knowledge not only about the topic but also the shared attitudes and conventions that color a piece of writing.

Our children can learn this information only by being taught it. [18] Shared literate information is deliberately sustained by national systems of education in many countries because they recognize the importance of giving their children a common basis for communication. Some decades ago a charming book called *1066 and All That* appeared in Britain. It dealt with facts of British history that all educated Britons had been taught as children but remembered only dimly as adults. The book caricatured those recollections, purposely getting the "facts" just wrong enough to make them ridiculous on their face. Readers instantly recognized that the book was mistaken in its theory about what Ethelred-the-Unready was unready for, but, on the other hand, they couldn't say precisely what he *was* unready for. The book was hilarious to literate Britons as a satire of their own vague and confused memories. But even if their schoolchild knowledge had become vague with the passage of time, it was still functional, because the information essential to literacy is rarely detailed or precise.

This haziness is a key characteristic of literacy and cultural literacy. [19] To understand the *Washington Post* extract literate readers have to know only vaguely, in the backs of their minds, that the American legal system permits a court decision to be reversed by a higher court. They would need to know only that a judge is empowered to tell the executive branch what it can or cannot do to farmers and other citizens. (The secretary of agriculture was barred from foreclosing a Missouri farm.) Readers would need to know only vaguely what and where Missouri is, and how the department and the secretary of agriculture fit into the scheme of things. None of this knowledge would have to be precise. Readers wouldn't have to know whether an appeals panel is the final judicial level before the U.S. Supreme Court. Any practiced writer who feels it is important for a reader to know such details always provides them.

Much in verbal communication is necessarily vague, whether we [20] are conversing or reading. What counts is our ability to grasp the general shape of what we are reading and to tie it to what we already know. If we need details, we rely on the writer or speaker to develop them. Or if we intend to ponder matters in detail for ourselves, we do so later, at our leisure. For instance, it is probably true that many people do not know what a beanball is in baseball. So in an article on the subject the author conveniently sets forth as much as the culturally literate reader must know.

> Described variously as the knockdown pitch, the beanball, the duster and the purpose pitch—the Pentagon would call it the peacekeeper— this delightful stratagem has graced the scene for most of the 109 years the major leagues have existed. It starts fights. It creates lingering grudges. It sends people to the hospital.... "You put my guy in the dirt, I put your guy in the dirt."

To understand this text, we don't have to know much about the partic- ular topic in advance, but we do require quite a lot of vague knowledge about baseball to give us a sense of the whole meaning, whether our knowledge happens to be vague or precise.

21   The superficiality of the knowledge we need for reading and writ- ing may be unwelcome news to those who deplore superficial learning and praise critical thinking over mere information. But one of the sharpest critical thinkers of our day, Dr. Hilary Putnam, a Harvard phi- losopher, has provided us with a profound insight into the importance of vague knowledge in verbal communication.

> Suppose you are like me and cannot tell an elm from a beech tree.... [I can nonetheless use the word "elm" because] *there is a division of lin- guistic labor....* It is not at all necessary or efficient that everyone who wears a gold ring (or a gold cufflink, etc.) be able to tell with any reli- ability whether or not something is really gold.... Everyone to whom the word "gold" is important for any reason has to *acquire* the word "gold"; but he does not have to acquire the *method of recognizing* if something is or is not gold.

22   Putnam does acknowledge a limit on the degrees of ignorance and vagueness that are acceptable in discourse. "Significant communica- tion," he observes, "requires that people know something of what they are talking about." Nonetheless, what is required for communication is often so vague and superficial that we can property understand and use the word *elm* without being able to distinguish an elm tree from a beech tree. What we need to know in order to use and understand a word is an initial stereotype that has a few vague traits.

> Speakers are *required* to know something about (stereotypic) tigers in order to count as having acquired the word "tiger"; something about elm trees (or anyway about the stereotype thereof) to count as having acquired the word "elm," etc.... The nature of the required minimum level of competence depends heavily upon both the culture and the topic, however. In our culture speakers are not ... required to know the fine details (such as leaf shape) of what an elm tree looks like. English speakers are *required by their linguistic community* to be able to tell tigers from leopards; they are not required to be able to tell beech trees from elm trees.

When Putnam says that Americans can be depended on to distin- 23
guish tigers and leopards but not elms and beeches, he assumes that
his readers will agree with him because they are culturally literate. He
takes for granted that one literate person knows approximately the
same things as another and is aware of the probable limits of the other
person's knowledge. That second level of awareness—knowing what
others probably know—is crucial for effective communication. In order
to speak effectively to people we must have a reliable sense of what
they do and do not know. For instance, if Putnam is right in his example, we should not have to tell a stranger that a leopard has spots or a
tiger stripes, but we would have to explain that an elm has rough bark
and a beech smooth bark if we wanted that particular piece of information conveyed. To know what educated people know about tigers but
don't know about elm trees is the sort of cultural knowledge, limited in
extent but possessed by all literate people, that must be brought into
the open and taught to our children.

Besides being limited in extent, cultural literacy has another trait 24
that is important for educational policy—its national character. It's true
that literate English is an international language, but only so long as
the topics it deals with are international. The background knowledge of
people from other English-speaking nations is often inadequate for
complex and subtle communications within our nation. The knowledge required for national literacy differs from country to country, even
when their national language is the same. It is no doubt true that one
layer of cultural literacy is the same for all English-speaking nations.
Australians, South Africans, Britons, and Americans share a lot of
knowledge by virtue of their common language. But much of the
knowledge required for literacy in, say, Australia is specific to that
country, just as much of ours is specific to the United States.

For instance, a literate Australian can typically understand Ameri- 25
can newspaper articles on international events or the weather but not
one on a federal appeals panel. The same holds true for Americans who
read Australian newspapers. Many of us have heard "Waltzing Matilda," a song known to every Australian, but few Americans understand or need to understand what the words mean.

> Once a jolly swagman camped by a billy-bong,
> Under the shade of a kulibar tree,
> And he sang as he sat and waited for his billy-boil,
> "You'll come a-waltzing, Matilda, with me."

Waltzing Matilda doesn't mean dancing with a girl; it means walking
with a kind of knapsack. A *swagman* is a hobo, a *billy-bong* is a brook or
pond, a *kulibar* is a eucalyptus, and *billy-boil* is coffee.

26   The national character of the knowledge needed in reading and writing was strikingly revealed in an experiment conducted by Richard C. Anderson and others at the Center for the Study of Reading at the University of Illinois. They assembled two paired groups of readers, all highly similar in sexual balance, educational background, age, and social class. The only difference between the groups was that one was in India, the other in the United States. Both were given the same two letters to read. The texts were similar in overall length, word-frequency distribution, sentence length and complexity, and number of explicit propositions. Both letters were on the same topic, a wedding, but one described an Indian wedding, the other an American wedding. The reading performances of the two groups—their speed and accuracy of comprehension—split along national lines. The Indians performed well in reading about the Indian wedding but poorly in reading about the American one, and the Americans did the opposite. This experiment not only reconfirmed the dependence of reading skill on cultural literacy, it also demonstrated its national character.

27   Although nationalism may be regrettable in some of its worldwide political effects, a mastery of national culture is essential to mastery of the standard language in every modern nation. This point is important for educational policy, because educators often stress the virtues of multicultural education. Such study is indeed valuable in itself; it inculcates tolerance and provides a perspective on our own traditions and values. But however laudable it is, it should not be the primary focus of national education. It should not be allowed to supplant or interfere with our schools' responsibility to ensure our children's mastery of American literate culture. The acculturative responsibility of the schools is primary and fundamental. To teach the ways of one's own community has always been and still remains the essence of the education of our children, who enter neither a narrow tribal culture nor a transcendent world culture but a national literate culture. For profound historical reasons, this is the way of the modern world. It will not change soon, and it will certainly not be changed by educational policy alone.

The Decline of Teaching Cultural Literacy

28   Why have our schools failed to fulfill their fundamental acculturative responsibility? In view of the immense importance of cultural literacy for speaking, listening, reading, and writing, why has the need for a definite, shared body of information been so rarely mentioned in discussions of education? In the educational writings of the past decade, I find almost nothing on this topic, which is not arcane. People who are introduced to the subject quickly understand why oral or written communication requires a lot of shared background knowledge. It's not the

difficulty or novelty of the idea that has caused it to receive so little attention.

Let me hazard a guess about one reason for our neglect of the sub-ject. We have ignored cultural literacy in thinking about education—certainly I as a researcher also ignored it until recently—precisely because it was something we have been able to take for granted. We ignore the air we breathe until it is thin or foul. Cultural literacy is the oxygen of social intercourse. Only when we run into cultural illiteracy are we shocked into recognizing the importance of the information that we had unconsciously assumed.

To be sure, a minimal level of information is possessed by any nor-mal person who lives in the United States and speaks elementary English. Almost everybody knows what is meant by *dollar* and that cars must travel on the right-hand side of the road. But this elementary level of information is not sufficient for a modern democracy. It isn't suffi-cient to read newspapers (a sin against Jeffersonian democracy), and it isn't sufficient to achieve economic fairness and high productivity. Cul-tural literacy lies *above* the everyday levels of knowledge that everyone possesses and *below* the expert level known only to specialists. It is that middle ground of cultural knowledge possessed by the "common reader." It includes information that we have traditionally expected our children to receive in school, but which they no longer do.

During recent decades Americans have hesitated to make a deci-sion about the specific knowledge that children need to learn in school. Our elementary schools are not only dominated by the content-neutral ideas of Rousseau and Dewey, they are also governed by approxi-mately sixteen thousand independent school districts. We have viewed this dispersion of educational authority as an insurmountable obstacle to altering the fragmentation of the school curriculum even when we have questioned that fragmentation. We have permitted school policies that have shrunk the body of information that Americans share, and these policies have caused our national literacy to decline.

At the same time we have searched with some eagerness for causes such as television that lie outside the schools. But we should direct our attention undeviatingly toward what the schools teach rather than toward family structure, social class, or TV programming. No doubt, reforms outside the schools are important, but they are harder to accomplish. Moreover, we have accumulated a great deal of evidence that faulty policy in the schools is the chief cause of deficient literacy. Researchers who have studied the factors influencing educational out-comes have found that the school curriculum is the most important controllable influence on what our children know and don't know about our literate culture.

It will not do to blame television for the state of our literacy. Televi-sion watching does reduce reading and often encroaches on home-

29

30

31

32

33

work. Much of it is admittedly the intellectual equivalent of junk food. But in some respects, such as its use of standard written English, television watching is acculturative. Moreover, as Herbert Walberg points out, the schools themselves must be held partly responsible for excessive television watching, because they have not firmly insisted that students complete significant amounts of homework, an obvious way to increase time spent on reading and writing. Nor should our schools be excused by an appeal to the effects of the decline of the family or the vicious circle of poverty, important as these factors are. Schools have, or should have, children for six or seven hours a day, five days a week, nine months a year, for thirteen years or more. To assert that they are powerless to make a significant impact on what their students learn would be to make a claim about American education that few parents, teachers, or students would find it easy to accept.

34   Just how fragmented the American public school curriculum has become is described in *The Shopping Mall High School,* a report on five years of firsthand study inside public and private secondary schools. The authors report that our high schools offer courses of so many kinds that "the word 'curriculum' does not do justice to this astonishing variety." The offerings include not only academic courses of great diversity, but also courses in sports and hobbies and a "services curriculum" addressing emotional or social problems. All these courses are deemed "educationally valid" and carry course credit. Moreover, among academic offerings are numerous versions of each subject, corresponding to different levels of student interest and ability. Needless to say, the material covered in these "content area" courses is highly varied.

35   Cafeteria-style education, combined with the unwillingness of our schools to place demands on students, has resulted in a steady diminishment of commonly shared information between generations and between young people themselves. Those who graduate from the same school have often studied different subjects, and those who graduate from different schools have often studied different material even when their courses have carried the same titles. The inevitable consequence of the shopping mall high school is a lack of shared knowledge across and within schools. It would be hard to invent a more effective recipe for cultural fragmentation.

36   The formalistic educational theory behind the shopping mall school (the theory that any suitable content will inculcate reading, writing, and thinking skills) has had certain political advantages for school administrators. It has allowed them to stay scrupulously neutral with regard to content. Educational formalism enables them to regard the indiscriminate variety of school offerings as a positive virtue, on the grounds that such variety can accommodate the different interests and abilities of different students. Educational formalism has also conveniently allowed school administrators to meet objections to the tradi-

tional literate materials that used to be taught in the schools. Objectors have said that traditional materials are class-bound, white, Anglo-Saxon, and Protestant, not to mention racist, sexist, and excessively Western. Our schools have tried to offer enough diversity to meet these objections from liberals and enough Shakespeare to satisfy conservatives. Caught between ideological parties, the schools have been attracted irresistibly to a quantitative and formal approach to curriculum-making rather than one based on sound judgments about what should be taught.

Some have objected that teaching the traditional literate culture means teaching conservative material. Orlando Patterson answered that objection when he pointed out that mainstream culture is not the province of any single social group and is constantly changing by assimilating new elements and expelling old ones. Although mainstream culture is tied to the written word and may therefore seem more formal and elitist than other elements of culture, that is an illusion. Literate culture is the most democratic culture in our land: it excludes nobody; it cuts across generations and social groups and classes; it is not usually one's first culture, but it should be everyone's second, existing as it does beyond the narrow spheres of family, neighborhood, and region.

37

Appendix: What Literate Americans Know

paragraph
Paraguay
parallelogram
parameter
paranoia
paraphrase
parapsychology
parathyroid
parenthesis
pariah
Paris (city)
Paris (greek myth)
parity price
Parkinson's disease
Parkinson's Law
parliament
parliamentary system
Parnassus
parody
Parthenon (image)
participle
particle accelerator
Parting is such sweet sorrow.

partition (politics)
partnership (economics)
parvenu
passé
passim
passive voice
Passover
pass the buck
Pasteur, Louis
pasteurization
pastoral (literary genre)
patience of Job
patience of Penelope
patriarchy
patronage
Patton, General George
Paul, Saint
Pauling, Linus
pauper
pax romana
pay the piper
Peace Corps, the
peaceful coexistence

Pearl harbor
pearl of great price
peasant
pediatrics
peeping Tom
Pegasus
Peking
pell-mell
Peloponnesian War
Penelope
penicillin
peninsula
penis
penis envy
pen is mightier than the sword, The
Penn, William
Pennsylvania
Pennsylvania Dutch
penny saved is a penny earned, A
pension
Pentagon
Pentagon Papers
People's Republic of China
per capita
percentage
per diem
perfectibility of man
Pericles
perimeter
periodic table of the elements
Perón, Eva
Perón, Juan
perpetual motion machine
Pershing, General John (Black Jack)
Persian Empire
Persian Gulf
person (first, second, third)
personal pronoun
persona non grata
perspective (optics)
Peru
Peter, Saint
Peter Pan
Peter Piper (text)
Peter the Great (Peter I)
Petrified Forest
pertrochemical
pH
phallic symbol

phallus
Pharoah
Pharisees
Phi Beta Kappa
Philadelphia, Pennsylvania
Philippine Islands
Philistines
philistinism
philosopher king
philosopher's stone
philosophy
phloem
phobia
Phoenicia
Phoenix, Arizona
phoenix (mythology)
photoelectric cell
photon
photosynthesis
phrase
phylum
physics
pianissimo
piazza
Picasso, Pablo
piccolo
Pickwickian
pièce de résistance
Pied Piper of Hamelin, The (title)
pie in the sky
Pierce, Charles Sanders
Pietà (image)
pig in a poke, buy a
Pike's Peak
Pilate, Pontius
pilgrims
Pilgrim's Progress (title)
pill, the
Pinocchio (title)
pistil
Pitt, William (Elder)
Pitt, William (Younger)
Pittsburgh, Pennsylvania
pituitary gland
placenta
plagiarism
plague
plagues of Egypt
Planck, Max

Planck's constant   planetarium
plane geometry   planets

◆ Discussion Questions

1. In paragraph 11, E. D. Hirsch, Jr., says that Thomas Jefferson and Martin Luther King both envisioned "a society founded...on personal merit." Is it possible to define "personal merit" without cultural or class bias? How do you suppose Hirsch would define it? What objections might be raised to his definition? Is it reasonable to expect those who fall short of that (or any other) definition to regard themselves as less meritorious?

2. As a rule, Hirsch is careful to refute opposing opinions with specific facts. In the last paragraph of this excerpt, however, he merely contradicts those who view his appeal for a mainstream culture as an attempt to impose the norms of an elite. Should this be viewed as an oversight or blunder, or as a wise argumentative strategy?

3. Are you familiar with everything in the excerpt from Hirsch's list? Is there anything that you think should be added to it?

Alan C. Purves

General Education and the Search for a Common Culture

———————◆———————

Predictably, the views expressed by E. D. Hirsch, Jr., in the preceding selection have been controversial. In the following short essay, Alan C. Purves, a professor of English at the State University of New York, offers a critique of those views. Purves's essay is the preface to a collection of essays titled Cultural Literacy and the Idea of General Education, *published by the National Society for the Study of Education.*

> Turning and turning in a widening gyre,
> The falcon cannot hear the falconer;
> Things fall apart, the center cannot hold.
>
> W. B. Yeats "The Second Coming"

1   General education might best be defined as the purposeful attempt to provide a particular group of students with a common core of knowledge, skills, and values. The term "general" refers not to the people who will undergo that education, but to the substance that is imparted. Paradoxically, general education, in many cases, is "caviar to the general," and is not to be equated with common schooling or basic education. At times it has been equated with "liberal education," that which traditionally includes training in the modes of thought of the humanities, including foreign languages, the natural and physical sciences, and the social sciences. At times it has been seen as encompassing a broader set of studies. General education, as applied to colleges and universities, appears to be a peculiarly American conception. It is often viewed as also the province of secondary schools, particularly by those who recall the fact that many universities ran their own preparatory schools to provide students with sufficient "general education" to be ready to begin specialized university training. Such schools no longer exist, but the very idea of university entrance or high school graduation requirements may be seen as vestiges of this earlier state of affairs.

General Education and Cultural Literacy

2   The idea of general education is related to the idea of culture, which is something to which people are affiliated as opposed to their

natural filiation. General education has come into the news during the 1980s, thanks to an article by E. D. Hirsch, Jr. and the addition of a measure of cultural knowledge in the National Assessment of Educational Progress. The idea of culture goes back at least as far as the eighteenth century and was spurred in the nineteenth century by the nationalist impetus. Culture may best be defined as Edward Said has defined it: "[C]ulture is used to designate not merely something to which one belongs but something that one possesses, and along with that proprietary process, culture also designates a boundary by which the concepts of what is extrinsic or intrinsic to the culture comes into forceful play." Anthropologists tend to see culture somewhat differently from literary people, but this root definition of possession and being possessed seems to apply both to those societies that operate through what might be called natural filiation (a system of intergenerational and familial relationships), and those that operate through affiliation to some arbitrarily instituted set of relationships. Current "American" culture is a culture of affiliation, whether it be the culture of Hawthorne and Harriet Beecher Stowe, the culture of Black Studies, the culture of feminism, or the culture of "hard science." Some have argued that the idea of general education came to America in its attempt to define itself as America and to define American culture. Others have seen general education as an attempt by American educational institutions to ensure that the European heritage remained part of the American culture.

Any culture serves to isolate its members from other cultures and 3
any culture is elitist in some senses. As Said points out, "What is more important in culture is that it is a system of values saturating downward almost everything within its purview, yet paradoxically culture dominates from above without at the same time being available to everything and everyone that it dominates." Cultures are exclusionary by definition; people who have a culture see others as outside or beneath them, and certainly very few people transcend cultures or are full members of more than one culture, although they may be members of several subcultures, such as that of mycologists, joggers, or film aficionados as well as of the broader culture of "generally educated" Americans.

To be a member of a culture, one must possess a fair amount of 4
knowledge, some of it tacit, concerning the culture: its rules, its rituals, its mores, its heroes, gods, and demigods. This knowledge lies at the heart of cultural literacy, and such knowledge is brought into play when people read and respond to a text that comes from the same culture. It is such knowledge that, in fact, enables them to read that text and is brought into play when we read and write as social beings within a particular community. The lack of such knowledge keeps us outside, as witness the problems of visitors to a national or disciplinary culture who often suffer trifling embarrassments or serious misunderstandings.

5   Cultural literacy may be thought of as language learning, for the study of any discipline or field of knowledge involves the learning of a language which represents a mode of thought culturally appropriate to the discipline. Judit Kádár-Fülop has written that there are three major functions of the language curriculum in school (and by extension the curriculum in any discipline) that accord with the definitions of language functions proposed by Uriel Weinreich. The first of these functions is the promotion of cultural communication so as to enable the individual to communicate with other members of the culture or discipline. Such a function clearly calls for the individual to learn the cultural norms of semantics, morphology, syntax, text structure, and pragmatics and some common procedural routines so as to operate within those norms and be understood. The second function is the promotion of cultural loyalty or the acceptance and valuing of those norms and routines and the inculcation of a desire to have them remain. A culturally loyal literate in physics, for example, would have certain expectations about how texts are to be written or to be read as well as what they should look like, and would expect others in the culture to follow those same norms. The third function of language education may be the development of individuality. Once one has learned to communicate within the culture and developed a loyalty to it, then one is able to become independent of it. Before then, independence of those norms and values is seen as naive, illiterate, or childish. As Lev Vygotsky wrote (1956): "In reality a child's thought progresses from the social to the individual not from the individual to the socialized."

6   When writers such as Hirsch speak of cultural literacy they are clearly advocating the first two goals set forth by Kádár-Fülop and restrict the sense of the term to literacy in a particular culture, as did William Bennett in his report, *To Reclaim a Legacy,* or that segment of general education which is defined as "the humanities" or "American classics." Hirsch and other advocates of cultural literacy refer to a definite body of knowledge (although Hirsch might not include specific titles, the National Assessment suggested that specific titles are necessary) that enables readers to read certain kinds of texts—notably texts that are shared by a group that one might define as "highly literate Americans." These would be people, for example, who can read the *New York Times* with understanding and can also read books and such journals as the *Atlantic Monthly.*

7   The argument for this sort of cultural literacy is the argument that supported the Chicago Great Books Program, Harvard's General Education proposal, and Columbia's Humanities and Contemporary Civilization program in the early part of this century: such literacy brings together a disparate immigrant population and helps the melting pot do its job. Such proposals bore with them the arguments of Matthew Arnold that a common culture based on the western heritage forged

society into unity through affiliation and prevented anarchy and mob-ocracy. It does so not without cost. Again to cite the comments of Edward Said: "When our students are taught such things as 'the humanities' they are almost always taught that these classic texts embody, express, represent what is best in our, that is, the only, tradition. Moreover, they are taught that such fields as the humanities and such subfields as "literature" exist in a relatively neutral political element, that they are to be appreciated and venerated, that they define the limits of what is acceptable, appropriate, and legitimate as far as culture is concerned."

The Limitations of the Equation of General Education and Cultural Literacy

But it is at this point that the similarity between the concern for general education and the current definitions of cultural literacy begin to break down, for those who advocate cultural literacy appear to think of the culture primarily in belle-lettristic terms. Such a conception seems hardly appropriate in an age of American culture in which science and technology play so large a part. One must consider the nature of American culture in broader terms.... Some of the points raised in the debate include the following:

8

1. Given a comprehensive secondary and initial tertiary educational system, more diverse groups with their distinctive cultural heritages are now passing through the system and we must attend to the needs and values of those groups. The current conception does not adequately address these minority groups.
2. Education should meet the functional needs of the students and the workplace; there is little room in life for the sort of culture that is implied by any of the definitions of general education.
3. Any concept of general education must recognize the technological and scientific nature of our society. The emphasis on the humanities must be lessened, otherwise American society will lose out to the technologically more sophisticated nations.
4. In current academic practice, general education exists in the curriculum of both higher and secondary educational institutions. It is often defined in terms that resemble a menu in a mediocre Chinese restaurant; a person has attained a general education if the requisite number of hours have been spent in certain portions of the course catalog, instead of particular kinds of knowledge, skill, or attitude. It is also generally defined in terms of a limited number of academic fields (literature and history, with the social, natural, and physical sciences playing a secondary role). Yet one could easily make the argument that the fine arts,

physical education, and the practical and technical arts should be included in general education. These areas, too, are constituents of our culture.

5. At the same time the very notion of the culture that a general education was to support has come to be challenged on a number of fronts: the culture appears too "Western" and too masculine and in defining itself has excluded much of the world in which Americans play an important but perhaps small part; the culture appears to have excluded the tremendous flow of information and the social and intellectual changes brought about by the new technologies; the culture has neglected the fact that people in various occupations have had to become so specialized in order to keep up with the occupation that they have "no time" to be cultured, and in many cases it has tended to see people in those occupations as without culture.

9   These are but some of the challenges to those planning general education for the students of the next century. To meet these challenges, educational planners and policymakers must face issues that are intellectual, political (both nationally and within the various educational institutions), and practical.

✦ Discussion Questions

1. In paragraph 2, Alan Purves refers to one scholar's view of culture (as defined by Matthew Arnold and E. D. Hirsch, Jr.) as "something that one possesses"—a form of capital, a commodity. Carefully rereading this selection, try to locate words and phrases (beginning with the reference to caviar in paragraph 1) that echo such a view.

2. Carefully reread paragraph 5 and try to paraphrase (restate in your own words) each of three supposed functions of the language curriculum in school. Try to cite specific schooling experiences that exemplify each of these three functions.

3. Purves says that current American culture is "a culture of affiliation." He cites black studies, feminism, and science as examples. Make a list of the affiliations that comprise your social identity and, if possible, compare your list with those of two or three classmates. Is it possible to arrange your list hierarchically—to determine which affiliations are most important?

John U. Ogbu

Minority Status and Literacy in Comparative Perspective

◆

The preceding selection, a critique of cultural literacy, addresses the technical feasibility of implementing its aims. In paragraph 7, however, the author, Alan Purves, refers to Edward Said's argument that issues involving literacy do not "exist in a relatively neutral political element." In the following selection, John U. Ogbu, a professor of anthropology, pursues that argument by looking at the effects of minority status on literacy and education. Ogbu's essay, from which this is an excerpt, was originally published in a book titled Literacy: An Overview by Fourteen Experts.

In many contemporary plural societies racial and ethnic minorities lag behind members of the dominant groups in acquisition of literacy and numeracy, that is, in school performance. It is well known that in the United States many minorities do not perform as well as the dominant white Americans. Similar gaps in school performance between minorities and the dominant groups are also found in Britain, Japan, and New Zealand, to mention only a few. At the same time, however, some other minorities perform as well as the dominant groups or even surpass them. In this essay I seek to explain why certain minority groups do not do particularly well in school while certain other minority groups do relatively better....

Anthropologists ... have concentrated on the effects of cultural differences, broadly defined, in the belief that the problem is caused by cultural differences and cultural conflicts. Where children receive their education in a learning environment different from the one familiar to them at home, they have difficulty acquiring the content and style of learning presupposed by the curriculum and the teaching methods. Cultural conflicts occur when non-Western children attend Western-type schools and also when immigrant children, minority children, and lower-class children attend schools controlled by middle-class members of the dominant group in an urban industrial society like the United States.

The conflict may be in language and communication, cognition, cognitive style, social interaction, values, or teaching and learning techniques. For example, it has been claimed that Puerto Rican children living on the mainland experience learning difficulties because they do

29

not interpret eye contacts as their white middle-class teachers do. The Oglala Sioux Indian children's learning difficulties seem also to stem from cultural miscommunication with white teachers. The Indians, it is said, resist the teachers' attempts to teach them because they are not used to a situation in which adults control child-adult communication. Warm Springs Indian children in Oregon fail to learn under white teachers because they require the use of rules of speech in the classroom different from those with which the children are familiar in their community. Similar situations exist among black children.

4   While I agree that cultural differences and cultural conflicts cause real difficulties for non-Western children in Western-type schools and for minority children in the U.S. public schools, studies suggest that the persistent disproportionate school failure rates of blacks and similar minorities are not caused simply by conflicts in cognitive, communication, social interaction, teaching, and learning styles. In any case, such theories fail to explain why certain minorities cross cultural boundaries, why others seem to have greater difficulties in crossing them. All three theories fail to take account of the incentive motivation in a minority's pursuit of education.

5   In our attempt to understand the school performance of minority children, the field is dominated by what may be called "improvement research," or "applied research," studies designed to search for "what works" or "does not work" in minority education. These studies focus on the microsetting events of classroom, school, or home and sometimes on the biographies of minority children. Such events are rarely analyzed in the context of the minority group's history or its structural position in society. My view is that what goes on inside the classroom and school is greatly affected by the minority group's perceptions of and responses to schooling, and that is related to its historical and structural experience in the larger society.

6   In my research on minority education I have found it useful to classify specific groups as autonomous minorities, immigrant or voluntary minorities, and castelike or involuntary minorities.

7   *Autonomous minorities,* represented in the United States by Jews and Mormons, for example, are found also in most developing nations in Africa and Asia. While these minorities may be victims of prejudice or pillory, stratification does not define their position. Their separate existence is rarely based on a special economic, ritual, or political role; they generally employ a cultural frame of reference which encourages success.

8   *Immigrant* or *voluntary minorities* are those who have more or less chosen to move to the United States or to some other society, in the belief that this change will lead to an improvement in their economic well-being or to greater political freedom. These expectations influence the way they perceive and respond to white Americans and to institu-

tions controlled by whites. The Chinese in Stockton, California, and the Punjabi in Valleyside, California, are representative examples.

Castelike or *involuntary minorities* are people initially brought into the United States through slavery, conquest, or colonization. Resenting the loss of their former freedom and perceiving the social, political, and economic barriers against them as part of an undeserved oppression, American Indians, black Americans, Mexican Americans, and native Hawaiians are characteristic American examples. Similar minorities exist in Japan—the Buraku outcastes and the Koreans—and in New Zealand—the Maoris.

By comparing the historical, structural, and psychological factors influencing school-adjustment problems of immigrants (i.e., voluntary minorities) with those of nonimmigrants (i.e., involuntary minorities) one can show why the latter are plagued by persistent poor academic performance while the former are not.

The cultural and language differences of various minorities vis-à-vis white American culture and language are not qualitatively the same. Such differences can be a significant factor in school adjustment, in the academic performance of a specific minority group. One must distinguish between primary and secondary cultural differences. *Primary cultural differences* are those that existed before two specific populations came into continuous contact. For example, before Punjabis emigrated from the Punjab to California, they spoke Punjabi, often wore turbans, accepted arranged marriages, and practiced the Sikh, Hindu, or Muslim religion. They also had their distinctive child-rearing practices. In California these immigrants maintained these beliefs and practices to some degree.

A better understanding of the nature of primary cultural differences may be gained by studying the situation of non-Western children introduced to Western-type education in their own societies. The Kpelle of Liberia, who attend schools established by Americans on an American model, were studied by John Gay and Michael Cole, who were interested in finding out how Kpelle culture and language affected the learning of the American mathematical system. The study focused on the kinds of mathematical knowledge, concepts, and activities found in Kpelle culture: indigenous arithmetical concepts, knowledge of geometry, systems of measurement, and Kpelle logic or reasoning all figured.

While the arithmetical concepts were similar in some ways, they were different in others. For example, like Americans, the Kpelle classify; unlike Americans, they do not carry out such classificatory activities explicitly or consciously. The Kpelle counting system does not include the concepts of "zero" or "number." Nor do the Kpelle recognize such abstract operations as addition, subtraction, multiplication, and division, though they do add, subtract, multiply, and divide. Lacking any terms for such operations, Kpelle culture has few geometrical concepts, which are generally used imprecisely. For example, when they were asked to name circular things, a pot, pan, frog, sledge hammer, tortoise, water turtle, and rice farmer were all mentioned. For the shape of a triangle, a tortoise shell, arrowhead, monkey's elbow, drum, and bow seemed relevant. The Kpelle measure length, time, volume, and money; but they lack measurements for weight, area, speed, and temperature. Such differences between American and Kpelle culture in mathematical knowledge and concepts existed before the Kpelle were introduced to American-type education.

14   Such primary cultural differences are found among many immigrant minorities. Immigrant minority children confront problems because of such primary cultural differences. The problems may range from interpersonal relations with teachers and other students, to academic work. Under favorable conditions, immigrant children are generally able to overcome such problems in the course of time.

15   *Secondary cultural* and *language differences* are those which arise after two populations have come into contact, or after members of one population have begun to participate in an institution controlled by members of another. Secondary cultural and language differences develop as a response to such contact, often involving the domination of one group by another.

16   In the beginning, the minorities and the dominant group will usually show primary cultural and language differences. In the course of time, a new type of cultural and language difference may emerge, reflecting the way the minorities are treated by the dominant group and the way they have come to perceive, interpret, and respond to that treatment. For example, when slavery was common, white Americans used legal and extralegal means to discourage black Americans from acquiring literacy and the associated behaviors and benefits. After the abolition of slavery, whites created barriers in employment and in other areas of life, effectively denying blacks certain social and economic benefits, but also the incentives associated with the education whites made available to them. Such barriers extended to places of residence, public accommodations, and political and legal rights. Blacks, like other involuntary minorities, developed new or "secondary" cultural ways of coping, perceiving, and feeling in relating to whites and to the public schools controlled by whites....

17   The public schools cannot be relied on to provide minority children with "the right education." Involuntary minorities find no justification for the prejudice and discrimination they find in school and society, which appears to be institutionalized, and enduring.

18   On the expressive side, involuntary minorities are characterized by secondary cultural systems, in which cultural differences arise or are reinterpreted after the groups have become involuntary minorities.

They develop certain beliefs and practices, including particular ways of communicating or speaking, as coping mechanisms in conditions of subordination. These may be new creations or simply reinterpretations of old ones. The secondary cultural system, on the whole, constitutes a new cultural frame of reference, an ideal way of believing and acting which affirms one as a bona fide member of a group. Involuntary minorities perceive their cultural frames of reference not merely as different from but as opposed to the cultural frames of reference of their white "oppressors." The cultural and language differences emerging under these conditions serve as boundary-making mechanisms. Involuntary minorities do not interpret language and cultural differences encountered in school or society as barriers to overcome; they interpret such differences as symbols of their identity. Their culture provides a frame of reference that gives them a sense of collective or social identity, a sense of self-worth.

Involuntary minorities develop a new sense of peoplehood or social identity after their forced incorporation into American society, because of the ways they interpret the discrimination they are obliged to endure. In some instances, involuntary minorities may develop a new sense of peoplehood because of their forced integration into mainstream society. Many appear to believe that they cannot expect to be treated as white Americans, whatever their ability, training or education; whatever their place of origin, residence, economic status, or physical appearance. These involuntary minorities know that they cannot escape from their birth-ascribed membership in subordinate and disparaged groups by "passing" or returning to their "homelands." They do not see their social identity as different from that of their white "oppressors," but as opposed to the social identity of white Americans. This oppositional identity, combined with their oppositional or ambivalent cultural frames of reference, makes cross-cultural learning, the "crossing of cultural boundaries," very problematic. Crossing cultural boundaries, behaving in a manner regarded as falling under the white American cultural frames of reference, is threatening to their minority identity and security, but also to their solidarity. Individuals seeking to behave like whites are discouraged by peer group pressures and by "affective dissonance." 19

Factors affecting minority children's acquisition of literacy and numeracy came from "the system" and from "the minority community." In American folk terminology, "the system" is made up of the public schools, of the powers-that-be in the wider society. Before 1960, the United States, like other urban industrial societies, did not provide equal educational opportunity for minorities. Even today, minorities do not enjoy equal educational opportunity, partly because vestiges of past discriminatory educational policies and practices survive. However, in some instances, significant improvements have been made to 20 equalize the education provided minorities with that of the dominant group.

21   Denial of equal educational opportunity shows up in the denial of equal access to desirable jobs, to positions in adult life that require good education, where education clearly pays off. Generations of black Americans were regularly denied equal employment opportunity through a job ceiling. Blacks with school credentials comparable to those of their white peers were not hired for similar jobs, were not paid equal wages, were not permitted to advance on the basis of education and ability. By denying minorities the opportunity to enter the labor force, by denying them equal rewards, American society discouraged whole generations, especially involuntary minorities (blacks and Indians, for example), from investing time and effort in education to maximize their educational accomplishments. The experience may have discouraged such minorities from developing a strong tradition of striving for academic achievement. . . .

22   Given this circumstance, such minority parents have tended to teach their children contradictory things about getting ahead through schooling. In my own ethnographic research among blacks and Mexican Americans in Stockton, California, I have observed parents telling their children to get a good education, encouraging them verbally to do well in school, while the actual texture of their own lives, with their low-level jobs, underemployment, and unemployment have provided a different kind of message, contradicting all their verbal exhortations. Unavoidably, such minority parents discuss their problems with "the system," with their relatives, friends, and neighbors in the presence of their children. The result, inevitably, is that such children become increasingly disillusioned about their ability to succeed in adult life through the mainstream strategy of schooling.

23   The folk theory of involuntary minorities stresses other means of getting ahead, survival strategies both within and beyond the mainstream. Such strategies tend to generate attitudes and behaviors in students that are not conducive to good classroom teaching or learning. Sometimes they convey contradictory messages about schooling itself. For example, when survival strategies are used, such as the collective struggle among black Americans to succeed in increasing the pool of jobs and other resources, they may indeed encourage certain minority youths to work hard in school. They may also lead such youths to blame "the system," even to rationalize their lack of serious school effort.

24   Clientship, or Uncle Tomming (Tio Tacoing), does not create role models for school success through good study habits and hard work. Instead, clientship teaches minority children manipulative attitudes and trains them in the knowledge and skills used by their parents to deal with white people and white institutions. As the children become

familiar with other survival strategies, including hustling and pimping as well as drug dealing, their attitudes toward schooling are adversely affected. For example, in the norms that support such survival strategies, like hustling, the work ethic is reversed by the insistence that one ought to be able to make it without working, especially without "doing the white man's thing," which includes doing schoolwork. Furthermore, for students who are engaged in hustling, social interactions in the classroom are seen as opportunities to exploit, opportunities to gain prestige by putting others down.

Because survival strategies can become serious competitors with schooling as ways of getting ahead, leading young people to channel their time and efforts into nonacademic activities, particularly as minority children become older, more aware of how certain adults in their communities "make it" without mainstream school credentials and employment, this shift is dangerous. There is evidence, for example, that among young black Americans, many see sports and entertainment, rather than education, as the way to get ahead. Their perceptions are reinforced by the realities they observe in the community, in society at large, as represented by the media. Blacks, for example, are overrepresented in such lucrative sports as baseball, basketball, and football. The average annual salary in the National Basketball Association is over $300,000; in the National Football League, it is over $90,000. Many of the superstars who earn between $1 million and $2 million a year are black; many have had little education. While the number of such highly paid athletes is low, the media make them, together with black entertainers, more visible than black lawyers, doctors, engineers, or scientists. There is preliminary evidence to suggest that black parents, imagining that such activities will lead to careers in professional sports, encourage their children's athletic activities.

To summarize, while such children, like their parents, may verbally express interest in doing well in school, in obtaining school credentials for future employment in the mainstream economy, they do not necessarily match their wishes and aspirations with effort. Black and Mexican-American students in Stockton, California, for example, correctly explained that Chinese, Japanese, and white students are more academically successful because they expend more time and effort in their schoolwork, both at school and at home. The lack of serious academic attitudes, of substantial effort, appears to increase as these students grow older, become more aware of their own social reality, and accept the prevailing beliefs that as members of disparaged minority groups they have limited opportunities to get good jobs, even with a superior education. They increasingly divert their time and effort from schoolwork into nonacademic activities.

The symbolic or expressive responses of involuntary minorities contribute greatly to their school-adjustment and performance problems. Because they appear to interpret cultural and language differences as markers or symbols of group identity to be maintained, not as barriers to be overcome, they do not appear to make a clear distinction, as immigrants do, between what they have to learn or do to enhance their school success (such as learning and using standard English and standard behavior practices) and what they must do to maintain a cultural frame of reference distinct from that of their "oppressors."

28   Involuntary minorities perceive or interpret learning certain aspects of white American culture, behaving according to white American cultural standards, as detrimental to their own cultures, languages, and identities. The equating of standard English and standard school practices with white American culture and white identity often results in conscious or unconscious opposition, showing itself in ambivalence toward learning. Those minority students who adopt the attitudes and behaviors conducive to school success, who use standard English and behave according to standard school practices, are accused by their peers of "acting white" or, in the case of black students, of being Uncle Toms. They are said to be disloyal to the cause of their groups; they risk being isolated from their peers.

29   Furthermore, as one authority has noted, even in the absence of peer pressures, such minority students appear to avoid adopting serious academic attitudes, persevering in their academic tasks. They have internalized their groups' interpretations of such attitudes and behaviors; also, they are uncertain, even if they succeed in learning to "act white," whether they will be accepted by whites. Minorities are afraid to lose the support of their own groups.

30   The dilemma of such students, as one observer has pointed out, is that they are compelled to choose between academic success and maintaining their minority identity and cultural frame of reference, a choice that does not arise for the children of immigrants. Those who wish to achieve academic success are compelled to adopt strategies that will shield them from peer criticism and ostracism.

31   Involuntary minorities tend to compare their schools with white schools, especially schools in the white suburbs; they usually end up with the negative judgment that they are being provided with an inferior education for which there is no justification. Since they mistrust the public schools and the whites who control them, the minorities are generally skeptical that the schools can educate their children well. This skepticism of parents, together with that of other members of the minority communities, is communicated to the children through family and community discussions, but also in public debates over minority education in general and debates on particular issues, such as school desegregation.

32   Another factor discouraging academic effort is that such minorities—parents as well as students—tend to question the schools' rules

for behavior and their standard practices, the perception being that they represent the imposition of a white cultural frame of reference which does not necessarily meet their real educational needs. . . .

Some black youths obviously become more or less imprisoned in 33 peer orientation and activity that are hostile to academic striving. These youths not only equate school learning with "acting white," but make no attempt to "act white." They refuse to learn, to conform to school rules of behavior and standard practices; these are defined as being within the white American cultural frame of reference.

To promote a greater degree of school success among the less aca- 34 demically successful minorities, it is essential to recognize and remove certain obstacles from the larger society, but also from within the schools. The obstacles within the minority communities need also to be acknowledged, which manifest themselves in specific perceptions and strategies of schooling.

✦ Discussion Questions

1. John Ogbu's argument is based on a view of culture different from the one held by E. D. Hirsch, Jr., in "Literacy and Cultural Literacy." How do those views differ, and what are some of the practical implications of the difference?

2. Does Ogbu raise any ideas that Hirsch has neglected to consider? If not, how do you suppose Hirsch would attempt to refute Ogbu's claims?

3. What remedies do you suppose Ogbu would favor in addressing the problems he perceives?

F. Nyi Akinnaso

Literacy and Individual Consciousness

◆

John Ogbu recognizes that literacy and culture are intertwined. However, he argues that given a history of racism and oppression, teaching literacy in the context of mainstream American culture carries political consequences for African Americans. Whereas E. D. Hirsch, Jr., views the connection between culture and literacy as a warrant for uniformity, Ogbu urges greater respect for diversity.

In each of the next three reading selections, specific individuals talk about literacy in personal terms—how they acquired it, how they use it in specific contexts, its impact on their lives. Together, these selections show how gender, social class, and ethnicity all influence the ways people learn to read and write as well as their uses of literacy. As the author of the first selection, F. Nyi Akinnaso, explains:

> *Literacy defies monolithic definition. Rather, it is conceived of as a range of socially constructed practices, values, and competencies regarding reading and writing activities as well as certain ways of speaking. The quality and quantity of these activities are hopelessly variable, as are their effects on participants.*

In the following excerpt from an essay, Akinnaso, a professor of linguistics, describes the Nigerian village where he was reared. Akinnaso's essay appears in the collection Literate Systems and Individual Lives: Perspectives on Literacy and Schooling.

1   I want...you to go along with me to Ajegunle-Idanre in southwestern Nigeria, the village in which I was born and raised in the early nineteen-forties. Located about ten miles away from the town of Idanre, Ajegunle was a small agricultural community with fewer than five hundred inhabitants in 1954 when I started going to school. I was already more than ten years old then and had seven siblings, two of whom were older than myself. The others were much younger, being between one and three years old. Father had four wives. Like others in the village, he was a farmer in cocoa, yams, plantain, and maize, while the women maintained secondary plantations for vegetable crops. We used to work on the farm for several weeks, sometimes months, at a

stretch before ever going to the town where Father owned what looked to us then like a mansion.

Father had several cocoa plantations scattered in different locations within a radius of about ten miles, the nearest to the village being about three miles. Plantations for other crops were located in appropriate places within this area, but usually away from the cocoa farms. Except for cocoa, farming was by shifting cultivation, meaning that a new plot was cultivated for new seedlings after each harvest season. Our routine was fairly regular. Typically, we would wake up early in the morning, usually around 5:00 A.M. There was no clock in the house (and no one could read a clock, anyway) but Father knew when it was time to wake up. The crowing of the cock and the activities of certain birds or rodents were good indicators. Father would ensure that everyone got up from bed and would assist us in preparing for the day's work. An important aspect of this preparation was walking us to the farm on which we were going to work for the day. We usually arrived at the farm between 7:00 and 8:30 A.M., depending on distance from the village, and would work until about 12:00 noon before the first day's meal. Time was determined either by the nature of some shadow or, sometimes, by Father's intuition. We usually closed for the day's work between 4:00 and 5:00 P.M. Our next meal was dinner, which was served around 7:00 P.M.

Father was a devoted worshipper of *ifa*, the Yoruba god of divination. Although he did not learn to divine by himself, he owned the divination apparatus which he inherited from his father, who was a professional diviner. There was an annual festival in our home that usually took place in the month of January. The festival was a combination of ancestor worship, thanksgiving for the passing season, and renewed devotion to *ifa*. Professional diviners were always invited to conduct the festival, which lasted seven days. A key feature of the festival was divination for each member of the family in order to find out what was in store for each person for the new year, and what to do in order to ensure the promised blessing or avert evil, depending on the diviner's predictions. Shortly after I was born, it was predicted during one such divination session that I was going to be a diviner. A few years later, it was also predicted that Father should beware of *esin alejo*, "the religion of strangers," which might divert my life course from divination.

As it turned out, this prediction "came to pass" as Father converted to Christianity around 1948, although without forsaking the worship of *ifa*. By 1950, most elders in the village had partially converted to Christianity. Because there was no church in the village, villagers had to go to the town every other Sunday for worship.

A few years later, a branch of the Cooperative Union for cocoa farmers was established in the village. Partly because he often had a very high annual yield of cocoa and partly because of his perceived stature in the village, Father was appointed the first Treasurer of the Union. Of all members of the executive of the Union, only the Secretary was literate in the sense of being able to read and write and do simple calculations. Two other adults had learned how to read simple messages in Yoruba and sign their names. One of them, who was a devoted Jehova Witness, could read and possibly write in English. . . .

6   Perhaps because of his close contact with invoices and books of account, books (as defined below) and any piece of paper, for that matter, were very important, almost sacred, to Father. He already knew that you could store and retrieve knowledge from books. The absence of a bookstore in town also added to their sacred quality. You had to go somewhere else to get them. In local terms, it was like going in search of a knowledgeable diviner. Indeed, the importance of books to my people is vividly captured in local vocabulary about literacy and literate activities. Thus, as you can see, the base word in the following terms is *iwe* "book":

ka'we	ka	+	iwe			
	count	+	book			"read"
ko'we	ko	+	iwe			
	scratch	+	book			"write"
koowe	ko	+	iwe			
	learn	+	book			"learn, study"
akowe	a	+	ko	+	iwe	
	–er	+	scratch	+	book	"writer, secretary, stenographer, literate person, etc."
omo ile iwe	ile	+	iwe			
	house	+	book			"school"
omo ile iwe	omo	+	ile	+	iwe	
	child	+	house	+	book	"pupil/student"

The word *iwe* itself is a highly generalized lexicon, covering anything from a scrap of paper to a dictionary or an encyclopedia. Invoices and letters are also *iwe*. Indeed, so basic is the word *iwe* in local usage that primary and secondary school diplomas are curiously referred to as *iwe meefa* "six books" and *iwe meewa* "ten books," respectively (I have yet to discover the logic behind the numbers). Interestingly, however, the word for teacher is not a derivative of *iwe*. Rather, it derives from the word *ko* (note the high tone) "to learn" (*iko*, noun, "learning"). Thus a teacher is known as *oluko* (o + ni + iko) "one who owns learning." It would appear that the word *ko* (without the high tone) as opposed to *ko* derives from the vocabulary of learning associated with traditional knowledge such as *ifa* divination. Thus the phrase *ko'fa* (ko + ifa [learn

+ ifa]) "to learn ifa" is analogous to *koowe* (ko + iwe [learn + book]) "to learn or study."

To go back to Father, books, and me, it is important to note that the nearest bookstore was the CMS (Church Missionary Society) bookstore, located ten miles away, in Akure, then the Divisional Headquarters of the colonial administration. While in primary school, Father always went with me to Akure to purchase necessary books and stationery for the new school year. Our purchases were often based on a booklist I had brought home from school at the end of the preceding school year. Father always allowed me to buy books outside the list once I or (sometimes) the bookseller convinced him that they would add to my knowledge. Indeed, after I was promoted to Primary Six, Father voluntarily gave me extra money to buy any additional books I wanted, partly because I took first position in the promotional examination and partly because I was going to be preparing for the Primary School Leaving Certificate, a major achievement by local standards. 7

With some of the extra money, I bought various books, three of which I can now remember as a book on letter writing and simplified editions of *Tales of the Arabian Nights* and Shakespeare's *The Tempest*, the latter two being recommended by the bookseller. But perhaps the most spectacular purchases for me then were postage stamps. I had learned in school about letter writing (which was why I bought the book on letter writing) and pen pals. I had also come in contact with Langfield's and Lennard's Catalogs and known that I could order clothes and shoes from England. I had also learned a curious word in school, the word "hobby." I had chosen photography as my hobby, partly because a professional photographer was, at that time, a tenant in our family house in town. With the book on letter writing, Langfield's Catalog, postage stamps, and additional funds from my mother, I could order a camera from England. Well, I did, but my first order was returned with a note that I was required to send a "money order" and not cash. Actually, I read that requirement somewhere in the catalog, but I thought that a money order meant an order backed up with money (i.e., cash)! Anyway, I went back to the post office to straighten that out and my camera arrived some two months later. 8

By this time, when I was literate enough to order a camera from England, I had become a local celebrity in our village. I had successfully communicated with the White Man in his own language through the medium of *iwe*. My father took pride in telling his friends about my accomplishments. I myself began to feel important and self-confident. My participation in local affairs increased tremendously as I became an "authority" in preparing sales agreements, reading invoices of cocoa sales and calculating necessary sums, recording minutes of meetings of local associations, explaining to local farmers how to use insecticides, writing letters and keeping records on various issues for local villagers, 9 and so on. More importantly, I was occasionally invited to the executive meeting of the local branch of the Cooperative Union to be the "eye" of nonliterate members. In fact, my attendance at these meetings became frequent (especially during vacations) after audit reports indicated that the Secretary of the Union had cheated and embezzled some funds. When I first read the report (of course I had to translate from English to the local dialect) to Father and a small group of friends (who were also members of the Union), they were very appreciative. It was as if I discovered the fraud myself. The farmers later banded together and protested to the Head Office of the Union in town, calling for the replacement of the Secretary, and they won. The Secretary was replaced at the end of the farming season.

10   From these early beginnings, my involvement with literacy and literacy education grew into teaching in the local high school (after my high school diploma), at a Nigerian university (after a college degree) and in various other universities in Nigeria and the United States after the doctorate. Many readers can now begin to fill in much of the remaining detail in this autobiographical account, especially since I became a member of their professional group, circulating my vita, which contains a great deal of what I have been doing since I left college. For the remainder of this essay, I want to concentrate on how I acquired literacy in a nonliterate environment and the influence it has had on me and people in my immediate environment at the early stages of my literacy education.

11   First of all, it has to be noted that I had no reading partner at home. There was no one to read to me and almost no one to read to. In the absence of domestic literacy, much of my learning in the early years took place in school. Our teachers were painstaking and instruction was highly repetitive at the beginning. Moreover, homework was minimal, perhaps in the realization that there would be no one to assist us at home. I was already leaving primary school by the time the next person in my family went to school.

12   I can recall vividly now that after mastering the Yoruba alphabet and learning how to read, I was eager to find someone to read to. Fortunately one Sunday evening, Father requested that I read the Bible to him. He had listened to a sermon in church about Paul, the apostle, visiting a governor. He wanted me to read that story to him. I searched in vain for the passage. Father could not understand why I could not pick out the story from the Bible, thus questioning my claim to readership. Without exactly succeeding in convincing him that it was difficult to locate a passage you never read before (especially when there were no prompts or clues), I elected to read the creation story from Genesis that I had read in school. In no time, father fired another query: Why couldn't I read the story in our dialect? I told him the Bible was not written in our dialect, but in the dialect of Yoruba we learn at school.

Then another question: What did the Bible say about *Oodua (Oduduwa)*, the ancestral founder of Yorubaland? I told him that the Bible does not contain stories about the Yoruba people. And yet another question: How could a creation story leave out *Oodua* and the Yoruba people? The only response I could give then was that the writers of the Bible probably did not know about the Yoruba people. I wish I had the anthropological insight at that time to tell him that every culture has its own creation myth and that the story in Genesis is just one of such myths.

We probably had three or four Bible reading sessions thereafter. But soon after the initial reading trials, my desire to read the Bible to Father waned considerably, largely because the medium of instruction in school had now switched completely to English. I wanted to read in English but there was no one in my family to read to in English. I needed an outlet and reinforcement for my learning. In retrospect, it is not unlikely that this need was partly accountable for what was considered an abnormal behavior that nearly led to my withdrawal from school: I was told that I began to speak English in my dreams. When my grandmother first noticed this behavior, she was hysterical. I was prevented from going to school the following morning. Instead, she took me to the family diviner. The complaint was that I was communicating with my "colleagues" in the other world, which meant that I might soon die, like three other siblings before me. Fortunately, however, Father came to town that weekend and convinced grandmother that my "English dreams" were an extension of my school experience. Father could relate to the *sheme-sheme* (Grandmother's expression for my strange English language) because he had interacted with literate people in the Cooperative Union. He knew that *sheme-sheme* was their language and that the Secretary of the Union and I had spoken such language before. And, fortunately too, as I now recall, my "English dreams" did not last long enough to give Grandmother continued concern.

I eventually resorted to writing letters to pen pals in the United States, England, and Australia. The Langfield Catalog orders also provided me with a necessary outlet. And I loved reading. But my reading was limited to whatever books I owned because there was neither a library in my primary school nor a bookstore in town. There was a library in town within the premises of the local government offices, but children could not go there, let alone borrow a book.

I had a friend and classmate in primary school who came from a different village but was living with his aunt one block or so away from my grandmother's house, where I stayed during the greater part of my primary school years. My friend and I shared similar interests in reading but his family could not afford to buy extra books for him. I shared my *Tempest* and *Arabian Nights* with him. He loved both of them as we shared our impressions about the stories. We both agreed to buy other

Shakespearean plays, most of which were listed on the back cover of *The Tempest*. We approached my mother for extra money to buy some important books we thought might make us pass well in school and she obliged. I can now remember that my friend and I both rode on the same bicycle to Akure where we bought several books, including a map of the world and several simplified editions of Shakespeare's plays, including *Hamlet, King Lear,* and *Romeo and Juliet.*

16   For me, the most outstanding purchase this time was the world map, because it enabled me to locate the countries of my pen pals. My world suddenly enlarged. I was no longer a small village boy, but one who "knows" the world! My pen pals gave me that feeling, too. They were real people, unlike Prospero and King Lear (not to mention Ariel, the spirit) that I read about in books. I felt as though I really knew my pen pals and that they knew me. They encouraged me to write and to write better. My American pen pal even sent a dictionary to me, but I could not use it because the spellings confused me. Nevertheless, I found in these pen pals and the Langfield Catalogs (which I received regularly from England for several years) a literate community, the kind of community that my immediate environment could not provide. Thus, my ability to read and write had transformed me beyond my immediate environment. . . .

17   While I became very sensitive to language and certainly developed more metalinguistic awareness than my nonliterate colleagues in the village, language was not necessarily the most significant aspect of my consciousness affected by literacy, especially in regard to my relationship with people around me. Rather, it was what I and my friends used to talk about and how we talked about them. I had two very close friends when I was in primary school. One (B), male, was my classmate in primary school, the same boy who shared my books and the bicycle ride to Akure. My other close friend was (F), female, a cousin. F never went to school and, therefore, was in the village whenever I went back there on weekends and vacations. Since she lived only two houses away from mine, we sort of grew up together, and I continued my pre-school close relationship with her. I was always eager to see her whenever I went back to the village. However, once she fed me, in about five minutes or so, with details of local events that happened while I was away in school in the city, there was little else to talk about. At first, after I learned to read well, I would tell her stories from my books. But I soon stopped doing that when I noticed that she could not respond. She knew neither Prospero nor Ariel and she could not relate to the story of Ali Baba and the forty thieves because their exploits did not happen in the village. Moreover, they were very different from the tortoise exploits and other folktales she knew.

18   In contrast, B and I would share the same stories with excitement, talk about the characters, and, on many occasions, refer to the appro-

priate pages in the books to explore interesting points of detail. While my conversations with F were always in the Idanre dialect of Yoruba, my conversations with B often involved extensive codeswitching: one, two, or all of the Idanre dialects, standard Yoruba, and English would be used, depending on topic and context. It soon became very evident from my interaction with B and F that I was living in two separate worlds and that B and F were symbols of the two. B knew and was part of my literate world, whereas F knew and was part of my nonliterate world. I soon learned that I needed to keep both worlds separate in my daily interactions with people around me. I had to select the appropriate audience for my "book" stories just as I had to choose appropriately between speaking in English (which was considered an overt symbol of literacy) and speaking in (which dialect of) Yoruba. Because of his encounter with literate activities, while being nonliterate himself, Father provided me with some sort of bridge (certainly not a very strong one) between both worlds. A clear example of this mediating role was his intervention during the "English dreams" episode. All the writing that I did for Father was done in either standard Yoruba or English, depending on topic and audience. However, after the Bible reading encounter, I began to read such writing back to Father in the Idanre dialect as often as possible.

Admittedly, nonliterate bilinguals are also faced with the problem   19
of matching language choice with audience and topic. The peculiar problem for me was that English had superseded my native tongue as the medium in which much of my knowledge was being acquired. While this is not a literacy issue *per se,* the point is that much of this knowledge came from books when reading became my preferred way of knowing. At first, I did not pay much attention to the differences between my book and nonbook knowledge. However, differences began to emerge and became more and more significant as my literacy advanced. My readings of George Orwell's *Animal Farm* provide a useful illustration. I use the word *readings* (in the plural) advisedly because I read *Animal Farm* at least four times. I first read the simplified edition in primary school. It was no more than a story about pigs and it was not substantially different from the folktales I knew even before I went to school. At that stage, the story blended well with my experience, although I knew then that my nonliterate friends did not know the story.

The story was substantially richer when I read it again in high   20
school. This time, we read the full, rather than an abridged, edition. The teacher was a Scot whose dialect of English differed significantly from that of my previous teachers. Since he was my first white teacher and the first white that I encountered at close range, I thought that all white men spoke that way. In any case, the issue here was that he introduced to my consciousness the second level of meaning that *Animal*

Farm was all about. The word "satire" came to my vocabulary, as well as a hazy connection between the story and the idea of revolution. I did not know the full meaning of satire and the connection between the animals' actions and the nature of rebellion or revolution, however, until my third reading of *Animal Farm.* At this time, I had just completed high school training and was preparing myself for the London GCE (General Certificate of Education). I was now on my own, as it were, and started reflecting on all my readings to date. Then I began to make connections I failed to make before. I began to "read" beyond the story. This new notion of reading characterized my approach to my studies when I eventually went to the university. Thus, when I encountered Animal Farm again, it was easy for me to go beyond the story to reading critical commentaries and discussing (an important literacy event!) *Animal Farm.* This critical attitude was sharpened later in that year by my encounter with Beckett's *Waiting for Godot* and Kafka's *Metamorphosis,* neither of which makes much sense if read literally.

21   The critical attitude that I began to develop in high school had grave consequences for my relationship with Father and others in the village. I made the first mistake when I began to question Father about the need for the annual *ifa* festival. I began to ask direct questions about the art of divination. I cannot recall now whether my intention was to question the authenticity of divination, but I do remember that Father read that meaning into my questions. Since I could not show up for the festival at the end of that year (I was writing the GCE examinations in Akure), Father concluded that I had rebelled against him and our tradition. To complicate matters, villagers began to complain to Father that I was no longer as helpful as before because I was becoming more and more unreachable.

22   On the instigation of his friends, Father invited me to the village after I informed him of my admission to the university. He and his friends took turns to praise me for my achievement and for what I had done for them, imploring me to continue in that way. One of them even expressed the group's optimism that I would become the Secretary of the Cooperative Union someday. I immediately recognized the discourse strategy, a strategy that could be described as "praise before you blame." When an errant boy is being called to order by a group of elders, they usually begin by praising him before he is told about his errors or wrongdoings. And I was right; by the end of the meeting, each of them had stressed the uselessness of any literacy that has no direct benefits for the recipient's village. Each of them had told me that the god of divination brought me to the world and has been guiding me since birth. Father did not send me to school to question the origins of my being! One of them even added that the Secretary of the Union who went to school before me (I am sure the farmers did not know that he had only primary education) never once questioned the validity of our

customs. Although Father was never as harsh as some of his friends on this occasion, it was clear that some tension had developed between us. The "usefulness" of my literacy had been called to question.

Of course, Father did not buy the idea of my becoming Secretary of the Union, as he later confided in me, but he wanted me to be close to the people and not raise doubts about our tradition. But by now I had developed certain habits which were not congruent with those prevalent in our tradition. I had developed a critical attitude and a sense of detachment or aloofness. I needed and valued privacy in order to carry out my studies. At first, Father thought that these were mere idiosyncrasies and he took steps to correct me; but my actions were later corroborated by those of two new tenants in our house in the city. The tenants were teachers who had just been transferred to teach in the local primary schools. One of them was, in fact, assigned to my primary school. These two teachers reinforced Father's encounter with literacy and, especially, talk about literacy. They assured Father that I was a very good student and that I needed every assistance from him to be able to continue to do well. Father was skeptical of their comments and, typically, demanded to know how they could evaluate me when they never taught me. One of them replied that they had looked up my records in the primary school and had also heard good reports about me from my high school teachers. The testimony and advice of these teachers and the fact that I won a government scholarship for university education persuaded Father to finally "let me go." For me, it was only partial freedom, because Father kept making sure that I did not forsake my roots. He kept consulting a diviner during every major transition I had to make, even until I went to graduate school.

Father's gratification eventually came when I graduated from college and took a teaching position in the local high school where I had graduated a few years back. To crown it all, I bought a car, through a combined loan from the high school where I was teaching and the village branch of the Cooperative Union, the latter loan being granted in Father's name. My sphere of operation now shifted from the village to the city, as I joined the small group of educated elite in the city. Since my degree was in English, I was invited by politicians and even the king of Idanreland to prepare "welcome addresses" for visiting eminent politicians and to draft petitions on behalf of the king or local government.

By this time, the bush path leading to Ajegunle village had been widened into a manageable motorway and I was able to commute as frequently as needed to resume my old scribal duties. But it turned out that I was not seriously needed for these functions any more because many younger children, including my own siblings, had been sent to school and had assumed those scribal duties. Nevertheless, a rousing reception was held for me during my first visit in my new car. At the end of the reception, a new role was assigned to me. The village had been involved in a boundary dispute with a neighboring village for some time. The dispute centered on the encroachment of farmers in one village on the farming land of the other, a dispute aggravated by the adoption of such perennial crops as cocoa and coffee that made it difficult, if not impossible, for encroaching farmers to move their crops as they would move a yam plantation the following planting season. Thus, arable land, especially near a stream or river (where water could be obtained easily for spraying insecticides on cocoa), became a prized possession. My duty was to use my political connections in the city to ensure a favorable settlement, since the matter had now gone up to the local government level. Thus, my village duties shifted from scribal to political functions.

26   While pursuing this new assignment, a delegation of cocoa farmers from the village, including Father, approached me. They wanted me to join them in negotiating the upgrade of the village branch of the Cooperative Union to a weighing station so that farmers would no longer have to take their cocoa to the city for weighing. Apart from saving costs, the upgrade meant higher ranking for the village branch of the Union. I obliged, but the obligation did not end there. I later took the delegation in my car to Ibadan, some 150 miles away, to submit the application to the headquarters of the Cooperative Union and also meet the head of the cocoa "examiners," as they were called. His duty was to interview the Secretary, Treasurer, and President of the branch seeking upgrade and examine their books. It turned out that the person to see was a colleague in the university and a good friend of mine. Instead of an interview, he took us all out to lunch. We got a positive response on the spot! The farmers were elated. *Akowe* (writer, literate person, etc.) has done it again!...

27   In contrast to villagers' conceptions about literacy, by the time I completed college, literacy had come to mean, for me, a way of life, a way of knowing, a way of talking, and a way of doing. It gave me pleasure and stimulation. It widened my horizon. More importantly, literacy made me engage in thinking as a deliberate, planned activity. The observation and description of regularities and irregularities in patterning became a conscious activity. Certainly, literacy had practical benefits, but I already took those for granted. What Ajegunle farmers considered to be the primary functions of literacy were almost its secondary functions for me.

✦ Discussion Questions

1. In "Minority Status and Literacy in Comparative Perspective," John Ogbu suggests that developing literacy involves a great deal more than acquiring a set of instrumental skills (encoding and decoding

sounds and words, memorizing rules, and so forth). How did the introduction of literacy alter the culture and consciousness of Nyi Akinnaso, his family, and others in his native village? Was anything lost in the process?

2. Does Akinnaso present any evidence that might support the views that E. D. Hirsch, Jr., expresses in "Literacy and Cultural Literacy"? How do you suppose Akinnaso might respond to those views?

3. What were Akinnaso's incentives for developing literacy? Does his case offer any kind of a model for American educators who grapple with illiteracy?

4. Toward the end of this passage (paragraphs 17–21), Akinnaso talks about a transition from functional literacy (reading and writing to meet practical everyday needs) to a more advanced type of literacy. Are the consequences of this transition just as profound as those involved in moving from illiteracy to functional literacy?

Rosa M. Torruellas, Rina Benmayor, Anneris Goris, and Ana Juarbe

Affirming Cultural Citizenship in the Puerto Rican Community

◆

The following selection describes the experience of two participants in an adult education program. The authors explain the history and purpose of that program:

> *In September 1985, the Language Policy Task Force of the Centro de Estudios Puertorriqueños, Hunter College, CUNY, initiated a research-educational project in the Puerto Rican community of East Harlem....*
> *Today, "the literacy project" has evolved into El Barrio Popular Education Program, a full-fledged community-based organization in which the participants are taking increasing directive responsibilities.*
>
> *The Program was incorporated as a nonprofit corporation in May 1987. It has a nine-member board of directors, which includes four Program participants and five Latino scholars and educators. Student decision-making power has also been formalized by the creation of a steering committee. This is the major directive body regarding the day-to-day operation of the Program. It is composed of six student representatives and the staff. The planning, organizing, and development of Program activities are more and more in the hands of the participants.*

The selection is an excerpt from an essay in the book Literacy as Praxis: Culture, Language, and Pedagogy.

Esther Huertas

1   Esther Huertas grew up in Jayuya, in the mountainous coffee region of Puerto Rico. Her family lived in the conditions of extreme poverty typical of the rural areas in the 1940s and 1950s. A number of her 18 brothers and sisters died during childhood. None of the survivors was able to attend school. Esther went to school for one week at the age of 12. But even as a child, her development was secondary to family

needs. As the oldest daughter she was responsible for taking care of the home and younger siblings while her parents did agricultural work, so she was not allowed to return. Like her parents and grandparents, Esther reached adulthood without knowing how to read and write.

As a young woman she worked the coffee harvest and migrated periodically to the bigger towns to do domestic work. Esther was expected to contribute most of her earnings to her family, saving only a small portion for herself. She does not recall needing literacy skills for her job as a domestic. Her resourcefulness and good memory helped her along. She would remember the items on a grocery list read to her by her employer, and relied on recognizing the labels in the store. And when her employer sent her and her cousin, who worked across the street, to prepare for their first communion, they both managed to learn the catechism even though they could not read it.

It was during a stroll in a nearby park after the evening lessons, that Esther met her husband-to-be, an acquaintance from her home-town. After several months of courting, he asked her to go back home to Jayuya, since he did not want her to work as a domestic anymore. He remained in Bayamón finishing an electrician's training program. This separation awakened in Esther a desire to learn how to read and write. Since she could not do it herself, she had to rely on a friend to read and write her love letters. She still vividly remembers the sense of dependency and lack of privacy she experienced at that time. Ironically, her efforts to obtain an education would be thwarted repeatedly by her husband.

Esther migrated to New York in the late 1960s as a young bride. Soon after she arrived, her sister-in-law encouraged her to enroll in a literacy program in the neighborhood. After the first week, her husband forbade her to go. He told her:

> I didn't marry you so you could go off to school and leave the baby in someone else's care. I come home from work and have to be all alone!

Although she had enjoyed the class thus far, she complied with his wishes, setting her own aspirations aside. Several years went by. Esther put all her energies into being the good mother and wife she had been raised to be: "Me dediqué a él y a mi hijo y se acabó." [I devoted my life to him and my son and that was it.] Her husband was the provider, on whom the family depended for economic survival. Since he was a high school graduate he took care of writing or reading letters, a fact that only exacerbated the power he had over her.

Esther remembers having very few friends at that time, going out only to take the children to and from school. She weighed over 200 pounds, but felt content since she was fulfilling the prescribed gender role expectations. Looking back, however, she describes the drudgery of the daily routine: doing household chores all day and running home after picking up the kids in order to have dinner ready by four or five P.M. Her husband would come home, eat, and go to sleep. And that was it, until the next day.

6   Around this time a Jehovah's Witness offered to teach her to read so she could read the Bible. The lady visited Esther every day for a week, accompanied by a male Witness. Her husband arrived from work one afternoon and was upset when he saw them: "Aquí el único hombre que puede entrar soy yo." [The only man allowed to enter my house is me.] Esther complied again, asking the woman not to come back "para no causar problemas y pasar bochorno" [to avoid problems and embarrassment]. This time, however, she longed to have another opportunity: "Si Dios quiere yo algún día podré ir a una escuela y quedarme." [God willing, someday I'll be able to go to school and stay there.]

7   Although Esther was not able to advance her own formal education, she became actively involved in her children's schooling. She describes sitting with them every afternoon while they did their homework, although she could not tell whether they were doing it correctly or not. The purpose, in any case, was not to "correct" their assignments, but to instill in them the importance of education:

> I would dictate the letters [to them] even though I didn't know if they were writing them down correctly.... I always sat down with them until they finished their homework. I'd talk to them about how important it was to study, knowing that I never had the chance....

The picture we get from Esther at this point in her life is quite different from that of earlier years. Active support of her children's education opened up avenues for her own development. It gave her an incentive to go out and start expanding her own social network. She started volunteering at her children's school and assisted the teachers in the lower grades:

> I would have breakfast and lunch in school. I'd help take the kids to the bathroom, tell them a funny story when it was nap time.... I was the first to be present at school activities.

When they were older, she checked on them regularly, visiting their school and making sure they were attending and doing well:

> I always stopped by school. I would say I was going to get a letter and they would let me in. I would ask the teacher or principal, "I am here to find out how my son, Bernardino Huertas, is doing." They would tell me I was doing the right thing, because there were parents who would not show up even after being sent letters.

Esther's participation in school activities won her the position of treasurer of the PTA. Her natural resourcefulness and wit are evident again in her ability to get ahead and around her illiteracy. She recalls with some amusement how she would memorize the accounts and then confidently stand up and give a financial report in the parents' meeting: "Ay madre, ¡yo no sabía leer y escribir y era tesorera de la 121!" [Oh God! I was treasurer of PS 121 and I didn't know how to read or write!] A plaque she received from the school district hangs on her living room wall, and reads in part: "for her contribution to the East Harlem community." Esther's example challenges the stereotype that Latino parents do not support their children's education due to lack of educational credentials or interest.

It was at this specific juncture of her life, when her youngest child   8 was already 10 and she in her late 30s, that Esther decided it was now her turn to obtain an education. She was cashing a check endorsed with a cross and commented how bad it was to be unable to read or write. The cashier woman told her about a literacy program nearby. She enrolled. A few months later, a teacher in the district office encouraged her to go to a new educational program being offered at PS 72, a local school. In the Fall of 1985, she and a group of her female peers joined El Barrio Popular Education Program. This time she would stay.

A critical turning point in the process of becoming literate is the   9 ability to communicate one's thoughts and idea's into writing. This is a practice the women in the program often describe as "escribir de la mente" [writing from the mind]. For Esther this process has been driven by a strong motivating goal: writing her life history "de mi puño y letra" [in my own hand]. The Program has provided a context and a medium for reflection and validation of the participants' lived experience that has encouraged Esther to see her own story as a valuable source of knowledge to share. Esther's willingness to take part in this study is related to the desire to leave a legacy that her children and grandchildren can enjoy in the future. She says that her children are enthusiastic about her writing a book about her life.

> My son tells me that he wants me to write my book and that it should have my picture in the front. Then when he gets married and has children, he will show it to them.

Esther conceives her autobiography not just as a personal document, but as having historical and didactic significance. She wants to record the sharp contrasts between the rural Island environment where she was formed and the New York City housing projects where her children are growing up.

> In Puerto Rico we used to walk barefoot. Sometimes when I was going to town I would hang the shoes around my neck and put them on

when I arrived. And we wore rags for clothing. And now you [the sons] want $60 tennis shoes when the ones you have are still in good condition. And I have never worn shoes that cost more than $30 or $40.

But what might be interpreted as a typical intergenerational discourse acquires class-specific significance in this context. Although by many standards present material conditions seem better than in the past, poverty is still the underlying oppressive reality. Esther wants her children to be well aware of this fact and to learn to fight for what they want.

10   Despite the negative image shed on the poor in this country, Esther is not ashamed of her origins. Her class identity is strong, often expressed in a collective way, "Nosotros los pobres" [We, the poor]. This identity emerges in a context where the traditional values guiding social interaction were "dignidad" and "respeto" [dignity and respect], allowing a measure of self-worth to all. She wants to transmit this knowledge to her children, as a way to prepare them for the tough challenges that lie ahead.

> I remember when I was little.... There was a lot of poverty and suffering . . . but despite everything, we were happy. You could see the happiness. . . . Not like now. Then, with five cents we could buy a loaf of bread and eat. . . . We didn't care how we dressed or that we had to go barefoot, because everyone got along well and everything was fine. Not anymore.

11   When Esther joined the Program she had barely learned how to sign her name. Now she regularly brings in compositions of her own inspiration, written at home, and shares them with her peers in class. Although her compositions are still short and written phonetically, they reflect the expressive capacity that signal mastery of literacy. Within the last six months, she has started writing about her child's bout with meningitis.

> I am going to tell the story of one of my children, the second of my four sons. His name is Edgar, and he was born in Morrisania Hospital in the Bronx, on the 18th of July, 1969. When he was six months old he came down with meningitis. He was in a coma for three months, in a hospital on 14th Street, the New York Infirmary. The doctors would not guarantee his survival. It seemed as if he were dead. He would not move or eat. But I kept my faith, and I promised God that if He saved him, I would go from the hospital to the church on my knees. One day I went to see him and I saw him move, and he started living again. I thought I would go crazy when I saw him. I later fulfilled my promise. Edgar was in the hospital for a year and two weeks. But the illness affected his leg and arm. He continued treatment and therapy in a hospi-

tal closer to home. And despite everything, thank God, he is 19 today and he graduated from high school with outstanding grades, even though he limps with his right leg, and his right arm is atrophied. But despite everything, he leads a normal life. He likes to do household chores and has four football trophies. This is my story for now. Next time there will be more. Esther. (11/6/88)

Esther's educational development is a highly collective family experience. She keeps a pad and pencil on her night table. After cleaning up the kitchen at night she likes to climb into bed and read or write. Her sons often help her with her homework, sitting around her while she works. They read and help correct her compositions despite their limited knowledge of Spanish. When she gets frustrated for not being able to express something correctly, they tell her to write it anyway and to ask for help in the class the next day. Her children are returning the support she has given them, and want her to continue in school. This process has very important implications for reinforcing the importance of education in the home. Two of the children have already graduated from high school.

Writing has become an effective, sometimes cathartic, vehicle for expressing her thoughts and feelings: "Uno se desahoga." [It's a release]. Recently, Esther shared with me a poem she had written one night when she was very depressed. Her children saw her crying and wanted to know what was wrong. They encouraged her to write about it, since they know it helps her feel better. The poem is very lyrical, and concerns love, life and death: 12

> to be deeply loved
> by someone gives you
> strength
>
> but to love someone
> deeply gives you
> courage
>
> I'm not afraid to die
> but I'd rather not be there
> when it happens
>
> but when I dream that
> I'm alive, it seems like I'm dead
> when I awaken.

Esther 9/29/88

Esther's writing expresses the conflicting emotions that accompany the process of transformation. As soon as Esther joined the Program her husband tried to make her quit again. But this time she refused. He reacted violently to her demands for respect, accusing her of becoming "fresh" and "possessed by the devil." He has since left her and Esther is now raising their children on her own.

13   Esther says that people who know her comment that she has changed a lot, and she herself recognizes this has occurred overnight, "de la noche a la mañana." She attributes her new-found assertiveness to participation in the Program:

> One thing I've learned is to demand respect. I've come to realize that I used to let people take advantage of me, even my friends.... They would step all over me and I would say nothing.... Not anymore!

Having a strong support network in the Program has been a tremendous source of power during these difficult times. It has helped Esther deal with her sense of loss, move ahead in her struggle to fulfill her self-defined needs, and to believe in herself as a person with much knowledge to contribute to her community.

14   Esther has formed a particularly tight network with two other women who entered the Program with her. Since they all live in the same block of housing projects, they wait for each other and walk together to and from the Program. They also work together in class, checking each other's writings and providing answers to doubts. Learning is a highly collective process in this context as well, as the women take increasing responsibility not just for their own but for their peers' learning.

15   The staff encourages this collective interaction as the basis where real learning takes place. Esther and her two friends, Rosario and Lila, were illiterate when they started. The three of them have advanced to the intermediate level, and they can all "write from the mind." These accomplishments have raised the women's self-esteem enormously and changed the goals they set for themselves. They also attach a different meaning to their educational process than they did three years ago. When they began they were ashamed of admitting to others that they were attending a literacy class. During a recent case study with Esther I had the opportunity to observe first hand an empowering development.

16   While walking with the three women to the Program several different neighbors greeted them, in some way making reference to the fact that they were going to school. It is quite clear that the experience of getting an education is now shared with other community members as well. Learning how to read and write is no longer a shameful fact to be hidden from all but the immediate family. It is an activity to be proud of.

17   Esther aims to go to college and become a teacher. As she recently wrote:

[If] I had not gone to school I would not be able to write my experiences. I am happy because I have learned to read and write a bit, and I never give up hope that some day I'll be able to go to college. That is all for now. (Oct., 1988)

There is little doubt that she is ready to fight against any circumstance that threatens the realization of this dream.

Minerva Torres Rios

Age 83, Minerva Torres Ríos' self-appointed nickname in the Program is "la nena" [the baby]. This is not just a playful twist on the fact that she is the eldest but that she is one of the most energetic, socially engaged, and joyous participants in the Program. Minerva was born in Guayanilla, on the Caribbean coast of Puerto Rico, in 1905. At age 16, she completed the eighth grade, which for that time constituted a substantial educational achievement. She then went to work in a local home garment shop, embroidering linens, lingerie, and blouses until 1929, when she migrated to New York City. El Barrio became her home for fifty-odd years; the Amalgamated Clothes laundry her place of work for 40.

Upon retirement eighteen years ago, Minerva joined the Senior Citizens' Center at Casita María, a former "settlement house" in East Harlem. She has since enrolled in all the special interest courses offered at the Center and so, when El Barrio Popular Education Program came to Casita, she signed up. She did not need literacy training. As she puts it:

In Puerto Rico, one comes out of the third grade knowing how to read and write. I don't understand what the problem is here.

So, what did this Program have to offer a woman who reads and writes fluently, who is not in search of better employment or of an avenue to higher education?

Rather than empowering her to propose new life goals, the Program has provided Minerva with a formal context of validation. It has offered her the opportunity to define and fulfill a special role within the collective, that of the "Historian":

I don't know, Rina. At this Center they've had many programs and I've enrolled in them all. But, I think this Program is really extraordinary. Every time Felix (the teacher) gives us something to write, it jogs my memory. The other day he showed us a painting of women washing down by a river. Immediately, my mind flashed on the people washing on the riverbank [in my hometown], singing and washing in the river.

This Program, as distinct from the others, has offered Minerva a context for bridging the gap between past and present, allowing memory to become more than personal nostalgia. This has enabled her to reclaim and rename as "history" the experience of living in a bygone period of Puerto Rican culture. Her class essays deliberately document various aspects of her times, for example: "Mi primera enseñanza" [My First Lesson], "Remembranzas" [Remembrances], "El baquiné" [Child Burial]. She frequently qualifies statements with: "hablo de mi tiempo" [I'm speaking about my times], and has expressed the desire to write the history of her hometown.

21   However, her passion for history is motivated by more than a desire to *document* the past. Because the essays are always read aloud and discussed in the class, they are produced for an "audience," the younger Puerto Rican women in the Program. So, she conceives her writing not as an exercise for improving literacy skills or a vehicle for self-evaluation, but as a contribution of knowledge to her community.

22   Elsewhere in the interview, I asked Minerva if she had ever thought of being a teacher, to which she replied:

> I might have become a journalist because I love to write. Even at my age I love to write.

But writing is not the only strategy through which Minerva expresses her historical and cultural ambassadorship. She actively constructs spaces for political practice. Since retirement, she has become an ardent advocate for the Hispanic elderly and often travels to the state capital to lobby. She sits on all the major committees at Casita Maria, has served on the Program's Steering Committee, volunteers on a daily basis in the seniors' lunchroom, collects money, distributes tickets, keeps records, and—together with her equally active 90-year-old friend, Mr. Burgos—periodically volunteers to teach elementary school children about Puerto Rican life and culture.

23   Again, Minerva does all this not just to keep herself busy, to have company, or to improve the quality of her own life. Her role is predicated on a sense of connectedness. For example, my case study notes of November 16, 1988, record these observations from an informal chat on the subject of benefits for the elderly:

> Then, Burgos came along to put four cans of Goya beans into a cart for needy families for Thanksgiving. Minerva pointed out that the two of them are the representatives from Casita María on the Concilio de Personas Mayores Hispanas (the Council for the Hispanic Elderly). They have been active for a long time in this organization, which has been responsible for acquiring benefits for senior citizens. Both Burgos and Minerva stated that they were doing this not for themselves but for the generations to come, so that they would have it easier in their old age.

Both "upstairs," in the El Barrio Popular Education Program and "downstairs," in Casita Maria,* Minerva encounters and organizes contexts in which validation and self-worth are organically linked to the shared terrain of community.

What historical, social, and personal factors helped shape this sense of social commitment? Life history as a method offers us valuable clues. Minerva was delighted to sit down and record her life experiences. We agreed that, together, we would turn her testimony into a little book, as a legacy for future generations. As she constructed this narrative, certain life-cycle chapters—childhood, migration and work—revealed the discourse that organizes her values, identities, and practice.   24

Childhood in Puerto Rico occupies a major part of her 200-page life history transcript. Although my first elicitation was in part responsible—"Minerva, tell me about your youth in Puerto Rico"—I had obviously hit a central nerve. Minerva projects her childhood in idyllic terms, in which poverty and exploitation are tempered by the physical beauty of the environment and by structures of respect, morality, and order in social life: 25

> Our lives were poor but happy because there was no violence. Boys and girls used to go swimming together in the river with old clothes on [and nothing ever happened].

> I used to love going to the beach. We'd get up early, around 5 am and walk down there in a group. Just as we arrived, the dawn would break. That dawn in Puerto Rico is beautiful, the sky gets lighter and lighter and then you see that sun, oh God!

Ever-present in her account is the contrast between then and now. This image of a carefree and wholesome past is reconstructed against the backdrop of fear and urban violence which surrounds Minerva today and which she perceives to be developing even in Puerto Rico. Her own physical safety is indeed a concern, but she is also preoccupied with social disintegration. The traditional structures of "respeto"—of children for parents, children for teachers, and parents for teachers— allow her to feel more securely anchored in the threatening and changing contemporary environment.

> My mother was a very serious person who brought us up very strictly. We had to respect our teachers. I couldn't come home and complain about the teacher because she would tell me that the teacher was right. She'd take me to school, and in front of all the kids give me a spanking.

---

*Casita María rents two floors in a low-income housing project in East Harlem. The ground floor houses Casita's senior citizens' center and the second floor, the Popular Education Program.

School is another major chapter in Minerva's testimony. With great fondness and precision of detail she paints a picture of a local, multi-grade school house, where children of the rich and poor studied together. She tells us how colonial rule meant that English became a language of instruction, that teachers were often "imported," and that the curriculum was largely defined in the United States:

> We had a book that was called *Rudiments of America* because at that time everything came from there [the U.S.]. At that time the Governor was American, the laws were American. From here they would send them over there [to the Island] and they [the laws] were all made here.

Puerto Rican children became well-versed in the major myths and chapters of United States history:

> I learned all the songs from the South in English. "Old Kentucky Home," "Oh Susana," "Old Black Joe," I know all those songs.... I know the story of Lincoln, from my schooldays there, they taught it to me in Puerto Rico; I know the story of Washington, Benjamin Franklin with his kite.... There were classes about Puerto Rico but there was no history book of Puerto Rico. They taught it orally, you know.

> There in Puerto Rico they never taught us about the Mayas, nor about the peoples of South America. I didn't know anything of that. I'm learning it now, because Felix gives us that history, about the Mayan Indians.

Minerva's present involvement in the Program has undoubtedly led her to recall and emphasize her grade-school experience. Yet, it was also a part of her life that imbued her with a tremendous sense of achievement and self-confidence, as well as with skills and frameworks of knowledge, even though these were not to translate into fulfilling work.

26   Migration to New York City at the age of twenty-four was a decisive step. Also significant was the moment of her arrival—the onset of the Great Depression. Minerva's words cut a sharp contrast between life "here" and "there:"

> I was growing up and life was getting more expensive. So I said, "Well, I'm going to go to New York and at least I'll be able to help the family financially." So I did. My cousin sent me a ticket and I came. The trip took five days and I was in New York. That's when hard times *really* began.

After several months working in a scarf factory, she managed to insure herself against the perils of seasonal work by finding a stable job. She recounts with humor and some irony how she bypassed a clerical job in a hospital, commensurate with her level of schooling, because she would have to work Sundays, a factor that at the time she equated with exploitation. As a single woman with no other source of financial support, she opted to work in a commercial laundry because this was steady work. Consequently, she spent forty years pressing cuffs and collars on men's shirts.

> I earned ten dollars a week. Welfare and unemployment insurance didn't exist. It was the Depression. But with those ten dollars I survived until Roosevelt passed the minimum wage law, and I started to earn fourteen dollars. I worked Saturdays, all day, with no extra pay. I worked from 8 am to 7 or 8 at night.

The contrast was further marked by what I suspect was an anecdote of unintentional irony. Filling in details of daily life in Puerto Rico, she waxed poetic on how much she loved to iron as a young girl, peppering her narrative with expressive gestures:

> I'd set up a charcoal stove and heat up three irons. Then, I'd set up a board in front of the window. I would take my iron and "lalalala" begin to sing and iron. I loved to iron! And when the iron got cold, you'd put it to heat and grab the other one and test it: "Tá! It's ready."

Work in the laundry was to have a politicizing impact. Six years after coming to work at Amalgamated Clothes, Minerva found herself involved in a mass effort to unionize laundry workers. The success of this action brought her increases in pay, benefits and job protection, convincing her of the importance of standing on a picket line and fighting for one's rights. This experience contrasts with the idyllic way in which Minerva recalls her first job in Puerto Rico embroidering for doña María Rodríguez, whom she describes as a benevolent local entrepreneur.

If Minerva's sense of class and national identity is very much marked by childhood in another time and place, her political outlook and, I would propose, social practice are governed by the New Deal era that brings Social Security and welfare into being. To this day she sees such programs as positive safety nets for the poor. So, she subscribes to the notions of socially responsible government and the need for public pressure in the claiming of rights. Contrary to most post-World-War-II Puerto Rican migrants, she understands how institutional structures of government and community work in the United States and believes that one must work with or through them. [27]

Minerva cuts her *social* profile through this life-history account. She is less eager to talk about questions of gender and sexuality. She never had children of her own, but does have many nieces and nephews here in New York. About her first marriage she wrote a composition [28] recounting the story of how she eloped with her boyfriend but eventually separated on her mother's insistence. About her second marriage, many years later, she offers little information, quickly pulling the conversation back to topics about life during "her times."

29   Wanting to account for these silences, I first thought that in gender struggles Minerva may feel less successful, less proficient in dealing with its structures of domination. However, on closer consideration, it is also apparent that these episodes do not fit into Minerva's conception of history and her role as transmitter. They are personal dimensions of her life that in her estimation do not bear the weight of useful or important public knowledge. And so, they do not deserve the same attention. However, silences do provide important clues as to how people perceive the contribution of their life history and how they in turn selectively organize its contents.

30   The Popular Education Program has given Minerva the opportunity to write, an activity she dearly loves. It has satisfied some of her curiosity and thirst for knowledge. But, more importantly, it has strengthened an identity rooted in class and national consciousness. The Program has provided the space for Minerva to be a *teacher* of Puerto Rican culture for the younger women. She reminds them, through her extraordinary memory, that she is a witness of history. She also shows how through their daily life and commitment to community people also become actors in history. On a more personal note, I asked Minerva if remembering the past makes her sad. She replied:

> To the contrary. It gives me joy, it gives me life. I don't feel at all close to death.

Memory is a strategy for life and for building the future.

✦ Discussion Questions

1. The stated purpose of El Barrio Popular Education Program is to "mobilize individual and collective resources for empowerment and change." How have Esther Huertas and Minerva Torres Rios used literacy to empower themselves?

2. Do you feel that Huertas and Torres Rios have achieved the type of cultural literacy envisioned by E. D. Hirsch, Jr., in "Literacy and Cultural Literacy"? What specific evidence can you find to indicate that they have or have not? Is the literacy they have acquired more or less complex (or both) than what Hirsch seems to have in mind?

3. Do the practices of El Barrio offer any suggestions about how literacy might best be taught to all persons at all educational levels?

4. Race, gender, ethnicity, age, and social class all come into play at El Barrio. Is it possible to say that any one or two of these variables is more important than the others in the development and practice of literacy?

Amy Ling

Creating One's Self: The Eaton Sisters

———————◆———————

Previous selections have shown how cultural history affects the acquisition and uses of literacy. In the next reading, Amy Ling describes a more unusual circumstance: instances in which highly literate individuals, gifted storytellers, have literally rewritten their cultural identities. Ling, an English professor at the University of Wisconsin, published her essay in the collection Reading the Literatures of Asian America.

1   Feminist scholars...iterate what has by now become almost a truism: that the self is not a fixed entity but a fluid, changing construct or creation determined by context or historical conditions and particularly by power relationships.

2   Nowhere do we find this phenomenon more clearly, even literally, demonstrated than in the choice of identity made by persons of mixed race. Unhampered by physical features which may declare a particular exterior identity at odds with interior realities, mixed-race people, particularly those combining Caucasian and Asian races, are free to choose the identity or identities that suit a particular historical moment. Not only are more choices open to them than to people of monoracial ancestry, but these choices are fluid and may change during one lifetime. The story of the Eaton sisters provides a striking illustration of identity as a conscious creation of the self.

3   As far as our research has uncovered to date, Asian American fiction may be said to have had its beginning with the publication of Sui Sin Far's first short story, "The Gamblers," in the February 1896 issue of *Fly Leaf* and with Onoto Watanna's first novel, *Miss Nume of Japan*, in 1899. If we use an author's ethnic origin as an identifying criterion to classify her writing, then we may say, without qualms that Chinese American fiction began with Sui Sin Far, but we may not say that Japanese American literature began with Onoto Watanna. In fact, we would have to say that *Miss Nume of Japan* was the first Chinese American novel and that the twelve other "Japanese" novels of Onoto Watanna should be classified, despite their themes and settings, as Chinese American fiction (Cheung and Yogi ix), for Sui Sin Far and Onoto Watanna were two of the fourteen children of a Chinese woman, Grace Trefusis, and her English husband, Edward Eaton. Sui Sin Far was the

pseudonym of Edith Maude Eaton, and Onoto Watanna was her younger sister (Lillie) Winnifred Eaton (Babcock) (Reeve). Thus, it is a fact that the two texts named above were published in the years cited and that Asian American fiction, as far as we know, had its start with those texts, but it is also a fact that the ethnicity of one of the authors was very much a fiction.

The lesson of the Eaton sisters is a lesson in the permeability of the boundaries of the self. In *Between Worlds: Women Writers of Chinese Ancestry,* I have traced the context and historical conditions of the turn of the century as background to a discussion of the Eaton sisters' autobiographical and fictional writing. A brief review may be necessary and useful, but this paper will focus on the creation of the sisters' separate identities through their individual choices of pseudonyms and personae. Setting Winnifred Eaton into the context of contemporaneous pseudonymous writers will shed new light on their choice of a persona and enable us to read this choice as a biographical enactment of the literary trickster.   4

The choice of a pseudonym is an act of self-creation, a choice of identity. Pseudonyms are chosen for a variety of reasons, as Joseph Clarke has pointed out in the brief introduction to his reference book on the subject. In theater and film, a stage name is chosen because it conveys more glamour, a more attractive image than the name one was born with, such as Marilyn Monroe for Norma Jean Mortenson and Cary Grant instead of Archibald Leach. In politics, one may be motivated by fear of persecution or discovery, as was Dzhugashvili when he took the name Stalin. Among writers, particularly prevalent in the nineteenth century, one could change one's sex and be more readily published. More women took men's names, of course, than vice versa; however, Clarke mentions one William Sharp who published romantic novels as Fiona Macleoud. Sharp fabricated a biographical entry for Macleoud that was published in *Who's Who* at the turn of the century, as Winnefred Eaton would later do for Onoto Watanna. Literary historian Karl Miller has described the 1880s and 1890s as "an age tormented by genders and pronouns, by pen-names, by the identity of authors" (209).   5

For both of the Eaton sisters, the choice of a pseudonym was a cloak to mask their patronymic and to emphasize their matronymic and for both, even Edith, though to a lesser extent than her sister, the pen-name was a contextual construct. Though biologically half Chinese through their mother, the Eaton sisters were culturally English and Canadian. In her 1909 autobiographical essay, "Leaves from the Mental Portfolio of an Eurasian," Edith relates that their mother as a child was adopted by an English couple, educated in English schools and always dressed in Western clothes. Edith and five siblings were born in England before the family immigrated to America, arriving in Hudson City, New York, in the early 1870s and finally settling in Mont-   6 real, Quebec, where Winnifred was born. Edith writes that at age six when she saw her first Chinese workmen, "uncouth specimens of their race, dressed in working blouses and pantaloons with queues hanging down their backs, I recoiled with a sense of shock" (126). In their childhood home in Montreal, their mother read them Tennyson's *Idylls of the King*; the children took parts and performed minidramas. Several children wrote poetry, but all communication within the family was in English. Edith notes that when she began her work in the Chinese community, one drawback was that "save for a few phrases, I am unacquainted with my mother tongue." Furthermore, "the Americanized Chinamen actually laugh in my face when I tell them that I am of their race" (131).

7   Nonetheless, since only three Chinese women resided in Montreal in the 1870s, Grace Eaton's ethnicity colored all, and the perception of outsiders was that this was a Chinese family. To be Chinese at this period and for several preceding decades was to be considered subhuman by the dominant society. After the Civil War had abolished black slave labor, workers by the thousands were imported from China to complete the transcontinental railroad and to supply agricultural labor. However, in the 1870s, when an economic depression ensued, Chinese laborers became the scapegoat. The ambivalence of North America's attitude toward the Chinese is clear in the words of a Montana journalist, published in *The Montanian*, March 27, 1873: "We don't mind hearing of a Chinaman being killed now and then, but it has been coming too thick of late. . . . Soon there will be a scarcity of Chinese cheap labor in the country. . . . Don't kill them unless they deserve it, but when they do—why kill 'em lots" (Lyman 165). On the one hand, the Chinese were desirable as cheap labor; on the other hand, they were like vermin, deserving of extermination.

8   In this hostile climate, prevalent throughout Canada and the United States, the Eaton sisters grew to maturity. Perceived as Chinese, they were subject to all the abuse heaped on that group. One sister, Grace, reported that a girl at school refused to sit next to her because she was Chinese. A young man in their dancing class said he'd "rather marry a pig than a girl with Chinese blood in her veins" (Far 130). Years later, a dinner conversation recorded in Edith's autobiographical essay demonstrates the continued persistence of sinophobia. Edith, then in the United States, had just obtained a position "in a little [midwest] town away off on the north shore of a big lake." Among those at the dinner table were her new employer, her new landlady, the town clerk, and a young girl. A trainload of Chinese workers passing through the town sparked the ensuing conversation:

> My employer shakes his rugged head. "Somehow or other," says he, "I cannot reconcile myself to the thought that the Chinese are humans

like ourselves. They may have immortal souls, but their faces seem so utterly devoid of expression that I cannot help but doubt."

"Souls," echoes the town clerk. "Their bodies are enough for me. A Chinaman is, in my eyes, more repulsive than a nigger."

"They always give me such a creepy feeling," puts in the young girl with a laugh.

"Now I wouldn't have one in my house," declares my landlady.

"Now the Japanese are different altogether. There is something bright and likeable about those men," continues Mr. K. (Far 129)

Edith, though tempted to keep silent after this conversation, spoke out, identified herself as Chinese and left that town—an act of courage and defiance. She made it her life's work to defend her mother's much maligned race, and a Chinese pen-name served her purpose well. Winnifred, however, chose to be the admired "oriental." 9

To understand why the Japanese were admired, we have only to look at a few facts of history. First, there were few Japanese in the United States in the late nineteenth century and therefore they were not an alternate labor source posing an economic threat to white workers. Second, Japan, an island empire, had fought and defeated two large continental nations—China in 1895 and Russia in 1905. Japanese militarism was seen as the noble embodiment of the samurai tradition until it was directed against the United States decades later, at Pearl Harbor. 10

Since the Chinese and Japanese were indistinguishable to Western eyes and since Edith was already mining the Chinese vein, Winnifred Eaton chose to be Japanese. Her choice paid off, in the form of astonishing success. She published hundreds of short stores in national magazines and two dozen novels that were nearly all best sellers, most published by Harpers. Several novels were translated into many European languages. Her second novel, *A Japanese Nightingale* (1901), was adapted as a play and performed on Broadway in 1903 to compete with David Belasco's long-running *Madame Butterfly*. From 1924 to 1931 Onoto Watanna wrote scripts for Hollywood and for a period was chief scenarist for Universal Studios. She had a play produced in Paris, "The Road to Honor," and worked on such early films as "Show Boat," "Phantom of the Opera," and "Shanghai Lady" before retiring with her second husband, Francis Reeve, to Calgary, Alberta. 11

Winnifred Eaton was the author of her own life story in supplying *Who's Who* with the following "facts": born in 1879 in Nagasaki, Japan, to a Japanese noblewoman. Her actual birth year was 1875, her birthplace Montreal and her mother, of course, Chinese. In a very literal way, Winnifred created herself, drawing no distinctions between her books and her life, extending her fiction-making skills into her life. Her keen marketing instinct and sense of timing were precisely accurate, for orientalism was in full flower at the turn of the century. Her sense of 12 the importance of ethnic validity as manifested in a name, however, was so strong that it overshadowed her belief in her imagination and her storytelling powers, both of which were considerable. In midcareer, for example, Winnifred submitted a novel in Irish American dialect, *The Diary of Delia,* under the name Winnifred Mooney. The publisher, Doubleday, chose to publish this book under her well-known pseudonym, Onoto Watanna. Thus, for the first, and undoubtedly only, time in literary history, we have a novel written in Irish American dialect by a Chinese Eurasian Canadian published under a Japanese name. (In so blatantly disregarding boundaries and facts, she has given literary scholars a major headache: how do we classify this anomaly?)

13   In her excellent study, *Dark Twins: Imposture and Identity in Mark Twain's America,* Susan Gillman differentiates between British writers whose pen-names were neutral and innocuous, such as George Eliot or Acton, Currer and Ellis Bell, and Americans who chose names that dramatized and fostered a personality cult, such as Artemus Ward, Petroleum V. Nasby, Josh Billings, and Mark Twain. She quotes Walter Benjamin, who criticized this tendency still manifested in our present-day film industry: "The cult of the movie star... preserves not the unique aura of the person but 'the spell of the personality,' the phony spell of a commodity" (29). Clearly Onoto Watanna's name had become a commodity too valuable to ignore.

14   Sui Sin Far is Cantonese for narcissus, also known as "Chinese Lily." Onoto Watanna sounds Japanese but is not a legitimate Japanese name. Each sister selected a pseudonym to authenticate the subject matter she had chosen to make her own. It was a choice not all of their siblings made. With English names and racially indeterminate facial features, the racial identification of the Eaton offspring, on reaching adulthood, varied. The eldest son, Edward, denied his Chinese heritage, marrying an aristocratic white woman who had little to do with her parents-in-law and joining a Montreal rifle club whose members were exclusively Anglo-Canadian. One sister, May, is believed to be the Eurasian described in "Leaves" in this fashion:

> Her face is plastered with a thick white coat of paint and her eyelids and eyebrows are blackened so that the shape of her eyes and the whole expression of her face is changed.... Living for many years among the working class, she had heard little but abuse of the Chinese. It is not difficult in a land like California, for a half Chinese, half white girl to pass as one of Spanish or Mexican origin. This the poor child does, tho she lives in nervous dread of being "discovered." (131)

Though their specific choices differed, all of the Eaton children were responding to the same hostile environment. Despite the differences in their specific choices—passing as Mexican, as English, as Japanese, as

Chinese—there were essentially only two responses to their embattled position: resistance or accommodation. Edith was the only one among fourteen children to choose resistance, the more difficult and more noble path.

Conventional wisdom decrees that "honesty is the best policy,"   15 that integrity and truthfulness are noble while lying and accommodation are cowardly and condemnable. And yet, should accommodation always be condemned? If we look more closely at the situation, can we not deconstruct this hierarchy?

We can begin by noting that in nature and in warfare, for example,   16 the fittest survive, and survival depends on adaptation to one's environment. Camouflage is not only a legitimate strategy but a clever and critical one. Was it not the British soldiers' red coats and straight military lines that made them easy targets during the Revolutionary War? Is not the broad-leaved, thick-trunked oak that stands firm against the wind more easily blown over and uprooted than the thin, pliant, hollow-centered bamboo? Ironically, Edith in asserting her Chinese ancestry was like the English oak, while Winnifred, in assuming a Japanese persona, was more like the bamboo, regarded by the Chinese as a symbol of nobility. What Rosenblatt noted as true of Afro-Americans like Malcolm X also held true for Asian Americans like Winnifred Eaton: "Recognizing an elusive and unpredictable situation, they adapt to it for survival, becoming masters of both physical and psychological disguise, in part to avoid their hunters" (175).

In *Dark Twins*, Gillman represents "that process of continual self-con-   17 struction and destruction by someone who is both critic and child of his culture" (13). Though Gillman is writing of Samuel Clemens, this was equally true of Winnifred Eaton. In assuming a Japanese persona, and making liberal use of orientalist materials in her novels, she was a child of her culture and yet, since all was a conscious fantasy and in time a disillusionment, she was a critic of it as well. The dark twin is a trope for the Other within the Self, and the pseudonym is a manifestation of that inner split. Though Gillman recognizes the moral dimensions of imposture, she sees it primarily as a useful strategy for the writer:

> Since "posture" already implies posing or faking, "imposture" is the pose of a pose, the fake of a fake. The word implies no possible return to any point of origin. Synonyms for imposture complicate this ambiguity by distinguishing degrees of intentionality on the part of the impostor. "Deceit" is strongly condemnatory because it refers to "purposeful" deceiving or misleading, whereas "counterfeit" and "fake" may or may not condemn "depending on culpable intent to deceive." Thus imposture raises but does not resolve complex connections between morality and intentionality. Its multiple confusions leave room for lawyers, confidence men, and, ultimately, the writer himself to

erase boundaries and circumvent the law, making suspect the premise
that knowledge is possible—by legal or any other means. (6)

Further, Gillman writes: "The confidence man presides over the comic
tale as hero, not villain. Simon Suggs, a character created by Johnson J.
Hooper, another humorist, proclaims in his favorite motto, 'It is good
to be shifty in a new country'" (22).

18   It is crucial to remember that the trickster figure from the perspective of the disempowered is a hero, not a villain. In situations when
power is unequal and legally obtained justice is impossible, outsmart-
ing the system is the only means of resistance available. In folk tales of
Native Americans and African Americans, the trickster figure—despite
what would normally be considered faults—chicanery, cheating, and
lying—has the sympathy of the audience because it is through this
clever deviousness and deception that unjust situations too large and
too difficult for the small person to handle are overcome and victory or
a balance of the scales is achieved. In this inversion of established
power, the powerless person may take vicarious delight. Furthermore,
in contrast to the flexibility and variousness of the trickster, the morally
sanctioned stance of his/her opponent at the top of the established
hierarchy appears foolishly rigid. Thus, we may read the novels of
Onoto Watanna as the brain children of Asian America's first trickster
hero.

19   Undoubtedly Suggs was not the only person who realized that a
new country provides a fresh start, releasing one from the constraints
of the past, from the restraints of family and of history. One has the
freedom to create oneself anew, and the West, both in Canada and the
United States, in the late nineteenth and early twentieth centuries was
still a relatively "new" country. Under the big tolerant skies of the prai-
ries, and in valleys protected by tall mountains, anything seemed possible; one had only to assert it. Winnifred Eaton had at least two well-
known contemporaries in Western Canada who, like her, assumed personae unsubstantiated or not wholly substantiated by facts.

20   The first of these was Grey Owl (1888–1938). He claimed to be the
son of an Apache Indian and a Scot and achieved an international reputation as a writer/naturalist, whom the London *Times* called a Canadian Thoreau. Unlike Thoreau, who spent only two years at Walden
Pond and was always within walking distance of Concord, Grey Owl
lived much of his adult life far from civilization and in close harmony
with the animals of the woods, particularly beavers. His love of beavers and their regard for him were captured, incredibly, on film that
showed the beavers swimming back and forth bringing sticks to repair
his cabin. Initially a trapper, he was convinced by his Iroquois wife,
Anahareo, of the need for conservation, the central theme of his writing
and of their work. The couple's success in creating a sanctuary for bea-

vers in northern Quebec, described in Grey Owl's book, *Pilgrims of the Wild* (1930), attracted the attention of the Canadian government, which then appointed him Honorary Park Warden and built a home for Anahareo, Grey Owl, and their beavers at Lake Ajawaan in Prince Albert National Park, Saskatchewan. His many articles and four books were so popular that he made two highly successful lecture tours of England and the United States in 1935–36 and 1937–38, concluding with a lecture before the royal family at Buckingham Palace. After his death in 1938, a great public furor followed the discovery that Grey Owl had had no Indian blood at all and was born Archibald Stansfeld Belany in Hastings, England.

Reared by two maiden aunts and his grandmother, Belany had an unhappy childhood and a passion for North American Indians. In his late teens, he immigrated to Canada, became a guide and packer in Northern Ontario, and lived six years with a band of Ojibwa Indians on Bear Island in Lake Temagami. By his own account, he was adopted into this tribe and given the name Grey Owl. In 1910 he married an Ojibwa woman, Angela Eguana, but left the tribe in 1912 to serve in World War I and was wounded in service. While recuperating in England in 1917, he married his childhood sweetheart, Constance Holmes. This marriage was brief, for he soon returned to Canada, where, in 1926, he married Anahareo. This marriage was the turning point of his life. After his death, Anahareo wrote two books about him, *My Life with Grey Owl* (1940) and the more revealingly titled *Devil in Deerskins* (1972). His grave is beside his cabin on Lake Ajawaan in Prince Albert National Park. The original cross with his English name was replaced with a stone bearing the name Grey Owl, as if to assert that the identity he had chosen and created was of greater lasting significance than the one thrust upon him at birth. 21

The other notable persona of this period was Long Lance, another celebrated Indian, whose years (1919–27) in Calgary overlapped with Winnifred's. He, like Sui Sin Far, began as a journalist. In Calgary, he discovered his calling when he began to visit Indian reserves in the outskirts of Calgary and then published articles about the plight of the various Indian tribes of western Canada. In 1922 he was adopted into the Blackfoot tribe and given the name Buffalo Child, a warrior known for his bravery. In 1923, Long Lance staged a kidnapping of the mayor of Calgary as a publicity stunt for the Calgary Stampede. His biographer, Donald Smith, describes the event in this way: 22

> Long Lance with seven chiefs and a healthy assortment of Blackfoot, Stoney and Sarcee warriors all painted and feathered and mounted on war ponies charged down 7th Avenue to City Hall. Led by Long Lance, they entered the mayor's office, ordered him to vacate his chair and installed Running Rabbit (who spoke no English) as mayor. Pho-

tographers recorded the "event." Mayor Webster was tied to a horse and ridden to the center of the city (8th Avenue and 1st Street West). The Indian mayor officially adopted the captive white mayor as Blackfoot, naming him Chief Crowfoot, and then returned the charge of the city to the white chief who was now one of them. (110)

23   Though one cannot help thinking of this as an elaborate charade invented and relished by boys who have refused to grow up, Long Lance carried off the stunt with such aplomb that the story "made a great splash in Eastern Canada" and in the United States (Smith 106). He had himself photographed astride an Indian pinto attired in white buckskins, mocassins, and full feather war headdress. When an Indian was sought to play the starring role in "The Silent Enemy," a silent film about Indians, Long Lance was called to Hollywood. Despite his public high jinks and celebrity, his private life was unfulfilled; he never married, cut himself off from his family, had no close friends, and shot himself on March 20, 1932, at the estate of Anita Baldwin, a rich philanthropist, outside Los Angeles. He was forty-two years old.

24   Long Lance was born Sylvester Long in Winston-Salem, North Carolina, on December 1, 1890, to parents who claimed exclusively white and Indian blood. His mother was three-quarters white and one-quarter Croatan. Despite the family's denial, however, photographs of his father and brother show them to have strongly African features, though Long Lance himself, in the photographs, seemed to have straight hair. Smith explains that discrimination against black people in the American south was so oppressive that Sylvester Long "got out and asserted his Indian heritage." Claiming Cherokee blood, Sylvester Long gained admission to Carlyle Indian School, though when Carlyle School investigated further, the Cherokee nation disclaimed any knowledge of him. After graduation, he applied to West Point but decided instead to join the Royal Canadian Air Force. Here, again, he ran into difficulties concerning his claim of an Indian identity and finally decided to go west in search of his fortune.

25   What all four—Mark Twain, Onoto Watanna, Grey Owl, and Long Lance—had in common, in addition to the use of pseudonyms, of course, was the means by which all made their living. To be a good writer, one must be a good storyteller. Where does one draw the boundary between fiction and lying? And, to play the devil's advocate, why must storytelling cease when one's own life is concerned? Who among us does not enjoy the pleasures of "hamming it up" and role-playing?

26   Furthermore, according to William James humbugging may be a universal trait. In "Final Impressions of a Psychic Researcher," James asserts that the medium's "will to personate" raises "questions about our subconscious constitution and its curious tendency to humbug." He tentatively concludes that far from being uncommon, "every sort of

person is liable to it [humbugging], or to something equivalent to it" (Gilman 163–64). Is this statement an indictment of the human race or a description of one of our imaginative and unique pleasures? Is the assumption of a persona merely telling a useless lie or is it pointing out a useful truth about the values of the society in which we live?

I would argue that, in cases where no harm to others is done by the deception, assuming a persona is a form of defiance to free one's self from the fetters applied by a society concerned with the insignificancies of skin color and eye shape. To exploit, consciously and cynically, the prejudices and stereotypes of the dominant society in its misperceptions of the racial minority in its midst is one step toward exploding the prejudices. As the grandfather in Ellison's *Invisible Man* advised his grandson, "Agree 'em to death and destruction" (497). Clearly, though her own personal stance differed from her younger sister's, Edith Eaton wrote in her defense in "Leaves":

> The Americans, having for many years manifested a much higher regard for the Japanese than for the Chinese, several half Chinese young men and women, thinking to advance themselves, both in a social and business sense, pass as Japanese. They continue to be known as Eurasians; but a Japanese Eurasian does not appear in the same light as a Chinese Eurasian. The unfortunate Chinese Eurasians! Are not those who compel them to thus cringe more to be blamed than they? (Far 131)

Edith Eaton makes a strong and irrefutable point. The creation of a more acceptable identity, particularly in the cases of Winnifred Eaton/ Onoto Watanna and Sylvester Long/Long Lance, is indeed a defensive reaction to an unacceptable embattled situation: the rejection and devaluation of the biological self. For this provocation, the society that made such harsh judgments in the first place should be called to account.

WORKS CITED

Clarke, Joseph F. *Pseudonyms*. Nashville: T. Nelson, 1977.

De Laurentis, Teresa. *Feminist Studies/Critical Studies*. Bloomington: Indiana University Press, 1988.

Ellison, Ralph. *Invisible Man*. New York: Signet, 1952.

Far, Sui Sin. "Leaves from the Mental Portfolio of an Eurasian." *Independent*, January 21, 1909. 125–32.

Gillman, Susan. *Dark Twins: Imposture and Identity in Mark Twain's America*. Chicago: University of Chicago Press, 1989.

Kondo, Dorinne. *Crafting Selves: Power, Gender, and Discourses of Identity in a Japanese Workplace*. Chicago: University of Chicago Press, 1990.

Ling, Amy. *Between Worlds: Women Writers of Chinese Ancestry*. New York: Pergamon Press, 1990.

Lyman, Stanford. "Strangers in the City: The Chinese in the Urban Frontier." In *Roots: An Asian American Reader*, ed. Amy Tachiki, Eddie Wong, Franklin Odo, and Buck Wong. Los Angeles: University of California, Los Angeles, Asian American Studies Center, 1971. 159–87.

Miller, Karl. *Doubles: Studies in Literary History.* New York: Oxford University Press, 1985.

Oxford Companion to Canadian Literature, ed. William Toye. New York: Oxford University Press, 1983.

Rosenblatt, Roger. "Black Autobiography: Life as the Death Weapon." In *Autobiography: Essays Theoretical and Critical,* ed. James Olney. Princeton, N.J.: Princeton University Press, 1980.

Scott, Joan Wallach. *Gender and the Politics of History.* New York: Columbia University Press, 1988.

Smith, Donald. *Long Lance: The True Story of an Imposter.* Lincoln: University of Nebraska Press, 1983.

Watanna, Onoto. *The Diary of Delia.* New York: Page, 1907.

_____. *A Japanese Nightingale.* New York: Harper, 1901.

_____. *Marion: A Story of an Artist's Model by Herself and the Author of Me.* New York: Watt, 1916.

_____. *Me, A Book of Remembrance.* New York: Century, 1915.

_____. *Miss Nume of Japan.* Chicago: Rand, McNally, 1899.

✦ *Discussion Questions*

1. Amy Ling offers two contradictory judgments of the Eaton sisters. On one hand, Edith might be seen as the more admirable because of her courage and integrity. On the other hand, Winnifred might be seen as the more admirable for her shrewd survival skills. Try to make the strongest possible argument for each of these positions.

2. In paragraphs 17–18, Ling describes the trickster as a recurrent figure in fables, legends, and folklore. Does such a figure appear in any of the stories shared within the circle of your immediate family? If so, what are some of the forces against which she or he contends?

3. One of the critics quoted by Ling makes reference to "the phony smell of a commodity." Do you feel that Winnifred Eaton, Grey Owl, and Long Lance made commodities of themselves, the cultures with which they tried to affiliate themselves, or both?

4. Do you feel there is a useful distinction to be made between a writer like Joel Chandler Harris, a white southerner who transcribed African folk tales and published them for profit, and the literary "impostors" to whom Ling refers? If so, what is that distinction?

WRITING SUGGESTIONS

1. Write the history of your own emerging literacy, placing it, if possible, within some cultural context that has shaped it. You might share your history with those of selected classmates, then write an essay that generalizes about the group.

2. Write an essay in which you contrast popular depictions of some group to which you belong with the way members of that group might wish to define themselves. Try to speculate on whether and how members of this group use literacy to define themselves in opposition to popular stereotypes.

3. Referring to ideas and details from readings in this chapter, write a critique of E. D. Hirsch's argument for the teaching of cultural literacy.

4. Referring to ideas and examples found in the last four readings in this chapter, write an essay that shows how ethnic minorities in the United States use literacy both to assimilate themselves into mainstream American culture and to affirm their differences from that culture.

2

The Macho Myth

———————◆———————

It is a sign of the times that "dumb male" jokes are replacing the "dumb blonde" jokes that used to be prevalent before women's liberation and before consciousness raising about the effect of such jokes. The punch line of one dumb male joke plays on the stereotype that men are not truthful in intimate relationships. "How can you tell when a man is lying?" one woman asks another. "When his lips are moving," goes the sexist punch line.

The reading selections in this chapter examine stereotypic macho behavior. Frank Pittman explores concepts of masculinity and what he refers to as an unseen male chorus that encourages men to be macho at the expense of their humanity. Pittman claims that we need to raise a better generation of fathers if we are to free men from the "masculine mystique." Lorenzo Carcaterra describes his boyhood experience with a macho father. As he stands in the funeral parlor awaiting his father's cremation, Carcaterra remembers this man as both his "dreaded enemy" and "most trusted friend." William Raspberry comments on peer pressure and macho behavior at Ballou High, a school in Washington, D.C. where intelligence and success rarely win approval from male peers; In fact, some top students prefer to fail classes rather than run the risk of being labeled good students.

In "Rape and the Boxing Ring," Joyce Carol Oates examines male experiences that glorify violence and encourage macho behavior in its most negative form—violent sporting events. She also examines the guilty verdict in Mike Tyson's prosecution on rape charges. Recruitment of young males for gangs is the focus, in part, of Fredric Dannen's "The Revenge of the Green Dragons."

The final three selections discuss changes in traditional male and female roles. Margaret Edwards's essay suggests that the new man cannot win; in adopting new male behavior, he runs the risk of being called a wimp. Warren Farrell, in the next selection, questions a feminist perspective on masculinity. The last word is from Joseph Campbell, who seems accepting of changing roles for men and women.

Reading Strategies and Reading Journals

To write well requires conscious understanding of the connections between reading and writing. Forming reading groups and keeping reading journals can help make those connections clear. Further, the reading process is particularly facilitated by rereadings of complicated texts. Through a series of reading, writing, and revising activities, readers often re-envision these texts in interesting ways. In this chapter, therefore, we introduce a number of strategies for reading (and rereading) the texts presented here.

First, we invite you to keep two types of entries in your reading journal: freewriting and analytic entries. These entries serve as the basis for negotiation in your reading groups as differences in interpretation and in reading strategies arise. We suggest that you freewrite in your journals as you read, responding with questions and comments to the content of each selection—to central ideas or to some particular detail that draws your attention. You may discuss these freewrites in reading groups, using them to negotiate meaning at a broad level.

Next, we suggest that you respond to complicated readings analytically, perhaps with a scratchline entry in your reading journals (not all texts, of course, are complicated enough to require such close readings). A *scratchline* is an informal list of central ideas, events, or characters in a reading. For example, a scratchline for the first reading in this chapter, Frank Pittman's "Beyond the BS and Drumbeating," might appear in a journal as follows:

> problem with "heavy dose of masculinity"
> The problem—the masculine mystique
> not biological
> masculinity—mostly cultural not biological
> article mainly about writer's struggle with masc. myst.
> examines young boys' behavior
> > act like boys not girls
> > can't be mama's boy
> > puberty unsettling
> next, initiation rites to masculinity
> men and women relating generally
> mating v. "partnering" next
> What causes problem—absent fathers
> solution? men free themselves of masculine myst.

A scratchline (or other notes) becomes the basis for writing a summary, a literal response to a reading. Group members can compare scratchlines before summarizing to further negotiate their understandings of the reading. Such activities, if repeated often enough, allow readers to recognize two important points about reading:

1. Readings can be *exuberant* (to use Jose Ortega y Gasset's term). Readers often fill in a text, adding to the writer's ideas, by reading between the lines from their own experience with the subject matter.
2. Readings can be *deficient* (again Ortega y Gasset's term, meaning "less than," not "defective"). Readers often read less into a text, missing some of the writer's explicit or implicit points on a first or even second reading.

Following the freewriting and analytic tasks, we introduce critical reading sections with focused questions. Of course, you can ask many more questions. You might consider some interrelated factors that A. L. Becker, rhetorician and linguist, suggests influence the reading process:

1. The cultural context and what may be unsaid or unsayable in a text
2. The interpersonal relationships between writer and reader (of purpose, audience, organization and development, for example)
3. The relationships between characters/events or the relationship of ideas in a text
4. the medium and its effect on the shaping of meaning
5. the meaning carried by rhetorical and syntactic structure
6. the influence of prior knowledge in the reading process

For example, you might focus productively only on interpersonal relations between writer and reader and what that tells you about the text. You might focus on language choice: key words that trace and introduce different topics. Or you might focus on relationships among specific ideas, events, or characters.

Frank Pittman

Beyond the BS and Drumbeating: Staggering Through Life as a Man

◆

In the following selection, published in Psychology Today, *Frank Pittman, MD, argues that we need to raise a better generation of fathers, men who will be more effective role models for their sons.*

Pittman has also written Private Lies, Infidelity and the Betrayal of Intimacy *(1990) and* Turning Points: Treating Families in Transition and Crisis *(1987).*

Men aren't doing very well. In alarming numbers, we drink ourselves sick, take drugs, work ourselves to death, run away from home, live on the streets, kill other people, and kill ourselves. Those still alive enough to be aware of what it feels like to be a man these days tell me they feel lonely, isolated from other men, and peripheral to their family while they trudge along wasting their lives in meaningless work, with very little sense of who they are or what they are living for.

Masculinity has become a problem, not just for the men who spend their lives in mortal struggle with its demands, but also for those who must share the world with them. The qualities that were useful in protecting primitive society from saber-toothed tigers have few practical functions these days. Cities full of men stomping around flexing their muscles and growling manly noises at one another have become our modern jungles. Men fight for turf and wrestle for control over people and things, whether through warfare, armed robbery, or corporate takeovers.

Heavy doses of masculinity are unquestionably toxic. But that's not the problem. The problem is the masculine mystique—the veneration and exaggeration of all that is masculine. It stems not from the testicles but from what our culture *defines* as masculinity, and how men develop it.

We like to think of masculinity as biologically determined, but most of its origins are cultural and historical and so vary from time to time and place to place. It doesn't exist just in the mind of an individual man; it's a view of life shared by other men.

5   Masculinity includes the symbols and the uniforms and the chants and the plays that make this the boys' team rather than the girls' team. And as a guy develops and practices his masculinity, he is accompanied and critiqued by an invisible male chorus of all the other guys who hiss or cheer as he attempts to approximate the masculine ideal, who push him to sacrifice more and more of his humanity for the sake of his masculinity, and who ridicule him when he holds back. The chorus is made up of all of man's models of masculinity: his comrades and rivals, his buddies and bosses, his male ancestors, and—above all—his father, who may have been a real person in the boy's life, or who may have existed for him only as the myth of the man who got away.

6   I will tell you what I know about man's battle with the masculine mystique, from the experience of my son and nephews, my friends and patients, but especially from my own struggle.

A Portrait of the Man as a Young Boy

> Snips and snails and puppy dogs' tails; that's what little boys are
> made of.
>
> —Anonymous

7   We know from the beginning that we're supposed to be boys, but somehow the Y chromosome doesn't show. For the first part of our life, the only visible sign of our maleness is a useless little peanut we're told to keep hidden.

8   So we wear boy clothes and try to act like boys act. We practice being cowboys or soldiers or football players or space jockeys when the other boys are with us. We piss off porches, roll in the mud, and do whatever we can think of that boys do and girls don't. We don't want to be mistaken for girls. We avoid answering the telephone because our voice isn't a man's voice and callers might think we are our mother when we say "hello." As much as we love our mother, as much as we depend on her, as much as we enjoy her company, we don't want to be seen with her. We don't want anyone to think we like doing the sorts of things girls do, so if anyone is looking, we have to act uncomfortable around Mom. We want to be seen with Dad, hanging out with men and doing manly things.

9   We go around pretending that we're big, powerful men, but our mothers keep reminding us that we are still little boys. When we're prepared to test our bravery against the forces of darkness in the night, Mom tells us to brush our teeth and go to bed. Our mother treats us as if she, not we, owned our bodies and our lives. She isn't even fazed by our magic peanut. We're still her baby, and as much as we love that when we need her, she can bring us back from the soaring fantasy world of masculinity to the inglorious life of a child.

As boys, we long for our father. We wear his clothes, and literally   10
try to fill his shoes. Anything of his is charmed and can endow us with
his masculinity. We hang on to him, begging him to teach us how to do
whatever is masculine... to throw balls or be in the woods or go see
where he works.

But we spend so much more time with our mother that we begin to   11
fear she will stifle the masculinity we know we must develop, that she
will civilize us and tame us and destroy us as the wild animals we
know we must be. We want our fathers to protect us from coming too
completely under the control of our mothers. We'll do anything with a
man, but we fear that femininity might be contagious, and we don't
want it to rub off on us.

We practice our masculinity, trying to develop enough of it. We feel   12
a bit foolish with it, like impostors, so we practice it in front of mirrors,
trying to learn how to swagger, trying to mimic the men we admire. We
always overdo it. We aren't big yet, or strong, and we can't make our
muscles grow very much, so we substitute recklessness. We take risks,
daring one another to do whatever frightens us all most: stealing
things, jumping off bridges, picking fights, or swallowing live frogs.
We talk dirty. We show off for the older boys.

The less we know of real men, the more daring we seem to become   13
in our efforts to be masculine. If we have a father (or uncle or grandfather) we admire, and we can find some of him in ourselves, we can imitate him. If we don't, we may have to imitate movie stars or sports
heroes. We look to other boys our own age to tell us when we're over-
doing it, and they may be battling just as fiercely and desperately to
flex their masculinity at the world. So we bounce our absurdly puffed-
up masculinity off one another and think we are preparing ourselves
for manhood.

A Boy and His Pecker Face Puberty

> I wonder why men get serious at all. They have this delicate thing
> hanging outside their bodies which goes up and down by its own
> free will. If I were a man, I would always be laughing at myself.
>
> —Yoko Ono

A boy's puberty is a strangely unsettling transition, perhaps not   14
quite as dramatic and definitive as menarche (though a boy's first ejac-
ulation can be as frightening as a girl's first menstruation). Before puberty, the bodies of boys and girls are similar enough to be easily
interchangeable—except for the insignificant little genitals. Much is
made of those little genitals from birth, or nowadays even before birth,
and they become the determinant of everything in life.

15   But for the first 10 or 12 years they have little significance except as predictors of future events. Early on, girls begin to menstruate, which is dramatic but not immediately obvious to their playmates. For boys, puberty comes later, sometimes much later, and its delay is humiliating. While the tall, round girls are getting themselves up like grown women, the prepubescent boys, with their featureless, hairless bodies, are just little kids who could almost pass for the children of the grown-up-looking girls.

16   The genitals are the first part to change. First, there is a little pubic hair, and then, with alarming suddenness, the penis blossoms into its full glory, utterly inappropriate to the little-boy body from which it dangles. A boy's penis seems so enormous and hard to hide, far too big yet still too small, always too small.

17   The boy has little control over it, and for a few years it is not clear who is in charge of whom. He pushes it down constantly, but it simply springs back up just when it is least expected. Yet when it is needed, it is nowhere to be found; with any anxiety it will run away and hide. The boy has become one element of a pair of Siamese twins, with this other independent being attached to his body—a constant, unreliable companion, a source of comfort and entertainment when alone, but a steady embarrassment in public.

18   While the boy is preoccupied, learning to break this willful creature, thick hair has started at the ankles and moves relentlessly up—as if a furry monster—to swallow him. All this remains concealed from the outer world until his voice changes and his pants, one morning, are a foot short. The hair reaches the pimply face, and the body exudes goat-like odors. The muscles bulge—though never enough, of course—and he bears no resemblance to who he was a year ago or even yesterday.

19   Parts of his body look like a man's, and impatient girls who reached puberty before him expect him to act like a man. Yet he doesn't *feel* like a man, and his parents don't treat him like one. They have no idea what has happened inside his body and inside his mind. And he certainly doesn't know how to talk to them about it. At the beginning, he clings to other boys who are experiencing the same exciting, terrifying changes, and they form a separate society, a very intimate one, alternately avoiding and examining the sexuality that obsesses them and passing on fantasies, fears, and fallacies about sex.

20   From the day this man's organ sprouts from this boy's body, the two are in a struggle over who is in charge and whose needs will prevail. Boys with models of masculinity can learn to keep their penises under control, but a boy without models may turn control over to his penis—which at this most sensitive stage of life seems so much more masculine than the rest of him—and then spend the rest of his life a slave to an insensitive, noncommunicative, unreliable, utterly self-centered, spineless piece of flesh.

Losing Our Cherry

> *I was never to see her again. Nor was I ever to learn what became of*
> *her. . . . Life is made up of small comings and goings, and, for every-*
> *thing we take with us, there is something we leave behind. In the*
> *summer of '42 . . . in a very special way, I lost Hermie—forever.*
> —Herman, *reflecting on his lost virginity, in* Summer of '42

I failed my own prescribed masculinity test: I didn't play football   21
past the eighth grade, which meant I wasn't a real man. I had to gain acceptance by getting drunk throughout my teens, engaging in activities
requiring more bravado than brains, and making obligatory sexual efforts with women I didn't know, didn't like, and didn't want. These initi-
ations were not pleasant, but they weren't crippling either, and I'm glad
I learned to play the macho games well enough to survive adolescence.

The scariest step in a boy's quest for manhood is sexual. Hot and   22
ready since puberty, he feels it is time for the twins to make it with girls.
They may not want to get close to girls yet, but the point may be to
remove the homophobic barrier: to prove you're straight so that you
won't have to feel unmasculine in your closeness to other boys.

At first we need girls who don't scare us or threaten our budding   23
virility. We feel safest with smaller, weaker girls, perhaps damsels in
distress who make us feel strong and important. Yet our male chorus
may propel us toward girls who are "popular" and beautiful, trophies
that announce our masculinity to our fellows.

A virginal 15-year-old boy's wet-dream Wonder Woman might be a   24
beautiful, popular, undersize, slightly dim-witted, depressed, 14-year-
old anorectic (with big tits), who is running away from an abusive
family.

These experiences are at least as traumatic and crucial for the girls   25
as for us, yet we're barely aware of our partners as we go through this
experience physically together and emotionally apart. Back in my day,
in the sexual Dark Ages when virginity was valued (for girls and
nerds) and pregnancy feared, there were a few girls who could be had;
but since they'd had boys with far more expertise than we, it took guts
to expose our amateurish efforts to their possible ridicule.

But "nice" girls set limits on where they could be touched and on   26
just how far the efforts could go—i.e. touching only above the waist or
through the panties, sticking it in only partway.

In those days a nice girl would try to hold on to us by holding us   27
off. She somehow knew that the audience for these sexual experiments
was still the other boys and the invisible male chorus, and all that we
wanted was to get in her pants, and her primary power lay in frustrating us. How tortured we were, and how grotesquely we overvalued
sex as a result. We might have even thought we were in love with whatever girl most maddeningly frustrated us.

Mating

> Woman is the sun, an extraordinary creature, one that makes the
> imagination gallop. Woman is also the element of conflict. With
> whom do you argue? With a woman, of course. Not with a friend,
> because he accepted all your defects the moment he found you. Be-
> sides, woman is mother—have we forgotten?
>
> —Marcello Mastroianni

28   We men need women for many reasons: to take care of us, to bear
children for us, to point out reality to us. Once we've passed the hurdle
of our own virginity, we don't really need women for sex. We might
prefer them, but we can do that for ourselves, and we do. Mostly we
need women to affirm our masculinity. They can do so by responding
to us sexually; by assuring us that we are strong and powerful; and by
loving and nurturing us as our reward for being masculine enough—or
as our solace if we're not.

29   When we choose a mate, a partner for a lifetime, should we choose
the woman who makes us feel good or the one who makes us look
good to our relentless male chorus? The chorus demands that we honor
our masculinity before we consider our comfort, our humanity, and our
soul. So we must consider which woman will make us seem more masculine—perhaps someone younger, dumber, poorer, more scared. Or
we can try for status. Or we may protect our masculinity by clutching
our balls and escaping each eligible candidate just before the wedding
bells. Can we have a real partner, or will that just make us look pussy-
whipped? Do we want a girl just like the girl who married dear old
Dad, or more like the type of girl dear old Dad eventually ran off with?

30   Our ability to fall in love, to go into that most revered of sacred
insanities, requires enough comfort with our masculinity to join it with
someone's femininity and feel enhanced. In order to marry, we must
find a woman who doesn't scare us. If our mother scared us by
depending upon us too much, or because we depended on her too
much, or if we felt her to be a threat to our freedom to be men, we have
to find someone very different from her: someone less seductive or
more so, less manipulative, more direct, sexier, quieter—the opposite of
whatever it is that seemed to make our mother a threat.

31   But if our mother made us feel secure and proud in our masculinity, then we want to find that again in our wife. If we are really comfortable with our mother, we can even marry a woman who is a friend
rather than an adversary, and form a true partnership. The boy still
inside us is one of the voices in our chorus and helps influence whether
we seek either a woman who will take care of us, a woman whom we
can take care of, or, in the best of worlds, a coupling of equals where we
look after one another.

What we need most in a mate is someone who can enable us to see   32
and understand all those things to which our masculinity blinds us.
Dare we find in a woman the lost part of ourselves, and by marrying
become whole? Or are we still just measuring peckers with the other
boys?

Living with A Wife

Man must partly give up being a man when he is with womenfolk.
                                                        —Robert Frost

Mating with a woman is one thing; partnering with a woman is   33
quite another. One steady refrain from the men's chorus reminds us
that our balls will fall off if we come under the control of a woman. The
choir keeps singing music from *Samson and Delilah,* warning us that a
woman can shear us from our masculine glory and thus rob us of our
strength. We approach each woman as if she is our mother come to
punish us for our independence by taking away our puberty.

The average man feels fully masculine only if he can attract   34
women, thus granting women terrifying power. And not only must he
win her, he must also satisfy her. A woman can utterly deflate a man by
refusing to be aroused, or, if things get to that point, by refusing to be
satisfied. And a woman's anger terrifies men. It returns us to our childhood with Mom.

I don't think it off the wall to speculate that most of the problems   35
between men and women are related to a man's panic in the face of a
woman's anger. A woman who misunderstands the male display of
power may assume the man is trying to dominate her because he does
not respect her enough. But a display of female anger, however justified, will only frighten the man into a more garish hormonal display. In
men whose male chorus permits it, this might erupt as violence—the
failing man's last-ditch effort to show enough masculinity to drown
out her anger.

When we do marry, we play a new role, discovering the female   36
perspective and the limitations of being male. Are we able to partner
with someone whose views are different from our own and ultimately
achieve binocular vision—seeing life from both his and her perspectives? Or do we choose to protect our maleness from her femaleness,
playing our male role to her female role, going through life obeying our
militant chorus?

Our macho chorus might not let us hear her wishes and desires: We   37
may ask our father, our clergyman, or all our friends how to deal with
marriage, but completely refuse to talk with the woman, our ostensible
partner. Protecting ourselves from her anger comes before learning
how to make her happy.

38   We've been taught that masculinity has little to do with being married. Being a husband means more than the act of being macho. To be a husband means "to take thrifty care of domestic affairs." Much of what we've learned about being male involves escape from female control and the civilizing influence of women so we could join the company of other men out there in the wild.

39   Some of us, mostly those whose dads fathered well, can adapt to marriage despite previous conditioning. Others, less fortunately fathered, must be dragged, kicking and screaming, into marriage—and in due time, into counseling. These guys have devoted their lives to becoming men, despite their lack of domestic models; now they are asked to unlearn, and they're scared. They have yet to learn that masculinity and marriage are compatible.

What Went Wrong: A Generation without Fathers

> *How sad that men should base an entire civilization on the principle of paternity, upon the legal ownership and presumed responsibility for children, and then never really get to know their sons and daughters very well.*
>
> —Phyllis Chesler

40   When looking for answers as to how men got so messed up in regard to their masculinity, it is easiest (and probably most logical) to cite our society's bizarre attempt to raise our sons without fathers—or at least without someone to serve as grown-up models for growing boys. After three decades of working with men who can't live in comfort with women, I'm increasingly convinced that the problem is not in the relationship with the woman, or with the man's mother, or with society, but in the boy's relationship with his father—or rather, its absence.

41   Boys know they're supposed to grow up to be like their fathers, and if Dad is there and the boy is malleable, he will become a man just like his father. If the boy finds something in the father that doesn't appeal to him, he may be able to correct it in himself. But most boys nowadays are growing up with fathers who spend little, if any, time with them. Ironically, when the boy most needs to practice being a man, his father is off somewhere playing at being a boy.

42   Theories of human development keep assuming that fathers are there, actually living in the same house with the rest of the family, performing some useful functions, interacting emotionally with wife and children, playing a role in a son's life, being a model for the boy. Such blissful days, if they ever existed, have now passed, and fathers wield their influence not by their presence, but by their absence. Instead of real-life fathers, boys grow up with myths of fathers, while mothers, whatever their relative significance out there in the world, reign supreme at home and in the life of the boy.

If fathers have run out on mothers, in any of the many ways men   43
use to escape women, then boys can't imagine that their masculinity is
sufficient until they too run away from women and join the world of
men. The fathers may have used work, sports, war, other women, alcohol or drugs, or whatever they could come up with to escape home;
and their sons would then equate masculinity with whatever they
imagined their fathers to be doing that was more important then being
at home with their sons. Boys who don't have fathers they know and
love don't know how much masculinity is enough.

Fathers have the authority to let boys relax the requirements of the   44
masculine model: If our fathers accept us, then that declares us masculine enough to join the company of men. In effect, boys then have their
diplomas in masculinity and can go on to develop other skills. If the
father is dead, the boy can invent whatever mythology suits him and
imagine his acceptance, but if the father is alive but gone, then it seems
the boy can only feel his lack of acceptance.

A boy may spend his entire life seeking that acceptance, the love   45
and approval of his father, and with it a reprieve from the masculine
striving. If boys can't get acceptance from their fathers, then they are
dependent on the company of other men to overwhelm the father's
rejecting voices or the echoing sounds of paternal silence.

Few girls grow up without mothers or some other woman as a   46
mother stand-in, but boys often see very little of their fathers and have
no other man in the family who is involved enough to demonstrate
proper masculinity. Most likely the fathers didn't get much fathering
either, and the mothers got even less; so no one is alarmed by the fact
that boys are being raised by mothers and that fathers are not teaching
boys how to be men, much less teaching boys how to be men with
women.

It's hard to imagine how we can raise a better generation of sons   47
until we have created a better generation of fathers. The miracle in
what seems like a hopeless paradox is what can happen to a man when
he becomes a father—not just a sperm donor or a landlord but a man
who nurtures his children over time. If a man, even a fatherless father,
will let himself learn from child-raising rather than just trying to control or perfect his children, they can carry him through all the stages of
human development from the other side and help make him aware of
how men and women develop, how masculinity and femininity are
taught and learned, and how to become a more complete human being.

But if he is a fatherless father, having grown up without ordinary   48
domestic models of men, he may see child-raising as "women's work,"
and he may distance himself from the mysterious job of fathering and
the disconcertingly enlightening process of child-raising. Thus, while
he lurks at the periphery of the family, protecting his precious masculinity from questioning its roots, he may miss his last chance.

Saving Yourself from Being a Total Asshole All Your Life

> All men are not slimy warthogs. Some men are silly giraffes, some
> woebegone puppies, some insecure frogs. But if one is not careful,
> those slimy warthogs can ruin it for all the others.
>
> —Cynthia Heimel

49   For the last 30 years I've been trying to free men, including myself,
from the spell of the masculine mystique. Luckily I found and married
a woman who stayed very sane with me. I still felt I wasn't masculine
enough, and when we had a son, I was afraid I couldn't be the man he
needed as a father. I went into psychoanalysis and complained about
my mother's failure to make me feel manly enough. My analyst was a
man whose masculinity I respected, and he declared me masculine
enough, and I got on with my life.

50   Wherever I turned in my profession as a therapist, I found men
who feared they were not masculine enough, so I did what my analyst
had done for me and what my father had failed to do: I assured them
that they were real men. I like to bring men face-to-face with their
fathers while there is still time. I find that what men most want to talk
about, when the atmosphere is safe and it isn't too embarrassing to cry,
is their failure to get close to their fathers. Just try keeping dry-eyed in
an audience of men watching *Field of Dreams*.

51   I've sent male clients to see movies such as *City Slickers, Born on the
Fourth of July,* and *When Harry Met Sally...*—all of which gave them a
different message than the one they've been getting from Rambo or
Rocky, or some shoot-em-up that glorifies men when they die for their
masculinity. I'm not trying to give these guys wimp models or heroes
of unmasculinity. I'm trying to show them that society is giving them
permission to expose and question the models they already have. All
men need a variety of ways to be a man, so we can be free to do whatever life requires of us, and particularly to do whatever our marriage
and our family require of us.

Reading and Writing Activities

PRELIMINARY RESPONSE

Notes.   As you read, record your reactions (questions or comments) to
"Beyond the BS and Drumbeating" in your reading journal. You may
react to a number of factors in the reading: the ideas, the language
(especially vocabulary choice), the rhetorical structure, the unspoken
assumptions, and the relationship between writer and reader (audience, purpose, organization, development). Your prior experience of

masculinity or femininity will also be a factor in your reaction to Pittman's essay. You need not, however, attempt to react to all of these factors in the essay at this time.

Discussion.   In class, compare your reactions in reading groups of five or six. Appoint a recorder to keep track of similarities or differences, consensus or disagreement, arising from the discussion. The recorder may summarize your group discussion for the rest of the class later.

Freewriting.   After the class discussion, freewrite for 10 to 15 minutes about Pittman's claim that defining masculinity has become a problem. Read your freewriting in groups of two to four.

SUMMARIZING

1. Create a scratchline of the ideas that Pittman introduces to develop his essay. Note shifts in topics as the essay progresses: from the introduction of problems with current definitions of masculinity through discussion of "man's battle with the masculine mystique."
2. Write a summary paragraph or two, from your scratchline or other preliminary work, of central topics that Pittman introduces to develop his point of view on the way culture, not biology, defines masculinity.
3. Read the summaries in your reading groups. Compare the focus of each summary. How do the summaries differ? How are they the same? What evidence does Pittman introduce to support his claims about men and masculinity?

FOCUSED CRITICAL READING

1. Frank Pittman claims that an "invisible male chorus" made up of "comrades and rivals, buddies and bosses, male ancestors and—above all—his father" influences an American male's masculinity. How do you respond to the notion of this male chorus that Pittman describes?
2. Pittman claims that boys need to learn to control sexual urges or be controlled by these urges all their lives. He goes on to say that boys need effective role models to learn control. How do men who suffer from an absence of effective role models behave towards women, according to Pittman?
3. What is the major difference in the socializing process of girls and boys, according to Pittman?

Lorenzo Carcaterra

Loving Your Enemy

◆

Lorenzo Carcaterra reflects on his relationship with his father in the following essay published in The New York Times Magazine. *Now a successful writer and editor of a television series,* Top Cop, *Carcaterra examines the complexity of that relationship as he attends his father's last rites in the funeral home where the body will shortly be cremated. Carcaterra has written a memoir of his father called* A Safe Place.

1   The last time I saw my father, he had his eyes closed and his hands across his chest. He was in the middle of a dank room with frayed wall-to-wall carpeting and a dim overhead light. My father was stretched out inside a large four-ply cardboard box, a white sheet folded to the center of his bare chest. He had been dead less than 48 hours and in three hours would be cremated.

2   My mother stood in front of him, thin hands gripping the edge of the box. "It didn't have to be like this," my mother said to her husband. "Didn't have to end this way. Foolish. Always so foolish."

3   I paced the back of the room, hands inside the pockets of my jeans jacket, trying not to cry over the death of my father, trying to ignore my sadness at the loss of a man who had, over the course of my lifetime, become my most dreaded enemy.

4   And most trusted friend.

5   My father was a violent man with a short fuse, quick to attack verbally, quicker still to lash out physically. He beat my mother often, for the silliest and simplest offenses. I was not spared his blows either. By age 10, I had 35 stitches on my body, the majority caused by his hands.

6   He was a con man, a sharp-talking dreamer skilled at duping dollars from the wallets of working men, promising riches in return for hard-earned table money. He seldom concerned himself about his own ability to pay back.

7   My father was also a convicted murderer. In late October 1946, his temper fueled by a jealous rage, he held a pillow against the face of his first wife and kept it there until the life was snuffed from her 24-year-old body. He walked out of the hotel on the West Side of Manhattan where he had left her and within three days was in the hands of the law. "I may be a rat," he said at his arrest, "but now no other rat can have her."

He was convicted of manslaughter in the second degree and sentenced to a 5-to-15-year term in a state penitentiary. He was 29. Less than seven years after the murder, he was again a free man. 8

I found out about my father's crime when I was 14 years old, on an island in southern Italy, visiting my mother's family for the first time. It was my mother who told me. 9

Until that moment, my father and I had been virtually inseparable. It had become easy for me to ignore his violent mood swings and vicious beatings, for in the streets of the neighborhood we lived in my father was no different from many of the men who called Hell's Kitchen home. 10

Those West Side streets served as a haven for dockworkers and butchers, hard hats and steam fitters, printers and truckers, all tough men who lived tough lives. Most cheated on their wives, quite a few had served prison time and all were comfortable around violence. 11

Like most of the neighborhood men, my father treated me not as a child but as an equal. He would take me to Yankee Stadium and there, under the lights of a twi-night doubleheader, our mouths crammed with hot dogs, he talked about Joe D., Ted Williams and Harmon Killebrew. He took me to Madison Square Garden for weekly fights and monthly wrestling matches, our seats always in the front rows. 12

My father was a man who cursed in every sentence he spoke, but never allowed an ethnic or racial slur to be used in our home. He loved music and would talk for hours about how much better Gene Krupa was than Buddy Rich and how nobody could touch Chick Webb when it came to the art of playing drums. 13

My father laughed at the Three Stooges and the Marx Brothers, cried at the most vapid movie melodrama and smiled whenever he heard my mother singing a Neapolitan love ballad. He loved watching Cagney, Bogart and Robinson on television and hated opera, talk shows and soccer. He didn't drink much and smoked even less, never voted in any elections and ate pasta every day of his free life. He also wolfed down steak-and-egg breakfasts at 4 in the morning, in front of a rusty barrel filled with crackling wood at the 14th Street meat market where he worked as a butcher. 14

But most of all, my father loved me. 15

These images filled my mind as I looked at my father in that box in the funeral home in the northeast Bronx, waiting to be turned to ashes. I remembered how our lives had changed after I found out about the murder, how my initial shock had grown into hate. I remembered all the years I had ignored him, turned my back to his pleas for money or even conversation. 16

All those years I was more concerned about what the murder meant to me. I thought nothing of what it had meant to him. I had 17 helped pay his debts and had covered up many of his lies, but I found it impossible to return his love. I knew he had killed a woman and had seen him beat my mother into a ruin. I could not bring myself to forgive him for either act.

18   I moved closer to his body, staring at the waxlike glaze of his skin, amazed at how the cancer had eaten at his once formidable bulk. I put my left hand on top of his head, bald and cold to the touch. My mother, still standing by my father's side, began to cry—loving tears shed over a man she had so much reason to hate.

19   I stared down at my father and knew now that he neither wanted nor cared about my forgiveness. He was a hard man and the dark hours of his life were his alone to bear. What he *did* want from me was a son's love. I had been more than willing to give him that during the first 14 years of my life. I never could on any day after.

20   I put a hand under my mother's arm and nudged her from the box, away from her husband.

21   "We should go," I said.

22   My mother wiped at the corners of her eyes with the edge of a white tissue. She buttoned her wool coat.

23   "You should have told him," she said.

24   "Told him what?"

25   "That you loved him," my mother said. "It was all he wanted."

26   "I know," I said.

27   "It's not too late," my mother said. "Stay with him a while longer. I'll wait outside."

28   "Mom, there's not much time," I said. "They have to take him away."

29   "They can wait," my mother said.

30   I stood in the center of the room, alone with my father, my back and chest wet with sweat. Five more hesitant steps and I was staring once again at his silent features. I bit my lower lip and fought back tears. I held the side of the cardboard box and shook my head.

31   "You bastard," I said to my father. "You dirty bastard."

32   Then I sank to my knees and cried over the body of the one man I loved more than any other.

Reading and Writing Activities

PRELIMINARY RESPONSE

Notes.   As you read, record your reactions (questions or comments) to "Loving Your Enemy" in your reading journal.

Remember, again, that you may react to one or two of a number of factors in the reading: the ideas, the language (especially vocabulary choice), the rhetorical structure, the unspoken assumptions, and the relationship between writer and reader (audience, purpose, organization, development). Your prior experience with family relationships will also be a factor in your reaction to Carcaterra's essay. You need not, however, attempt to react to all of these factors in the essay at this time.

Discussion. In class, compare your reactions in reading groups of five or six. Appoint a recorder to keep track of similarities or differences, consensus or disagreement, arising from the discussion. The recorder may summarize your group discussion for the rest of the class later.

Freewriting. After the class discussion, freewrite for 10 to 15 minutes about Carcaterra's love of his abusive father. Read your freewriting in groups of two to four.

SUMMARIZING

1. Create a scratchline or cluster representation of the progression of topics as Carcaterra reflects on his relationship with his father. Note the shift in topics as he contrasts his feelings about his father before and after he discovers that his father is a convicted killer.
2. Write a summary paragraph or two, from your scratchline or other preliminary work, of Carcaterra's portrayal of his father.
3. Read the summaries in your reading groups. Compare the focus of each summary. How do the summaries differ? How are they the same?

FOCUSED CRITICAL READING

1. Lorenzo Carcaterra gives details that show his father to be a complex individual. But he leaves some things unsaid about his father's ethnic heritage. Where in the essay do you have to read between the lines to construct your image of Carcaterra's father?
2. What do you know of the relationship between Carcaterra's mother and father? What about Carcaterra's relationship to his mother?
3. What do you think about the ability to separate forgiveness and love? Is Carcaterra able to forgive his father?
4. Frank Pittman claims that boys need involvement with their fathers to be good fathers themselves. What kind of father do you think Carcaterra can be, given Pittman's claims about father-son relationships?

William Raspberry

What You See . . .

◆

William Raspberry's article, "What You See," is a response to an article by Ron Suskind, "Against All Odds," which appeared in the Wall Street Journal. *Raspberry reports for the* Washington Post, *and his columns are syndicated nationally.*

1   "What you see," Flip Wilson's "Geraldine" character used to remind us, "is what you get."

2   The phrase was intended as a declaration of simple straightforwardness. No complications, no hidden agendas, no false airs: What you see *is* what you get.

3   But there is another meaning: You cannot accomplish anything that is beyond your ability to imagine.

4   A limited vision limits achievement because it limits hope. If you can't see it—at least with your mind's eye—you can't get it. What you can see is what you get.

5   It's this second meaning I've been thinking about—nearly crying about—ever since I read Ron Suskind's page one story in the May 26 *Wall Street Journal.*

6   The stars of Mr. Suskind's extraordinary piece are Cedric Jennings, a 16-year-old A student at Washington's Ballou High School, with visions of a career as a scientist; Phillip Atkins, 17, the class clown who has learned not to be too smart; and Delante Coleman, a 17-year-old gang leader whose "crew" likes to harass the "goodies" like Cedric.

7   There's drama in the *Journal* account: Will Cedric win acceptance into a special MIT program? Will Phillip follow his academically determined sister or his street-wise and school-dumb peers? Will Delante come to grips with the self-doubts and frustrations that are behind his harassment of Cedric?.

8   But there is also the pervasive sense of limited vision.

9   Phillip, as bright as Cedric, has learned the lessons taught by his father (Don't aim *too* high) and by his survival instinct. ("The best way to avoid trouble is to never get all the answers right on a test.").

10   Delante is bright, too. As a sophomore, he scored above 12th grade level nationally on the math portion of a standardized test, making the same score as Cedric. But in school, his last report included two Fs.

In a statement that might have been crafted by a scriptwriter, 11
Delante explains his contempt for Cedric and the other "goodies" who
study and strive for grades:

"Everyone knows they're trying to be white, get ahead in the white 12
man's world. In a way, that's a little bit of disrespect to the rest of us."

I spent hours being angry with Delante—both for his assaults on 13
the "goodies" and for wasting his own intelligence.

But then I wanted to shake him awake, plead with him, explain to 14
him in words capable of cutting through his resistance, that neither he
nor the rest of us can afford for him to waste his intellectual gifts.

The minidrama Ron Suskind captured at Ballou is being played in 15
high schools and playgrounds and streets across America. Thousands
of young black men—and growing numbers of young black women as
well—are coming of age without the vision of a satisfying place for
themselves in the world.

The athletically gifted may dream of riches earned from profes- 16
sional sports; the musically talented may picture themselves as top-tier
entertainers.

But the academically gifted—unless they are discovered by the 17
likes of A Better Chance or the Black Student Fund and sent off to prep
school—have trouble seeing themselves as successful in a world where
intellect counts.

A few, like Cedric, survive the anti-intellectualism of their neigh- 18
borhoods, though at a social cost that must be stupendous. A handful
of nerds, weirdos or gays draw strength and freedom from their ostracism and allow themselves to see bigger things for themselves.

But too many young people, including some with the potential to 19
elevate themselves, rescue their families or change the world, allow
themselves to be dragged down by the curse of low expectations.

Countless thousands succumb so completely to the curse that they 20
imagine that they are *supposed* to fail. Indeed, some, like Delante, see
the refusal to fail as a sort of racial treason.

The question we need to answer is how to broaden the vistas of 21
these hopeless children, to get them to see not just race-based impedi-
ments but also opportunity. After all, they cannot strive for what they
cannot see.

"Where there is no vision," says the Book of Proverbs, "the people 22
perish."

True enough. So is this: "What you *see* is what you get." 23

Reading and Writing Activities

PRELIMINARY RESPONSE

Notes. As you read, record your reactions (questions or comments) to William Raspberry's article about peer pressure among young African-American males at Ballou High in Washington, D.C.

Your experience with peer pressure, both negative and positive, in and out of school, will give you a special frame of reference in reacting to this article.

Discussion. In class, compare your reactions in reading groups of five or six. Appoint a recorder to keep track of similarities or differences, consensus or disagreement, arising from the discussion. The recorder may summarize your group discussion for the rest of the class later.

Freewriting. After the class discussion, freewrite for 5 to 10 minutes about the kind of peer pressure the males in this article deal with every day in school. What do you know from personal experience about peer pressure? Read your freewriting in groups of two to four.

SUMMARIZING

1. Create a preliminary analysis of "What You See" by noting the progression of characters and events that Raspberry introduces in his report. Note also how these characters and events are connected. What central point about peer pressure is the writer making? How do you know what the point of the story is?
2. Write a summary paragraph or two, from your preliminary analysis.
3. Read the summaries in your reading groups. Compare the focus of each summary. How do the summaries differ? How are they the same? Check to see if you are *reacting and responding* to the story instead of summarizing it.

Joyce Carol Oates

Rape and the Boxing Ring

◆

The following selection concerns Mike Tyson's rape conviction. One of America's most prolific writers, Joyce Carol Oates (born in Lockport, New York, on June 16, 1938) has almost thirty novels, twenty collections of short stories, fourteen poetry collections, seven book-length nonfiction selections, and eight plays to her credit.

In addition to the O. Henry Award in 1967 for "In the Region of Ice" and again in 1973 for "The Dead," she has received several National Book Award nominations. This prestigious award was given to Oates in 1970 for the novel Them.

Mike Tyson's conviction on rape charges in Indianapolis is a minor 1
tragedy for the beleaguered sport of boxing, but a considerable triumph for women's rights. For once, though bookmakers were giving 5–1 odds that Tyson would be acquitted, and the mood of the country seems distinctly conservative, a jury resisted the outrageous defense that a rape victim is to be blamed for her own predicament. For once, a celebrity with enormous financial resources did not escape trial and a criminal conviction by settling with his accuser out of court.

That boxing and "women's rights" should be perceived as opposed 2
is symbolically appropriate, since of all sports, boxing is the most aggressively masculine, the very soul of war in microcosm. Elemental and dramatically concise, it raises to an art the passions underlying direct human aggression; its fundamentally murderous intent is not obscured by the pursuit of balls or pucks, nor can the participants expect help from teammates. In a civilized, humanitarian society, one would expect such a blood sport to have died out, yet boxing, sponsored by gambling casinos in Las Vegas and Atlantic City, and broadcast by cable television, flourishes: had the current heavyweight champion, Evander Holyfield, fought Mike Tyson in a title defense, Holyfield would have earned no less than $30 million. If Tyson were still champion, and still fighting, he would be earning more.

The paradox of boxing is that it so excessively rewards men for 3
inflicting injury upon one another that, outside the ring, with less "art," would be punishable as aggravated assault, or manslaughter. Boxing belongs to that species of mysterious masculine activity for which

anthropologists use such terms as "deep play": activity that is wholly without utilitarian value, in fact contrary to utilitarian value, so dangerous that no amount of money can justify it. Sports-car racing, stunt flying, mountain climbing, bullfighting, dueling—these activities, through history, have provided ways in which the individual can dramatically, if sometimes fatally, distinguish himself from the crowd, usually with the adulation and envy of the crowd, and traditionally, the love of women. Women—in essence, Woman—is the prize, usually self-proffered. To look upon organized sports as a continuum of Darwinian theory—in which the sports-star hero flaunts the superiority of his genes—is to see how displays of masculine aggression have their sexual component, as ingrained in human beings as any instinct for self-preservation and reproduction. In a capitalist society, the secret is to capitalize upon instinct.

4   Yet even within the very special world of sports, boxing is distinct. Is there any athlete, however celebrated in his own sport, who would not rather reign as the heavyweight champion of the world? If, in fantasy at least, he could be another Muhammad Ali, or Joe Louis, or indeed, Mike Tyson in his prime? Boxing celebrates the individual man in his maleness, not merely in his skill as an athlete—though boxing demands enormous skill, and its training is far more arduous than most men could endure for more than a day or two. All athletes can become addicted to their own adrenaline, but none more obviously than the boxer, who, like Sugar Ray Leonard, already a multimillionaire with numerous occupations outside the ring, will risk serious injury by coming back out of retirement; as Mike Tyson has said, "Outside of boxing, everything is so boring." What makes boxing repulsive to many observers is precisely what makes boxing so fascinating to participants.

5   This is because it is a highly organized ritual that violates taboo. It flouts such moral prescriptions as "Thou shalt not kill." It celebrates, not meekness, but flamboyant aggression. No one who has not seen live boxing matches (in contrast to the sanitized matches broadcast over television) can quite grasp its eerie fascination—the spectator's sense that he or she is a witness to madness, yet a madness sanctioned by tradition and custom, as finely honed by certain celebrated practitioners as an artist's performance at the highest level of genius, and, yet more disturbing, immensely gratifying to the audience. Boxing mimics our early ancestors' rite of bloody sacrifice and redemption; it excites desires most civilized men and women find abhorrent. For some observers, it is frankly obscene, like pornography; yet, unlike pornography, it is not fantasy but real, thus far more subversive.

6   The paradox for the boxer is that, in the ring, he experiences himself as a living conduit for the inchoate, demonic will of the crowd: the expression of their collective desire, which is to pound another human being into absolute submission. The more vicious the boxer, the greater

the acclaim. And the financial reward—Tyson is reported to have earned $100 million. (He who at the age of 13 was plucked from a boys' school for juvenile delinquents in upstate New York.) Like the champion gladiators of Roman decadence, he will be both honored and despised, for, no matter his celebrity, and the gift of his talent, his energies spring from the violation of taboo and he himself is tainted by it.

Mike Tyson has said that he does not think of boxing as a sport. He   7
sees himself as a fantasy gladiator who, by "destructing" opponents, enacts others' fantasies in his own being. That the majority of these others are well-to-do whites who would themselves crumple at a first blow, and would surely claim a pious humanitarianism, would not go unnoted by so wary and watchful a man. Cynicism is not an inevitable consequence of success, but it is difficult to retain one's boyish naiveté in the company of the sort of people, among them the notorious Don King, who have surrounded Tyson since 1988, when his comanager, Jim Jacobs, died. As Floyd Patterson, an ex-heavyweight champion who has led an exemplary life, has said, "When you have millions of dollars, you have millions of friends. "

It should not be charged against boxing that Mike Tyson *is* boxing   8
in any way. Boxers tend to be fiercely individualistic, and Tyson is, at the least, an enigma. He began his career, under the tutelage of the legendary trainer Cus D'Amato, as a strategist, in the mode of such brilliant technicians as Henry Armstrong and Sugar Ray Robinson. He was always aware of a lineage with Jack Dempsey, arguably the most electrifying of all heavyweight champions, whose nonstop aggression revolutionized the sport and whose shaved haircut and malevolent scowl, and, indeed, penchant for dirty fighting, made a tremendous impression upon the young Tyson.

In recent years, however, Tyson seems to have styled himself at   9
least partly on the model of Charles (Sonny) Liston, the "baddest of the bad" black heavyweights. Liston had numerous arrests to his credit and served time in prison (for assaulting a policeman); he had the air, not entirely contrived, of a sociopath; he was always friendly with racketeers, and died of a drug overdose that may in fact have been murder. (It is not coincidental that Don King, whom Tyson has much admired, and who Tyson has empowered to ruin his career, was convicted of manslaughter and served time in an Ohio prison.) Like Liston, Tyson has grown to take a cynical pleasure in publicly condoned sadism (his "revenge" bout with Tyrell Biggs, whom he carried for seven long rounds in order to inflict maximum damage) and in playing the outlaw; his contempt for women, escalating in recent years, is a part of that guise. The witty obscenity of a prefight taunt of Tyson's—"I'll make you into my girlfriend"—is the boast of the rapist.

Perhaps rape itself is a gesture, a violent repudiation of the female,   10
in the assertion of maleness that would seem to require nothing beyond

physical gratification of the crudest kind. The supreme macho gesture—like knocking out an opponent and standing over his fallen body, gloves raised in triumph.

11   In boxing circles it is said—this, with an affectionate sort of humor—that the heavyweight champion is the 300-pound gorilla who sits anywhere in the room he wants; and, presumably, takes any female he wants. Such a grandiose sense of entitlement, fueled by the insecurities and emotions of adolescence, can have disastrous consequences. Where once it was believed that Mike Tyson might mature into the greatest heavyweight of all time, breaking Rocky Marciano's record of 49 victories and no defeats, it was generally acknowledged that, since his defeat of Michael Spinks in 1988, he had allowed his boxing skills to deteriorate. Not simply his ignominious loss of his title to the mediocre James (Buster) Douglas in 1990, but subsequent lackluster victories against mediocre opponents made it clear that Tyson was no longer a serious, nor even very interesting, boxer.

12   The dazzling reflexes were dulled, the shrewd defensive skills drilled into him by D'Amato were largely abandoned: Tyson emerged suddenly as a conventional heavyweight like Gerry Cooney, who advances upon his opponent with the hope of knocking him out with a single punch—and does not always succeed. By 25, Tyson seemed already middle aged, burnt out. He would have no great fights after all. So, strangely, he seemed to invite his fate outside the ring, with sadomasochistic persistence, testing the limits of his celebrity's license to offend by ever-escalating acts of aggression and sexual effrontery.

13   The familiar sports adage is surely true, one's ultimate opponent is oneself.

14   It may be objected that these remarks center upon the rapist, and not his victim; that sympathy, pity, even in some quarters moral outrage flow to the criminal and not the person he has violated. In this case, ironically, the victim, Desiree Washington, though she will surely bear psychic scars through her life, has emerged as a victor, a heroine: a young woman whose traumatic experience has been, as so few traumas can be, the vehicle for a courageous and selfless stand against the sexual abuse of women and children in America. She seems to know that herself, telling *People* magazine, "It was the right thing to do." She was fortunate in drawing a jury who rejected classic defense ploys by blaming the victim and/or arguing consent. Our criminal-justice system being what it is, she was lucky. Tyson, who might have been acquitted elsewhere in the country, was unlucky.

15   Whom to blame for this most recent of sports disgraces in America? The culture that flings young athletes like Tyson up out of obscurity, makes millionaires of them and watches them self-destruct? Promoters like Don King and Bob Arum? Celebrity hunters like Robin Givens, Tyson's ex-wife, who seemed to have exploited him for his

money and as a means of promoting her own acting career? The indulgence generally granted star athletes when they behave recklessly? When they abuse drugs and alcohol, and mistreat women?

I suggest that no one is to blame, finally, except the perpetrator 16 himself. In Montieth Illingworth's cogently argued biography of Tyson, "Mike Tyson: Money, Myth and Betrayal," Tyson is quoted, after one or another public debacle: "People say 'Poor guy.' That insults me. I despise sympathy. So I screwed up. I made some mistakes. 'Poor guy,' like I'm some victim. There's nothing poor about me."

Reading and Writing Activities

PRELIMINARY RESPONSE

Notes. As you read, record your reactions (questions or comments) to "Rape and the Boxing Ring" in your reading journal. Is the central point or points stated or implied?

Discussion. In class, compare your reactions in reading groups of five or six. Appoint a recorder to keep track of similarities or differences, consensus or disagreement, arising from the discussion. The recorder may summarize your group discussion for the rest of the class later.

Freewriting. After the class discussion, freewrite for 10 to 15 minutes about the connection Oates makes between boxing and women's rights especially as these rights refer to protection against male violence. Think about sports and violent behavior. Do particular sports encourage violence? How common are gestures of triumph over an opponent in sports other than boxing? How do you react to such gestures? Are women prone to similar behavior as they play professionally? Read your freewriting in groups of two to four.

SUMMARIZING

1. Develop a preliminary analysis of "Rape and the Boxing Ring." How many times does Oates change topics as she develops her point of view? How does she arrange those topics? How does she signal, if she does signal, a change in topic?
2. Write a summary paragraph or two, from your preliminary analysis, of the perspectives Oates presents on masculine behavior and the topics she introduces to develop that perspective.
3. Read the summaries in your reading groups. Compare the focus of each summary. How do the summaries differ? How are they the

same? Again, check to see if you are *reacting and responding* to the essay instead of summarizing the central topics.

FOCUSED CRITICAL READING

1. Speculate about what might cause a group of readers to compose different versions of their reading of this report on Mike Tyson? Can there be agreement on central events?
2. Can there be agreement on Oates's interpretation of those events?

Fredric Dannen

Revenge of the Green Dragons

———————◆———————

The following selection is only an excerpt from "Annals of Crime: Revenge of the Green Dragons" published in The New Yorker *in November 1992. Here Fredric Dannen describes the chilling function of gangs and their culture as well as the Chinese culture within which the gangs operate and recruit new members. He claims that "Asian gangs engage in a recognizable pattern of racketeering, the bedrock crime being extortion. It is difficult to find a restaurant in Chinatown that is not shaken down for protection money by one gang or another on a regular basis."*

Fredric Dannen also wrote Hit Men: Power Brokers and Fast Money Inside the Music Business (1990).

Around seven o'clock on the night of July 16, 1989, Anthony Gallivan went out drinking. He was joined by his wife, Christine, and another couple. The Gallivans, who were both in their early thirties, were born in Ireland, but at present they lived in Jackson Heights, Queens. It was wet and windy, so the two couples took a cab to the Liffey Pub, an Irish bar in Elmhurst. They laughed and talked and drank Guinnesses until after nine, and then decided they were hungry for Chinese food.

This was a commodity not hard to come by in Elmhurst. In two decades, Elmhurst, Flushing, and other sections of Queens within a two-mile radius of Shea Stadium have become a second Chinatown, cleaner and more prosperous than the one in lower Manhattan. (The No. 7 subway train to Flushing has been dubbed the Orient Express.) The Gallivans and their friends ducked into the Tien Chau, a Taiwanese restaurant just a short jog from the Liffey Pub. They had planned to order takeout, but now it was raining heavily, so they sat down at a table for four.

The Tien Chau was a small restaurant, with only about a dozen tables, and at nine-thirty on a wet night it was almost empty. Seated near the cash register, Gregory Hyde and his Chinese-American wife, Carol Huang, were getting ready to leave. When they got up to pay the check, two well-dressed Chinese boys were arguing with the manager, a thirty-five-year-old Taiwanese named Mon Hsiung Ting. Well, Greg figured, we might as well sit down and let them finish their discussion. Moments later, Greg heard what sounded like firecrackers. When he turned around, one of the boys was crouching, his feet spread apart. He was firing a pistol.

4   "Carol, duck!" Greg yelled. Carol dived under the table, her eyes on the shooter. The boy caught her looking at him. She later estimated that they made eye contact for two or three seconds—long enough for her to fix an image in her mind of a handsome young man with spiky hair, huge eyes, and, for an Asian, very fair skin. He wore a black suit and a white shirt with black pinstripes. He appeared quite calm. Then he fired in Carol's direction, and she instinctively covered her face with her hands.

5   Greg Hyde was struggling to get under the table as well. His back was to the shooter. He tried to slide out of his chair, but it was stuck, and when he pushed back hard he was forced upright. Suddenly, his legs gave way under him, and he knew that he had been shot. Hyde fell to the floor, face forward, on his arm. He tried to move, but his legs were paralyzed. He could feel his body going into shock.

6   At her table toward the rear of the restaurant, Christine Gallivan looked over to her left and saw her dish fall. Her husband clutched his chest and said, "Christine, I think I've been hit!" She glanced up and saw a young man with a small, "James Bond-type" gun, his arms bouncing in recoil after each shot. Blue smoke rose in the background. Tony Gallivan was sliding off his chair. One of his friends grabbed him and laid him on the ground on his back. There was blood on his T-shirt in the middle of his chest, a dot the size of a pen top. It was an exit wound; the bullet had entered his back on the right side and passed through his heart. Christine was screaming. She later recalled, "I held him in my arms, and his eyes rolled and his color changed. And I figured he died then."

7   The restaurant manager, Mon Hsiung Ting, staggered out from behind the cash register and collapsed, dead, in the middle of the floor. His blood was splattered on the wall mirrors, and gushed out of holes in his body. He had been shot nine times, by both boys.

8   The second boy grabbed his companion in the black suit and pulled him out the door. Carol got up from under the table and screamed at a waitress to open the cash register for a quarter to phone 911. She returned to her husband's side, and Greg said an Act of Contrition. He believed he was dying. He would live, though, crippled for life; a bullet had entered his shoulder and damaged his spine. Carol had escaped unharmed, and she had seen so much that in time the boy in the black suit would regret not having killed her.

9   About four miles south of the Tien Chau restaurant, in an apartment on Eighty-seventh Road in Woodhaven, Queens, the man who

had ordered the shooting was debriefing the two assassins. His name was Chen I. Chung, and he was the *dai lo*, or big brother, of a Chinese gang called the Green Dragons. *Dai lo* is a term of respect accorded to one's elders, or to a boss, in a gang, and Chen I. Chung was both a boss and an older gang member. He was twenty.

The Green Dragons were based in Elmhurst, and their principal competition in the borough of Queens was a Flushing gang known as the White Tigers. The Dragons and the Tigers maintained an uneasy truce, and on occasion ranking members of the two gangs would sit down in a restaurant or a night club and attempt to resolve territorial disputes. Besides mutual animosity, the Green Dragons and the White Tigers had something else in common: both were patterned after established gangs in Manhattan's Chinatown. Youth gangs started to emerge in Chinatown in the sixties and seventies, and they have a distinctive culture—a bizarre mixture of traits borrowed from the Hong Kong triads (secret criminal societies) and the clichés of American and Chinese gangster movies. Gang members dress all in black and have their chests and arms tattooed with dragons, serpents, tigers, and sharp-taloned eagles. They can be as young as thirteen. Once enlisted, a gang member loses contact with family and school; the gang becomes both. Members live in safe-house apartments, often several to a room. Gangs have territories—certain streets, certain hangouts—and the appearance of a rival gangster in the wrong place can lead to bloodshed.

It would be simplistic to compare gangs such as the Green Dragons and the White Tigers, as some have tried, to the Jets and the Sharks of "West Side Story," or even to the color gangs of Los Angeles. They are not youth gangs in the usual sense but, rather, a young form of organized crime. They have a clearly defined hierarchy, and junior members will obey the instructions from the *dai lo* or someone else of high rank even if the order is to kill for reasons not explained. Asian gangs engage in a recognizable pattern of racketeering, the bedrock crime being extortion. It is difficult to find a restaurant in Chinatown that is not shaken down for protection money by one gang or another on a regular basis.

The Green Dragons and the White Tigers imported this tradition into Queens. Sometimes the restaurants would put up a fight. This was not something that Chen I. Chung could allow. If word were to get around that a restaurant had successfully refused to pay the Green Dragons, no one would take the gang seriously. According to the testimony of former gang members (a prime source of information for this account), Chen I. Chung repeatedly complained that the manager of the Tien Chau, Mon Hsiung Ting, was "hardheaded." Finally, he decided to send a pair of Dragons to kill Ting. One of the boys he selected was Alex Wong, who had been the goodlooking boy in the black suit. The other killer was Joseph Wang. Both boys were sixteen.

13   Now Alex and Joe were reporting back to Chen I. Chung after the shooting, and the *dai lo* was satisfied, with one reservation. Alex said that the customers had ducked when the shooting started—all except one man. He had stood up, so Alex had fired at him. (That was Gregory Hyde.) Alex perhaps did not realize that he had shot and killed Anthony Gallivan, but he knew that the man he had hit was Caucasian. Chen I. Chung did not like that part of the story. Victimizing a non-Asian might bring heat from law enforcement. Gangs did not think American justice cared much about Asians, and the Asian community seemed to agree, for most extortions and many armed robberies went unreported.

14   Chen I. Chung was Taiwanese. He was familiarly called I. Chung (with "I" pronounced like "E"). I. Chung had immigrated to Waco, Texas, in 1981, at thirteen, along with two older sisters and an older brother, and had moved to Chicago before settling in Queens. His parents opened a Chinese restaurant in Buffalo. He was about five foot seven and skinny, with a tattoo of a tiger on his left shoulder and a gold ring in his left ear. His face was catlike. On Christmas Eve, 1987, two Asian youths opened fire on I. Chung as he sat in his car, at a red light. He managed to drive to the hospital with a bullet lodged in his skull. Since then, I. Chung experienced severe headaches at times of stress. After eight years in America, he spoke almost no English. He had been with the Green Dragons from its inception, in 1985, and had moved steadily up the ladder. As *dai lo,* he had his own apartment and a platinum American Express card. It is commonly thought that gang members kill mostly one another. The Green Dragons dispelled that myth: they preyed on the innocent.

15   With two dozen active members at most, the Green Dragons was a relatively small gang compared with Chinatown gangs such as the Ghost Shadows and the Flying Dragons. It was also more autonomous, since the Chinatown gangs must answer to a more senior criminal hierarchy. Chinatown, which was established in the eighteen-hundreds, operates on a system of tongs, or fraternal societies, which constitute, quite literally, the local government. (The Hip Sing, with headquarters on Pell Street, is the largest and most powerful tong; next in line is the On Leong, on Mott Street; and then the Tung On, on Division Street. A fourth, the Fukien American Association, on East Broadway, is a comer.) The tongs control Chinatown's commerce, and allegedly profit from drug trafficking, gambling, and prostitution. Each tong enjoys the allegiance of a youth gang. The fear that gangs inspire in merchants is enormously useful to the tongs, which govern the community through intimidation.

16   The tongs and the gangs are often equated with Mafia enterprises, but a far better analogy is to the Black Hand, the precursor of the American Mafia which in the early part of the century also preyed on its own ethnic group—first-generation Italian immigrants who spoke lit-

tle English and did not trust American law enforcement to protect them. Most of Chinatown's population is also foreign-born, and regards police and prosecutors with the same skepticism.

The government has exerted far more effort against "traditional" organized crime in America—the Mafia—than against Asian crime, which has existed here just as long. Prosecutors have a lot of catching up to do. While RICO, the Racketeer Influenced and Corrupt Organizations Act, has been used effectively against Mafia families, no successful RICO case has ever been brought against a tong. The government has been more successful in prosecuting the gangs. In 1985, Nancy Ryan, of the Manhattan District Attorney's Jade Squad, convicted twenty-five members of the Ghost Shadows of numerous acts of racketeering, including thirteen murders. The Ghost Shadows serve the On Leong tong. A few years ago, the Flying Dragons, the gang overseen by the Hip Sing tong, was infiltrated by a police officer, David Chong. Today a lieutenant in the New York Police Department and the highest-ranking Asian on the force, Chong fooled the Flying Dragons so thoroughly that he rose to the status of *dai lo* and became a street lieutenant, with a crew of twelve soldiers. Recently, Chong spoke about one of the most deplorable jobs of a *dai lo,* recruiting new gang members. This is typically done at school. 17

"I drove a Corvette, I had handfuls of money, the prettiest girls, the best jewelry, so you know what I would do?" Chong said. "I would have my kids go to a high school in Chinatown and look for the turkey right off the boat. You want him in ninth or tenth grade, he can't speak English, he's got a stupid haircut. And when you find this kid, you go beat the shit out of him. Tease him, beat him up, knock him around. We isolate this kid; he's our *target.* What will happen, one day I'll make sure I'm around when this kid is getting beaten up, and I'll stop it with the snap of my finger. He'll look at me—he'll see that I have a fancy car, girls, I'm wearing a beeper—and I'll turn around and say, 'Hey kid, how come these people are beating on you?' I'm gonna be this kid's hero, this kid's guru—I'm gonna be his *dai lo.* I'll take the kid for a drive, take him to a restaurant, order him the biggest lobster, the biggest steak. Eventually, I'll take him to the safe house where I keep kids and guns. Then I slowly break him in." 18

Reading and Writing Activities

PRELIMINARY RESPONSE

Notes. As you read, record your reactions (questions or comments) to this excerpt from "Revenge of the Green Dragons" in your reading journal.

Remember, you may react to a number of factors in the reading: the ideas, the language (especially vocabulary), the rhetorical structure, the unspoken assumptions, and the relationship between writer and reader (audience, purpose, organization, development). You need not, however, attempt to react to all of these factors in the essay at this time.

Discussion.   In class, compare your reactions in reading groups of five or six. Appoint a recorder to keep track of similarities or differences, consensus or disagreement, arising from the discussion. The recorder may summarize your group discussion for the rest of the class later.

Freewriting.   After the class discussion, freewrite for 10 to 15 minutes about your response to this piece of writing. Read your freewriting in groups of two to four.

SUMMARIZING

1. Create a preliminary analysis of the structure of "Revenge of the Green Dragons" by focusing on the parts of the excerpt that make up the whole. Capture those parts in a scratchline, outline, cluster diagram, or other strategy for presenting a parts-whole analysis. Focus on key words that help you mark the introduction of a new topic.
2. Write a summary paragraph or two, from your scratchline or other preliminary analysis.
3. Read the summaries in your reading groups. Compare the focus of each summary. How do the summaries differ? How are they the same? Is any member of the group reacting to the essay, making comments or evaluations, rather than summarizing?

FOCUSED CRITICAL READING

1. The opening section of the "Green Dragons" excerpt is highly dramatic. What rhetorical shift does Fredric Tannen make after he introduces gang activity in this first scene?
2. What is Dannen's purpose in describing in detail the culture that produced both the *dai lo* at age 20 and the two other gang members at age 16?
3. How is masculinity implicitly defined in this "second Chinatown" in New York?
4. The Green Dragons recruit young Chinese boys who are isolated by culture and language from mainstream cultures. Why might this recruitment be successful?

Margaret Edwards

But Does the New Woman Really Want the New Man?

Margaret Edwards is a professor of English at the University of Vermont. In the following article, originally published in Working Woman *in 1985 and later reprinted in the collection* Gender Identity: The Changing Rules of Dating and Marriage, *Edwards examines the evolution of American males from "Macho Men" to "New Men."*

It used to be that the man would telephone the woman and ask for a date. This was in the days before running shoes (there were only tennis shoes), when "Made in Japan" was a synonym for "shoddy." The man's bad luck was to have to screw up his courage and ask. The woman's bad luck was to have to stifle her hopes and wait. 1

But times change. 2

Recently, when a young male colleague in my office mentioned a woman whom he liked, I suggested, "Why don't you two drop by my place for a drink the next time you invite her on a date?" 3

"Oh, we don't *date*," he said. "We sort of hang out." 4

I have since made further discreet inquiries among the under-30 singles on our staff and have confirmed that dating as I once knew it is indeed dead. Fashion houses may be reviving the 1950s style of ball gowns, but the date, I've been assured, remains moribund. 5

Going back to the first source of my information, I asked who had made the crucial phone call to arrange the first meeting. His answer gave no hint of a new protocol. In this particular case, while idly conversing with the young woman—both of them having stopped to stretch their muscles at the same bend in a jogging trail—he mentioned he was going to a reggae concert. She remarked that she had a ticket to the same event. 6

It so happened that they bumped into each other afterwards, and in the company of numerous mutual friends, they walked downtown to a favorite bar. 7

"But that seems too whimsical and uncertain," I said. "Suppose she hadn't had a ticket to the same concert? Would you have gotten hold of her phone number to call her up and say, 'I've got an extra ticket; do you want to come?'" 8

No. Definitely not. He confessed, though, that he might have said, "I've got an extra ticket; do you want to buy it?" 9

10   "Can you tell me what's wrong," I asked, "with letting a woman know you're interested?" I began recalling with a certain nostalgia the brave, gruff voices on telephones that had wondered if I were free on Saturday night. My friend looked uncomfortable and evasive.

11   "If I let a woman know I'm interested," he said, "she might expect too much."

12   His face said it all: She might expect a regular and increasing familiarity. Marriage? Well, not quite that. But all too soon, books and stereos would be packed in cartons, a lease would have been jointly signed, and two sets of parents would begin looking pained but hopeful on Christmas holidays.

13   "Women make marvelous friends," he affirmed.

14   And I thought how often that's been said, in the same tone, about dogs.

New Men, Wimps and Wormboys

15   Are men getting weaker as women get stronger? This question seems to be preoccupying feminists lately. In the *New York Times,* Barbara Ehrenreich characterized the evolution of Macho Man into New Man as a mutation from tyrant to fop. She praised the new-found domestic independence of the male—he can fix his own quiche—but lamented the "narcissism" that makes him prefer to eat it alone or with a series of pretty companions. She praised his budding sensitivities—he enjoys a shopping spree, he keeps his body trim, he cries—but deplored his self-absorption. There is no commitment in the New Man. He's not out to enslave or dominate a female. In fact, what's wrong with him now is that he feels little urge to create a longstanding or passionate bond with any woman. Bachelorhood, freed of its gay stigma, has become his prime and perpetual state. He accepts that women have joined him on the fast track, yet their paths seem to be parallel, not intersecting.

16   "So it is not enough, anymore, to ask that men become more like women," concluded Ehrenreich. She tried to give a helpful directive: "We should ask that they become more like what both men and women might be"—cultivating in themselves both "masculine" and "feminine" virtues, plus a capacity for commitment and "a broad and generous vision of how we all might live together."

17   What Ehrenreich advocates is close to a wholesale change in human nature. It would surely call a truce in the war between the sexes. (It might even bring peace among nations as well.) But is it realistic to expect this? Are men going to redouble their efforts to be the best sort of people they can be? Pessimists among us may find the litmus of our predictions turning a shade darker.

18   Deborah Laake's article "Wormboys"—widely published last year in a number of newspapers—put forth the woman's position bluntly:

"As the clock keeps ticking and I'm neither younger nor more firmly settled in love than when I began my research, a primitive inner force wants to wind things up and have a life with someone. But something stops me. And that something is that I'm surrounded by wimps." She coined another word for wimps—wormboys.

These are men who shrink from marriage, from having children, [19] even from the simplest assertion, such as deciding where to go and what to do on a weekend. They are "lazy," unambitious in their work and unashamed of letting women pay. They do not embrace the roles of provider, arbiter, analyst, manager or leader. They avoid anything the least bit unpleasant. If a confrontation looms, they run and hide.

Laake advised women to assess what it means if they, not the men [20] they spend time with, "comb the entertainment sections of local periodicals" and then choose what to do with leisure time. What does it mean if women allow themselves to be accompanied by men who have offered no suggestions about where to go and are content to "just go along"?

The male ideal in feminist minds is no longer what it was, yet has [21] taken no definite subsequent shape. A superficial makeover of yesteryear's he-man won't do. John Wayne with a developed culinary talent will still think it's his woman's role to wash his dishes.

For serious feminists, there is no way back to the style of commit- [22] ment the he-man was half of—a style requiring the man's providence in exchange for the woman's subservience.

Yet the New Woman, in querulous moments, seems angry with the [23] new possibilities. If a feminist is offered the converse of the old style of commitment—that is, a union in which *she* will provide and *he* will serve—she balks. It's a bond that, by the logic of inverted tradition, ought to have a chance of strength.

Laake's article described her breakup with a so-called wormboy. "I [24] was overwhelmed," she wrote, "by the responsibilities falling to me in our union—those of principal breadwinner, head of the entertainment committee, business manager and mother of souls." Yet think of the years that men were expected to take on this same "overwhelming" role! All as a matter of course. And what was their reward? There was one. It was A Wife of One's Own.

Does a Woman Really Want a Wife?

Laake's pseudonymous boyfriend Henry is a hirsute version of [25] what has been the time-honored, much-idealized Little Woman, with "velvet sheathing the steel demurely." When Laake asked him exactly what he would contribute to their relationship, he replied, "I've observed that I seem to function as an invisible support system."

Invisible support—that's what the more retiring member of a cou- [26] ple offers. This is not the visible cash on the table or paycheck in the mailbox or gold card at the restaurant, but it's support nonetheless. It used to be called "what money can't buy" (although money kept it fed and housed), and it still takes amorphous forms: the shoulder to cry on, the home-cooked dinner that's waiting for you (still hot), the calm in the midst of your daily storm.

27   Laake admitted that she had enjoyed this kind of support from her Henry. To him, she had confided fears and fantasies. From him, she had received encouragement, understanding, sympathy and attention. She acknowledged that often he would talk to her in rambling and irrelevant monologues, but the talk itself provided support. "I'd [be] alternately absorbed in and comforted by it," she wrote, "the way I sometimes actually watch a TV show and other times just flip on the set and feel glad for the company."

28   Customarily men have felt "glad for the company" of women offering only invisible support. Why can't women be glad for the same? Perhaps it's bizarre and maybe a little scary to find oneself head of a household that includes an able-bodied man.

Did we feminists really expect that, as a norm, two equally ambitious careerists could form an amicable partnership under the same roof?

29   "Yes!" comes the chorus. "That's what we did expect. Why haven't we gotten it?"

30   Putting the question of sexual differences aside for the moment, I've asked myself: Are the strong couples I know made of partners who are alike or partners who are complimentary?

31   My answer: complimentary. A logical mate for a person full of energy and drive and purpose is someone offering that valuable old-fashioned commodity, "invisible support." Tractability (let's not keep calling it passivity) and an amenable disposition, a domestic focus (not necessarily being "lazy" about work) and an enjoyment of being coddled, indulged and led (despite being bright and full of his own opinions)—why aren't these traits considered valuable in a man? For a self-willed, adventurous woman, they might be the traits to look for if she wants to form a strong bond with someone who suits her.

32   Unfortunately, women don't yet admire in men what have been known as the "feminine virtues." It took women so long to get out from under these virtues that one can hardly blame them for still being suspicious of them. Maxims such as "They also serve who only stand and wait" seemed designed to keep women at home. Rather than standing and waiting, and being content to change diapers and fix the dinners for movers and doers, some women have wanted to be the movers and doers themselves.

33   It is all to the good and only fair that society seems to be moving in the direction of letting temperament and talents, rather than sex and

race, determine employment and compensation. But the old maxim still holds true, for those who "also serve" by giving "invisible support" are a vague "they," neither male nor female.

Little Women vs. New Women

When will we feminists stop feeling disappointed that the high-salaried mates willing to support families often prefer the Little Women types? They seem happier with them in fundamental ways. Those Little Women, despite Betty Friedan's debunking of their "mystique," are still the ones who willingly pack and move at their husband's decree, who are free to go on business junkets at short notice, who stay home to mind the children and run the errands. We all know by now that each Little Woman is taking a big chance, going at it with that combination of foolhardiness and courage peculiar to the motorbike racer who doesn't wear a helmet. If her marriage crashes, the damage to her will be inevitable and severe, for she's got very little protection. And the statistics are against her. 34

The New Woman, the mover and doer, is simply carving out new spheres of risk, "We are becoming the men we wanted to marry," *Ms.* editor Gloria Steinem told a large gathering of women. Right now, the "neither younger nor more firmly settled" New Woman may feel that her heaviest liability is a likelihood of winding up alone. The chances of marrying a man like herself seem slim and getting slimmer. 35

Yet our old dream dies hard. The prince must come and kiss the sleeping beauty. She is still under a dark spell, though this time not a spell of prudery or parents or her own pitiful ineptitude. What currently immobilizes her is loneliness. She feels paralyzed by the work of living up to her own vaunted promise, by the late nights and by the dumb dullness that creeps into any career. She has her independent self and nobody else—nobody else in the bed, nobody else across the breakfast table—at least nobody steady enough, ever-present enough, and promised as a part of each day. A prince must arrive who is willing to banish her loneliness permanently, to share half the housework, to become a "participating" father *and* to bring home a full share of income. Is that so much to ask of a man? The answer is that it must be, given how men seem to flee such commitment. 36

"She might expect too much" echoes beyond the revealing conversation I had with that man at the office. "You won't believe the guy I went out with last week..." begins a story I am told by an attractive single woman. "He was so afraid of commitment he checked the fire exits in the restaurant before we sat down!" A contemporary greeting card carries the message "To get a prince, you have to kiss a lot of frogs"—and today's unmarried women can get tired of kissing frogs. 37

Fewer Frogs, More Fish

38   Fewer frogs, and more fish, appear in the pool of available men if a feminist is willing to consider forming a serious alliance with the sort that the macho tradition taught her to spurn.

39   What about the man of gentle and unassuming temper? The man of erratic and skimpy income? The man shorter than she? The man less educated? The man from a less privileged background? Or, the man much younger?

40   A lot of misunderstanding between men and women comes from our believing the two sexes are inherently polarized. Actually, they're closer to an androgynous human mean. Men are cursed with the same conflicts we experience—and should not be envied and therefore reviled. The men I know, like the women I know, find it hard to choose between modern life's contraries: the safe routine and the adventurous possibility, the vocation and the avocation, the thrill of affairs and the comforts of marriage, the time they spend alone and the time they spend with others, the satisfaction in being free of children and the urge to have kids. If you talk to a man who is worried about his life, he sounds exactly like the worried woman—as if he's being torn along the same seams as she. He even ends a conversation as she does, by saying, "There's nobody free in this city. They're all married. I can't meet anyone."

41   So far, it seems that the work-directed and undomesticated New Woman doesn't like the look of the New Man. But should those of us who have asked to ride the horse turn petulant when we're hoisted astride and handed the reins? There are sincere pleasures in taking command. If a woman calls a new tune because she's earned enough to pay the piper, it doesn't mean she has to dance unpartnered. The New Woman may have to take a chance on living with the type of man who benefits from her energy rather than duplicates it, who admires her clear sense of purpose and doesn't thwart it, who feels inclined not so much to lead her as to enjoy where she leads. She may have to look past the classic knight on the white charger to find the next hero—the one on the dark horse.

Reading and Writing Activities

PRELIMINARY RESPONSE

Notes.   As you read, record your reactions (questions or comments) to "But Does the New Woman Really Want the New Man?" in your reading journal.

Remember, again, you can react to one or two of a number of related factors that shape meaning: the ideas, the relationships among ideas, the language used to present those ideas; the relationship of writer to readers; the relationship of medium to the message; the relationship of what is said to what is unsaid or unsayable in our culture about male behavior.

Discussion.   In class, compare your reactions in reading groups of five or six. Appoint a recorder to keep track of similarities or differences, consensus or disagreement, arising from the discussion. The recorder may summarize your group discussion for the rest of the class later.

Freewriting.   After the class discussion, freewrite for 10 to 15 minutes about the characteristics of the new man. Read your freewriting in groups of two to four.

SUMMARIZING

1. Create a preliminary analysis of Edwards's essay. Note the major claims. What is the central point Edwards makes in this essay?
2. Write a summary paragraph or two, from your preliminary analysis, of Edwards's claims and the way she develops those claims.
3. Read the summaries in your reading groups. Compare the focus of each summary. How do the summaries differ? How are they the same? Again, check to see if you are *reacting and responding* to the essay instead of summarizing the claims and development of those claims.

FOCUSED CRITICAL READING

1. What is the problem for feminists with the evolution of the New Man? How do you respond to their criticism of the New Man?
2. What were the specific problems for some women with the "he-man" style of commitment—a style "requiring the man's providence in exchange for the woman's subservience."
3. What are the problems, according to Edwards, of "two equally ambitious careerists" forming an "amicable partnership under the same roof"?
4. How do you respond to the suggestion that women be willing to "consider forming a serious alliance with the sort [of man] that the macho tradition taught her to spurn"?

Warren Farrell

Why Men Are the Way They Are

◆

Based in San Diego, Warren Farrell, Ph.D., is the only man in the United States to have been elected three times to the board of the National Organization for Women in New York City. In addition to "Why Men Are the Way They Are," he has published The Myth of Male Power *(1993). In the following selection, Farrell analyzes the social pressure exerted on men to behave the way they do.*

1   For thousands of years, marriages were about economic security and survival. Let's call this Stage I in our culture's conception of marriage. Beginning in the 1950s, marriages became focused on personal fulfillment and we entered into the era of the Stage II relationship. In Stage II, love was redefined to include listening to each other, joint parenting, sexual fulfillment, and shared decision-making. As a result, many traditional marriages consummated in Stage I failed under the new Stage II expectations. Thus we had the great surge of divorces beginning in the '60s.

2   The increasing incidence of divorce altered the fundamental relationship between women, men, and the workplace. Before divorce became common, most women's income came from men, so discrimination in favor of a woman's husband benefited her. But, as the divorce rate mushroomed, the same discrimination often hurt her. Before divorce became a common expectation, we had two types of inequality —women's experience of unequal rights in the workplace and men's experience of unequal responsibility for succeeding in the workplace. To find a woman to love him, a man had to "make his mark" in the world. As women increasingly had to provide for themselves economically, we confined our examination of inequality between the sexes to inequality in the workplace. What was ignored was the effect of inequality in the homeplace. Also ignored was a man's feeling that no woman would love him if he volunteered to be a full-time househusband instead of a full-time provider. As a result, we falsely assumed that the experience of inequality was confined to women.

3   Because divorces led to a change in the pressures on women (should she *become* a doctor, marry a doctor, or have a career and marry a doctor?), that change became "news" and her new juggling act got

attention in the media. Because the underlying pressures on men did not change (women still married men who earned more than they did), the pressure on men to succeed did not change, and, therefore, received no attention. With all the focus on discrimination against women, few understood the sexism directed against men.

The feminist perspective on relationships has become like fluorine in water—we drink it without being aware of its presence. The complaints about men, the idea that "men are jerks," have become so integrated into our unconscious that even advertisers have caught on. After analyzing 1,000 commercials in 1987, researcher Fred Hayward found that when an ad called for a negative portrayal in a male-female interaction, an astonishing 100 percent of the time the "bad guy" was the man.   4

This anti-male bias isn't confined to TV commercials. A sampling of the cards in the "Love and Friendship" section of a greeting card store revealed these gems: 5

"If they can send one man to the moon, why can't they send them all?"   6

"When you unzip a man's pants...his brains fall out."   7

"If we can make penicillin out of moldy cheese...maybe we can make men out of the low-lifes in this town."   8

A visit to the bookstore turns up titles like *No Good Men.* Imagine *No Good Women* or *No Good Jews.* And what do the following titles have in common? *Men Who Can't Love; Men Who Hate Women and the Women Who Love Them; Smart Women/Foolish Choices; Successful Women, Angry Men; Peter Pan Syndrome.*   9

Feminism-as-fluoride has left us acknowledging the working mother ("Superwoman") without ever being aware of the working father. It is by now well recognized that, even among men who do more housework or more childcare than their wives, almost never does the man truly share the 24-hour-a-day psychological responsibility of ministering to everyone's needs, egos, and schedules.   10

But it is not so widely recognized that, despite the impact feminism has had on the contemporary family, almost every father still retains 24-hour-a-day psychological responsibility for the family's financial well-being. Even women who earn more than their husbands tell me that they know their husbands would support their decision to earn as much or as little as they wish. If a woman marries a successful man, then she knows she will have an option to work or not, but not an obligation. Almost all men see bringing home a healthy salary as an obligation, not an option.   11

A woman today has three options.   12
Option 1: Full-time career.
Option 2: Full-time family.
Option 3: Some combination of career and family.

13   A man sees himself as having three "slightly different" options:
Option 1: Work full time.
Option 2: Work full time.
Option 3: Work full time.

14   The U.S. Bureau of the Census explains that full-time working males work an average of eight hours more per week on their jobs than full-time working females.

15   Since many women now earn substantial incomes, doesn't this relieve the pressure on men to be a wallet? No. Why? Because successful women do exactly what less-successful women do—"marry up," that is, marry a man whose income is greater than her own. According to statistics, if a woman cannot marry up or marry someone with a high wage-earning potential, she does not marry at all. Therefore, a man often reflexively backs away from a woman he's attracted to when he discovers she's more successful than he is because he senses he's only setting himself up for rejection. Ultimately, she'll dump him for a more successful man. She may sleep with him, or live with him, but not marry him unless she spots "potential." Thus, of top female executives, 85 percent don't get married; the remaining 15 percent almost all marry up. Even successful women have not relaxed the pressure on men to succeed.

16   Ask a girl in junior high or high school about the boy whom she would "absolutely love" to ask her out to the prom and chances are almost 100 percent that she would tell you her fantasy boy is *both* good-looking *and* successful (a jock or student leader, or someone who "has potential"). Ask a boy whom he would absolutely love to ask out to the prom and chances are almost 100 percent his fantasy girl is good-looking. Only about 25 percent will also be interested in a girl's "strong career potential" (or her being a top female jock). His invisible curriculum, then, taught him that being good-looking is not enough to attract a good-looking girl—he must be successful *in addition* to being good-looking. This was his experience of inequality: "Good-looking boy does not equal good-looking girl." Why are boys willing to consider themselves unequal to girls' attention until they hit their heads against 21 other boys on a football field?

17   In part, the answer is because boys are addicted. In all cultures, boys are addicted to the images of beautiful women. And in American culture this is enormously magnified. Boys are exposed to the images of beautiful women about 10 million times per year via television, billboards, magazines, etc. In the process, the naturally beautiful girl becomes a *genetic celebrity.* Boys become addicted to the image of the quasi-anorexic female. To be the equal of this genetic celebrity, the adolescent boy must become an *earned celebrity* (by performing, paying on dates, etc.) Until he is an earned celebrity, he feels like a groupie trying to get a celebrity's attention.

18   Is there an invisible curriculum for girls and boys growing up? Yes. For girls, "If you want to have your choice among boys, you had better

be beautiful." For boys, it's "You had better be handsome *and* success-ful." If a boy wants a romantic relationship with a girl he must not only be successful and perform, he must pay and pursue—risk sexual rejec-tion. Girls think of the three Ps—performing, paying, and pursuing—as male power. Boys see the three Ps as what they must do to earn their way to female love and sexuality. They see these not as power, but as compensations for powerlessness. This is the adolescent male's experi-ence of inequality.

Reading and Writing Activities

PRELIMINARY RESPONSE

Notes.   As you read, record your reactions (questions or comments) to Warren Farrell's essay "Why Men Are the Way They Are" in your read-ing journal.

You may react to his central ideas, the relationships he discusses or implies exist between men and women, the clarity of the presentation of his ideas, the persona he creates through his writing, or the experi-ence you have with ideas or experiences he describes.

Discussion.   In class, compare your reactions in reading groups of five or six. Appoint a recorder to keep track of similarities or differences, consensus or disagreement, arising from the discussion. The recorder may summarize your group discussion for the rest of the class later.

Freewriting.   After the class discussion, freewrite for 10 to 15 minutes about Farrell's suggestion that men have a 24-hour responsibility to be providers and women do not.

SUMMARIZING

1. Create a preliminary analysis of the progression of claims that Farrell makes.
2. Write a summary paragraph or two, from preliminary work, of the central claims and the evidence or support Farrell presents to elabo-rate those claims.
3. Read the summaries in your reading groups. Compare the focus of each summary. How do the summaries differ? How are they the same? Are there claims that everyone in the group records? Are there supporting details that some members of the group summa-rize and other members do not? What is the significance, if any, of differences in summaries?

Joseph Campbell

Marriage and Feminism

◆

Joseph Campbell was a noted scholar, teacher and writer. Before his death in 1987, he electrified the television audience in a series of interviews with Bill Moyers on PBS, with his interpretations of legends, myths, and religions. Later, The Power of Myth, *a book of transcripts of these Campbell-Moyers interviews, became a* New York Times *bestseller.*

In the following selection from another set of interviews on public radio with Michael Toms, he talks, among other things, of the changing roles of men and women. He seems unfettered by a "male chorus" that makes other men resist this change. He says, "We're in a marvelous moment with respect to the state of women, and it's a moment just as crucial for men because the archetypology of just wife and mother is gone."[1]

1   *Michael:* You once said you have to risk in order to find life, that so often people go into work thinking of making money instead of looking for something that will inspire them to life action. Have you ever done anything in your life primarily for money?

2   *Joseph:* No. Absolutely not. I would have, I think, but I came back from Europe about two weeks before the crash, and I didn't have a real job for five years. But I found—I don't know whether it would work now—that a young unmarried man didn't need much money; I could take care of myself pretty well for almost nothing. My decision to follow this course came one day in Paris while I was sitting in the little garden of Cluny, where the Boulevards St. Michel and St. Germain come together. It suddenly struck me: What in heaven's name am I doing? I don't even know how to eat a decent, nourishing meal, and here I'm learning what happened to vulgar Latin when it passed into Portuguese and Spanish and French. So I dropped work on the Ph.D. On my return, I found a place in upstate New York and read the classics for twelve hours a day. I was

[1]Joseph Campbell, in John M. Maher and Dennie Briggs, eds., *An Open Life: Joseph Campbell in Conversation with Michael Toms* (New York: Harper & Row, 1989), p. 126.

enjoying myself enormously, and realized I would never finish my degree because it would have required me to do things that I had already outgrown. In Europe, the world had opened up: Joyce, Sanskrit, the Orient, and the relationship of all these to psychology. I couldn't go back and finish up that Ph.D thesis; besides, I didn't have the money. And that freewheeling, maverick life gave me a sense of the deep joy in doing something meaningful to me.

When, after five years, I was invited to teach at Sarah Lawrence   3
College, I found that they were very excited by what I wanted to do. I would not have taken a job otherwise, just as I wouldn't take the Ph.D. I don't know how it would have been had I been married with a child. I can't speak to that point. But it wasn't by accident that I wasn't married because it was my notion that before a commitment like that, I should be prepared to take care of the situation.

Michael: You have been married for some forty years now—   4

Joseph: Forty-six years [1984].   5

Michael: —to Jean Erdman. During that time, we've gone from a tradi-   6
tional patriarchal ideal of woman to the feminist movement and the assertion of women's power—a return of the goddesses, if you will. What's happening in these changes of the past couple of decades?

Joseph: We're in a marvelous moment with respect to the state of wom-   7
en, and it's a moment just as crucial for men because the archety-pology of just the wife and mother is gone. Many a man, when he thinks of marriage, imagines that archetype, and he is unwilling or unable to face the fact of a female personality. Men have had a wid-er range of life courses enabling them to develop their potentials, but women have been condemned to one style, one system of inter-ests and concerns. That's not true anymore; the world has opened up to them. Now there are very few models for them. The immedi-ate model is the men's world, and many women move into that in competition.

But the great thing is the emerging possibility of the female   8
personality as the guiding image of the women's own life. And then her husband has to match that. He's in dialogue now with an unpredictable presence, because the sexes are deeply mysterious to each other—really and wonderfully so.

You see, the whole thing in marriage is the relationship and   9
yielding—knowing the functions, knowing that each is playing a role in an organism. One of the things I have realized—and peo-ple who have been married a long time realize—is that marriage is not a love affair. A love affair has to do with immediate person-

al satisfaction. But marriage is an ordeal; it means yielding, time and again. That's why it's a sacrament: you give up your personal simplicity to participate in a relationship. And when you're giving, you're not giving to the other person: you're giving to the relationship. And if you realize that you are in the relationship just as the other person is, then it becomes life building, a life fostering and enriching experience, not an impoverishment because you're giving to somebody else. Do you see what I mean?

10   This is the challenge of a marriage. What a beautiful thing is a life together as growing personalities, each helping the other to flower, rather than just moving into the standard archetype. It's a wonderful moment when people can make the decision to be something quite astonishing and unexpected, rather than cookie-mold products.

11 *Michael:* Do you think the high divorce rate comes from failure to recognize that?

12 *Joseph:* Partly. And to be able to continue the adventure. Because no matter whom you tie your life to, you're going to find the person mysterious. There will be a lot that you didn't know about, and even the person himself didn't know about. And remember, the person is having the same problem in relation to you.

13 *Michael:* And both are changing all the time.

14 *Joseph:* All the time.

15 *Michael:* So often we want to freeze the other person into a position.

16 *Joseph:* Naturally. People have a notion of what a marriage ought to be, and the marriage that they want. You can't have that and have the adventure of a love marriage. It's got to be one or the other. And wherever love takes you, there you are.

17 *Michael:* And that's the adventure.

18 *Joseph:* That *is* the adventure! I see marriage in two stages. One is that wonderful impulse stage of youth where everything is "coming up roses" and the birds are singing and all that. Then there comes a time when those vital energies aren't there, but at the same time there is an awakening of a spiritual relationship. When that doesn't happen, you see people getting divorced. I've been shocked at the number of my friends who brought up a family, everything seems wonderful, the kids are gone, and they get divorced!

19   You know the story about the priest, the minister, and the rabbi who ask when life begins? The priest says, "It begins at conception." The minister says, "Oh, it begins after twenty days or something like that." And the rabbi says, "It begins when the children

have graduated and the dog has died." And that's just the time when people tend to grow apart. They all need things that bond them together, the physical things—the joy of bringing up the family. And with all that gone, what next?

Michael: In some sense, too, all those things have become walls to pre- 20 vent us from really asking the question "Why am I here?"

Joseph: Yes. 21

Michael: What's it all about? 22

Joseph: You've got a lot of reasons just to have two cars, you know? Win 23 the lottery, or something like that, but for heaven's sake, what's the adventure? And it gets to be more and more adventurous the longer you live. I can tell you that much!

Michael: I'd believe it, Joseph, coming from you. It has to be true! 24

Joseph: [laughs]: You'll get there, Michael. 25

Reading and Writing Activities

PRELIMINARY RESPONSE

Notes.　　As you read, record your reactions (questions or comments) to Joseph Campbell's interview with Michael Toms.

Discussion.　　In class, compare your reactions in reading groups of five or six. Appoint a recorder to keep track of similarities or differences, consensus or disagreement, arising from the discussion. The recorder may summarize your group discussion for the rest of the class later.

Freewriting.　　After the class discussion, freewrite for 5 to 10 minutes about similarities or differences in your group reading of the interview. Read your freewriting in groups of two to four.

SUMMARIZING

1. Write a summary paragraph or two of the topics Campbell covers in his interview.
2. Read the summaries in your reading groups. Compare the focus of each summary. How do the summaries differ? How are they the

same? Again, check to see if you are *reacting and responding* to the interview instead of summarizing the topics,

FOCUSED CRITICAL READING

1. Campbell responds to Michael Toms's questions with a series of stories. How might you categorize these stories?
2. In response to a question asking if he had ever done anything in his life "primarily for money," Campbell responds, "No." How easy or difficult was it for him to achieve such a life, according to what he says in this interview?
3. How does he view the changing roles of men and women?

WRITING SUGGESTIONS

1. Freewrite for about 10 minutes on friendships between men and women. Has it been easier for you to maintain friendships with men or with women? Read your freewrites in pairs, then revise and extend. Cite Pittman's claims about male relationships, if appropriate, to extend your revised draft to an essay (2–3 pages).
2. Freewrite a paragraph or two about family values or traditions. This freewriting need not reflect your family relationships (pre-sent or past) but may reflect a specific value or tradition you inherited from your family that you hope to pass on to your children. Or freewrite a paragraph or two about the men or women you would like your children and grandchildren to have as role models.
3. Write a short essay in which you respond to Pittman's views about the role of fathers in changing the "masculine mystique."
4. Read Joyce Carol Oates's "Rape and the Boxing Ring."

   From the information in this article, present your point of view on boxing in an essay (2–3 pages). Speculate about the forming of Mike Tyson's character and the influences that may have contributed to his conviction. Use information from the article to support your speculations. How difficult or easy is it for you to understand Mike Tyson's behavior?
5. Freewrite about changes you see in different generations of men in your family. Are the younger men "New Men," as Margaret Edwards describes them? Finish with a generalization about the behavior of

men you know toward women. Use this generalization to write an essay on the topic of evolving male behavior. Include information from the readings in this chapter in your essay, if appropriate.

6. Freewrite a paragraph or two about the men or women you find attractive. Has your idea of attractiveness changed over the years? Or write an essay in which you respond to the claims and information presented in Margaret Edwards's and Warren Farrell's essays. Be sure to summarize those ideas in your essay before you start responding.

3

Sexual Relationships: Romantic Love, Courtship, Marriage

◆————————

In 1963, psychologist Erik Erikson reaffirmed his belief that the crucial task of adolescence is developing the capacity for intimate heterosexual relationships.* Although many people, including some of the writers presented in this chapter, would dispute that notion, nearly everyone growing up in America has felt some pressure to initiate and remain involved in a heterosexual relationship. Readings in this chapter examine some of the conflicts and controversies that arise from this pressure.

Expanding on the notion of focused freewriting in Chapter 2, this chapter opens with an explanation and illustration of *collaborative response*. The negotiations of a small reading group are modeled through the interactions of three experienced readers who respond to Lawrence Stone's critical look at romantic love. These three readers use group inquiry as a way of expanding and refining their initial responses to a text, thus initiating more methodical analysis.

Richard Stengel extends Lawrence Stone's critique of romantic love, proposing a reconsideration of arranged marriage as a preferable alternative. Stengel's essay is followed by two recent cover stories from *Time* disputing the belief that romantic love is an artificial construct

*Erik Erikson, *Childhood and Society,* 2nd ed. (New York: Norton, 1964), pp. 265–66.

126

unique to Western culture. Both articles report recent research suggesting a chemical or biological basis for romantic passion.

The last four readings look at problems and issues related to courtship, marriage, and family life. Michael Lerner derides the popular expectation that a loving domestic environment should provide a safe haven from the frustrations of work. Venny Villapando examines the exploitation of Asian women brought to America by men seeking submissive, obedient wives. Finally, Maulana Karenga argues that problems often attributed to relationships between African-American men and women must be viewed within the context of the dominant American culture and its traditions of racism, sexism, and materialism.

Analyzing a Text Through Group Inquiry

Chapter 2 introduced freewriting as a response to reading. This chapter describes an effective way of extending and refining that spontaneous, often personal type of response, moving toward a more deliberate and public interpretation. Specifically, we show how three experienced readers enriched their understanding of a text by sharing and discussing each other's freewritten response in a reading group.

After a first reading of "A Short History of Love" by Lawrence Stone (pages 129–32), Janet, Alex, and Agnes shared the brief, unfocused responses they had recorded in their reading journals. Then, having read and discussed those responses, they freewrote for 5 to 10 minutes on each of five specific features of Stone's text:

Purpose: What Stone may have wanted to accomplish—how he hoped to influence listeners or readers.

Audience: The persons toward whom Stone directs his aims.

Main idea: The basic point Stone is driving at.

Development: The kinds of evidence (facts, examples, personal experience, research findings, casual observation, abstract reasoning, and so forth) that Stone presents.

Organization: The sequence or arrangement of evidence within the text.

As you will see, all three readers agreed about a few broad issues of interpretation—that Lawrence Stone is critical of romantic love, that he seems to issue a stern warning to his audience—but they also noted and responded very differently to specific details in the text.

Janet, Alex, and Agnes duplicated their freewritten responses so that each had a copy. All three read their writing aloud while their partners took notes, recording any reactions or associations that entered their minds. The methods they used to take notes during this reading differed as much as their freewritten responses. As he listened to his partners read, Alex wrote phrases and short sentences in the margins. Beside Janet's comments about development, for instance, he wrote: "Your view of audience and purpose seems to shift as you get further along." Next to Agnes's observation that Stone does not say how and why love-based marriages replaced arranged marriages in the 1700s, Alex asked: "Because of the rise of democracy?" In contrast to Alex, Agnes preferred to circle key words and phrases in her partners' responses. For example, she circled *more critically, examine,* and *question* in Janet's first paragraph. Janet was a bit more methodical than Alex and Agnes. She used check marks to note ideas she considered interesting or unusual, wrote "yes" next to those she agreed with, placed a question mark beside anything she found confusing or doubtful, and inserted an exclamation mark whenever she took exception to something one of her partners had written.

Take a few moments now to read the following selection by Lawrence Stone, professor of history at Princeton University. The selection is an excerpt from a paper that Stone delivered to professional colleagues at a 1987 conference cosponsored by the Columbia University Psychoanalytic Center and the Association for Psychoanalytic Medicine. After you have read Stone's text, look at the freewritten responses composed by Janet, Alex, and Agnes.

Lawrence Stone

A Short History of Love

◆

Historians and anthropologists are in general agreement that romantic love—the usually brief but intensely felt and all-consuming attraction toward another person—is culturally conditioned. Love has a history. It is common only in certain societies at certain times, or even in certain social groups within those societies, usually the elite, which have the leisure to cultivate such feelings. Scholars are, however, less certain whether romantic love is merely a culturally induced psychological overlay on top of the biological drive for sex, or whether it has biochemical roots that operate quite independently from the libido. Would anyone in fact "fall in love" if they had not read about it or heard it talked about? Did poetry invent love, or love poetry? 1

Some things can be said with certainty about the history of the phenomenon. The first is that cases of romantic love can be found in all times and places and have often been the subject of powerful poetic expression, from the Song of Solomon to Shakespeare. On the other hand, as anthropologists have discovered, neither social approbation nor the actual experience of romantic love is common to all societies. Second, historical evidence for romantic love before the age of printing is largely confined to elite groups, which of course does not mean that it may not have occurred lower on the social scale. As a socially approved cultural artifact, romantic love began in Europe in the southern French aristocratic courts of the twelfth century, and was made fashionable by a group of poets, the troubadours. In this case the culture dictated that it should occur between an unmarried male and a married woman, and that it either should go sexually unconsummated or should be adulterous. 2

By the sixteenth and seventeenth centuries, our evidence becomes quite extensive, thanks to the spread of literacy and the printing press. We now have love poems, such as Shakespeare's sonnets, love letters, and autobiographies by women concerned primarily with their love lives. The courts of Europe were evidently hotbeds of passionate intrigues and liaisons, some romantic, some sexual. The printing press also began to spread pornography to a wider public, thus stimulating the libido, while the plays of Shakespeare indicate that romantic love was a concept familiar to society at large, which composed his audience. 3

Whether this romantic love was approved of, however, is another question. We simply do not know how Shakespearean audiences 4 reacted to *Romeo and Juliet*. Did they, like us (and as Shakespeare clearly intended), fully identify with the young lovers? Or, when they left the theater, did they continue to act like the Montague and Capulet parents, who were trying to stop these irresponsible adolescents from allowing an ephemeral and irrational passion to interfere with the serious business of politics and patronage?

5   What is certain is that every advice book, every medical treatise, every sermon and religious homily of the sixteenth and seventeenth centuries firmly rejected both romantic passion and lust as suitable bases for marriage. In the sixteenth century, marriage was thought to be best arranged by parents, who could be relied upon to choose socially and economically suitable partners. People believed that the sexual bond would automatically create the necessary harmony between the two strangers in order to maintain the stability of the new family unit. This assumption is not, it seems, unreasonable, since recent investigations in Japan have shown that there is no difference in the rate of divorce between couples whose marriages were arranged by their parents and couples whose marriages were made by individual choice based on romantic love.

6   In the eighteenth century, orthodox opinion about marriage began to shift from subordinating the individual will to the interests of the group, and from economic or political considerations toward those of well-tried personal affection. The ideal marriage was one preceded by three to six months of intensive courting by a couple from families roughly equal in social status and economic wealth; that courtship, however, took place only with the prior consent of parents on both sides. But it was not until the Romantic movement and the rise of the novel, especially the pulp novel in the nineteenth century, that society accepted a new idea—that it is normal and indeed praiseworthy for young men and women to fall passionately in love, and that there must be something wrong with those who fail to have such an overwhelming experience sometime in late adolescence or early adulthood. Once this new idea was publicly accepted, the arrangement of marriage by parents came to be regarded as intolerable and immoral.

7   Today, the role of passionate attachments between adults is obscured by a new development: the saturation of the whole culture—through every medium of communication—with the belief that sexuality is the predominant and overriding human drive, a doctrine whose theoretical foundations were provided by Freud. In no past society known to me has sex been given so prominent a role in the culture at large, nor has sexual fulfillment been elevated to such preeminence in the list of human aspirations—in a vain attempt to relieve civilization of its discontents. We find it scarcely credible today that in most of Western Europe in the seventeenth century, in a society in which people usually married in their late twenties, a degree of chastity was prac-

ticed that kept the illegitimacy rate—without contraceptives—as low as 2 or 3 percent. Today, individualism is given such absolute priority in most Western societies that people are virtually free to act as they please, to sleep with whom they please, and to marry and divorce when and whom they please. The psychic (and, more recently, the physical) costs of such behavior are now becoming clear, however, and how long this situation will last is anybody's guess.

Here I should point out that the present-day family—I exclude the poor black family in America from this generalization—is not, as is generally supposed, disintegrating because of the very high divorce rate—up to 50 percent. It has to be remembered that the median duration of marriage today is almost exactly the same as it was 100 years ago. Divorce, in short, now acts as a functional substitute for death: both are means of terminating marriage at a premature stage. The psychological effects on the survivor may well be very different, although in most cases the catastrophic economic consequences for women remain the same. But the point to be emphasized is that broken marriages, stepchildren, and single-parent households were as common in the past as they are today.   8

The most difficult historical problem regarding romantic love concerns its role among the propertyless poor. Since they were propertyless, their loves and marriages were of little concern to their kin, and they were therefore more or less free to choose their own mates. By the eighteenth century, and probably before, court records make it clear that the poor often married for love, combined with a confused set of motives including lust and the economic necessity to have a strong and healthy assistant to run the farm or the shop. It was generally expected that they would behave "lovingly" toward each other, but this often did not happen. In many a peasant marriage, the husband seems to have valued his cow more than his wife. Passionate attachments among the poor certainly occurred, but how often they took priority over material interests we may never know for certain.   9

Finally, we know that in the eighteenth century—unlike the seventeenth—at least half of all brides in England and America were pregnant on their wedding day. But this fact tells us more about sexual customs than about passionate attachments: sex began at the moment of engagement, and marriage in church came later, often triggered by the pregnancy. We also know that if a poor servant girl was impregnated by her master, which often happened, the latter usually had no trouble finding a poor man who would marry her, in return for payment of ten pounds or so. Not much passion there.   10

Passionate attachments between young people can and do happen in any society as a by-product of biological sexual attraction, but the social acceptability of the emotion has varied enormously over time and class and space, determined primarily by cultural norms and prop-   11 erty arrangements. We are in a unique position today in that our culture is dominated by romantic notions of passionate love as the only socially admissible reason for marriage; sexual fulfillment is accepted as the dominant human drive and a natural right for both sexes; and contraception is normal and efficient. Behind all this lies a frenetic individualism, a restless search for a sexual and emotional ideal in human relationships, and a demand for instant ego gratification.

12   Most of this is new and unique to our culture. It is, therefore, quite impossible to assume that people in the past thought about and experienced passionate attachments the way we do. Historical others—even our own forefathers and mothers—were indeed other.

Three Freewritten Responses to
A Short History of Love

JANET'S RESPONSE

Purpose: Stone wants us to think more critically about romantic love, perhaps even to view it as unnecessary. Too many of us assume that living without romantic love is to be deprived. Stone wants us to examine and question that assumption.

Audience: Stone addresses readers familiar with Shakespeare and Freud and comfortable with terms like *orthodox opinion* and *ego gratification.* He assumes an audience already a bit cynical about romance and passionate love. I think the reader most receptive to Stone's ideas has lost his or her idealism about such matters and is someone willing to believe that passion is not necessary, maybe unhealthy, in long-term relationships. The essay is for people more likely to sneer at Valentine's Day than to search for just the right greeting card.

Main Idea: Stone's point is that passion, romance, and sexual fulfillment are less crucial to happiness than our culture conditions us to believe. He argues that poets and playwrights created romantic love and that Freud added the notion that sex is an overriding drive. The presumed need for passionate attachments has been constructed by a culture in which the individual comes first and the needs of the group are relegated to a distant second. Stone warns that addiction to romance places us at peril, and he lists the increase of sexually transmitted diseases, divorce, depression, and even mental illness among the results.

Development: Stone supports his ideas with evidence from history, with particular attention to the mass publication of novels, the Romantic Movement, and the influence of Freud. There's a gradual change in tone as the reading progresses. After the first few paragraphs, I expected a scholarly, informative piece with no earthshaking point to it. But by the time I was finished, I realized that Stone was kind of up on a soapbox. As the essay develops, I get the picture of an embittered prude manipulating history to argue against something he either doesn't want or can't have.

Organization: Stone organizes this piece chronologically. He shows the development of romantic love over the centuries, down to the current frenzy for instant gratification and the sexual and emotional ideal. But even though this chronological progression is easy to follow and serves well as an organizational blueprint, I detect a move from scholarly detachment to preachy moralizing.

ALEX'S RESPONSE

Purpose: Stone asks readers to consider a cultural norm in a fundamentally different and unconventional way. The trappings of romantic love so permeate our daily lives, that we assume there's something wrong with an adolescent or young adult who doesn't experience the feeling. So Stone asks us to set aside this conditioning for a moment and to entertain the idea that a thing we all "know" to be natural and proper really isn't. Also he wants us to see that there's something at stake. I'm not sure he wants to alarm us and alter patterns of behavior, but he does want us to think about the consequences of our beliefs and to get a debate going.

Audience: I think Stone is addressing a well-educated, broad-minded audience—the sort of people who subscribe to *Psychology Today*. Ironically, that type of reader, like the people who perpetuated the concept of romantic love prior to the eighteenth century, are an elite. An essay like this is probably leisure reading for such persons. I think Stone envisions a reader who prides herself on being an independent, tough-minded skeptic—someone who isn't taken in by bunk just because it's popular or "nice." An iconoclast, I guess you could say. I'm not sure Stone is *addressing* this type of audience so much as he is *conjuring it up*.

Main Idea: I think there are two important ideas. First, Stone says that love may be (or is? he's inconsistent on that point) a kind of learned behavior. Second, because of historical developments (democracy and individualism, invention of mass media, Freudian psychology), romantic love has run rampant and introduces certain dangers.

Development: Stone cites sources from history and anthropology—both the scholarship in those fields and other documents like autobiographies, love letters, medical treatises, sermons, and even pornography. Stone seems well read outside his field, citing literary works as well. But I see contradictions in the evidence. In paragraph 1, Stone mentions the uncertainty of "scholars" (psychologists maybe?) about whether love is "culturally induced" or "has biochemical roots." If it's the latter, then aren't historians and anthropologists mistaken in the view that Stone attributes to them? Or are psychologists less certain about this than scholars in other fields? Has Stone expressed himself poorly, or am I reading his first paragraph carelessly?

Stone introduces more specific support in paragraph 5, when he refers to the divorce rate in Japan. It's interesting, though, that he relies on emotionally charged language in his last sentence, with words like *frenetic, restless,* and *demand.* This seems out of keeping with the rest of the essay, which sounds more scholarly.

Organization: A quick look shows that the essay is chronologically ordered, tracing the history of romantic love. But beneath that, I see a question-answer approach. Stone opens with a problem or dilemma, and the first paragraph ends with two questions. The next paragraph opens with "some things can be said with certainty," and Stone lists those things. Paragraph 4 then opens with "another question," and that question leads to two others. Paragraph 5 goes back to certainty, beginning with "What is certain is that. . . ."

AGNES'S RESPONSE

Purpose: Stone reminds an audience of psychoanalysts of the history of romantic love. He assesses where we stand today, with tremendous social pressures for people to seek and insist upon sexual fulfillment. For me, the essay doesn't make clear whether Stone sees romantic love and sexual love as the same thing. Stone fails, probably on purpose, to give a detailed explanation of how "love" took the place of arranged marriages and how, through the "saturation of the whole culture," sexual gratification was encouraged, even idealized. The chips seem to go down when he examines the influences of Freud. Is he trying to discredit the Freudian theory of human sexuality, now taken for granted in some circles? (When he speaks of "relieving society of its discontents," he alludes to Freud's justification of neurosis, *Civilization and Its Discontents*.) Stone seems to say that we pay a heavy price for license and excess. Is he trying to upset the Freudians? to urge therapists to stress social values rather than individual desires as they guide their patients out of a self-induced wilderness?

Audience: Stone is speaking to a group of professionals interested in new ways of thinking about mental illness and its treatment. The allusion to *Romeo and Juliet* isn't so important, since every high schooler has read the play. The Troubadors are less familiar, but anyone who's heard of Bing Crosby or Perry Como has heard the term. So I think Stone is flattering his audience without really demanding much of them. It seems scholarly, but is it really? His tone is earnest, though bias slips in near the end. There's not a great deal of hard evidence. Frankly, I think this essay could be adapted for the *Parade* section of the Sunday paper with only minimal editing. After all, we're all interested in what makes us tick, and all the emphasis on the demons of instant gratification, license, and unfettered individualism would hit home with people trying to figure out what's gone wrong with their relationships. Why not say something about the psychic toll taken by adulterous liaisons or arranged marriages?

Main Idea: Stone salts his essay with variations of his main idea, echoing in the process. It gathers weight, ending in a condemnation of our current value system. Stone turns from chronicler to prophet of doom. I have problems with the title. A person can be passionately attached to anyone—a child, a friend of the same sex.

Development: Stone writes at a level somewhere between broad generalization and concrete particulars. He sums up the events of centuries in a few sentences, making it sound like fact. Though he probably has done extensive research, I don't sense that it's been recently. He deals with the printing press and pornography in a sentence, something an undergraduate history major could do. Perhaps this is enough detail for his audience of non-historians.

Organization: Stone uses a time order, easy to follow, especially when the ideas begin to gather upon themselves. You can almost hear him saying, "Once upon a time there never was a Cinderella. Now we have Cinderella in lycra." Words like *today* at the beginning of paragraph 7 do a lot of the work.

After Janet, Alex, and Agnes had read their freewritten responses aloud, all three discussed ideas and observations that made an impact on them. For example, Alex remarked on Janet's belief that as Lawrence Stone gets farther into his topic he begins to sound more like a soapbox orator than a scholar. Alex connected that belief with something he had written about Stone's development—that "emotionally charged language" appears in paragraph 5 of "A Short History of Love." Janet's observation thus helped Alex see the language in that paragraph in terms of a broader pattern. Janet, on the other hand, benefited from Alex's narrower focus on words in a specific segment of the text. Not only was her perception reinforced by what Alex noted; she also had supporting evidence for what had been only a vague impression about tone.

As the group proceeded to discuss each other's responses, a number of similar transactions occurred. Agnes took issue with Janet's and Alex's notion that Stone hopes to alter public behavior. She reminded her partners that Stone delivered his paper at an academic conference and that his primary audience was psychoanalysts rather than a randomly selected group of single men and women. Acknowledging that they had lost sight of that fact, Janet and Alex modified their understanding of Stone's purpose. Later, Janet took note of her partners' doubts about Stone's authority in fields other than history and became more skeptical herself.

In short, group interaction enriched the responses of these experienced readers, causing them to modify and extend their interpretations of "A Short History of Love."

Questions and exercises that follow reading selections in this book often ask you to engage in group inquiry. Sometimes we recommend that you work in groups of five or six, pursuing a narrower focus—a specific issue or problem of interpretation. Other times we suggest that you work in smaller groups, expanding your focus to the overall aims, content, and structure of a particular text. Regardless of the circumstances, however, you should keep these general guidelines in mind:

1. Read the text at least a day before your group gets together.
2. Record an initial response in your reading journal immediately after a first reading of the text. Subsequent freewriting may be influenced by group or class discussion.
3. Approach writing and group discussion as ways to open various plausible interpretations, not as ways to reach a single correct understanding of a text.
4. Bring your writing to the group (in multiple copies if possible) and be prepared to read it aloud. Never "tell about" what you have written, and discourage other group members from doing so.

Richard Stengel

No More MoonJune:
Love's Out

◆

After reading the following essay, you will be asked to carry out processes of writing and group discussion explained on pages 127–28 and modeled on pages 132–36. The author of this essay, Richard Stengel, has been associated with Time *since he became a staff writer in 1981. He has also written for other periodicals, including* Vanity Fair, GQ, *and* Rolling Stone. *"No More MoonJune," first published in* The New York Times, *takes Lawrence Stone's critique of romantic love a bit further, proposing an alternative to relationships formed on that basis.*

Romantic love is a supreme fiction, marriage for love the conse-   1
quence of that fiction, and divorce the painful evidence of that initial delusion.

The history of romantic love is the continuing ironic testimony of   2
the power of our minds to mesmerize our bodies, while romantic marriage is the most recent and least successful evolutionary stage in the history of matrimony.

Now that the Census Bureau has estimated that more than one in   3
three marriages will end in divorce, it is apparent that the solution to the troubled state of matrimony is a return to the tradition of arranged marriages.

The sentimental sanctity of love was the invention of the Provençal   4
poets of the twelfth century, and they saw it as the exotic refinement of a bored aristocracy. Since then, however, love has democratized itself and is no longer the luxury of a courtly minority but the expectation of every man and woman. Indeed, the joys of romantic love are the birthright of every American, for the Framers of the Declaration of Independence declared "the pursuit of happiness" to be the inalienable right of all men and women.

Love, though, is neither a right nor an instinct, but a learned form   5
of behavior; it is not a spontaneous feeling but an artificial ritual. It is a response that we have learned from literature, and its contemporary handmaidens, the news media.

As lovers, we are all actors—we imagine ourselves most spontane-   6
ous when we are most imitative. We learn how to love from movies,

television, novels, magazines, and advertisements. We learn to adore love, to idolize love, to fall in love with love.

7   To most Americans, love is romantic love. It is a drive or state of tension induced by our prevailing romantic myths. The lover's nourishment is the expectation of bliss. Love is a competitive and covetous game: Competition for a mate brings out the best in an individual. To be alone is not considered a self-imposed choice but evidence of failure in the contest of love.

8   During the Industrial Revolution, arranged romantic marriages succumbed to individual love matches. The monotony of work and the impersonality of the city led people to escape monotony in personal relations and retreat from impersonality to the "emotional fortress" of marriage. Urbanization caused the "privatization" of marriage so that the intimacy of wedlock became a sanctuary from a world where all intimacy was excluded.

9   Yet, romantic marriage was the cradle of its own demise. More and more pressure was forced on marriage to be "a haven in a heartless world." As the temptations of the outside world were becoming more varied, the standards of marital fidelity became more exigent. Opportunity multiplies, morality declines: The pressure on marriage increased geometrically. Between 1870 and 1920 the number of divorces multiplied fifteenfold.

10   In the past, when society was more structured, married partners were externally oriented, and did not have to rely exclusively on each other for emotional gratification. They could find that elsewhere. Romantic passion had always existed *outside* of the marriage but it had nothing to do with wedlock. Contemporary society forces couples to depend on each other for permanence and stability, functions that were formerly provided by a large familial and social network.

11   Today, marriage has not lost its function; it suffers from a surfeit of functions. The marriage partner must not only be a lover, but a friend, a colleague, a therapist, and a tennis partner. Indeed, the standards of romantic marriage—unquestioned fidelity and undiminished passion—are merely an ideal to be approximated, not a universal precept to be obeyed.

12   Traditionally, the selection of mates has been determined by social, political and economic considerations directed either toward establishing new ties or reaffirming old ones. Every arranged marriage was the formation of a new society—a merger of a network of familial and social relationships. Marriage was a duty. Its *raison d'être* was procreation. Children were best raised in a congenial home, and a congenial home was best created by a reasonable arrangement between congenial people. Marriage was contracted according to a principle other than the self-interest of the participants, and emotional satisfaction was neither the origin nor purpose of marriage.

The concept of arranged marriage is based on a positive view of   13
human nature. Its guiding principle is that marriage requires a more
durable foundation than romantic love, that wisdom is more important
in the choosing of a partner than passion, and that everyone can find
something to "love, honor, and cherish" in anyone else.

Romantic love, however, is fundamentally narcissistic; we either   14
choose someone who resembles ourself, the self we'd like to be or think
we are, or we choose someone who complements us. The former is
incestuous, the latter entropic. If love means touching someone outside
of ourselves, then romantic love is solipsistic while arranged marriage
is altruistic.

Romantic love allows the reverie of imagining what the other per-   15
son is like, whereas arranged marriage forces us to acknowledge truly
another human being. Instead of falling in love with an ideal-image, an
arranged marriage teaches us how to live with an actual individual.
The myth of romantic love teaches us how to fall in love. Perhaps when
marriages are arranged, we will learn *how* to love.

Reading and Writing Activities

PRELIMINARY RESPONSE

Notes.　As you read, record your reactions (questions or comments) to
"No More MoonJune: Love's Out" in your reading journal.

You may react to one or more of a number of factors in the reading.
You might, for example, compare Richard Stengel's purpose with that
of Lawrence Stone in "A Short History of Love." Or you might respond
to Stengel's tone or *persona* (the way he presents himself as a thinker
and writer).

Discussion.　In class, compare your reactions in reading groups of five
or six. Appoint a recorder to keep track of similarities and differences,
consensus or disagreement, arising from the discussion. The recorder
may summarize your group discussion for the rest of the class later.

Freewriting.　Freewrite for 5 to 10 minutes on each of the five areas of
response presented on page 127. If possible, make three duplicate copies of your freewriting and bring them to class. Read your freewriting
in groups of two to four. As others are reading, take written note of
areas of agreement or disagreement, questions that arise in your mind,
and ideas that might be qualified or extended. After everyone has read,
appoint a recorder to keep track of similarities or differences, consen-

sus or disagreement, that arise in the ensuing discussion. The recorder may summarize your group discussion for the rest of the class later.

SUMMARIZING

1. Create a brief, preliminary analysis of "No More MoonJune"—one that reflects your consideration of the freewriting and discussion of group members.
2. Write a summary paragraph or two, using your preliminary analysis, to address Stengel's arguments about romantic love and arranged marriage, the evidence he cites to support those arguments, and, possibly, the ways he hopes to influence readers.
3. Read summaries in groups. Compare the focus of each summary. How do the summaries differ? How are they the same? Again, check to see if you are *reacting and responding* to the essay instead of summarizing the central topics.

FOCUSED CRITICAL READING

1. In his first sentence, Stengel seems to come out fighting. Why do you suppose he opens his essay this way?
2. Stengel was 24 years old when he wrote "No More MoonJune" in 1979. Does that information alter your response to the essay? If so, how and why?
3. Psychologist Charlotte Kasl says: "I doubt that flirting is based entirely on genetic instincts. I suspect that some flirting is an attempt to compensate for feelings of fear, awkwardness, and inadequacy." In "No More MoonJune," Stengel says: "Love . . . is neither a right nor an instinct, but a learned form of behavior; it is not a spontaneous feeling but an artificial ritual. It is a response we have learned from literature and its contemporary handmaidens, the news media."

   Putting aside the fact that flirting and romantic love are not exactly the same thing and ignoring any inclination you may have to disagree with one writer or the other, try to characterize the difference in tone and persona embodied in these two statements. What are the consequences of that difference in terms of your response as a reader?

Paul Gray

What Is Love?

———————◆———————

The two following articles were cover stories in the February 15, 1993, issue of Time. *They report on research undertaken after 1987, when Lawrence Stone wrote "A Short History of Love."*

> *What is this thing called love? What? Is this thing called love?*
> *What is this thing called? Love.*

However punctuated, Cole Porter's simple question begs an answer. Love's symptoms are familiar enough: a drifting mooniness in thought and behavior, the mad conceit that the entire universe has rolled itself up into the person of the beloved, a conviction that no one on earth has ever felt so torrentially about a fellow creature before. Love is ecstasy and torment, freedom and slavery. Poets and songwriters would be in a fine mess without it. Plus, it makes the world go round.

Until recently, scientists wanted no part of it.

The reason for this avoidance, this reluctance to study what is probably life's most intense emotion, is not difficult to track down. Love is mushy; science is hard. Anger and fear, feelings that have been considerably researched in the field and the lab, can be quantified through measurements: pulse and breathing rates, muscle contractions, a whole spider web of involuntary responses. Love does not register as definitively on the instruments; it leaves a blurred fingerprint that could be mistaken for anything from indigestion to a manic attack. Anger and fear have direct roles—fighting or running—in the survival of the species. Since it is possible (a cynic would say commonplace) for humans to mate and reproduce without love, all the attendant sighing and swooning and sonnet writing have struck many pragmatic investigators as beside the evolutionary point.

So biologists and anthropologists assumed that it would be fruitless, even frivolous, to study love's evolutionary origins, the way it was encoded in our genes or imprinted in our brains. Serious scientists simply assumed that love—and especially Romantic Love—was really all in the head, put there five or six centuries ago when civilized societies first found enough spare time to indulge in flowery prose. The task of writing the book of love was ceded to playwrights, poets and pulp novelists.

5   But during the past decade, scientists across a broad range of disciplines have had a change of heart about love. The amount of research expended on the tender passion has never been more intense. Explanations for this rise in interest vary. Some cite the spreading threat of AIDS; with casual sex carrying mortal risks, it seems important to know more about a force that binds couples faithfully together. Others point to the growing number of women scientists and suggest that they may be more willing than their male colleagues to take love seriously. Says Elaine Hatfield, the author of *Love, Sex, and Intimacy: Their Psychology, Biology, and History.* "When I was back at Stanford in the 1960s, they said studying love and human relationships was a quick way to ruin my career. Why not go where the real work was being done: on how fast rats could run?" Whatever the reasons, science seems to have come around to a view that nearly everyone else has always taken for granted: romance is real. It is not merely a conceit; it is bred into our biology.

6   Getting to this point logically is harder than it sounds. The love-as-cultural-delusion argument has long seemed unassailable. What actually accounts for the emotion, according to this scenario, is that people long ago made the mistake of taking fanciful literary tropes seriously. Ovid's *Ars Amatoria* is often cited as a major source of misreadings, its instructions followed, its ironies ignored. Other prime suspects include the 12th century troubadours in Provence who more or less invented the Art of Courtly Love, an elaborate, etiolated ritual for idle noblewomen and aspiring swains that would have been broken to bits by any hint of physical consummation.

7   Ever since then, the injunction to love and to be loved has hummed nonstop through popular culture; it is a dominant theme in music, films, novels, magazines and nearly everything shown on TV. Love is a formidable and thoroughly proved commercial engine; people will buy and do almost anything that promises them a chance at the bliss of romance.

8   But does all this mean that love is merely a phony emotion that we picked up because our culture celebrates it? Psychologist Lawrence Casler, author of *Is Marriage Necessary?*, forcefully thinks so, at least at first: "I don't believe love is part of human nature, not for a minute. There are social pressures at work." Then falls a shadow over this certainty. "Even if it is a part of human nature, like crime or violence, it's not necessarily desirable."

9   Well, love either is or is not intrinsic to our species; having it both ways leads nowhere. And the contention that romance is an entirely acquired trait—overly imaginative troubadours' revenge on muddled literalists—has always rested on some teetery premises.

10   For one thing, there is the chicken/egg dilemma. Which came first, sex or love? If the reproductive imperative was as dominant as Darwinians maintain, sex probably led the way. But why was love hatched in

the process, since it was presumably unnecessary to get things started in the first place? Furthermore, what has sustained romance—that odd collection of tics and impulses—over the centuries? Most mass hallucinations, such as the 17th century tulip mania in Holland, flame out fairly rapidly when people realize the absurdity of what they have been doing and, as the common saying goes, come to their senses. When people in love come to their senses, they tend to orbit with added energy around each other and look more helplessly loopy and self-besotted. If romance were purely a figment, unsupported by any rational or sensible evidence, then surely most folks would be immune to it by now. Look around. It hasn't happened. Love is still in the air.

And it may be far more widespread than even romantics imagined. Those who argue that love is a cultural fantasy have tended to do so from a Eurocentric and class-driven point of view. Romance, they say, arose thanks to amenities peculiar to the West: leisure time, a modicum of creature comforts, a certain level of refinement in the arts and letters. When these trappings are absent, so is romance. Peasants mated; aristocrats fell in love.   11

But last year a study conducted by anthropologists William Jankowiak of the University of Nevada–Las Vegas and Edward Fischer of Tulane University found evidence of romantic love in at least 147 of the 166 cultures they studied. This discovery, if borne out, should pretty well wipe out the idea that love is an invention of the Western mind rather than a biological fact. Says Jankowiak: "It is, instead, a universal phenomenon, a panhuman characteristic that stretches across cultures. Societies like ours have the resources to show love through candy and flowers, but that does not mean that the lack of resources in other cultures indicates the absence of love."   12

Some scientists are not startled by this contention. One of them is anthropologist Helen Fisher, a research associate at the American Museum of Natural History and the author of *Anatomy of Love: The Natural History of Monogamy, Adultery and Divorce,* a recent book that is making waves among scientists and the general reading public. Says Fisher: "I've never *not* thought that love was a very primitive, basic human emotion, as basic as fear, anger or joy. It is so evident. I guess anthropologists have just been busy doing other things."   13

Among the things anthropologists—often knobby-kneed gents in safari shorts—tended to do in the past was ask questions about courtship and marriage rituals. This now seems a classic example, as the old song has it, of looking for love in all the wrong places. In many cultures, love and marriage do not go together. Weddings can have all the romance of corporate mergers, signed and sealed for family or territorial interests. This does not mean, Jankowiak insists, that love does not exist in such cultures; it erupts in clandestine forms, "a phenomenon to be dealt with."   14

15   Somewhere about this point, the specter of determinism begins once again to flap and cackle. If science is going to probe and prod and then announce that we are all scientifically fated to love—and to love preprogrammed types—by our genes and chemicals, then a lot of people would just as soon not know. If there truly is a biological predisposition to love, as more and more scientists are coming to believe, what follows is a recognition of the amazing diversity in the ways humans have chosen to express the feeling. The cartoon images of cavemen bopping cavewomen over the head and dragging them home by their hair? Love. Helen of Troy, subjecting her adopted city to 10 years of ruinous siege? Love. Romeo and Juliet? Ditto. Joe in Accounting making a fool of himself around the water cooler over Susan in Sales? Love. Like the universe, the more we learn about love, the more preposterous and mysterious it is likely to appear.

Anastasia Toufexis

The Right Chemistry

◆————————◆

O.K., let's cut out all this nonsense about romantic love. Let's bring some scientific precision to the party. Let's put love under a microscope.

When rigorous people with PhDs after their names do that, what they see is not some silly, senseless thing. No, their probe reveals that love rests firmly on the foundations of evolution, biology and chemistry. What seems on the surface to be irrational, intoxicated behavior is in fact part of nature's master strategy—a vital force that has helped humans survive, thrive and multiply through thousands of years. Says Michael Mills, a psychology professor at Loyola Marymount University in Los Angeles: "Love is our ancestors whispering in our ears."

It was on the plains of Africa about 4 million years ago, in the early days of the human species, that the notion of romantic love probably first began to blossom—or at least that the first cascades of neurochemicals began flowing from the brain to the bloodstream to produce goofy grins and sweaty palms as men and women gazed deeply into each other's eyes. When mankind graduated from scuttling around on all fours to walking on two legs, this change made the whole person visible to fellow human beings for the first time. Sexual organs were in full display, as were other characteristics, from the color of eyes to the span of shoulders. As never before, each individual had a unique allure.

When the sparks flew, new ways of making love enabled sex to become a romantic encounter, not just a reproductive act. Although mounting mates from the rear was, and still is, the method favored among most animals, humans began to enjoy face-to-face couplings; both looks and personal attraction became a much greater part of the equation.

Romance served the evolutionary purpose of pulling males and females into long-term partnership, which was essential to child rearing. On open grasslands, one parent would have a hard—and dangerous—time handling a child while foraging for food. "If a woman was carrying the equivalent of a 20-lb. bowling hall in one arm and a pile of sticks in the other, it was ecologically critical to pair up with a mate to rear the young," explains anthropologist Helen Fisher, author of *Anatomy of Love*.

While Western culture holds fast to the idea that true love flames forever (the movie *Bram Stoker's Dracula* has the Count carrying the

145

torch beyond the grave), nature apparently meant passions to sputter out in something like four years. Primitive pairs stayed together just "long enough to rear one child through infancy," says Fisher. Then each would find a new partner and start all over again.

7   What Fisher calls the "four-year itch" shows up unmistakably in today's divorce statistics. In most of the 62 cultures she has studied, divorce rates peak around the fourth year of marriage. Additional youngsters help keep pairs together longer. If, say, a couple have another child three years after the first, as often occurs, then their union can be expected to last about four more years. That makes them ripe for the more familiar phenomenon portrayed in the Marilyn Monroe classic *The Seven-Year Itch*.

8   If, in nature's design, romantic love is not eternal, neither is it exclusive. Less than 5% of mammals form rigorously faithful pairs. From the earliest days, contends Fisher, the human pattern has been "monogamy with clandestine adultery." Occasional flings upped the chances that new combinations of genes would be passed on to the next generation. Men who sought new partners had more children. Contrary to common assumptions, women were just as likely to stray. "As long as prehistoric females were secretive about their extramarital affairs," argues Fisher, "they could garner extra resources, life insurance, better genes and more varied DNA for their biological futures. Hence those who sneaked into the bushes with secret lovers lived on— unconsciously passing on through the centuries whatever it is in the female spirit that motivates modern women to philander."

> Love is a romantic designation for a most ordinary biological—or, shall we say, chemical?—process. A lot of nonsense is talked and written about it.
>
> —Greta Garbo to Melvyn Douglas in *Ninotchka*

9   Lovers often claim that they feel as if they are being swept away. They're not mistaken; they are literally flooded by chemicals, research suggests. A meeting of eyes, a touch of hands or a whiff of scent sets off a flood that starts in the brain and races along the nerves and through the blood. The results are familiar: flushed skin, sweaty palms, heavy breathing. If love looks suspiciously like stress, the reason is simple: the chemical pathways are identical.

10   Above all, there is the sheer euphoria of falling in love—a not-so-surprising reaction, considering that many of the substances swamping the newly smitten are chemical cousins of amphetamines. They include dopamine, norepinephrine and especially phenylethylamine (PEA). Cole Porter knew what he was talking about when he wrote "I get a kick out of you." "Love is a natural high," observes Anthony Walsh,

author of *The Science of Love: Understanding Love and Its Effects on Mind and Body.* "PEA gives you that silly smile that you flash at strangers. When we meet someone who is attractive to us, the whistle blows at the PEA factory."

But phenylethylamine highs don't last forever, a fact that lends 11 support to arguments that passionate romantic love is short-lived. As with any amphetamine, the body builds up a tolerance to PEA; thus it takes more and more of the substance to produce love's special kick. After two to three years, the body simply can't crank up the needed amount of PEA. And chewing on chocolate doesn't help, despite popular belief. The candy is high in PEA, but it fails to boost the body's supply.

Fizzling chemicals spell the end of delirious passion; for many peo- 12 ple that marks the end of the liaison as well. It is particularly true for those whom Dr. Michael Liebowitz of the New York State Psychiatric Institute terms "attraction junkies." They crave the intoxication of falling in love so much that they move frantically from affair to affair just as soon as the first rush of infatuation fades.

Still, many romances clearly endure beyond the first years. What 13 accounts for that? Another set of chemicals, of course. The continued presence of a partner gradually steps up production in the brain of endorphins. Unlike the fizzy amphetamines, these are soothing substances. Natural painkillers, they give lovers a sense of security, peace and calm. "That is one reason why it feels so horrible when we're abandoned or a lover dies," notes Fisher. "We don't have our daily hit of narcotics."

Researchers see a contrast between the heated infatuation induced 14 by PEA, along with other amphetamine-like chemicals, and the more intimate attachment fostered and prolonged by endorphins. "Early love is when you love the way the other person makes you feel," explains psychiatrist Mark Goulston of the University of California, Los Angeles. "Mature love is when you love the person as he or she is." It is the difference between passionate and compassionate love, observes Walsh, a psychobiologist at Boise State University in Idaho. "It's Bon Jovi vs. Beethoven."

Oxytocin is another chemical that has recently been implicated in 15 love. Produced by the brain, it sensitizes nerves and stimulates muscle contraction. In women it helps uterine contractions during childbirth as well as production of breast milk, and seems to inspire mothers to nuzzle their infants. Scientists speculate that oxytocin might encourage similar cuddling between adult women and men. The versatile chemical may also enhance orgasms. In one study of men, oxytocin increased to three to five times its normal level during climax, and it may soar even higher in women.

One mystery is the prevalence of homosexual love. Although it 16 would seem to have no evolutionary purpose, since no children are produced, there is no denying that gays and lesbians can be as romantic as anyone else. Some researchers speculate that homosexuality results from a biochemical anomaly that occurs during fetal development. But that doesn't make romance among gays any less real. "That they direct this love toward their own sex," says Walsh, "does not diminish the value of that love one iota."

A certain smile, a certain face

—Johnny Mathis

17   Chemicals may help explain (at least to scientists) the feelings of passion and compassion, but why do people tend to fall in love with one partner rather than a myriad of others? Once again, it's partly a function of evolution and biology. "Men are looking for maximal fertility in a mate," says Loyola Marymount's Mills. "That is in large part why females in the prime childbearing ages of 17 to 28 are so desirable." Men can size up youth and vitality in a glance, and studies indeed show that men fall in love quite rapidly. Women tumble more slowly, to a large degree because their requirements are more complex; they need more time to check the guy out. "Age is not vital," notes Mills, "but the ability to provide security, father children, share resources and hold a high status in society are all key factors."

18   Still, that does not explain why the way Mary walks and laughs makes Bill dizzy with desire while Marcia's gait and giggle leave him cold. "Nature has wired us for one special person," suggests Walsh, romantically. He rejects the idea that a woman or a man can be in love with two people at the same time. Each person carries in his or her mind a unique subliminal guide to the ideal partner, a "love map," to borrow a term coined by sexologist John Money of Johns Hopkins University.

19   Drawn from the people and experiences of childhood, the map is a record of whatever we found enticing and exciting—or disturbing and disgusting. Small feet, curly hair. The way our mothers patted our head or how our fathers told a joke. A fireman's uniform, a doctor's stethoscope. All the information gathered while growing up is imprinted in the brain's circuitry by adolescence. Partners never meet each and every requirement, but a sufficient number of matches can light up the wires and signal, "It's love." Not every partner will be like the last one, since lovers may have different combinations of the characteristics favored by the map.

20   O.K., that's the scientific point of view. Satisfied? Probably not. To most people—with or without PhDs—love will always be more than the sum of its natural parts. It's a commingling of body and soul, reality and imagination, poetry and phenylethylamine. In our deepest hearts, most of us harbor the hope that love will never fully yield up its secrets, that it will always elude our grasp.

Reading and Writing Activities

PRELIMINARY RESPONSE

Notes. As you read, record your reactions (questions or comments) to "What Is Love?" and "The Right Chemistry" in your reading journal.

You may react to one or more of a number of factors in the readings. You might, for example, respond to how the two articles contradict or qualify claims made by Lawrence Stone in "A Short History of Love" and echoed by Richard Stengel in "No More MoonJune."

Discussion. In class, compare your reactions in reading groups of five or six. Appoint a recorder to keep track of similarities and differences, consensus or disagreement, arising from the discussion. The recorder may summarize your group discussion for the rest of the class later.

Freewriting. After the class discussion, freewrite for 10 to 15 minutes about the debate over what causes people to fall in love. Try to assess the validity of the notion that love is a form of learned behavior and of the contrary belief that love is a matter of instinct and chemical reactions. Read your freewriting in groups of two to four. As others are reading, take written note of areas of agreement or disagreement, questions that arise in your mind, and ideas that might be qualified or carried further. After everyone has read, appoint a recorder to keep track of similarities or differences, consensus or disagreement, that arise in the ensuing discussion. The recorder may summarize your group discussion for the rest of the class later.

SUMMARIZING

1. Make a scratchline, cluster representation, or notes indicating the progression of ideas in "The Right Chemistry."
2. Write a summary paragraph or two using your scratchline, cluster representation, or notes.
3. Read summaries in groups. Compare the focus of each summary. How do the summaries differ? How are they the same? Again, check to see if you are *reacting and responding* to the essay instead of summarizing the central topics.

FOCUSED CRITICAL READING

1. In paragraph 9 of his article, Paul Gray asserts that "love either is or is not intrinsic to our species; having it both ways leads nowhere."

Does Anastasia Toufexis contradict that assertion in her final paragraph? If so, which point of view do you feel is better supported?

2. In paragraph 11 of his article, Gray shows that viewing romantic love as a form of learned behavior might be a "Eurocentric and class-driven" attitude. Look again at paragraph 9 of "A Short History of Love" and paragraph 4 of "No More MoonJune" and try to determine whether either of those passages demonstrates the type of bias to which Gray refers.

3. In paragraph 17 of her article, Toufexis sets forth the explanation for romantic love provided by evolution and biology. Do the generalizations about men and women found in that paragraph accord with your experience and observation? If they do, would it follow that attempts to alter such patterns are unnatural and doomed to failure?

Michael Lerner

The Frustration in Family Life

---◆---

In "No More MoonJune" Richard Stengel speaks of how the "monotony of work and the impersonality of the city" have led people to view marriage as "an emotional fortress . . . a haven in a heartless world." According to this view, family members are expected to provide one another with consolation and emotional support, relieving occupational stress and disappointment. The following selection, an excerpt from the book Surplus Powerlessness: The Psychodynamics of Everyday Life, *examines the pressures that work places on family life. Its author, Michael Lerner, argues that these pressures can be traced to the widely held belief that society's rewards are distributed according to merit and that those without wealth and power have their own inferiority to blame.*

1   One reason why people don't get more upset about the pain of work is because they tend to accept the myth that Personal Life will make up for it all. Personal Life will be their compensation for the frustration of work, for the powerlessness they experience in their unions and in the political arena, and for the absence of any larger sense of purpose and meaning in life. "Don't worry about this area of Public Life," we are told, "because you can't expect anything in that sphere. But there will be a magical reward, a terrific Relationship that will make up for all your other deprivations."

2   The locus of the fantasy that someone will come along and make everything OK changes with age. In the teen years, it tends to be identified with movie stars, sports heroes, rock musicians, or "Miss Wonderful" or "Mr. Right." In the years of early adulthood it tends to be identified with a partner or series of partners. In the thirties and sometimes early forties it can be identified with actual or possible children. The content of the fantasy, however, remains constant. We are going to have a very deep and meaningful relationship with some person who will make the pain go away, who will make up for all the crap we have had to suffer through in the rest of our lives.

Reprinted from Tikkun Magazine, a bi-monthly Jewish Critique of Politics, culture, and society. Subscriptions are $31.00 per year from Tikkun, 251 West 100th Street, 5th floor, New York, NY 10025.

3   People deeply believe that Personal Life will make up for every-thing else that is so frustrating and unfulfilling, that it will be a "safe space," a "haven in a heartless world," a "shelter from the storm," a place unaffected by the cruelty and insensitivity that surrounds us all day in the world of work.

4   In the years 1977–85 researchers at the Institute for Labor and Mental Health interviewed several thousand working people from a wide variety of work situations, representing a cross-section of workers in manufacturing, transportation, service, government, high technology, and educational enterprises. These were people whose lives were not "in crisis." They were workers who were facing the normal stresses of the work world, and they came to us only after we had engaged in extensive work to assure them that this was not a service for "people in trouble," but for people facing the normal stresses at work. What we discovered was that there is a very widespread pain in Personal Life, a pain that pervades thousands of families whose outward appearance is often very much that of a family which has no problems and is working very well. Beneath the surface, we found that in these "normal families" the level of pain was quite intense.

5   The fantasy of finding a haven in Personal Life is rarely fulfilled. Most people end up with relationships which do not meet these expectations. For a variety of reasons most people in this society fail to find the magical relationship that will compensate for the alienation of the world of work and the frustrations of the public world. But instead of understanding the way that the original fantasy could not be fulfilled, they then turn on themselves....

6   People typically return home from work feeling tense, often upset, sometimes depressed, almost always with a deep sense of frustration at what they perceive as their own failure to create a fulfilling life for themselves. They blame themselves for the frustrations at work. They are often filled with rage that has had to be suppressed all day and they are often afraid that this rage might get out of hand. They suspect that their anger is itself proof that they deserve the pain of their lives. Typically, these feelings are layered over by a surface level of calm and relief at getting home. Most workers attempt to present themselves as not "letting it get to them." They try to pretend that they are unaffected by stupid bosses, arrogant supervisors, new techniques or processes that they aren't quite sure they can master and feel they must, sales that didn't go through, people whom they aren't sure they have impressed enough, co-workers with whom they must compete for praise or pro-motions, changes in the economy that may make their product less desirable, or people whom they work with who aren't doing their part of the work competently and who thereby make it harder for everyone else. "Oh no—nothing is going to get to us—we can just leave it all at work." Most frequently I found that people don't want to know about

the psychic costs of work, or even begin to think about them. They tell themselves that all this can be quickly forgotten in some form of "relaxation" at home.... They try a wide variety of strategies to bury these feelings and keep themselves unaware of the huge burden they are bringing home into their Personal Life. Among these strategies are the following activities.

1. People try to bury their pain through watching TV. Nothing seems to do it quite as well as TV. People are able to sit and watch program after program, sometimes allowing themselves to experience some limited set of feelings evoked by the programs, but mostly numbing themselves to all feelings. The rapid succession of programs does not allow for time to reflect or get too deeply attached to the meanings and feelings of any one program. The rapid pace in each particular show forces them to pay so much attention to what is happening that there is no chance to distance, to think, to deeply feel. The beauty, the vivid colors, the quick movements, the rapid succession of images all help to re-create a world of fantasy within which non-work hours can be lived. The narcotizing effect is powerful. People can escape the self-paralyzing feelings they have brought home from work by living through this new fantasy world. 7

2. People also use alcohol or drugs—the "royal road" to forgetting the frustrations at work. Alcohol and drugs deaden the pain, suppress the memories, and create a new emotional reality based on artificial stimulations. The importance of these narcotics lies precisely in their ability to contain the anger that we feel at our world and at ourselves. The narcotic allows us to let the feelings pass, and inclines us to pretend that the pain and anger are gone. 8

Sometimes the narcotics or alcohol are not strong enough to repress the feelings of anger and pain. They come out anyway. But in this situation, we can blame the outbursts of anger on the drug or alcohol. "It wasn't me who said all those things—I was drunk, I was stoned, and it was the substance that took me over." This is a frequently used strategy by people who are terrified of their own real feelings, and who think that their anger is further confirmation of "how bad" they really are. They can release the anger but blame the drug or alcohol. Similarly, there may be secondary gains of this sort when a person moves from light or social drinking to overt alcohol abuse. The sense of failure that many people have about their work life and their family life may now be attributed to the alcohol or drug—"My life is a failure because I became an alcoholic." This attribution, difficult as it is, sometimes feels safer to some people who would otherwise attribute their failure to their own personal failings as a person (given their persistent belief that the world is a Meritocracy and that they should have done better). 9

10   Ironically, those who try to combat alcoholism or drug abuse often engage in therapies that are aimed at reinforcing the very dynamics that led to the abuse in the first place. Patients are taught to "take responsibility" for their addictions, and take charge of their lives. While this may sometimes work to cure the abuser of drugs or alcohol, it actually tends to reinforce the underlying dynamics that led to the alcohol or drugs in the first place. Denying the social roots of our personal problems thus leads to an ongoing drama in which one attempt to bury the pain may fail, and will then be replaced by some other denial mechanism. Of course, getting people away from addiction is a valuable thing to do—but to the extent that the method reinforces the underlying dynamic, we have little reason to be hopeful that other self-destructive behaviors will not recur at later points.

11   3. People sometimes engage in frenetic activity in sports, religion, politics. Too often these activities serve a destructive function for working people because they are used as ways of escape from the feelings of pain of the world of work. This is particularly true of people who throw themselves into these activities, allowing their entire emotional lives to be consumed and leaving no space for reflection, self-introspection, or time to calm themselves down from the stresses of the work world. Many people feel that their athletic programs are forms of stress reduction. They will report that their jogging, bowling, baseball, political meetings, PTA, scouts, or church activities actually serve to calm them down. For some this may be true, but for many more all they do is divert attention from the pains of the work world. The pains don't go away; they persist and function on an unconscious level. They will sometimes re-emerge in the form of aggressive competitiveness with other people. The anger that they have felt all day at work gets directed at the "opponent" on the sports field, the "politically misdirected foe," or the "Russians who are about to invade us," or some religious grouping that doesn't share our approach and is therefore "keeping us all from salvation." In this way these frenetic activities allow some people to remain completely out of touch with their underlying feelings of anger and upset, and still let some of them out through a symbolic acting out of aggression. While this displacement of aggressive feelings may sometimes seem safe (e.g., when we are cheering on a particular sports team), they are not so safe when they begin to shape what candidates we back for office, what foreign policy we support, or what religious groups we revile. Nor are they safe when they get played out in the form of angry hostilities in our churches or schools or community organizations, when one group pushes for its policy with a level of insensitivity that tramples on all others around them. Yet because we are expecting people to have magically transcended the anger and frustration at work, we act surprised when it shows up in church or politics or

social life, and then see this as somehow confirming our worst fears that everyone around us is just naturally bad or aggressive.

4. They try sexual "acting out" or "profligacy." The decline of rigid standards of sexual behavior has had mixed results. On the one hand, sexual experimentation has permitted many people to try "living together." Sexual contact before marriage gives them a much better idea of their potential compatibility. The rejection of notions that implied sex was "dirty" or was solely for procreation has created a potential for new levels of pleasure and freedom. On the other hand, sexuality itself has become a new form of escape from feelings generated in the world of work. At work itself people spend a huge amount of time fantasizing about sex so that they can avoid thinking about how unfulfilling their work feels. Then they return into Personal Life with the hope that a myriad of sexual experiences will drown out the pain and frustration of their working lives.
12

Through an endless and all-consuming quest for new social alliances and sexual conquests, the emotionally battered worker seeks to forget about the daily assaults on his/her dignity and worth at work. Whether it be through illicit affairs, or through an endless sequence of new sexual connections, or through nightly partying in the search of Mr. or Ms. Right, the worker experiences a pseudo liberation that would be more real if a deep emotional contact with other human beings could be made. That contact is precluded by a desperation generated in part by the feelings that one is wasting one's life at work, so one must find some peak satisfaction immediately and constantly in "Personal Life." Yet ironically the very pain that one seeks to escape guarantees failure by making sex incomplete and unfulfilling. . . .
13

It would be foolish to argue that all families share all these dynamics to the same extent. There is a wide variability in family life. And there are ways that some families have managed to escape these dynamics. Not every workplace is equally stressful. Not every person has equally bought into the idea of the Meritocracy. Some people have had the benefit of political activism, the women's movement, or other experiences that help them understand that personal problems are often a reflection of social realities and not their own faults. Some people have learned better than others how to deal with their anger—and not to fear it. Some couples have learned to recognize that the tensions they generate are often a reflection of external realities—so they can have a good fight, and then use that as a springboard to deeper levels of intimacy. Some families are rooted in ethnic minority cultures in which they have learned to recognize the phoniness of the dominant culture, and are able to use that sense of the difference between appearance and reality as a frame through which they can understand their
14

own tendencies towards falseness in family life. Some families have learned how to consciously process their own developments—so that when there is a tendency towards withdrawal and hiddenness, it can be recognized and named without causing fear and emotional hiding. These are all important qualifications on all that has been said, and they pull for the need to recognize the richness and diversity in family life.

15   But while there is great variety in family life, and while the dynamics I have described apply differently and to different extents in different families, there is nevertheless a very widely shared reality of pain in family life that is usually underplayed or acknowledged in the same passing way that I have acknowledged the mitigating factors in the previous paragraph. The central dynamic facing American families is the wide range of pain they face, and the fact that underlying much of this pain is a set of emotional dynamics that has been generated in the world of work and then brought home. The way that people have been shaped all day in the world of work has a profound impact on how they will be in their family life. It is unrealistic to expect that these dynamics can be overcome through individual or family therapy—they require, instead, a massive restructuring of the world of work. And a first step in that is for us to recognize how the pain, rather than being a badge of individual shame and failure, is a reflection of a social reality we did not construct and which we as individuals cannot change without the creation of a very large movement for social change.

Reading and Writing Activities

PRELIMINARY RESPONSE

Notes.   As you read, record your reactions (questions or comments) to "The Frustration in Family Life" in your reading journal.

You may react to one or more of a number of factors in the reading. You might, for example, respond to Michael Lerner's claim that people's inability to deal with their frustrations through therapy demonstrates the need for a massive restructuring of society.

Discussion.   In class, compare your reactions in reading groups of five or six. Appoint a recorder to keep track of similarities and differences, consensus or disagreement, arising from the discussion. The recorder may summarize your group discussion for the rest of the class later.

Freewriting.   After the class discussion, freewrite for 10 to 15 minutes about Lerner's analysis of work, emotional pain, and family life. Read your freewriting in groups of two to four. As others are reading, take written note of areas of agreement or disagreement, questions that arise in your mind, and ideas that might be qualified or carried further. After everyone has read, appoint a recorder to keep track of similarities or differences, consensus or disagreement, that arise in the ensuing discussion. The recorder may summarize your group discussion for the rest of the class later.

SUMMARIZING

1. Make a scratchline, cluster representation, or notes indicating the progression of ideas in "The Frustration in Family Life." Note in particular the way Lerner enumerates and describes unsuccessful and destructive ways of responding to frustration.
2. Write a summary paragraph or two using your scratchline, cluster representation, or notes.
3. Read summaries in groups. Compare the focus of each summary. How do the summaries differ? How are they the same? Again, check to see if you are *reacting and responding* to the essay instead of summarizing the central topics.

FOCUSED CRITICAL READING

1. Like some of the other writers in this chapter, Lerner argues that romantic love and the expectations it arouses place a heavy burden on marriage. Lerner, however, places most of the blame on conditions in the workplace. Do you think Lerner believes that if work were more rewarding, marriage would better fulfill the expectations aroused by romantic love? Or is he suggesting that if work were more fulfilling, we would expect less from family life?
2. In this excerpt, Lerner twice refers to *Meritocracy.* What does he mean by that term, and how do you suppose it contributes to people's dissatisfaction with work?
3. How do you think Lerner is trying to influence readers in the last two paragraphs of this selection?

Venny Villapando

The Business of Selling Mail-Order Brides

---◆---

While many Americans view arranged marriage as an anachronism, the following selection deals with its survival in the present. Venny Villapando, a Filipino journalist who lives in Hawaii, describes the business of bringing mail-order brides into the United States and other English-speaking countries. Villapando's essay reveals the tacit racism of this enterprise as well as its view of women as commodities.

1   The phenomenon is far from new. Certainly in the Old West and in other frontier situations such as the labor camps at the sugar farms in Hawaii, the colonization of Australia, or even in the early Irish settlements of New York, there were always lonely men who would write to their homeland for a bride. These women would come on the next train or on the next boat to meet their husbands for the very first time.

2   For Japanese immigrants traditional marriages were arranged in Japan between relatives of the man and the prospective bride. Information was exchanged between the two families about the potential union, and photographs were exchanged between the couple. If both parties agreed, then the marriage was legalized in the home country, and the bride came to America.

3   While these marriages occurred in less than ideal situations, a number of them were successful. For example the Japanese sugar worker who once waited at the Honolulu pier for the arrival of his picture bride, today enjoys the company of a family clan that spans at least two generations. That is indeed an achievement considering the picture bride of yesteryear, just like the contemporary mail-order bride, has always been at a disadvantage. She comes to the marriage from far away, without the nearby support of her family or a familiar culture. The distance that she has traveled is measured not so much in nautical as in emotional miles. She is not quite the happy bride who has been courted and wooed, freely choosing her groom and her destiny.

4   Today's mail-order brides are products of a very complex set of situations and contradictions. They are confronted by far more complicated conditions than the picture brides of years past. They do not quite fit the simple pattern of a marriage between a lonely man stranded in a foreign land and a woman who accepts him sight unseen.

158

In the present matches brides-to-be are generally Asian and hus- 5
bands-to-be are Caucasians, mostly American, Australian, and Canadian. A majority of the women are poor and because of economic
desperation become mail-order brides. Racial, as well as economic, factors define the marriage however. The new wife is relegated to a more
inferior position than her picture bride counterpart. Plus the inequity of
the partnership is further complicated by the mail-order bride's immigrant status. Consequently she is a foreigner not only to the culture, language, and society, but to her husband's race and nationality as well.

Why Men Choose Mail-Order Brides

"These men want women who will feel totally dependent on 6
them," writes Dr. Gladys L. Symons of the University of Calgary. "They
want women who are submissive and less intimidating." Aged
between thirty and forty, these men grew up most likely before the rise
of the feminist movement, adds Symons. She partially attributes the
resurgence of the mail-order bride to a backlash against the 1980s high-
pressure style of dating.

Dr. Davor Jedlicka, a sociology professor from the University of 7
Texas, notes in his study of 265 subscribers of mail-order bride catalogues that "very many of them had extremely bitter experiences with
divorce or breakups or engagements." His research also shows the
median income of these men to be higher than average—65 percent of
them had incomes of over $20,000. According to Jedlicka, the average
age was 37, average height five feet seven inches, and most were college educated. Only five percent never finished high school.

The Japanese American Citizens League, a national civil rights 8
group, confirms this general profile of the typical male client and adds
other findings. According to its recent position paper on mail-order
brides, the group found that the men tend to be white, much older than
the bride they choose, politically conservative, frustrated by the
women's movement, and socially alienated. They experience feelings
of personal inadequacy and find the traditional Asian value of defer-
ence to men reassuring.

In her interview in the *Alberta Report*, Symons points out that the 9
men are also attracted to the idea of buying a wife, since all immigration, transportation, and other costs run to only about two thousand
dollars. "We're a consumer society," says Symons. "People become
translated into commodities easily." And commodities they are.

Gold at the End of the Rainbow

Contemporary traders in the Asian bride business publish lists 10
sold for twenty dollars for a catalogue order form to twenty thousand

dollars for a deluxe videotaped presentation. Perhaps the most success-ful company is Rainbow Ridge Consultants run by John Broussard and his wife Kelly Pomeroy. They use a post office box in Honakaa, Hawaii. Explains Broussard:

> Basically, we just sell addresses.... We operate as a pen pal club, not a front for the slave trade, although some people get the wrong idea. We're not a Sears catalogue from which you buy a wife. You have to write and win the heart of the woman you desire.

For providing this service, Broussard and Pomeroy reported a net profit in 1983 of twenty-five thousand dollars, which catapulted to sixty-five thousand in 1984.

11   Rainbow Ridge Consultants distribute three different publications, of which the top two are *Cherry Blossoms* and *Lotus Blossoms.* These dif-fer from the Sears catalogue only because an issue is only twenty-eight pages long, not several hundred, and photos are black and white, not glossy color. A typical entry reads: "If you like'em tall, Alice is 5'9", Filipina, social work grad, average looks, wants to hear from men 25–40. $4." For the stated dollar amount, interested men can procure an address and a copy of her biographical data.

12   Broussard and Pomeroy's sister publication *Lotus Blossoms* has twice the number of names, but Broussard admits that *Lotus* is a "sec-ond string" brochure, offering pictures of women who do not have the same looks as those in *Cherry Blossoms.*

13   Six months of subscription to the complete catalogues of Rainbow Ridge will cost the wife-seeker $250. A special service will engage Broussard and Pomeroy in a wife hunt at the rate of $50 per hour and includes handling all details, even writing letters and purchasing gifts when necessary. Should the match succeed, the business pockets another fee of $1,000.

14   Kurt Kirstein of Blanca, Colorado, runs Philippine-American Life Partners, which offers one thousand pictures of Filipino women looking for American men. Louis Florence of the American Asian Worldwide Service in Orcutt, California, provides men with a similar catalogue for $25; another $630 will permit the bride-seeker to correspond with twenty-four women, of whom any fifteen will be thoroughly investi-gated by the service. The California business reports an annual gross income of $250,000.

15   Selling Asian women is a thriving enterprise because the number of American men who seek Asian brides continues to grow. Broussard estimates the total number of daily inquiries is five hundred. In 1984 the Gannett News Service reported that seven thousand Filipino women married Australians, Europeans, and Americans. The *Wall*

Street Journal noted that in 1970, only 34 Asians were issued fiancée-petitioned visas; while in 1983, the figure jumped dramatically to 3,428.

Broussard says that he receives one hundred letters a day from 16
Asian and other women. He publishes about seven hundred pictures every other month in his catalogues. Still, Broussard reports that the chances of a man finding a wife through his service is only about one in twenty.

When he receives a letter and the appropriate fees from a prospec- 17
tive groom, Broussard sends off a catalogue. One of his correspondents describes the process: "I selected fourteen ladies to send introductory letters to. To my amazement, I received fourteen replies and am still corresponding with twelve of them." One of the reasons why letters so often succeed is the detailed coaching both parties receive. For instance Broussard and Pomeroy publish a 130-page pamphlet entitled "How to Write to Oriental Ladies." There is also one for women called "The Way to an American Male's Heart."

The Japanese American Citizens League points out the disadvan- 18
tage to women in these arrangements because of the inequality of information disseminated. Under the traditional arranged marriage system, family investigation and involvement insured equal access to information and mutual consent. Now only the women must fill out a personality evaluation which asks very intimate details about their life style and history, and is then shared with the men. Prospective grooms do not have to submit similar information about themselves. Some companies, in fact, even discourage their male clients from disclosing certain types of personal facts in their correspondence, including such potentially negative characteristics as being black or having physical disabilities.

The Economics of Romance

Coaching or no coaching, the mail-order brides business succeeds 19
partly because it takes advantage of the economic deprivation faced by women in underdeveloped Asian countries. The Broussard brochure categorically states:

> We hear lots of stories about dishonest, selfish and immature women
> on both sides of the Pacific. Perhaps women raised in poverty will
> have lower material expectations and will be grateful to whoever res-
> cues them and offers a better life.

One Caucasian man who met his wife through the mail says: "They 20
don't have a whole lot of things, so what they do have they appreciate very much. They appreciate things more than what the average Amer-

ican woman would." In other words, they are properly grateful for whatever the superior male partner bestows on them.

21   "Filipinas come because their standard of living is so low," asserts Pomeroy. In 1984 the per capita income in the Philippines was $640. "Most of the women make no secret of why they want to marry an American: money." An Australian reporter who has studied the influx of Filipino mail-order brides to her country agrees: "Most Filipinas are escaping from grinding poverty." Indeed most Asian governments that are saddled with chronic unemployment, spiraling cost of living, malnutrition, and political turmoil, are faced with the problem of emigration and a diminishing labor force. In contrast, Japan, the economic and technological leader of Asia, has very few women listed in mail-order catalogues.

22   The *Chicago Sun-Times* describes Bruce Moore's visit to the family home of his mail-order bride, Rosie, in Cebu, Philippines:

> 'All of a sudden, we were driving through the jungle. There was nothing but little huts. I really started worrying about what I got myself into.'... The house turned out to be an unpainted concrete building with no doors, plumbing or electricity.... Rosie had worked in a factory, eight hours a day, making 75 to 80 cents a day.

23   Because the Filipinas who avail themselves of mail-order bride service may not have much, Broussard's instructional brochures advise men to use caution in describing their financial status. The woman may turn out to be a "con artist after your money or easy entry into the United States." Despite the poverty, though, many of the women are truly sincere in their responses. The Broussard customer who is still writing to twelve of the fourteen women who wrote him notes:

> They all appeared genuine, and not one has asked me for money or anything else. In fact, in two instances, I offered to help with postage, and in both cases, it was declined. One of the ladies said she could not accept postal assistance, as that would lessen the pleasure she felt in the correspondence.

24   Regardless of the sincerity of the parties involved, one women's rights group in the Philippines has denounced the promotion of relationships through "commerce, industry, negotiation or investment." Their protests, however, do not seem to affect the business.

Racial Images and Romance

25   Added to economic exploitation, a major cornerstone of the mail-order bride business, is the prevalence of racial stereotypes. They have a widespread effect on the treatment of women and influence why so

many men are attracted to mail-order romance. "These men believe the stereotypes that describe Oriental women as docile, compliant and submissive," says Jedlicka. His 1983 survey showed that 80 percent of the respondents accept this image as true.

One Canadian male, who asked not to be identified, was quoted as saying: "Asian girls are not as liberated as North American or Canadian girls. They're more family-oriented and less interested in working. They're old-fashioned. I like that." 26

The California-based American Asian Worldwide Service perpetuates the stereotypes when it says in its brochure: "Asian ladies are faithful and devoted to their husbands. When it comes to sex, they are not demonstrative, however, they are inhibited. They love to do things to make their husbands happy." 27

This company began after owner Louis Florence began his search for a second wife. He says that friends had touted how their Asian wives "love to make their men happy" and finally convinced him to find a wife from Asia. 28

Another mail-order pitch describes Asian women as "faithful, devoted, unspoiled and loving." Broussard confirms this popular misconception by saying these women are "raised to be servants for men in many Oriental countries." Referring to the Malaysian and Indonesian women who have recently joined his list of registrants, Broussard insists: "Like the Filipinas, they are raised to respect and defer to the male.... The young Oriental woman...derives her basic satisfaction from serving and pleasing her husband." 29

Virginity is a highly sought virtue in women. Tom Fletcher, a night worker in Ottawa, Canada, who dislikes American women because they "want to get out [of the house] and work and that leads to break-ups," is especially appreciative of this sign of purity. "These women's virginity was a gift to their husbands and a sign of faithfulness and trust." One mail-order service unabashedly advertises virginity in a brochure with photos, home addresses, and descriptions of Filipino women, some of whom are as young as seventeen. "Most, if not all are very feminine, loyal, loving...and virgins!" its literature reads. 30

Many of the Asian countries affected by the revived mail-order bride business have a history of U.S. military involvement. Troops have either fought battles or been stationed in Korea, the Philippines, and countries in Southeast Asia. During their stays, the soldiers have often developed strong perceptions of Asian women as prostitutes, bargirls, and geishas. Then they erroneously conclude that Asian American women must fit those images, too. Consequently the stereotype of women servicing and serving men is perpetuated. 31

The Japanese American Citizens League objects to the mail-order bride trade for that very reason. "The marketing techniques used by the catalogue bride companies reinforce negative sexual and racial ste- 32 reotypes of Asian women in the U.S. The negative attitude toward Asian women affects all Asians in the country." Further, the treatment of women as "commodities" adds to the "non-human and negative perception of all Asians."

Romance on the Rocks

33   A marriage made via the mail-order bride system is naturally beset by a whole range of problems. In her testimony before the U.S. Commission on Civil Rights, Professor Bok-Lim Kim, then with the University of Illinois, noted that negative reactions and attitudes toward foreign Asian wives "exacerbates marital problems," which result in incidences of spouse abuse, desertion, separation, and divorce. In addition, writes an Australian journalist, most of the men they marry are social misfits. "Many of them drink too much; some beat their wives and treat them little better than slaves."

34   The Japanese American Citizens League asserts:

> Individually, there may be many cases of couples meeting and marrying through these arrangements with positive results. We believe, however, that for the woman, there are many more instances in which the impetus for leaving their home countries and families, and the resulting marriage relationships, have roots and end results which are less than positive.

35   Many of the Caucasian men who marry what they believe are stereotypical women may be in for some surprises. Psychiatry professor Joe Yamamoto of the University of California at Los Angeles says: "I've found many Asian women acculturate rather quickly. These American men may get a surprise in a few years if their wives pick up liberated ways."

36   One legally blind and hard-of-hearing American, married to a Korean woman, was eventually bothered by the same problems that plague other couples: in-laws and lack of money. "She gets frustrated because I don't hear her," complains the man about his soft-spoken Asian wife. In response, she says, "The main problem is [his] parents. I can't adapt to American culture. I was going to devote my life for him, but I can't."

37   Another area which specifically affects foreign-born brides is their immigrant status. According to the Japanese American Citizens League, "these foreign women are at a disadvantage." This civil rights group targets the women's unfamiliarity with the U.S. immigration laws as one of the most disturbing aspects of the business. "As a result [of the ignorance], they may miss an opportunity to become a naturalized citizen, forfeit rights as a legal spouse, or live under an unwar-

ranted fear of deportation which may be fostered by their spouse as a means of control."

Conclusion

Despite the constant stream of criticism, the mail-order bride sys-   38
tem will prevail as long as there are consumers and profit, and as long as underdeveloped countries continue failing to meet the economic, political, and social needs of their people. Indications show the business is not about to collapse now.

Erroneous ideas continue to thrive. An Asian woman dreams she   39
will meet and marry someone rich and powerful, someone to rescue her and free her from poverty-stricken bondage. She hopes to live the rest of her life in a land of plenty. An American male dreams he will meet and marry someone passive, obedient, nonthreatening, and virginal, someone to devote her entire life to him, serving him and making no demands. Only a strong women's movement, one tied to the exploited underdeveloped country's struggle for liberation and independence, can challenge these ideas and channel the aspirations and ambitions of both men and women in a more positive and realistic direction.

Reading and Writing Activities

PRELIMINARY RESPONSE

Notes.   As you read, record your reactions (questions or comments) to "The Business of Selling Mail-Order Brides" in your reading journal.

You may react to one or more of a number of factors in the reading. You might, for example, respond to Venny Villapando's tone and attitude toward his subject: whether and how he shows disapproval and how his approach influences readers.

Discussion.   In class, compare your reactions in reading groups of five or six. Appoint a recorder to keep track of similarities and differences, consensus or disagreement, arising from the discussion. The recorder may summarize your group discussion for the rest of the class later.

Freewriting.   After the class discussion, freewrite for 10 to 15 minutes about the attitudes and conditions that sustain the mail-order bride business. Read your freewriting in groups of two to four. As others are reading, take written note of areas of agreement or disagreement, questions that arise in your mind, and ideas that might be qualified or carried further. After everyone has read, appoint a recorder to keep track of similarities or differences, consensus or disagreement that arises in the ensuing discussion. The recorder may summarize your group discussion for the rest of the class later.

SUMMARIZING

1. Make a scratchline, cluster representation, or notes indicating the progression of ideas in "The Business of Selling Mail-Order Brides." Note in particular the way Villapando begins by examining the motives and methods of male clients, entrepreneurs, and prospective brides.
2. Write a summary paragraph or two using your scratchline, cluster representation, or notes.
3. Read summaries in groups. Compare the focus of each summary. How do the summaries differ? How are they the same? Again, check to see if you are *reacting and responding* to the essay instead of summarizing the central topics.

FOCUSED CRITICAL READING

1. Villapando suggests that the practices he describes are worse than the "traditional arranged marriage system." Do you agree with that appraisal?
2. A source quoted in this essay says that men who choose mail-order brides "want women who will feel totally dependent on them." How does that attitude resemble and how does it differ from the dependency often found in more traditional types of courtship and marriage?
3. Do you think Michael Lerner (author of "The Frustration in Family Life") would see the patterns described by Villapando as a further manifestation of Americans' frustrations with work and family life?

Maulana Karenga

Black Male/Female Relations

◆

A young black man interviewed by Robert Staples in his book The World of Black Singles[2] *maintains that "the only place where a black man can experience real power, the only time he can be totally in control of the situation, is with a black woman, but we tend to abuse that." In the following selection, Maulana Karenga argues that problems faced by many black couples must be examined within the context of the dominant American culture—specifically its sexism, racism, and materialism.*

Karenga is Professor and Chair of the Department of Black Studies and heads the President's Task Force on Multiculturalism and Campus Diversity at California State University, Long Beach. He is chairman of Us and the director of the African American Cultural Center and the Kawaida Institute of Pan-African Studies, Los Angeles. Moreover, he is the creator of Kwanzaa and the author of numerous scholarly articles and eight books, including Kwanzaa: Origins, Concepts, Practice *(1977); and* Selections from the Husia: Sacred Wisdom of Ancient Egypt *(1984).*

One of the earliest and most important texts of Black womanist or feminist discourse is Anna Julia Cooper's *A Voice from the South*. In this seminal volume she criticizes racism, sexism and classism and argues that "there is a feminine as well as masculine side to truth, that these are related, not as inferior or superior, not as better or worse, not as weaker or stronger, but as complements—complements in one necessary and symmetric whole." Moreover, Cooper argues against elevation of the personal over the collective saying, "we too often mistake individual honor for race development and are so ready to substitute petty accomplishments for sound sense and purpose." She recognized and noted the dual character of her oppression and possibilities as both Black and woman and the essential role women must play in defining "an ideal manhood and womanhood" free from racist, classist and sexist flaws. Maintaining that the women's cause in this epoch of crisis and struggle is a universal one which will free not only Africans, but Native Americans and other oppressed peoples, she says "To be a woman in such an age carries with it a privilege and opportunity never

[2]Robert Staples, *The World of Black Singles: Changing Patterns of Male/Female Relations* (Westport, CT: Greenwood, 1981), p. 74.

implied before. But to be a woman of the (African) race in America and to grasp the deep significance of the possibilities of the crisis is to have a heritage, it seems to me, unique in the ages." Finally, Cooper challenges Black men to build a partnership of equals in love and struggle for liberation and a higher level of human life for "nature never meant the ideals and standards of the world should be dwarfing and minimizing ones, and men should thank us for requiring of them the richest fruits they grow." It is this equal partnership in love and struggle that Afrocentric womanists would later pose as the key and priority focus in male/female relationships and womanist discourse.

2   ...[T]he 70's marked a flourishing of discourse around the issue of Black male/female relations. The discourse originally rose from within the ranks of activist women who had worked in the Black Freedom Movement and who, in looking back on their experiences, remembered painful encounters with sexism, marginalization and disappreciation of their contributions. Writings and narratives by key women in the Black Movement such as Toni Cade Bambara, Frances Beale, Ella Baker and Septima Clark bear important witness to these problems. In an essay titled "On the Issue of Roles," Toni Cade (Bambara) outlined some of the basic criticisms of sexism in the Movement: 1) assignment of silencing and servile roles to women; 2) focusing on problematic notions of manhood and womanhood rather than progressive concepts of "Blackhood"; and 3) talking revolutionary rhetoric about "picking up the gun" rather than facing "the task of creating a new identity, a (new) self" which synthesized the best of both woman and man "via commitment to struggle."

3   Inherent in Bambara's concerns is a set of charges and challenges which have consistently informed Black women's discourse concerning men's approaches to male/female relationships and relations. Among the major points of focus are: 1) the tendency to define roles which are unequal, exploitative, oppressive, and unresponsive to the demands of equality, reciprocity and mutual benefit; 2) the tendency to subordinate gender issues to racial (people) issues and using calls to unity to suppress difference, critique and challenge; 3) failing to define the terms and goals of the struggle, so that freedom is a collective project and practice and current relations prefigure the new society and community struggled for; 4) resistance to redefining and reconstructing Black masculinity and Black femininity in and for the liberation struggle; 5) inadequate sensitivity to Black women's pain—current and historical—and the need to bear witness to it and have it acknowledged and ended; and 6) frequent unwillingness to be self-critical and self-corrective and to practice partnership in equality rather than relationship in dominance.

4   The ongoing dialogue around these issues in the 60's was not always conducted in a full, free, frank and principled manner and it

began to take an ominous turn in the 70's. Key developments in this dialogue were the publication and resultant discourse around Ntozake Shange's play, *For Colored Girls Who Have Considered Suicide When the Rainbow is Enuff* and Michele Wallace's *Black Macho and the Myth of the Super Woman*. Major publications in the Black community such as the *Black Scholar, Black Books Bulletin* and *Freedomways* provide ample space for the ongoing debate; and the debate was wide-ranging in the community. Toni Morrison's *The Bluest Eye* and *Beloved* and Gloria Naylor's *Women of Brewster Place* among other works by African American women in the 80's not only continued to express the painful and intense conflict between Black men and women, but also revealed the development of Black women's literature as a major, perhaps the primary, way in which this conflict was defined and pursued. Black men writers like Ishmael Reed in *Reckless Eyeballing* and Trey Ellis in *Platitudes* responded strongly to this genre of literature and its negative representation of Black men. Other men, on campus and in the community, joined in the criticism and challenge. Thus, the debate around Wallace's work had essentially yielded a series of issues and a pattern of public and private encounters that would repeat themselves in the 80's and 90's. Such exchanges intensified and expanded in the debate around Alice Walker's *The Color Purple* and culminated in a very bitter and difficult discourse around the Clarence Thomas-Anita Hill confrontation in 1991. Terry McMillan's *Waiting to Exhale,* however, tends to take a different turn and appeared to many men as a call to responsible and principled partnership between Black women and men rather than the condemnatory project they perceived much of other Black women's literature to be.

As it was possible to glean from Toni Cade Bambara's concerns a   5 basic set of charges and challenges posed by Black women concerning men's approaches to male/female relations, it is also possible to extract a similar set of concerns from the discussion by Black male writers and other Black men around Black women's literature. Among the major points of focus are: 1) the tendency towards monolithic and reductive characterizations of Black men; 2) the failure to contextualize the problem and critique race, class and gender relations in the context of oppression; 3) subordination of race, community and collective issues to gender and personal ones rather than linking them in a mutually beneficial way; 4) consciously or unconsciously providing the established order and racists in general with negative images of Black men, women and families which they appropriate and use to their advantage against all; 5) the failure to develop an Afrocentric approach to the question of male-female relations and thus an over-reliance on white feminists for both essential categories and concepts; and 6) the unwillingness to be self-critical and self-corrective, moving from an overabundant discourse on victimization and oppression to one of agency and the practice of freedom. It is important to note here that within the Black women's study project and the Black Women's Movement in general, there exist two intellectual and political tendencies. The first is the Afrocentric womanist tendency which as Stewart notes "embraces the field's (Black Studies') long-standing cultural nationalist ideology" and focuses on "forging a new partnership between Africana men and women in pursuit of previously articulated intellectual and political objectives." Moreover, this body of scholars and activists consider alliances with white feminists problematic at best and use of their theories and practices inappropriate in defining the Black woman's experience and approaching Black male/female relations. On the contrary, they pose rootedness in Black culture as indispensable to creating the new partnership between women and men, free of racist, classist and sexist assumptions and practices."

6   The other tendency which may be called either Black womanist or Black feminist "elevates feminism to a higher ideological status than cultural nationalism...tends to be more directly connected to traditional disciplines...and, more specifically, they are clustered in the areas of literary criticism and creative writing." Moreover, they are both critical of and collaborative with white feminists, often building alliances with them, but usually trying to maintain a measure of distinctiveness. In fact, the category womanist introduced by Alice Walker is an expression of this desire for distinction. However their priority focus on gender issues and criticism of race focus often finds them unable to establish a clear distinction conceptually between Black and white feminism.

The Question of Quality Relations

7   Perhaps, then, a definition of the importance of quality Black male/female relations is in order. Many others have discussed this importance. Building on these insights, male/female relationships can be seen as a fundamental and enduring concern and has importance for several reasons: 1) they have a species character, i.e., they are indispensable to the maintenance and development of the species; 2) they are a measurement of our humanity, i.e., how far humans are from the animal world; 3) they are a measurement of the quality of social life of any given society, i.e., the treatment of women in relationships and by extension in society becomes as Toure notes, "...a mirror that reflects the economic and social conditions, the level of political, cultural and moral development of a given country;" 4) they are a measurement and mirror of personal development and identity, i.e., a revelation of who persons really are; and finally, 5) they are a measurement of a people's capacity for struggle and social construction, for as a fundamental unit of the nation, their strengths and weaknesses determine the nation's capacity to define, defend and develop its interest.

No one can honestly deny that there are substantive problems concerning Black male/female relationships. This is true whether one focuses on sexism or the scarcity of men, or the games one plays to begin and sustain relationship, or the self-destructiveness and racist targeting of Black men. For in the final analysis, it is the quality of relations that is a key and continuing question and challenge. And this challenge requires serious and sober reassessment and reconstruction of and by both men and women in order to lay the basis for more proactive and mutually beneficial exchanges and relationships.

However, in discussing the problems of Black male/female relationships, it is important to keep in mind at least four fundamental facts. First, Black male/female relationships, like Black families, are no more problem-ridden or pathological than white families and male/female relationships, but given our moral claims and liberational struggle, we are morally compelled to create a context for maximum human flourishing. Secondly, it is important to recognize that real life unavoidably involves problems and problem-solving. The point, then, is not to be without problems, but to be resourceful in devising solutions. Thirdly, it is important to recognize that not all Black male/female relationships are in turmoil and trouble. However, there are enough relationships in turmoil and trouble and enough persons without relationships to make the question of Black male/female relationships necessary for discussion. Finally, it is of equal importance to realize that any criticism of Black male/female relationships is at the same time and in equal measure a criticism of U.S. society which has shaped them to fit and function "properly" in it. For social conditions create both social consciousness and social conduct and failure to recognize this can lead one to see racial defects where social ones are more real and relevant.

It is this final contention that serves as a key point of departure for any serious analysis of Black male/female relationships. For to say we are products of our social conditions is to say the same thing about our relationships. Analyses of the major defects in Black male/female relationships clearly reveal their social rather than genetic or purely personal basis. Thus, to understand the negatives of our relationships we must understand the negative characteristics of society which have shaped them.

These negatives of U.S. society are defined by and derived from three major structural and value systems: capitalism, racism and sexism. *Capitalism is a socio-economic system defined by private ownership of the means to satisfy human needs and the ruthless and continuous pursuit of profit which turns virtually everything into a commodity, i.e., an object for sale and purchase. Racism is a system of denial and deformation of a people's history and humanity and right to freedom based primarily or exclusively on the specious concept of race and racial hierarchies. Sexism is the social practice of using gender or sex as the key determinant in establishing, maintaining and explaining relationships and exchanges.* In others words, it is a system of assumptions and acts, theories and practices which imply and impose unequal, oppressive and exploitative relationships based on gender or sex.

12 Capitalism, then, turns relationships and parts of relationships into commodities and utilitarian arrangements. Racism engenders self-hate, self-doubt and pathological fixation on the white paradigm. And sexism encourages artificial personal power over women as a substitute for real social power over one's destiny and daily life. The result of these three structural and value strains on Black male/female relationships expresses itself as a transformation of the relationships into what can be best described as connections. A connection is a short-term or tentative association which is utilitarian and alienated and is designed primarily for the mutual misuse of each other's body. A quality relationship on the other hand is a long-term, stable association defined by its positive sharing and its mutual investment in each other's happiness, well-being and development.

The Connections

13 There are four basic connections which plague male/female relationships in the U.S.: 1) the cash connection; 2) the flesh connection; 3) the force connection; and 4) the dependency connection. The cash connection grows out of the commodity character of society. It is informed by several capitalistic assumptions among which are: 1) everything and everyone has a price; 2) anything you can't buy ain't worth having anyhow; 3) what you invest money or material assets in is yours; and 4) money is the measure of and solution to everything.

14 In such a context, mothers tell their daughters to look for and marry someone who can "take care" of them, as if they were disabled; women sell themselves to men, exchanging sex for economic security and call it marriage; teenage men invest materially in young women with a movie and a Mac burger and demand their bodies in exchange; and male idiots claim the right to rule and ruin the lives of their wives and children on the basis of the money they bring in. Money and material consideration, then, form the basis for the cash connection and diminish the chances for a quality relationship which is conscious of, but not ruled by, material consideration. It often leads to women collaborating in their own oppression.

15 The flesh connection grows out of the pornographic character of society and is defined as an association based purely or predominantly on the pursuit of sex. This connection focuses on the body and all the perverse things one can do with all or selected parts of it. Pornography, as a definite social thought and practice and as the essence and source of the flesh connection, expresses itself in five basic ways: 1) as species alienation, i.e., man alienated from and oblivious of his species half;

2) objectification of the species half, turning a natural partner into an object of use and disuse; 3) fragmentation of the body, i.e., hacking the body into usable pieces and rejecting the wholeness of the human personality; 4) brutalization, most viciously expressed in the sado-masochistic vulgarities society at its most violent and alienated level has produced; and 5) a sexual commodity form, i.e., the joining of the cash and flesh connection through the packaging and peddling of the human body.

A third connection is the force connection which rises out of the violent and oppressive character of society. Historically, men have used their greater physical strength to subdue women and win arguments they would otherwise lose. Moreover, the flesh and force connection merge in the act of rape which is not so much sexual as it is psychocultural and physical. For above all, it is an act of domination practiced by husbands, friends and strangers.   16

Also, there is social or ideological coercion which forces women, through censure and labelling, into roles which degrade and silence. As Vivian Gordon notes, "we are all familiar with the denigrating labels which confront the Black woman who strikes out and dares to maintain a valued self; such women are variously viewed to be: domineering, aggressive, probably non-threatening to the man, bad looking/bad acting women that no man wants." The tragedy, she says is that many Black women have accepted these stereotypes but fortunately "the majority of Black women have managed to maintain positive self-identifies." The force connection also expresses itself in economic coercion. This operates on the principle that whoever controls the means to satisfy human needs controls at the same time the humans with those needs.   17

The fourth and final connection which challenges and often prevents quality Black male/female relationships is the dependency connection. This connection is the logical and inevitable result of the others. After a woman has been transformed into a commodity, reduced to parts of her body and physically or ideologically whipped into compliance, she can only be dependent. Like all enslaved persons and servants, she becomes a set of reactions to her slaveholder, a defender of his definitions and treatment of her. Thus, interdependence, a key value in quality relationships, becomes impossible and the connection becomes the model rather than the deviance.   18

Toward Solutions

Given the seriousness of the problem, it is only logical to ask, what is the solution? The solution like the problem has both a personal and social dimension and requires transformation on both levels. Although, one can argue that conditions create consciousness, consciousness and the social practice that it engenders can and often do create conditions.   19

Certainly, capitalism, racism and sexism shape our relationships, but they are systems created and maintained by humans and they can be changed and rebuilt by humans. Without such a proactive conception of human possibility, neither personal nor social change is possible.

20   But the struggle to change systems must begin with the struggle of a people to change themselves, i.e., their own views and values and the negative and non-productive ways they have organized and live their daily life. Only then can they self-consciously rebuild their relationships and begin to change the social conditions which deform and deny these relationships.

21   The solution to deficient relations, then, is rooted in the creation, acceptance and practice of a new value system. Both Ladner and Staples argue the need for a value system which rejects and counters the standards of the dominant society. "We must seek other alternative and more viable standards," Ladner asserts. For the U.S. model "which purports to be the exemplary one" is not only negative to Black interest, but also "is in the process of internal destruction, and there is little within it which seems worthy of salvaging." This requires an alternative value system which calls for a redefinition of reality in Blacks' own interest and image, for a new definition of man and woman and the kind of relationships they ought to have.

22   Real relationships must begin with terms clearly stated, and then grow and are reinforced by common values, common interests and aspirations, quality commitment, support structures, continuous renewal, and common struggle for liberation and a higher level of human life. For in the final analysis, the call for an end to deformed and defective relationships must be a call for an end to the social conditions which created and sustain them. One must begin with a *moral minimum* that cannot be compromised, a set of values which are resistant to revision because they are at the very roots of the relationship. Prohibition against violence; full, free and frank discussion; egalitarian exchange; collective decision-making; and shared responsibility in love and struggle must be a part of that moral minimum, if a relationship is to be real and mutually beneficial. Moreover, it is important that women continue to define and fight for the freedom, equality and the kind of relationships they need and want, that they reconstruct their supportive links with each other and speak their own African truth of what it means to be a woman-in-community. Likewise, men must stand upright, assume a moral posture on the personal and the political level and reconstruct themselves in relationship with and in consideration of women.

23   It is important to repeat that any solution that evolves must be a collective and community-affirming solution, one that honors the moral demands of equality, mutual respect and reciprocity. It is this conception of person-in-community, being of equal worth, rights and respect that stands at the center of any Afrocentric conception of man/

woman relations. Rodgers-Rose in her early work on the Black woman reaffirmed this location and rootedness in community, saying the authors of articles in her book "stress the point that the history and lives of Black women cannot be separated from the history and lives of Black men and black children." Thus, the need became one of studying and reconstructing relations among them to achieve maximum human flourishing.

When Alice Walker says in her definition of womanist that a womanist is one "committed to the survival and wholeness of an entire people, male and female," she repeats this theme of person-in-and-for-community. Also Vivian Gordon reaffirms this when she states that "African women are in a partnership struggle with Black men for the emancipation of their communities." Defining a fundamental aspect of Afrocentric feminism, Clenora Hudson-Weems argues that "The Africana womanist...perceives herself as the companion to the Africana man, and works diligently toward continuing their established union in the struggle against racial oppression." But the community cannot stifle, cannot impose silence or abusive conformity. On the contrary, if it stifles voices, it stifles itself and will wither and decay morally and culturally. Maximum freedom is the basis for maximum human flourishing, and social freedom as well as social oppression are ultimately expressed or exposed in the quality of human relations.   24

This, however, is just a beginning and an outline of possibilities. The realities will be built by those *New Africans* in U.S. society who dare to be other than their immediate and social conditions encourage them to be. Staples has correctly observed that, "Now we stand at the crossroads of a major decision about which way we will proceed to order our lives." The choice is clearly between the continuation of the current social and personal state of things or self-conscious intervention to change it and build a better society and more life-affirming moral and meaningful relationships. And as Staples concludes, "Whatever the decision may be, we should not be deluded into believing that the consequences are individual ones. The future of the race may be at stake."   25

Reading and Writing Activities

PRELIMINARY RESPONSE

Notes.   As you read, record your reactions (questions or comments) to "Black Male/Female Relations" in your reading journal.

You may react to one or more of a number of factors in the reading. You might, for example, respond to Maulana Karenga's belief that problems in male-female relationships reflect broader societal problems.

Discussion.   In class, compare your reactions in reading groups of five or six. Appoint a recorder to keep track of similarities and differences, consensus or disagreement, arising from the discussion. The recorder may summarize your group discussion for the rest of the class later.

Freewriting.   After the class discussion, freewrite for 10 to 15 minutes about how Karenga's text helps to clarify traditional relationships between men and women: black, white, or both. Read your freewriting in groups of two to four. As others are reading, take written note of areas of agreement or disagreement, questions that arise in your mind, and ideas that might be qualified or carried further. After everyone has read, appoint a recorder to keep track of similarities or differences, consensus or disagreement, that arise in the ensuing discussion. The recorder may summarize your group discussion for the rest of the class later.

SUMMARIZING

1. Make a scratchline, cluster representation, or notes indicating the progression of ideas in "Black Male/Female Relations." Note in particular various relationships among the "negatives of U.S. society...defined by and derived from three major structural and value systems" and the "four basic connections which plague male/female relationships."
2. Write a summary paragraph or two using your scratchline, cluster representation, or notes.
3. Read summaries in groups. Compare the focus of each summary. How do the summaries differ? How are they the same? Again, check to see if you are *reacting and responding* to the essay instead of summarizing the central topics.

FOCUSED CRITICAL READING

1. In a few places, Karenga departs from the type of language we are accustomed to expect in academic writing. For example, he uses *"ain't"* in paragraph 13 and refers to "male idiots" in paragraph 14. Why do you think Karenga makes these unusual choices? Do they have the effect that he may intend?
2. How would you characterize Karenga's persona in this selection?

WRITING SUGGESTIONS

1. Write a brief report on the case against romantic love, synthesizing the views of Lawrence Stone in "A Short History of Love" and those of Richard Stengel in "No More MoonJune." One possible structure for such a report might be a paragraph summarizing Stone's text as an academic treatment of the case and another paragraph summarizing Stengel's text as an attempt to propose and advocate a practical response to the case as Stone presents it.

2. Write a brief report that objectively sets forth two opposing points of view about romantic love: that it is a form of learned behavior/that it is a function of biology and chemistry that transcends culture. Quote or paraphrase appropriate passages from some or all of the first four readings in this chapter.

3. Write a brief report on the pros and cons of arranged marriage, synthesizing the views of Richard Stengel in "No More MoonJune" on one hand and the evidence presented by Venny Villapando in "The Business of Selling Mail-Order Brides" on the other hand. One possible structure for such a report might be a paragraph summarizing Stengel's claims and another paragraph examining the validity of those claims in the light of Villapando's text.

4

The Beauty Myth

---◆---

Despite what one might hear to the contrary, being beautiful really does count for something. Women (and men) may hear messages that beauty is only "skin deep," that beauty is in the "eye of the beholder," and believe them for a little while.

But other messages for women are at work in our culture. In the well-known fairytales of Cinderella, Sleeping Beauty, and Snow White and the Seven Dwarfs, just to name a few, young women grow up hearing the message that beauty is all important in being chosen, in winning the handsome prince. Alice Walker, in her essay "Beauty: When the Other Dancer Is the Self," suggests that this message is internalized at a very young age. At age 2½, the narrator in Walker's essay says to her father, "Take me, Daddy, I'm the prettiest."

The chapter begins with a news report on the subject of Barbie dolls and Marge Piercy's poem "Barbie Doll." In the first essay that follows, Lavonne Adams suggests that even very young children can be pressured by the image of ideal beauty. Her essay locates a place—the beauty contest—where ideal beauty is defined publicly in our culture. The next essay, Alice Walker's "Beauty: When the Other Dancer Is the Self," addresses cultural perceptions of female beauty and the loss of self-esteem with a loss of beauty.

The selections following connect beauty, power, and control. "Bootstrap Feminism" examines changing perceptions about women, beauty, and power presented by Naomi Wolf, author of *The Beauty Myth* (1991). Richard Selzer's "Fetishes" conveys another message about beauty and control. This essay depicts a woman powerless in her struggle to maintain her particular beauty myth without the permission of the men around her. Ynestra King's "The Other Body" introduces the issue of identity and the disabled. King reminds us that "of all the ways of becoming 'other' in our society, disability is the only one that can happen to anyone, in an instant, transforming that person's life and identity forever."

In the final selection, "Sitting Pretty," Margo Kaufman deals, in a very understated way, with reconstructive surgery after a mastectomy—cosmetic surgery that many women have had to consider.

178

Creating a Synthesis of Ideas

Chapters 2 and 3 introduced group inquiry and dialectical approaches to reading and writing to suggest that you read and reread complicated texts for academic purposes. We continue to emphasize this dialectical approach to reading and writing throughout the book. In this chapter, additionally, we focus on *using writing extensively in reading for academic purposes* for those times when group discussion is not possible.

For example, Sam, a writing class student, was asked to summarize a number of essays in this chapter before writing an essay presenting his *informed* view on the issue of beauty and American culture. In presenting his view, he integrated information from summaries of readings. Sam wrote two of the summaries with the help of group inquiry. Several others he wrote on his own. After writing extensively and revising summaries with his group, he took a similarly systematic approach when reading and writing on his own. After a first reading during which he took notes, he produced a *freewritten response* to the content of the articles he was reading. He responded to the content again using an *analytic reading guide.*

What central point(s) do you think the writer makes—implicitly or explicitly?

If explicit, is the point stated at the beginning or end of the text?

If only implied, how did you decide the central point for yourself?

In other words, what textual evidence can you draw on to support your reading of this text?

What is the writer's purpose, audience, means of development?

How does the writer arrange the parts of this text?

How many major parts are there?

Are there key words that help you follow a pattern of changing topics?

How do the topics relate to one another?

Can you identify methods of developing ideas in this article that are especially effective?

Finally, in writing a final draft of his summaries, the end product of this preliminary and analytic writing, Sam started with a sentence or two about the central point the writer made, then summarized the content of each major topic. He took care to state the central point of each topic, as he understood that point, and summarized the information the writer presented to elaborate, explain, or otherwise develop each major point. In other words, Sam used writing extensively to help him

closely analyze each reading in order to produce a *complex summary.*
Finally, he responded critically to the readings, using his earlier writings to make connections and draw inferences. During all these processes, Sam constantly revised; he reported that the more he wrote, the
more he revised what he had originally thought were key points in a
reading. As his ideas about key points changed, so did his earlier reactions and interpretations.

In drafting his essay, Sam created an introduction section from his
summaries of Alice Walker's "Beauty: When the Other Dancer Is the
Self" (one of the readings in this chapter) and Terry McMillan's "What
Is Perfect Anyway? Simply Being Beautiful?" Before drafting his introduction, Sam had already decided he wanted to write an essay in favor
of cosmetic surgery. To develop his point of view, he synthesized information from summaries of three other essays (in addition to the Walker
and McMillan selections), one from this chapter and two he discovered
in the library.

Here is Sam's introduction:

> In her essay, "Beauty: When the Other Dancer Is the Self," Alice Walker
> discusses the importance she has always placed on beauty and how
> she came to terms with the scarring of her eye. Walker recounts several
> memories of different events in her life that reflect her feelings about
> herself before and after the "accident."
>
> The essay opens with Walker's recollection of being chosen by her
> father to go to the fair with him because she was the prettiest. She also
> tells of giving a speech at church for Easter Sunday. She recalls how the
> members of the congregation admired and complimented her (24). The
> next memory is of how she was shot in the eye with a BB gun and
> scarred for the rest of her life (25).
>
> After that she had many memories of how other children were
> cruel and treated her differently because of her eye. She writes that she
> started to do poorly in school, had few friends, and very low self es-
> teem. She says she constantly looked down because of self-conscious-
> ness about her eye. Then, when she was fourteen she visited her
> brother in Boston, and he had a doctor remove most of the scarred tis-
> sue, leaving only a small bluish mark. After that her feelings of self-
> consciousness disappeared, and her life turned around. She did better
> in school, became valedictorian, and the most popular student of her
> graduating class (27).
>
> Terry McMillan, in her essay "What Is Perfect Anyway? Simply
> Being Beautiful?" discusses her thoughts on the aging process, and
> how these thoughts affect her in her daily life. She relates that al-
> though she knows she is gifted in several areas, there are still many
> things she would like to change about herself. McMillan writes about
> the possibilities of cosmetic surgery, and she sees nothing wrong with
> it if it makes you feel better about yourself (32). In closing, the author
> shows that she realizes that the effects of time on the body are natural,
> and she has come to terms with this fact.

> While these two authors have some different views, I think both would agree that cosmetic surgery can be a valuable alternative to going through life unhappy about what may be even the most minor of physical flaws.

Sam begins the development section with a transition paragraph, then draws on a synthesis of information from two more of his sources as he continues:

> These days people place a strong value on beauty; this value is in our society and cannot be changed or eliminated. Since this is the case, quite a few people have begun to change their appearance instead— with cosmetic surgery.
>
> While there is quite a bit of controversy over whether or not cosmetic surgery for aesthetic reasons is a psychologically healthy thing to do more and more experts are beginning to believe that it is. Annette C. Hamburger in her article "Beauty Quest," states that studies made in 1949, described "megalomaniac thinking," "latent homosexuality," "incestuous and sadistic behavior," and narcissism in patients [that requested cosmetic surgery] " (29). More recently, though, these ideas have changed, John Camp states in his article "The Importance of Being Pretty." He states that "the opinions of psychologists are catching up [with the rest of society]. A pleasing appearance . . . has a positive effect on personal relationships, experts now concede." He also writes that "there is, in fact, a good deal of evidence that an attempt to change a noticeably bad feature might represent distinctly rational behavior" (82).

To add support to the argument that "by looking and feeling better, patients often feel a lot better about themselves, brimming with new confidence and self-esteem," Sam draws on a particularly telling description of renewed self-esteem from Walker's essay:

> I become a different person from the girl who did not raise her head. Or so I think. Now that I've raised my head I win the boyfriend of my dreams. Now that I've raised my head I have plenty of friends. Now that I've raised my head classwork comes from my lips as faultlessly as Easter speeches did, and I leave high school as valedictorian, most popular student, and queen. (27)

Sam also shows that he is aware of conflicting perspectives, counter claims, when he writes:

> This is not meant to say that cosmetic surgery is for everyone with a self-esteem problem. In his article "Buying the Perfect Body," Steven Findlay writes, "a person who hopes that a straighter nose or a fuller bust line will jump start a stalled love life or provide a lift to a flagging

career is virtually sure to be disappointed" (75). He quotes psychologist Mary Ruth Wright, a counselor for cosmetic surgery patients, as saying "by itself, cosmetic surgery won't make you happy, popular or successful. It won't save a marriage or a career, and it probably won't change other people's opinion of you" (75).

Experts agree that "good candidates for cosmetic surgery have definite goals and realistic expectations," and that "people who do not have a clear understanding of the possibilities of cosmetic surgery and who have unrealistic expectations are not good candidates" (Hamburger 30).

Next, Sam presented his draft on the advantages of cosmetic surgery to his writing group. He made a copy of his four-page essay for each member of the group. As he read his essay to the group, members could respond with questions and comments. They noted some responses on their copies of Sam's paper. Sam took time, also, to note reminders to himself of suggestions he received and any other revisions that occurred to him during the reading. At the end of this writing workshop, members of the group gave Sam back the copies of his paper with their written responses.

Similarly, in some of the reading and writing activities following this chapter, we ask you first to draft essays from an informed viewpoint, presenting a synthesis of information from systematic analyses of readings, then to present these drafts in writing workshop.

Doll of Easy Inches Is More Realistic Model

The following, a New York Times news service report, appeared in newspapers across the United States in August, 1991.

It's turning out to be a rough year for Barbie.

Last year Mattel celebrated her 30th anniversary, a gala affair with a black-tie dinner and great new clothes. But in February, the world's most popular plastic teen-ager faced some stiff competition: a line of Miss America dolls, made by the Miss America Pageant and Kenner products, with up-to-date names like Devon, Tanya, Justine and Raquel.

Now Barbie's got troubles of a different nature. A new doll about the same size is poised to make her debut. She is the "Happy to Be Me" doll, who prides herself on being very different.

The Happy to Be Me doll is a sort of politically correct Barbie, a doll with a social agenda. Her mission is to help girls develop realistic body images and accept themselves as they are.

While Barbie is known for her extraordinary proportions, the Happy to Be Me doll is shaped more like an average woman, with a wider waist, larger feet, shorter neck and shorter legs. Assuming a bust measurement of 36 inches, Barbie's proportions would be 36-18-33, while the Happy to Be Me doll would be content with 36-27-38.

The new doll, which has a nine-piece wardrobe, compared with Barbie's more than 100 new outfits a year, also has bendable arms and legs.

This makes her easier to dress and pose in action, "like active women who enjoy and get involved in life," said the doll's creator, Cathy Meredig, the president of High Self-Esteem Toys Corp. in Wood-bury, Minn., a suburb of Minneapolis.

"The whole thing came about after a conversation I had with my friends," said Ms. Meredig, who has a background in industrial engineering and computer software design.

"No matter how much they had accomplished in life, if they had successful careers or were good mothers, none of them felt good about themselves. The conversation stuck in my head, I just kept wondering why."

She then began reading about children and body image. Among other things, she learned that 2 percent of girls in the United States become anorexic, 15 percent become bulimic and 70 percent viewed themselves as fat. Then she thought of the impact of the Barbie doll. She decided to market a doll with a more realistic body.

Christopher Athas, vice president of the National Association of Anorexia Nervosa and Associated Disorders in Highland Park, Ill., said he considered the creation of an anatomically realistic doll a much-needed development.

"In America there is a false conception of the female form that is repeated over and over in thousands of ways," said Mr. Athas, whose fellow member include more than 2,000 therapists who specialize in eating disorders.

Marge Piercy

Barbie Doll

———————◆———————

Marge Piercy has said about her work that it is her hope that "readers will find poems that speak to and for them, will take those poems into their lives and say them to each other and put them upon the bathroom wall and remember bits and pieces of them in stressful or quiet moments." Born in Detroit in 1936, she has long been involved in civil rights causes, including the women's movement. Her writing, both fiction and verse, reflect her activism. The following poem appeared in Circles on the Water *(1973).*

1 This girlchild was born as usual
and presented dolls that did pee-pee
and miniature GE stoves and irons
and wee lipsticks the color of cherry candy.
Then in the magic of puberty, a classmate said:
You have a great big nose and fat legs.

2 She was healthy, tested intelligent,
possessed strong arms and back,
abundant sexual drive and manual dexterity.
She went to and fro apologizing.
Everyone saw a fat nose on thick legs.

3 She was advised to play coy,
exhorted to come on hearty,
exercise, diet, smile and wheedle.
Her good nature wore out
like a fan belt.
So she cut off her nose and her legs
and offered them up.

4 In the casket displayed on satin she lay
with the undertaker's cosmetics painted on,
a turned-up putty nose,
dressed in a pink and white nightie.
Doesn't she look pretty? everyone said.
Consummation at last.
To every woman a happy ending.

Reading and Writing Activities

PRELIMINARY RESPONSE

Notes.   As you read, record your reactions (questions or comments) to Marge Piercy's poem in your reading journal.

You may react to one or two of a number of factors in the reading: the ideas, the language (especially vocabulary choice) the rhetorical structure, the unspoken assumptions, and the relationship between writer and reader (audience, purpose, organization, development). Your prior experience will also be a factor in your reaction at this point. You need not, however, attempt to react to all of these factors in the essay at this time.

Discussion.   In class, compare your reactions in reading groups of five or six. Appoint a recorder to keep track of similarities or differences, consensus or disagreement, arising from the discussion. The recorder may summarize your group discussion for the rest of the class later.

Freewriting.   After the class discussion, freewrite for 10 to 15 minutes about similarities or differences in your group's preliminary reading of the poem. Read your freewriting in groups of two to four.

SUMMARIZING

1. Create a preliminary analysis of the Piercy poem.
2. Write a summary paragraph or two, from your preliminary analysis, of the perspectives Piercy presents on standards that define beauty.
3. Read the summaries in your reading groups. Compare the focus of each summary. How do the summaries differ? How are they the same?

FOCUSED CRITICAL READING

1. How does Marge Piercy represent the subject of the poem, the "girl-child?" What picture does she give us of the subject?
2. How does she represent the "others" in this poem—the "classmate," those who advised her to "play coy," those who admired her in death?

Lavonne Adams

The Holly Pageant

◆

Lavonne Adams is a graduate of the Creative and Professional Writing Program at the University of North Carolina at Wilmington. She is the mother of three daughters and was a member of the volunteer fire department in Holly Ridge when she wrote "The Holly Pageant." She now teaches in the English Department at the University of North Carolina at Wilmington while she continues writing.

1 Everything is ready. The fire trucks and ambulances have been moved outside, floors have been swept, chairs have been placed in orderly rows. At seven o'clock, the Holly Pageant is scheduled to begin.

2 Armed with a green metal cash box and a rubber stamp for the patron's hands, I take my seat behind the folding table to the left of the front door. I watch as the girls and their parents arrive, chattering excitedly, arms laden with garment bags, shoe boxes, makeup cases, curling irons. The mothers greet each other, size up the competition, push compliments from their tongues—"Oh, you look so pretty tonight!"— "What a beautiful dress"—"I love what you've done to your hair!"

3 Barbara, one of the pageant organizers, arrives. She is in charge of acquiring the judges from the "Certified Judges List," a product of the judging seminars held every year in Raleigh. Each year, she assiduously sets the judge's table with a white tablecloth, glasses of water, and bowls of snack foods. Once the judges arrive, she ushers them into the radio room where they remain sequestered until the pageant commences. She stands at that door, as anxious as a presidential bodyguard.

4 I have heard rumors of corrupt judges, bribed by overanxious mothers at other pageants, yet have been assured that these judges are not told the names of the contestants until they are handed the programs.

5 Barbara's four-year-old son runs up to her, yanks impatiently on her arm, whispers something in her ear. She glances around anxiously, frowns as she takes his hand, then disappears in the direction of the bathroom. The inner sanctum has been left unguarded. I take advantage of the opportunity. Unobtrusively, I walk toward the radio room, cautiously turn the knob, ease open the door, and slip inside. The judges look up, startled ... perturbed. Once I explain why I am interested in talking to them, they smile, settle back in their chairs, obvi-

ously relieved. They agree to let me interview them after the pageant. I slip back outside.

The Holly Pageant is a tradition in this small North Carolina town, a social event rivaled only by the yearly parish "reunion" at the town's largest Baptist church. The Holly Ridge Volunteer Fire Department and Rescue Squad officially adopted the pageant a few years ago, after a group of local citizens abandoned it. There was much debate that night. Since I was a new member, I felt unsure of my social standing, so kept my mouth firmly closed. The other female members had stars in their eyes, the men had dollar signs. "This," one of them declared "could be financially rewarding." He saw it as a means of breaking the endless cycle of barbecue dinners and bake sales. He was proven right: the department cleared approximately $1,400 that first year.   6

The theme for this year's program is "Rock Around the Clock." Mounted on the wall directly opposite the front door is a large black and white poster featuring a caricature of two "jitter-buggers," the male sporting a fashionable crew cut, the pony-tailed female wearing a poodle skirt, bobby socks, and saddle oxfords. The stage is done in a '50's motif, a reminder of an age of American innocence. Black 45-rpm records and oversized red musical notes are plastered on the white walls. All the props are surrounded with a gold tinsel garland, the kind used to decorate Christmas trees. Everything is supposed to shine in the harsh white glare of the spotlights.   7

I hear music, applause, the introduction of this year's emcee, a popular local disc jockey. The entertainment is beginning.   8

"Notice how carefully she walks—so ladylike," says the emcee. She is referring to Tiny Miss contestant number two, who is carefully placing one patent-leather clad foot in front of the other. With every step, her fluffy pink iridescent party dress shimmers.   9

The Tiny Miss contestants are three to five years old—there are four of them this year. Glenda, another of the pageant organizers, told me that there was no contestant number one; she dropped out after the third night of practice—simply refused to continue.   10

"It's time for our former Tiny Miss Holly to present her portrait to Chief Duane Longo. Duane?" calls out the emcee.   11

Traditionally, each of the outgoing queens presents the department with a framed photograph—twinkling eyes, smile, and crown preserved for posterity. Duane walks toward the stage, bouquet of roses lying awkwardly across his left arm. Each footstep resounds from the plywood platform that functions as the stage. The Tiny Miss Holly is staring at his knee caps. He kneels. They look at each other uncertainly for just a moment, then swap the flowers for the photo. The little girl wraps her free arm around his neck, briefly buries her face against his shoulder.   12

"Awww," I hear from a woman in the audience, "isn't that sweet!"   13

14   Duane leaves the stage a flattering shade of crimson.

15   The four Tiny Miss contestants return to the stage. One is hiding behind the emcee; the rest are waiting expectantly, anxious smiles frozen on their faces.

16   "And your new, 1991 Tiny Miss Holly is contestant number... three!"

17   The audience cheers, screams, whistles. A crown is placed upon a small head.

18   "When she grows up," the emcee tells the audience, "she wants to be a cheerleader."

19   I remember when they crowned last year's Tiny Miss Holly. One contestant, who stood to the winner's right, folded her arms across her chest, stamped her foot, eyebrows lowered over a fierce angry glare, bottom lip stuck out petulantly. For just an instant, I feared for the physical safety of the new little queen, afraid the other girl was going to hit her. As the twinkling crown was placed carefully upon the winner's blonde curls, her competitor burst into tears.

20   "How embarrassing for her mother," whispered a voice in the crowd.

21   There is a brief intermission. I see one of the defeated Tiny Miss contestants standing next to the stage. She's surrounded by friends and family. Her father is talking softly to her as she hangs her head dejectedly. I move closer, catch the funereal tones of the adult voices as her parents pat her shoulder consolingly. "You looked real pretty, honey"— "You did a good job"—"You'll be ready for them next year."

22   The pageant continues with the introduction of the Little Miss contestants, ages six to nine, a bit older than the Tiny Miss contestants. These young girls appear on stage one at a time wearing incredible concoctions of satin, lace, taffeta, beads, and rhinestones: fairy-tale visions from our youth. The women in the audience gasp, sigh, exclaim enthusiastically over the beauty of each dress. Contestant number one steps onto the stage wearing a stunning teal-green party dress, appliqued with a combination of rhinestones, pearls, and sequins.

23   "Contestant number one," reads the emcee, "enjoys shrimping with her daddy.

24   I sit down in a chair recently vacated by one of the covey of visiting queens, winners of other local pageants. To my left sits a stately, composed woman who is scrutinizing the proceedings. I ask her if she is the mother of the queen whose seat I just appropriated. "No," she answers, pointing to yet another queen who is getting ready to entertain the crowd, "That's my daughter."

25   As we discuss pageants in general, I ask her about the cost of the clothing.

"You can't wear a sack, you know. This is based on more than tal- 26 ent and poise. You can put the most talented, beautiful girl up there, but if her dress is not competitive... well...." She leaves the sentence unfinished, raises her eyebrows, looks at me knowingly. She then describes a dress she saw at another pageant: floor-length black velvet with white satin flowers, spaghetti straps, fifteen-dollar-a-yard rhinestone trim. Total cost, $2,500.

She points to the owner of that dress, who later entertains the 27 crowd with a "Dixie/Battle Hymn of the Republic" medley. Tonight she is wearing a royal-blue sequined cocktail dress. I am disappointed that she has not worn the black gown, as I've never seen a dress that cost $2,500.

My curiosity piqued, I head backstage to track down the owner of 28 the teal party dress. I walk into the combination meeting room and kitchen, now transformed into a massive dressing room, the smell of makeup, hairspray, perfume, and hot bodies hanging thick in the air. One teen contestant is in the kitchen area, practicing her tap routine on a sheet of plywood meant to protect the new linoleum floor, purchased with the proceeds from last year's pageant. I look around the room, searching for that particular child, or rather that particular dress, in the confusion. I spot her on the far side of the room. As I work my way toward her, I dodge the hyperactive contestants and the tense chaperons who dress the girls and have them on stage at all the appropriate times. Once I catch up to her, I ask the woman I assume to be her mother, "If it's not too personal, would you mind telling me how much you spent on that dress?" I pause to gauge her reaction, then add encouragingly, "It's absolutely gorgeous."

To the mother's right stands a woman who has been acknowl- 29 edged periodically throughout the evening as being instrumental in helping several contestants with both their dance routines and their hairdos. She is dressed in a pink lace, pearl-studded tea gown, blonde hair and makeup flawless. The mother pauses uncertainly, looks to this woman for support.

"Why do you want to know?" the woman growls. A feral look 30 comes into her eyes; her demeanor becomes aggressive, yet with an oddly defensive undertone.

I catch myself taking a step backward, totally unprepared for the 31 hostility in her voice. I straighten my back, refuse to be intimidated, wonder if she thinks I'm a spy for a competitor. I explain. "I'm a writer. I'm working on a story."

I wait as she stares me up and down, then nods to the mother 32 before once again turning her back on me.

"Three hundred and fifty dollars," states the mother. 33

34   While Glenda stressed that this year's parents have not been as competitive as those in years past, by the time you figure in the costumes and the dance lessons, it's about a $2,000 per contestant investment. This year the pageant has a total of fifteen contestants.

35   Before the crowning of the new Little Miss, the former Little Miss makes her final appearance on stage. Tradition. With tears in her eyes, she waves farewell to her admirers. Well-wishers step forward with balloons and bouquets of flowers as a pre-taped message plays, "I want to thank God for giving me the opportunity to be Little Miss Holly...and to Uncle Roger for letting me use his Corvette to ride in the parades."

36   My daughter says that several years ago the winner of that year's Little Miss competition wore her full-length dress to school the first day after the pageant.

37   "And she wore her crown, too!" she adds emphatically.

38   "The sash?" I ask.

39   "Yep," she says. "Her Daddy stayed with her all day. He even spread out napkins across her lap at lunch. And her friends had to hold up her skirts during recess because the playground was muddy and the grass was all wet. But she still climbed on the monkey bars."

40   We have another brief intermission, then the visiting queens go up on stage one by one to introduce themselves. Our newly crowned Tiny Miss and Little Miss are allowed to join the throng. When the Tiny Miss steps up to the microphone, she says, "Hi. I'm...." She panics, has obviously forgotten what to say, looks around like a cornered mouse. "Mommy!" she calls out in a frightened voice. Her mother steps up to the stage with an indulgent smile and prompts her daughter. The little girl returns to the microphone and announces her name.

41   Glenda chuckles, "If that wasn't precious!"

42   Most of the older girls, the Pre-teens and the Teens, have been in pageants before. They're familiar with the routine, know all the ins and outs, understand how to play up to the judges, an art in itself.

43   Teen contestant number one, for instance, seems to be a house favorite. She does a clogging routine entitled "Texas Tap" that brings down the house. Her talent is undeniable, her exuberance contagious. I find myself smiling and clapping in time to the music along with the rest of the audience. Unfortunately, when it comes time for her prepared speech, this contestant forgets what she was going to say, stumbles verbally. She mumbles, "Oh God," then continues the best she can.

44   A young woman to my right shakes her head, turns to me and says with resignation, "She would have had a hard time, anyway. Her gown is red."

45   My face must reflect my bewilderment.

46   "With her red hair?" she adds with implied significance.

Obviously, the contestant is unenlightened. Redheads don't wear   47
red. *Faux pas.* One just doesn't do these things.

Some rules in the pageant circle are even more specific. Wearing   48
black shoes with the evening gown is forbidden, as are hats, parasols,
and elbow-length gloves. Rules are rules. I have heard that one mother,
in another pageant, tried to add an extra row of lace to her daughter's
socks. It was specified that only two rows of lace would be allowed.
The pageant's organizers solemnly handed this mother a seam-ripper.

According to Glenda, this pageant has done away with collective   49
judging, the commonly accepted practice of simultaneously lining up
the girls on stage, having them turn, pose in front of the judges. "We
don't want them compared to one another. They stand on their own
merit."

Teen contestant number one does not win.   50

The pageant over, I weave through the departing crowd toward the   51
radio room, anxious to talk to the judges. There is a long line. Accompanied by their mothers, the contestants are each given the opportunity
to discuss her performance with the judges, find out what cost her the
competition, where she lost those valuable points. It is a quiet cluster.

To my left stands one of the winners. Her mother is not waiting   52
with her, not monitoring her behavior. One of her friends walks by,
teases, "Hey, you won this year. Why are *you* waiting to see the
judges?"

This victor smiles, puffs out her chest with pride, swings her right   53
hand up to her forehead. She nods toward the closed door. "I just want
to tell them . . .(with a saucy salute). . . thanks!"

A mother and her daughter, one of the defeated contestants, try to   54
slip past unnoticed. Another mother looks up, asks, "Aren't you going
to conference with the judges?"

"No, I'm afraid I might start crying," the first mother answers. Her   55
daughter says nothing, but her eyes are red.

After a thirty-five minute wait, I am finally able to talk to one of the   56
judges, a man named John. He's wearing a black tuxedo, sporting a
diamond stud in his ear, has a red carnation pinned to his lapel. He's a
hairdresser, has done hair for lots of the pageants—that's how he got
"hooked." Most of the judges, he explains, become involved when
either friends or their own children enter a pageant. These judges don't
get paid for their work; instead, they receive a small gift.

"Why do you do it, then?" I ask.   57

"I like to see the girls have a good time," he answers.   58

Every year I'm asked if I'm going to enter my two little girls in the   59
pageant. Every year I say no.

"Mommy," asks my youngest, "don't you think I'm pretty enough   60
to win?"

Reading and Writing Activities

PRELIMINARY RESPONSE

Notes.   As you read, record your reactions (questions or comments) to Lavonne Adams's essay in your reading journal.

Discussion.   In class, compare your reactions in reading groups of five or six. Appoint a recorder to keep track of similarities or differences, consensus or disagreement, arising from the discussion. The recorder may summarize your group discussion for the rest of the class later.

Freewriting.   After the class discussion, freewrite for 10 to 15 minutes about similarities or differences in your group's preliminary reading of the essay. Read your freewriting in groups of two to four.

SUMMARIZING

1. Create a preliminary analysis of the Adams essay. A scratchline or clustering representation of central topics may be useful at this point. Or you may want to refer to the analysis questions that can guide your preliminary analysis presented at the beginning of this chapter.
2. Write a summary paragraph or two, from your preliminary analysis, of the perspectives Adams presents on beauty pageants.
3. Read the summaries in your reading groups. Compare the focus of each summary. How do the summaries differ? How are they the same? Check to see if you are *reacting and responding* to the essay instead of summarizing the central topics.

FOCUSED CRITICAL READING

1. How does Adams represent the culture of the beauty pageant?
2. How does she represent the principal "others" in this contest— the mothers who prepare and bring their children to compete?
3. How does she represent the other adults—the organizers and the judges?
4. What can you tell about the audience at the specific beauty pageant that Adams presents?

Alice Walker

Beauty: When the Other Dancer Is the Self

◆

Alice Walker is well known as the author of the novel The Color Purple *(1982). She published the following essay, "Beauty: When the Other Dancer Is the Self," in her collection* In Search of Our Mothers' Gardens *(1983). Since then, it has been reprinted in many anthologies. In her novels, short stories, and poems, Walker writes about African-American women and their struggle to survive.*

It is a bright summer day in 1947. My father, a fat, funny man with beautiful eyes and a subversive wit, is trying to decide which of his eight children he will take with him to the county fair. My mother, of course, will not go. She is knocked out from getting most of us ready: I hold my neck stiff against the pressure of her knuckles as she hastily completes the braiding and then beribboning of my hair.   1

My father is the driver for the rich old white lady up the road. Her name is Miss Mey. She owns all the land for miles around, as well as the house in which we live. All I remember about her is that she once offered to pay my mother thirty-five cents for cleaning her house, raking up piles of her magnolia leaves, and washing her family's clothes, and that my mother— she of no money, eight children, and a chronic earache—refused it. But I do not think of this in 1947. I am two and a half years old. I want to go everywhere my daddy goes. I am excited at the prospect of riding in a car. Someone has told me fairs are fun. That there is room in the car for only three of us doesn't faze me at all. Whirling happily in my starchy frock, showing off my biscuit-polished patent-leather shoes and lavender socks, tossing my head in a way that makes my ribbons bounce, I stand, hands on hips, before my father. "Take me, Daddy," I say with assurance; "I'm the prettiest!"   2

Later, it does not surprise me to find myself in Miss Mey's shiny black car, sharing the back seat with the other lucky ones. Does not surprise me that I thoroughly enjoy the fair. At home that night I tell the unlucky ones all I can remember about the merry-go-round, the man who eats live chickens, and the teddy bears, until they say: that's enough, baby Alice. Shut up now, and go to sleep.   3

4   It is Easter Sunday, 1950. 1 am dressed in a green, flocked, scalloped-hem dress (handmade by my adoring sister, Ruth) that has its own smooth satin petticoat and tiny hot-pink roses tucked into each scallop. My shoes, new T-strap patent leather, again highly biscuit-polished. I am six years old and have learned one of the longest Easter speeches to be heard that day, totally unlike the speech I said when I was two: "Easter lilies/pure and white/blossom in/the morning light." When I rise to give my speech I do so on a great wave of love and pride and expectation. People in the church stop rustling their new crinolines. They seem to hold their breath. I can tell they admire my dress, but it is my spirit, bordering on sassiness (womanishness), they secretly applaud.

5   "That girl's a little *mess*," they whisper to each other, pleased.

6   Naturally I say my speech without stammer or pause, unlike those who stutter, stammer, or, worst of all, forget. This is before the word "beautiful" exists in people's vocabulary, but "Oh, isn't she the *cutest* thing!" frequently floats my way. "And got so much sense!" they gratefully add . . . for which thoughtful addition I thank them to this day.

7   *It was great fun being cute. But then, one day, it ended.*

8   I am eight years old and a tomboy. I have a cowboy hat, cowboy boots, checkered shirt and pants, all red. My playmates are my brothers, two and four years older than I. Their colors are black and green, the only difference in the way we are dressed. On Saturday nights we all go to the picture show, even my mother; Westerns are her favorite kind of movie. Back home, "on the ranch," we pretend we are Tom Mix, Hopalong Cassidy, Lash LaRue (we've even named one of our dogs Lash LaRue); we chase each other for hours rustling cattle, being outlaws, delivering damsels from distress. Then my parents decide to buy my brothers guns. These are not "real" guns. They shoot "BBs," copper pellets my brothers say will kill birds. Because I am a girl, I do not get a gun. Instantly I am relegated to the position of Indian. Now there appears a great distance between us. They shoot and shoot at everything with their new guns. I try to keep up with my bow and arrows.

9   One day while I am standing on top of our makeshift "garage"—pieces of tin nailed across some poles—holding my bow and arrow and looking out toward the fields, I feel an incredible blow in my right eye. I look down just in time to see my brother lower his gun.

10   Both brothers rush to my side. My eye stings, and I cover it with my hand. "If you tell," they say, "we will get a whipping. You don't want that to happen, do you?" I do not. "Here is a piece of wire," says the older brother, picking it up from the roof; "say you stepped on one end of it and the other flew up and hit you." The pain is beginning to start. "Yes," I say. "Yes, I will say that is what happened." If I do not say

this is what happened, I know my brothers will find ways to make me wish I had. But now I will say anything that gets me to my mother.

Confronted by our parents we stick to the lie agreed upon. They place me on a bench on the porch and I close my left eye while they examine the right. There is a tree growing from underneath the porch that climbs past the railing to the roof. It is the last thing my right eye sees. I watch as its trunk, its branches, and then its leaves are blotted out by the rising blood.

I am in shock. First there is intense fever, which my father tries to break using lily leaves bound around my head. Then there are chills: my mother tries to get me to eat soup. Eventually, I do not know how, my parents learn what has happened. A week after the "accident" they take me to see a doctor. "Why did you wait so long to come?" he asks, looking into my eye and shaking his head. "Eyes are sympathetic," he says. "If one is blind, the other will likely become blind too."

This comment of the doctor's terrifies me. But it is really how I look that bothers me most. Where the BB pellet struck there is a glob of whitish scar tissue, a hideous cataract, on my eye. Now when I stare at people—a favorite pastime, up to now—they will stare back. Not at the "cute" little girl, but at her scar. For six years I do not stare at anyone, because I do not raise my head.

Years later, in the throes of a mid-life crisis, I ask my mother and sister whether I changed after the "accident." "No," they say, puzzled. "What do you mean?"

What do I mean?

I am eight, and, for the first time, doing poorly in school, where I have been something of a whiz since I was four. We have just moved to the place where the "accident" occurred. We do not know any of the people around us because this is a different county. The only time I see the friends I knew is when we go back to our old church. The new school is the former state penitentiary. It is a large stone building, cold and drafty, crammed to overflowing with boisterous, ill-disciplined children. On the third floor there is a huge circular imprint of some partition that has been torn out.

"What used to be here?" I ask a sullen girl next to me on our way past it to lunch.

"The electric chair," says she.

At night I have nightmares about the electric chair, and about all the people reputedly "fried" in it. I am afraid of the school, where all the students seem to be budding criminals.

"What's the matter with your eye?" they ask, critically.

When I don't answer (I cannot decide whether it was an "accident" or not), they shove me, insist on a fight.

22   My brother, the one who created the story about the wire, comes to my rescue. But then brags so much about "protecting" me, I become sick.

23   After months of torture at the school, my parents decide to send me back to our old community, to my old school. I live with my grandparents and the teacher they board. But there is no room for Phoebe, my cat. By the time my grandparents decide there is room, and I ask for my cat, she cannot be found. Miss Yarborough, the boarding teacher, takes me under her wing, and begins to teach me to play the piano. But soon she marries an African—a "prince," she says—and is whisked away to his continent.

24   At my old school there is at least one teacher who loves me. She is the teacher who "knew me before I was born" and bought my first baby clothes. It is she who makes life bearable. It is her presence that finally helps me turn on the one child at the school who continually calls me "one-eyed bitch." One day I simply grab him by his coat and beat him until I am satisfied. It is my teacher who tells me my mother is ill.

25   My mother is lying in bed in the middle of the day, something I have never seen. She is in too much pain to speak. She has an abscess in her ear. I stand looking down on her, knowing that if she dies, I cannot live. She is being treated with warm oil and hot bricks held against her cheek. Finally a doctor comes. But I must go back to my grandparents' house. The weeks pass but I am hardly aware of it. All I know is that my mother might die, my father is not so jolly, my brothers still have their guns, and I am the one sent away from home.

26   "You did not change," they say.

27   *Did I imagine the anguish of never looking up?*

28   I am twelve. When relatives come to visit I hide in my room. My cousin Brenda, just my age, whose father works in the post office and whose mother is a nurse, comes to find me. "Hello," she says. And then she asks, looking at my recent school picture, which I did not want taken, and on which the "glob," as I think of it, is clearly visible, "You still can't see out of that eye?"

29   "No," I say, and flop back on the bed over my book.

30   That night, as I do almost every night, I abuse my eye. I rant and rave at it, in front of the mirror. I plead with it to clear up before morning. I tell it I hate and despise it. I do not pray for sight. I pray for beauty.

31   "You did not change," they say.

32   I am fourteen and baby-sitting for my brother Bill, who lives in Boston. He is my favorite brother and there is a strong bond between

us. Understanding my feelings of shame and ugliness he and his wife take me to a local hospital, where the "glob" is removed by a doctor named O. Henry. There is still a small bluish crater where the scar tissue was, but the ugly white stuff is gone. Almost immediately I become a different person from the girl who does not raise her head. Or so I think. Now that I've raised my head I win the boyfriend of my dreams. Now that I've raised my head I have plenty of friends. Now that I've raised my head classwork comes from my lips as faultlessly as Easter speeches did, and I leave high school as valedictorian, most popular student, and *queen,* hardly believing my luck. Ironically, the girl who was voted most beautiful in our class (and was) was later shot twice through the chest by a male companion, using a "real" gun, while she was pregnant. But that's another story in itself. Or is it?

"You did not change," they say.   33

It is now thirty years since the "accident." A beautiful journalist   34
comes to visit and to interview me. She is going to write a cover story for her magazine that focuses on my latest book. "Decide how you want to look on the cover," she says. "Glamorous, or whatever."

Never mind "glamorous," it is the "whatever" that I hear. Sud-   35
denly all I can think of is whether I will get enough sleep the night before the photography session: if I don't, my eye will be tired and wander, as blind eyes will.

At night in bed with my lover I think up reasons why I should not   36
appear on the cover of a magazine. "My meanest critics will say I've sold out," I say. "My family will now realize I write scandalous books."

"But what's the real reason you don't want to do this?" he asks.   37

"Because in all probability," I say in a rush, "my eye won't be   38
straight."

"It will be straight enough," he says. Then, "Besides, I thought   39
you'd made your peace with that."

And I suddenly remember that I have.   40

I remember.   41

I am talking to my brother Jimmy, asking if be remembers anything   42
unusual about the day I was shot. He does not know I consider that day the last time my father, with his sweet home remedy of cool lily leaves, chose me, and that I suffered and raged inside because of this. "Well," he says, "all I remember is standing by the side of the highway with Daddy, trying to flag down a car. A white man stopped, but when Daddy said he needed somebody to take his little girl to the doctor, he drove off."

I remember.   43

I am in the desert for the first time. I fall totally in love with it. I am   44
so overwhelmed by its beauty, I confront for the first time, consciously, the meaning of the doctor's words years ago: "Eyes are sympathetic. If

one is blind, the other will likely become blind too." I realize I have dashed about the world madly, looking at this, looking at that, storing up images against the fading of the light. *But I might have missed seeing the desert!* The shock of that possibility—and gratitude for over twenty-five years of sight—sends me literally to my knees. Poem after poem comes—which is perhaps how poets pray.

On Sight

I am so thankful I have seen
The Desert
And the creatures in the desert
And the desert Itself.

The desert has its own moon
Which I have seen
With my own eye.
There is no flag on it.

Trees of the desert have arms
All of which are always up
That is because the moon is up
The sun is up
Also the sky
The stars
Clouds
None with flags.

If there *were* flags, I doubt
the trees would point.
Would you?

45   *But mostly, I remember this:*

46   I am twenty-seven, and my baby daughter is almost three. Since her birth I have worried about her discovery that her mother's eyes are different from other people's. Will she be embarrassed? I think. What will she say? Every day she watches a television program called "Big Blue Marble." It begins with a picture of the earth as it appears from the moon. It is bluish, a little battered-looking, but full of light, with whitish clouds swirling around it. Every time I see it I weep with love, as if it is a picture of Grandma's house. One day when I am putting Rebecca down for her nap, she suddenly focuses on my eye. Something inside me cringes, gets ready to try to protect myself. All children are cruel about physical differences, I know from experience, and that they don't always mean to be is another matter. I assume Rebecca will be the same.

47   But no-o-o-o. She studies my face intently as we stand, her inside and me outside her crib. She even holds my face maternally between

her dimpled little hands. Then, looking every bit as serious and lawyer-like as her father, she says, as if it may just possibly have slipped my attention: "Mommy, there's a *world* in your eye." (As in, "Don't be alarmed, or do anything crazy.") And then, gently, but with great interest: "Mommy, where did you *get* that world in your eye?"

For the most part, the pain left then. (So what, if my brothers grew   48
up to buy even more powerful pellet guns for their sons and to carry real guns themselves. So what, if a young "Morehouse man" once nearly fell off the steps of Trevor Arnett Library because he thought my eyes were blue.) Crying and laughing I ran to the bathroom, while Rebecca mumbled and sang herself off to sleep. Yes indeed, I realized, looking into the mirror. There *was* a world in my eye. And I saw that it was possible to love it: that in fact, for all it had taught me of shame and anger and inner vision, I *did* love it. Even to see it drifting out of orbit in boredom, or rolling up out of fatigue, not to mention floating back at attention in excitement (bearing witness, a friend has called it), deeply suitable to my personality, and even characteristic of me.

That night I dream I am dancing to Stevie Wonder's song   49
"Always" (the name of the song is really "As," but I hear it as "Always"). As I dance, whirling and joyous, happier than I've ever been in my life, another bright-faced dancer joins me. We dance and kiss each other and hold each other through the night. The other dancer has obviously come through all right, as I have done. She is beautiful, whole and free. And she is also me.

Reading and Writing Activities

PRELIMINARY RESPONSES

Notes.   As you read, record your reactions (questions or comments) to Alice Walker's essay in your reading journal.

You may want to relate what Walker is saying about her experience to your own experience as a member of a family.

Discussion.   In class, compare your reactions in reading groups of five or six. Appoint a recorder to keep track of similarities or differences, consensus or disagreement, arising from the discussion. The recorder may summarize your group discussion for the rest of the class later.

Freewriting.   After the class discussion, freewrite for 10 to 15 minutes about similarities or differences in your group's preliminary reading of the article. Read your freewriting in groups of two to four.

SUMMARIZING

1. Create a preliminary analysis of Walker's essay. A scratchline or clustering representation of central topics may be useful at this point.
2. Write a summary paragraph or two, from your preliminary analysis, of the perspectives Walker presents on the effects of changes in her appearance.
3. Read the summaries in your reading groups. Compare the focus of each summary. How do the summaries differ? How are they the same? Check to see if you are *reacting and responding* to the essay instead of summarizing the central topics.

FOCUSED CRITICAL READING

1. How does Alice Walker show you differences in the way she perceived herself before the accident and after the accident?
2. How does she perceive herself as "other" because of her disfigurement.
3. How does she define a principle "other" in this essay—the dominant culture?

David Futrelle and Leora Tanenbaum

Bootstrap Feminism

◆

David Futrelle is an editor for In These Times; *Leora Tanenbaum is a writer who lives in New York.* In These Times, *published in Chicago by The Institute for Public Affairs, is a publication listed in the Alternative Press Index and the Left Index. The following selection, a review of new books written by three very different women, focuses on Naomi Wolf's changing radicalism as she shares the spotlight with "two decidedly un-radical regulars on the lunch-and-lecture circuit."*

At first glance, it seems an unlikely sight, Naomi Wolf, author of *The Beauty Myth,* a feminist polemic describing how women are hurt by the perpetual and inherently unfulfillable quest for physical perfection, is smiling winsomely in an ad for... pantyhose. You know, those nylon torture devices that make a 90-degree day seem like a 100-degree one, that push in the gut and mask unsightly veins. Liberated women who have conservative jobs and wear pantyhose with their skirted suits can't wait to rush home and tear them off. Yet Wolf has been named the "No Nonsense American Woman" for the month of July, so chosen (the ad copy explains) because she "challenges us to embrace a more open-minded feminism—one that respects a woman's heart and individuality while it promotes her power!"

The radical rage that filled Wolf's first book has given way, it appears, to a complacent commercialism. These days, Wolf seems less concerned with feminism than femininity. So perhaps it should come as no surprise that while on tour for her book *Fire with Fire* last fall, Wolf was able to quite comfortably share a podium at New York's posh 21 club with two decidedly unradical regulars on the lunch-and-lecture circuit, each pushing a new book: trophy-wife-turned-cosmetics-entrepreneur Georgette Mosbacher and New Age guru Marianne Williamson. The group of society women who had gathered for the lunch expected to hear vastly different opinions and witness a sharp debate—after all, you would hardly think that there would be much common ground among a strident feminist, a maven of mascara and a celebrity psyche healer.

Mosbacher, best known as the wife of Texas oilman and former Secretary of Commerce Robert Mosbacher, was there to promote an autobiography of sorts called *Feminine Force*. With her perfectly coiffed dyed red hair and thick encrustations of jewelry, she seemed the very embodiment of the Beauty Myth that Wolf once so diligently attempted to deconstruct. Indeed, in *Feminine Force*, Mosbacher's book-length paean to the powers of femininity, she warns unwary women to "look out for the theoreticians of anger who argue that beauty is a myth perpetuated to keep us down." Williamson, for her part, seems uninterested in such earthly squabbles. "Feminine beauty is not a function of clothes or hair or makeup," she writes in *A Woman's Worth*, which has now become a bestseller. "Beauty is an internal light.... When we are truly aware of our spiritual glory, a varicose vein or two is not that big a deal."

4   But it was more than the perversity of fate that brought these three women together. Despite some obvious differences on the surface, all preach a similar message—promoting a distinctly individualistic brand of female empowerment, an up-by-the-bootstraps model of personal success. And they've displayed remarkable savvy in marketing their message. At a moment when nearly all American women support the goal of gender equality—yet when polls show that only a third of them embrace the label "feminist"—these three women have promoted their brand of empowerment as the ultimate form of do-it-yourself therapy.

5   At the same time that most Americans associate feminism with the excesses of Andrea Dworkin, a vague rhetoric of female empowerment has infiltrated even the most seemingly apolitical places in our popular culture—daytime talk shows, romance novels and self-help books designed especially for women. It's a rhetoric that owes as much to Helen Gurley Brown as to Robin Morgan; as much to Horatio Alger as to Susan B. Anthony. Advertisers, quick to sense profit in the appropriation of anything with a potentially big market share, have increasingly directed their attention to a new generation of revved-up power females. Nike encourages women to "just do it"; a recent ad for Diet Coke portrays an office full of young women lustily ogling a shirtless construction worker—making him the focus of a post-feminist female gaze as objectifying as the legendary male gaze itself.

6   This new rhetoric of female empowerment has now become the raw material for self-described feminists—like Wolf—as well as for semifeminists like Mosbacher and Williamson. Each of the three, in her own way, shuns the notion of women as victims, preferring to appeal to women's innate power. All acknowledge the dangers of sexism and the power of sexist institutions, but without advocating messy or difficult strategies for change. Low self-esteem, inequitable salaries and abusive partners are very real problems—but happily they can all be repaired and redeemed through *sheer feminine will*. It is no wonder that the three find inspiration in Scarlett O'Hara—the epitome of feminine willfulness.

Traditionally, feminists have looked upon such expressions of   7
female individualism with a degree of suspicion: feminism, after all, is
a political movement for the collective empowerment of women as a
class—not a cheering section for individually powerful women. But it
has always been tempting for such women—who look upon their
unsuccessful sisters with a degree of pity and embarrassment—to turn
their backs on a movement that talks so much of victimization. "Since
admitting . . . unfreedom is painful and anxiety provoking," social critic
Ellen Willis has suggested, "organized feminism has always had to
contend with women insisting that they can liberate themselves and
don't need a movement, thank you." And so Mosbacher tells her readers to cease their whining; she's "dismayed when I see women focus on
the idea that as women, we are victims." Williamson is similarly dis-
tressed by those who dwell too much on the negative, letting her readers in on a "magical secret . . . No one is stuck who chooses not to be."

It is relatively easy for Mosbacher and Williamson to dispense with   8
the notion of victimhood; they, after all, don't claim to be feminists.
Wolf *does,* and so her task is a bit harder. She has to distinguish her version of feminism (she calls it "power feminism") from "victim feminism"—the ideology of those who have "charge[d] women to identify
with powerlessness even at the expense of taking responsibility for the
power that they do possess." Sexism is no longer the real problem, Wolf
maintains; what holds women back is old-style *feminism*—the ideological, uncompromising and unfeminine variety. Blaming men, masculinity or male institutions for women's unequal status is passé. Instead,
feminists should "develop a vision of femininity in which it is appropriate and sexy for women to use power." Power, to Wolf, means
upward economic mobility within the present system, with no need to
subvert it.

Ah, the joy of success! Wolf celebrates the novels of Judith Krantz,   9
Jackie Collins and, yes, Ivana Trump, whose books tell the stories of
bold female entrepreneurs intent on the accumulation of wealth and
power. She even glorifies the readers of the fast-growing specialty magazine *Women & Guns,* who share "the pioneer feminism of women who
know that no one will take care of them but themselves."

In their celebration of individual advancement, Wolf and Mos-   10
bacher are reacting against the fuzzy notion that there is a natural and
innate connection among all women. That impulse is good: the utopian
vision of women as a global class with fundamental commonalities is
simplistic, and is predicated on the false assumption that all women are
similarly united by the experience of sexist subjugation.

But in their total rejection of the notion of sisterhood, Wolf and   11
Mosbacher go too far. The fact is that there *is* some truth to the notion of
female universality. After all, no man, however sensitive or feminist he

tries to be, can give birth. All women, by contrast, are in some way bound by their reproductive capacity. Most women do eventually become mothers—and even those women who don't are expected somehow to possess an inherently feminine, nurturing nature. Women who stray too far from the motherly role—one thinks of Leona Helmsley, the "Queen of Mean"—tend to be denigrated as cold, power-hungry bitches.

12   To admit these realities would mean espousing an ideological feminism that attempts to subvert the status quo—yet none of these writers are willing to critique the American Dream, or the individualism underlying it. Indeed, they celebrate it. Mosbacher proudly relates her immigrant heritage: her feisty great-grandmother Baba emigrated from Austria and settled in a small town in Indiana. She couldn't read or write, yet never wasted a moment dwelling on her shortcomings. Baba, who pulled "all of her resources together and boldly took control of her life," is for Mosbacher "the essence of Feminine Force."

13   Wolf similarly argues that feminists need to "replace the sentimentalized model of sisterhood with a pragmatic model: that of the immigrant connection. The immigrant succeeds because she breaks ties with the old country and learns to assimilate into the new culture." Sexual inequality, too, Wolf claims, "which we think of as being the texture and taste of femininity itself, can begin to become a quaint memory of the old country—if we are not too attached to let it go." Women must stop thinking of themselves as victims and start thinking of themselves as victors. They must hone a "psychology of female power to match their new opportunities" and "learn to imagine and enjoy winning." It's that easy. Attitude is everything.

14   *Fire with Fire* is an exercise in positive thinking from start to finish, a celebration of the "genderquake" that, Wolf says, has transformed American politics over the last few years. The backlash against feminism, according to Wolf, is history—a relic of the '80s. It ended in the fall of 1991. Then a new era began, initiated by the Supreme Court's confirmation hearings for Clarence Thomas, which "performed the same alchemy on the aura of patriarchy" that Joseph Welch's challenge to Joe McCarthy during the Army-McCarthy hearings had done to the aura of anticommunism.

15   A churlish critic might suggest that the effects of the genderquake have been more symbolic than real. You may recall that Clarence Thomas did in fact make it to the Supreme Court. But advertisers (who know well the power of symbolism) are far ahead of feminist theorists on this point. "The great leaders are those who know how to...use symbols that resonate unconsciously as well as literally," Wolf explains. "In this view, a DKNY ad that shows the swearing in of a woman president can have as much power to advance women's historical progress on the psychic level as can the passage of the ERA on the political level."

Just as advertisers have learned (in their way) from Anita Hill, feminists need to learn a lesson or two from them. "Feminism lacks positive imagery," Wolf complains, "even something as basic as a widely understood, positive logo."   16

For Wolf, psychic victories are at least as important as victories in the real world. Indeed, she's hard-pressed to tell the difference between the two, chiding those who see the new emphasis on self-esteem as misguided solipsism with the thought that "we in the First World have reached the point at which [the] distinction between inner and outer life is obsolete."   17

This faith in faith is something Wolf shares with her empowered sisters. Williamson is just as enthusiastic about the power of positive thinking. "Women are not powerless," she writes. "We just pretend we are." In her search for positive energy, she finds inspiration in greeting cards, and picks up her spiritual slogans from coffee mugs—quite literally. "Someone once gave me a coffee mug on which it is printed ENTERTAIN NO NEGATIVITY," she writes. "if only I could be so strong."   18

Mosbacher similarly explains that success is, quite simply, "the process of not accepting failure." Those with "guts of steel" are destined to win. "The Feminine Force," Mosbacher writes, "is my way of describing the intangible but indelible powers or energies that all women are born with but that many of us lose somewhere along life's way." To Mosbacher, the boundaries that limit women are self-imposed. You can recreate yourself—through makeup, hair dye and a little cosmetic surgery. "When I look my personal best," she proudly writes, "I am powerful." No wonder she fills her book with some two dozen photos of herself—half of them in color. "What can I say?" one photo caption reads. "I love getting dressed up . . . and I love being a girl."   19

Femininity, for Mosbacher, is not only fun; it's a means of self-advancement. Even catching and winning the right man, if done properly, can be an act of enpowerment—and Mosbacher offers detailed instructions to help her readers along. She admits that "hard-core feminists may not like" some of her techniques—which include suggestions about how to steer a conversation toward a man's main interest (himself), how to master the art of flattery and how to cultivate "the look," that is, a gaze that makes a man feel "as though everything he says is brilliant."   20

And even the mystical Williamson stops to offer some practical man-catching advice of her own: women need to get their "spiritual chops down," she argues, so that they can attract the right kind of man. In a chapter entitled "Embracing the Goddess," she offers what is essentially a postfeminist New Age dating guide. "[D]aughters of God," she explains, "don't brake for jerks." Once a woman transforms herself from a mere "princess" into a "goddess," Williamson writes,   21 she will be ready to fall in love with a masculine man; and this process, she informs us with a presumably straight face, will change the world. For all her talk of empowerment, and for all of her theological flights of fancy, Williamson's message is an old one: A "woman's worth" is inseparable from her relationship with her Significant Other. That's not a message of liberation; that's what Betty Friedan, 30 years ago, rightly denounced as the Feminine Mystique.

22   It's hard not to be reminded of Marabel Morgan's legendary '70s guide to self-improvement-through-self-abasement, *The Total Woman.* Born-again Morgan suggested that her readers should give up trying to improve their mates; to be happy, she suggested, women had to learn to "accept," "admire," "adapt" and "appreciate" their husbands as they were. But if she could not see her way out of a system that left women dependent on unreliable men, she did at least suggest how women could improve their position within it.

23   The first step in Morgan's style of empowerment was a kind of "interior decorating" remarkably similar to Gloria Steinem's idea of "revolution from within," "Perhaps it sounds self-centered to love yourself," Morgan wrote, "but it's most necessary if you're going to love others, including your husband. When you do, you will have a good image of yourself. That means you like being you. You will function properly and accomplish what you set out to do. You will have a sense of well-being within." Sound familiar?

24   Feminists, of course, shouldn't leave the subject of self-esteem to the Marabel Morgans of the world: a truly empowering feminism needs to promote confidence. Underappreciating oneself, after all, goes hand in hand with staying in an abusive relationship, shunning the beach on a perfect summer day and passively accepting a salary without negotiating. Without a doubt, drive and ambition are positive traits—though not inherently feminist ones. Yet Wolf, in a moment of rash enthusiasm, suggests affixing the feminist label to "every woman who is operating at her full speed"—forgetting that antifeminists such as Phyllis Schlafly and Marilyn Quayle are every bit as "empowered" as she and Susan Faludi.

25   In their own ways, Mosbacher, Williamson and Wolf are the very models of self-made womanhood. And so it is hardly surprising that these three women—whose new books were written after they had each achieved a certain success—would be drawn to the Scarlett O'Hara prototype, eager to celebrate the resilience and power of women who have fought hard to get somewhere in the world.

26   Yet in doing so each has forgotten that the primary barriers to success are external ones—and that the lessons of their own admittedly exceptional cases do not apply to all. The glorification of female success on the individual level is, at best, an extraordinarily limited form of

feminism; at worst, it's a repudiation of the feminist ideal of collective empowerment.

But why should we let mere ideology spoil this new message of success? There's no need to worry about sexual harassment, abortion waiting periods and inequitable hiring practices. Just freshen your lipstick, smooth the wrinkles on your chic power suit, pick up a stylish bra holster for your cute pink handgun, and you're on your way to new horizons. *Just do it.*   27

Reading and Writing Activities

PRELIMINARY RESPONSE

Notes.   As you read, record your reactions (questions or comments) to "Bootstrap Feminism" by David Futrelle and Leora Tanenbaum.

Discussion.   In class, compare your reactions in reading groups of five or six. Appoint a recorder to keep track of similarities or differences, consensus or disagreement, arising from the discussion. The recorder may summarize your group discussion for the rest of the class later.

FOCUSED CRITICAL READING

1. How do these two writers, David Futrelle and Leora Tanenbaum, view the growing acceptance of female empowerment even in unlikely, apolitical situations?
2. What stance do they adopt, in this review, towards the three women whose work they are reviewing?
3. How do you react to this review of "bootstrap feminism"?

Richard Selzer

Fetishes

———————◆———————

*Richard Selzer was born in Troy, New York, in 1928. Selzer was employed
as a physician and surgeon for twenty years before his first book, a collection of short stories, was published in 1974. His writing, both fiction and
nonfiction, vividly describes the details of human anatomy as well as the
procedures of surgery. Another of Selzer's concerns is the psychological
responses of patients to surgery, disease, and impending death. The following selection is from his book,* Taking the World in for Repairs, *published in 1986.*

1   There is Audrey. And there is Leonard. Audrey had waited until
she was thirty-two to marry. Not by choice; no one had asked her. But
all the time she had never given up hope. So that when Leonard
Blakeslee had come along, she had at once reached out her hands for
him as though he were an exotic foreign dish whose very strangeness
captured her appetite completely. "You'll love me?" she asked him, and
never once in all these years had he given her reason to doubt it. The
fact that no children had come along was briefly regretted by both of
them, then accepted. Somehow, it suited them.

2   Leonard is an anthropologist. Every so often he goes off to New
Guinea on an expedition among the Asmat. It is the only time they are
separated. When he is away Audrey feels only half intact, bisected.
And Leonard too, as he wrote in a letter (she has saved them all), is
"never done with wanting you at my side, where you ought always to
be, my darling." She loved that "ought always to be." It was courtly.
When he is not going on in that vein, his letters are anthropological,
having to do with the language of the tribe for which he is compiling a
dictionary, the artifacts he is collecting, the myths and mores of the people, all of which Audrey reads with affection and even genuine interest.
Leonard and his artifacts, she would say to her sister, Violet, with an
indulgent smile. Not that Audrey is beautiful. No one but Leonard
could accuse her of that. But what she had she had and that was the
true love of her husband.

3   Another thing Audrey has right now is a ten-centimeter cyst on her
right ovary which the doctors can't say for certain is benign, and so it
will have to come out. Thank heavens Leonard isn't off on one of his
expeditions, she thought.

Fifteen years ago, she had been forty-two then, every one of her 4
upper teeth had been extracted while Leonard was in New Guinea.
Pyorrhea, the dentist had said. Said it severely. "You've let it go. They
are all rotten and ready to fall out on their own."

Audrey was flabbergasted. "I have to think," she had said. "My 5
husband isn't here. He's in New Guinea." She remembered the man's
contemptuous little smile. On the way home, she said to Vi, "But...
Leonard..."

"Leonard is not a dentist," said Violet. 6

And so a few days later Audrey had gone through with it. She 7
hadn't been out of that dentist's office ten minutes when she knew
that she had made a dreadful mistake. Vi drove her home afterward.
Lying down on the backseat of the car, her mouth numb, her cheeks
stuffed with pledgets of cotton, she wondered what Leonard would
think, how he would feel. And she recalled something she had heard
him say to one of his students, she couldn't remember why: "No one,"
Leonard had said to the student, "can take your dignity away from
you; you might throw it away yourself, but no one can take it away
from you." Then and there Audrey decided that Leonard didn't have
to know.

"You all right?" Vi asked from behind the wheel, and turned round 8
to see at every red light.

Right from the start, Audrey had refused to take the denture out of 9
her mouth, no matter the pain. There were dark blisters on her gums;
she lisped. But she was determined. Leonard would be coming home
in two months. Audrey persevered so that with weeks to spare, she had
gotten used to the "prosthesis," as they called it, incorporated it. It had
become second nature.

Oh, she had had to steel herself against the first times it had to 10
come out, be cleaned, then reinserted. But she had surprised herself.
She was calm, curious, even, as she turned it over in her hand, examining. Like a pink horseshoe, she decided, and how wise she was to have
avoided the vulgarity of pure white. Ivory was more natural. Ivory has
endured; ivory has kept faith. In time her palate had molded itself to
fit, her gums were snug and secure in the hollow trough. Never, never
would she remove her teeth anywhere but in a locked bathroom. She
would keep them in at night. It was a myth that you had to take your
dentures out at night. Before long, she had no qualms, didn't mind at
all. The denture had become for her a kind of emblem of personal dignity, like one of those Asmat artifacts with magic properties, but this
having to do with the one thing that mattered most to Audrey:
Leonard. "It isn't really cheating," she told Violet.

"You're lucky," said Vi. "You're one of those people who don't 11
show their teeth when they smile."

12   When at last Leonard burst into the room, gathered her in his arms and kissed her, she smiled as much from triumph as with happiness. "You never cease to charm me," he had said, and she knew then that she had done it. Leonard would never know.

13   But now it was fifteen years later. "Total abdominal hysterectomy," the surgeon announced. "A clean sweep." As though she were a kitchen floor. "What does that include?" she asked him. "The uterus, both ovaries, both tubes," he told her. "Why my uterus?" She insisted upon the personal pronoun. "Why my left ovary? My tubes?" He then explained, rather too patiently, she thought, that she didn't need her reproductive organs anymore, that the risk of getting cancer in one of those organs was "not inconsiderable." Human beings do not talk like that, she thought. That is not human speech. "And," the surgeon went on, "as long as we are going to be in there anyway..." In there! Audrey could not keep her hand from passing lightly across her abdomen. Then he spoke about the small additional risk of the larger operation, said it was "negligible." But Audrey already knew what it was to go through life missing something. She wished fervently that she had been able to keep her cyst a secret, like her teeth. You would think it would be easier since the ovaries were inside and safely hidden. Imagine having to carry them in a bag between your legs, like testicles. And as for the risk of getting cancer... is that a reason to have your organs taken out? All of life is a risk. Living in California is a risk; there might be an earthquake. First, her teeth, and now her... her womanhood, yes, it was nothing short of that. All at once the operation seemed part of a plot to take her body apart. And she remembered the clink of coins years ago, as that dentist stirred the change in his pocket, stirred it on and on, enjoying the sound of it before he took up the syringe and injected her with novocaine.

14   On the wall in back of the surgeon's desk was a colored diagram of the female organs. Altogether, it resembled a sweet-faced cow's head rising to the gentle curve of the horns.

15   "No," she said, closing down. "No, that cannot be. Only my ovary, the one with the cyst. Nothing else, unless there is cancer." She would sign permission only for that. In the end, she had capitulated. "You're doing the right thing, I assure you, Mrs. Blakeslee," said the surgeon as she signed the permission sheet.

16   At the hospital, Leonard and Audrey followed the nurse into the room. "Get undressed and into this." The nurse held up a knee-length shirt open at the back. She did and over it put on the pale green brocade bed jacket Leonard had given her the night before. It had been arranged that Leonard was to wait in the solarium outside the operating rooms. The surgeon would talk to him there, let him know what he had found. Afterward, he would wait for Audrey to be wheeled down from the recovery room a few hours later.

"Visiting hours are over," commanded the page operator. "Will all 17
visitors please leave now."

"Good luck," said Leonard with a smile that was much too bright 18
for him. He's frightened, she thought, and felt tears filming her eyes.
After Leonard had left, Audrey lay on the bed, thinking of him—the
silky feel of the black hairs on his forearms, his smell of permanence,
the sound of his singing. Leonard sang bass. It was her favorite. At
sixty-one, his voice was as rich as ever. Sometimes, listening in church
to that submarine vibrato, she would have moments of unecclesiastical
commotion. Once, when she confessed it, Leonard reproached her with
a waggle of his finger. Ah, but his was a magic throat.

"I'm Dr. Dowling." The man had knocked and come in at the 19
same time. It is what happens in hospitals, she thought. She was glad
to be wearing the green bedjacket. So long as she had it on, there was
protection.

"The anesthesiologist," he explained. "I'll be putting you to sleep 20
tomorrow. Any questions?"

Audrey shook her head. He had an important sort of face, florid, 21
with jowls made even more congressional by the white political hair
that escaped from beneath his green surgical cap. He was wearing a
scrub suit of the same color and, over that, a white laboratory coat. The
strings of a mask dangled.

"Open your mouth wide as you can." He peered in. 22

"I see you have an upper plate. Out it comes in the morning before 23
you leave this room. The nurse will mind it for you."

Mute shadows of words trembled at her lips. 24

"But I never take it out, only to clean..." 25

"Well, you cannot go to the operating room with it in. I cannot put 26
you to sleep with a foreign body in your mouth."

Foreign body! Audrey felt the blood leave her head. Gongs could 27
not have sounded louder in her ears. Then a final cold ticking.

"For how long...?" 28

"Until you are fully awake. Certainly till evening." 29

"But you don't understand..." she began. Her voice trailed off. The 30
doctor waited, turned his head, looked at her from the corner of an eye.

"Yes ?" 31

"It is... My husband does not know that I have a denture. He has 32
been unaware of it for fifteen years. I would not want him to see me
without it. Please," she said very quietly. "It is important to me." She
waited for the walls to burst.

"Pride," said the man. "No room for it here. Like modesty. Suppose 33
we had to get at your trachea, your windpipe, in a hurry, and then we
had to waste time fishing those teeth out. Suppose they came loose in

the middle of the operation. There are a hundred supposes." He started to go.

34   "It isn't pride," she managed.

35   "What, then?"

36   "It's dignity." Perhaps it had been pride at the very beginning, but it had grown. And something else: Audrey understood that the connubial apparatus of a man is more delicate than a woman's. She saw no need to put it to the test.

37   "Come now. Mrs. Blakeslee, is it?" He consulted the name on the chart to make sure. Audrey struggled to fend off his voice. "You are making too much of it."

38   All right, then, she would calculate, be a cat.

39   "Don't you…" she began. "Don't you have a little something hidden away that you wouldn't want anyone to know about?" She smiled, laying it on in almost visible slabs. The doctor was taken off guard.

40   "No, actually not." But he had hesitated for the fraction of a second, and so she knew.

41   "How boring," she said, smiling, giving it to him right in his face. "And, of course, I don't for a minute believe you." This doctor could not know it, but Audrey was fighting for her life. But now she saw that he had retreated a vast safe distance behind his lips.

42   "In any case, you may not keep them in. And that's that." He stood abruptly and walked to the door.

43   "Have a good night," he called over his shoulder.

44   After he had left, Audrey felt her heart go small in her chest. Again there was the clink of coins being stirred in a pocket. With a sudden resolve, she decided that there was no longer any need for tact. The situation didn't call for tact. It called for defiance. I'll sign myself out of the hospital, she thought. Against medical advice, as they say. That cyst on her ovary, it might well be benign. They don't know. Leaving it in would be just one more risk. A risk infinitely smaller than having Leonard see her without her denture. Her mouth caved in, wrinkled like a drawstring pouch. She tried to imagine herself saying to Leonard afterward: "All right, then. You have seen what you have seen. Now accept it. Or not." But she could not. That way lay death. Hers or that of something far more delicate and valuable. No, she thought. No. Never again would she cultivate a belief in inevitability.

45   Audrey reached for the telephone, dialed.

46   "Leonard, don't come to the hospital at all tomorrow."

47   "But why?" He was startled. "Of course I'm coming to see you."

48   "That's just the point, Leonard, please…" She heard her voice flapping about her, out of control. "Please." She was imploring him.

49   "Don't come. Promise me."

50   "I'm sorry, Audrey. I'm just not going to agree to that. So forget it." His tone was severe, as with a child.

51   "I don't want you to see me like that."

"Like what?" He smiled with his voice. "I have seen it all before, you know." Oh, but you haven't, she thought. You shouldn't. 52

"What is it, Audrey? You sound distraught. Shall I come right over? I'll make them let me in." 53

"I just wanted to spare you," she said harshly. "There are times when people need to be alone." 54

"No," said Leonard. "I'll be there." 55

Violet managed the gift shop in the lobby of the hospital. She was two years older than Audrey—a big woman, divorced once, widowed once. Violet did not use makeup. I have nothing to hide, she said. Still, she dyed her hair. For business reasons. When you have to meet the public, gray hair automatically dismisses you. Fifteen years before, they had been closer, when Violet had brought her home from the dentist's office and Audrey had sworn her to a lifetime of silence. But somewhere between then and now Vi had become the kind of woman who sat herself down with ceremony in a deep chair to receive the secrets of others. She would be coming up to the room after she closed the gift shop. Audrey would ask her for a ride home. She would deal with Leonard later. 56

"I'll do no such thing," said Violet. "Do you mean to lie there and tell me that Leonard still doesn't know about your false teeth?" Vi made a point of never saying "denture." "False teeth" had a balder sound and they had drifted too far apart for softness. The venules on Vi's cheeks dilated with indignant blood. Audrey reached for the light switch, flicked it off. It was something to do. 57

"May I turn off the light?" she asked then. In the dark she could see the glossy mound of her sister's hair. 58

"Listen, Audrey, this has become a sick obsession with you." Her vehemence was reiterated by flashes of gold at neck and earlobes. 59

"There are madder things," said Audrey. And she lamented the weakness that made her let down her guard before this stranger who was her sister. 60

"Besides, it's a lie. People shouldn't lie, whatever." 61

"Oh, lies," said Audrey. "That's where you're wrong. People don't lie enough. When people tell the whole truth, that's when things fall apart. Most relationships are like some plants, I think. They need to be kept partly in the shade or they wither." A nurse came in and turned on the light. In the sudden glare Violet leaped up at her. 62

"Now, Audrey, don't be stupid," she said, standing to leave. "Behave yourself" Violet's teeth would never fall out, Audrey thought. They chew words, worry them; the way they buckle up her mouth. 63

Almost at once there was a hesitant knock at the door. Oh, God. Now who? 64

"My name is Dr. Bhimjee. I am the intern on this ward." An Indian or Pakistani, she thought. And lame. He limped toward the bed using his head and one arm in the act of locomotion. 65

66   "Mrs. Blakeslee, I see that our names both end with two *e*'s." His face was dark, she suspected, more from fatigue than from racial coloring. More than anything else he resembled an ungainly parcel, something bulgy and ill-wrapped. His hair was almost too thick, too black, but relieved by a single swatch of white near the crown. He is not young, Audrey decided. What has he endured and with how much patience? All at once, a fence came down. Who, after all, is to say where, in whom, one places trust?

67   "I have false teeth," she said, firing the words into his hair. She was shocked at the ease with which the forbidden words had come. The intern gazed down at her.

68   "Many people do," he said. The slate-colored skin set off the perfection of his own very white teeth. He is beautiful, she thought. And she threw herself further upon his mercy.

69   "I have had them for fifteen years. My husband has never seen me without them. He doesn't know that I have them. The anesthetist was here. He says I must leave them here in the room tomorrow. My husband will be waiting for me to come back from the recovery room. He will see me. I can't do that. Please, please." The last words rose like echoes. For a long moment they looked at each other, during which something, a covenant perhaps, Audrey did not know, was exchanged. Audrey lashed her gaze to his long gracile fingers. Then, all at once, deep called unto deep. A rush of profound affection came over her. It was nothing like her feeling for Leonard, but for all she knew, it might have been love.

70   "Do not worry." The *r*'s rolled very slightly. "In the morning, put them in the nightstand. There is a container. I will take them with me to the operation. I am assigned to your case, so I will be there too. Before you leave the recovery room, I will put them back into your mouth. Do not worry."

71   Later, when she awoke in the recovery room, the pain of her incision was the second thing that Audrey felt. The first was the denture which she explored with her tongue. Only then came the pain which, so help her, she did not mind. In spite of it, she curled up like a cat in a basket. Once, when she opened her eyes, she saw, or thought she saw, a dark face above her, a white swatch in a tumble of black hair, like a plume of smoke clinging to the chimney of a snug cottage.

72   "Don't worry," he was saying softly. "Your teeth are in. Take a deep breath. Again." He listened with his stethoscope. "You will be awake soon." He checked her pulse, and was gone. For a long time his voice lingered, lapsing, returning, drifting into darkness. And then there was Leonard, holding her hand, leaning over the bed to kiss her. "The doctor says it was benign." Audrey smiled up at him within the limits of morphine.

73   During the days that followed, Audrey found herself thinking about Dr. Bhimjee as much as she did about Leonard. There was a peacefulness

about him. Not resignation so much as acceptance. No, definitely not resignation. Resignation suggests defeat. Acceptance, rather. Where had he
found it? Wrested it, she supposed, barehanded from a tangle of thorns.
He had no need to deceive. It had not been given to him to deceive. She
saw him differently now from the way she had that first desperate night.
What she had thought was fatigue became the sum total of all the suffering he had experienced. It had worn his face down to the bone. The sock-
ets of his eyes were dark cabins of it. Audrey would have liked to take
the bony parcel in her arms, to breathe in his dreams.

And soon it was the hour of Audrey's discharge from the hospital.   74
The intern had come to say good-bye.

"My wife tells me that you have been very kind to her," said   75
Leonard. Audrey could not take her gaze from the two men.

"Not at all."   76

"I want you to know that I will always remember your" —she saw   77
that Leonard was struggling—"your courtesy."

"Please, it was nothing."   78

"Nevertheless," said Leonard. "Nevertheless," he repeated, "I   79
want you to have this." He held out a small reddish stone.

"What is that?"   80

"Just a stone that has been dyed red by the Asmat people of New   81
Guinea. See? It has a monkey carved on one side, a parrot on the other.
A shaman gave it to me. He's a sort of doctor too. It wards off melan-
choly, brings good luck. Please, take it." The doctor hesitated.

"I want you to have it," said Leonard. There was in his voice some-   82
thing vivid, mighty. Maybe it was the sun probing between the slats of
the venetian blinds, but from her wheelchair it seemed to Audrey that,
at the exact moment when the red stone left the white hand of one and
entered the dark hand of the other, something flared up that looked for
all the world like fire.

Reading and Writing Activities

PRELIMINARY RESPONSE

Note. As you read, record your reactions (questions or comments) to
Richard Seltzer's story "Fetishes" in your reading journal.

Discussion. In class, compare your reactions in reading groups of five
or six. Appoint a recorder to keep track of similarities or differences,
consensus or disagreement, arising from the discussion. The recorder
may summarize your group discussion for the rest of the class later.

Freewriting. After the class discussion, freewrite for 10 to 15 minutes about similarities or differences in your group's preliminary reading of the selection. Read your freewriting in groups of two to four.

SUMMARIZING

1. Create a preliminary analysis of Seltzer's story. A scratchline or clustering representation of central topics may be useful at this point. Or you may want to refer to the analysis questions that can guide your preliminary analysis presented at the beginning of this chapter.
2. Write a summary paragraph or two, from your preliminary analysis, of this perspective on the beauty myth and control that Selzer presents.
3. Read the summaries in your reading groups. Compare the focus of each summary. How do the summaries differ? How are they the same? Check to see if you are *reacting and responding* to the essay instead of summarizing the central topics.

FOCUSED CRITICAL READING

1. How does Selzer represent Audrey in this story? Does she have power or control in her interactions with her dentist, doctor, or husband?
2. How does he represent Audrey's husband, Leonard?
3. What is the relationship between Audrey and the intern who is in charge of her case?
4. Does cultural conditioning partly account for Audrey's desire to maintain her image?

Ynestra King

The Other Body: Reflections on Difference, Disability and Identity Politics

◆

Ynestra King has written a number of books, including Ecofeminism and the Reenchantment of Nature (1990). *The following selection appeared in the March/April 1993 issue of* Ms *magazine.*

Disabled people rarely appear in popular culture. When they do, 1
their disability must be a continuous preoccupation overshadowing all other areas of their character. Disabled people are disabled. That is what they "do." That is what they "are."

My own experience with a mobility impairment that is only 2
minorly disfiguring is that one must either be a creature of the disability, or have transcended it entirely. For me, like most disabled people (and this of course depends on relative severity), neither extreme is true. It is an organic, literally embodied fact that will not change—like being a woman. While it may be possible to "do gender," one does not "do disability." But there is an organic base to both conditions that extends far into culture, and the meaning that "nature" has. Unlike being a woman, being disabled is not a socially constructed condition. It is a tragedy of nature, of a kind that will always exist. The very condition of disability provides a vantage point of a certain lived experience in the body, a lifetime of opportunity for the observation of reaction to bodily deviance, a testing ground for reactions to persons who are readily perceived as having something wrong or being different. It is fascinating, maddening, and disorienting. It defies categories of "sickness" and "health," "broken" and "whole." It is in between.

Meeting people has an overlay: I know what they notice first is that 3
I am different. And there is the experience of the difference in another person's reaction who meets me sitting down (when the disability is not apparent), and standing up and walking (when the infirmity is obvious). It is especially noticeable when another individual is flirting and flattering, and has an abrupt change in affect when I stand up. I always make sure that I walk around in front of someone before I accept a date, just to save face for both of us. Once the other person perceives the disability, the switch on the sexual circuit breaker often pops

off—the connection is broken. "Chemistry" is over. I have a lifetime of such experiences, and so does every other disabled woman I know.

4   White middle-class people—especially white men—in the so-called First World have the most negative reactions. And I always recognize studied politeness, the attempt to pretend that there's nothing to notice (this is the liberal response—Oh, you're black? I hadn't noticed). Then there's the do-gooder response, where the person falls all over her/himself, insisting on doing everything for you; later they hate you; it's a form of objectification. It conveys to you that that is all they see, rather like a man who can't quit talking with a woman about sex.

5   In the era of identity politics in feminism, disability has not only been an added cross to bear, but an added "identity" to take on—with politically correct positions, presumed instant alliances, caucuses to join, and closets to come out of. For example, I was once dragged across a room to meet someone. My friend, a very politically correct lesbian feminist, said, "She's disabled, too. I thought you'd like to meet her." Rather than argue—what would I say? "I'm not interested in other disabled people," or "This is my night off"? (The truth in that moment was like the truth of this experience in every other moment, complicated and difficult to explain)—I went along to find myself standing before someone strapped in a wheelchair she propels by blowing into a tube with a respirator permanently fastened to the back of the chair. To suggest that our relative experience of disability is something we could casually compare (as other people stand by!) demonstrates the crudity of perception about the complex nature of bodily experience.

6   My infirmity is partial leg paralysis. I can walk anywhere, climb stairs, drive a car, ride a horse, swim, hang-glide, fly a plane, hike in the wilderness, go to jail for my political convictions, travel alone, and operate heavy equipment. I can earn a living, shop, cook, eat as I please, dress myself, wash and iron my own clothes, clean my house. The woman in that wheelchair can do none of these fundamental things, much less the more exotic ones. On a more basic human level I can spontaneously get my clothes off if I decide to make love. Once in bed my lover and I can forget my disability. None of this is true of the woman in the wheelchair. There is no bodily human activity that does not have to be specially negotiated, none in which she is not absolutely "different." It would take a very long time, and a highly nuanced conversation, for us to be able to share experiences as if they were common. The experience of disability for the two of us was more different than my experience is from the daily experience of people who are not considered disabled. So much for disability solidarity.

7   With disability, one is somewhere on a continuum between total bodily dysfunction—or death—and complete physical wholeness. In some way, this probably applies to every living person. So when is it

that we call a person "disabled"? When do they become "other"? There are "minor" disabilities that are nonetheless significant for a person's life. Color blindness is one example. But in our culture, color blindness is considered an inconvenience rather than a disability.

The ostracization, marginalization, and distorted response to disability are not simply issues of prejudice and denial of civil rights. They reflect attitudes toward bodily life, an unease in the human skin, an inability to cope with contingency, ambiguity, flux, finitude, and death.

Visibly disabled people (like women) in this culture are the scapegoats for resentments of the limitations of organic life. I had polio when I was seven, finishing second grade. I had excelled in everything, and rarely missed school. I had one bad conduct notation—for stomping on the boys' blocks when they wouldn't let me play with them. Although I had leg braces and crutches when I was ready to start school the next year, I wanted desperately to go back and resume as much of the same life as I could. What I was not prepared for was the response of the school system. They insisted that I was now "handicapped" and should go into what they called "special education." This was a program aimed primarily at multiply disabled children, virtually all of whom were mentally retarded as well as physically disabled. It was in a separate wing of another school, and the children were completely segregated from the "normal" children in every aspect of the school day, including lunch and recreational activities. I was fortunate enough to have educated, articulate parents and an especially aggressive mother; she went to the school board and waged a tireless campaign to allow me to come back to my old school on a trial basis—the understanding being that the school could send me to special education if things "didn't work out" in the regular classroom.

And so began my career as an "exceptional" disabled person, not like the *other* "others." And I was glad. I didn't want to be associated with those others either. Apart from the objective limitations caused by the polio, the transformation in identity—the difference in worldly reception—was terrifying and embarrassing, and it went far beyond the necessary considerations my limitations required.

My experience as "other" is much greater and more painful as a disabled person than as a woman. Maybe the most telling dimension of this knowledge is my observation of the reactions of others over the years, of how deeply afraid people are of being outside the normative appearance (which is getting narrower as capitalism exaggerates patriarchy). It is no longer enough to be thin; one must have ubiquitous muscle definition, nothing loose, flabby, or ill defined, no fuzzy boundaries. And of course, there's the importance of control. Control over aging, bodily processes, weight, fertility, muscle tone, skin quality, and movement. Disabled women, regardless of how thin, are without full bodily control.

12   I see disabled women fight these normative standards in different ways, but never get free of negotiating and renegotiating them. I did it by constructing my life around other values and, to the extent possible, developing erotic attachments to people who had similar values, and for whom my compensations were more than adequate. But at one point, after two disastrous but steamy liaisons with a champion athlete and a dancer (during which my friends pointed out the obvious unkind truth and predicted painful endings), I discovered the worlds I had tried to protect myself from: the disastrous attraction to "others" to complete oneself. I have seen disabled women endure unspeakably horrible relationships because they were so flattered to have such a conventionally attractive individual in tow.

13   And then there's the weight issue. I got fat by refusing to pay attention to my body. Now that I'm slimming down again, my old vanities and insecurities are surfacing. The battle of dieting can be especially fraught for disabled women. It is more difficult because exercising is more difficult, as is traveling around to get the proper foods, and then preparing them. But the underlying rage at the system that makes you feel as if you are your body (female, infirm) and that everything else is window dressing—this also undermines the requisite discipline. A tempting response is to resort to an ideal of self as bodiless essence in which the body is completely incidental, and irrelevant.

14   The wish that the body should be irrelevant has been one of my most fervent lifelong wishes. The knowledge that it isn't is my most intense lifelong experience.

15   I have seen other disabled women wear intentionally provocative clothes, like the woman in a wheelchair on my bus route to work. She can barely move. She has a pretty face, and tiny legs she could not possibly walk on. Yet she wears black lace stockings and spike high heels. The other bus occupants smile condescendingly, or pretend not to notice, or whisper in appalled disbelief that this woman could represent herself as having a sexual self. That she could "flaunt" her sexual being violates the code of acceptable appearance for a disabled woman. This woman's apparel is no more far out than that of many other women on our bus—but she refuses to fold up and be a good little asexual handicapped person.

16   The well-intentioned liberal new campaigns around "hire the handicapped" are oppressive in related ways. The Other does not only have to demonstrate her competence on insider terms; she must be better, by way of apologizing for being different and rewarding the insiders for letting her in. And the happy handicapped person, who has had faith placed in her/him, must vindicate "the race" because the politics of tokenism assumes that there are in fact other qualifications than doing the job.

This is especially prejudicial in a recession, where there are few 17
social services, where it is "every man for himself." Disabled people
inevitably have greater expenses, since assistance must often be paid
for privately. In the U.S., public construction of the disabled body is
that one either is fully disabled and dysfunctional/unemployable (and
therefore eligible for public welfare) or totally on one's own. There is
no in-between—the possibility of a little assistance, or exceptions in
certain areas. Disabled people on public assistance cannot work or they
will lose their benefits. (In the U.S. ideology that shapes public attitudes and public policy, one is either fully dependent or fully autonomous.) But the reality of human and organic life is that everyone is
different in some way; there is no such thing as a totally autonomous
individual. Yet the mythology of autonomy perpetuates in terrible
ways the oppression of the disabled. It also perpetuates misogyny—
and the destruction of the planet.

It may be that this clear lack of autonomy—this reminder of mortal 18
finitude and contingency and embeddedness of nature and the body—is
at the root of the hatred of the disabled. On the continuum of autonomy
and dependence, disabled people need help. To need help is to feel
humiliated, to have failed. I think this "help" issue must be even harder
for men than women. But any disabled person is always negotiating
both the provisionality of autonomy and the rigidity of physical norms.

From the vantage point of disability, there are some objective and 19
desirable aspects of autonomy. But they have to do with independence.
The preferred protocol is that the attendant or friend perform the task
that the disabled person needs done in the way the disabled person
asks it to be done. Assistance from friends and family is a negotiated process, and often maddening. For that reason most disabled people prefer
to live in situations where they can do all the basic functions themselves, with whatever special equipment or built-ins are required.

It's a dreadful business, this needing help. And it's more dreadful 20
in the U.S. than in any place in the world, because our heroes are
dynamic overcomers of adversity, and there is an inevitable cultural
contempt for weakness.

Autonomy is on a continuum toward dependency and death. And 21
the idea that dependency could come at any time, that one could die at
any time, or be dismembered or disfigured, and still have to live
(maybe even *want to live*) is unbearable in a context that understands
and values autonomy in the way we moderns do.

I don't want to depict this experience of unbearability as strictly 22
cultural. The compromising of the human body before its natural time
is tragic. It forces terrible hardship on the individual to whom it occurs.
But the added overlay of oppression on the disabled is intimately
related to the fear of death, and the acknowledgment of our embedded-

ness in organic nature. We are finite, contingent, dependent creatures by our very nature; we will all eventually die. We will all experience compromises to our physical integrity. The aspiration to human wholeness is an oppressive idealism. Socially, it is deeply infantilizing.

23   It promotes a simplistic view of the human person, a static notion of human life that prevents the maturity and social wisdom that might allow human beings to more fully apprehend the human condition. It marginalizes the "different," those perceived as hopelessly wedded to organic existence—women and the disabled. The New Age "human potential movement"—in the name of maximizing human growth—is one of the worst offenders in obscuring the kind of human growth I am suggesting.

24   I too believe that the potential for human growth and creativity is infinite—but it is not groundless. The common ground for the person—the human body—is a place of shifting sand that can fail us at any time. It can change shape and properties without warning; this is an essential truth of embodied existence.

25   Of all the ways of becoming "other" in our society, disability is the only one that can happen to anyone, in an instant, transforming that person's life and identity forever.

Reading and Writing Activities

PRELIMINARY RESPONSE

Notes.   As you read, record your reactions (questions or comments) to Ynestra King's essay in your reading journal. You may want to focus on points Ynestra King makes about disability and identity that you are hearing for the first time.

Discussion.   In class, compare your reactions in reading groups of five or six. Appoint a recorder to keep track of similarities or differences, consensus or disagreement, arising from the discussion. The recorder may summarize your group discussion for the rest of the class later.

Freewriting.   After the class discussion, freewrite for 10 to 15 minutes about King's disability, how she perceives herself, and how she copes with other people's reaction to her disability. Read your freewriting in groups of two to four.

SUMMARIZING

1. Create a preliminary analysis of King's essay. A scratchline or clustering representation of central topics may be useful at this point. Or you may want to refer to the analysis questions that can guide your preliminary analysis presented at the beginning of this chapter.
2. Write a summary paragraph or two, from your preliminary analysis, of King's central points.
3. Read the summaries in your reading groups. Compare the focus of each summary. How do the summaries differ? How are they the same? Check to see if you are *reacting and responding* to the essay instead of summarizing the central topics.

FOCUSED CRITICAL READING

1. King talks about disability and control in a number of places in this essay. What, according to King, are the issues for women with disabilities and what are the degrees of control that she discusses?
2. What does King refer to when she talks about the "other" in her essay?
3. Why do we expect men and women with disabilities to be asexual, according to King?

Margo Kaufman

Sitting Pretty

——————◆——————

The following selection appeared in The New York Times Magazine, *April 18, 1993. Margo Kaufman is also the author of 1-800-Am-I-Nuts? (1992)—a collection of essays published by Random House.*

1 My mother is the Vince Lombardi of beauty. Looking good isn't everything, it's the only thing. If she passed along one truth when I was growing up, it was that I had an obligation to take care of myself, and she didn't mean it in a feminist kind of way. Years before I reached puberty, she began what she called my "Gigi lessons," after the scene in the movie where Isabel Jeans teaches Leslie Caron how to eat ortolans. "Life is not one big drudge," Mom explained.

2 While her curriculum covered fine food (eating, not cooking, it) and helpful hints on choosing and graciously accepting expensive jewelry (a skill that has, alas, gotten rusty), the bulk of her instruction focused on the fine art of body maintenance. Some women have warm fuzzy memories of bonding with Mom in the kitchen, but I get misty when I see the red door of Elizabeth Arden. By the age of 14, I had been introduced to facials, pedicures, manicures, brow waxing, lash tinting, custom-blended makeup and, of course, the psychological advantages of an expert wash and set.

3 "When you look in the mirror and you look good, you feel good," Mom told me. "I always think you should be the best and the prettiest you can be." Wasn't 12 a little young to introduce a make-over as a coping mechanism, I wondered aloud recently. "Not if it made you feel better about yourself," Mom replied.

4 Inevitably, as soon as she packed me off to college with a suitcase full of Pantene shampoo, Yardley lip gloss and Neutrogena soap, I rebelled. I let my hair grow wild and frizzy, stopped plucking my eyebrows and began biting my nails, all the while smugly reminding myself that it's what's inside that counts. My fall lasted a couple of years, until the morning I looked in the mirror, got hideously depressed and instinctively sought asylum at Vidal Sassoon. While in theory I believed that looks shouldn't matter, in fact they mattered to me. (This is not to suggest that I'm a fanatic or anything. I don't go in for herbal wraps, liposuction, highlights, low lights or even waxing—at least not yet.)

"Obviously your insides have to be more than fluff," Mother scoffed, 20 years later, when she learned I was writing this. She hoped that she hadn't given me the wrong impression: the look she liked was Eleanor Roosevelt on the inside and Grace Kelly on the outside. "If you've got a pretty inside and you're smart, then why not look good outside too?"

Why not? It certainly gives us a safe topic of conversation. Whatever our differences, we can always swap tips on hair, clothes and makeup, the way fathers and sons talk sports. And I don't have to waste a lot of time reading fashion magazines. Mother, soignée to the fourth power, has the beauty equivalent of the Rand Corporation on call.

Last week, for example, I happened to mention that I was thinking of cutting my long hair short. Instantly, Mother went on red alert. "You've got to come to New York," she said urgently, flipping through her Rolodex trying to decide which stylist-of-the-moment could give me the best look. I assured her there was no shortage of hair stylists in Los Angeles, but she was skeptical. "Promise you won't do anything until I make a few calls."

I promised. A year ago, we had practically the same conversation about a more serious beauty problem. I had found a tiny malignant granule in my right breast, in the scar of a four-year-old lumpectomy. It was my worst nightmare come true. Granted, as bad news goes it wasn't awful: every doctor I spoke to assured me that a recurrence in the scar did not significantly alter my chances of being cured. But they all recommended mastectomy. This was a devastating prospect to a women whose mood fluctuates with the size of her thighs.

My husband went out of his way to assure me that he would love me no matter how I looked. I knew he meant it too, but I've been vain for over 30 years and I wasn't sure I'd pass that kind of character test. I demanded simultaneous reconstruction. Mother was totally supportive. "I didn't raise my daughter of mine to scrimp on plastic surgery," she said.

Mom consulted her beauty cabal and came up with a short list. The top scalpel was booked for a month, but she somehow—I really don't want to know how—convinced him to squeeze me in. He recommended a mind-bogglingly difficult surgical procedure called a free gluteal flap. It would take seven or eight hours, but through the miracle of microsurgery, I'd wake up with a new breast, made of my own tissue.

I asked myself: Am I really vain enough to put myself through this? It was then I knew that I was my mother's daughter. I didn't hesitate. I booked the operation and tried not to panic.

There wasn't time to panic because every day, via Federal Express from New York, Mother infused me with her version of chicken soup: beauty CARE packages that included a spectrum of eye shadows, matte foundations, blushers, lipsticks, miracle shampoo, magical hair polisher, bath salts from the Dead Sea, pajamas, negligees, camisoles and peignoirs. "Where do you think I'm going?" I asked, "the Golden Door?" "It's important that you feel glamourous," she said, citing a little known principle of psychoneuroimmunology.

13   I knew I was in trouble the day I received a pair of lace and beribboned earplugs along with a note saying I could use them to drown out the sound of her voice. The Beauty Queen had decided to fly out to California to "coordinate" my surgery. "We'll have such a good time," she said. I couldn't imagine having a blast when I was going to be flat on my back in a special "flap ward" for five days, but her enthusiasm was contagious. I almost began to look forward to the event.

14   The day before I went to the hospital, Mother arrived bearing nightgowns, hair ornaments, moisturizers and the *coup de main*—what every patient needs going into surgery—a full-length mink coat, left to her by an elderly relative. "When this is all over, you'll come to New York and we'll go out on the town," Mom promised. Then she escorted me to a preoperative eyelash tint (since I'd be too weak to use mascara) and haircut.

15   Waking up after seven hours of surgery, the first face I saw was Mother's. I knew she must have been worried sick because her hair was a mess. For days she sat by my bedside, adjusting my surgical stockings, untangling my hair, coaching me through breathing exercises to fill my lungs with air. When I was finally ambulatory, she helped me out of hospital garb into a dainty gown. Instantly, I felt better. Then she pulled out a bottle of Chanel polish. "Lie down," she ordered. "Let me do your toes."

16   Now, when I look back (blessedly healthy and intact, with just a few fading scars) on what could have been a hideous ordeal, I remember Mother's secret beauty remedies with gratitude and indulgence. So when she called last week with a short list of au courant hairdressers, I dropped what I was doing and drove to Beverly Hills. The top scissors advised reshaping instead of cutting and, not surprisingly, did an excellent job.

17   "When you come to New York, if you still want it short, I can take you to my people," Mother said.

18   "Sounds like fun," I replied.

Reading and Writing Activities

PRELIMINARY RESPONSE

Notes. As you read, record your reactions (questions or comments) to Margo Kaufman's "Sitting Pretty" in your reading journal.

You may want to respond to what Kaufman leaves unsaid in this article about her husband and father, and why.

Discussion. In class, compare your reactions in reading groups of five or six. Appoint a recorder to keep track of similarities or differences, consensus or disagreement, arising from the discussion. The recorder may summarize your group discussion for the rest of the class later.

Freewriting. After the class discussion, freewrite for 10 to 15 minutes about Kaufman's mother and why Kaufman chose to present the subject of reconstructive surgery through a detailed description of her relationship with her mother. Read your freewriting in groups of two to four.

SUMMARIZING

1. Create a preliminary analysis of the Kaufman reading selection. A scratchline or clustering representation of central topics may be useful at this point.
2. Write a summary paragraph or two, from your preliminary analysis, of Kaufman's essay.
3. Read the summaries in your reading groups. Compare the focus of each summary. How do the summaries differ? How are they the same? Check to see if you are *reacting and responding* to the essay instead of summarizing the central topics.

FOCUSED CRITICAL READING

1. What is Kaufman's attitude toward her mother?
2. Who is the audience for this article, and what is its purpose?
3. Is there anything particularly effective or ineffective about the organizational structure of this article?

WRITING SUGGESTIONS

1. Use your summary of the characters and events depicted in Marge Piercy's poem to write an introduction to a short essay in response to the poem. Finish the introduction with a sentence or two that summarizes your interpretation of the poem. You can then develop your response in a page or two, supporting your response directly by referring to sections of the poem.

A *writing workshop* would be a useful way to work with drafts of essays written in response to reading selections in this chapter or in other chapters. In a writing workshop, one writer's draft can be reviewed by four or five peers who comment and ask the writer questions about the content and organization of the draft. (A peer review for editing purposes is probably more effective if done in pairs—the writer and one editor.)

Ask your reading-writing group to review a draft of your essay in response to this assignment. You need to provide a copy for each member of the group. As you read your paper aloud, ask your reviewers to read along with you and stop you if they have questions, comments, or suggestions. Ask them to stop you any time there is a problem with a claim you have made or with the evidence you use to support that claim. You will also probably see things in your draft as you read it aloud in public that may not have struck you in a private reading. Your reviewers should jot down their remarks on the copies of your paper. You may also want to make a note of what is being said or of any revisions that occur to you during the workshop. At the end of the reading, collect the copies of your paper from your group.

2. Use your summary of the characters and events depicted in Lavonne Adams's "The Beauty Pageant" to write an introduction for an essay about beauty pageants. Finish the introduction with a sentence or two that summarizes your interpretation of the essay. Develop your interpretation in a page or two, supporting that interpretation directly by referring to sections of the Adam's essay. Extend your interpretation with primary research. For example, survey your friends and family, or the students in one of your classes, for their opinions on the subject of child and teenage beauty pageants. Or observe the pageant process, if possible. Note how Adams reports her primary research (her observations of the local beauty pageant). Report your results and conclusions.

Or you might survey popular magazines and clothing catalogues for defining characteristics of beauty, implicit or explicit, in the ads for these magazines and catalogues. Are there class specific definitions? For example, does a particular "look" vary according to a magazine or catalogue's possible audience? Is the L. L. Bean look different from the look in other catalogues that advertise similar merchandise? Compare three fashion magazines or catalogues representing three distinct audiences based on special interests, social class, or ethnicity.

Share your findings in your reading-writing groups, then write an essay that presents your findings and interpretation from your survey. You may be able to compile a small data bank of all your findings.

Share your essays in writing workshops. You will need a copy for each member of your group. Collect the copies after the workshop.

3. Reread Alice Walker's essay about her disability (and disfigurement) after an accident. Reflect on the similarities and differences

between Walker and King as they write on the issue of beauty and disability from different perspectives and experiences. What do you know about the way agencies in your community (schools, churches, businesses, or government agencies, for example) treat those with disabilities? Interview, if you can, local community leaders about this subject. What conclusions can you draw from what you learn? Present your findings in draft form (3–4 pages) to your writing group. You may use the Walker and King essays to introduce the topic and issue of disability. You may also want to use summaries of the essays in the development section of your report.

4. Write a documented essay that focuses on the relationship between self-image and power. You may want to use the Selzer short story to introduce the topic. Most of the selections in this chapter would be fruitful in developing this essay.

5

Family Images

———————◆———————

Imagine the beginning of a movie. The camera slowly pans over characters and locations as the titles roll and the movie begins. In this chapter, we pan over images of families in America. We invite you to add to these images from your knowledge of families in your communities.

The first three readings present aspects of working-class families. In "Scales," an excerpt from her novel *Love Medicine* (1984), Louise Erdrich depicts families living in poverty amid cross-cultural conflicts. Rosario Morales, in "The Day It Happened," tells another fictional story, one of spousal abuse; in dramatic detail she shows us the consequences of that abuse. And Scott Russell Sanders describes the real-life men he knew "as a boy growing up on the back roads of Tennessee and Ohio."

Mixing fiction and nonfiction again, we turn our camera on upper-class families. We begin with Stephen Birmingham, who, in "Telling Them Apart," describes distinguishing features of an American upper class. To make a case for an American aristocracy, he compares the language and behavior of white upper-class Americans with the language and behavior of British aristocrats. William B. Gatewood, in his prologue to "Color, Culture, and Behavior," describes a black aristocracy situated in Washington, D.C. at the turn of this century. He also describes the solid middle-class community of African Americans of that era. Joyce Carol Oates gives us a fictionalized (and chilling) view of upper-middle-class families in white suburbia; in "Is Laughter Contagious?" Oates shows us a family without compassion.

Families in two immigrant groups, both well-established in America, are introduced next. In "The Invisible Immigrants," Joel Dreyfuss describes middle- and working-class Haitian families, contrasting these communities of immigrants to recent Haitian refugee boat people. Another immigrant group is the subject of Deborah Dash Moore's "New York Jews." Describing that group, she says: "Since the beginning of the twentieth century, roughly half of all American Jews have lived in New York City. Indeed, they constitute the largest concentration of Jews in history."

The final selection of this chapter features stories of men and women who lack family support altogether. In "Long Island Shelter," Eugene Richards describes a homeless shelter through the eyes of one of its long-term residents.

Rhetorical Structure and Meaning

One strategy for analyzing texts is to determine if a text is reader friendly. By *reader friendly,* we mean that the writer makes it easy for us to see the rhetorical structure of the text and its transition points so that we can make connections between structure and meaning.

Whether or not a text is reader friendly, you can begin an analysis of its structure by identifying *transition points* (those places in a text where one topic ends and another begins) and key words that trace the development of topics. Once you identify transition points, you can examine what the writer is doing (rhetorically) and begin to follow how he or she is constructing meaning immediately before and after each transition point. We believe that identifying these transition points helps you establish the writer's purpose and central ideas, even when those ideas are unstated. This procedure also lets you quickly determine if the writer's strategies of development are helping or hindering your understanding of the text. Often, as you identify transition points, the subtle messages a writer is making also emerge.

For example, as we identified what we took to be significant transition points in the fourth essay in this chapter, Steven Birmingham's "Telling Them Apart," we agreed that, for us, this essay is reader friendly. Birmingham signals topic shifts throughout. We could see that Birmingham devotes the first six paragraphs to the following topics: one paragraph contrasting American upper- and lower-class vocabulary; one paragraph describing what the upper classes do not talk about, two paragraphs on secret rules of upper-class behavior, and two on mastering an upper-class accent. Once Birmingham describes the American upper class in this way, he makes a major shift, devoting the next six paragraphs to a single topic: a comparison of American and British aristocracies.

It was not immediately clear to us, however, what Birmingham is up to here, in terms of making his point. Right after this transition point, he proceeds as if he has already established that the American upper class *is* an aristocracy, referring to the "two aristocracies" throughout this section of his essay. At the same time, however, he is still making his case that the American upper class is indeed aristocratic by showing that the American upper class behaves just like the British aristocracy. Paying attention to transition points, and what happens before and after these transition points, helped our analysis of the meaning of Birmingham's text. In this way an analysis of the rhetorical structure of any text helps to clarify its meaning.

To practice the analytic strategy that we have just modeled, we ask you, in this chapter, to identify transition points in the essays you read, summarize, and synthesize. You can identify transition points in group discussion or on your own as you work with individual assignments. Once you have identified these points, examine what the writer is doing as he or she develops each section of the text. As you write your own essays, think about making the structure of your writing reader friendly, too—and think about how structure helps or hinders meaning.

Louise Erdrich

Scales

---◆---

The daughter of a Chippewa, Louise Erdrich grew up in North Dakota and is married to Michael Dorris, who is also part Native American. Her stories have won several awards and are included in some important anthologies. Love Medicine *(1984), Erdrich's first novel, won both the National Book Critics Circle Award for Fiction and the* Los Angeles Times *award for best novel of 1985. Erdrich has since published three more novels:* The Beet Queen *(1986),* Tracks *(1988), and* Tales of Burning Love *(1996). The following selection comes from* Love Medicine.

Albertine Johnson

I was sitting before my third or fourth Jellybean, which is anisette, grain alcohol, a lit match, and small wet explosion in the brain. On my left sat Gerry Nanapush of the Chippewa Tribe. On my right sat Dot Adare of the has-been, of the never-was, of the what's-in-front-of-me people. Still in her belly and tensed in its fluids coiled the child of their union, the child we were waiting for, the child whose name we were making a strenuous and lengthy search for in a cramped and littered bar at the very edge of that Dakota town. 1

Gerry had been on the wagon for thirteen years. He was drinking a tall glass of tonic water in which a crescent of soiled lemon bobbed, along with a Maraschino cherry or two. He was thirty-five years old and had been in prison, or out of prison and on the run, for almost half of those years. He was not in the clear yet nor would he ever be, that is why the yellow tennis player's visor was pulled down to the rim of his eyeglass frames. The bar was dimly lit and smoky; his glasses were very dark. Poor visibility must have been the reason Officer Lovchik saw him first. 2

Lovchik started toward us with his hand on his hip, but Gerry was over the backside of the booth and out the door before Lovchik got close enough to make a positive identification. 3

"Siddown with us," said Dot to Lovchik, when he neared our booth. "I'll buy you a drink. It's so dead here. No one's been through all night." 4

Lovchik sighed, sat, and ordered a blackberry brandy. 5

"Now tell me," she said, staring at him, "honestly. What do you think of the name Ketchup Face?" 6

7   It was through Gerry that I first met Dot, in a bar like that one only denser with striving drinkers, construction crews who had come into town because a new interstate highway was passing near it. I was stuck there, having run out of money and ideas of where to go next. I was twenty-two and knew I'd soon have to do something different with my life. But no matter what that would be, I had to make some money first.

8   I had heard Gerry Nanapush was around, and because he was famous for leading a hunger strike at the state pen, as well as having been Henry Lamartine's brother and some kind of boyfriend to Aunt June, I went to look for him. He was not hard to find, being large. I sat down next to him and we struck up a conversation, during the long course of which we became friendly enough for Gerry to put his arm around me.

9   Dot entered at exactly the wrong moment. She was quick-tempered anyway, and being pregnant (Gerry had gotten her that way on a prison visit six months previous) increased her irritability. It was only natural then, I guess, that she would pull the barstool out from under me and threaten my life. Only I didn't believe she was threatening my life at the time. I had a false view of pregnant women. I thought of them as wearing invisible halos, not committing mayhem.

10   "I'm gonna bend you out of shape," she said, flexing her hands over me. Her hands were small, broad, capable, with pointed nails. I used to do the wrong thing sometimes when I was drinking, and that time I did the wrong thing, even though I was stretched out on the floor beneath her. I started laughing at her because her hands were so small (though strong and determined looking—I should have been more conscious of that). She was about to dive on top of me, six-month belly and all, but Gerry caught her in midair and carried her, yelling, out the door. The next morning I reported for work. It was my first day on the job, and the only other woman on the construction site besides me was Dot Adare.

11   That day Dot just glared toward me from a distance. She worked in the weigh shack, and I was hired to press buttons on the conveyor belt. All I had to do was adjust the speeds on the belt for sand, rocks, or gravel and make sure it was aimed toward the right pile. There was a pyramid for each type of material, which was used to make hot-mix and cement. Across the wide yard, I saw Dot emerge from the little weigh shack from time to time. I couldn't tell whether she recognized me, but I thought, by the end of the day, that she probably didn't. I found out differently the next morning when I went to the company truck for coffee.

12   She got me alongside of the truck somehow, away from the men. She didn't say a word, just held the buck knife out where I could see it, blade toward me. She jiggled the handle, and the tip waved like the pointy head of a pit viper. Blind. Heat seeking. I was completely aston-

ished. I had just put the plastic cover on my coffee and it steamed between my hands.

"Well, I'm sorry I laughed," I said. She stepped back. I peeled the 13 lid off my coffee, took a sip, and then I said the wrong thing again.

"And I wasn't going after your boyfriend." 14

"Why not?" she said at once. "What's wrong with him?" 15

I saw that I was going to lose this argument no matter what I said, 16 so for once I did the right thing. I threw my coffee in her face and ran. Later on that day Dot came out of the weigh shack and yelled, "Okay then!" I was close enough to see that she even grinned. I waved. From then on things were better between us, which was lucky, because I turned out to be such a good button presser that within two weeks I was promoted to the weigh shack, to help Dot.

It wasn't that Dot needed help weighing trucks, it was just a for- 17 mality for the state highway department. I never quite understood, but it seems Dot had been both the truck weigher and the truck-weight inspector for a while, until someone caught wind of this. The company hired me to actually weigh the trucks, and Dot was hired by the state to make sure I recorded accurate weights. What she really did was sleep, knit, or eat all day. Between truckloads I did the same. I didn't even have to get off my stool to weigh the trucks, because the arm of the scale projected through a rectangular hole and the weights appeared right in front of me. The standard back dumps, bellydumps, and yellow company trucks eased onto a platform built over the arm next to the shack. I wrote their weight on a little pink slip, clipped the paper in a clothespin attached to a broom handle, and handed it up to the driver. I kept a copy of the pink slip on a yellow slip that I put in a metal filebox. No one ever picked up the filebox, so I never knew what the yellow slips were for. The company paid me very well.

It was early July when Dot and I started working together. At first I 18 sat as far away from her as possible and never took my eyes off her knitting needles, although it made me a little dizzy to watch her work. It wasn't long before we came to an understanding, though, and after this I felt perfectly comfortable with Dot. She was nothing but direct, you see, and told me right off that only three things made her angry. Number one was someone flirting with Gerry. Number two was a cigarette leech, someone who was always quitting but smoking yours. Number three was a piss-ant. I asked her what that was. "A piss-ant," she said, "is a man with fat buns who tries to sell you things. A Jaycee, an Elk, a Kiwanis." I always knew where I stood with Dot, so I trusted her. I knew that if I fell out of her favor she would threaten me and give me time to run before she tried anything physical.

By mid-July our shack was unbearable, for it drew heat in from the 19 bare yard and held it. We sat outside most of the time, moving around the shack to catch what shade fell, letting the raw hot wind off the beet-fields suck the sweat from our armpits and legs. But the seasons change fast in North Dakota. We spent the last day of August jumping from foot to numb foot before Hadji, the foreman, dragged a little column of bottled gas into the shack. He lit the spoked wheel on its head, it bloomed, and from then on we huddled close to the heater, eating, doz-ing, or sitting mindless in its small radius of dry warmth.

20   By that time Dot weighed over two hundred pounds, most of it peanut-butter cups and egg-salad sandwiches. She was a short, broad-beamed woman with long yellow eyes and spaces between each of her strong teeth. When we began working together, her hair was cropped close. By the cold months it had grown out in thick quills—brown at the shank, orange at the tip. The orange dye job had not suited her col-oring. By that time, too, Dot's belly was round and full, for she was due in October. The child rode high, and she often rested her forearms on it while she knitted. One of Dot's most peculiar feats was transforming that gentle task into something perverse. She knit viciously, jerking the yarn around her thumb until the tip whitened, pulling each stitch so tightly that the little garments she finished stood up by themselves like miniature suits of mail.

21   I thought that the child would need those tight stitches when it was born. Although Dot as expecting mother lived a fairly calm life, it was clear that she had also moved loosely among the dangerous elements. The child, for example, had been conceived in a visiting room at the state prison. Dot had straddled Gerry's lap in a corner the closed-circuit TV did not quite scan. Through a hole ripped in her pantyhose and a hole ripped in Gerry's jeans they somehow managed to join and, miraculously, to conceive. Not long after my conversation with Gerry in the bar, he was caught. That time he went back peacefully, and didn't put up a fight. He was mainly in the penitentiary for breaking out of it, anyway, since for his crime of assault and battery he had received three years and time off for good behavior. He just never managed to serve those three years or behave well. He broke out time after time, and was caught each time he did it, regular as clockwork.

22   Gerry was talented at getting out, that's a fact. He boasted that no steel or concrete shitbarn could hold a Chippewa, and he had eellike properties in spite of his enormous size. Greased with lard once, he squirmed into a six-foot-thick prison wall and vanished. Some thought he had stuck there, immured forever, and that he would bring luck, like the bones of slaves sealed in the wall of China. But Gerry rubbed his own belly for luck and brought luck to no one else, for he appeared, suddenly, at Dot's door, and she was hard-pressed to hide him.

23   She managed for nearly a month. Hiding a six-foot-plus, two-hundred-and-fifty-pound Indian in the middle of a town that doesn't like Indians in the first place isn't easy, A month was quite an accom-

plishment, when you know what she was up against. She spent most of her time walking to and from the grocery store, padding along on her swollen feet, astonishing the neighbors with the size of what they thought was her appetite. Stacks of pork chops, whole fryers, thick steaks disappeared overnight, and since Gerry couldn't take the garbage out by day, sometimes he threw the bones out the windows, where they collected, where dogs soon learned to wait for a handout and fought and squabbled over whatever there was.

The neighbors finally complained, and one day, while Dot was at work, Lovchik knocked on the door of the trailer house. Gerry answered, sighed, and walked over to their car. He was so good at getting out of the joint and so terrible at getting caught. It was as if he couldn't stay out of their hands. Dot knew his problem and told him that he was crazy to think he could walk out of prison and then live like a normal person. Dot told him that didn't work. She told him to get lost for a while on the reservation or to let his mother, Lulu, who had a long successful history of hiding men, keep him under cover. She told him to change his name, to let the straggly hairs above his lip grow, disguising his face. But Gerry wouldn't do any of that. He simply knew he did not belong in prison, although he admitted it had done him some good when he was younger, hadn't known how to be a criminal, and so had taken lessons from professionals. Now that he knew all there was to know, however, he couldn't see the point of staying in a prison and taking the same lessons over and over. "A hate factory," he called it once, and said it manufactured black poisons in his stomach that he couldn't get rid of although he poked a finger down his throat and retched and tried to be a clean and normal person in spite of everything.

Gerry's problem, you see, was he believed in justice, not laws. He felt he had paid for his crime, which was done in a drunk heat and to settle the question with a cowboy of whether a Chippewa was also a nigger. Gerry said that the two had never settled it between them, but that the cowboy at least knew that if a Chippewa was a nigger he was sure also a hell of a mean and lowdown fighter. For Gerry did not believe in fighting by any rules but reservation rules, which is to say the first thing Gerry did to the cowboy, after they squared off, was kick his balls.

It hadn't been much of a fight after that, and since there were both white and Indian witnesses, Gerry thought it would blow over if it ever reached court. But there is nothing more vengeful and determined in this world than a cowboy with sore balls, and Gerry soon found this out. He also found that white people are good witnesses to have on your side, because they have names, addresses, social security numbers, and work phones. But they are terrible witnesses to have against you, almost as bad as having Indians witness for you.

Not only did Gerry's friends lack all forms of identification except their band cards, not only did they disappear (out of no malice but simply because Gerry was tried during powwow time), but the few he did manage to get were not interested in looking judge or jury in the eyes. They mumbled into their laps. Gerry's friends, you see, had no confidence in the United States judicial system. They did not seem comfortable in the courtroom, and this increased their unreliability in the eyes of judge and jury. If you trust the authorities, they trust you better back, it seems. It looked that way to Gerry, anyhow.

28   A local doctor testified on behalf of the cowboy's testicles, and said his fertility might be impaired. Gerry got a little angry at that, and said right out in court that he could hardly believe he had done that much damage since the cowboy's balls were very small targets, it had been dark, and his aim was off anyway because of two, or maybe it was three, beers. That made matters worse, of course, and Gerry was socked with a sentence that was heavy for a first offense, but not bad for an Indian. Some said he got off lucky.

29   Only one good thing came from the whole experience, said Gerry, and that was that maybe the cowboy would not have any little cowboys, although, Gerry also said, he had nightmares sometimes that the cowboy did manage to have little cowboys, all born with full sets of grinning teeth, Stetson hats, and little balls hard as plum pits.

30   So you see, it was difficult for Gerry, as an Indian, to retain the natural good humor of his ancestors in these modern circumstances. He tried though, and since he believed in justice, not laws, Gerry knew where he belonged—out of prison, in the bosom of his new family. And in spite of the fact that he was untrained in the honest life, he wanted it. He was even interested in getting a job. It didn't matter what kind of job. "Anything for a change," Gerry said. He wanted to go right out and apply for one, in fact, the moment he was free. But of course Dot wouldn't let him. And so, because he wanted to be with Dot, he stayed hidden in her trailer house even though they both realized, or must have, that it wouldn't be long before the police came asking around or the neighbors wised up and Gerry Nanapush would be back at square one again. So it happened. Lovchik came for him. And Dot now believed she would have to go through the end of her pregnancy and the delivery all by herself.

31   Dot was angry about having to go through it alone, and besides that, she loved Gerry with a deep and true love—that was clear. She knit his absences into thick little suits for the child, suits that would have stopped a truck on a dark road with their colors—Bazooka pink, bruise blue, the screaming orange flaggers wore.

32   The child was as restless a prisoner as its father, and grew more anxious and unruly as the time of release neared. As a place to spend a nine-month sentence in, Dot wasn't much. Her body was inhospitable. Her skin was loose, sallow, and draped like upholstery fabric over her short,

boardlike bones. Like the shack we spent our days in, she seemed jerry-built, thrown into the world with loosely nailed limbs and lightly puttied joints. Some pregnant women's bellies look like they always have been there. But Dot's stomach was an odd shape, almost square, and had the tacked-on air of a new and unpainted bay window. The child was clearly ready for a break and not interested in earning its parole, for it kept her awake all night by pounding reasonlessly at her inner walls or beating against her bladder until she swore. "Kid wants out, bad," poor Dot would groan. "You think it might be premature?" From the outside, any-way, the child looked big enough to stand and walk and maybe even run straight out of the maternity ward the moment it was born.

The sun, at the time, rose around seven, and we got to the weigh shack while the frost was still thick on the gravel. Each morning I started the gas heater, turning the nozzle and standing back, flipping the match at it the way you would feed a fanged animal. Then one morning I saw the red bud through the window, lit already. But when I opened the door the shack was empty. There was, however, evidence of an overnight visitor—cigarette stubs, a few beer cans crushed to flat disks. I swept these things out and didn't say a word about them to Dot when she arrived. 33

She seemed to know something was in the air, however; her face lifted from time to time all that morning. She sniffed, and even I could smell the lingering odor of sweat like sour wheat, the faint reek of slept-in clothes and gasoline. Once, that morning, Dot looked at me and narrowed her long, hooded eyes. "I got pains," she said, "every so often. Like it's going to come sometime soon. Well, all I can say is he better drag ass to get here, that Gerry." She closed her eyes then, and went to sleep. 34

Ed Rafferty, one of the drivers, pulled in with a load. It was over-weight, and when I handed him the pink slip he grinned. There were two scales, you see, on the way to the cement plant, and if a driver got past the state-run scale early, before the state officials were there, the company would pay for whatever he got away with. But it was not illicit gravel that tipped the wedge past the red mark on the balance. When I walked back inside I saw the weight had gone down to just under the red. Ed drove off, still laughing, and I assumed that he had leaned on the arm of the scale, increasing the weight. 35

"That Ed," I said "got me again." 36

But Dot stared past me, needles poised in her fist like a picador's lances. It gave me a start, to see her frozen in such a menacing pose. It was not the sort of pose to turn your back on, but I did turn, following her gaze to the door, which a man's body filled suddenly. 37

Gerry, of course it was Gerry. He'd tipped the weight up past the red and leapt down, cat-quick for all his mass, and silent. I hadn't 38 heard his step. Gravel crushed, evidently, but did not roll beneath his tight, thin boots.

39   He was bigger than I remembered from the bar, or perhaps it was just that we'd been living in that dollhouse of a weigh shack so long that everything else looked huge. He was so big that he had to hunker one shoulder beneath the lintel and back his belly in, pushing the door-frame wider with his long, soft hands. It was the hands I watched as Gerry filled the shack. His plump fingers looked so graceful and artistic against his smooth mass. He used them prettily. Revolving agile wrists he reached across the few inches left between himself and Dot. Then his littlest fingers curled like a woman's at tea, and he disarmed his wife. He drew the needles out of Dot's fists, and examined the little garment that hung like a queer fruit beneath.

40   "S'very, very nice," he said, scrutinizing the tiny, even stitches. "S'for the kid?"

41   Dot nodded solemnly and dropped her eyes to her lap. It was an almost tender moment. The silence lasted so long that I got embarrassed and would have left had I not been wedged firmly behind his hip in one corner.

42   Gerry stood there, smoothing black hair behind his ears. Again, there was a queer delicacy about the way he did this. So many things Gerry did might remind you of the way that a beautiful courtesan, standing naked before a mirror, would touch herself—lovingly, conscious of her attractions. He nodded encouragingly. "Let's go then," said Dot.

43   Suave, grand, gigantic, they moved across the construction site and then, by mysterious means, slipped their bodies into Dot's compact car. I expected the car to belly down, thought the muffler would scrape the ground behind them. But instead they flew, raising a great spume of dust that hung in the air a long time after they were out of sight.

44   I went back into the weigh shack when the air behind them had settled. I was bored, dead bored. And since one thing meant about as much to me as another, I picked up her needles and began knitting, as well as I could anyway, jerking the yarn back after each stitch, becoming more and more absorbed in my work until, as it happened, I came suddenly to the end of the garment, snipped the yarn, and worked the loose ends back into the collar of the thick little suit.

45   I missed Dot in the days that followed, days so alike they welded seamlessly to one another and took your mind away. I seemed to exist in a suspension and spent my time sitting at the window watching nothing until the sun went down, bruising the whole sky as it dropped, clotting my heart. I couldn't name anything I felt anymore, although I knew it was a kind of boredom. I had been living the same life too long.

I did jumping jacks and pushups and stood on my head in the little shack to break the tedium, but too much solitude rots the brain. I wondered how Gerry had stood it. Sometimes I grabbed drivers out of their trucks and talked loudly and quickly and inconsequentially as a madwoman. There were other times I couldn't talk at all because my tongue had rusted to the roof of my mouth.

Sometimes I daydreamed about Dot and Gerry. I had many choice daydreams, but theirs was my favorite. I pictured them in Dot's long tan trailer house, both hungry. Heads swaying, clasped hands swinging between them like hooked trunks, they moved through the kitchen feeding casually from boxes and bags on the counters, like ponderous animals alone in a forest. When they had fed, they moved on to the bedroom and settled themselves upon Dot's king-size and sateen-quilted spread. They rubbed together, locked and unlocked their parts. They set the trailer rocking on its cement-block-and-plywood foundation and the tremors spread, causing cups to fall, plates to shatter in the china hutches of their more established neighbors.

But what of the child there, suspended between them. Did it know how to weather such tropical storms? It was a week past the week it was due, and I expected the good news to come any moment. I was anxious to hear the outcome, but still, I was surprised when Gerry rumbled to the weigh-shack door on a huge and ancient, rust-pocked, untrustworthy-looking machine that was like no motorcycle I'd ever seen before.

"She asst for you," he hissed. "Quick, get on!"

I hoisted myself up behind him, although there wasn't room on the seat. I clawed his smooth back for a handhold and finally perched, or so it seemed, on the rim of his heavy belt. Flylike, glued to him by suction, we rode as one person, whipping a great wind around us. Cars scattered, the lights blinked and flickered on the main street. Pedestrians swiveled to catch a glimpse of us—a mountain tearing by balanced on a toy, and clinging to the sheer northwest face, a scrawny half-breed howling something that Dopplered across the bridge and faded out, finally, in the parking lot of Saint Adalbert's Hospital.

In the waiting room we settled on chairs molded of orange plastic. The spike legs splayed beneath Gerry's mass but managed to support him the four hours we waited. Nurses passed, settling like field gulls among reports and prescriptions, eyeing us with reserved hostility. Gerry hardly spoke. He didn't have to. I watched his ribs and the small of his back darken with sweat. For that well-lighted tunnel, the waiting room, the tin rack of magazines, all were the props and inevitable features of institutions. From time to time Gerry paced in the time-honored manner of the prisoner or expectant father. He made lengthy trips to the bathroom. All the quickness and delicacy of his movements had disappeared, and he was only a poor tired fat man in those hours, a husband worried about his wife, menaced, tired of getting caught.

51   At last the gulls emerged and drew Gerry in among them. He visited Dot for perhaps half an hour, and then came out of her room. Again he settled, the plastic chair twitched beneath him. He looked bewildered and silly and a little addled with what he had seen. The shaded lenses of his glasses kept slipping down his nose. Beside him, I felt the aftermath of the shock wave traveling from the epicenter deep in his flesh outward from part of him that had shifted along a crevice. The tremors moved in widening rings. When they reached the very surface of him, and when he began trembling, Gerry stood suddenly. "I'm going after cigars," he said, and walked quickly away.

52   His steps quickened to a near run as he moved down the corridor. Waiting for the elevator, he flexed his nimble fingers. Dot told me she had once sent him to the store for a roll of toilet paper. It was eight months before she saw him again, for he'd met the local constabulary on the way. So I knew, when he flexed his fingers, that he was thinking of pulling the biker's gloves over his knuckles, of running. It was perhaps the very first time in his life he had something to run for.

53   It seemed to me, at that moment, that I should at least let Gerry know it was all right for him to leave, to run as far and fast as he had to now. Although I felt heavy—my body had gone slack, and my lungs ached with smoke—I jumped up. I signaled him from the end of the corridor. Gerry turned, unwillingly turned. He looked my way just as two of our local police—Officers Lovchik and Harriss—pushed open the fire door that sealed off the staircase behind me. I didn't see them and was shocked at first that my wave caused such an extreme reaction in Gerry.

54   His hair stiffened. His body lifted like a hot-air balloon filling suddenly. Behind him there was a wide, tall window. Gerry opened it and sent the screen into thin air with an elegant chorus-girl kick. Then he followed the screen, squeezing himself unbelievably through the frame like a fat rabbit disappearing down a hole. It was three stories down to the cement and asphalt parking lot.

55   Officers Lovchik and Harriss gained the window. The nurses followed. I slipped through the fire exit and took the back stairs down into the parking lot, believing I would find him stunned and broken there.

56   But Gerry had chosen his window with exceptional luck, for the officers had parked their car directly underneath. Gerry landed just over the driver's seat, caving the roof into the steering wheel. He bounced off the hood of the car and then, limping, a bit dazed perhaps, straddled his bike. Out of duty, Lovchik released several rounds into the still trees below him. The reports were still echoing when I reached the front of the building.

I was just in time to see Gerry Nanapush, emboldened by his god-like leap and recovery, pop a wheelie and disappear between the neat shrubs that marked the entrance to the hospital. 57

Two weeks later Dot and her girl, who was finally named Shawn, like most girls born that year, came back to work at the scales. Things went on as they had before, except that Shawn kept us occupied during the long hours. She was large, of course, and had a sturdy pair of lungs she used often. When she cried, she screwed her face into fierce baby wrinkles and would not be placated with sugar tits or pacifiers. Dot unzipped her parka halfway, pulled her blouse up, and let her nurse for what seemed like hours. We could scarcely believe her appetite. Dot was a diligent producer of milk, however. Her breasts, like overfilled inner tubes, strained at her nylon blouses. Sometimes when she thought no one was looking, Dot rose and carried them in the crooks of her arms, for her shoulders were growing bowed beneath their weight. 58

The trucks came in on the hour, or half hour. I heard the rush of air brakes, gears grinding only inches from my head. It occurred to me that although I measured many tons every day, I would never know how heavy a ton was unless it fell on me. I wasn't lonely now that Dot had returned. The season would end soon, and we wondered what had happened to Gerry. 59

There were only a few weeks left of work when we heard that Gerry was caught again. He'd picked the wrong reservation to hide on—Pine Ridge. As always, it was overrun with federal agents and armored vehicles. Weapons were stashed everywhere and easy to acquire. Gerry got himself a weapon. Two men tried to arrest him. Gerry would not go along, and when he started to run and the shooting started, Gerry shot and killed a cleanshaven man with dark hair and light eyes, a state trooper, a man whose picture was printed in all the papers. 60

They sent Gerry to prison in Marion, Illinois. He was placed in the control unit. He receives visitors in a room where no touching is allowed, where the voice is carried by phone, glances meet through sheets of Plexiglas, and no children will ever be engendered. 61

Dot and I continued to work the last weeks together. Once we weighed baby Shawn. We unlatched her little knit suit, heavy as armor, and bundled her in a light, crocheted blanket. Dot went into the shack to adjust the weights. I stood there with Shawn. She was such a solid child, she seemed heavy as lead in my arms. I placed her on the ramp between the wheel sights and held her steady for a moment, then took my hands slowly away. She stared calmly into the rough distant sky. She did not flinch when the wind came from every direction, wrapping us tight enough to squeeze the very breath from a stone. She was so 62 dense with life, such a powerful distillation of Dot and Gerry, it seemed she might weigh about as much as any load. But that was only a thought, of course. For as it turned out, she was too light and did not register at all.

Reading and Writing Activities

PRELIMINARY RESPONSE

Notes. As you read, record your reactions (questions or comments) to Louise Erdrich's narrative about two people who cannot prosper in a community that does not share or understand their value system. How familiar or unfamiliar is this community to you? If it is unfamiliar, what, if anything, strikes you as difficult to understand?

Discussion. In class, compare your reactions in groups of five or six. Appoint a recorder to keep track of similarities or differences, consensus or disagreement, arising from the discussion. The recorder may summarize your group discussion for the rest of the class later.

Freewriting: After discussion, freewrite for 10 to 15 minutes about similarities or differences in preliminary readings of the story. Read your freewriting in groups of two to four.

SUMMARIZING

1. Create a preliminary analysis of the Erdrich reading selection with a scratchline of characters and events.
2. Write a summary of the story as you understand it. Note how the story unfolds before and after transition points. What explicit message do you get from this story? What is the implicit message? How much do you, the reader, have to infer?
3. Compare the summaries in your groups.

FOCUSED CRITICAL READING

1. How would you describe Dot's value system? What does she care about?
2. How would you describe Gerry's value system? What does he care about?
3. How would you describe the narrator?

Rosario Morales

The Day It Happened

———————◆———————

Rosario Morales has coauthored a collection of poetry and prose, Getting Home Alive *(1986). Her work has appeared in many anthologies and literary journals. The following short story was published in* Callaloo *in 1992.*

The day it happened I was washing my hair. I had long hair then that went halfway down my back and I washed it once a week and rinsed it with lemon juice "to bring out the blond highlights" Mami said. Then I'd set it into pincurls that took an age to do because there was so much to wind around and around my finger. But if Mami was in a good mood, and she looked like she might be that day, she curled the back for me. I usually did all this on Saturday so I would look great for church on Sunday, and for a date Saturday night if I ever had one. ¡ojala!

Naturally the moment when it all began I was rinsing the big soapy mess. Nosy Maria was leaning out the window drying her dark red fingernails in the breeze when Josie stepped out of our apartment house doorway with a suitcase in her hand. Maria sucked in her breath so hard the sound brought my mother who took one look, crossed herself, or so Maria says, and started praying. Someone needed to pray for Josie. It was five o'clock and Ramón was due home any minute.

I wouldn't have known anything about any of this if Olga next door hadn't rung our doorbell and banged on the door just when Mami was too deep in prayer to hear and Maria was leaning out over the sill with her eyes bugging out. I cursed, very quietly of course, because if Mami or Papi heard me curse I'd get a slap across my face. I wrapped my sopping head in a towel and opened the door to Olga's "Oh my goodness, oh my dear. Oh honey, did you see? Look out the window this minute. I wouldn't have believed it if I hadn't seen it with my own two eyes. That poor little kid. I hate to think..." and on and on as we crossed the apartment to look out on the street.

Little Mikey from across the way was telling the rest of the kids how he'd found a taxi for Josie the minute he'd hit Southern Boulevard and how he'd hailed it and how the driver had let him ride back to Brook Street in the front seat—even though all of them had seen him arrive and step out with his back stiff with pride. Meantime Josie was back down in the street with Doña Toña from across the hall and Betty Murphy upstairs right behind her, all of them loaded down with two

1

2

3

4

lamps, a typewriter and a big box of books. Doña Toña was muttering something we couldn't hear up here on the second story but it was probably either the prayer I was hearing on my right or the "...hurry oh hurry oh God he'll be here any minute are you mad girl, are you mad" that came at me from the left.

5   It was hard not to be scared as well as glad that Josie was packing up and leaving Ramón. They'd been married only six months but already they were in a pattern, like the Garcias down the block who did everything the same way on the same day, all year. Ramón worked late till seven every week day and five on Saturday. When he arrived he expected a good dinner to be on the table at the right temperature exactly five minutes after he walked in the door. He yelled if she didn't get it right and sometimes even if she did.

6   Saturday evening they went out to a party or the bar down the avenue, both of them dressed up and Ramón looking proud and cheerful for a change. Josie always looked great. She's so cute. Small and plump with long lashes on her dark eyes and, get this, naturally curly hair. She smiled a lot when she was happy but she hadn't been happy much lately and not at all since she got pregnant. I wasn't supposed to know this. God, I was almost thirteen! But Maria, who was fourteen and a half and thought she was twenty, listened in on conversations in the living room by opening the door a sliver and she told me all about it.

7   Saturday nights there was sure to be a fight. Either it was that Josie was "no fun, a man can't be a man with such a wet rag around." Or it was that Josie was "a tramp. Why else was that guy staring at you, eating you up with his eyes?" The first time it happened, soon after they moved in, it woke me up from a deep sleep and I was so scared I crept into Maria's bed. I'd never heard such yelling in my life. When my parents fight it's during the day and in angry whispers. It sounds like a snake convention in my parents' bedroom. That's bad enough. Maria and I get real nervous and nothing's right until they make up and talk in normal voices again. But Ramón could be heard right through the floor at two in the morning. And then he took to throwing things and then he started hitting her. The first time that happened Josie didn't go to morning mass at St. Francis and Mami went down to her apartment to see if she was sick or something. Josie came to the door with a big bruise on her face. After that Mami went to fetch her every Sunday and stayed with her if she was too ashamed to go to church.

8   After she found out she was pregnant Josie had talked it over with Doña Toña and Doña Toña had talked it over with Mami and by and by we all knew she was scared he would hurt the little baby growing inside of her and worried about the child growing up with Ramón for a father. He expected too much of everyone and little kids hurt so when a parent thinks whatever they do is all wrong. Ha! Tell that to Mami and Papi, will you.

I don't think there was anyone in the neighborhood on Ramón's   9
side not even Joe who liked to bully his wife and daughters but didn't
realize he did or Tito who talked all the time about "wearing the pants
in this family." Ramón was too much, even for them. Josie was so
clearly a fine person, a quiet homebody, a sweetypie. Ramón was out of
his mind, that's what most of us thought. I mean you had to be to be so
regularly mean to a person who adored you. And she did, at least at
first. You could see it in the way she looked at him, boasted about his
strength, his good job, his brains. The way she excused his temper. "He
can't help himself. He doesn't mean it."

And now she was packed up and sitting in the taxi. Waiting for   10
him to come home, I guess. That was too much for Mami and she
scooted out the door with Olga, Maria, Papi, no less, and me right
behind her with that soaked blue towel wrapped sloppily around my
head. "Ai Mamita! Jesus, Maria y José. Jesus Maria y José" came faintly
up the stairs in the front of the hurrying line. I knew Mami and I knew
she meant to stand in front of Josie to protect her from that bully and,
sure as shooting, Papi was going to protect Mami who was going so
fast in her house slippers she almost fell down except that Olga
gripped her hard and kept her upright.

When we streamed out the door into the small crowd that had   11
gathered by now it was to see Ramón coming down the street with a
sour look on his face. He looked up once or twice but mostly just stared
at his feet as he strode up the block. He swept past us and almost into
the house the way he did when he came home weary from the shipyard
and the long ride home. He would have missed seeing Josie for sure, as
I was praying he would, except that she called to him.

"Ramón," she said in her soft voice, stepping out of the taxi.   12
"Ramón." He looked up and around then, took in the crowd, the taxi
with a tall lamp lying on the back seat and Josie in her good suit. He
stood looking at all this and especially at Josie for a long time. When he
spoke it was only to Josie, as if we weren't there at all. He had to clear
his throat to say "Josie?"

I was totally surprised and confused. He sounded so small, you   13
know. So uncertain. It was Josie looked tall now and hard. If I hadn't
known what I knew I would've said Josie was the bully in the family.
She looked him straight in the eye and said stiffly, as if they were lines
someone had given her to memorize, "I warned you. I said I would
leave if you ever hit me again. I am not safe with you. Our child is not
safe with you. I'm going now. I left arroz con pollo on the stove and the
electric bill on the table." He didn't answer so she turned to hug Doña
Toña and Mami before sitting herself back down. It was then that
Ramón acted. Before I could blink he'd hurled himself at her, thrown
himself on his knees and gripped her around her stockinged legs. "No!
No te vayas. Tu no comprendes. Eres muy joven para comprender. Tu

no puedes dejarme asi. Estamos casados para la vida. Te amo para siempre, para siempre. Josita, mi amor, no te vayas. Si te vas me mato. Te lo juro. No te puedes ir. No te puedes ir..." and on and on in a hoarse voice while Josie stood there frozen, fear on her face. There was no sound but Maria whispering occasional translations into Olga's impatient ear "Don't go." "You're too young to understand." "We're married for life." "I'll love you always." "I'll kill myself, I swear it."

14   It went on forever, Josie standing there, Ramón kneeling, all of us listening, tears running down my face, Josie's face, Mami's face. It was Olga who ended it, who walked up to Ramón, knelt down beside him, put an arm around him, and started talking, telling him Josie was a mother now and had to think about what was best for her baby, that it was his baby too, that he had to let her go now so she could bear a baby healthy in body and soul, that she knew he loved Josie, that his love would let him do what was best for them all. He was crying now, arguing with her while he slowly let go while he said he never could let her go that she was his whole life, that he would die without her, while Josie kissed Toña quickly on the cheek and climbed in next to the taxi driver who sat there looking the way I probably looked, dazed, like he'd stumbled into a movie screen and couldn't get out. She had to tell him to drive off.

Reading and Writing Activities

PRELIMINARY RESPONSE

Notes.   As you read, record your reactions (questions or comments) to Rosario Morales's narrative about the roles of women and men in her community. How familiar or unfamiliar is this community to you? If it is unfamiliar, what, if anything, strikes you as difficult to understand?

Discussion.   In class, compare your reactions in groups of five or six. Appoint a recorder to keep track of similarities or differences, consensus or disagreement, arising from the discussion. The recorder may summarize your group discussion for the rest of the class later.

Freewriting.   After discussion, freewrite for 10 to 15 minutes about similarities or differences in the preliminary readings of "The Day It Happened." Read your freewriting in groups of two to four.

SUMMARIZING

1. Create a preliminary analysis of the Morales story with a summary of characters and events.
2. Note how the story unfolds before and after transition points. Summarize Morales's central points and means of development from your notes so far. What explicit message do you get from this story? What is the implicit message? How much do you have to infer?
3. Compare summaries of characters and events in your groups.

FOCUSED CRITICAL READING

1. Rosario Morales tells a familiar story about patterns of spousal abuse. Describe the pattern of behavior between Josie and Ramon.
2. How much does Morales tell us about the community that shaped Josie's and Ramon's values?
3. How much does Morales tell us about the role of women in that community?
4. Speculate about Josie's life after leaving her community.

Scott Russell Sanders

The Men We Carry in Our Minds... and How They Differ from the Real Lives of Most Men

———————◆———————

Scott Russell Sanders has received an impressive number of awards for fiction and nonfiction. He won the Associated Writers Program Award for Creative Nonfiction in 1986 for The Paradise of Bombs, *the American Library Association Award in 1987 for* Bad Man Ballad, *and the PEN Syndicated Fiction Award in 1988.*

The following selection, "The Men We Carry in Our Minds," was first published in the literary journal The Milkweed Chronicle *in 1984 and reprinted in* The Utne Reader.

1   This must be a hard time for women," I say to my friend Anneke. "They have so many paths to choose from, and so many voices calling them."

2   "I think it's a lot harder for men," she replies.

3   "How do you figure that?"

4   "The women I know feel excited, innocent, like crusaders in a just cause. The men I know are eaten up with guilt."

5   "Women feel such pressure to be everything, do everything," I say. "Career, kids, art, politics. Have their babies and get back to the office a week later. It's as if they're trying to overcome a million years' worth of evolution in one lifetime."

6   "But we help one another. And we have this deep-down sense that we're in the *right*—we've been held back, passed over, used—while men feel they're in the wrong. Men are the ones who've been discredited, who have to search their souls."

7   I search my soul. I discover guilty feelings aplenty—toward the poor, the Vietnamese, Native Americans, the whales, an endless list of debts. But toward women I feel something more confused, a snarl of shame, envy, wary tenderness, and amazement. This muddle troubles me. To hide my unease I say, "You're right, it's tough being a man these days."

"Don't laugh," Anneke frowns at me. "I wouldn't be a man for anything. It's much easier being the victim. All the victim has to do is break free. The persecutor has to live with his past." 8

How deep is that past? I find myself wondering. How much of an inheritance do I have to throw off? 9

When I was a boy growing up on the back roads of Tennessee and Ohio, the men I knew labored with their bodies. They were marginal farmers, just scraping by, or welders, steelworkers, carpenters; they swept floors, dug ditches, mined coal, or drove trucks, their forearms ropy with muscle; they trained horses, stoked furnaces, made tires, stood on assembly lines wrestling parts onto cars and refrigerators. They got up before light, worked all day long whatever the weather, and when they came home at night they looked as though somebody had been whipping them. In the evenings and on weekends they worked on their own places, tilling gardens that were lumpy with clay, fixing broken-down cars, hammering on houses that were always too drafty, too leaky, too small. 10

The bodies of the men I knew were twisted and maimed in ways visible and invisible. The nails of their hands were black and split, the hands tattooed with scars. Some had lost fingers. Heavy lifting had given many of them finicky backs and guts weak from hernias. Racing against conveyor belts had given them ulcers. Their ankles and knees ached from years of standing on concrete. Anyone who had worked for long around machines was hard of hearing. They squinted, and the skin of their faces was creased like the leather of old work gloves. There were times, studying them, when I dreaded growing up. Most of them coughed, from dust or cigarettes, and most of them drank cheap wine or whiskey, so their eyes looked bloodshot and bruised. The fathers of my friends always seemed older than the mothers. Men wore out sooner. Only women lived into old age. 11

As a boy I also knew another sort of men, who did not sweat and break down like mules. They were soldiers, and so far as I could tell they scarcely worked at all. But when the shooting started, many of them would die. This was what soldiers were *for*, just as a hammer was for driving nails. 12

Warriors and toilers: those seemed, in my boyhood vision, to be the chief destinies for men. They weren't the only destinies, as I learned from having a few male teachers, from reading books, and from watching television. But the men on television—the politicians, the astronauts, the generals, the savvy lawyers, the philosophical doctors, the bosses who gave orders to both soldiers and laborers—seemed as remote and unreal to me as the figures in Renaissance tapestries. I could no more imagine growing up to become one of these cool, potent creatures than I could imagine becoming a prince. 13

14   A nearer and more hopeful example was that of my father, who had escaped from a red-dirt farm to a tire factory, and from the assembly line to the front office. Eventually he dressed in a white shirt and tie. He carried himself as if he had been born to work with his mind. But his body, remembering the earlier years of slogging work, began to give out on him in his fifties, and it quit on him entirely before he turned 65.

15   A scholarship enabled me not only to attend college, a rare enough feat in my circle, but even to study in a university meant for the children of the rich. Here I met for the first time young men who had assumed from birth that they would lead lives of comfort and power. And for the first time I met women who told me that men were guilty of having kept all the joys and privileges of the earth for themselves. I was baffled. What privileges? What joys? I thought about the maimed, dismal lives of most of the men back home. What had they stolen from their wives and daughters? The right to go five days a week, 12 months a year, for 30 or 40 years to a steel mill or a coal mine? The right to feel every leak in the roof, every gap in the fence, every cough in the engine as a wound they must mend? The right to feel, when the layoff comes or the plant shuts down, not only afraid but ashamed?

16   I was slow to understand the deep grievances of women. This was because, as a boy, I had envied them. Before college, the only people I had ever known who were interested in art or music or literature, the only ones who read books, the only ones who ever seemed to enjoy a sense of ease and grace were the mothers and the daughters. Like the menfolk, they fretted about money, they scrimped and made do. But, when the pay stopped coming in, they were not the ones who had failed. Nor did they have to go to war, and that seemed to me a blessed fact. By comparison with the narrow, ironclad days of fathers, there was an expansiveness, I thought, in the days of mothers. They went to see neighbors, to shop in town, to run errands at school, at the library, at church. No doubt, had I looked harder at their lives, I would have envied them less. It was not my fate to become a woman, so it was easier for me to see the graces. I didn't see, then, what a prison a house could be, since houses seemed to me brighter, handsomer places than any factory. I did not realize—because such things were never spoken of—how often women suffered from men's bullying. Even then I could see how exhausting it was for a mother to cater all day to the needs of young children. But if I had been asked, as a boy, to choose between tending a baby and tending a machine, I think I would have chosen the baby. (Having now tended both, I know I would choose the baby.)

17   So I was baffled when the women at college accused me and my sex of having cornered the world's pleasures. I think something of my bafflement has been felt by other boys (and by girls as well) who grew up in dirt-poor farm country, in mining country, in black ghettos, in

Hispanic barrios, in the shadows of factories, in Third World nations—any place where the fate of men is just as grim and bleak as the fate of women.

When the women I met at college thought about the joys and privileges of men, they did not carry in their minds the sort of men I had known in my childhood. They thought of their fathers, who were bankers, physicians, architects, stockbrokers, the big wheels of the big cities. They were never laid off, never short of cash at month's end, never lined up for welfare. These fathers made decisions that mattered. They ran the world.   18

The daughters of such men wanted to share in this power, this glory. So did I. They yearned for a say over their future, for jobs worthy of their abilities, for the right to live at peace, unmolested, whole. Yes, I thought, yes yes. The difference between me and these daughters was that they saw me, because of my sex, as destined from birth to become like their fathers, and therefore as an enemy to their desires. But I knew better. I wasn't an enemy, in fact or in feeling. I was an ally. If I had known, then, how to tell them so, would they have believed me? Would they now?   19

Reading and Writing Activities

PRELIMINARY RESPONSE

Notes.   As you read, record your reactions (questions or comments) to Scott Russell Sanders's essay "The Men We Carry in Our Minds" in your reading journal.

You may react to his central ideas, the relationships he discusses or implies exist between men and women, the clarity of the presentation of his ideas, the persona he creates through his writing, or the experience you have with ideas or experiences he describes.

Discussion.   In class, compare your reactions in reading groups of five or six. Appoint a recorder to keep track of similarities or differences, consensus or disagreement, arising from the discussion. The recorder may summarize your group discussion for the rest of the class later.

Freewriting: After the class discussion, freewrite for 10 to 15 minutes on the point that Sanders is making about men and women from working-class families.

SUMMARIZING

1. Create a preliminary analysis of the progression of claims that Sanders makes.
2. Write a summary paragraph or two, from preliminary work, of the central claims and the evidence or support Sanders presents to elaborate those claims.
3. Read the summaries in your reading groups. Compare the focus of each summary. How do the summaries differ? How are they the same? Are there claims that everyone in the group notes? Are there supporting details that some members of the group summarize and other members do not? What is the significance, if any, of differences in summaries?

Stephen Birmingham

Telling Them Apart

◆

Stephen Birmingham, born in Hartford, Connecticut in 1932, writes novels, short stories, and nonfiction. In "Telling Them Apart," the opening chapter of America's Secret Aristocracy *(1987), Birmingham discusses characteristic features of American upper-class behavior and language.*

Whenever you hear an American speak of a *terrace* rather than a   1
patio, of a *house* rather than a *home* or an *apartment,* of a *sofa* rather than a *davenport* or *couch,* of *curtains* rather than *drapes,* of *guests for dinner* rather than *company,* of a *long dress* rather than a *formal,* of a *dinner jacket* rather than a *tuxedo,* and of *underwear* rather than *lingerie,* chances are you are in the presence of a member of the American upper class. Upper-class Americans use the toilet, not the lavatory or the commode or the facilities or the loo or the little boys' room. Upper-class Americans go to boarding schools, not prep schools, where they earn grades, not marks. Upper-class Americans are either rich (not wealthy) or poor (not less well-off), and the prices they pay for things are either high (not expensive) or cheap (not inexpensive). Upper-class Americans say "Hello," not "Pleased to meet you," and "What?" not "Pardon me?" Upper-class American women do not have bosoms. They have breasts, or even tits when they are among their own kind, when other vulgarisms frequently emerge. The familiar four-letter word for sexual intercourse is a perfectly acceptable upper-class expression.

Brevity, simplicity, and the avoidance of euphemism are the chief   2
hallmarks of the upper-class American vocabulary. When an upper-class American feels sick, he says just that, and never "I feel ill" or "I feel nauseous." Cuteness is anathema. Thus in an upper-class American house you would never find a den or a rumpus room or a family room, though you might find a library or a playroom. Upper-class Americans do not own bedroom suites or dining room suites or any other kind of suites, or "suits." They own furniture, and if it is particularly good furniture, it is often simply called wood. Pretentiousness is similarly shunned. Thus to an upper-class American a tomato is a toma*y*to, not a toma*h*to. Upper-class Americans write "R.S.V.P." on the corners of their invitations, never "The favor of a reply is requested." Upper-class Americans give and go to parties, never to affairs, and if the affair being talked about is of the romantic variety, it is always, specifically, a love affair.

3   But, most important, the American upper class never talks about the upper class, or about any other sort of class, for that matter. Partly this is a question of delicacy and taste. It is simply not upper class to talk about class. Also, in a constitutionally classless society where an upper class has managed to emerge anyway, there is a feeling among members of the upper class that they are a somewhat illicit entity, a possibly endangered species. If one were to go about boasting of being upper class, who knows what sort of angry mob from below might rise up and challenge the precious barricades? So you will never hear a member of the upper class talk of "the right people," or "nice people," or even "the people we know." Instead it will be "our friends," or, more often, "our family and friends." This way, the polite illusion is created that the American aristocracy is a private, even secret, club, whose members all know each other and whose rules are observed without ever having to be written down or otherwise made public. Most frequently, when the American aristocracy speaks of itself in a general sense, it is in terms of "people," as in, "What will people say?" And if a member of the upper class behaves—as can happen—in a non-upper-class way, the reaction is "People just don't *do* that!"

4   In an upwardly mobile society, in which nearly everybody dreams of elevating himself to a higher social or economic stratum, there are some rules of upper-class behavior that are easy to learn. For example, when upper-class women swim, they do the Australian crawl, never the breaststroke or backstroke. It is easy to remember that the finger bowl has no function whatsoever—certainly not to dabble one's fingers in—and is to be removed, with the doily, and set at the upper left of one's plate, after which the dessert spoon and fork are to be removed from the service plate and placed on either side of it. It is easy to remember that it is acceptable to eat asparagus with one's fingers (if no tongs have been provided), while it is not acceptable to pick up the chop or the chicken leg in the same manner, unless one is dining *en famille*. It is never proper to squeeze the juice from a grapefruit half into a spoon.

5   But there are other more subtle, arcane codes by which members of the American aristocracy recognize each other and send signals to each other and that are more difficult to learn—which, it might be added, is the whole unwritten point of there being such codes. In addition to language and vocabulary, recognition is by name and by the association of name with place. Thus one should be able to remember that Ingersolls and Cadwaladers and Chews and *some* Morrises are from Philadelphia, while other Morrises are from New York and New Jersey, and so when meeting a Morris it is important to find out which family he or she represents. Livingstons, Jays, Bownes, Lawrences, Schieffelins, Iselins, Schuylers, and Fishes are from New York, while Otises, Saltonstalls, and Gardners are from Boston. Gardiners are from New York. Hoppins

and Browns are from Providence, Pringles and Pinckneys are from Charleston, Des Loges are from St. Louis, Stumpfs are pre-oil Texas, and Chandlers are Los Angeles.

Over the past generation, America's upper-class boarding schools and colleges have become thoroughly democratized, but members of the upper class can still send signals to one another by the way they designate their schools. An upper-class Yale alumnus, for example, would never say that he had graduated "from Yale." He would say that he had studied "at New Haven." Following is a list of other upper-class schools and colleges, with their special upperclass designations:

Actual Name	*Upper-Class Designation*
The Taft School	Watertown
The Hotchkiss School	Lakeville
St. Mark's School	Southborough
St. Paul's School	Concord
Miss Porter's School	Farmington
The Foxcroft School	Virginia
The Ethel Walker School	Simsbury
Choate-Rosemary Hall School	Wallingford
Smith College	Northampton
Vassar College	Poughkeepsie

But even more important and difficult than remembering names and their ancient associations with cities is mastering the American upper-class accent. Just as in England, where class is defined by accent, the American aristocracy has developed an accent peculiar to itself. It is a curious hybrid derived, in part, from the flat vowel sounds of New England, as well as from the New York accent that is sometimes described as "Brooklynese," with random borrowings from the drawl of the antebellum South. From the South comes a tendency to drop final consonants—as in "somethin'" or "anythin'"—or to elide initial letters in words such as "them," which makes a statement such as "I can't think of anything to give them" sound very much like "I cahnt think o' anythin' to give 'em." Final *r*'s are also dropped, whereby *paper* comes out "papuh," and *rear* is "reah." Interior *r*'s are elided as well, so that *apart* becomes "apaht," and *church* becomes "chuhch." Final *s*'s are almost, but not quite, lisped, so that the word *birds* is pronounced something like "budzh." Perhaps most difficult to master are the vowel sounds in simple words like *were*, where the audible vowel sound of the *e* almost sounds like the *i* in *prism*. On top of this, particularly among men, there has long been something called the boarding school stammer, a speech pattern whose origins are unclear but which may descend from the British public school stammer: "I—uh—oh, I say—wha-what would you say to—uh—," et cetera.

8   In perfecting an American upper-class accent, one rule to remember is the upper-class injunction to keep a stiff upper lip. The upper lip moves very little in American upper-class speech. But of course members of the American upper class do not have to be taught how to speak this way. They learn it from the cradle.

9   A comparison of the aristocracies of America and Great Britain is useful, for the American uppermost class has always looked to the British class system as its most satisfactory model. Even at the time of the American Revolution this was true, and many of the American "heroes" whose signatures grace the Declaration of Independence signed this document with great misgivings, distrusting the Revolutionary movement and not at all agreeing with Thomas Jefferson's notion that "all men are created equal." A number of American families have aristocratic forebears who managed to be conveniently "out of town" or otherwise unavailable when that document was being signed, and as we shall see, there are American families today who are just as proud of ancestors who failed, or refused, to sign as are those with ancestors who were Signers. Particularly in New York, Pennsylvania, and Maryland, enthusiasm for the Revolution was lukewarm at best, while in Boston, the Revolutionary cradle, it was intense. Even today, these philosophical differences between Boston and the rest of the East Coast more than two hundred years ago are expressed in a certain antipathy between the upper classes of New York, Philadelphia, and Baltimore and the upper class of the Bay Colony.

10   Like the British, many members of the American aristocracy are exceedingly rich while, like some British, some are not, though all manage to live in considerable style. How this is accomplished is sometimes unclear. But it has a lot to do with a creed that one ought to live only "on the income from one's income," that one should sell property only under the most desperate circumstances, and the belief that, every generation or so, there is nothing wrong with obtaining a fresh infusion of money through a well-orchestrated marriage.

11   At the same time, like the members of the Royal House of Windsor since Victoria's time, American aristocrats in their private lives often convey the impression of being rather ordinary people, neither particularly intellectual nor witty, committed to their friends and to lives that are comfortable and familiar, people who are not remarkable for being anything other than what they are and were born to be—and who are remarkable only for not having to demonstrate, or prove, who they are.

12   Like the queen of England, women of the American aristocracy rarely change their hairstyles. Nor do they show much real interest in fashion. When they go out-of-doors—which they like to do—they bundle up and will choose a down-filled coat over a mink if the former is warmer. The American aristocracy, like the British, is generally sports-minded. From England, the American aristocracy brought golf and

tennis to this country. From Edward VIII's example, the American upper crust took up skiing. Now these sports have become too popular to still be classified as upper class, though the upper class still enjoys them. The great American sports—baseball, football, hockey, basketball—have never been popular with the upper class, though baseball, the most gentlemanly of these sports, has always found a few adherents. Such English sports as rugby and soccer—and even cricket and beagling—have long been enjoyed by pockets of the American upper class.

Like the English queen and her family, the American aristocracy   13
has a passion for certain quadrupeds: dogs and horses. Since ancient times, the horse has been a mythic symbol of leadership. For centuries, kings and generals and emperors and caesars have had their portraits painted, and their images carved in bronze and marble, astride a horse. This of course is not to say that all members of the American aristocracy are superb equestrians, but it would be safe to assume that nearly all, at some point in their lives, have been taught to sit a horse properly in an English saddle. Fox hunting, the steeplechase, the point-to-point, polo—all popular with England's landed gentry, where they began centuries ago—remain popular with the American equivalent, who still buy their boots and riding attire in London.

And, just as the queen of England looks happiest surrounded by a   14
pack of yelping corgis, so do the American aristocrats love their dogs. They love dogs, furthermore, in numbers. In an informal survey in New York not long ago, at a gathering where a number of America's oldest families were assembled, the guests were asked what they were giving their spouses for Christmas. A surprising number said that the gift was going to be a new dog for the family collection—if not for a husband or wife, then for the children or for some other close family member. From this, the conversation turned to books about dogs. *Everyone's* favorite dog author, it so happened, was Albert Payson Terhune.

This affection for certain domestic animals does not, however,   15
extend to all forms of wildlife. Hunting, as it is in England, is a pastime enjoyed by the American aristocracy. But aristocrats of neither the English nor American variety would consider hunting squirrels, possum, or rabbits, or even killing the fox in the hunt. Birds, on the other hand, are a different matter—game birds: quail, pheasant, partridge, and grouse. Deer are hunted only when there is a specific ecological reason to do so. Mr. Robert David Lion Gardiner, for example, sixteenth lord of the manor of Gardiner's Island, which he owns, periodically takes small groups of friends on deer-hunting forays to his island in order to keep the deer population—which would starve if the island became defoliated by its numbers—under control. "It isn't a pleasant chore," he says, "but it simply must be done."

Like the British, the members of the American upper class are not   16
really prejudiced against Jews and Catholics, For one thing, it is not

upper class to express religious prejudice, though most members of the upper class would confess that they do not really "understand" Judaism or Catholicism. These religions are, after all, more demanding of their adherents and require the mastery of arcane languages, Hebrew and Latin. Over the years, a number of American upper-class families have intermarried with Jews and Catholics, but it was usually with the understanding that the outsider would convert to the prevailing Protestant mode—just to keep things simpler for future generations. In fact, most American upper-class families are proud of their long record of religious tolerance and of the fact that their aristocratic ancestors saw to it that an article guaranteeing religious freedom was written into the Constitution. When the Dutch colony of Nieuw Amsterdam became the British colony of New York, the old Dutch families did not suddenly become social pariahs. Of course, this is an additional reason why other upper-class Americans look on upper-class Bostonians as a somewhat special, peculiar breed. Puritan New Englanders hated— and tortured and hanged—people who rejected the tenets of their tiny sect.

17   In the early days of the Republic, the American aristocracy simply assumed that its members would run the new country—as presidents, governors, senators, cabinet members, ambassadors—just as the British aristocracy ran England. It was not until America's seventh president, the log cabin-born Andrew Jackson, that a man entered the White House who was neither a member of the old Virginia landed gentry nor an Adams from Boston. The aristocratic John Quincy Adams went so far as to call Jackson a "barbarian who could not write a sentence of grammar and hardly could spell his own name."

Reading and Writing Activities

PRELIMINARY RESPONSE

Notes.   As you read, record your reactions (questions or comments) to Birmingham's essay in your reading journal.

Discussion.   In class, compare your reactions in groups of five or six. Appoint a recorder to keep track of similarities or differences, consensus or disagreement, arising from the discussion. The recorder may summarize your group discussion for the rest of the class later.

Freewriting.   After discussion, freewrite for 10 to 15 minutes about your preliminary readings and discussion of the article. Read your freewriting in groups of two to four.

SUMMARIZING

1. Create a preliminary analysis of the essay "Telling Them Apart" with a scratchline of topics. Note explicit transition words, phrases, sentences, or paragraphs.
2. Note how Birmingham is developing his essay before and after transition points. Summarize his central point, purpose, and means of development from your notes so far. (Refer to the introduction to this chapter for a discussion of one reading of this essay's structure and meaning.)
3. Compare summaries in your groups.

FOCUSED CRITICAL READING

1. What are the central points Birmingham makes in his essay?
2. How does he develop each section of his essay, and how can you keep track of changes in topic?
3. How reader friendly does this essay appear to you?

William B. Gatewood

Prologue to "Color, Culture, and Behavior"

◆

William B. Gatewood, Alumni Distinguished Professor of History at the University of Arkansas, Fayetteville, has written nine books on the history of African Americans. In this selection from his book The Black Elite, 1880–1920 (1990), *he describes Blanche and Josephine Bruce, a husband and wife who "exemplified the culture, behavior, and life style of the nation's aristocrats of color." He says of the Bruces that they were "obviously aware of the acrimonious debate over the so-called color complex in the black community."*

1   A strikingly handsome couple, Blanche and Josephine Bruce exemplified the culture, behavior, and life style of the nation's aristocrats of color. Exhibiting the decorum, dignity, and restraint characteristic of the polite society of which they were a part, they abided by the prevailing canons of proper etiquette and avoided ostentatious display. They held membership in a variety of high-status social clubs and racial uplift organizations, affiliated with what some called "high-tone" churches, and were sufficiently affluent to enjoy the amenities of life denied most blacks. Devoted to the cause of education, they insisted on a classical curriculum for their son but considered vocational education appropriate for the black masses. Despite their support of the educational efforts of Booker T. Washington and their cordial personal relationship with him, the Bruces never embraced the Tuskegee formula of race relations but remained committed to the concept of black equality, especially as applied to blacks of their own class. Their approach was that of conservative assimilation.

2   The Bruces were obviously aware of the acrimonious debate over the so-called color complex in the black community. Critics denounced what they claimed to be the practice of utilizing color as a major stratifier, with fairer-skinned Negroes occupying places at the top of the social scale and darker people those at the bottom. While it does not appear that either the senator or his wife addressed the color issue in public, they knew from first-hand knowledge and experience that color could and indeed did "cut considerable figure in grouping Negroes.

3   Blanche Bruce was obviously a "mixed blood." Descriptions of him, especially by whites, rarely failed to mention his swarthy complexion

and even his hair, which one observer described as "wavy but parted and brushed like a white man's." While the senator, by the nature of his position, appeared frequently before audiences of dark-skinned Negroes and was associated in an official way with blacks exhibiting an infinite variety of color, his social life was largely confined to those whose complexion was rarely darker, and often fairer, than his own. In 1884 he and his wife served as witnesses at the private wedding ceremony of Frederick Douglass and Helen Pitts, a graduate of Mount Holyoke and a "plain, fortyish and efficient" white woman—a marriage that created outrage among blacks as well as whites. That the Bruces stood as witnesses meant that they did not share the disapproval voiced by the many blacks who viewed Douglass's act as one of racial treachery.

On perhaps no other occasion did the light complexion of Josephine Bruce create more difficulties than in her work with the National Association of Colored Women. She aspired to be president of the organization, and at the biennial convention in Detroit in 1906 it appeared that she would realize her ambition. Rather suddenly, she, or rather her color, became the center of the only serious dispute at an otherwise harmonious convention, for opposition to her candidacy centered on the fairness of her skin. Not since she arrived in Washington in 1878 as the bride of Senator Bruce had it prompted so much public comment. A large contingent of delegates felt that she was unacceptable because "the predominance of her Caucasian blood caused her to be considered a white woman," and that would be harmful to an organization that prided itself on being "directed and controlled entirely by women of the colored race." "We prefer," said one delegate, "a woman who is altogether a Negro, because, while the lighter women have been the greatest leaders and are among the most brilliant in the Association, their cleverness and ability is [sic] attributed to their white blood. We want to demonstrate that the African is as talented." 4

The controversy stirred by Mrs. Bruce's complexion became the subject of news stories from Detroit entitled "Colorline in Woman's Convention." White reporters interpreted this incident as "a new phase of color discrimination" since Josephine Bruce encountered opposition "not because she was too black, but because she was too white." Deeply embarrassed by the whole episode, Josephine Bruce withdrew from contention for the presidency. 5

The Bruces would undoubtedly have insisted that character and genteel conduct were infinitely more important than color. In their private and public lives they exhibited all the attributes of what Karen Halttunen has described as the genteel performance, "a system of polite conduct that demanded flawless self-discipline practiced with an apparently easy, natural sincere manner." Both the senator and his wife according to all accounts, possessed "elegant manners" and all the 6 attributes of "good breeding." Both were skilled in the art of conversation and practitioners of the most decorous behavior in public, marked by quiet dignity and politeness. They attached importance to proper dress that was conservative in taste and high in quality. In their manner of dress, as in their life style generally, the Bruces were not inclined toward conspicuous consumption.

7   Like other aristocrats of color, Mrs. Bruce was most likely to exhibit emotion in the form of anger or disgust when she encountered breaches in the genteel performance by those who knew better. For example, she was dismayed by the way the family of her future daughter-in-law, Clara Burrill, "paraded the engagement." In her view their behavior was simply a matter of bad taste and may well have accounted for her reluctance to approve the match.

8   Although Roscoe Bruce, the son of a United States senator and an honor graduate of Harvard, was obviously considered an ideal husband by the Burrill family, Clara subscribed to the same social code as did her future husband and his mother. She never equaled her mother-in-law in the practice of the genteel performance, but she shared many of the same social values and was no less concerned about proprieties and decorum. Like many aristocrats of color, Clara and her husband were disdainful of the materialism that they believed to be rampant among blacks as well as whites early in the twentieth century. Nor did either Roscoe or Clara Bruce approve of people who made an ostentatious display of their wealth. Such behavior automatically placed such persons outside the "charmed circle" and among the vulgar. From clothing and jewelry to household furnishings, the Bruces preferred "pretty things, simple but elegant."

9   Perhaps nothing was so indicative of one's degree of gentility as one's use of language. Any trace of what was called "dialect" placed one beyond the pale of polite black society. Despite the meagerness of his formal education, Senator Bruce possessed the vocabulary and language skills of an educated man. His wife not only was a gifted conversationalist, public speaker, and writer but also read French. Their son and daughter-in-law, both of whom enjoyed educational opportunities open to few Americans, regardless of race, were always conscious of correct usage of language. Clara Bruce, on first meeting George Washington Carver at Tuskegee, was appalled to hear him say, "he don't."

10   Throughout their residence in Washington both generations of Bruces were active in a variety of clubs and voluntary organizations. In addition to being identified with Republican party organizations, the senator figured prominently in several highly selective gentleman's clubs. Because of the prestige that Bruce enjoyed as a senator and as Register of the Treasury and Recorder of Deeds, social as well as philanthropic organizations eagerly sought to have his name associated with their cause. The presence of the Bruces at a purely social function

or charity benefit was indisputable evidence that it was an upper-class affair.

Both before and after the death of her husband, Josephine Bruce took an active part in the civic and club life of Washington's black community. In 1892 she was among the female aristocrats of color who founded the Colored Women's League, which sponsored a variety of activities to aid the disadvantaged of their race. After the League merged with similar organizations elsewhere to form the National Association of Colored Women, Josephine Bruce became a prominent figure in a nationwide federation of black women's clubs. In the years following the death of her husband in 1898, "Mrs. Senator Bruce" was almost invariably described as "a woman prominent in club affairs." [11]

Like most of those who belonged to their social circle, the Bruces were keenly interested in education. While the senator had relatively little formal schooling, he read widely and avidly throughout his life. According to a journalist who was often critical of upper-class blacks, Blanche Bruce was not only an "exceptionally cultured and refined man" but also "better read than most men of his class." In his lectures to black audiences throughout the United States Bruce emphasized the critical importance of education in promoting the "progress of the race." [12]

Josephine Bruce was reared in a home in which art, music, and literature received much attention. Following her graduation from Cleveland's Central High School in 1871, she took "the short course required of teachers" and secured a position at Mayflower School, one of the city's public elementary schools. Although she abandoned teaching following her marriage, Josephine Bruce continued to have a keen interest in black education. She and several other socially prominent women in Washington organized a campaign to establish a vocational or industrial high school for blacks in the District. Such a school was designed not for their children but for those of the less fortunate classes. Her experience at Tuskegee following her husband's death appears to have reinforced her commitment to industrial education as the most appropriate solution to the problem of educating the black masses. [13]

The Bruces provided their only child, Roscoe, with all the educational and cultural advantages enjoyed by upper-class Americans, regardless of race. He grew up in a home that bore all the attributes of culture and refinement and attended Washington's famous M Street High School, whose high academic standards attracted the children of aristocrats of color not merely from the District but from other parts of the United States as well. Following his graduation from Phillips Exeter Academy, he entered Harvard College and graduated with honors in 1902. The following year he married Clara Burrill, who was also a graduate of the M Street School and who had attended Radcliffe College. She was, according to one observer, "quite as cultured as her distinguished husband." [14]

15　　　　Booker T. Washington, who no doubt was fully aware of the prestige attached to the Bruce name and the Harvard degree, persuaded Roscoe to head the academic department at Tuskegee, where he remained from 1902 until 1906. Bruce assisted Washington in a thorough revision of the curriculum through a process known as "correlating" or "dovetailing." To obliterate "differences between the literary department and the industrial department," the revised curriculum required the practice of mathematics in carpentry classes and the writing of essays on plowing or other agricultural subjects in English courses. Although Bruce was at first Washington's principal agent in implementing the new curriculum, he became convinced that it was leading to a steady erosion of the academic component of the school. Regardless of differences that developed between them, Bruce remained on friendly terms with Washington. In 1906 he returned to Washington as principal of one of the Negro public schools. The following year he became assistant superintendent in charge of Negro schools in the District of Columbia, a coveted post that he secured with the aid of Booker T. Washington and held for fifteen years.

16　　　　The religious life of the Bruce family was, in many respects, typical of that of the aristocrats of color with whom they associated socially. They attended church, but it was not the institution around which their lives revolved. The denominations with which they were identified engaged in formal and liturgical worship and were generally perceived as high-status churches. As a major political figure, Blanche Bruce considered it appropriate to appear frequently before numerous black religious organizations and to attend Sunday worship at various black churches. There is little to suggest that he was especially devout or possessed a deep attachment to a particular creed or faith. Although Bruce joined a group of his close friends in organizing a Congregational church in Washington two years before his death, he was also identified with the Episcopal church during his residence in the city, largely because of his wife's influence. His funeral, in 1898, was perhaps indicative of his ecumenical approach to religion. It was held in the huge sanctuary of the Metropolitan A.M.E. Church in Washington to accommodate the large crowd. Sterling Brown, minister of the Congregational church that Bruce assisted in establishing, presided, while ministers of the Episcopal, Presbyterian, Baptist, and A.M.E. churches participated in the funeral service.

17　　　　Throughout her life Josephine Bruce remained attached to the Episcopal church, in which she had been reared, although she later joined her husband's Congregational church. In the late 1880s, when the Bruces lived in Indianapolis for eighteen months, they joined Saint Paul's Episcopal Church, a white church, where Mrs. Bruce's sisters, Mary and Victoria Wilson, teachers in the city's public schools, were members.

The decision of the Bruces to attend a white church prompted some   18
blacks to question why a former senator from Mississippi who claimed
to be a spokesman for Afro-Americans found no black church in the
city to his liking. A well-known black citizen of Indianapolis later
claimed that Bruce and his wife "alienated many colored people here"
because they did "not go to hear a colored preacher in a church
attended by colored people." Other prominent blacks, who identified
with predominantly white denominations, such as Congregational,
Presbyterian, and Methodist Episcopal churches, encountered similar
complaints.

Roscoe and Clara Bruce, like the elder Bruces, found the emotional   19
religion practiced in many black churches distasteful. During a visit to
Tuskegee in 1902 before he joined the faculty, Roscoe Bruce likened a
revival being conducted on campus to "a reversion to barbarism." "The
antics of the preacher and the students," he declared, "were disgusting.
Such nonsense ought to be stopped at once. I for one shall never attend
such a performance again."

Even though Blanche and Josephine Bruce, as well as their son and   20
daughter-in-law, participated in a variety of racial uplift causes, they
scarcely belonged among the vanguard of the civil rights activists of
their generation. Neither the senator nor his wife had experienced the
bitter realities of slavery or the frustrations of the common freedman.
Their encounters with social rebuffs and indignities were relatively
few. As a result, the Bruces, like others of their class, viewed the plight
of the black masses from a distance. White conservatives in Mississippi
liked the senator precisely because he was a "man of moderation and
integrity without brilliance or force."

Blanche Bruce and his wife early moved into the circle of Booker T.   21
Washington, whose influence spread rapidly following his Atlanta
Compromise speech in 1895. Five years earlier, Washington had invited
the ex-senator from Mississippi to deliver the commencement address
at Tuskegee. Profoundly impressed by what he observed at Washington's school during this visit, Bruce became an enthusiastic advocate of
industrial education as suitable for the educational needs of the black
masses.

While Bruce's support of Washington's educational endeavor lent   22
prestige to the Tuskegee idea of education, Washington's alliance with
the senator had its advantages for the Bruces. Bruce enlisted Washington's support in obtaining a political appointment in the McKinley
administration and in securing the admission of his son, Roscoe, to
Harvard. All the while, Josephine Bruce and Washington's wife
worked closely in launching the National Association of Colored
Women.

While Roscoe Bruce remained on cordial terms with Booker T.   23
Washington until the latter's death in 1915, he was also an early mem-

ber of the National Association for the Advancement of Colored People, which the Tuskegean viewed as an enemy and sought to undermine. In a sense Bruce, not unlike other upper-class blacks, became a casualty of his attempt to embrace two movements, one symbolized by Washington and the other by W. E. B. Du Bois. Part of his problem as head of the black schools in the District, according to one critic, was his effort "to please everybody" or at least to please two ideologically antagonistic factions in the black community.

24   Such a stance sprang from a basic ambivalence which Bruce shared with many of his upper-class associates. They embraced Du Bois's concept of the "Talented Tenth" and its implications, but, at the same time, they recognized and even admired the contributions of Booker T. Washington to the uplift of the black masses. An outspoken advocate of industrial education for the black majority, Bruce considered such a curriculum inappropriate for the elite, especially for his own children, who attended prestigious preparatory schools and liberal arts institutions. Though constantly reminded of racial barriers and restricted in career opportunities by their racial identities, Bruce and those of comparable status in the black community were reluctant to abandon the idea that blacks, especially educated and genteel blacks like themselves, would be assimilated into the larger society. They never doubted that they were indeed different from other blacks. "It is," Bruce's mother observed figuratively in 1902, "the several thousand years of development that makes the difference."'

25   As did others of his associates, Roscoe Bruce tended to think of himself in class, rather than racial, terms. That his son, Blanche and Josephine Bruce's grandson, shared such a perception was abundantly evident in a letter he wrote to his mother about sending Roscoe, Jr., to Exeter. "O, about Exeter, you know mama, little Bubsie [Roscoe, Jr.] would have no trouble of a racial character at all with those boys. They would never in the world *think* of him that way; he doesn't think of himself that way." Young Bruce may not have thought of himself within a racial context or may not have encountered any problems of a racial character among those "fine, clear-eyed, clean-souled New Englanders" at Exeter, but his race assumed great importance when he applied for a dormitory room at Harvard, his father's alma mater.

26   Bruce's attempt to reserve a room for his son in the freshman dormitory at Cambridge was personally denied by President A. Lawrence Lowell. "I am sorry to tell you," Lowell wrote, "that on the Freshman Halls, where residence is compulsory, we have felt the necessity of not including colored men." In a lengthy reply, Bruce expressed disappointment and dismay that his alma mater had inaugurated such a discriminatory policy, which diverged so sharply from that existing during his days as an undergraduate. "Few words in the English language, I submit," Bruce wrote, "are susceptible of more poignant abuse

than the two you have seen fit to employ. The first is 'race'; the second 'necessity.' As the one is often nothing more than a term of social convenience, so the other is quite as often a means to buttress prejudice. But, *Veritas* is less elusive." Bruce concluded by informing Lowell that "no son of mine will ever deny his name or his blood or his tradition" in order to enter Harvard. For Bruce, the "basis of sound nationality" was not race but culture.

The publication of the Bruce–Lowell correspondence in the daily press touched off a storm of protest. Although interviews with Harvard students indicated that they were sharply divided on what came to be known as Harvard's "Negro exclusion policy," the alumni bulletin opposed it as did numerous alumni who interpreted Lowell's action as "an ominous departure from Harvard traditions." James Weldon Johnson of the NAACP lodged a strong protest against Harvard's "Negro policy," describing it as nothing more than "putting into effect the program proclaimed by the notorious Ku Klux Klan." Even though Lowell at one point admitted that he felt like "Saint Sebastian, stuck full of arrows which people are firing at me," he refused to alter his position regarding the exclusion of blacks from Harvard's freshman dormitories.   27

Roscoe Bruce had rarely confronted such overt racial discrimination as that involved in the Harvard incident. It was all the more devastating because it affected his son. An upper-class black man who took great pride in his Harvard education and refinement, Bruce had, like others of his class, viewed himself as a cultural broker who spoke to blacks and for blacks to whites. Intimately acquainted with the culture of both races, Bruce had for most of his career functioned as a carrier of white culture into the black community. The refusal of his alma mater to extend to his son the same privileges that he had enjoyed twenty years earlier undoubtedly prompted him, as similar incidents did others of the upper class, to reassess his traditional place and role in a biracial society. As a result, their roles as cultural brokers underwent subtle changes, prompting a closer identity with and appreciation of black culture. Like Bruce, they tended to find greater significance in their black heritage—in their name, blood, and traditions as Afro-Americans.   28

Reading and Writing Activities

PRELIMINARY RESPONSE

Notes. As you read, record in your reading journal your reactions (questions or comments) to Gatewood's description of a black aristocracy in Washington, D.C. at the turn of this century.

Discussion.   In class, compare your reactions in groups of five or six. Appoint a recorder to keep track of similarities or differences, consensus or disagreement, arising from the discussion. The recorder may summarize your group discussion for the rest of the class later.

Freewriting.   After discussion, freewrite for 10 to 15 minutes about similarities or differences in preliminary readings of this selection. Read your freewriting in groups of two to four.

SUMMARIZING

1. Create a preliminary analysis of the Gatewood reading selection with a scratchline of topics. Note explicit transition words, phrases, sentences, or paragraphs.
2. Note what Gatewood does (rhetorically) at these transition points. Summarize his central point, rhetorical purpose, and means of development from your notes so far.
3. Compare summaries in your groups.

FOCUSED CRITICAL READING

1. What are the defining features of the black aristocracy Gatewood describes?
2. What was the attitude towards "mixed blood" in upper-class black society in the late nineteenth century?
3. How did attitudes towards "colored" men change in the early twentieth century, according to Gatewood?

Joyce Carol Oates

Is Laughter Contagious?

———◆———

The following short story originally appeared in Harper's *in 1991. For information about the author, turn to the prefatory note to "Rape and the Boxing Ring," page 97.*

Is laughter contagious? Driving on North Pearl Street, Franklin Village, Mrs. D. began suddenly to hear laughter on all sides, a wash of laughter gold-spangled like coins, just perceptibly louder issuing from the rear of her car, and she found herself smiling, her brooding thoughtful expression erased as if by force, on the verge of spontaneous laughter herself, for isn't there a natural buoyancy to the heart when we hear laughter? even, or particularly, the laughter of strangers? even an unexpected, inexplicable, mysterious laughter?—though Mrs. D. understood that the laughter surrounding her was in no way mysterious, at least its source was in no way mysterious, for, evidently, she had forgotten to switch off the car radio the last time she had driven the car, and the laughter was issuing from the radio's speakers, the most powerful of which was in the rear of the Mercedes.

What were they laughing about, these phantom radio-people?

Men's laughter?—and, here and there, the isolated sound of a woman's higher-pitched laughter?—delicious, cascading, like a sound of icicles touching?

Though laughing by this time herself, Mrs. D., who was a serious person, with a good deal on her mind—and most of it private, secret, not to be shared even with Mr. D.—switched the radio off, preferring silence.

There.

Christine Delahunt. Thirty-nine years old. Wife, mother. Recently returned to work—a "career." A woman of moral scruples, but not prim, puritanical, dogmatic. Isn't that how Mrs. D. has defined herself to herself? Isn't Mrs. D., in so defining herself, one of us?—determined, for no reason we can understand, to define ourselves to—ourselves?

As if we doubt that anyone else is concerned?

Mrs. D. was to tell us, certain of her friendly acquaintances. Last Thursday it seemed to begin. Did others in Franklin Village notice— that afternoon, sometime before six o'clock? The time of suburban car-errands, family-tasks, last-minute shopping, and pickups at the dry cleaners and drugstore, the pace of the waning day quickening, yes and Thursday is the day-preceding-Friday, when the week itself notoriously quickens, a panic-sensation to it, as a river seemingly placid and navigable begins to accelerate, visibly, as it approaches a cataract—though there is, yet, no clear sign of danger? no reason for alarm?

9   Outbursts of laughter. Gay infectious laughter. In the Franklin Food Mart, our "quality" grocery store, at one of the checkout counters when the deaf-and-dumb packer wearing the badge FRITZ (pasty-skinned, in his fifties; the Franklin Food Mart is one of several area businesses that have "made it a policy" to employ the handicapped) spilled a bag of fresh produce onto the floor, and Washington State winesaps, bright-dyed Florida navel oranges, hairy-pungent little kiwi-fruit, several pygmy-heads of Boston lettuce, a dozen Idaho red potatoes, a single California melon—all went tumbling, rolling, startling yet comical as the deaf-and-dumb packer gaped and blinked, standing frozen in a kind of terror that for all its public expression seemed to us, witnessing, to be private, thus somehow funnier, and the very customer who had paid extravagant prices for these items laughed, if a bit angrily; and other customers, seeing, burst into laughter, too; and the checkout cashier, and other cashiers, and employees of the store, peering over, craning their necks to see what the commotion is, their laughter tentative at first since the look in poor Fritz's eyes *was* terror wasn't it?—then exploding forth, an honest, candid, gut-laughter, not malicious surely, but, yes, *loud*?

10   Mrs. D. was at an adjacent checkout counter, methodically making out a check to the Franklin Food Mart, a weekly custom this is, perhaps it might better be called a blood-sacrifice, this week's check for—how can it be? $328.98 for an unexceptional week's shopping? for a family of four? no supplies for a dinner party? no beer, wine, liquor? not even any seafood? making out the check with resigned fingers when she heard the strange laughter rising around her, rising, erupting, childlike raucous laughter, and turning, smiling, wanting to join in, Mrs. D. saw the cause—a bag of groceries had overturned, things were rolling on the floor, and that look on that poor man's face, it *was* amusing, but Mrs. D. suppressed laughter for, oh dear, really it *wasn't* amusing, not at all, that poor man backing off and staring at the produce on the floor, paralyzed as everyone laughed so cruelly, what are people thinking of? how can it be? in the Franklin Food Mart of all places?

11   Are the Delahunts neighbors of ours? Not exactly.

12   We don't have "neighbors," in the old sense of that word, in Franklin Village. Our houses are constructed on three- and four-acre lots, which means considerable distance between houses, and with our elaborate landscaping (trees of all varieties, shrubs, twelve-foot redwood fences, electrically charged wire-mesh "deer-deterrent" fences)

it's possible for the residents of one house to be unable to glimpse even the facade of the house next door, certainly it's possible to go for years without glimpsing the faces of the people who live next door, unless, of course, and this is frequently the case, we encounter one another socially—on neutral territory, you might say. Nor have we sidewalks in residential Franklin Village. Nor have we streets, in the old sense of that word—we have "lanes," we have "drives," we have "passes," "circles," "courts," even "ways," but we do not have "streets."

Are Mr. and Mrs. Delahunt friends of ours? Not exactly. 13

We don't have "friends," in the old sense of that word, in Franklin 14 Village. Most of us are relatively new here, and a number of us are scheduled to move soon. Spring is the busiest time for moving! (Of course there are residents in this area who are known as "old-time." Who can recall, for instance, when the Franklin Hills Shopping Mall was nothing but an immense tract of open, wild, useless land, and when Main Street in the Village was residential from Pearl Street onward, and when Route 26 was a mere country highway!) Thus the majority of us make no claims to have (or to be) "friends"—but we *are* "friendly acquaintances" of one another and we *are* social. Very!

The Delahunts, Mr. and Mrs., became friendly acquaintances of 15 ours within days of their arrival. They are highly respected, warmly regarded, attractive, energetic, invited almost immediately to join the Franklin Hills Golf Club and the yet more prestigious Franklin Hills Tennis Club. Mr. D. moved his family here three years ago from Greenwich, Connecticut—or was it Grosse Pointe, Michigan?—when he became sales director at W.W.C. & M., and Mrs. D. has recently begun public relations work part-time, for our Republican Congressman Gordon Frayne—Gordon's the man whom the papers so frequently chide, urging him to "upscale" his image. The Delahunts live in a six-bedroom French Normandy house on Fairway Circle, their fourteen-year-old daughter, Tracey, and their eleven-year-old son, Jamey, both attend Franklin Hills Day School. Mrs. D., like many of us, tries to participate in parent-teacher activities at the school, but—when on earth is there *time?*

"Upscaling" Gordon Frayne's image is a challenge, Mrs. D. laugh- 16 ingly, if somewhat worriedly, confesses. But Gordy Frayne—some folks even call him Gordo—wins elections. He's a big-hearted ruddy-faced shooting-from-the-hip character, often in the headlines and on television, one or another controversy, last year he was interviewed on network television and made a statement warning that "ethnic minorities" had better man their own oars "or the venerable Ship of State's gonna capsize and sink"—which naturally led to protests from certain quarters but a good deal of support from other quarters. Mrs. D., like other associates and friendly acquaintances of Gordon Frayne's, has learned to frown as she smiles at his witticisms, just slightly reprovingly, as

Franklin Village women often do, she has unconsciously mastered this response, this facial expression, as adroitly as any professional actress—"Oh Gordy! Oh *really!*" It was at a party on Saturday night (the Saturday following the Thursday) that Gordy launched into one of his comical diatribes, the guy could have been a stand-up comedian for sure, cruel but ingenious mimicry of Jesse Jackson (an old routine, but a favorite), and the latest of his AIDS jokes . . . and most, though not all, of the company laughed, Mrs. D. among them, shocked, yes, but not wanting to be a prude, or to seem a prude; but smiling, shaking her head, avoiding the others' eyes as in a communal complicity, but thinking why, why, why, and what will come of this?

17   Five girls from the Franklin Hills Day School jogging on Park Ridge Road, Monday after school, pumping legs and arms, high-held heads, shorts and loose-fitting school T-shirts and identical expensive jogging shoes, and according to the girls' testimonies after the "vehicular assault" they were running single file, they were keeping to the left side of the road, facing oncoming traffic, careful to keep off the road itself and to run on the asphalt-paved shoulder. As usual one of the girls was falling behind, there were three girls running close together, then, a few yards behind them, the fourth, and approximately twenty feet behind her the fifth, poor Bonnie, Bonnie S., fourteen years old, second year in the "upper form" at the Day School. Bonnie S. is a few pounds overweight, not fat, the most accurate word would be plump but who wants to be plump? who can bear to be plump? fourteen years old and plump in Franklin Village, New York?—poor Bonnie S., whom the other girls like well enough, feel sort of sorry for, she's sweet she tries so hard she's so generous but it's pathetic, Bonnie trying to keep up with the tall thin girls, the girls she envies, letting it be known at school that her problem isn't overeating it's glandular it's "genetic— like fate," and maybe that's true since none of Bonnie's classmates ever sees her eating anything other than apples, carrot sticks, narrow slices of honeydew melon, she'll devour fleshy-fruit and rind both—poor Bonnie S.! (But *is* her weight problem "glandular"? Maybe she binges?—in secret?—tries to stick her finger down her throat and vomit it up?—but can't quite *succeed*?—enough to make a difference?) In any case, there was Bonnie S. running fifth in the line of girls, breathless, clumsy, a sweaty sheen to her round flushed face, a glazed took to her damp brown eyes, and the carload of boys swerved around the curve, that curve just beyond Grouse Hill Lane, six older students from the Day School jammed together in a newly purchased white Acura. The girls could hear the radio blasting heavy-metal rock even before the car came into sight, they could hear the boys yelling and laughing as the car bore down upon them, they saw the faces of the boys in the front seat clearly, wide grins, gleeful, malicious eyes, a raised beer can or

two, then the girls were screaming, scattering. It was Bonnie S. who was the target, poor Bonnie arousing male derision pumping away there twenty feet behind the others, poor plump sweaty Bonnie S. with her expression of incredulous shock and terror as the white car aimed for her, boyish-prankish braying laughter, she threw herself desperately to the left, the car skidded by, missing the screaming girl by perhaps a single inch, then righted itself, regained the road, on shrieking tires it sped away and there was Bonnie S., lying insensible in the shallow concrete drainage ditch like something tossed down, bleeding so profusely from a gash in her forehead that the first of her friends to reach her nearly fainted.

Tracey Delahunt tells her mother afterward, she'll confess to her mother solely, knowing her mother will understand, or, failing to understand—for who after all *can* understand?—will sympathize with the hungry wish to understand. "It happened so fast—oh God!—we looked back and there was Bonnie sort of *flying* off the road like something in a kid's cartoon—and it was horrible—it was just, just horrible, but—" lowering her teary eyes, thick-lashed tawny-green eyes Mrs. D. thinks are far more beautiful than her own, though closely resembling her own, "—sort of, in a way—oh God!—*comical* too."   18

Pressing her fingertips hard against her lips but unable to keep from bursting into a peal of hysterical laughter.   19

Three days later, the most upsetting incident of all.   20

Not that Mrs. D. allowed herself to think of it very much afterward. Certainly not obsessively. She isn't that type of mother—the obsessive, neurotic mother. Fantasizing about her children, worrying, suspicious.   21

She'd entered the house from the rear, as usual. About to step into the kitchen when she'd overheard, coming up from the basement, the "family room" in the basement, the sound of juvenile laughter, boys' laughter, and ordinarily she would not have paused for a moment since Jamey and his friends often took over that room after school to watch videos, yes some of the videos the boys watched were questionable, yes Mrs. D. knew and, yes, she'd tried to exercise some restraint while at the same time she'd tried not to be, nor even to appear to be, censorious and interfering, but that day there was something chilling about the tone of the boys' laughter, and wasn't there, beneath it, another sound?—as of a creature *bleating?*—a queer high-pitched sound that worried Mrs. D. so she went to the door of the family room (which was shut) and pressed her ear against it, hearing the laughter, the giggling, more distinctly, and the other sound too, and carefully, almost timidly—she, Christine Delahunt, nearly forty years old, wife, mother, self-respecting surely?—self-determined surely?—opening a door timidly in her own house?—and saw there a sight that froze her in her tracks even as, in that instant, she was already shoving it from her,   22 banishing it from her consciousness, denying its power to qualify her love for her son: for there were Jamey and several of his boy friends, eighth-graders at the Day School whose faces Mrs. D. knew well, Evan, Allen, Terry, red-haired impish Terry, and who was there with them? a girl? a stranger? and *strange*?—slightly older than the boys, with dull coarse features, eyes puckered at the corners, wet-dribbly mouth, no one Mrs. D. knew or had ever glimpsed before, and this girl was sprawled on her back on the braided "colonial"-style carpet in front of the fireplace, in the Delahunts' family room, her plump knees raised, and spread, naked from the waist down, and what was red-haired Terry doing?—poking something (too large to be a pencil, an object plastic and chunky, was it a child's play baseball bat?), or trying to poke something, into the girl's vagina?—while the other boys, as if transfixed, crouched in a circle, staring, blinking, grinning, giggling.

23   Mrs. D. cried, without thinking, "Oh what are you doing! Boys! Jamey! And you—you filthy, disgusting *girl*!"

24   Her voice was unlike any voice she'd ever heard springing from her. Breathless, disbelieving, angry, wounded.

25   She slammed the door upon the children's startled-guilty-grinning faces and fled. Upstairs.

26   That evening, at dinner, not a word! not a word! not a word! to Jamey, who, frightened, subdued, ate his food almost shyly, and cast looks of appeal to Mrs. D., who behaved as—as usual?—knowing that the child *knew*.

27   "I'm so afraid."

28   Mrs. D. was sitting, yes in the family room, which Mr. D. preferred to call the "recreation" room, with a drink in her hand. Her voice was quiet, apologetic.

29   Mr. D. sipped his drink. Peered at the newspaper. Said, vague, but polite, "Yes?"

30   "Harry. I'm so afraid."

31   "Well, all right."

32   Mr. D. was scanning the paper with increasing impatience.

33   "Christ, it's always the same! AIDS, crack, crime! 'Ghetto!'" He squinted at a photograph of several black youths being herded into a police van, he laughed harshly. "*I'm* a subscriber, for Christ's sake, d'you think these punks subscribe? Why the hell am I always reading about *them*?"

34   Upstairs a telephone rang. Tracey's private number.

35   Mrs. D. raised her glass to her lips but did not sip from it. She feared the taste of it—that first slip-sliding taste. She pressed her fingertips to her eyes and sat very still.

After a few minutes Mr. D. inquired, glancing in her direction even as his attention remained on the newspaper, "Chris—are you all right?" 36

"I'm so afraid." 37

"Cramps, eh? Migraine?" 38

"I'm *afraid.*" 39

Mr. D. was scanning the editorial page. A sudden smile illumi- 40 nated his face. He nodded, then, suddenly bored, let the newspaper fall. "Everyone has an *opinion*. 'Put your money where your mouth is' my father used to say."

Mr. D. rose—majestically. A solid figure, ham-thighed, with a 41 faintly flushed face, quick eyes. At its edges Mr. D.'s face appeared to have eroded but his mouth was still that "sculpted" mouth which Mrs. D., a very long time ago, so long ago now as to seem laughable, like a scene in a low-budget science-fiction film, had once avidly, ravenously, *insatiably* kissed.

Mr. D. said, walking away, "Two Bufferin. That'll do it." 42

After dinner, rinsing dishes and setting them carefully into the 43 dishwasher, Mrs. D. smiled tentatively at her reflection in the window above the sink. Why was she afraid? Wasn't she being a bit silly? Where, so often recently, she was thinking of what she was *not* thinking of, now, abruptly, she was *not* thinking of what she was *not* thinking of.

Elsewhere in the house, issuing from the family room, and from 44 Tracey's room upstairs, laughter rippled, peaked—television laughter by the sound of it.

Simple boredom with the subject, maybe. 45

Which subject? 46

Mr. H., father of one of the girls who had been jogging on Park 47 Ridge Road on the day of the infamous "vehicular assault," telephoned Mr. D. another time, and, another time, Mr. D. took the call in private, the door to his study firmly shut; and, as they were undressing for bed that night, when Mrs. D. asked cautiously what had been decided, Mr. D. replied affably, "We don't get involved."

Mrs. D. had understood from the very first, even as Tracey was 48 sobbing in her arms, that, given the litigious character of Franklin Hills, this would be the wisest, as it was the most practical, course of action; she gathered too, as things developed, despite Tracey's protestations and bouts of tears, temper, and hysteria, that Tracey concurred, as her girl friends, apart from Bonnie, concurred, perhaps even before their worried parents advised them, yet she heard herself saying weakly, "Oh Harry—if Tracey *saw* those boys' faces, Tracey wants to *say*," and Mr. D., yawning, stretching, on his way into his bathroom, nodded vaguely in her direction and said, "Set the alarm for 6:15, hon, will you?—the limo's picking me up at 6:45."

49   Tracey no longer discusses the incident with Mr. and Mrs. D. *Ugly!—horrible!—nightmare!—never never forget!*—she restricts all discussions of it to her girl friends, as they restrict their discussions of it too.

50   That is, the girls who were witnesses to the incident, not Bonnie S., to whom it happened. Not pathetic Bonnie S., to whom they no longer speak, much, at all.

51   For weeks, red-haired Terry was banished from the Delahunts' house. Not that Mrs. D. spoke of such a banishment, or even suggested it to Jamey, who watched her cautiously, one might say shrewdly, his gaze shifting from her if she chanced to look at him.

52   No need to chastise and embarrass the poor child, Mrs. D. has begun to think. He's a good decent sensitive civilized child, he *knows* how much he has upset me.

53   Poor Mrs. K.!—poor "Vivvie"!

54   Since the start of her problem eighteen months ago, the first mastectomy, and the second mastectomy, and then the chemotherapy treatments, her circle of friendly acquaintances has shrunken; and those who visit her, primarily women, have had difficulties.

55   Yes it's so sad it's *so* sad.

56   Vivvie Kern of all women.

57   A few of us visited her at the hospital, some of us waited to visit her at home, it's awkward not knowing what to do or to say, it sometimes seems there isn't anything *to* do or to say, and there's the extra burden of having to exchange greetings with Mr. K., who appears almost resentful, reproachful, that's how men are sometimes in such cases, husbands of ex-prom-queen-type women, and Mrs. K. was, a bit boastfully, one of these. Of course it's wisest to avoid *the subject,* but how can you avoid *the subject* with that poor man staring at you unsmiling?—just *staring*?

58   But it's lovely in their new solarium, at least. So much to look at, outside and in, and you aren't forced to look at *her,* I mean exclusively at *her,* poor thing! chattering away so bravely!—and that gorgeous redblond hair she'd been so vain about mostly fallen out now, the wig just sort of *perches* there on her head, and her eyebrows are drawn on so crudely, and with her eyelashes gone it's *naked eyes* you have to look at if you can't avoid it, but in such close quarters and with the woman leaning toward you sometimes even gripping your arm as if for dear life how can you avoid it?—except by not visiting poor Mrs. K. at all?

59   (Of course, some in our circle have stopped seeing her, and it's embarrassing, how painful, Mrs. K. joking to disguise her bitterness. Saying, "My God, it isn't as if I have AIDS after all, this isn't *contagious,* you know!")

Visiting Mrs. K. in late June, having procrastinated for weeks, Mrs. 60
D. was nervously admiring the numerous hanging plants in the solarium, listening to Mrs. K. speaking animatedly of mutual acquaintances, complaining good-naturedly of the Hispanic cleaning woman she and Mrs. D. shared, perhaps half-listening was more accurate, not thinking of what she was not thinking but she *was* thinking of the ceremonies of grief, death, mourning, how brave of human beings yet how futile, how futile yet how brave, for here was a terminally ill woman now speaking aggressively of regaining her lost weight—"muscle tone" she called it—and returning to the Tennis Club, and Mrs. D. smiled at the woman's wide smiling mouth, a thin mouth now and the lips garishly crimson, yes but you must keep up the pretense, yes but you must be brave, and smile, and nod, and agree, for isn't it too terrible otherwise?

Sharp-eyed, Mrs. K. has noticed that Mrs. D. has another time 61
glanced surreptitiously at her wristwatch, as a starving animal can sense the presence of food, however inaccessible, or even abstract, so does Mrs. K, sense her visitor's yearning to escape, thus she leans abruptly forward across the glass-topped table, nearly upsetting both their glasses of white wine, she seems about to bare her heart, *oh why does Vivvie do such things! with each of us, as if for the first and only time!* seizing Mrs. D.'s hand in her skeletal but strong fingers and speaking rapidly, intensely, naked bright-druggy eyes fixed upon Mrs. D.'s, thus holding her captive.

"...*can't* bear to think of leaving them...abandoning them...poor 62
Gene! poor Robbie!...devastated...unmoored...already Robbie's been having...only thirteen...the counselor he's been seeing...specializes in adolescent boys...says it's a particularly sensitive age...traumatic... for a boy to lose...a mother."

Mrs. D., though giving the impression of having been listening 63
closely, and being deeply moved, has, in fact, not been listening to Mrs. K.'s passionate outburst very closely. She has been thinking of, no she has *not* been thinking of. What?

With a startled, gentle little laugh, Mrs. D. says, "Oh—do you 64
really think so? *Really?*"

Frightened, Mrs. K. says, "Do I really think—what?" 65

Calmly and unflinching, Mrs. D. looks the doomed woman in the 66
face for the first time.

"That your husband and son will be 'devastated' when you die? 67
That they will even miss you, much? I mean, after the initial shock— the upset to their routines?"

A long moment. 68

A *very* long moment. 69

Mrs. K. is staring incredulously at Mrs. D. Slowly, her fingers relax 70
their death-grip on Mrs. D.'s fingers. Her bright lips move, tremble— but no sound emerges.

71   It's as if, in this instant, the oxygen in the solarium is being sucked out. There's a sense of something, an invisible flame, a radiance, about to go *out*.

72   "Oh, my goodness!" Mrs. D. exclaims, rising. "I must leave, I still have shopping to do, it's after *six*."

73   She would tell us, confide in us, yes we'd had similar experiences lately, unsettling experiences, sudden laughter like sneezes, giggles like carbonated bubbles breaking the surface of something you'd believed was firm, solid, permanent, unbreakable, the way in her car that day, fleeing Mrs. K., Mrs. D. found herself driving like a drunken woman, dizzy-drunk, scary-drunk, but also *happy*-drunk as she never is in real life, she was hearing laughter in the Mercedes, washing tickling over her, so funny! so wild! you should have seen that woman's face! that bully! that bore! how dare she! intimidating us! touching us! like that! how dare! as if I wasn't, for once, telling the truth!

74   Hardly a five-minute drive from the Kerns' house on Juniper Way to the Delahunts' house on Fairway Circle, but Mrs. D. switched on the radio to keep her company.

75   *There.*

Reading and Writing Activities

PRELIMINARY RESPONSE

Notes.   As you read, record your reactions (questions or comments) to the short story "Is Laughter Contagious?" in your reading journal.

Discussion.   In class, compare your reactions in groups of five or six. Appoint a recorder to keep track of similarities or differences, consensus or disagreement, arising from the discussion. The recorder may summarize your group discussion for the rest of the class later.

Freewriting.   After discussion, freewrite for 10 to 15 minutes about similarities or differences in preliminary reading of the story. Read your freewriting in groups of two to four.

SUMMARIZING

1. Create a preliminary analysis of the Oates short story with a scratchline of characters and events. Note explicit transition words, phrases, sentences, or paragraphs.

2. Summarize the central characters and events in her story.
3. Compare summaries in your groups.

FOCUSED CRITICAL READING

1. What are the physical characteristics of the "other," the outsider, in each of the narratives in "Is Laughter Contagious?"
2. What are the physical characteristics of the "subjects," the insiders, in these narratives?
3. How does the type of laughter in each of the narratives help shape meaning in the text?
4. What is the extent of the narrator's involvement with family and acquaintances?

Joel Dreyfuss

The Invisible Immigrants: Haitians in America Are Industrious, Upwardly Mobile and Vastly Misunderstood

———————◆———————

Joel Dreyfuss emigrated to the United States from Haiti in the 1950s. His family settled in New York, where, according to Dreyfuss, the community of Haitian immigrants "was small, consisting mostly of mixed-race members of the so-called elite"; he adds that his family was "typical of the ethnic stew that prevailed in Haiti's middle class." The following article was published in The New York Times Magazine *in 1993.*

1   "Where are you from?" In multiethnic America, the question is a way to classify you: to embrace or dismiss you. For those of us who came to America from Haiti 20 or 30 years ago, the question is usually a signal to brace ourselves. If our interrogators knew anything about our native land just a few hundred miles south of Miami, it was not likely to be very positive. "Aha!" people would say once we had answered, "Voodoo. Poverty. Papa Doc." It was a snapshot that, denying the complexity of our country, imprisoned us in a stereotype. Today the response is "Aha! AIDS. Boat People."

2   For 12 years, the news media have dutifully reported the thousands of black people packed to the gunwales of leaky boats trying to make their way to Florida or, once there, quarantined because they are H.I.V. positive.

3   Despite the stereotypes and our having come from the poorest country in the Western Hemisphere, we Haitians have established ourselves in the United States as an industrious, upwardly mobile immigrant group with a strong work ethic. We are cabdrivers and college professors, schoolteachers and police officers, stockbrokers and baby sitters, soldiers and politicians, bankers and factory workers. "By and large, one can compare the Haitian immigration experience in the United States to that of other, more celebrated, immigrant groups," says Michel S. Laguerre, an anthropologist of Haitian origin who teaches at the Univer-

sity of California at Berkeley. "They are young, aggressive, even pushy, and to that extent, not very different from other immigrants."

There are about 290,000 who claimed Haitian ancestry in the 1990 census, but that does not include the tens of thousands who are here illegally or second- and third-generation Haitian-Americans who simply identify themselves as black, Laguerre explains. Even legal immigrants may not want to admit to roots that go back to a Caribbean nation so often associated with superstition and poverty. Laguerre, who has written extensively about Haitians in America, estimates that as many as 1.2 million people in the United States are of Haitian ancestry.

The two largest communities are in Southern Florida (300,000) and the New York metropolitan area (500,000), with smaller communities in Boston and Chicago. Yet, for the most part, Haitians are invisible immigrants, hidden by the banality of success. Detailed data from the 1990 census has not yet been released, but experts say that few Haitian immigrants are on welfare. And police say that even fewer get in trouble with the law.

This is not to suggest that all is wonderful for Haitians in America. Many are undocumented, trapped in fear and dead-end jobs. Behind the facade of pride and achievement, there is a litany of social problems: battered women, homeless families, economic exploitation. But like most immigrants, Haitians busy themselves in the pursuit of the American dream.

"Even some of those who came on boats are homeowners now," says the Rev. Thomas Wenski, director of the Pierre Toussaint Haitian Catholic Center in the Little Haiti district of Miami. "It's a tribute to the Haitians' resourcefulness and their self-discipline."

My own family settled in New York in the 1950's. The Haitian community was small, consisting mostly of mixed-race members of the so-called elite. Many could be mistaken easily for white or Hispanic. Back then, when New Yorkers learned we were Haitian, the reaction was mostly bewilderment. Most had never heard of Haiti, and they knew even less about it. "Tahiti?" I was asked more than once. We were proud to tell them about the world's first black republic, about our own struggle for independence and about Alexandre Dumas, the author of "The Three Musketeers" and the son of a Haitian general.

We had to explain that Haiti's middle and upper middle classes had their unique melting pot: Africans, Europeans, Arabs, Asians, Jews. That yes, most light-skinned Haitians were members of the elite, but so were some very dark-skinned Haitians. Status back home was a matter of history and family and circumstance, much more complex than the simplistic racial definitions in the United States. But we had no easy explanation for the sharp disparities of power and income back home, of the even sharper division among social classes—and of the treacherous politics that had forced us to America.

10   My family was typical of the ethnic stew that prevailed in Haiti's middle class. Emmanuel Dreyfuss, a Jew from Amiens, France who had served in the French Army in Indochina, sailed west in the 1880's in a wave of European emigrants and landed in Haiti. He would never confirm any relation to Capt. Alfred Dreyfus, the French officer whose anti-Semitic persecution had outraged the world and bitterly divided France, but my father remembered that mere mention of the case was enough to set his father's pince-nez quivering and his hands shaking. Dreyfuss married into a fair-skinned and class-conscious family of South American and French origin, which traced its roots in Haiti back to the 1700's.

11   My mother came from an equally haughty black family in Haiti's north, where Henri Christophe, one of the three leaders of the struggle for independence, had ruled. In fact, one of my great-great-grand-fathers had helped build the Citadelle, Christophe's mountaintop fortress in the early 1800's, and another, Jean-Baptiste Riché, who had been a general in Christophe's army, served as a president of Haiti in the 1840's. But all that history and all that pride counted for naught in America. I remember well as a 7- or 8-year-old my bewilderment when my mother tried to explain why a cab wouldn't pick us up at the Miami airport because we were "colored." America—at least on matters of race—was a great social leveler.

12   Our community was centered on the West Side of Manhattan, mostly around 86th Street along Broadway and Amsterdam Avenue (West End Avenue and Riverside Drive landlords would not often rent to blacks—even exotic, light-skinned foreigners with French accents). A number of families managed to congregate at the Bretton Hall on 86th and Broadway and the Oxford Hotel at 88th and Amsterdam. My sisters and I went to the local Catholic schools. As in most families, our parents spoke French to us, Creole to each other, and did their best to preserve the memories of home. The nostalgia was most obvious at the loud Sunday dinners with steaming dishes of our savory foods from home—spicy chicken and goat, rice and djondjon, a dried mushroom—Haitian music, loud arguments in Creole and French and much laughter.

13   Some of our neighbors came from other highly respected Haitian families, but in New York, they were just blacks who took care of other people's children, cleaned other people's apartments, worked in the garment factories around 34th Street or drove cabs. The weekend gatherings were an opportunity to regain self-respect, to cast off the burden of being black in a white world and to recall what they had lost: privilege, status, servants, warm weather. Few from that old middle and upper class had plans to set down roots in America.

14   The first hint that our stay might be long came when the nature of the Haitian community began to change in the 1960's. Since François Duvalier had taken power in 1957, many of my parents' friends had

expected him to be ousted in a matter of weeks or months. After all, that was the pattern for Haitian presidents. But his regime, swept into office on a vague platform of "black power," became unusually tenacious. Duvalier instituted a reign of terror uncommon even for Haiti. Schoolchildren were bused to public executions. Opponents, real or imagined, were beaten or killed with impunity. Those who had stayed behind lived in daily fear of arbitrary arrest. The Tontons Macoutes, Duvalier's vicious militia, swaggered through the towns and villages in dark glasses and denim suits, with pistols tucked in their belts.

New arrivals to our community from Haiti were now politicians   15
and professionals who had finally grasped the scope of Duvalier's brutality. One frequent Sunday guest was a former Senator who had been forced to flee after running afoul of the regime. He came from a prominent political family and he lived for politics. He and his cronies crowded the benches on a Broadway traffic island on weekends, naming each other to hypothetical cabinets and reading position papers out loud in flawless French, waiting for the change of Government. But on weekdays, the Senator pushed a hand truck through the bustling traffic of the garment district. Sharp-tongued Haitians were merciless. "Make way for the Senator," they shouted as he maneuvered down Seventh Avenue. "Make way for Senator Broadway."

After "Papa Doc" Duvalier died in 1971 and his 19-year-old son,   16
Jean-Claude, was placed at the head of the government as "President-for-Life," the exodus accelerated. Many of the new arrivals were working-class Haitians, chased out by the realization that no improvement in their lives was likely under a regime led by a boy more interested in fast cars and women than in public works and budgets. The stream of refugees became a flood, many of them illegals who came on tourist visas. They were not "people we know," the elite sniffed.

The West Side was no longer the Haitian haven. Gentrification had   17
priced the neighborhood out of reach. People began moving to Flushing and Elmhurst, in Queens. The new, poorer arrivals settled around Nostrand and Flatbush avenues in Crown Heights. Florida, with employment opportunities at Miami Beach resorts and weather reminiscent of Haiti's, became a new center of Haitian activity.

"The boat people are a tragic aspect of Haitian life," says one Hai-   18
tian immigrant. "But most of us are not boat people and we hate being lumped with them." I can understand his anger. The majority of Haitians arrive in the United States by plane. The daily American Airlines Flight No. 658 between Port-au-Prince and Kennedy Airport disgorges passengers who reflect the range of Haitians living in the United States. There are those who are returning from visiting relatives back home: the prosperous upper-middle-class Haitians are deliberately casual in their designer jeans and resort wear; the working-class immigrants wear their Sunday best and carry the bags of food from home that they hope

to slip by alert customs officials. Then there are the new arrivals, often shivering in their thin suits and dresses and glancing about with open anxiety for the relatives and friends who are supposed to meet them.

19   In the Haitian enclaves of New York and Miami, a strong entrepreneurial spirit has spawned grocery stores, barbershops, restaurants, real-estate firms and medical clinics. Bustling shopping districts have taken on a strong Caribbean flavor, laced with Haiti's African-inflected Creole and driven by the beat of merengues and compas. Haitian weekly papers report the minutiae of political maneuverings back home. Radio and cable television programs air heated political debates and, increasingly, instructions on coping with life in America. Farther north, the computer boom along Route 128 in Massachusetts has created plenty of factory jobs for Haitians.

20   The latest wave of Haitian immigrants comes on the bicentennial of the first. Haiti, then called St. Domingue, was the richest of the French colonies. In the 1790's, the black population of the island revolted against slavery and there was a panicked exodus. Thousands of whites, free blacks and slaves fled to American seaports, contributing to large French-speaking communities in New Orleans, Norfolk, Va., Baltimore, New York and Boston.

21   Immigrants from Haiti who made their mark in the United States during the 18th and 19th centuries include Jean Baptiste Point du Sable, a trapper who settled on the shore of Lake Michigan and became the founder of the city of Chicago. There was also Pierre Toussaint, whom the Vatican is considering naming the first black saint from the United States. Toussaint, a devout Catholic, came to New York as the slave of a French family in 1787. He became a prominent hairdresser to New York's rich, and a major fund-raiser who helped the sick and the destitute.

22   France remained the center of the universe for most educated Haitians. Only a few middle-class Haitians chose the United States, which the elite saw through Francophile eyes as a nation bursting with energy but lacking in civilization. My own father was considered something of a rebel when he decided to come to America in 1927 to accept a scholarship to graduate school at Yale. During World War II, with access to Europe cut off by the war, growing numbers of Haitian scholars came here. Felix Morisseau-Leroy, a renowned poet and playwright, lived at the International House on Riverside Drive with a half-dozen men and women who would be Haiti's brightest literary stars in the postwar years. Morisseau-Leroy recalls few racial incidents. "We were treated well," he says. "We had the feeling that the Americans had been told to be nice to us."

23   The slow migration of Haitians to the United States might have remained unnoticed by most Americans had not the first bodies washed up on the Florida coast in 1979. The very poor were now deter-

mined to escape the dictatorship of Baby Doc, which had changed the emphasis of Government from terror to just plain larceny. Blaise Augustin, a native of St. Louis-du-Nord, an impoverished town in Haiti's northwest, saved enough money to take a boat to the Bahamas in 1977. When the newly independent island began expelling Haitians, Augustin headed for Florida. He was one of several dozen Haitians pushed off an overcrowded boat by a panicked smuggler. A woman and her four children drowned. Augustin managed to make it to the Florida shore. The son of peasant farmers, Augustin is a small-boned slim man with an uncanny resemblance to exiled President Jean-Bertrand Aristide. Like many boat people, he has unusual energy.

Policy makers argue about whether the Haitians are economic or political refugees. Augustin's description of the obstacles he faced back home explain why a simple answer is difficult. "If you saved some money and bought some cement blocks to add to your house or opened a small grocery story, everyone noticed," he says. "Sooner or later, the local Tontons Macoutes or chef de section (a regional military chieftain) approached you for a loan. If you refused, he might denounce you as an opponent of the Government and have you arrested. 24

"In Haiti, it's very hard to move up," says Augustin. "The U.S. is a country with a lot of complications, but if you're smart, you can get ahead." 25

Today, Augustin is an outreach worker for a Catholic church in Pompano Beach, 20 miles north of Miami. He owns his home and a car. He and his wife have opened a small variety store to serve the town's growing Haitian population. He has taken a course in photography and now takes pictures at weddings and baptisms. The store shares a tiny mall with a sleepy Haitian restaurant and a Haitian doctor's office. It stocks Haitian foods, records and tapes. An employee helps Augustin's wife with the store while he is engaged in church business. "I have a vision of becoming a business man," says Augustin, modestly. 26

Augustin's story—and his ambition—are repeated again and again in south Florida. Dr. David Abellard, who lives a few miles farther north along the Florida coast, is a fine example of the immigrant success story Americans like to celebrate. As a boy growing up in a hilltop village, he woke before dawn and walked miles in bare feet to attend school. On Saturdays, he helped his peasant mother sell vegetables in the market. Today, he has a profitable medical practice in Lake Worth, 60 miles north of Miami. A steady stream of affluent patients passes through his waiting room. Abellard has no nostalgia about home. "I had influential friends," he says, citing connections made in high school and at the University of Haiti, where he earned degrees in law and medicine. "I could have been a minister. But it would have been very unstable. I might have been shot." 27

28 Little Haiti, which tourist-conscious Miami officials have touted as an example of immigrant entrepreneurship, may have passed its peak. The several blocks of shops, restaurants, travel agencies, community centers, law offices and doctors' clinics that display signs in French, Creole and English seem worse for wear. A bad imitation of Port-au-Prince's famous Iron Market sits seedy and half-empty.

29 Haitians in New York have also begun to abandon their traditional enclaves in Manhattan, Queens and Brooklyn. The ads in Haiti-Observateur, the largest Haitian paper in the United States, with a circulation of 30,000, are directed to Haitians in northern New Jersey, Spring Valley, N.Y., Nassau and Suffolk counties in New York, Boston and Montreal.

30 Radio and television are the glue that holds these geographically dispersed communities together. Programs like "Moment Creole," which airs every Sunday on WLIB-AM from 10 A.M. to 4 P.M., and "Eddy Publicité" on WNWK-FM, offer a mix of Haitian music, news and a discussion of community issues. There is even a radio "underground," subcarrier stations that require a special radio, but offer freewheeling discussion, call-in shows, news, gossip and nuts-and-bolts services like death announcements. Radio Tropical (50,000 subscribers) and Radio Soleil d'Haiti (10,000 subscribers) both broadcast 24 hours a day over special radios that the stations sell to listeners for between $75 and $120. Several cable television programs have also begun to target Haitian audiences. Some focus on community or health issues—or politics. Others simply show videos made by Haitian performers.

31 The ability of broadcast media to reach an audience of a half a million interests Wilner Boucicault, 43, whose A&B Furniture & Appliances in Brooklyn is one of the largest Haitian-owned businesses in New York.

32 He has ambitions to help propel Haitian immigrants to the next important stage in their Americanization—politics. "Haitians are ready," says Boucicault, who came to New York from Haiti at age 19, attended New York University and eventually opened the store with a partner. "Since Aristide, Haitians have developed a political consciousness. They have to organize themselves here." He and other Haitians trace their American political awakening to April 20, 1990. That was the day more than 50,000 Haitians marched across the Brooklyn Bridge to City Hall. They were protesting the most damaging label yet attached to Haitians. The Centers for Disease Control and the American Red Cross had ruled that no Haitians could give blood because all Haitians were AIDS risks. That ruling, the only one ever applied to one nationality, was later rescinded.

33 The size of the march, and the ability of Haitian leaders to organize it, stunned New York's political establishment—and the organizers themselves. "We told the police we expected 5,000 people, but we hoped 25,000 would turn up," says Fritz Martial, a vice president at Inner City

Broadcasting. "When we saw the size of the crowd, we ran to the front of the line in panic." Now Martial, Boucicault and others are looking for a Haitian candidate to back for City Council from Brooklyn, which has the highest concentration of Haitians in New York.

Bringing no historical baggage to their American relationships, Haitians tend to get along with neighbors from different ethnic backgrounds. In Crown Heights, where American-born blacks and Hasidic Jews have been at odds, Haitians mention Jews as a model of effective political organization. Haitian stores sit side by side with shops owned by Dominicans and British West Indians. On Sundays, neatly dressed Jamaicans and Trinidadians, flow out of Methodist and Evangelical churches, shouting to their children in English patois. On the same streets, Haitians pour out of the Catholic churches, shouting caution in French and Creole to their suited and ribboned children. 34

Even Haitians like me, who have been in America far longer than in Haiti, retain a close identification with our native land. We agonize over the political turmoil there, and we rage over United States inaction. But while we look for ways to help, we have no plans to go back. Ghislain Gouraiges Jr., 34, and his family left Haiti when he was 8 years old. Gouraiges grew up in Albany, where his father taught at the State University. Today Gouraiges works for Citibank in Miami, where he manages the accounts of multimillionaires and looks the part: well-tailored pinstripes, suspenders, two-tone shirts and gold cufflinks. There is no trace of Haiti in his English and he has no ambition to return there. Yet, "I feel Haitian," he says. "One of the reasons I moved here was to be closer to Haiti." 35

For those who have difficulties grabbing the first rung of the ladder of American success, a group of self-help programs and social agencies is evolving. Haitian-Americans United for Progress sits in a nondescript storefront on a section of Linden Boulevard in Queens dominated by Haitian businesses. On a Saturday morning, the Haitian-American Women's Advocacy Network is meeting. They have contacted American feminist groups for advice and are drawing up a constitution and a charter. "Many Haitian women need help integrating themselves into American society," says Marie Thérèse Guilloteau, one of the organizers. "They have a different role here." 36

In Brooklyn, a community organizer, Lola Poisson, just won a $400,000 New York City grant to provide mental health services to Haitians and other Caribbean immigrants. Poisson says she wants to provide an "extended family" for Haitians, who often feel emotionally lost in New York. 37

At the Haitian Information Center on Flatbush Avenue, the entire staff is unpaid. Daniel Huttinot, one of the founders, says the organization was started to counter misinformation about Haiti and Haitians, but its staff soon learned that Haitians had more pressing needs. They 38 switched gears and now offer help with immigration problems, teaching language classes and courses in computers. In Miami, the Pierre Toussaint Haitian Catholic Center offers literacy classes, Sunday school, preparation for the high-school equivalency exam and help in job placement.

39   Getting these services is hardly unusual for new immigrants. What is remarkable is the involvement of Haitians, who came from a country where social services and philanthropy are usually left to foreign missionaries. In a way, this charity is a sign of their Americanization.

40   A subject of ambiguity for Haitians is race. Most are eager to talk about their country's role as the first independent black nation in the modern era. Even middle-class Haitians are now willing to acknowledge the deep African roots of Haitian culture. But they are less sure about the value of being categorized with African-Americans. Most will acknowledge that many of the obstacles they face are racial. "They want to force us to live in black neighborhoods by pricing us out of the white areas," complains Augustin, the young entrepreneur in Pompano Beach. "We need the help of black Americans to help save Haiti, and to help against what whites do to us here."

41   Yet, almost as quickly, he begins to delineate the differences he perceives between African-Americans and Haitians. "We have a different culture. We are completely different," says Augustin, echoing comments I hear frequently in discussions with Haitians. What these perceived differences are depends on what experience the Haitians have had with black Americans. Those in Miami's Little Haiti, which abuts impoverished Liberty City, often talk in stereotypes. "The blacks" are not clean, they say. They do not work. they don't care about their homes. When pressed, Haitians acknowledge that they have heard about the black middle class. But living near poor black neighborhoods that most successful blacks escaped long ago, many Haitians say they don't know any "good blacks."

42   Most Haitian-Americans seek a middle ground between assimilation and ethnic isolation. Edeline Léger, 15, and her sister Edna, 13, live in Lincroft, a New Jersey suburb. They were both born in the United States. Their father, Eddy, is a settlements manager for the brokerage firm of Kidder Peabody. Although the two girls have never been to Haiti, they are its staunch defenders. They write book reports in school on Haitian topics and don't hesitate to speak in defense of the country they've never seen. "We're not ashamed of Haiti," Edeline says. "We tell everybody we're Haitian."

43   I suspect that being Haitian teen-agers in a predominantly white suburb makes them exotic, as we were decades earlier. But I find myself comforted by their self-assertion. Haitians will change in America and they will learn to flex their new economic and political muscle. They are now moving more deeply into the mainstream, away from

Little Haiti to the Miami suburbs, from Brooklyn to Westchester, from the West Side to Long Island and New Jersey, from Boston to Newton and Brookline. But they seem in no danger of losing their identity. No one says "Tahiti?" any more when we say Haiti, and even the boat people label and the AIDS label will pass too. Someday the other Americans will even appreciate our role as a new link in the long chain of hyphenated Americans.

Reading and Writing Activities

PRELIMINARY RESPONSE

Notes. As you read, record your reactions in your reading journal (questions or comments) to "The Invisible Immigrants."

Discussion. In class, compare your reactions in groups of five or six. Appoint a recorder to keep track of similarities or differences, consensus or disagreement, arising from the discussion. The recorder may summarize your group discussion for the rest of the class later.

Freewriting. After discussion, freewrite for 10 to 15 minutes about similarities or differences in the preliminary readings of the essay. Read your freewriting in groups of two to four.

SUMMARIZING

1. Create a preliminary analysis of the Dreyfuss essay with a scratchline of topics. Note explicit transition words, phrases, sentences, or paragraphs.
2. Note what Dreyfuss does (rhetorically) at transition points. Summarize his central points, purpose, and means of development from your notes so far.
3. Compare summaries in your groups.

FOCUSED CRITICAL READING

1. In "The Invisible Immigrants," Joel Dreyfuss discusses different groups of Haitian immigrants in America. What might be his rhetorical purpose in telling the story of each group?
2. What might be Dreyfuss's rhetorical purpose in introducing the first group of immigrants, those who left Haiti in the 1700s, almost at the end of the essay?

3. Do you get a sense from Dreyfuss that the Haitians who have been in the United States for a comparatively long period of time have assimilated into mainstream American culture? Why or why not?
4. What role do the mass media play, according to Dreyfuss, in uniting Haitians? What might his purpose be in talking about the role of the media?

Deborah Dash Moore

New York Jews

◆

Deborah Dash Moore teaches in the Department of Religion at Vassar College. In 1981 she published At Home in America: Second Generation New York Jews, *from which the following selection has been excerpted.*

Second generation Jews developed a relationship of intimacy with the city; many even conducted a clandestine love affair with it. They succeeded in wedding their experiences as New Yorkers to their existence as Jews. Through the process of becoming New Yorkers—and by extension, also Americans—second generation Jews redefined the meaning of Jewishness. As they built new neighborhoods, pursued secular education in the public schools, organized their religious and philanthropic institutions, and entered the political system, they established the limits of their assimilation into American society. Participation in the myriad aspects of New York culture did not mark the decline of Jewish group life—as some had feared and others had hoped. Rather, as they became middle-class New Yorkers, second generation Jews created the framework for their persistence as an ethnic group. Most New York Jews persisted in associating with each other in secular and sectarian settings. They remained Jews and brought their children up as Jews. Only a few chose to intermarry and dissociate from the group, while an articulate handful struggled to secure recognition legitimating Jewish separateness.

Out of the second generation's encounter with the city emerged a new American Jew, one whose Jewishness was shaped by the city's peculiar dynamic. This Jew saw himself a part of and yet apart from New York. Irving Howe remembers the irony of this experience: "New York did not really exist for us as a city, a defined place we felt to be our own. Too many barriers intervened, too many kinds of anxiety." And yet, Howe admits, "while we thought of ourselves as exposed to the coldest winds of the coldest capitalist city—and in many, many ways we were—we still lived in a somewhat sheltered world." The protection came from the comforting shadows cast by neighborhood Jewish communities in the Bronx and Brooklyn. For if Jews felt uneasy in cosmopolitan Manhattan—if they thought of New York as an alien city—they also felt at home on the streets of their own neighborhoods. There they reconstructed Jewishness, shaping it to fit an American middle-class mode, adjusting it to the rigors of urban life, imbuing it with Jewish sentiments learned from their immigrant parents, and attaching it to the chain of Jewish history. The style and ethos of their ethnicity developed as the second generation acclimated itself to the fertile matrix of New York.

3   New York's multi-ethnic environment, its character as an immigrant entrepôt, and the changing interests of its ethnic groups, nourished this ethnicity. In New York, white Protestants struggled to uphold their American norm against succeeding waves of immigrants. A majority at the turn of the century, by 1935 they ranked third in population behind Catholics and Jews. Like Jews, New York Catholics dissented from the Protestant American norm. New York City Catholics supported parochial schools, acquiesced in the Church's ban against intermarriage, and maintained separate charitable and social organizations. Thus Irish Catholics, who persisted as an ethnic group in the city, established protective precedents for Jews who wanted to preserve Jewish group life. The New York situation supported Rabbi Mordecai M. Kaplan's observation that "a second environmental factor which indirectly yet effectively makes for the conservation of Jewish life in America is the presence in the body politic of a large and powerful group that insists upon remaining unassimilable." Referring to the Catholics, Kaplan argued that they "constitute a minority of the American people, but a minority too large, too well organized and too safely entrenched to have any apprehension about succumbing to attrition by the majority."

4   The city's neighborhood structure also facilitated the development of diverse ethnic cultures and organizations. Ethnic groups clustered in various sections of the city, endowing these areas with a distinctive character. Groups promoted their own associations in the ethnic enclaves; and New York Jews, too, evolved their particular ethnic pattern within these multi-ethnic, parochial boundaries. The city's neighborhood structure helped ethnic groups to synthesize their cultural values and associational patterns with their social and economic group interests. "The informal and formal social groupings that make up these communities are strengthened by the fact that Jews can talk about the garment business, Irish about politics and the civil service, Italians about the state of the trucking or contracting or vegetable business," Nathan Glazer and Daniel Patrick Moynihan point out. The confluence of the immigrant heritage and American environment in New York stimulated the growth of ethnic groups. New Yorkers in turn incorporated the ethnic character of their social associations into the city's social structure: its politics, economic activities, and residential patterns. Common job experiences, neighborhood living, and reliance on similar institutions crystallized ethnicity in New York City and reinforced the diverse patterns of association at its core. Ethnicity depended no less on

the strength of personal associational patterns than on the assumption of a common heritage.

If the city's social structure encouraged ethnic diversity and persis- 5
tence, the masses of Jews in the city sustained the vitality of a pluralist Jewish ethnicity. In New York there were many ways to be a Jew. Even within the immigrant milieu, Jews elaborated a wide range of alternatives, eschewing any consensus. As Howe astutely argues, "east European Jews brought with them considerable experience in creating 'secondary associations' that would cut through the confines, and limit the authority, of family and synagogue." Immigrant Jews "filled out the social spaces between family and state with a web of voluntary organizations." These secondary associations institutionalized a pluralist Jewish life. Immigrants had many choices among social groups which preserved a sense of peoplehood, "the essence of ethnicity." Initially an immigrant often grounded his Jewish identity through association with a *landsmanshaft,* an organization of fellow Jews from the same town or region of Europe. But increasingly immigrants discarded such parochial old-world commitments: many chose to build a Jewish life through socialism. Socialism offered them membership in an idealogical community that transcended the boundaries of local concerns even though it linked Jews through such institutional ties as the Workmen's Circle (a fraternal organization) and the garment workers' unions. Even immigrants eager to become Americans frequently discovered Jewish organizations directing the Americanization programs. These Jews often Americanized within a Jewish milieu: they studied with fellow Jews and were taught how to become Americans from Jewish immigrants who had preceded them. "Tacitly but shrewdly, the immigrant Jews improvised a loose pattern for their collective existence," Howe writes.

> Most wanted to maintain a distinctive Yiddish cultural life while penetrating individually into American society and economy; most wanted to insure their survival as a people while feeling free to break out of the ghetto; and most hoped for cultural and religious continuity while opting for a weak, even ramshackle community structure. Before the term became fashionable they made their way to a sort of "pluralism"—and the later decades proved them right.

Jewish residential concentration, since it threw masses of Jews 6
together in close confines, encouraged ideological disputes among groups who vied to shape the Jews' future. Immigrant Jews brought with them across the ocean multiple Jewish value systems. What enabled Zionists to debate Socialists, Anarchists to attack Orthodox, Americanizers to compete with Survivalists, Bundists to oppose Universalists, and Yiddishists to struggle with Hebraists was their com-

mon situation as Jewish immigrants in New York City. They shared the same streets and parceled out the street corners. Within these boundaries they succeeded in transplanting through secondary social structures a common realm of discourse.

While a huge immigrant quarter like the Lower East Side was divided into many smaller sections, the area appeared to have a certain unity, especially from the outside. Sociologist Peter Rose calls it "an urban equivalent of the shtetl," the small towns which immigrant Jews left behind in Europe. The New York immigrant quarter "came to be called ghetto, not by those who lived and worked and played out life's dreams there, but by the outsiders who peered into these 'exotic' and 'oriental' enclaves." Yet the term ghetto was a misnomer, for "a ghetto connotes forced residential permanence, entrapment." Immigrant Jews were free to move throughout the city. Indeed, as new tenement construction created opportunities to live elsewhere, Jewish immigrants availed themselves. By 1910 many Jewish immigrants lived in Harlem, in the Bronx, and in Williamsburg and Brownsville and Brooklyn. While the Lower East Side community did not disappear, its seeming permanence belied the transiency of its residents. As older immigrants moved out, new arrivals rapidly filled their places. Estimates suggest that between 1905 and 1915, two-thirds of the Jews living on the Lower East Side left the area. Nevertheless, if residential stability eluded Jewish immigrants, residential concentration continued to characterize Jewish life.

Immigrant Jews' residential concentration and mobility complemented their occupational concentration and mobility. Most Jewish immigrants earned their livelihood in the garment shops located on the Lower East Side and in the other immigrant sections. Here the confluence of work and residence transformed the public character of the streets. Jewish workers found jobs through the curbside employment markets, while pushcarts placed commerce on the sidewalks. But the immigrant areas housed both lower-class workers and the beginnings of a bourgeoisie. Thus the bitter battles between bosses and workers staged on the streets of the Lower East Side engaged the emotions of all Jewish immigrants. Class struggles ranging from garment worker walk-outs to rent strikes often became communal conflicts in the immigrant quarter. Despite their commitment to class solidarity, immigrant Jews declined to remain lower-class workers. Jewish immigrants' social mobility paralleled their residential restlessness. "Jews found the New York economy fluid and open," and they moved into white-collar positions rapidly. Yet as the earlier arrivals among the immigrants improved their economic position—and after 15 to 25 years in the United States half achieved white-collar status—more recent immigrants filled their vacated jobs. A Jewish working class endured in New York even as a Jewish middle and upper class flourished.

The immigrant generation necessarily lived in two worlds, the old 9
and the new. Immigrant Jews remembered their ties to the towns of
eastern Europe and with their *landslayt* strove to plant that culture in
America. The second generation appreciated these experiences, at best,
as abstract ideals. In reacting to the city environment, immigrant Jews
referred to both Europe and America; their children knew only America. The immigrant generation remained a transitional generation.
Nevertheless, this immigrant experience triggered a cultural explosion
and released creative powers among many Jews. With these energies
Jewish immigrants shaped a moral community, which comprised "a
sense of identity and unity with one's group and a feeling of involvement" and commitment by the individual. The second generation
received the community—sustained less by common consensus or
authority than by "visions of collective fulfillment and ambitions for
personal ascent"—as its Jewish inheritance. "It was the unspoken hope
of the immigrants that their visions and ambitions, the collective dream
of Jewish fulfillment and the personal wish to improve the lot of sons
and daughters, could be satisfied at the same time." While "too radical
a break in actual life patterns of generations had made the personal and
concrete experiences of the immigrant fathers inaccessible to the sons,"
second generation Jews accepted their parents' goal of linking "spiritual fulfillment with material gratification." But the second generation
turned to existing American institutions to fashion their own moral
community. Indeed, the ability of second generation Jews to recast
available institutions into instruments of self-perpetuation marks their
important contribution to Jewish and to American history.

Reading and Writing Activities

PRELIMINARY RESPONSE

Notes.   As you read, record your reactions (questions or comments) to
Deborah Dash Moore's description of New York Jews in your reading
journal.

Discussion.   In class, compare your reactions in groups of five or six.
Appoint a recorder to keep track of similarities or differences, consensus or disagreement, arising from the discussion. The recorder may
summarize your group discussion for the rest of the class later.

Freewriting.   After discussion, freewrite for 10 to 15 minutes about
similarities or differences in preliminary readings of "New York Jews."
Read your freewriting in groups of two to four.

SUMMARIZING

1. Create a preliminary analysis of the Moore reading selection.
2. Summarize the central point of this selection and note any transition points.
3. Compare summaries in your groups.

FOCUSED CRITICAL READING

1. Moore refers to "ethnic enclaves," including Irish Catholic enclaves, in New York City neighborhoods. She describes Catholic immigrants as being already "entrenched, well-organized, unassimilated." What is Moore's purpose in describing these Irish Catholic neighborhoods?
2. What does Moore mean when she talks about socialism and fraternal organizations replacing "old-country" ties?
3. Moore makes a point about New York Jews as forming a moral community. What, according to her, makes a community moral?
4. How do the second-generation Jews differ from the first generation of immigrant Jews?

Eugene Richards

Long Island Shelter, Boston, Massachusetts

◆

Eugene Richards is a professional photographer. His book Exploding
into Life *received the Nikon Award for best photography book of 1986. In
1987, he won the International Center of Photography Journalism Award
for* Below the Line: Living Poor in America, *from which the following
selection is taken.*

Vinnie Bono: I'm fifty-seven. I was born in the North End of Bos-   1
ton. I lost my parents when I was six.

I had an uncle. He was my father's brother and he was in love with   2
my mother. She was in love with my father. In other words, there was a
jealousy there.

So when I was six years old, I was in the hospital—I had scarlet   3
fever—and that's when my uncle sneaked into the house. We had a
cold-water flat then and he went up the fire escape, went in the house
and shot my mother and father. He didn't catch my brother. My brother
was asleep in the next room.

My uncle was arrested. He did life in the Charlestown State Prison.   4
They put me and my brother in what today they call the House of Little
Wanderers. I was raised there until I was seventeen. It was wonderful.
It was run by the nuns in the Catholic diocese. They raised us up, boys
and girls without families. We went to school, just like a regular, you
know, just like having your own, living at home.

So I grew up. The only thing was, I seen people come and adopt   5
from there. That hurt. I figured why not me? Is there something wrong
with me? I grew up with that feeling. It took me thirty-odd years—'til I
came here to the shelter—to find out that people did care.

I've been in this shelter since '81. I'm a night supervisor with the   6
live-in staff. I make sixty dollars a week and my job is to make sure the
people get showers and food and a bed to sleep in. I work from one to
nine, five days a week.

When I was seventeen, I went in the service, and that's how my   7
drinking problem started. I went to boot camp in 1949. Like any GI,
you get in with your buddies. They used to sneak me drinks 'cause I
was underage. I used to go out and get pissed.

8   I was in the Green Berets. They had a demolition school, so I went to learn how to make bombs, blowing up bridges and all that.

9   We went to Korea. They taught us how to kill. They learned you one thing, it's him or you. So I kept that in mind. I made sure it was him. That's how I kept onto life.

10   Sometimes we'd blow something up, caves or something. Every time I'd be doing something, when them other guys all had canteens of water, I would make sure my canteen was full of booze. They never knew it. Half of us were all either junkies, on dope, or drunks.

11   Then one day I had a patrol. We had this guy from Tennessee on the rear point and as we're going by, we seen this North Korean girl doing something, probably taking a piss. The next thing, there was a yell and a shot and the Tennessee guy was dead. He had decided he wanted to rape the girl and she shot him. She was a North Korean soldier.

12   The North Koreans came and the next thing we knew, we were captured. They blindfolded us and put us on a truck. It was the most frightening day of my life. I thought I was gonna be dead right there. But they only took us prisoners and that's how I started my term in the prisoner-of-war camp.

13   In my compound, we were about fifty. Only thirty survived. They used to work us from sunrise to sundown. Digging ditches and working the wheel. They had the wheel to get water, and you had to go on it barefooted to run it. Many times your feet would come out bleeding. For food, they used to give us a bowl of rice and you had to take them maggots out. I got out on July 19, 1955. They called a truce. There was a bridge that connected the North and South. It's called the Bridge of No Return. We crossed that bridge when they exchanged prisoners.

14   There was this one captain who used to be in the compound. He was no good. He had a bamboo rod and he used to always come in and whip our feet after working on that wheel. So I made a promise to myself, if I ever got a chance, I was gonna kill him. So when we were crossing over the bridge, there was this South Korean had a .45 automatic on his hip. So I stopped and took the .45, cocked it, and blew that North Korean's head off. I was crazy anyway. I didn't give a shit for life then. I figured nobody cared for me, or they wouldn't have let us stay in that camp that long. It wouldn't have taken six years.

15   After that, I was taken to a psycho ward. From there the Americans sent me to a hospital in Honolulu. I stayed there for six months and then they discharged me. It was an honorable discharge. Later they gave me, I think, the Congressional Medal of Honor.

16   We got our back pay. It was about fifteen thousand dollars, but I had no place to go. I stopped in a store and bought some civilian clothes and I went in a barroom and I started drinking. I was drinking, drinking, having a good time. I went to the airport. I asked a stewardess, where's that plane going? She says Aruba. I don't remember get-

ting on the plane, but when I woke up I was in Aruba. I took a room. Then I found out there was gambling in Aruba, so I went to the casino and I lost all my money, all fifteen thousand dollars. It took me a couple days. I was drinking. I just didn't give a shit.

I got a job on a yacht on the galley, going back to Florida. When we got to Miami Beach, the captain paid me off, about $250. What the hell, first thing I did was go to the nearest bar. Three days later, I woke up on the streets, broke, sick. I was twenty-six. I started hitchhiking. That's how my life on the road started. I was twenty years on the road. Or thirty. I don't remember.

17

The first place I went was Abilene, Texas. Got a job picking fruit. Then drank and panhandled. Nickels and dimes. I went from Texas to New York and went down the Bowery. Seen all the people there sleeping on the streets.

18

On the streets, I had to learn one thing, survival. My teacher was old Foxy, from Boston. He learned me all the ways of the streets. He learned me how to do the telephone boxes; he learned me how to panhandle.

19

First thing you learn, you have to con your way. Like a street person, he'll never ask you for a dollar, he'll never ask you for fifty cents, he'll always ask for a quarter. 'Cause he's damn sure you have a quarter in your pocket. He's like a vulture waiting for the pickings. I know, I've been there. I think me and Foxy wrote the book on that.

20

I myself, I don't give no quarters to street people. They tell me they're hungry, that's a lot of crap. Don't believe it. A street person knows where to go, where there's churches and missions. I kept on traveling. I went to Trenton, I hitchhiked to Arizona. I had a woman now and again. Only when I was sober though. Then every time I would drink, I would get sick. I didn't know what was happening inside me. I would throw it up and drink it down again. It was getting so there was no taste to it.

21

Then I seen this railroad, I seen guys getting on the boxcars, I said, why don't I try that? So I went down the embankment and I seen my first hobo jungle. They took me in, made me wash up. They showed me how to jump on the boxcars, how to get off. We used to go into town, look for work and panhandle. And when we made something, we'd bring it back. We'd share everything we made.

22

I was a hobo for ten years. Sometimes I stayed four or five days on a boxcar. You make your own ventilation. I always carried a knife and I used to make holes. But you couldn't cook, you'd burn the car up. You ate cold beans, things like that.

23

Then one February, I hitchhiked up to Boston. When I got here, I was hurting inside. It was eighteen above zero and I had only a short sleeve shirt on, Bermuda shorts, and sandals. Everybody was looking at me like I was crazy. Then a cruising car pulled up and the police

24

asked me what I was doing, dressed like that. I said, "Oh, I'm walking up to go to the hospital." And when I said that, I passed out.

25   When I woke up, I was in the hospital. I had been in a coma for fourteen days and they told me I was going through what they call the d.t.'s. I was hemorrhaging, I was passing blood. My liver was infected and everything.

26   After I was better, the doctor told me, "You've got no place, why don't you go to the shelter?" That's when I started a brand-new life, a new living. I went to the shelter at the Boston City Hospital. There was fifty, sixty people, all on one floor. The women would sleep on one side and the men would sleep on the other.

27   I used to go there at night, come out during the day. So one time I asked the director, I says, "Can I help out?" He says, yeah, okay, and he gave me a job, helping around the shelter, cleaning it up and everything. He saw I took an interest.

28   I wasn't drinking no more. 'Cause I had no money and I wanted to stop. What changed me was coming close to dying.

29   Then they moved the shelter out here, to Long Island Hospital, and the director told me, "I want you to go down and help clean the building and so forth." So I went and I been here ever since. We live in a dorm. I got nice clean clothes. I enjoy the work. It's a regular job and it ain't that hard. These people are my family. We're all from the same streets.

30   When I'm feeling depressed, angered, uptight, I go down to the statue. It's a statue of the Blessed Mother. I sit down there and just look at it, and after awhile, it makes me feel good. My depression goes away, my anger's gone.

31   I saw the Blessed Mother when I was going through the d.t.'s. She was a ray of hope to me and she said, "If I cure you, you have to do a favor for me which is to help other helpless people." I kept it in my mind all the time and I've been doing it ever since. The only way I'm gonna stop is if they close this place.

32   We get about 360 people at the shelter, men and women. We have 40 percent mentally impaired people and 50 percent alcoholics and 10 percent just people who think you owe them a living. 'Cause a lot of them just don't want to work. They want things but they don't want to pay for it. They can get forty-two dollars every two weeks from the welfare, even if they don't have an address. So that's enough for them to get their booze on, their dope, and they can come out to the shelter free every night. This is not the people in their forties and fifties, this is the guys in their twenties, early thirties. Those same guys are the ones that'll rob you.

33   It's not dangerous in the shelter, though. It's quiet, people scatter around, watch TV, play cards, and talk. It's like any place else though. They see something that's not nailed down, they're gonna lift it.

A couple of years ago, I met a woman at the shelter and we got 34
married. Her name was Sharon. She was homeless, too. I just seen her,
hey, she looked so nice, it was something I wanted. I figured it would
make a nice something to get together and have a companionship.

We got married right here in the shelter. All the staff was here. Then 35
we got ourselves a little apartment in Dorchester and we was going
good for awhile. I wasn't drinking. I was clean. She was clean. We were
both working here. We paid the rent, we bought the food, we had a
bank account, about five hundred dollars.

Then one day I went home. I opened the door. Now, we had a radio 36
with the speakers on it. I don't see that. So I looked around and I see
her keys on the table. I said, oops, something happened.

What she did was took her paycheck and the five hundred dollars 37
and left. See, a homeless person will never settle down.

She never came back. She just went. I felt hurt. I said, "Lord, what 38
do I do?," and the good Lord says, "Don't touch the booze, just keep
going forward. . . ." So here I am back at the shelter.

Reading and Writing Activities

PRELIMINARY RESPONSE

Notes. As you read, record your reactions in your reading journal
(questions or comments) to "Long Island Shelter."

Discussion. In class, compare your reactions in groups of five or six.
Appoint a recorder to keep track of similarities or differences, consensus or disagreement, arising from the discussion. The recorder may
summarize your group discussion for the rest of the class later.

Freewriting. After discussion, freewrite for 10 to 15 minutes about
similarities or differences in preliminary readings of "Long Island Shelter." Read your freewriting in groups of two to four.

SUMMARIZING

1. Create a preliminary analysis of the Richards selection with a
   scratchline of characters and events in the essay. Note explicit transition words, phrases, sentences, or paragraphs.
2. Summarize the events in the story.
3. Compare summaries in your groups.

FOCUSED CRITICAL READING

1. What do you know about the people Vinnie Bono spent time with during his lifetime?
2. What does Vinnie Bono's story tell you about friendship or love that he has experienced?
3. Vinnie Bono has painted a very general picture of his life. What details can you fill in that he has omitted?

WRITING SUGGESTIONS

1. Write an analysis (1–2 pages) of the voice Stephen Birmingham adopts in "Telling Them Apart." Refer to specific language Birmingham uses to support your analysis.

2. Interview friends and family about behavior that "just isn't done" in your home community. Present your findings in a short essay (2–3 pages).

3. Write a 3–4-page critique of the structure and content of "The Invisible Immigrants." You might reconsider some of the following questions: What are the major transition points? What is Dreyfuss's rhetorical purpose before and after those transition points? Is he introducing an additional example or a contrasting example? Is he making a major topic change? How smoothly does he change topics? How effective is the rhetorical structure of this essay?

4. Think about the roles of the women in "Scales" and in "The Day It Happened." Use a synthesis of both stories to develop and support your point of view about the roles of these women. (Refer to Chapter 4 for reminders of how to create a synthesis of information to develop a point-of-view essay.)

5. Compare the defining characteristics of the American aristocracy that Stephen Birmingham describes in "Telling Them Apart" and the black aristocracy that William B. Gatewood describes in his prologue to "Color, Culture, and Behavior." Write a brief comparison of similarities and differences between the two groups.

6. Present a comparison of different classes in America using information from a number of essays in this chapter. For example, you could take the point of view that there is, in fact, a large class gap in America and develop that view with extended examples. You could synthesize information from the selections by Birmingham, Gatewood, and Oates.

You could also use information from earlier selections about working-class families by Erdrich or Morales.

(In a complex synthesis of this kind, you need to pay close attention to your transition points, to what you are doing before and after those transition points.)

7. Compare the two immigrant communities Deborah Dash Moore and Joel Dreyfuss describe in "New York Jews" and "The Invisible Immigrants." Dreyfuss describes well-established Haitians as "industrious, upwardly mobile and vastly misunderstood." How does his description of this Haitian community compare with Moore's description of the New York Jewish community?

8. Research a group of immigrants who arrived in the United States in the 1950s. Compare this group to the description in this chapter of Haitian immigrants or Jewish immigrants or both who arrived here in the 1950s. Suggest why these groups have had similar or different experiences as immigrants in this country.

9. Research the issue of AIDS and the homeless. Do a careful reading of the sources of information you find in the library or elsewhere. (*Note:* In writing suggestions 8 and 9, use writing when you are doing a close reading: freewrites, notes, clustering, scratchlines, summaries.)

Think about how you will present your findings.

If appropriate, structure your introduction so that your point of view on the issue is stated at the end of the introduction, after you have introduced the topic and issue. (Refer to Chapter 4, page 180 for guidelines on introducing topic and issue in a documented essay.) It may be more appropriate as you explore this issue to state your point of view in the concluding section of your essay.

Think about how you will structure your essay. Check some of the reading selections in this chapter (or other chapters) for ideas on effective structure and development.

6

Work, Social Class, and Ethnicity: Sharing the American Dream

◆

Originality and the feeling of one's own dignity are achieved only through work.

Fyodor Dostoevsky

Far and away the best prize that life offers is the chance to work hard at work worth doing.

Theodore Roosevelt

These two quotations highlight the relationship among work, identity, and self-esteem. Readings in this chapter examine work within the contexts of social class and ethnicity, both of which influence the way people perceive themselves in relation to others.

Historically, many Americans have viewed work idealistically, particularly in their public utterances. For example, Benjamin Franklin's widely read autobiography is usually seen as a statement of the *work ethic*—the belief that anyone can succeed financially through determined effort. Subscribing to that belief, many Americans revere "self-made" men and women as leaders and role models. At times the work ethic has also been used as a way of dismissing the economic effects of ethnocentrism and class bias. Convinced that we live in an egalitarian, classless society, most Americans disclaim ethnic biases and resist discussions of social class, which they regard as subversive or in poor taste. By the end of the 1980s, however, most Americans were forced to reexamine their assumptions about work, class, and ethnicity. This resulted in part from a series of economic recessions and in part from a gradual shift in employment opportunities from manufacturing to service occupations.

Chapter 6 begins with a look at what Nicholas Lemann calls the "Meritocratic Upper Class," persons prepared from early childhood for careers in law, medicine, finance, and higher education. Lemann's critique is followed by a feature article that examines the hardships and disillusionments of individuals who have aspired to permanent membership in this elite class—men and women who once considered themselves immune to the effects of recession.

Factory workers, on the other hand, have always been among the first to be affected by business cycles. The economic insecurity of a blue-collar career, along with the sense of powerlessness that hourly wage earners often feel, has therefore stigmatized manual labor in the eyes of many. Few children aspire to blue-collar careers, and many laborers hope to see their sons and daughters engaged in more prestigious lines of work. These issues are addressed in "The Blue Collar Blues," a feature article in *Newsweek*.

"On Dumpster Diving," by Lars Eighner, concerns the experience of a socioeconomic group often called the *underclass*—citizens overlooked by more prosperous Americans until a dramatic rise in homelessness made their presence difficult to ignore. Eighner treats begging and scavenging as lines of work, each with its own rules and procedures.

A final cluster of readings examines the role of work within specific ethnic communities. Some of these readings look at the oppression of minorities in the workplace; others consider the consequences of upward mobility within a historically ethnocentric social context.

Reading selections in Chapter 6 include both objective reports, such as feature stories and analytical essays, and first-person narratives. Though neither type of source, in isolation, may provide an authoritative view of socioeconomic realities, the dialectical interplay between them should complicate and enrich our understanding of the issues.

Distinguishing the Main Parts of a Text

In Chapter 5, we saw how an examination of transition points (those places in a text where one topic ends and another begins) can help reveal the structure of a text and thus guide a reader's interpretation. Key *transition words* (as well as phrases, sentences, or even brief paragraphs) often mark these transition points. Transition words, however, are only one type of clue that writers use to indicate changes in direction or emphasis. Others include explicit textual and typographical signals—numerals, headings and subheadings, a wider space between the end of one paragraph and the beginning of the next—as well as more subtle prompts such as repetition and contrast.

The first reading in this chapter, "Curse of the Merit Class: America's New Ruling Caste Is Bad News for the Country," by Nicholas Lemann, provides examples of both these kinds of clues. Lemann begins his article by quoting the former prime minister of Japan—a quotation that helps focus attention on an issue the author deems worthy of national concern. Noting that Prime Minister Miyazawa's statement was, uncharacteristically, critical of American professionals rather than factory workers or ethnic minorities, Lemann introduces his basic aim in this article—to profile a privileged class of people and to critique their role in American society.

Opening paragraph 3 with the word *today* suggests a comparison or contrast between something in the present and something comparable in the past. Accordingly, paragraphs 3–9 define the Meritocratic Upper Class by comparison to another class, the Protestant Establishment, which held similar power and influence in the past. Though Lemann's tone in these paragraphs is derogatory, criticism of the Meritocratic Upper Class is purely implicit.

By opening paragraph 10 with "Yet Miyazawa is right in accusing...," Lemann introduces explicit criticism, even blame, harkening back to the quotation cited in paragraph 1, a quotation that points to a national problem—perhaps even a curse, as the title of this article suggests. Thus, paragraphs 10–15 criticize the Meritocratic Upper Class, contrasting its defining characteristics with the diligence of the Lifer track and the skills of the Talent track.

The next shift in thought is signaled by a wide break between paragraphs 15 and 16, a helpful prompt since the first sentence of paragraph 16 carries no verbal evidence of transition. Paragraphs 16–19 explain how the Meritocratic Upper Class rose to prominence, comparing its belief in the moral basis of social and economic rewards to the idealism of the now-declining Protestant Establishment. The last two paragraphs of this section show how that idealism eventually undermined the status of the Protestant Establishment as Jews and a few other minorities began to benefit from increased emphasis on standardized test scores.

To open paragraph 20, Lemann returns to the transition word *today*. Predictably, paragraphs 20–24 offer another comparison-contrast with the Protestant Establishment. In these paragraphs, Lemann shows how the Meritocratic Upper Class is vulnerable to the same criticism as its precursor. He ends this section of his article by asking "whether the Meritocratic Upper Class—fair, open and efficient though it may consider itself to be—is on its way to becoming a caste."

The next section of Lemann's article is indicated by another enlarged space between paragraphs. In this portion of his text, Lemann considers the evidence in favor of the Meritocratic Upper Class (paragraph 25) and the case against it (paragraphs 26–27).

Finally, in his last five paragraphs, Lemann addresses the possibility of reforming the Meritocratic Upper Class. Though he concedes that such an idea may seem "a silly project," Lemann proceeds to argue that the best interests of the nation would be served by such reform.

We suggest that this method of analysis can contribute to an enhanced understanding of Lemann's essay. However, we offer a word of caution. Once you have seen (or composed) such a close analytical reading, it may seem logical to regard Lemann's meaning as fixed and determinant—to infer that the author deliberately planted textual clues to ensure that readers will experience his article exactly in the way he intended. In previous chapters, we have tried to complicate this familiar, though simplistic, notion of reading, showing how interpretation is often as much a matter of generating new understandings as it is one of retrieving or decoding preexistent meaning. One of the best ways to keep the process of interpretation open ended is provided by reading groups. Therefore, as you read the selections in Chapter 6, we invite you to share your perceptions of the main parts of each text with other readers.

Nicholas Lemann

The Curse of the Merit Class: America's New Ruling Caste Is Bad News for the Country

◆

The following selection appeared in the editorial pages of the Washington Post, *one of four or five American newspapers that have a national circulation. The author, Nicholas Lemann, serves as national correspondent for* Atlantic, *a prominent magazine of opinion. Lemann has also written* The Promised Land (1991), *a book that details the migration of African Americans from the rural South to the urban Northeast and Midwest between 1940 and 1970.*

1   We've gotten used to the idea that when Japanese officials get up to tell us what's wrong with American culture, we're going to be treated to an exercise in factory-worker bashing, at best, and at worst, minority bashing. So it was refreshing, in a way, when Prime Minister Kiichi Miyazawa decided the other day to lecture us about the shortcomings of the people at the *top* of our society. Miyazawa charged that American college graduates take jobs on Wall Street rather than running factories, "with the result," said Japan's prime minister, "that the number of engineers who produce goods has gone down quickly."

2   This is perfectly true, and it's only one aspect of a much larger change in this country: the steady rise to dominance, since World War II, of a group that might be called the Meritocratic Upper Class.

3   Today, the Meritocratic Upper Class is a distinctive group with its own values and own way of life—perhaps not as fully articulated, yet, as those of what E. Digby Baltzell once identified as the Protestant Establishment, but the Meritocratic Upper Class is still quite new. One day—after novelists and filmmakers memorably depict its culture—the distinctiveness of this class will be obvious. So will the problems it poses to the society as a whole.

4   The essential formative experience of members of the Meritocratic Upper Class is educational overachievement. Therefore, in the culture of the class, purely social or ethnic credentials don't matter much, but educational credentials matter a great deal (and adult status is mainly a function of the prestige of one's job). The stations of the cross for members of the Meritocratic Upper Class aren't Tap Day or the Assembly

Ball, they're the Princeton Review course and the day the admissions letters from college and graduate school arrive.

A social gaffe can't ruin a member of the Meritocratic Upper Class (as it did a member of the Protestant Establishment in John O'Hara's *Appointment in Samarra*), but a professional setback can. Grave career problems like accusations of malpractice or plagiarism transfix us because they have the power to destroy meritocrats' lives; and the faked résumé plays a part in modern America like that of a shameful bit of hidden lineage in Victorian novels.

The Meritocratic Upper Class is probably somewhat larger than the Protestant Establishment was. Its members live in metropolitan areas, particularly on the East and West coasts. (Yuppies, if they are literally young urban *professionals* rather than just affluent city dwellers, would be a subset of the Meritocratic Upper Class, most of whose members are former yuppies who have become suburban and middle-aged.) They marry within the class—Baltzell is right when he says that the dean of admissions is the new marriage broker—and usually form two-career couples. They work as what Robert Reich calls "symbolic analysts"—as lawyers, doctors, investment bankers, management consultants, professors, and, increasingly, in the fields of journalism, entertainment and information processing.

Members of the Meritocratic Upper Class have a distinctive taste in clothing, cars, architecture, books, movies and food. These tastes change regularly, but as a general rule, meritocrats prefer things that can be described with words like "authentic" or "understated" or "quality" or "old," so long as they aren't seedy; they also have a weakness for well-designed high-tech stuff.

They make a lot of money but don't accumulate "fortunes" in the manner of members of the Protestant Establishment in its great days. Partly for this reason, and partly because they've had to run a gauntlet to get where they are, meritocrats tend to feel somewhat aggrieved. For example, they very often complain about "stress" and feel that they don't live as well as they deserve to and that their taxes are too high.

Meanwhile, as Reich has observed, many members of the Meritocratic Upper Class have engineered an Ayn Randian exodus from any involvement with the public sector through the use of security guards, private schools and Federal Express. They don't serve in the military. Their taxes have been cut while almost everyone else's have gone up. And while they can't be absolutely certain of passing on their status and isolation to their children, their focus in childrearing is trying to maximize the odds of their kids' success by stressing education and the development of the psychological tools necessary for high achievement.

Yet Miyazawa is right in accusing the Meritocratic Upper Class of being concentrated in careers that don't promote economic productivity. Even its members who go into business are usually advisers and transaction arrangers, not managers or entrepreneurs. "Over the last 10 years," Miyazawa said "It seems that America has reached the point that the mind-set to produce things and create value has loosened sharply."

11   Perhaps it will help define the Meritocratic Upper Class more clearly if I mention two other classes that also play a part in running the country but are quite different. I'll call them "Lifers" and "Talent."

12   Lifers are people who, after completing their education, join large organizations—the military, corporations, the civil service—and spend their lives slowly rising through the ranks of management until, after many winnowings out, a few of them briefly attain great power. The talent class includes salesmen, entertainers, athletes, entrepreneurs and specialists in arcane financial fields like currency trading—they're people who perform (and are rewarded) at a high level in jobs where output can be precisely measured and who therefore don't need formal credentials.

13   Because the principle of risk reduction is at the top of meritocrats' minds as they choose careers, they tend to shun the Lifer and Talent tracks: In both, only a tiny percentage who enter will get to become big shots, while for the professionals the odds are a lot shorter. (And on the Talent track, even if you make it, you can become washed up later.)

14   In the case of the Lifer track, meritocrats stay away because over the last generation they've developed a contempt for organization life, and their dream of success is now symbolized by those ads in which the rich, handsome guy is sitting alone on a mountaintop with his notebook computer. Because of the meritocrats' avoidance of the Lifer track, government service, an acceptable career path for graduates of elite European universities, doesn't attract the Meritocratic Upper Class, and neither do big corporations.

15   As for the Talent track, it's stylistically too vulgar and showy for most meritocrats, whose tastes tend to be muted as a kind of tribute to the WASPs they displaced from power.

16   Anyone who has spent time around the Meritocratic Upper Class knows that it believes success is apportioned on a moral basis. Of course, as Baltzell reminds us in his latest collection of essays, "The Protestant Establishment Revisited," that ruling class also believed it was apportioning success in a profoundly fair way, rather than simply reserving all the goodies for Episcopalians who happened to have been born in the right hospital beds; it felt itself to be evaluating and rewarding people on the basis of, in Baltzell's words, "character and moral standards."

17   Indeed, within its strictly limited eligibility pool, the Protestant Establishment usually did confer the best positions on people who combined talent, diligence and decency. (I should acknowledge here that I realize that the president, secretary of state and secretary of the treasury are all White Anglo-Saxon Protestants born to secure upper-

class wealth and educated at boarding schools and Ivy League colleges. It is a WASP Trifecta not achieved at any other time in the past half-century. Still, the Protestant Establishment is dying or dead.)

But there were, of course, many victims of the Protestant Establishment's way of making personnel decisions, the best known being Jews, who, when the top jobs were being handed out, always seemed to be disqualified on the grounds of their shortcomings in the "character and moral standards" department—they were too ambitious, too pushy, insufficiently genteel.   18

The fight to replace the Protestant Establishment's standard with a meritocratic one based on academic performance and aptitude-test results was one that Jews joined in wholeheartedly, because they believed that the "character and moral standards" test was prejudiced and the meritocratic measurements inherently fair.   19

Today, with the meritocrats in dominance, the struggle over affirmative action and multiculturalism has a similar structure. What Jews (now joined by Asians) see as a personnel system in keeping with the highest ideals of American society, many of the post-World War II wave of ethnic new arrivals in metropolitan America, notably blacks, see as a way of rigging the race so that only people born in fortunate circumstances can win it.   20

The reason these issues stir up such strong passions is that universities, in addition to educating people, have become the most reliable distributors of success in America; decisions about admissions and hiring are decisions about who gets to be in the establishment.   21

The elite universities realize this full well and have been brilliant at hedging their bets during the current power struggle. The Protestant Establishment still has disproportionate power in the Ivy League, partly owing to its astute use of its capital to make gifts to alma mater in return for slightly eased admissions standards for its children; the meritocrats are essentially in the catbird's seat; and the universities are also careful to include "people of color," the new claimants to membership in the ruling class.   22

The advocates of affirmative action—that is, the opponents of the meritocracy as it's now run—are engaging, then, in a time-honored battle: the struggle of rising ethnic groups to revise the personnel system in such a way that it will reward more of them. Although this process takes place under the banner of the left, it can be justified on conservative grounds: Inclusion is the best means of self-preservation for the Meritocratic Upper Class, and changes in the composition of the elite almost always involve altering the standard of admission.   23

It is still worth asking, as Baltzell has done, whether the Meritocratic Upper Class—fair, open and efficient though it may consider itself to be—is on its way to becoming a caste. Is it weakening the country through the tenacity of its hold on power?   24

25   In favor of the Meritocratic Upper Class, it can be said that it is not nearly as prejudiced and cosseted as the Protestant Establishment was. Its social life is carried out in restaurants more than in private clubs (and to the extent that private clubs are still important, they're the more meritocratic ones, like the Century in New York and the Cosmos in Washington); some of its children go to public schools (though only in the suburbs, and even there, the number is probably decreasing); and it isn't mono-ethnic. Access to it is probably more open than access to the Protestant Establishment was, and its children's ultimate place in life is determined at birth to a lesser extent.

26   On the other hand, at this fairly early point in its history, the Meritocratic Upper Class is more Darwinian, more convinced of its superiority, than the Protestant Establishment was—the meritocrats made it by running the educational gauntlet and therefore qualify as self-made, don't they? Also, the Meritocratic Upper Class, already fairly isolated from the rest of the country, is becoming more so. Because of their taste in way of life, its members have very little spare time or money. All this breeds a lack of familiarity, empathy, concern and responsibility with respect to everybody else.

27   With any established upper class—especially if it becomes a caste—there is a danger that it will use its power to protect those aspects of the society from which it derives its position. To the extent that the Meritocratic Upper Class really does replenish its ranks by seeking out the talented from every nook and cranny of the country and bringing them together in the best universities, it then substantially wastes the talent by channeling it so heavily into the professions. In America today, this means we keep an excessive share of our resources tied up in the legal, medical and financial worlds, while business and government wither.

28   There is a temptation to regard the idea of reforming the Meritocratic Upper Class as a silly project—isn't reform supposed to be directed at solving people's problems rather than modifying the career paths of people whose lives are pretty cushy? But even those who don't believe there should be a coherent, quasi-hereditary upper class of any kind (let alone one that absorbs reformist energy) should realize that rectifying the shortcomings of the Meritocratic Upper Class is a noble cause, since to do so would be to make the Meritocratic Upper Class less coherent and less quasi-hereditary.

29   Its isolation is an easy problem to address, at least partially; it could be done by instituting compulsory national service. The problem of restricted access to the class could be solved in part by trying hard to find ways to make big personnel decisions later in life and on the basis of performance rather than credentials.

30   Lifer and Talent venues like the military, the corporate world, Hollywood and Silicon Valley tend to have more varied leadership groups

than the meritocratically controlled professions, because they don't have to decide who makes it and who doesn't before the age of 30, when inherited advantages are at the peak of their potency.

If we can move the professions in this direction, it will help solve 31 the Meritocratic Upper Class's economic productivity problem, too: If a six-figure income were no longer virtually assured for everyone who enters an elite law school or medical school and became instead merely a possibility, we'd stop seeing more than half the graduates of our best colleges becoming doctors and lawyers.

All this would certainly help stave off the Meritocratic Upper 32 Class's metamorphosis into a caste—and it might even, dream of dreams, broaden access so much that the country would be well led by an ever-changing group of people who were not members of a discernible class, or establishment, at all.

Reading and Writing Activities

PRELIMINARY RESPONSE

Notes.   As you read, record your reactions (questions or comments) to "The Curse of the Merit Class" in your reading journal.

You may react to one or more of a number of factors in the reading. You might, for example, consider whether or not meritocracy is a fair and effective way to distribute power and privilege. Or you might speculate on Nicholas Lemann's title: does it suggest that the Meritocratic Upper Class suffers a curse, that it has placed a curse on American society, or both?

Discussion.   In class, compare your reactions in reading groups of five or six. Appoint a recorder to keep track of similarities and differences, consensus or disagreement, arising from the discussion. The recorder may summarize your group discussion for the rest of the class later.

Freewriting.   Reread the last five paragraphs of "Curse of the Merit Class" and then freewrite for 10 to 15 minutes on Lemann's proposal to reform the Meritocratic Upper Class—both the desirability of reform and the likelihood of bringing it about. Read your freewriting in groups of two to four. As others are reading, take written note of areas of agreement or disagreement, questions that arise in your mind, and ideas that might be qualified or extended. After everyone has read, appoint a recorder to keep track of similarities or differences, consensus or disagreement, that arise in the ensuing discussion. The recorder may summarize your group discussion for the rest of the class later.

SUMMARIZING

1. Create a brief, preliminary analysis of "The Curse of the Merit Class"—one that reflects your consideration of the freewriting and discussion of group members. Note in particular Lemann's criticisms of the Meritocratic Upper Class, the evidence he uses to support those criticisms, and his proposals for reform.
2. Write a summary paragraph or two, using your preliminary analysis.
3. Read summaries in groups. Compare the focus of each summary. How do the summaries differ? How are they the same? Again, check to see if you are *reacting and responding* to the reading selection instead of summarizing the central topics.

FOCUSED CRITICAL READING

1. Do you agree with Lemann's assertion in paragraph 4 that "adult status is mainly a function of the prestige of one's job"? Who determines which jobs have the most prestige, and on what basis? Do any "low-prestige" jobs pay high salaries? Do any "high-prestige" jobs pay modest salaries?
2. Why do you suppose the Meritocratic Upper Class places so much value on privacy and isolation? Does this emphasis conflict with the desire for conspicuous consumption so often attributed to prosperous American families?
3. Since Lemann says that members of the Meritocratic Upper Class dominate the field of journalism, can we expect him, as a journalist, to shed the biases of that class sufficiently to analyze its values and shortcomings?
4. What do you make of Lemann's statement that members of the Meritocratic Upper Class work, by and large, as "symbolic analysts"? Does this assertion suggest that analysis is inherently elitist? Might it explain the emphasis that universities, the "most reliable distributors of success," place on analytical inquiry?
5. Do you agree with Lemann's contention that affirmative action can be justified on conservative grounds? How might that alignment complicate one's views on the issue?

Barbara Kantrowitz
(with Anetta Miller, Karen Springen, and Rita Pyrillis)

Young, Gifted and Jobless: For a Rising Number of Professionals, the Dream of Financial Security Is Gone

———————◆———————

Nicholas Lemann presents the Meritocratic Upper Class as a powerful force in conflict with democratic ideals. The following selection sees the members of that class as the unlikely, and perhaps undeserving, victims of economic hard times. The fact that this article was the cover story for a 1990 issue of Newsweek *shows that the editors of that magazine considered the subject a significant national trend.*

They all had a dream, once upon a time. It went something like this: good grades, the right schools, perhaps even an M.B.A. Then, after a few hard years of 12-hour days and total loyalty to the company, they would get the big prize—a hefty salary leading someday to a comfortable retirement. Now that dream of job security is like so many other youthful fantasies, just a memory. It has been replaced by job anxiety, a scary new vision filled with euphemisms like restructuring, downsizing and streamlining. Even respected members of once stable professions—banking, insurance, the law—have felt the ax.

In the old days, a pink slip wouldn't have been such a big deal for white-collar workers, many of whom have undergraduate and graduate degrees in technical areas. But with whole industries shrinking in a declining economy, even highly skilled professionals are likely to find that there are no new jobs in their field. They may spend months looking for work and then have to settle for something far below their previous jobs. Many of the victims of this recession are middle managers, often people in their 30s and early 40s. This was supposed to be the prime of their lives, their peak earning years. Instead, they find themselves weighted down by mortgages, young families, big bills and an increasingly uncertain future. Dan Lacey, editor of the newsletter *Workplace Trends*, estimates that 70 percent of this year's newly jobless will be white-collar workers. "It totals up to nearly 250,000 families who used to believe in lifetime job security," says Lacey. "These are the economic icon jobs. They are the Ozzie-and-Harriet jobs, the jobs that gave us the ability to buy a house in a nice neighborhood and drive two cars. They an the jobs that have made the American lifestyle possible."

3   When that dream dies, everyone grieves. Myles O'Dwyer, a 38-year-old former chief financial officer of a Los Angeles-area manufacturing company, lost his job last May when his firm went on a cost-cutting campaign. Six months later he's still out of work. "It's a terrible blow to your self-confidence," O'Dwyer says. "You feel worthless." With a wife and two young daughters to support, he's willing to look at positions that are a step down on the career ladder. His wife has suffered, too, he says. "When my wife has been on a high, I have been on a low and when she's been low, I've been feeling good. Each of us has had severe emotional depths to wade through." His daughters don't understand why Daddy doesn't go to the office anymore. "We went to Disneyland a few weeks ago and there was a wishing well that we threw our pennies into," he recalls. "My wife asked me what I wished for and I said, 'A new job,' and my daughter said, 'You can't do that, Daddy. That was my wish for you.'"

4   Blue-collar workers are more used to weathering such storms. In many industries, such as automobiles or steel, layoffs have come to be a part of the economic cycle. "That's the bump and grind of their life," says Margaret Morley, executive director of the Beacon Therapeutic Diagnostic and Treatment Center in Chicago. "The white-collar worker doesn't expect the bump and grind. It's an unusual assault." Professionals and managers also tend to have more of their identity tied up in their work. "If you ask somebody in a blue-collar job what he does, he'll say, 'I work at the plant or the factory,'" says Neil P. Lewis, a management psychologist in Atlanta who counsels businesses. "But if you ask a white-collar person, he'll say, 'I'm an accountant or a marketing person or a journalist.' When there's a layoff, it's not just losing a paycheck, but losing a bit of your self-concept." Linda Rie, a New York banker, has two master's degrees and is fluent in Russian. She thinks she would be a great asset to any company planning to expand into Eastern Europe. But after nearly a year of joblessness, she's deeply discouraged. "I know the homeless have it worse than we do," she says. "The people with AIDS have it worse than we do. But what am I supposed to do? I'm 40 years old. Am I supposed to retire for the next 40 years?"

5   Although some people see the warning signs, many are stunned to find themselves suddenly among the ranks of the jobless. Rich Briede worked for Donaldson, Lufkin & Jenrette, Inc. at the Midwest Stock Exchange in Chicago until last week. He found out he had lost his job when he received a certified letter on a Saturday informing him that his company was dropping his insurance coverage. The pink slip seems particularly unreal to employees who have felt successful and appreci-

ated at work. Rani Verma, 29, lost her job as a marketing manager at Sara Lee Bakery in Deerfield, Ill., on Oct. 4 when the company eliminated her department. Three weeks earlier she had had her annual review and received the highest possible raise in her level. When the boss called her in and told her she was losing her job, she started laughing. "I thought he was joking," she says. He wasn't. "My boss said, 'Please. Stop laughing.'"

Verma isn't laughing anymore. Like many of the newly unemployed, she went through a series of emotional stages that resemble common reactions to death and divorce—the two traumas psychologists say most closely resemble firing. After shock comes anger and grief and then finally an acceptance of the inevitable. "Some people go through it all in two days," says Lewis, the Atlanta psychologist. "Others take weeks and months. I think six to 12 hours of self-pity is OK, but after that you need to get on with it."   6

In recent months there has been a surge in membership of groups catering to dismissed workers. Forty Plus, a nationwide organization that specializes in job hunters 40 years of age and older, features a "job jury," where job hunters have their résumés critiqued by their peers. Church groups around the country have taken on the unemployed as a new ministry, offering emotional support, job-hunting assistance and personal-finance tips. Even state governments are getting into the act. California's Employment Development Department has a special program for white-collar managers and projects aimed at two major industries: aerospace and electronics. The programs offer moral support as well as practical advice.   7

As time passes and the severance pay runs out, families are forced to make drastic revisions in long-held life plans. David Johnson, 30, earned more than $100,000 as a Wall Street mutual-fund manager. When he was fired in late January, his wife, Cindy, 30, was on maternity leave from her job as a buyer at Bloomingdale's in Manhattan. Their son, Zachary, was just 2 months old and Cindy had been hoping to put off her return to full-time work to be home more with the baby. Instead, David has found himself playing Mr. Mom while Cindy has gone back to work full time at a Bloomingdale's branch near their New Jersey home. David has had a number of promising interviews but he's given up speculating about how long his search will take. Instead, he tries to concentrate on the positive: time with his son. "It's probably what has kept my spirits up," he says. "I see it as an opportunity to get to know him." They're living on savings; Cindy's salary covers no more than half of their monthly expenses, David says. Cindy sees their life as being in a kind of "holding pattern" and concedes that there have been moments of tension between them. "It's what we don't say to each other" in an effort to minimize strain, she says. "It's very stressful."   8

Long-term unemployment forces a major readjustment of a family's emotional balance. Although some couples, like the Johnsons, say   9 they are stronger for the experience, others find the mental strain is even worse than the financial strain. People who have lost jobs may be more susceptible to alcohol and drug abuse, says Stephen Pilster-Pearson, director of employee assistance at the University of Wisconsin at Madison. Feelings of anger and betrayal may lead to family violence or divorce. "Those feelings have to go somewhere," says Pilster-Pearson, "and one of those places, of course, is home." Couples may find themselves fighting over seemingly small issues and saying more than they mean to. Comments like "My mother said I should never have married you and she was right" represent deep frustration over a situation that seems out of control. "All those unresolved issues that have been sort of pushed aside get let loose because there's nothing to hold them back anymore," Pilster-Pearson says.

10   Even those still on the job are not immune to anxiety and stress. A recent study by Brooks International, a management-consulting firm, found that fewer than 24 percent of 11,000 workers surveyed expressed confidence in the long-term future of their jobs. Employee paranoia is sometimes carried to extremes. Some middle managers at one particularly beleaguered Wall Street brokerage firm are so fearful of losing their jobs that they arrange to be out of the office on Friday, the day on which they believe they are most likely to get the ax. "They think that if they aren't around, they might be able to dodge the pink slip for a while," says one consultant. Other anxious executives try to seek out advance warning. William Morin, chairman of Drake Beam Morin, an outplacement firm, says he gets as many as 10 calls a week from friends who want to know if they have been singled out to be canned. "They constantly ask, 'Am I on the list, Bill?' I've never seen anything like it during all the years I've been in business."

11   Fear isn't the only emotion stalking the office. Survivors of mass layoffs often feel guilty receiving a paycheck while their friends and ex-colleagues are down at the unemployment office. There's a feeling of "Why them and not me?" They also probably have to work even harder now that there are fewer people to share the load. All these issues demand special sensitivity from top management, says Joel Brockner of Columbia University's graduate school of business. Brockner, who has studied survivors' reactions, says managers should be careful to explain the economic reasons behind the layoffs. "We can accept things better when we understand why they occurred," he says. They should make sure that dismissals are handled "with dignity" and not callously. After the layoffs, they should emphasize the positive aspects of a newly streamlined organization: more opportunity for those still on board, new career paths, less bureaucracy and greater efficiency. It's also important for managers to "play it straight," Brockner says. If an employee asks about the possibility of future layoffs, "you

can say, 'None are planned. However, we can't say for sure. It depends on how things go.'"

Even with the best of management, there's no easy way to bridge the gap left by breaking a crucial clause in the unspoken contract between employee and employer. If loyalty and hard work no longer guarantee the payback of security, why should workers put the company's interests before their own? John Fetcho was let go with one day's notice last March after working more than a decade at a Chicago-area insurance-brokerage firm. Although he managed to find another job in only three months, Fetcho, 33, learned an important lesson: never count on an employer. "I make a point of interviewing every couple of months," he says, "more to keep my hand in it so it pushes me to keep a résumé updated and my interview skills." He has gained a new understanding of economic realities. "Unless you work for yourself, you're always subject to the whims of the people who employ you," he says. "If it's a publicly held company, then it's the bottom line" that counts, not years of dedicated service.

This newfound wisdom is one unanticipated benefit of joblessness; another plus is an unexpected opportunity to re-evaluate. Some white-collar workers may view joblessness as an opportunity to change professions and start over in a new direction at midlife. "People don't look at alternatives until they are forced to," says Laura Wada, who was fired in June from her $30,000-a-year administrative job after 11 years at GTE in Mountain View, Calif. "There is no time to re-evaluate your life when you're on the treadmill." At 40, she is planning to switch careers and is looking for a job in human resources after taking courses in the subject. "In the '90s," she says, "people have to learn to be more flexible."

As in most economic upheavals, there's always someone who profits. In this case, it's the outplacement firms hired to help laid-off professionals in their job search. The industry has grown by roughly a quarter in the past year; revenues are expected to hit $500 million, up from $400 million in 1989. "We may be turning out corporate America's lights," said William Morin. But even he strikes a cautionary note. "If we can't find people jobs, we could be the last ones out the door." No one is safe anymore.

Reading and Writing Activities

PRELIMINARY RESPONSE

Notes.   As you read, record your reactions (questions or comments) to "Young, Gifted and Jobless" in your reading journal.

You may react to one or more of a number of factors in the reading. You might, for example, speculate on whether and why the unemployment of the "young and gifted" could be considered more newsworthy than the unemployment of others. (This line of thought may lead you to consider any assumptions that underlie Barbara Kantrowitz's notion of giftedness.)

Discussion.   In class, compare your reactions in reading groups of five or six. Appoint a recorder to keep track of similarities and differences, consensus or disagreement, arising from the discussion. The recorder may summarize your group discussion for the rest of the class later.

Freewriting.   In a 10- to 15-minute freewrite, try to present the workers profiled by Kantrowitz from two very different points of view: first as victims who deserve compassion or pity; then as spoiled, self-pitying members of what Nicholas Lemann calls the Meritocratic Upper Class (note in particular the complaints about stress that Lemann highlights in paragraph 8 of "Curse of the Merit Class"). Read your freewriting in groups of two to four. As others are reading, take written note of areas of agreement or disagreement, questions that arise in your mind, and ideas that might be qualified or extended. After everyone has read, appoint a recorder to keep track of similarities or differences, consensus or disagreement, that arise in the ensuing discussion. The recorder may summarize your group discussion for the rest of the class later.

SUMMARIZING

1. Make a scratchline, cluster representation, or notes indicating the progression of ideas in "Young, Gifted and Jobless"—one that reflects your consideration of the freewriting and discussion of group members. Note in particular the way Kantrowitz contrasts the high expectations and current economic status of the workers she profiles.
2. Write a summary paragraph or two, using your scratchline, cluster representation, or notes.
3. Read summaries in groups. Compare the focus of each summary. How do the summaries differ? How are they the same? Again, check to see if you are *reacting and responding* to the reading selection instead of summarizing the central topics.

FOCUSED CRITICAL READING

1. Speaking of the unemployment caused periodically by economic cycles, Kantrowitz says that "blue-collar workers are more used to

weathering such storms." Does that make their efforts to do so less newsworthy—less appropriate as the topic of a *Newsweek* cover story?

2. Kantrowitz says that "everyone grieves" when dreams of the young and gifted die—dreams said to revolve around "Ozzie-and-Harriet jobs...that [provide] the ability to buy a house in a nice neighborhood and drive two cars." Do you agree? Why might others who have never had any realistic hope of achieving such dreams grieve?

3. Kantrowitz suggests that since "loyalty and hard work no longer guarantee the paycheck of security," many professionals do not put their employers' interests before their own. Do you think this attitude represents a change for most professionals? What about other kinds of workers? Do you suppose they would act differently if loyalty and hard work *did* guarantee security?

Richard Manning and
John McCormick

The Blue-Collar Blues: Hundreds of Thousands of Former Factory Workers Suddenly Constitute a Downwardly Mobile Class

◆

Like "Young, Gifted and Jobless," the following selection appeared, in June 1984, as a feature article in the business section of Newsweek. *(Unlike the former, however, it was not a cover story.) Together, these articles provide a disturbing glimpse of a society in which career opportunities and attitudes about work are undergoing profound and rapid change.*

1 Frank Burton goes to work in the dark and comes home in the dark, like his father and grandfather before him. For three generations they built tires from dawn to dusk as rubber rats in the acrid gum shops of Akron, Ohio. Now Burton works the graveyard shift at a convenience store, stocking shelves, ringing the register, keeping the books when his math skills seem up to it. He earns $7,000 a year, a minimum-wage fraction of the $30,000 he made before the plants shut down and Akron stopped making car tires for good. It is the irony of factory towns like Akron that Burton's new job is the same one he held 24 years ago when he graduated from high school. "The blue-collar work was good while it lasted," he sighs. "It just didn't last long enough for me."

2 There are hundreds of thousands of Frank Burtons in America today. They are the blue-collar refuse of industrial reorganization. While the nation's manufacturers have clawed their way back to prosperity, half a million industrial jobs have been lost along the way. Former factory workers are fighting a downward spiral of income and self-esteem in a society where upward mobility is preached from birth. Many blue-collar workers have retrained and entered the white-collar work force, but their new jobs pay only half of what the old ones did. Others languish in unskilled positions while many more wait for jobs that will never return. With few exceptions their lives have been dimin-

ished. Frank Burton has abandoned the dream of sending his children to college. Winnie Brink was forced to moth ball his family's second car. A union hall where rubber workers gathered to drink Stroh's beer and follow the exploits of the Cleveland Indians is now a day-care center; the TV set is gone.

They were the backbone of the blue-collar middle class. Their 3 proudest possession was a mortgage, and their savings allowed millions of other Americans to buy new homes as well. They packed the ballparks on summer Sundays and the softball diamonds after work. Above all, they dreamed of security and better lives for their children. A job at the factory could fulfill that promise for workers in blue-collar towns like Akron. But no longer.

Despite the swelter and the stench of its factories, Akron was an 4 industrial mecca in its prime. So prosperous were the times that the shop rats developed a taste for silk shirts, and simply threw them away at the slightest smudge. But there were soon to be smudges aplenty in Rubber City: management errors, decentralization, recession and a doubling of union wages each contributed to the decline. Today the factory façades along South Main Street are an aging monument to past prosperity. Fewer than 7,000 workers, many of them janitors, man the shops where 10 times as many worked in a different age.

Some men take any work they can get. Frank Burton studied 980 5 hours of computer science after Firestone laid him off three years ago, only to find that nobody in Akron needed his new skills. "I got my heart torn out," he remembers. "At 42 I should be reaching my top income potential." The convenience store took him on in part because, at 6 feet 2 and 260 pounds, he is a discouraging sight to would-be robbers. Burton suffers health problems and sold his pension rights to pay debts. Only his wife's clerical job allows them to meet the $300 mortgage. "A lot of guys would say this is demeaning," he says. "But there's nothing else out there."

The sooner laid-off factory workers realize that, the better, the 6 experts say. "The best message to give them may be that they're lucky they did so well for so long," says Dennis Ahlburg, a professor of industrial relations at the University of Minnesota. "For a lot of these people it really *is* over." Part of the problem is that organized labor is fighting old battles and cannot conceive of giving up past gains. "Spokesmen for the working class have tried to build a sense of self-pride in the dignity of labor," says University of Wisconsin urban historian Stanley Schultz. "But to keep mouthing old phrases—to attempt to breathe life into words no longer relevant to our present social vocabulary—will produce bitterness, frustration and possibly rising social disorder."

Any fall is hard, but Akron is suddenly confronting the conse- 7 quences of a 10-story plunge. "Many blue-collar workers didn't realize they were earning wages unsustainable in the face of growing competition from abroad," notes Wharton School economist Michael Wachter. "It's unfair to expect them to appreciate these broader themes. When you're getting hit over the head, you don't worry about who exactly is hitting you. Your main concern is getting your head patched up."

8   Some men patch up and retrain. Albert Marziale, 58, worked 18 years at Firestone before his plant closed. He had the foresight to see the end coming and went to night school to study drafting. Yet he was still unemployed for a year, bringing home $194 a week in jobless benefits. Finally he found work at an aerospace company, but his wage dropped by a fifth, and so did his benefits and vacations. Despite his fall from $11-an-hour grace, he is relieved. "I'm a lot happier now than I was at Firestone," he says. "There's a future here. There are no opportunities in rubber anymore."

9   Yet fundamental retraining is easier to praise than to practice. "We can talk about retraining, but I think it's fictitious," argues John Cumbler, an economic historian at the University of Louisville. "How can we retrain all these people in a meaningful way?" Besides, Cumbler insists, too many programs train people for technologies that are already obsolescent.

10   And some men never stop retraining in their search for work in a world without blue collars. Winnie Brink, 48, has gone through four programs in the last five years, transforming himself from maintenance man to computer operator and beyond. He still can't find steady work. He had hired into the Firestone One plant for the wages, the benefits and the security. "There would always be a Firestone," he recalls thinking. But instead of security and $9 an hour he got a second mortgage so he could pay bills and all his job-retraining tuition. "I could go to school forever and never get good-paying work," he says. "They want people age 31 with 10 years on the job. But I'm going to keep at it, looking for something that pays better than $5 an hour."

11   Workers who six years ago would have turned up their noses at minimum-wage work now flock to opportunities of any kind. When a job opened up recently for a janitor in a local housing project, 400 former tire builders applied—men who once thought that janitors were the lowest of the low. For others, hope may be the greatest enemy, causing them to put off retraining or the search for a more distant job. In Michigan, forlorn groups of furloughed industrial workers gather outside closed plants. At noon they open their lunch buckets. At what used to be quitting time they go home. "You can't expect workers to understand what's happening when they see an occasional plant reopening," says Minnesota's Ahlburg. "As long as there's one glimmer of light, they'll wait to get their jobs back."

12   Bill Ehmer, 42, worked for 15 years in machine shops that serviced rubber plants. His layoff came two years ago, and although he has held a series of minimum-wage spot jobs, he continues to wait for the callback notice. "I can do factory work," he insists. "I can do *any* of it if the

job is there." But the job is not there. Ehmer bought his house when he and his wife both had full-time work. Now they manage to pay the mortgage, but they slide on the utilities. It pains Ehmer that he can't afford presents for his granddaughter. But low-paying service jobs hold no appeal. "I could wear a tie and come home early," he says, "but it wouldn't pay enough. I want factory work."

Downward mobility can spread its chill over entire communities. 13 The shift from manufacturing to service has meant an income loss for greater Akron of $2.65 billion since 1974. While the number of service jobs has increased by 20 percent, the service payroll, in constant dollars, has actually declined. "It's a very unhealthy climate," says Keith Fletcher, a labor-market analyst at the Ohio Bureau of Employment Service's Akron office. "It precludes expansion. People don't buy, so businesses start to fail. City finances become tight. It's all tied together by the tentacles of doom."

Downward mobility can also chill the soul. "People tend to 14 entrench," says Louisville's Cumbler. "There is a potential for social meanness—a tendency to close in on what you've got at the expense of everybody else." And for many workers, making the switch to a new, poorer-paying industry exacts a psychological toll. "We define ourselves in terms of our jobs, and that identity permeates our families, especially in towns where one industry is prominent," says Walter Nord, a professor of organizational psychology at Washington University in St. Louis. "When you're suddenly working at a hamburger joint instead of Bethlehem Steel, that's a blow to your self-esteem. And the loss of health and other benefits has to have family-life consequences."

Some men die because the readjustment is too much to take. One 15 Akron rubber worker lost his job and watched his life shrivel. His wife divorced him and took the kids away. On the day his divorce became final, the man drove to her business and waited for her to leave work. Then he drew his car alongside hers and blew his brains out with a deer rifle. It's a tale told in whispers in the city's blue-collar bars and union halls.

Today's difficulties can only worsen as the already diminished 16 blue-collar work force shrinks from 30 percent of the labor market to as little as 10 percent in the next two decades. It is one of the most difficult social problems the country will face in the rest of this century, and precious little is being done about it. "We stand last among the major industrial and post-industrial nations in public expenditures on job training and retraining," says the University of Wisconsin's Schultz. "Because of trends in the economy, we must make a genuine national commitment to education and job retraining for many of our working-class citizens."

Mark Wasik used federal and county retraining funds to recast his 17 life. Wasik, 37, spend 18 years as a steelworker. This week he gets his nursing degree. After his layoff his wife went back to work and Wasik spent his days studying, cooking and cleaning house. When he becomes a nurse he will earn $6 an hour instead of $12. But Wasik doesn't mind. "I never wanted to leave the mill," he says, "but the choice wasn't mine. I had to trade in my work boots for white shoes and a smock. If you put all your resources together the shift can be made. It has to be."

Reading and Writing Activities

PRELIMINARY RESPONSE

Notes.   As you read, record your reactions (questions or comments) to "The Blue-Collar Blues" in your reading journal.

You may react to one or more of a number of factors in the reading. You might, for example, identify the causes to which Richard Manning and John McCormick attribute the "blue-collar blues," the persons and forces they blame, and the remedies they propose.

Discussion.   In class, compare your reactions in reading groups of five or six. Appoint a recorder to keep track of similarities and differences, consensus or disagreement, arising from the discussion. The recorder may summarize your group discussion for the rest of the class later.

Freewriting.   In a 10- to 15-minute freewrite, compare the success story that appears in the last paragraph of this article with the one found in the last two paragraphs of "Young, Gifted and Jobless." In particular, examine the values and personality traits that the writers of these two articles show to be necessary for survival during difficult times. Read your freewriting in groups of two to four. As others are reading, take written note of areas of agreement or disagreement, questions that arise in your mind, and ideas that might be qualified or extended. After everyone has read, appoint a recorder to keep track of similarities or differences, consensus or disagreement, that arise in the ensuing discussion. The recorder may summarize your group discussion for the rest of the class later.

SUMMARIZING

1. Make a scratchline, cluster representation, or notes indicating the progression of ideas in "The Blue-Collar Blues"—one that reflects your consideration of the freewriting and discussion of group members. Note in particular the way that Manning and McCormick contrast traditional, presumably outdated attitudes about blue-collar

work with attitudes they consider more realistic and constructive in view of present circumstances. Also note the article's structure, particularly the way it concludes with a success story.

2. Write a summary paragraph or two, using your scratchline, cluster representation, or notes.
3. Read summaries in groups. Compare the focus of each summary. How do the summaries differ? How are they the same? Again, check to see if you are *reacting and responding* to the reading selection instead of summarizing the central topics.

FOCUSED CRITICAL READING

1. What are the implications of referring to persons in particular types of occupations as the "working class"? Does this label suggest, for example, that the need to work is a class marker? That persons engaged in other types of occupations don't really work?
2. Manning and McCormick speak of a "downward spiral of income and self-esteem in a society where upward mobility is preached from birth." Do you think the time has come for everyone to abandon the ideal of upward mobility? Is it reasonable to expect some Americans to abandon it when others do not?
3. An economic historian quoted in paragraph 14 says that hard times create "a potential for social meanness." Can you cite any examples from experience, observation, or reading that support that view? Can you cite any examples that contradict it?
4. Janitors, the authors tell us, were once regarded as "the lowest of the low." Do you see any other connections made in this article between work and status?

Lars Eighner

On Dumpster Diving

◆

Lars Eighner, a writer from Austin, Texas, contributed the following article to The Threepenny Review, *a literary magazine published in Berkeley, California.*

1   I began Dumpster diving about a year before I became homeless.

2   I prefer the term "scavenging" and use the word "scrounging" when I mean to be obscure. I have heard people, evidently meaning to be polite, use the word "foraging," but I prefer to reserve that word for gathering nuts and berries and such which I do also according to the season and the opportunity. "Dumpster diving" seems to me to be a little too cute and, in my case, inaccurate because I lack the athletic ability to lower myself into the Dumpster as the true divers do, much to their increased profit.

3   I like the frankness of the word "scavenging," which I can hardly think of without picturing a big black snail on an aquarium wall. I live from the refuse of others. I am a scavenger. I think it a sound and honorable niche, although if I could I would naturally prefer to live the comfortable consumer life, perhaps—and only perhaps—as a slightly less wasteful consumer owing to what I have learned as a scavenger.

4   While my dog Lizbeth and I were still living in the house on Avenue B in Austin, as my savings ran out, I put almost all my sporadic income into rent. The necessities of daily life I began to extract from Dumpsters. Yes, we ate from Dumpsters. Except for jeans, all my clothes came from Dumpsters. Boom boxes, candles, bedding, toilet paper, medicine, books, a typewriter, a virgin male love doll, change sometimes amounting to many dollars: I acquired many things from the Dumpsters.

5   I have learned much as a scavenger. I mean to put some of what I have learned down here, beginning with the practical art of Dumpster diving and proceeding to the abstract.

6   What is safe to eat?

7   After all, the finding of objects is becoming something of an urban art. Even respectable employed people will sometimes find something tempting sticking out of a Dumpster or standing beside one. Quite a number of people, not all of them of the bohemian type, are willing to

brag that they found this or that piece in the trash. But eating from Dumpsters is the thing that separates the dilettanti from the professionals.

Eating safely from the Dumpsters involves three principles: using the senses and common sense to evaluate the condition of the found materials, knowing the Dumpsters of a given area and checking them regularly, and seeking always to answer the question "Why was this discarded?"

8

Perhaps everyone who has a kitchen and a regular supply of groceries has, at one time or another, made a sandwich and eaten half of it before discovering mold on the bread or got a mouthful of milk before realizing the milk had turned. Nothing of the sort is likely to happen to a Dumpster diver because he is constantly reminded that most food is discarded for a reason. Yet a lot of perfectly good food can be found in Dumpsters.

9

Canned goods, for example, turn up fairly often in the Dumpsters I frequent. All except the most phobic people would be willing to eat from a can even if it came from a Dumpster. Canned goods are among the safest of foods to be found in Dumpsters, but are not utterly foolproof.

0

Although very rare with modern canning methods, botulism is a possibility. Most other forms of food poisoning seldom do lasting harm to a healthy person. But botulism is almost certainly fatal and often the first symptom is death. Except for carbonated beverages, all canned goods should contain a slight vacuum and suck air when first punctured. Bulging, rusty, dented cans and cans that spew when punctured should be avoided, especially when the contents are not very acidic or syrupy.

1

Heat can break down the botulin, but this requires much more cooking than most people do to canned goods. To the extent that botulism occurs at all, of course, it can occur in cans on pantry shelves as well as in cans from Dumpsters. Need I say that home-canned goods found in Dumpsters are simply too risky to be recommended.

12

From time to time one of my companions, aware of the source of my provisions, will ask, "Do you think these crackers are really safe to eat?" For some reason it is most often the crackers they ask about.

13

This question always makes me angry. Of course I would not offer my companion anything I had doubts about. But more than that I wonder why he cannot evaluate the condition of the crackers himself. I have no special knowledge and I have been wrong before. Since he knows where the food comes from, it seems to me he ought to assume some of the responsibility for deciding what he will put in his mouth.

14

For myself I have few qualms about dry foods such as crackers, cookies, cereal, chips, and pasta if they are free of visible contaminates and still dry and crisp. Most often such things are found in the original packaging, which is not so much a positive sign as it is the absence of a negative one.

15

16   Raw fruits and vegetables with intact skins seem perfectly safe to me, excluding of course the obviously rotten. Many are discarded for minor imperfections which can be pared away. Leafy vegetables, grapes, cauliflower, broccoli, and similar things may be contaminated by liquids and may be impractical to wash.

17   Candy, especially hard candy, is usually safe if it has not drawn ants. Chocolate is often discarded only because it has become discolored as the cocoa butter de-emulsified. Candying after all is one method of food preservation because pathogens do not like very sugary substances.

18   All of these foods might be found in any Dumpster and can be evaluated with some confidence largely on the basis of appearance. Beyond these are foods which cannot be correctly evaluated without additional information.

19   I began scavenging by pulling pizzas out of the Dumpster behind a pizza delivery shop. In general prepared food requires caution, but in this case I knew when the shop closed and went to the Dumpster as soon as the last of the help left.

20   Such shops often get prank orders, called "bogus." Because help seldom stays long at these places pizzas are often made with the wrong topping, refused on delivery for being cold, or baked incorrectly. The products to be discarded are boxed up because inventory is kept by counting boxes: a boxed pizza can be written off; an unboxed pizza does not exist.

21   I never placed a bogus order to increase the supply of pizzas and I believe no one else was scavenging in this Dumpster. But the people in the shop became suspicious and began to retain their garbage in the shop overnight.

22   While it lasted I had a steady supply of fresh, sometimes warm pizza. Because I knew the Dumpster I knew the source of the pizza, and because I visited the Dumpster regularly I knew what was fresh and what was yesterday's.

23   The area I frequent is inhabited by many affluent college students. I am not here by chance; the Dumpsters in this area are very rich. Students throw out many good things, including food. In particular they tend to throw everything out when they move at the end of a semester, before and after breaks, and around midterm when many of them despair of college. So I find it advantageous to keep an eye on the academic calendar.

24   The students throw food away around the breaks because they do not know whether it has spoiled or will spoil before they return. A typical discard is a half jar of peanut butter. In fact non-organic peanut butter does not require refrigeration and is unlikely to spoil in any reasonable time. The student does not know that, and since it is Daddy's money, the student decides not to take a chance.

Opened containers require caution and some attention to the question "Why was this discarded?" But in the case of discards from student apartments, the answer may be that the item was discarded through carelessness, ignorance, or wastefulness. This can sometimes be deduced when the item is found with many others, including some that are obviously perfectly good.

Some students, and others, approach defrosting a freezer by chucking out the whole lot. Not only do the circumstances of such a find tell the story, but also the mass of frozen goods stays cold for a long time and items may be found still frozen or freshly thawed.

Yogurt, cheese, and sour cream are items that are often thrown out while they are still good. Occasionally I find a cheese with a spot of mold, which of course I just pare off, and because it is obvious why such a cheese was discarded, I treat it with less suspicion than an apparently perfect cheese found in similar circumstances. Yogurt is often discarded, still sealed, only because the expiration date on the carton had passed. This is one of my favorite finds because yogurt will keep for several days, even in warm weather.

Students throw out canned goods and staples at the end of semesters and when they give up college at midterm. Drugs, pornography, spirits, and the like are often discarded when parents are expected— Dad's day, for example. And spirits also turn up after big party weekends, presumably discarded by the newly reformed. Wine and spirits, of course, keep perfectly well even once opened.

My test for carbonated soft drinks is whether they still fizz vigorously. Many juices or other beverages are too acid or too syrupy to cause much concern provided they are not visibly contaminated. Liquids, however, require some care.

One hot day I found a large jug of Pat O'Brian's Hurricane mix. The jug had been opened, but it was still ice cold. I drank three large glasses before it became apparent to me that someone had added the rum to the mix, and not a little rum. I never tasted the rum and by the time I began to feel the effects I had already ingested a very large quantity of the beverage. Some divers would have considered this is a boon, but being suddenly and thoroughly intoxicated in a public place in the early afternoon is not my idea of a good time.

I have heard of people maliciously contaminating discarded food and even handouts, but mostly I have heard of this from people with vivid imaginations who have had no experience with the Dumpsters themselves. Just before the pizza shop stopped discarding its garbage at night, jalapeños began showing up on most of the discarded pizzas. If indeed this was meant to discourage me it was a wasted effort because I am native Texan.

For myself, I avoid game, poultry, pork, and egg-based foods whether I find them raw or cooked. I seldom have the means to cook what I find, but when I do I avail myself of plentiful supplies of beef which is often in very good condition. I suppose fish becomes disagreeable before it becomes dangerous. The dog is happy to have any such thing that is past its prime and, in fact, does not recognize fish as food until it is quite strong.

33   Home leftovers, as opposed to surpluses from restaurants, are very often bad. Evidently, especially among students, there is a common type of personality that carefully wraps up even the smallest leftover and shoves it into the back of the refrigerator for six months or so before discarding it. Characteristic of this type are the reused jars and margarine tubs which house the remains.

34   I avoid ethnic foods I am unfamiliar with. If I do not know what it is supposed to look like when it is good, I cannot be certain I will be able to tell if it is bad.

35   No matter how careful I am I still get dysentery at least once a month, oftener in warm weather. I do not want to paint too romantic a picture. Dumpster diving has serious drawbacks as a way of life.

36   I learned to scavenge gradually, on my own. Since then I have initiated several companions into the trade. I have learned that there is a predictable series of stages a person goes through in learning to scavenge.

37   At first the new scavenger is filled with disgust and self-loathing. He is ashamed of being seen and may lurk around, trying to duck behind things, or he may try to dive at night.

38   (In fact, most people instinctively look away from a scavenger. By skulking around, the novice calls attention to himself and arouses suspicion. Diving at night is ineffective and needlessly messy.)

39   Every grain of rice seems to be a maggot. Everything seems to stink. He can wipe the egg yolk off the found can, but he cannot erase the stigma of eating garbage out of his mind.

40   That stage passes with experience. The scavenger finds a pair of running shoes that fit and look and smell brand new. He finds a pocket calculator in perfect working order. He finds pristine ice cream, still frozen, more than he can eat or keep. He begins to understand: people do throw away perfectly good stuff, a lot of perfectly good stuff.

41   At this stage, Dumpster shyness begins to dissipate. The diver, after all, has the last laugh. He is finding all manner of good things which are his for the taking. Those who disparage his profession are the fools, not he.

42   He may begin to hang onto some perfectly good things for which he has neither a use nor a market. Then he begins to take note of the things which are not perfectly good but are nearly so. He mates a Walkman with broken earphones and one that is missing a battery cover. He picks up things which he can repair.

At this stage he may become lost and never recover. Dumpsters are full of things of some potential value to someone and also of things which never have much intrinsic value but are interesting. All the Dumpster divers I have known come to the point of trying to acquire everything they touch. Why not take it, they reason, since it is all free. 43

This is, of course, hopeless. Most divers come to realize that they must restrict themselves to items of relatively immediate utility. But in some cases the diver simply cannot control himself. I have met several of these pack-rat types. Their ideas of the values of various pieces of junk verge on the psychotic. Every bit of glass may be a diamond, they think, and all that glitters, gold. 44

I tend to gain weight when I am scavenging. Partly this is because I always find far more pizza and doughnuts than water-packed tuna, nonfat yogurt, and fresh vegetables. Also I have not developed much faith in the reliability of Dumpsters as a food source, although it has been proven to me many times. I tend to eat as if I have no idea where my next meal is coming from. But mostly I just hate to see food go to waste and so I eat much more than I should. Something like this drives the obsession to collect junk. 45

As for collecting objects, I usually restrict myself to collecting one kind of small object at a time, such as pocket calculators, sunglasses, or campaign buttons. To live on the street I must anticipate my needs to a certain extent: I must pick up and save warm bedding I find in August because it will not be found in Dumpsters in November. But even if I had a home with extensive storage space I could not save everything that might be valuable in some contingency. 46

I have proprietary feelings about my Dumpsters. As I have suggested, it is no accident that I scavenge from Dumpsters where good finds are common. But my limited experience with Dumpsters in other areas suggests to me that it is the population of competitors rather than the affluence of the dumpers that most affects the feasibility of survival by scavenging. The large number of competitors is what puts me off the idea of trying to scavenge in places like Los Angeles. 47

Curiously, I do not mind my direct competition, other scavengers, so much as I hate the can scroungers. 48

People scrounge cans because they have to have a little cash. I have tried scrounging cans with an able-bodied companion. Afoot a can scrounger simply cannot make more than a few dollars a day. One can extract the necessities of life from the Dumpsters directly with far less effort than would be required to accumulate the equivalent value in cans. 49

Can scroungers, then, are people who *must* have small amounts of cash. These are drug addicts and winos, mostly the latter because the amounts of cash are so small. 50

51   Spirits and drugs do, like all other commodities, turn up in Dumpsters and the scavenger will from time to time have a half bottle of a rather good wine with his dinner. But the wino cannot survive on the occasional finds; he must have his daily dose to stave off the DTs. All the cans he can carry will buy about three bottles of Wild Irish Rose.

52   I do not begrudge them the cans, but can scroungers tend to tear up the Dumpsters, mixing the contents and littering the area. They become so specialized that they can see only cans. They earn my contempt by passing up change, canned goods, and readily hockable items.

53   There are precious few courtesies among scavengers. But it is a common practice to set aside surplus items: pairs of shoes, clothing, canned goods, and such. A true scavenger hates to see good stuff go to waste and what he cannot use he leaves in good condition in plain sight.

54   Can scroungers lay waste to everything in their path and will stir one of a pair of good shoes to the bottom of a Dumpster, to be lost or ruined in the muck. Can scroungers will even go through individual garbage cans, something I have never seen a scavenger do.

55   Individual garbage cans are set out on the public easement only on garbage days. On other days going through them requires trespassing close to a dwelling. Going through individual garbage cans without scattering litter is almost impossible. Litter is likely to reduce the public's tolerance of scavenging. Individual garbage cans are simply not as productive as Dumpsters: people in houses and duplexes do not move as often and for some reason do not tend to discard as much useful material. Moreover, the time required to go through one garbage can that serves one household is not much less than the time required to go through a Dumpster that contains the refuse of twenty apartments.

56   But my strongest reservation about going through individual garbage cans is that this seems to me a very personal kind of invasion to which I would object if I were a householder. Although many things in Dumpsters are obviously meant never to come to light, a Dumpster is somehow less personal.

57   I avoid trying to draw conclusions about the people who dump in the Dumpsters I frequent. I think it would be unethical to do so, although I know many people will find the idea of scavenger ethics too funny for words.

58   Dumpsters contain bank statements, bills, correspondence, and other documents, just as anyone might expect. But there are also less obvious sources of information. Pill bottles, for example. The labels on pill bottles contain the name of the patient, the name of the doctor, and the name of the drug. AIDS drugs and anti-psychotic medicines, to name but two groups, are specific and are seldom prescribed for any

other disorders. The plastic compacts for birth control pills usually have complete label information.

Despite all of this sensitive information, I have had only one apartment resident object to my going through the Dumpster. In that case it turned out the resident was a University athlete who was taking bets and who was afraid I would turn up his wager slips.

Occasionally a find tells a story. I once found a small paper bag containing some unused condoms, several partial tubes of flavored sexual lubricant, a partially used compact of birth control pills, and the torn pieces of a picture of a young man. Clearly she was through with him and planning to give up sex altogether.

Dumpster things are often sad—abandoned teddy bears, shredded wedding books, despaired-of sales kits. I find many pets lying in state in Dumpsters. Although I hope to get off the streets so that Lizbeth can have a long and comfortable old age, I know this hope is not very realistic. So I suppose when her time comes she too will go into a Dumpster. I will have no better place for her. And after all, for most of her life her livelihood has come from the Dumpster. When she finds something I think is safe that has been spilled from the Dumpster I let her have it. She already knows the route around the best Dumpsters. I like to think that if she survives me she will have a chance of evading the dog catcher and of finding her sustenance on the route.

Silly vanities also come to rest in the Dumpsters. I am a rather accomplished needleworker. I get a lot of materials from the Dumpsters. Evidently sorority girls, hoping to impress someone, perhaps themselves, with their mastery of a womanly art, buy a lot of embroider-by-number kits, work a few stitches horribly, and eventually discard the whole mess. I pull out their stitches, turn the canvas over, and work an original design. Do not think I refrain from chuckling as I make original gifts from these kits.

I find diaries and journals. I have often thought of compiling a book of literary found objects. And perhaps I will one day. But what I find is hopelessly commonplace and bad without being, even unconsciously, camp. College students also discard their papers. I am horrified to discover the kind of paper which now merits an A in an undergraduate course. I am grateful, however, for the number of good books and magazines the students throw out. . . .

Dumpster diving is outdoor work, often surprisingly pleasant. It is not entirely predictable; things of interest turn up every day and some days there are finds of great value. I am always very pleased when I can turn up exactly the thing I most wanted to find. Yet in spite of the element of chance, scavenging more than most other pursuits tends to yield returns in some proportion to the effort and intelligence brought to bear. It is very sweet to turn up a few dollars in change from a Dumpster that has just been gone over by a wino.

The land is now covered with cities. The cities are full of Dumpsters. I think of scavenging as a modern form of self-reliance. In any event, after ten years of government service, where everything is geared to the lowest common denominator, I find work that rewards initiative and effort refreshing. Certainly I would be happy to have a sinecure again, but I am not heartbroken not to have one anymore. . . .   65

Many times in my travels I have lost everything but the clothes I was wearing and Lizbeth. The things I find in Dumpsters, the love letters and ragdolls of so many lives, remind me of this lesson. Now I hardly pick up a thing without envisioning the time I will cast it away. This I think is a healthy state of mind. Almost everything I have now has already been cast out at least once, proving that what I own is valueless to someone.   66

Anyway, I find my desire to grab for the gaudy bauble has been largely sated. I think this is an attitude I share with the very wealthy— we both know there is plenty more where what we have came from. Between us are the rat-race millions who have confounded their selves with the objects they grasp and who nightly scavenge the cable channels looking for they know not what.   67

I am sorry for them.   68

Reading and Writing Activities

PRELIMINARY RESPONSE

Notes.   As you read, record your reactions (questions or comments) to "On Dumpster Diving" in your reading journal.

You may react to one or more of a number of factors in the reading. You might, for example, consider Lars Eighner's attitude toward scavenging, particularly his view of it as a respectable occupation with its own rules, procedures, and ethics.

Discussion.   In class, compare your reactions in reading groups of five or six. Appoint a recorder to keep track of similarities and differences, consensus or disagreement, arising from the discussion. The recorder may summarize your group discussion for the rest of the class later.

Freewriting.   In a 10- to 15-minute freewrite, try to explain and support the notion that scavenging, as a way of life, is compatible with such traditional values as thrift, conservation, and self-reliance. Read your freewriting in groups of two to four. As others are reading, take written note of areas of agreement or disagreement, questions that arise in your mind, and ideas that might be qualified or extended. After everyone has read, appoint a recorder to keep track of similarities or differences, consensus or disagreement, that arise in the ensuing discussion. The recorder may summarize your group discussion for the rest of the class later.

SUMMARIZING

1. Make a scratchline, cluster representation, or notes indicating the progression of ideas in "On Dumpster Diving"—one that reflects your consideration of the freewriting and discussion of group members. Note in particular Eighner's attitudes toward the more affluent and their attitudes toward him.
2. Write a summary paragraph or two, using your scratchline, cluster representation, or notes.
3. Read summaries in groups. Compare the focus of each summary. How do the summaries differ? How are they the same? Again, check to see if you are *reacting and responding* to the reading selection instead of summarizing the central topics.

FOCUSED CRITICAL READING

1. What kinds of obstacles do you suppose a homeless person would have to contend with in order to have his or her writing appear in a literary magazine published in a distant city? How do you suppose Eighner contended with such difficulties?
2. Do you believe Eighner when he says that he has "no special knowledge" about whether or not discarded food can be eaten safely? If you don't believe him, why do you suppose he disclaims such knowledge?
3. Eighner says that "many people...find the idea of scavenger ethics too funny for words." Would reading Eighner's essay be likely to change anyone's mind in this regard?

bell hooks

Homeplace: A Site of Resistance

◆

Gloria Watkins, who writes under the pen name of bell hooks, is a profes-sor of English and women's studies at Oberlin College. In the following selection, she examines the familiar notion that politics of the workplace should be kept separate from the home environment—a notion that leads many Americans to view home and family as a shelter from conflict and stress. Hooks considers this attitude a retreat into middle-class individu-alism, one that serves to advance white racism. In its stead, she proposes an alternative view of home as a place where political change is initiated.

1   When I was a young girl the journey across town to my grand-mother's house was one of the most intriguing experiences. Mama did not like to stay there long. She did not care for all that loud talk, the talk that was usually about the old days, the way life happened then—who married whom, how and when somebody died, but also how we lived and survived as black people, how the white folks treated us. I remem-ber this journey not just because of the stories I would hear. It was a movement away from the segregated blackness of our community into a poor white neighborhood. I remember the fear, being scared to walk to Baba's (our grandmother's house) because we would have to pass that terrifying whiteness—those white faces on the porches staring us down with hate. Even when empty or vacant, those porches seemed to say "danger," "you do not belong here," "you are not safe."

2   Oh! that feeling of safety, of arrival, of homecoming when we finally reached the edges of her yard, when we could see the soot black face of our grandfather, Daddy Gus, sitting in his chair on the porch, smell his cigar, and rest on his lap. Such a contrast, that feeling of arrival, of homecoming, this sweetness and the bitterness of that jour-ney, that constant reminder of white power and control.

3   I speak of this journey as leading to my grandmother's house, even though our grandfather lived there too. In our young minds houses belonged to women, were their special domain, not as property, but as places where all that truly mattered in life took place—the warmth and comfort of shelter, the feeding of our bodies, the nurturing of our souls. There we learned dignity, integrity of being; there we learned to have

faith. The folks who made this life possible, who were our primary guides and teachers, were black women.

Their lives were not easy. Their lives were hard. They were black women who for the most part worked outside the home serving white folks, cleaning their houses, washing their clothes, tending their children—black women who worked in the fields or in the streets, whatever they could do to make ends meet, whatever was necessary. Then they returned to their homes to make life happen there. This tension between service outside one's home, family, and kin network, service provided to white folks which took time and energy, and the effort of black women to conserve enough of themselves to provide service (care and nurturance) within their own families and communities is one of the many factors that has historically distinguished the lot of black women in patriarchal white supremacist society from that of black men. Contemporary black struggle must honor this history of service just as it must critique the sexist definition of service as women's "natural" role.

Since sexism delegates to females the task of creating and sustaining a home environment, it has been primarily the responsibility of black women to construct domestic households as spaces of care and nurturance in the face of the brutal harsh reality of racist oppression, of sexist domination. Historically, African-American people believed that the construction of a homeplace, however fragile and tenuous (the slave hut, the wooden shack), had a radical political dimension. Despite the brutal reality of racial apartheid, of domination, one's homeplace was the one site where one could freely confront the issue of humanization, where one could resist. Black women resisted by making homes where all black people could strive to be subjects, not objects, where we could be affirmed in our minds and hearts despite poverty, hardship, and deprivation, where we could restore to ourselves the dignity denied us on the outside in the public world.

This task of making homeplace was not simply a matter of black women providing service; it was about the construction of a safe place where black people could affirm one another and by so doing heal many of the wounds inflicted by racist domination. We could not learn to love or respect ourselves in the culture of white supremacy, on the outside; it was there on the inside, in that "homeplace," most often created and kept by black women, that we had the opportunity to grow and develop, to nurture our spirits. This task of making a homeplace, of making home a community of resistance, has been shared by black women globally, especially black women in white supremacist societies.

I shall never forget the sense of shared history, of common anguish, I felt when first reading about the plight of black women domestic servants in South Africa, black women laboring in white homes. Their stories evoked vivid memories of our African-American past. I remember that one of the black women giving testimony complained that after traveling in the wee hours of the morning to the white folks' house, after working there all day, giving her time and energy, she had "none left for her own." I knew this story. I had read it in the slave narratives of African-American women who, like Sojourner Truth, could say, "When I cried out with a mother's grief none but Jesus heard." I knew this story. I had grown to womanhood hearing about black women who nurtured and cared for white families when they longed to have time and energy to give to their own.

8   I want to remember these black women today. The act of remembrance is a conscious gesture honoring their struggle, their effort to keep something for their own. I want us to respect and understand that this effort has been and continues to be a radically subversive political gesture. For those who dominate and oppress us benefit most when we have nothing to give our own, when they have so taken from us our dignity, our humanness that we have nothing left, no "homeplace" where we can recover ourselves. I want us to remember these black women today, both past and present. Even as I speak there are black women in the midst of racial apartheid in South Africa, struggling to provide something for their own. "We ... know how our sisters suffer" (Quoted in the petition for the repeal of the pass laws, August 9, 1956). I want us to honor them, not because they suffer but because they continue to struggle in the midst of suffering, because they continue to resist. I want to speak about the importance of homeplace in the midst of oppression and domination, of homeplace as a site of resistance and liberation struggle. Writing about "resistance," particularly resistance to the Vietnam war, Vietnamese Buddhist monk Thich Nhat Hahn says:

> ... resistance, at root, must mean more than resistance against war. It is a resistance against all kinds of things that are like war. ... So perhaps, resistance means opposition to being invaded, occupied, assaulted and destroyed by the system. The purpose of resistance, here, is to seek the healing of yourself in order to be able to see clearly. ... I think that communities of resistance should be places where people can return to themselves more easily, where the conditions are such that they can heal themselves and recover their wholeness.

9   Historically, black women have resisted white supremacist domination by working to establish homeplace. It does not matter that sexism assigned them this role. It is more important that they took this conventional role and expanded it to include caring for one another, for children, for black men, in ways that elevated our spirits, that kept us from despair, that taught some of us to be revolutionaries able to struggle for freedom. In his famous 1845 slave narrative, Frederick Douglass

tells the story of his birth, of his enslaved black mother who was hired out a considerable distance from his place of residence. Describing their relationship, he writes:

> I never saw my mother, to know her as such more than four or five times in my life; and each of these times was very short in duration, and at night. She was hired by Mr. Stewart, who lived about twelve miles from my house. She made her journeys to see me in the night, traveling the whole distance on foot, after the performance of her day's work. She was a field hand, and a whipping is the penalty of not being in the field at sunrise.... I do not recollect ever seeing my mother by the light of day. She was with me in the night. She would lie down with me and get me to sleep, but long before I waked she was gone.

After sharing this information, Douglass later says that he never 10 enjoyed a mother's "soothing presence, her tender and watchful care" so that he received the "tidings of her death with much the same emotions I should have probably felt at the death of a stranger." Douglass surely intended to impress upon the consciousness of white readers the cruelty of that system of racial domination which separated black families, black mothers from their children. Yet he does so by devaluing black womanhood, by not even registering the quality of care that made his black mother travel those twelve miles to hold him in her arms. In the midst of a brutal racist system, which did not value black life, she valued the life of her child enough to resist that system, to come to him in the night, just to hold him.

Now I cannot agree with Douglass that he never knew a mother's 11 care. I want to suggest that this mother, who dared to hold him in the night, gave him at birth a sense of value that provided a groundwork, however fragile, for the person he later became. If anyone doubts the power and significance of this maternal gesture, they would do well to read psychoanalyst Alice Miller's book, *The Untouched Key: Tracing Childhood Trauma in Creativity and Destructiveness.* Holding him in her arms, Douglass' mother provided, if only for a short time, a space where this black child was not the subject of dehumanizing scorn and devaluation but was the recipient of a quality of care that should have enabled the adult Douglass to look back and reflect on the political choices of this black mother who resisted slave codes, risking her life, to care for her son. I want to suggest that devaluation of the role his mother played in his life is a dangerous oversight. Though Douglass is only one example, we are currently in danger of forgetting the powerful role black women have played in constructing for us homeplaces that are the site for resistance. This forgetfulness undermines our solidarity and the future of black liberation struggle.

12   Douglass's work is important, for he is historically identified as sympathetic to the struggle for women's rights. All too often his critique of male domination, such as it was, did not include recognition of the particular circumstances of black women in relation to black men and families. To me one of the most important chapters in my first book, *Ain't I a Woman: Black Women and Feminism,* is one that calls attention to "Continued Devaluation of Black Womanhood." Overall devaluation of the role black women have played in constructing for us homeplaces that are the site for resistance undermines our efforts to resist racism and the colonizing mentality which promotes internalized self-hatred. Sexist thinking about the nature of domesticity has determined the way black women's experience in the home is perceived. In African-American culture there is a long tradition of "mother worship." Black autobiographies, fiction, and poetry praise the virtues of the self-sacrificing black mother. Unfortunately, though positively motivated, black mother worship extols the virtues of self-sacrifice while simultaneously implying that such a gesture is not reflective of choice and will, rather the perfect embodiment of a woman's "natural" role. The assumption then is that the black woman who works hard to be a responsible caretaker is only doing what she should be doing. Failure to recognize the realm of choice, and the remarkable re-visioning of both woman's role and the idea of "home" that black women consciously exercised in practice, obscures the political commitment to racial uplift, to eradicating racism, which was the philosophical core of dedication to community and home.

13   Though black women did not self-consciously articulate in written discourse the theoretical principles of decolonization, this does not detract from the importance of their actions. They understood intellectually and intuitively the meaning of homeplace in the midst of an oppressive and dominating social reality, of homeplace as site of resistance and liberation struggle. I know of what I speak. I would not be writing this essay if my mother, Rosa Bell, daughter to Sarah Oldham, granddaughter to Bell Hooks, had not created homeplace in just this liberatory way, despite the contradictions of poverty and sexism.

14   In our family, I remember the immense anxiety we felt as children when mama would leave our house, our segregated community, to work as a maid in the homes of white folks. I believe that she sensed our fear, our concern that she might not return to us safe, that we could not find her (even though she always left phone numbers, they did not ease our worry). When she returned home after working long hours, she did not complain. She made an effort to rejoice with us that her work was done, that she was home, making it seem as though there was nothing about the experience of working as a maid in a white household, in that space of Otherness, which stripped her of dignity and personal power.

Looking back as an adult woman, I think of the effort it must have   15
taken for her to transcend her own tiredness (and who knows what
assaults or wounds to her spirit had to be put aside so that she could give
something to her own). Given the contemporary notions of "good
parenting" this may seem like a small gesture, yet in many post-slavery
black families, it was a gesture parents were often too weary, too beaten
down to make. Those of us who were fortunate enough to receive such
care understood its value. Politically, our young mother, Rosa Bell, did
not allow the white supremacist culture of domination to completely
shape and control her psyche and her familial relationships. Working to
create a homeplace that affirmed our beings, our blackness, our love for
one another was necessary resistance. We learned degrees of critical consciousness from her. Our lives were not without contradictions, so it is
not my intent to create a romanticized portrait. Yet any attempts to critically assess the role of black women in liberation struggle must examine
the way political concern about the impact of racism shaped black
women's thinking, their sense of home, and their modes of parenting.

An effective means of white subjugation of black people globally   16
has been the perpetual construction of economic and social structures
that deprive many folks of the means to make homeplace. Remembering this should enable us to understand the political value of black
women's resistance in the home. It should provide a framework where
we can discuss the development of black female political consciousness, acknowledging the political importance of resistance effort that
took place in homes. It is no accident that the South African apartheid
regime systematically attacks and destroys black efforts to construct
homeplace, however tenuous, that small private reality where black
women and men can renew their spirits and recover themselves. It is
no accident that this homeplace, as fragile and as transitional as it may
be, a makeshift shed, a small bit of earth where one rests, is always subject to violation and destruction. For when a people no longer have the
space to construct homeplace, we cannot build a meaningful community of resistance.

Throughout our history, African-Americans have recognized the   17
subversive value of homeplace, of having access to private space where
we do not directly encounter white racist aggression. Whatever the
shape and direction of black liberation struggle (civil rights reform or
black power movement), domestic space has been a crucial site for
organizing, for forming political solidarity. Homeplace has been a site
of resistance. Its structure was defined less by whether or not black
women and men were conforming to sexist behavior norms and more
by our struggle to uplift ourselves as a people, our struggle to resist
racist domination and oppression.

That liberatory struggle has been seriously undermined by con-   18
temporary efforts to change that subversive homeplace into a site of

patriarchal domination of black women by black men, where we abuse one another for not conforming to sexist norms. This shift in perspective, where homeplace is not viewed as a political site, has had negative impact on the construction of black female identity and political consciousness. Masses of black women, many of whom were not formally educated, had in the past been able to play a vital role in black liberation struggle. In the contemporary situation, as the paradigms for domesticity in black life mirrored white bourgeois norms (where home is conceptualized as politically neutral space), black people began to overlook and devalue the importance of black female labor in teaching critical consciousness in domestic space. Many black women, irrespective of class status, have responded to this crisis of meaning by imitating leisure-class sexist notions of women's role, focusing their lives on meaningless compulsive consumerism.

19   Identifying this syndrome as "the crisis of black womanhood" in her essay, "Considering Feminism as a Model for Social Change," Sheila Radford-Hill points to the mid-sixties as that historical moment when the primacy of black woman's role in liberation struggle began to be questioned as a threat to black manhood and was deemed unimportant. Radford-Hill asserts:

> Without the power to influence the purpose and the direction of our collective experience, without the power to influence our culture from within, we are increasingly immobilized, unable to integrate self and role identities, unable to resist the cultural imperialism of the dominant culture which assures our continued oppression by destroying us from within. Thus, the crisis manifests itself as social dysfunction in the black community—as genocide, fratricide, homicide, and suicide. It is also manifested by the abdication of personal responsibility by black women for themselves and for each other. . . . The crisis of black womanhood is a form of cultural aggression: a form of exploitation so vicious, so insidious that it is currently destroying an entire generation of black women and their families.

20   This contemporary crisis of black womanhood might have been avoided had black women collectively sustained attempts to develop the latent feminism expressed by their willingness to work equally alongside black men in black liberation struggle. Contemporary equation of black liberation struggle with the subordination of black women has damaged collective black solidarity. It has served the interests of white supremacy to promote the assumption that the wounds of racist domination would be less severe were black women conforming to sexist role patterns.

21   We are daily witnessing the disintegration of African-American family life that is grounded in a recognition of the political value of constructing homeplace as a site of resistance; black people daily per-

petuate sexist norms that threaten our survival as a people. We can no longer act as though sexism in black communities does not threaten our solidarity; any force which estranges and alienates us from one another serves the interests of racist domination.

Black women and men must create a revolutionary vision of black   22
liberation that has a feminist dimension, one which is formed in consideration of our specific needs and concerns. Drawing on past legacies, contemporary black women can begin to reconceptualize ideas of homeplace, once again considering the primacy of domesticity as a site for subversion and resistance. When we renew our concern with homeplace, we can address political issues that most affect our daily lives. Calling attention to the skills and resources of black women who may have begun to feel that they have no meaningful contribution to make, women who may or may not be formally educated but who have essential wisdom to share, who have practical experience that is the breeding ground for all useful theory, we may begin to bond with one another in ways that renew our solidarity.

When black women renew our political commitment to home-   23
place, we can address the needs and concerns of young black women who are groping for structures of meaning that will further their growth, young women who are struggling for self-definition. Together, black women can renew our commitment to black liberation struggle, sharing insights and awareness, sharing feminist thinking and feminist vision, building solidarity.

With this foundation, we can regain lost perspective, give life new   24
meaning. We can make homeplace that space where we return for renewal and self-recovery, where we can heal our wounds and become whole.

Reading and Writing Activities

PRELIMINARY RESPONSE

Notes.   As you read, record your reactions (questions or comments) to "Homeplace: A Site of Resistance" in your reading journal.

You may react to one or more of a number of factors in the reading. You might, for example, consider the ways in which bell hooks challenges or affirms your notions of home life.

Discussion.   In class, compare your reactions in reading groups of five or six. Appoint a recorder to keep track of similarities and differences, consensus or disagreement, arising from the discussion. The recorder may summarize your group discussion for the rest of the class later.

Freewriting.   In a 10- to 15-minute freewrite, try to articulate the contrasting views of home on which hooks bases her argument. (It might help to reread paragraph 18 carefully before you start freewriting.) Read your freewriting in groups of two to four. As others are reading, take written note of areas of agreement or disagreement, questions that arise in your mind, and ideas that might be qualified or extended. After everyone has read, appoint a recorder to keep track of similarities or differences, consensus or disagreement, that arise in the ensuing discussion. The recorder may summarize your group discussion for the rest of the class later.

SUMMARIZING

1. Make a scratchline, cluster representation, or notes indicating the progression of ideas in "Homeplace"—one that reflects your consideration of the freewriting and discussion of group members. Note in particular the ways that hooks argues for a type of home life that contests institutionalized racism and sexism.
2. Write a summary paragraph or two, using your scratchline, cluster representation, or notes.
3. Read summaries in groups. Compare the focus of each summary. How do the summaries differ? How are they the same? Again, check to see if you are *reacting and responding* to the reading selection instead of summarizing the central topics.

FOCUSED CRITICAL READING

1. In paragraph 15, hooks says that "contemporary notions of 'good parenting'" might diminish the value of what her mother did for her family. Why?
2. In paragraph 1, hooks tells us that her mother disliked "all that loud talk, the talk that was usually about . . . how we lived and survived as black people, how the white folks treated us." Yet she goes on to say that she "learned degrees of critical consciousness" from her mother. How do you account for this apparent contradiction?
3. Does hooks's essay offer any insight or guidance about home life within white mainstream culture?

Yoichi Shimatsu and Patricia Lee

Dust and Dishes: Organizing Asian American Workers

———————◆———————

This selection addresses the vexed and painful conflict that forces many Asian Americans to pose their exploitation as workers against the oppression of racism, to weigh the advantages of union membership against a history of discrimination within the labor movement. Yoichi Shimatsu is a freelance writer and consultant to the Pacific and Asian American Center for Theology and Strategies. He lives in Berkeley, California, where he coordinates an immigrant counseling program for local churches. Patricia Lee is a San Francisco union leader who, since 1973, has worked aggressively for the rights of women and immigrant workers. She is currently a representative of the Hotel Employees and Restaurant Employees Union.

On Nob Hill the Christmas holidays are a fancy affair. Limousines glide past antique cable cars to deliver partygoers to grand hotels. Inside, the pastry chefs have constructed a life-sized gingerbread house for the children.

The resplendence comforts even the busiest minds as thoughts of oilfields and mergers, inheritances and mining rights are soon forgotten. Sprinkled throughout the lobby, foreign tourists and Midwestern couples pop flashbulbs in the glamorous setting of the recent television series, "Hotel." Even the staff at the front desk and in the dining rooms strongly resemble the wholesome cast of the show.

Behind the scenes, however, Asians and other immigrants carry on the more mundane work of operating a major hotel. Every morning at sunrise, Asian workers trudge up the steep grade from neighboring Chinatown or nearby bus stops to clock in at employee entrances. Inside cavernous kitchens, cooks fire up ovens and start the coffee while businesspersons prepare table settings of china, flowers, and real silverware. Room cleaners push their carts by linen stations to pick up fresh sheets and towels. Before any of the guests wake up, another workday has begun.

Nob Hill owes its reputation for opulent wealth to an earlier generation of Asian workers. On this hill above San Francisco Bay, the railroad barons built their mansions after amassing a fortune from the steel track laid by Chinese contract laborers. A century later the jetliner has surpassed the transcontinental railroad, and luxury hotels have replaced the old mansions. Asian immigrants, however, continue to fill the ranks of labor.

5   Unsuk Perry, a Korean American room cleaner, recalled her first day on the job at a downtown hotel. "I had never been employed before, so I was ready for anything. I didn't expect the work to be so hard physically, especially turning over the mattresses. It took a long time to get used to such work. The other employees were friendly and helped me along. Most of them were immigrants, too, so they understood how I felt."

6   Perry had married an American employed in South Korea and came with her husband to San Francisco in 1963. After nine years at the Hilton, she transferred to the Fairmont Hotel's housekeeping department. As a union shop steward, she frequently translates for her Korean co-workers. "During lunch breaks, I explain to them our union's medical and dental plan for their families. It takes about five years for the newer non-English-speaking women to fully adjust to their jobs and fit in with the rest of the employees," she noted. Perry's ability to help her colleagues stems not only from her years of experience, but also from leadership training and counseling that she received from a community-based group which helps Asian immigrant women working in entry-level jobs.

Historical Animosity

7   Though Perry is active with her union, Asians have not always felt welcome among the groups representing workers' interests. This tension has its roots in the anti-Chinese agitation of over a century ago. With the completion of the railroad, Chinese laborers scattered throughout the West in search of other employment. Their willingness to take jobs shunned by others led to the perception of the white working class that they were cheap foreign competition undercutting wages in a limited market. The image then led to hostility, beatings, arson, and even murder. Populist labor organizations, such as the Workingmen's Party, made opposition to Asian immigration its central rallying point. The Federation of Organized Trades (forerunner of the American Federation of Labor) provided the driving force behind the Chinese Exclusion Act of 1882, which severely curtailed immigration from China.

8   To their credit, however, some of the early California union leaders spoke out against the anti-Asian policies. The San Francisco culinary unions, for example, opened their membership to Asians at a time when most other labor organizations excluded Asians. During the 1920s and 1930s Waiters Union president Hugo Ernst, himself an immi-

grant, often spoke out as the lone voice against the anti-Asian bias in the Central Labor Council. In return, during the 1934 San Francisco general strike, all 150 Chinese union members, including female elevator operators, walked the picket lines. All this transpired before the International Union convention finally eliminated its official "color line" in 1936.

Hotel and Restaurant Workers

Employment patterns within the hotel business are similar to those   9
of other industries. Job categories are basically divided into two tracks: the "back of the house" or less visible, lower paying positions, such as room cleaner, buspersons, and dishwashers; and the "front of the house" or high visibility, tipped jobs and skilled crafts, including bartenders, food and cocktail servers, and chefs. The wage gap between the two tracks can be extremely wide, with chefs earning double the pay of room cleaners. There exists a corresponding hierarchy in social status where white Americans and Europeans are clustered in the higher ranking positions.

The inequity in wages and social status was the main cause of the   10
organizing movement among San Francisco Asian and Latina room cleaners in the late 1970s. Although physically isolated from each other on the job, the room cleaners maintained a high level of camaraderie at impromptu meetings in the employees' cafeteria and women's locker room.

Though the women hoped the union would confront their employ-   11
ers, their hopes were stifled by an entrenched local union leadership which had failed to keep up with the rapidly changing ethnic composition of the work force. Comprising over 30 percent of the total local membership by 1980, Asians had special problems of language, immigration status, and discrimination, all of which the union was unwilling to address.

Following the merger of five craft unions, the International Union   12
imposed a trusteeship in 1978 to control dissent in the unified local. Hotel room cleaners played a major role in the rank and file movement which eventually resulted in a court order overturning the trusteeship and returning control to the local members. The defeat of the old-line leadership opened the way to a new round of negotiations.

During the two-year period of arbitration and contract negotiation   13
from 1978 to 1980, the Asian and Latina room cleaners won a series of victories, including an unprecedented 44 percent wage increase, a reduction of workload by one room per day, free meals, a grievance procedure, and a shop steward system. One main problem remained: what the women workers felt to be the management's overbearing atti-

tude towards them. The local press described the 1980 hotel strike which followed as a fight for "dignity and respect." After the month-long strike, the room cleaners returned to work with an improved sense of worth and self-esteem, and with hopes that they would never again be discounted by either the management or the union.

14   Other Asian women in the hotels have also developed affirmative-action strategies to challenge sex and race barriers. Behind a gleaming stainless steel counter, Filipina American cook Lina Abellan decorates trays of small cakes with floral designs of whipped cream and choco-late frosting. As a *garde manger,* or garnish chef, she applies her artistry to fancy relishes, ice carvings, and other ornamental arrangements.

15   She is also fighting for fair promotions at her downtown hotel. "Hotel management has this mistaken idea that it's classier to have European or white American chefs. Whenever there's an opening for a sous chef's position, managers will usually pass up a qualified minor-ity applicant even if they have to hire from the outside," she explained. "Other minority cooks and I have applied unsuccessfully for a chef's position, myself five times. Frankly, we are getting tired of training inexperienced outsiders who were supposed to supervise us."

16   A black shop steward advised her to file a complaint with the state Fair Employment and Housing Commission. After reviewing her case, the commission authorized her to initiate a civil lawsuit under Title VII of the Civil Rights Act, which prohibits employment discrimination. With the assistance of an Asian American community legal group, Abellan and her co-workers are preparing a class action suit. "Filipino and other minority cooks don't really want to 'rock the boat,' but some-times you don't have any other choice. Whatever it takes—in the union or in court—we must make sure that everyone is treated fairly and equally," she said.

17   Abellan has demonstrated the same level of commitment and lead-ership within her union. In early 1985 she successfully ran for the exec-utive board with a multi-ethnic reform slate which was attempting to dislodge the incumbent administration. "The election campaign was very difficult since the rank and file were divided. In only a few months' time we had to build a campaign organization, raise money, publish literature, and hold meetings. Without any outside help or full-time staff, we ran a strong race and positioned ourselves for the future. If you don't try, you'll never learn," said the garnish chef.

18   One of just a handful of Asian American women union leaders, Abellan admits she still has much to learn. "Parliamentary procedure, financial matters, policy issues . . . these are all very new to me. It's a big responsibility to represent such a large membership. Now I can appre-ciate the importance of support from the rank and file." Since Local 2 of the Hotel and Restaurant Workers Union is the city's largest labor orga-nization, with thirteen thousand members, her leadership role has a

direct influence on the future of many San Francisco–area working women.

Department Store Activists

"Coming from a business background, I never dreamed that I 19 would ever become involved in a union," mused Eiko Mizuhara, who for most of her life was a middle-class housewife married to the owner of a San Francisco drugstore. Planning to return to college, Mizuhara found a part-time job at San Francisco's Emporium-Capwell department store in order to pay her tuition. A retail clerk at the cosmetics counter, she handled a wide selection of colognes and perfumes.

"Then one day, it happened. My colleague, another sales clerk, was 20 detained by a security guard for over four hours. She wasn't even allowed to make a phone call. Whatever she might have done, her civil rights were clearly violated." Mizuhara instinctively took action in defense of the detained woman by gathering signatures of her co-workers on a petition to the management. She presented copies of the petition to the company's board of directors, several managers, and to her union, the Department Store Employees' Local 1100.

"I often wondered why I reacted so forcefully. Looking back, I 21 think that my camp experience had a lot to do with my present involvement." Mizuhara was seven years old when she was relocated with her family to an internment camp in Poston, Arizona, and later at Tule Lake, California. At the outbreak of World War II, her father, the manager of Otagiri import/export company, was forced to close the prosperous business and move the family out of their home in Japantown, San Francisco.

"Our sense of justice was just routed. We were incapable of doing 22 anything to protect our rights. Who would have guessed that my feelings would surface forty years later? The main difference between then and now is that I am finally in a position to *do something*," said the clerk.

When the contract expiration date approached in May 1984, Mizu- 23 hara joined the rank and file negotiating committee and observed the bargaining process firsthand. "Being from a Japanese American background, I was appalled by the lack of even small courtesies. Since management and labor must depend on each other, I expected there to be a give-and-take attitude on both sides. The pure greed was shocking, especially considering the monumental profits made the previous year."

Departing from an era of labor-management cooperation, the 24 department store negotiators adopted a hard-line stance against the union. Taking their cue from other industries, the store's management proposed a staggering list of "take-aways," including employee contributions toward medical insurance; a lower wage scale for new hires;

and greater management control over rules determining schedules, shifts, and job descriptions.

25   "When store employees voted to strike Macy's, Emporium-Capwell locked us out. Even though they are fierce competitors, the two companies decided to combine their forces against the union," observed Mizuhara.

26   During the breaks in the negotiating sessions, Mizuhara and other committee members picketed the downtown stores. "Some of the Asian women clerks would refuse to picket because their husbands thought it was undignified. A few single women continued to work... because they had no other source of income.... The majority of Asian workers did show up for picket duty. Most of them, however, kept very quiet out of their sense of decorum. In contrast, I tried to be vocal when attempting to convince shoppers not to patronize the store. I was personally very disappointed with Asian American shoppers [who] crossed the picket lines of Asian strikers," she recalled.

27   Though she felt that the strike generally encouraged many more women to become involved in union activity, Mizuhara also acknowledged that the conditions of the final settlement led to a major crisis for her local. After striking for six weeks, the employees voted to accept many concessions and to work. As a result of staggering financial losses due to the lengthy strike, the International Union removed the local's popular president.

28   For the union membership, these unfortunate repercussions underlined the need to reorganize and revitalize their local. "At this point, trade unions must start looking for new directions. With the decline of blue-collar industrial jobs, service-oriented unions are becoming the main base for organized labor," Mizuhara noted. "The labor movement must once again become the social conscience of America, bringing together all the different unions and reaching out to our communities and involving broader constituencies."

Crossing Barriers

29   For Asian American women, the push into mainstream economy began shortly after World War II. Bertha Chan, a Chinese American retail clerk, has seen much progress over the decades since she first become a union member in the early 1950s. She recalled the lack of employment alternatives for her parents. "Although they were both second-generation Chinese Americans, my father and mother remained farmworkers all their lives. Outside of farm labor or Chinatown's small businesses, there simply weren't many opportunities for Asians."

30   Chan spent her early childhood in Isleton, California, in the Sacramento River delta region. Her parents followed the harvests on an annual circuit through the orchards and vegetable farms of the San

Joaquin and Sacramento Valleys. Asian farmworkers like the Chan family have played a crucial role in developing the vast agricultural economy of the Western states and Hawaii.

Working as a retail clerk in mainstream department stores offered not only better wages but also a new way of life. After her marriage, Chan found a job in a department store packing room to help support her family. "Asians were *not* in retail in those days immediately after the Second World War. Oh, you could find a job in a factory, cafeteria, or a restaurant, but never in a sales position dealing with Caucasian customers. At the department store, we worked out of sight in the back. The Asian women would always have to pack the heavier merchandise like lamps and suitcases. On my first day, I knew there was discrimination when all the Asians were assigned lockers on the very bottom by the floor," she remembered. 31

Dissatisfied with this blatantly unequal treatment, in the early 1950s she moved on to H. Liebes, a family-owned department store, where she began work as an elevator operator, a job rarely seen anymore. Elevators with manual switches were run by Asian American women dressed in high-collared Chinese silk dresses and white gloves. During the postwar years, this kind of service was considered an exotic attraction. "Of course, I wasn't complaining about being stereotyped. A position as an elevator runner was seen as an opportunity to work with the public. From there, Asian women were able to gradually work their way to sales." 32

Breaking the color line was less traumatic than Chan had expected. White employees and customers, and her new union, Janitors' Local 87, proved generally favorable to the new Asian clerks. 33

When the Liebes family sold their business six years later, Chan landed a sales position at Livingston's, a large San Francisco–based chain, and transferred over to the Department Store Employees Union. During the 1960s department stores were becoming large corporate-owned entities. "As department stores expanded in size and the number of employees multiplied, it became even more important to belong to a union," asserted Chan. "A lot of times, management would try to cheat you out of overtime pay or holidays. Then it became very important that someone was there to support and protect you." 34

Even as late as 1980 Chan, in her late fifties, continued her union work, this time serving on the negotiating committee which successfully gained pay increases and an extra holiday for the workers. She hopes that the future will bring unions to unorganized department stores, and she advises younger employees to assume a greater role in the union's decision-making process. "If you're interested in what's going on, get involved! We always expect someone else to do the legwork. If you just criticize and do not attend any meetings, there's only yourself to blame if things don't turn out right." 35

Conclusion

36   As the primary institutions representing the interests of workers, unions have been society's trendsetters in the area of working conditions. Benefits include vacations, sick leave, holiday pay and other paid leave, unemployment and disability compensation, and comparable worth. The traditional opponents of labor unions have been employers, but the government is also included in that group now. Tightening economies, changing political policies, and social priorities have contributed to an atmosphere in which many employee-oriented rights and benefits have fallen by the wayside: the government exhibits a reluctance to increase the minimum wage at a rate commensurate with cost-of-living increases and has reduced its enforcement of labor and occupational safety regulations.

37   The unions face a growing internal challenge, too. As the workforce changes and includes more women and more immigrants, especially at the entry and middle levels, unions find that their survival may be contingent on an ability to adapt programs and priorities to the needs of their new constituents. They must be willing to develop more allies, including the growing immigrant and minority communities. Immigration laws and access to bilingual information may not have been big issues twenty years ago, but they are certainly being discussed now.

38   Unfortunately, like many bureaucracies, unions can be slow to recognize the need for change. Some may even take positions antithetical to what immigrants express as being in their best interest. This means that Asian American women and other immigrants must be even more willing to participate vigilantly in the unions in order to raise concerns effectively. As Bertha Chan observed, "If we are going to succeed as a group, there has to be more participation by every one of us."

Reading and Writing Activities

PRELIMINARY RESPONSE

Notes.   As you read, record your reactions (questions or comments) to "Dust and Dishes: Organizing Asian American Workers" in your reading journal.

You may react to one or more of a number of factors in the reading. You might, for example, consider the ways that Asian American workers have had to contend with both unfair working conditions imposed by employers and the insensitivity of some labor unions.

Discussion.   In class, compare your reactions in reading groups of five or six. Appoint a recorder to keep track of similarities and differences, consensus or disagreement, arising from the discussion. The recorder may summarize your group discussion for the rest of the class later.

Freewriting.   In a 10- to 15-minute freewrite, try to account for the commitment to unionism (especially apparent in the conclusion of their article) expressed by Yoichi Shimatsu and Patricia Lee, in spite of the history of racism within the labor movement. Read your freewriting in groups of two to four. As others are reading, take written note of areas of agreement or disagreement, questions that arise in your mind, and ideas that might be qualified or extended. After everyone has read, appoint a recorder to keep track of similarities or differences, consensus or disagreement, that arise in the ensuing discussion. The recorder may summarize your group discussion for the rest of the class later.

SUMMARIZING

1. Make a scratchline, cluster representation, or notes indicating the progression of ideas in "Dust and Dishes"—one that reflects your consideration of the freewriting and discussion of group members. Note in particular the ways that Asian American workers have had to confront racism from both employers and unions.
2. Write a summary paragraph or two, using your scratchline, cluster representation, or notes.
3. Read summaries in groups. Compare the focus of each summary. How do the summaries differ? How are they the same? Again, check to see if you are *reacting and responding* to the reading selection instead of summarizing the central topics.

FOCUSED CRITICAL READING

1. What predictions about audience and purpose might be made from reading the first four paragraphs of "Dust and Dishes"? Are those predictions borne out by the rest of the text?
2. What do the final three paragraphs of this essay suggest about the authors' audience and purpose?
3. In paragraph 13, we are told that Asian and Latina hotel and restaurant workers conducted, and apparently won, a struggle for "dignity and respect." What sorts of concessions do you suppose they were able to extract from their employers?

Felicia Lowe

Asian American Women in Broadcasting

◆───────

Though relatively few in number, broadcast journalists are widely recognized and respected as professionals. The following selection looks at the involvement of Asian Americans in this field, tracing its history while examining problems and conflicts. Felicia Lowe, who has worked as a broadcast journalist for commercial and public television stations, produces and directs documentary films.

1   For those of us Asian American women in broadcast journalism, the story of our careers began around 1970, on the heels of the civil rights movement, Vietnam, student self-determination, the drug culture, women's liberation, the sexual revolution, rejection of traditional American values—anything that smacked of change. *Change* was the key word in those days, and in some convoluted amalgamation of what was happening then, the Federal Communications Commission ordered television stations across the country to begin hiring women and minorities.

2   Wherever there was a sizable Asian American population, many individuals and community groups added to the federal pressure by advocating affirmative action hiring of Asian American reporters and writers. Most opportunities turned out to be in the Northwest (Seattle and Portland); California (San Francisco, Sacramento, and Los Angeles); Hawaii; and some pockets on the East Coast.

3   A handful of independent souls also created their own training situations. On the East Coast, Connie Chung started out as a copyperson at WTTG-TV in Washington, D.C. Linda Shen, fresh out of Radcliffe, got her first production assistant job at WNEW-TV in New York, and at KOMO-TV in Seattle, Washington, Barbara Tanabe became the first Asian American female reporter. The year was 1971.

The Early Years

4   A steady stream of would-be reporters and anchors—trained by station-run programs, stipended by foundation and network grants,

and motivated by sheer determination—followed in the early years. Aspirants sometimes received inspiration from the few trailblazers on the air. Seattle native Wendy Tokuda, now a San Francisco news anchor, remembers, "When Barbara [Tanabe] was on, the whole family rushed to the television set.... Seeing her on air made me realize what was possible." After meeting personally with the reporter, Tokuda was even more encouraged by Tanabe's willingness to help in any way possible.

Most of us worked at entry-level positions or volunteered time at community newspapers and radio and television stations just for the exposure and the chance to absorb the many skills needed for broadcasting. As summarized by Connie Chung, "I was a schlep like everyone else."   5

By 1974 Asian faces on television were no longer a novelty. By then each of the San Francisco stations had their "first Asian American reporter"—usually a female. KRON-TV had Suzanne Joe; KPIX hired Linda Shen; at KGO I joined reporter David Louie as a vacation relief reporter.   6

Some names cropped up in other stations and locales; old names were replaced by new ones. In San Francisco KQED-TV hired Pamela Young away from KPIX's Public Affairs Department. In Los Angeles Tritia Toyota reported for KNBC, and Joanne Ishimine took over Linda Yu's trainee job when Yu moved to Portland, Oregon, for her first reporting and anchoring position. Tanabe, the first Asian American to anchor news, moved from Seattle to Honolulu, and at her old Seattle station, KING-TV, Tokuda landed her first media job as a production secretary in public affairs.   7

It was an intense period for us reporters and the Asian American communities we were hired to represent. Community people, especially the older generation, were happy and proud that the racial barrier had finally been broken in this highly visible and powerful medium. But learning how to trust and work with one another took time. We were often made to feel "suspect." Linda Shen recalls, "It was devastating to find the [San Francisco] community did not automatically support us. Since I was from Connecticut, it made it all the more difficult, even though I truly aspired to help."   8

I, too, remember a meeting in 1974, with community members who attacked me for "being an outsider who couldn't possibly understand the problems of the community." It was awkward and frustrating. I thought: here I am, born and raised in the Bay Area, moved to New York on my own to get training, and I return to find an unwelcome community. I responded by saying it was unfair to prejudge me and that a reporter's accountability to the community should be questioned only after he or she failed to generate more stories than had previously been reported.   9

Being Aggressive

10   Satisfying the community was just one requirement. Beyond that hurdle was another: learning the basics. We had to know where and how to get background information quickly, interview people efficiently, write clearly and concisely, use our voices effectively, and deliver information believably before the camera. Having to report two to four stories daily—always under deadline—helped hone those skills.

11   Almost all of us agree, however, that one of the most difficult aspects of reporting is overcoming a cultural tendency *not* to be aggressive. As Asian Americans, we are taught to be polite and to stay out of other people's business—tenets contrary to the requirements of the job. How to develop assertiveness on and off camera and how to be direct became our greatest challenges. Assertiveness went beyond obtaining the information needed for a story; it went to the very basis of survival in the business. As reporters we had to communicate what we wanted to the mostly male camera crew. Cooperation was not necessarily forthcoming. The older, more experienced technicians generally resented taking orders from young, inexperienced, minority women. Film editors, assignment editors, and writers often shared that attitude. We had to learn how to develop effective communication skills with our co-workers as well as the audience.

12   Chicago anchor Linda Yu says the work changed her. "People won't believe today that this person that I am used to barely speak above a whisper, always went to the back of the line, and glued herself to the wall. For a shy, retiring little girl, this is the one profession which got me out, forced me to stay outgoing and develop confidence."

13   We learned that self-confidence and a strong sense of ourselves are needed to sustain us in the field. Emerald Yeh, news anchor with a San Francisco station, and formerly a reporter for Cable News Network in Atlanta, Georgia, and a Portland, Oregon, station, says, "One has to become strong within—emotionally and psychologically. Being an anchor puts you on the line. You are an easy scapegoat if things aren't going well. But you can't let other people feel good or bad about you. You have to make your own judgment and do the best you can, based on *your* range of experience. Know yourself and be secure in that."

Conflicts on the Job

14   Television reporting is not for everyone, as some of us trailblazers soon discovered. After working as a reporter for CBS News in New York, Atlanta, and Chicago for nearly two years, Genny Lim eventually found the job unsuitable to her temperament. She recalls the excitement of covering the story of Wounded Knee, stealthily entering the

Indian compound that had been restricted to news personnel, and obtaining an exclusive interview with American Indian Movement leader Dennis Banks.

"CBS wouldn't run it. . . . They said the pieces were too sympathetic   15
to Indians, too slanted. I had no intention of doing that. I was reporting what I saw." But, the incident crystallized for Lim what she believed to be the racist, sexist, and paternalistic attitudes of the network. "I felt we [Asian American women] were ten years ahead of the times." She resigned. She took on some freelance assignments with East Coast educational stations and hosted a San Francisco public affairs show, but left television for good in 1977. Since that time Lim has concentrated on creative writing.

Roberta Wong, formerly with KRON-TV in San Francisco, has also   16
left television. Though she has been able to apply her reporting, writing, and broadcasting skills to her work in public relations, she prefers the economic freedom and less demanding schedule of her new job.

Linda Shen, now a small business entrepreneur, has harsh memo-   17
ries of her journalism work, which took her from New York to San Francisco and then Washington, D.C. "I was the '60s idealist. I wanted to work for social change but found few opportunities to do so. There were minor triumphs, but most of the stories I found despicable. . . . One time, I was sent out to interview a black welfare mother who had lost everything in a fire. On my return, the desk asked, 'Did you get her to cry on camera?' Personally, I was heartbroken because I had caused this woman public anguish. Even though I was handsomely rewarded, it wasn't worth it. I was miserable, and it wasn't made any better by office politics." In the end, Shen says, "Nobody's to blame. It was just a conflict of values."

But Shen also recalls some fonder moments. "There were aspects of   18
the job I liked. With my liberal arts background, reporting was perfect for the overeducated dilettante. You could dabble in this and that, then leave. You were exposed to different segments of society. I especially liked the visual experience and the teamwork involved in putting together stories."

Sherry Hu, a reporter for KPIX in San Francisco since 1980, also   19
loves these aspects of the job. "I love learning new things, meeting different people, and the pace. I've found a niche for myself. I feel fulfilled at the end of the day, and I love the people I work with."

Though the job is exciting, San Francisco reporter Linda Yee   20
quickly points out that "it's not a glamorous job. You work long, hard hours, and because of the visibility of the job, you lack some privacy outside of work." Public recognition, awards, speaking engagements, breaking news stories, and big money certainly sound glamorous, but these things alone could never sustain anybody in this high-pressure, competitive field where job security is nonexistent. The more enduring

traits, such as a love of the business and determination, are essential to survival in broadcast journalism.

21   One who intends to stay is Wendy Tokuda. "I am committed to the work and love what I do. There are aspects of the job that bother me. I find the tendency toward entertainment a matter of concern and am troubled that the medium being visual sometimes affects the kinds of stories that are reported, but I try to know the entire newscast, edit and write as much copy as possible, and maintain high journalistic standards."

Personal Life

22   Kaity Tong, WABC-TV News anchor in New York, formerly with Sacramento's KCRA and San Francisco's KPIX, has learned to live with critics, but she has had a harder time adjusting to job relocations. A Bryn Mawr graduate and native of the East Coast, Tong says being back in New York suits her, though professional moves have sometimes been hard on her personal life. She is married to Bob Long, a television producer whose work used to keep him in Los Angeles a great deal. The couple maintained two residences for many years, commuting back and forth from Sacramento. Her job in New York increased the commute by three thousand miles for nearly a year and a half. Her husband now lives in New York, but personal sacrifices had to be made in the name of professional ambition.

23   Linda Yu thinks that any woman who chooses a time-consuming and competitive career, such as journalism, must make some sacrifices when it comes to time for herself and her relationships. "I worked a lot of seven-day weeks, twelve- to fifteen-hour days for years until I met my husband and decided it was time to slow down to a more reasonable five- or six-day week, and occasionally eight-hour days."

24   For Wendy Tokuda, who anchored news at 6 P.M. and 11 P.M. for seven years, maintaining private time has become "like a career." She guards it judiciously so she has time to spend with her family. "Before I had the children, I concentrated on developing my career; there was some control in my life, but I had to relinquish those controls the minute Mikka was born." Though the birth of her second child initially caused Tokuda to doubt whether she could successfully "juggle another ring," Maggie's arrival helped Tokuda understand how much she wanted both family and career.

25   But Tokuda has had to make some major adjustments to balance the demands of children and work. "I try to do everything, but I realize I can't," she admits. For example, she has cut back some of her participation in time-consuming community benefits, and in 1987 she asked her station to relieve her of her late-night anchor slot. Though this cuts her exposure substantially, the new schedule yields two much-desired

results: she now can do reporting again and also spend more time with her two girls and husband, all of whom she happily acknowledges as the "best things that have happened to me." A live-in nanny provided help in the early days, but Tokuda largely credits her husband, independent producer Richard Hall, for his support and contribution in raising the family. "Richard and the girls... keep my life in balance," she says.

The schedule of street reporters generally is more time-consuming   26
and erratic than that of news anchors. Of the street reporters at KPIX in San Francisco who have had children in recent years, Sherry Hu points out that several have elected to work only part time. Shortly before the birth of her child, Linda Yu said, "I realize now that professional ambition isn't everything. Perhaps, I will feel again that I've made it [if] after my child is born, I learn to balance one more important element in life."

Future Trends

With the presence of Asian American women in the major televi-   27
sion stations across the country and our involvement in organizations such as the Asian American Journalists Association, which formed in the early 1980s to encourage professional development and to offer scholarships to aspiring journalists, the future looks promising to many. But some major problems remain.

Senior member of the broadcasting community, Barbara Tanabe, is   28
bothered that so few Asian American men are given a chance in the business. While less than a handful have co-anchored news in the smaller markets, including Seattle, Washington, where Ken Woo once anchored, and Honolulu, Hawaii, where Dalton Tanaoka recently began as a news anchor, no male has anchored in the larger markets. Veteran reporters, David Louie of KGO-TV in San Francisco and ABC correspondent Ken Kashiwahara both aspire to anchor, but neither has been approached. "It's been the women who have been nurtured for anchoring," says Louie.

The pressure applied in the early years was not about hiring Asian   29
men or women; it was applied to hiring Asians. Yet Asian females had an automatic edge. We were both minority and women, "two-point-ers," making us particularly attractive to television management. As a result, more job opportunities were open to Asian women and remain so today. Vic Lee, reporter for San Francisco's KRON-TV and former member of the management team at the station, has seen the issue from both sides. "Years ago when there were quotas, Asian females had the advantage of being minority and women. Then the consultants were brought in, and they conducted surveys which showed viewers found [white] male/minority female anchor teams acceptable but not the other way around. This makes it difficult for Asian males to find jobs, and with so few role models around, young men are discouraged."

30   In 1985 Asian American women anchored news in four out of the five largest markets in the country: Kaity Tong and Connie Chung in New York; Tritia Toyota and Joanne Ishimine in Los Angeles; Linda Yu in Chicago; and Wendy Tokuda and Emerald Yeh in San Francisco. It is the absence of Asian American male anchors in these major markets that is noteworthy.

31   This stark imbalance of females and males on television screens across the country raises questions about the greater and continued acceptability of Asian women by television management and viewers. The stereotypes attributed to Asian Americans have had a large part in establishing and perpetuating the pattern. The Asian male stereotype is less positive than the female's, says San Francisco reporter David Louie. "Asian men are seen as houseboys, cowering servants, not intellectual. We just don't fit in." Tokuda feels that the presence of Asian reporters and anchors has exposed viewers to another view of Asian women—as professionals—but admits there is ongoing testing as well. The stereotyping of Asian females as "exotic," "mysterious," "China dolls," "sex kittens" is not dead. But as one reporter points out, "You can play up that role as much as you want. Still you have to be good, if not better, at the job to keep it."

32   The call for social change in the 1970s inaugurated the presence of Asian women in the broadcast industry. But we still are constantly proving ourselves as competent veteran writers, reporters, and anchors in order to remain in the profession, and to open doors for other Asian Americans. At the same time, and like many other working women, we learn to survive in the business while balancing our family and personal lives. The challenges now before Asian American women journalists, and the chance for professional and personal fulfillment in today's electronic age, can and often do offset the conflicts we have all faced in the past fifteen years of broadcasting history. However, as long as there is the sex imbalance—the lack of Asian men in broadcasting—we have not reached equity. This situation is a bittersweet success for us as Asian American women.

Reading and Writing Activities

PRELIMINARY RESPONSE

Notes.   As you read, record your reactions (questions or comments) to "Asian American Women in Broadcasting" in your reading journal.

You may react to one or more of a number of factors in the reading. You might, for example, compare the image that most Americans hold of broadcast journalism with Felicia Lowe's inside view of the profession.

Discussion. In class, compare your reactions in reading groups of five or six. Appoint a recorder to keep track of similarities and differences, consensus or disagreement, arising from the discussion. The recorder may summarize your group discussion for the rest of the class later.

Freewriting. In a 10- to 15-minute freewrite, compare the costs and rewards for Asian American women who succeed in broadcast journalism. Read your freewriting in groups of two to four. As others are reading, take written note of areas of agreement or disagreement, questions that arise in your mind, and ideas that might be qualified or extended. After everyone has read, appoint a recorder to keep track of similarities or differences, consensus or disagreement, that arise in the ensuing discussion. The recorder may summarize your group discussion for the rest of the class later.

SUMMARIZING

1. Make a scratchline, cluster representation, or notes indicating the progression of ideas in "Asian American Women in Broadcasting"— one that reflects your consideration of the freewriting and discussion of group members. Note in particular Lowe's ambivalence about broadcast journalism and the achievements of Asian Americans in that field.
2. Write a summary paragraph or two, using your scratchline, cluster representation, or notes.
3. Read summaries in groups. Compare the focus of each summary. How do the summaries differ? How are they the same? Again, check to see if you are *reacting and responding* to the reading selection instead of summarizing the central topics.

FOCUSED CRITICAL READING

1. Why do you suppose television viewers are thought to be more content with a news anchor team that consists of a white male and a minority female?
2. Accused of biased reporting, former journalist Genny Lim responded that she "was reporting what she saw." Is it more difficult for a person from an oppressed minority to appear unbiased? Why or why not?

WRITING SUGGESTIONS

1. Write an analytical critique of meritocracy that synthesizes ideas from "Curse of the Merit Class" and Michael Lerner's "The Frustration in Family Life" in Chapter 3 (pages 151–56).

2. Critically assess the belief that good jobs and other economic rewards are distributed on a moral basis—that those who have the greatest wealth are most deserving and those who have the least are least deserving. Start by articulating objectively the basis of that belief and connecting it to any relevant personal experience or observation you may be able to apply.

3. Survey several consecutive issues of *Newsweek* or *Time* from the past two or three years, looking for cover stories that address broad national trends. After having located two or three such stories, compare them to "Young, Gifted and Jobless" in content, organization, and tone. You might consider, for example, how these cover stories cite specific cases, how the editors use sidebars (shorter pieces boxed in and surrounded by the featured article) to introduce related topics or conflicting interpretations, how "good news" and "bad news" are sequenced in relation to each other, and so forth. On the basis of your observations, compose one of the following:

   a. An essay that identifies and analyzes the distinguishing features of a cover story.
   b. An article that takes a similar approach in examining a trend on your campus or in your community.

4. Using the first two selections in this chapter as sources, write an essay that defines corporate executives and working professionals as a class. Address such matters as their ethnic and class background, their education, their values and expectations.

5. After reading the first three selections in this chapter, write an essay that argues one of the following positions:

   a. A hundred years from now, wealth and power in America will be held by people who have received the best education.
   b. A hundred years from now, wealth and power in America will be held by those who have inherited it from their parents.
   c. A hundred years from now, wealth and power in America will be held by an elite other than the Meritocratic Upper Class described by Nicholas Lemann.
   d. A hundred years from now, wealth and power in America will be distributed more or less equally among everyone.

6. Drawing on some of the ideas and details presented in the first two readings in this chapter, write an essay supporting the inference that newspaper and magazine articles often equate the interests and experiences of a relatively small class of affluent men and women with those of "Americans" or "people" in general.

7. Using "The Blue-Collar Blues" and either or both of the first two readings in this chapter as sources, write an essay demonstrating that profound changes in the American economy are causing hardships for both white-collar and blue-collar workers.

8. Write an essay addressing the apparent conflict between the view expressed in paragraph 14 of "The Blue-Collar Blues" and the one presented in paragraph 4 of "Young, Gifted and Jobless." Begin with a fair and objective articulation of each view.

9. Consider the following statements of expert opinion found in "The Blue-Collar Blues":

   a. "The sooner laid-off factory workers realize that [low-paying, 'demeaning' jobs are the only kind available to them], the better, the experts say. 'The best message to give them may be that they're lucky they did so well for so long,' says Dennis Ahlburg, a professor of industrial relations. . . ."
   b. "'Many blue-collar workers didn't realize they were earning wages unsustainable in the face of growing competition from abroad,' notes Wharton School economist Michael Wachter."
   c. "'We can talk about retraining, but I think it's fictitious,' argues John Cumbler, an economic historian at the University of Louisville. 'How can we retrain all these people in a meaningful way?'"

Note that in each case, a person from what Nicholas Lemann calls the Meritocratic Upper Class is speaking for others. (Observe in particular the contrast between "these people" and "us" implied in the last quotation.) Present in writing the strongest case for viewing this type of commentary as a way of understanding the subject at hand. Then present the strongest case for viewing it as a form of oppression.

10. Comparing "Young, Gifted and Jobless" and "The Blue-Collar Blues," show how feature stories in *Newsweek* can be said to follow a predictable structure.

11. Using any combination of readings from this chapter as sources, write an essay showing that many middle-income Americans resent the ways that both the wealthy and the destitute make their livings.

12. Write an essay that contrasts the views of bell hooks with those of Michael Lerner (as they are expressed in "The Frustration in Family Life" in Chapter 3, pages 151–56) in regard to home, work, and social change.

13. Write an essay that compares the experiences, attitudes, and expectations of the women profiled by Yoichi Shimatsu and Patricia Lee in "Dust and Dishes" with those of workers quoted in "The Blue-Collar Blues."

14. Using the last two readings in this chapter as sources, write an essay demonstrating the difficulties that many Asian-American women have faced in asserting themselves and their rights in the workplace, refusing to remain invisible.

7

Education, Social Class, and Ethnicity: Achieving Excellence and Equity

◆

Readings in previous chapters have shown that upward mobility is a cherished ideal of mainstream American culture. Several of the selections in Chapter 6 connect that ideal with the work ethic—the belief that diligent efforts result in financial rewards and social privilege. Another presumed avenue to upward mobility is education, often in the form of public schooling, to which all Americans, theoretically, have had access for more than a century.

Asked to provide opportunities for all, including the children of recent immigrants, public schools have done more than impart skills and factual knowledge. They have also tried to prepare young people for work and citizenship through a regimen of acculturation, patriotism, good manners (sharing, turn taking, waiting in line), personal hygiene, and a general conformity to white, middle-class norms. Over the years, however, these goals have become increasingly elusive as well as highly controversial.

Both critics and defenders of public education recognize that American schools must serve the needs of an increasingly diverse population. However, given their history of segregation by race, social class, and ability grouping, a record of past success can be deceptive: when students of previous generations failed, schools were rarely blamed. And even though equal access to public education may be official policy, many Americans remain convinced that school should be a place for screening out persons incapable or unworthy of success.

Several readings in this chapter refer to the Coleman Report, a study of the effects of poverty, social class, and racial integration. Issued in 1966 by the U.S. Office of Education, this report found that children from poor families and ethnic minorities do significantly better when enrolled in classes with more privileged students. (Researchers found, however, that many of these children also lost self-esteem.) The Coleman Report thus became an impetus for school busing, a logical response to social inequity.

Because school busing was not often accompanied by the most familiar indication of academic improvement (higher scores on standardized tests), disagreements arose that have yet to be resolved. Inevitably, some Americans pointed to a presumed lowering of educational standards and expectations; in their minds, social reform had not consistently translated into sound academic policy. On the other hand, studies subsequent to the Coleman Report blamed a more submerged and pervasive form of inequality in public schooling and in American life generally. (An excerpt from one such study, written in 1972 by Christopher Jencks and his associates, is included in this chapter.) The findings of a 1979 report by the Carnegie Council on Children, *Small Futures: Children, Inequality, and the Limits of Liberal Reform,* are summarized in the following excerpt from a story in the *New York Times:*

> Jimmy is in the second grade and he likes school. He pays attention in class and does well. He has an above average I.Q. and is reading slightly above grade level. Bobby is a second grader too. Like Jimmy, he is attentive in class, which he enjoys. His I.Q. and reading skills are comparable to Jimmy's.
>
> But Bobby is the son of a successful lawyer whose annual salary of more than $35,000 puts him within the top percentages of income distribution in this country. Jimmy's father, on the other hand, works from time to time as a messenger or a custodial assistant, and earns $4,800 a year.
>
> Despite the similarities in ability between the two boys, the differences in the circumstances to which they were born makes it 27 times more likely that Bobby will get a job that, by the time he is in his late 40's, will pay him an income in the top tenth of all incomes in this country. Jimmy has only about one chance in eight of earning even a median income. And Bobby will probably have at least four years more schooling than Jimmy.

Some have viewed recent criticism of public education as an indictment of misguided social reform, arguing that we should return to rigorous instruction in a single mainstream cultural tradition. Others contend that the evidence merely reveals a history of ethnocentrism, made more visible by the growing multiculturalism of American society.

Readings in Chapter 7 reflect these issues. The chapter begins with an article by Professors Allan Ornstein and David Levine, who survey the findings of recent research to arrive at ten painful realities about class, race, and education. The consequences of those realities are reflected in three readings that detail the experiences of groups and individuals shortchanged or disregarded by the educational system. The last two selections in Chapter 7 deal with very different proposals for addressing the effects of educational inequality. In "The Ghetto Preppies," Marcus Mabry examines an unusual program directed toward a few academically gifted black teenagers. Christopher Jencks and his associates at Harvard University, on the other hand, propose a restructuring of educational funding, forcing those who benefit most from schooling to contribute more proportionally to its costs.

The Believing Game

At the risk of oversimplifying, one could say that most of what college students do involves two complementary processes: *analysis,* the act of separating something (a text, a concept, an artifact, an organism) into components; and *synthesis,* the act of generating new ideas and products through creative combinations of facts, ideas, or physical matter. Likewise, much of the thinking students are asked to do in college courses involves skepticism, by which one examines ideas critically, looking for reasons to doubt; and belief, by which one often applies or extends an idea. Like analysis and synthesis, skepticism and belief should not be viewed as mutually exclusive activities; instead, they are best understood as powerful intellectual strategies that work best in tandem.

Perhaps unfortunately, people in academic culture are more likely to greet new ideas with initial skepticism. In the opinion of Peter Elbow, a well-known scholar and teacher of writing, many of us allow the believing "muscles" in our brains to atrophy. Elbow therefore recommends two deliberate procedures to enrich reading and interpretation: the Doubting Game and the Believing Game. In previous chapters, we have engaged the Doubting Game through the questions designated as "Focused Critical Reading" at the end of each selection. In Chapter 7, we invite you to engage in the Believing Game.

At the simplest level, Elbow's Believing Game means granting momentary assent to ideas that may be uncongenial to your beliefs, searching for truth rather than error. When an author relates an alien or distasteful experience, you try to empathize; if she makes a novel observation or reaches an outrageous conclusion, you pursue its implications in patient good faith. In Elbow's words, "It helps to think of [the Believing Game] as trying to get inside the head of someone who saw things this way. . . . Try to have the experience of someone who made this assertion." Since most readers will resist one or more of the selections in this chapter, there is ample opportunity to play the Believing Game at this level.

A more powerful use of the Believing Game emerges through the interactions of a reading group, particularly when its members are able to surrender the impulse for closure—the desire to arrive at the single "best," most authoritative reading of a text. In this situation, the function of the Believing Game, says Elbow, "is not to discredit a bad reading but to make better readings more available." This outcome is most likely to happen when each member of a group is concerned less with arguing the validity of a particular interpretation or presenting evidence to support it than with eliciting a variety of possible readings and making a concerted effort to *see* each one.

Allan C. Ornstein and Daniel U. Levine

Social Class, Race, and School Achievement: Problems and Prospects

———————◆———————

The following article appeared in the Journal of Teacher Education *in 1989. Its authors, both university professors, summarize and analyze the findings of research into the educational achievement of poor and minority children. Like many academic publications, Ornstein and Levine's article cites numerous sources, each of which is carefully documented according to the conventions recognized by scholars in the authors' field of study.*

Today, the term *working class* is more widely used than *lower class,* 1
but social scientists still generally use measures of occupation, education, and income to describe three to six levels of socioeconomic status (SES) ranging from upper class at the top to lower working class at the bottom. The UPPER CLASS is usually defined as including very wealthy persons having substantial property and investment; the MIDDLE CLASS includes professionals, managers and small business owners (upper middle) as well as technicians, sales personnel, and clerical workers (lower middle). The WORKING CLASS is generally divided into *upper working class* (skilled manual workers such as construction workers) and *lower working class* (unskilled manual workers such as those at hamburger restaurants). Skilled workers may be either middle class or working class, depending on their education and other considerations such as the community in which they live. In recent years, a number of observers also have identified an *underclass* which to some extent resembles the lower working class, but appears to be locked more permanently in a cycle of poverty and social disorganization (Auletta, 1988; Gelman, 1988; Vroman, 1988). Usually concentrated in the core slums of cities or in deteriorated rural poverty areas, members of the underclass frequently have little or no hope that their economic and social situation will ever improve. A large percentage are minority—mostly black and Hispanic.

Studies on Social Class and School Success

2   One of the first systematic studies investigating relations between class and achievement in the educational system was the Lynds' (1929) study of "Middletown" (a small midwestern city). The Lynds concluded that parents, regardless of social class level, recognize the importance of education for their children; however, working-class children do not come to school academically equipped to deal with the verbal skills and behavioral traits required for success in the classroom.

3   Thousands of studies have since documented the close relationship between social class and achievement in the educational system. For example, as reported by the National Assessment of Educational Progress and shown in Table 1, only 41 percent of students whose parents

Table 1
Reading and Science Scores of Thirteen-Year-Old Students by Social Class, 1977 and 1984

Parental Education	Average Percent Correct in Science, 1977	Percentage Reading at or above Intermediate Level, 1984[*]
Not graduated high school	53	41
Graduated high school	59	56
Attended postsecondary school	66	72

Type of Community	Average Percent Correct in Science, 1977	Average Reading Proficiency Score, 1984
Rural	56	254
Low-status metropolitan	48	237
High-status metropolitan	67	274
Main big city	57	253
Urban fringe	63	261
Medium city	61	257
Small communities	60	256

*Note: A reading proficiency score of 250 is considered "intermediate" (the student is able to recognize paraphrases of what he or she has read), and a score of 300 is considered "adept" (the student is able to understand complicated passages). "Low-status metropolitan" refers to urban areas with a low proportion of professional or managerial workers in cities of more than 200,000 population. "High-status metropolitan" communities in such cities have a high proportion of professionals or managers. "Main big city" communities also are in these large urban areas and are moderate in proportion of professionals and managers. "Medium cities" have between 25,000 and 200,000 residents, and "small communities" are urbanized areas with less than 25,000 persons.

Source: *The Condition of Education 1986* (p. 212), compiled by U.S. Government Printing Office (1986), Washington, DC.

had not graduated from high school (which is one measure of social class) had reading proficiency on scores at or above the "intermediate" level, compared with 72 percent of students whose parents had attended post-secondary institutions. Furthermore, the average proficiency score of seventeen-year-old students whose parents had not graduated from high school was almost identical to the average score of thirteen-year-old students whose parents had attended postsecondary institutions. Only 20 percent of seventeen-year-old students whose parents did not complete high school scored at or above the "adept" level, compared with 52 percent of those whose parents had a postsecondary education. Similar patterns were reported for science (NAEP, 1985, 1988).

School achievement also is correlated with type of community, which reflects the social class of persons who reside there. Also shown in Table 1, for example, the average reading score of thirteen-year-old students in high-status metropolitan (middle-class, suburban) locations is much higher than that of other students, and the average score of students in low-status metropolitan locations (with a high concentration of lower working-class and underclass families) is much lower. Students in mixed-class communities, such as rural areas and medium-sized cities that include substantial proportions of both working-class and middle-class families, have average scores in between those of wealthy, suburban, and inner-city, poverty communities. Similar patterns were found for science. Further evidence of the relationship between social class and school achievement can be found in studies of poverty neighborhoods in very large cities. Data on the performance of students in such neighborhoods have provided an almost unremittingly bleak picture of ineffective schooling for the past three decades (Levine and Havighurst, 1988; Ornstein, 1982). 4

Many educators also are particularly concerned about the achievement of low-status rural students, especially those who live in pockets of rural poverty. Although the average achievement of rural students is generally at about the national average, research indicates that poverty and inequality hamper the achievement of many rural students (Arends, 1987; DeYoung, 1987). 5

Race/Ethnicity and School Success

Patterns involving social class and educational achievement in the United States are further complicated by interrelationships among these variables and those of race and ethnicity (The term "ethnicity" refers to shared culture and background.) The nation's largest racial minority group—black Americans—is much lower in social class than is the white majority. Several other major ethnic groups—Mexican Americans and Puerto Ricans—are also disproportionately in the lower working class and under-class. In line with their lower social 6 class standing, these racial and ethnic minority groups are also low in academic achievement, high school and college graduation rates, and other measures of educational attainment.

7   The close association among social classes, racial/ethnic minority status, and school achievement is shown in Table 2, which represents average reading scores obtained by a nationally representative sample of high school students in 1980 and 1982. As shown in the table, black and Hispanic students have the lowest SES scores and also the lowest language, math, and science scores; non-Hispanic whites are highest on nearly all of these measures. Except for math scores among Asian-Pacific Americans, achievement scores parallel scores on socioeconomic status; the higher the SES score, the higher the academic scores. Black students, Hispanic students, and Native American students are much lower in SES than are non-Hispanic white and Asian-Pacific students and have much lower academic achievement scores.

8   However, data collected by the NAEP (1985) also indicate that black and Hispanic students have registered gains in reading, science, and math since 1971. Whereas proficiency scores for white students in these subject areas have remained "flat" or "constant," black and Hispanic students have registered about 10 to 15 percent increases over a 15 year period in reading (Rothman, 1988; U.S. Government, 1986). Some observers attribute these improvements partly to the effects of

Table 2

Language, Math, and Science Scores of High School Sophomores and Seniors, by Racial and Ethnic Group, 1980 and 1982

Racial/ Ethnic Group	Language Skills Score	Math Score	Science Score	Percent in Lowest 25%	Percent in College-Bound Program
Black	14.5	6.5	6.4	45	29
Hispanic	15.6	7.7	7.4	43	23
Native/American	18.5	7.8	8.8	36	23
Asian Pacific	25.2	16.6	11.0	22	47
White (non-Hispanic)	27.8	15.5	11.2	18	37

Note: Language scores are a combination of scores in vocabulary, reading, and writing. The maximum scores for language, math, and science skills were 57, 38, and 20, respectively. Social class is a composite measure of father's and mother's education, father's occupation, parental income, and types of items in the home. Language and math scores are for 1980 sophomores; science scores are for 1982 seniors.

Source: *High School and Beyond Study* (p. 56), compiled by U.S. Government Printing Office (1980), Washington, DC. *The Condition of Education 1985* (p. 58), compiled by U.S. Government Printing Office (1985), Washington, DC.

the federal Chapter 1 programs and/or some increase in school deseg-regation (Koretz, 1987). On the other hand, black and Hispanic students still score far below whites in reading and other subjects, and black and Hispanic seventeen-year-old students still have average reading scores at about the same level as the average white thirteen-year-old students.

In line with the achievement and social-class data shown in Table 2, non-Hispanic whites and Asian students (other than Vietnamese Americans) are much more likely to complete high school than are black and Hispanic students. As shown in Table 3, high school completion rates for black students have been rising since 1975, and rates for Hispanic students only have increased since 1983. (Cautions in interpreting the Hispanic scores are noted in the table.) Graduation rates for Asian students are higher than whites (Yao, 1987), but are not reported because they were not identified by the population survey data of the table.

In addition, high school dropout rates are still very high among black and Hispanic students in big-city poverty areas. Knowledgeable observers estimate that dropout rates range from 40 to 60 percent in some big cities and sometimes exceed 75 to 80 percent at schools enroll-ing mostly underclass students (Hahn, Danzerger, and Lefkowitz, 1987). Inasmuch as high school dropouts have rapidly diminishing opportunities to succeed in the economy, these considerations indicate that dropping out of urban schools has become a major problem in U.S. society, particularly among minority students.

Table 3
High School Completion by Ethnic Origin,
Persons 18 to 19, 1975 to 1985

Year	Total	White	Black	Hispanic (a)
1975	73.7%	77.0%	52.8%	50.0%
1977	72.9%	75.7%	54.9%	50.7%
1979	72.8%	75.3%	56.4%	53.7%
1981	72.5%	74.8%	59.6%	47.2%
1983	72.7%	75.6%	59.1%	50.3%
1985	74.6%	76.7%	62.8%	59.8%

Note: a = Year to year differences in completion rates for Hispanic are not statistically sig-nificant due to the small size of the Hispanic sample and to the fact that Hispanic stu-dents sometimes categorize themselves as white. Also, the number of immigrant Hispanic students steadily increases—perhaps masking real gains of American Hispan-ics who have been in the country for several years or even for second and third genera-tions.

Source: *The Condition of Education 1987* (p. 26), compiled by U.S. Government Printing Of-fice (1987), Washington, DC.

11   Regardless of whether an assessment of the situation in the inner city emphasizes poverty, segregation, social disorganization, or other social indicators, it is clear that educational achievement and attainment levels of inner-city children and youth are typically low, The extent of this ineffectiveness was underlined in an analysis of scores on the American College Testing (ACT) exam among high school seniors in the Chicago metropolitan area (Ornstein and Levine, 1989). After randomly selecting one-third of the schools for which data were available, the authors found that all but two of the twenty-six city high schools had average ACT scores below 15, and all but one of the thirty-six suburban schools had average scores above 15. Income and minority status accounted for a substantial portion of the outcomes; only three out of 36 suburban schools had more than 25 percent low-income students, whereas twenty of the city schools had more than 25 percent low-income students. (In addition, most of the city high schools were more than 75 percent black and/or Hispanic.)

12   The ACT is not a good measure of what has been learned in school, but it does provide a useful prediction of whether students are likely to succeed in traditional, four-year colleges. Thus, the overall pattern indicated that the large low-income population of seniors in Chicago high schools generally is not adequately prepared to succeed in traditional colleges, even though most of their lowest-achieving students already have dropped out or do not take the ACT. Comparable patterns undoubtedly would be found in many other metropolitan areas in which data are collected by city/suburban location.

13   Because social class, race/ethnicity, and school achievement are so closely interrelated, researchers frequently ask whether race and ethnicity are associated with performance in the educational system even after one takes into account the low socioeconomic status of blacks and other disadvantaged minority groups. In general, the answer has been that social class accounts for much of the variation in educational achievement by race and ethnicity. That is, if one knows the social class of a group of students one can predict with a good deal of accuracy whether their achievement, ability scores, and college attendance rates are high or low. This generalization also means that working-class and under-class white students as a group are low in achievement and college attainment (although their problems are often ignored because they are not well organized as a group and are not deemed newsworthy by the media).

Reasons for Low Achievement: Some Realities

14   Much research aimed at understanding and overcoming the problems of low-achieving students has been conducted during the past forty years, and a variety of explanations has been advanced to explain the academic deficiencies of low-achieving students in general and

low-achieving, lower working-class, and underclass students in particular. The reasons can be categorized, at least for our purposes, as
teacher-related (the first five reasons) and nonteacher-related (the last
five reasons).

Reality 1: Differences in teacher/student backgrounds

Teachers with middle-class backgrounds may experience particular   15
difficulties in understanding and motivating their working-class and
lower-class students. Problems of this nature may be particularly salient
and widespread in the case of white teachers working with disadvantaged minority students, in part because differences in dialect and
language background make it difficult for middle-class and/or non-
minority teachers to communicate effectively with minority students,
and even [may cause them] to reject the students' lifestyle and culture.

Reality 2: Teacher perceptions of student inadequacy

Based on low levels of achievement in their classrooms, many   16
teachers in working-class schools reach the conclusion that large numbers of their students are incapable of learning. This view becomes a
self-fulfilling prophecy because teachers who question their students'
learning potential are less likely to work hard to improve academic
performance, particularly since improvement requires an intense effort
that quickly consumes virtually all of a teacher's energy. Because students are influenced by their teacher's perceptions and behaviors, low
teacher expectations generate further declines in students' motivation
and performance.

Reality 3: Low standards of performance

The end result of this series of problems is that by the time low-   17
achieving students reach the upper elementary grades or the junior
high school, they are required to accomplish very little—low performance has become acceptable to their teachers. Whether in a lower
working-class or a mixed-status school, many working-class students
make little or no effort to meet demanding academic requirements by
the time they reach the secondary level. Not only do teachers add to the
situation by expecting little from such students, they sometimes wind
up praising them for below grade work and meaningless work so as
not to foster hopelessness.

Reality 4: Ineffective instructional grouping

Educators faced with large groups of low achievers frequently   18
address the problem of setting them apart in separate classes or sub-
groups in which instruction can proceed at a slower pace without
detracting from the performance of high achievers. Unfortunately, both
teachers and the students themselves tend to view concentrations of

lower achievers as "slow" groups or just plain "losers" for whom learning expectations are minimal.

19   On the other hand, individualized instruction in heterogeneous classes might make it possible for each student to make continual progress at his or her own rate, but individualization is extremely difficult to implement effectively and probably requires such costly and systematic change in school practices as to make it nearly impossible or impractical. Thus, teachers confronted with large heterogeneous classes in inner-city schools generally have not been able to work effectively with the low achievers in their classrooms.

Reality 5: Difficulty of teaching conditions

20   As lower working-class and underclass students fall further behind academically, and as both teachers and students experience frustration and discouragement, behavior problems increase in the classrooms, and teachers find it still more difficult to provide a productive learning environment. The terms "battle fatigue," "battle pay," and "blackboard jungle" have been used in the literature to describe the teaching conditions in some inner-city schools. One frequent result is that some teachers eventually give up trying to teach low achievers or seek less frustrating employment elsewhere.

Reality 6: Differences between parental and school norms

21   Lower working-class and underclass parents typically use physical punishment when their children actively misbehave or do not follow instructions; schools, on the other hand, tend to stress the middle-class approach, which emphasizes internalization of norms through inner controls and feelings of shame and guilt. Although the latter approach may be more productive in helping children internalize rules and expectations, differences between the home and the school make it difficult for many lower working-class students to follow rules and procedures when sanctions are not consistent with those imposed at home. In addition, even more than is the case among middle-class families, some working-class parents lack interest or are too preoccupied with their own lives to provide effective support for teachers.

Reality 7: Lack of previous success in school

22   Lack of academic success in the early grades not only detracts from learning more difficult material later, but also damages a student's perception that he or she is a capable learner who has a chance to succeed in school and in later life. Once students believe that they are inadequate as learners and lack control over their future (two characteristics of low-achieving students), they are less likely to work vigorously at overcoming learning deficiencies.

Reality 8: Negative peer pressure

Several researchers have studied peer influences in predominantly [23] inner-city schools and reported that academically oriented students frequently are ridiculed and rejected for accepting school norms. Strong antischool peer influence is attributed to black students as a "coping lifestyle" that is reinforced when children become disillusioned about their ability to succeed, less interested in or motivated by school, and less willing to exert the effort necessary to do well in school.

Reality 9: Inappropriate curriculum and instruction

Curriculum materials and instructional approaches in the primary [24] grades frequently assume that students are familiar with vocabulary and concepts to which lower working-class and underclass students have little or no exposure. As students proceed through school, terminology and concepts become increasingly abstract, and many lower working-class and underclass students fall further behind because their level of mastery is too rudimentary to allow for fluent learning. After grade three, much of the curriculum requires an increasing degree of reading skill that many low-achieving students have not yet attained; hence, they fall further behind in other subject areas.

Reality 10: Delivery-of-service problems

The problems we have described suggest that it is very difficult to [25] deliver educational services effectively in classes or schools with a high percentage of low achievers. If, for example, a teacher in an inner-city school has ten or fifteen low-achieving students in a class of twenty-five, the task of providing effective instruction is many times more difficult than that of a teacher who has only four or five low achievers in a middle-class school. Not only do teachers in the former situation need to spend virtually all their time remediating low achievers' learning problems, but the negative dynamics that result from students' frustration and misbehavior make the task that much more difficult.

Basically, the same observation can be offered regarding the func- [26] tioning of inner-city administrators, counselors, and other specialized personnel in such schools: so much time is spent dealing with the frequent occurrence of learning and behavior problems that little time may be left for delivering improved services for students. From this point of view, the working-class and especially underclass school can be called an overloaded institution in which a higher incidence of serious problems makes it very difficult for educators to function effectively. Indeed, in housing, private industry, and the military when conditions become too difficult the institution or operation is abandoned; in many schools, they just get worse.

Improving the Preparation of Teachers: Some Reforms

27   Given the difficulties teachers encounter in trying to enhance the performance of lower working-class and particularly underclass children and youth in big-city poverty areas, substantial improvements are imperative in preparing new teachers for success in overcoming the achievement patterns and problems described in the preceding pages. Possibilities for helping to bring about such improvements are discussed briefly in the remainder of this paper. They are geared only toward the first five teacher-related realities discussed in the previous section.

Increase the number of minority teachers. (Helps resolve problem reality #1.)

28   Only 10 percent of the current teaching force is black and Hispanic (NEA, 1987), and only 6 percent of the current teacher education majors are from these minority groups (Evangelauf, 1988). On the other hand, the percentage of black and Hispanic students in public schools has increased to 30 percent and is expected to exceed 35 percent by the year 2000 (Ornstein, 1984). Minority teachers will be increasingly underrepresented relative to the minority school population in the future. The problem is compounded by the fact that most of the states have introduced requirements that prospective teachers pass proficiency tests in basic skills, subject area specialization, and/or professional knowledge—in which black candidates fail more than twice and Hispanics 1½ times the rate of white candidates (Ornstein and Levine, 1989). Although the courts have upheld these tests as valid, the Educational Testing Service has announced that in 1991–92 it plans to replace the National Teacher Examination (now used by 30 states for licensing school teachers), and will rely less on pencil-pen tests and more on computer simulations and interactive videos. However, it will still require prospective teachers to take a test in reading, writing, and math during their sophomore year (Watkins, 1988).

29   In this connection, new programs should be initiated by the NEA and AFT in conjunction with colleges of education to attract minorities, including loans and scholarships, as well as compensatory and tutoring programs to enhance the number of well-prepared minority teacher education candidates.

Build in knowledge components focusing on effective instruction for low achievers. (Helps resolve problem realities #2,3,4.)

30   As researchers have pointed out, much has been learned concerning provision of success experiences, utilization of wait-time, direct or explicit instruction, introduction of cooperative learning, and mastery learning (Ornstein, 1987; Rosenshine, 1987; Slavin, 1988), and other approaches for improving the performance of low achievers, but many or most teacher education programs do little to help future teachers

acquire knowledge of what works so they can use an appropriate reper-
toire of these techniques effectively in real-world schools. Preservice
coursework would be more effective if research and theory were blended
with laboratory settings that can offer sufficient opportunity to practice
and master appropriate techniques (Berliner, 1985; Goodman, 1988).

*Improve practice teaching by making opportunities to practice a
systematic part of a larger learning experience. (Helps resolve problem
realities #2,3,4.)*

Reviews of research on practice teaching in general and student   31
teaching in particular have concluded that these experiences frequently
are too fragmented and isolated to allow for reliable acquisition of requisite teaching skills (Killian and McIntyre, 1988; Lanier and Featherstone, 1988). Even those student teachers who have had productive
methods have had little opportunity to develop their skills in a practical situation. Efforts should be made to help them negotiate the negative influences that sometimes function in the classrooms of
cooperating teachers. More efforts are needed, according to researchers
(Bunting, 1988; Evertson, 1986), in the training of cooperating teachers
in the strategies being taught at the teacher preparation level.

*Provide much greater assistance to teachers during their first years of
teaching. (Helps resolve problem realities #4,5.)*

One reason why many new teachers are unable or unwilling to uti-   32
lize potentially effective techniques is because they become dependent
on trial-and-error approaches acquired in isolation at the start of their
teaching careers (Corcoran and Andrew, 1988; McLaughlin, 1986). Such
methods have been demonstrated to be particularly ineffective in
working with low achievers. New teachers who work in inner-city
schools would receive greater and more meaningful assistance in the
future through the initiation of projects that assign successful teachers
to work as mentors or coaches (Anderson, 1987; Maeroff, 1988).

*Improve class management strategies for teachers. (Helps resolve
problem reality #5.)*

Of all the problems that concern beginning inner-city teachers and   33
cause anxiety and stress, the foremost is related to discipline. Discipline
has been considered the most important school problem with which
public school teachers must deal with in the last 12 out of 15 public surveys conducted by the Gallup organization for Phi Delta Kappa; it was
second the other three times (Gallup and Elam, 1988). Furthermore, in
only 39 percent of the public schools do teachers feel that student
behavior is positive, and in only 66 percent of the schools do they feel
in control of the classrooms (Ornstein, 1989b). Moreover, the percent-
ages are worse for inner-city teachers.

34   Beginning teachers must be educated in managing students and classrooms, especially in how to evoke preventive disciplinary measures and coping strategies when necessary. A research-based consensus of expert opinion on classroom management is evolving, and it must be incorporated into preservice and internship programs (Brophy, 1986; Brophy, 1988).

Consider several teacher effectiveness models in preservice and inservice education. (Helps resolve problem realities #4,5.)

35   The current research on teacher effectiveness tends to focus on a host of business-like, structured, and task-like behaviors, sometimes called teacher competencies. These behaviors are product oriented and easy to measure, yet they fail not only to consider different types of effective teachers, but also the fact that many effective teachers do not exhibit such direct behaviors (Ornstein, 1989a; Unks, 1986). Many experts jumped on this educational bandwagon, and many state departments and local school districts have developed "master teacher" and "merit pay" plans on the basis of these explicit behaviors. Even more questionably, teachers who do not exhibit these business-like and structured behaviors are often penalized, labeled as "marginal," and in some cases find their jobs are at stake (Conley, 1986; Holdzkom, 1987; Ornstein, 1988).

36   We must learn to accept that not all aspects of teaching are easy to measure. Teaching is part science and part art, and good teaching involves experience, values, insights, imagination, and appreciation. Much of teaching also involves creative ideas and inquiries, as well as artistic and philosophical appreciation, the kind of "stuff' that cannot be easily observed or quantified but corresponds with other research-based patterns of effective teachers: such as the warm-democratic, the creative-imaginative, and the problem solving-critical thinking teacher. The need is to recognize various types of "good" or "successful" teachers for inner-city schools as well as schools in general. When everyone involved with the schools can strip away the titles and come to realize that teaching and learning are a matter of people relating to each other and not a matter of tiny or sequenced prescriptions, we will have come a long way in training teachers and characterizing effective teaching.

Conclusion

The preceding analysis makes it clear that lower working-class and especially underclass students are educationally and economically disadvantaged, and that the interrelationships produce a host of problems for the schools. While some of these students are successful in the educational system, the general pattern has led some social scientists to question whether schools can indeed make any difference. Of course they can, but that will happen only when we provide improved preparation that helps teachers learn to deal with the problems and considerations that generate low achievement patterns among economically and socially disadvantaged students.

REFERENCES

Anderson, L. W. (1987). Staff development and instructional improvement. *Educational Leadership, 44* (5), 64–66.

Arends, J. H. (1987). *Building on excellence: Regional priorities for the improvement of rural, small schools.* Washington, DC: Council for Educational Development and Research.

Auletta, K. (1982). *The Underclass.* New York: Random House.

Berliner, D. C. (1985). Laboratory setting and the study of teacher education. *Journal of Teacher Education, 36* (6), 2–8.

Brophy, J. E. (1986). Classroom management techniques. *Education and Urban Society, 18* (2), 182–194.

Brophy, J. E. (1988). Educating teachers about managing classrooms and students. *Teaching and Teacher Education, 4* (1), 1–18.

Bunting, C. (1988). Cooperating teachers and the changing views of teacher certification. *Journal of Teacher Education, 39* (2), 42–47.

Conley, D. T. (1986). Certified personnel evaluation in Colorado. Unpublished doctoral dissertation, University of Colorado, Boulder.

Corcoran, E., & Andrew, M. (1988). A full year internship: An example of school-university collaboration. *Journal of Teacher Education, 39* (3), 17–24.

DeYoung, A. J. (1987). The status of American rural educational research. *Review of Educational Research, 57* (2), 123–148.

Evangelauf, J. (1988, January 3). Plan to encourage minority students to pursue teaching careers is proposed. *Chronicle of Higher Education,* p. 2.

Evertson, C. M. (1986). Do teachers make a difference? *Education and Urban Society, 18* (2), 195–210.

Gallup, A. M., & Elam, S. E. (1988). The 20th annual Gallup poll of the public's attitude toward the public schools. *Phi Delta Kappan, 70,* 33–46.

Gelman, D. (1988, March 7). Black and white in America. *Newsweek,* pp. 18–23.

Goodman, J. (1988). The political tactics and teaching strategies of reflective, active preservice teachers. *Elementary School Journal, 89* (1), 24–41.

Hahn, A., Danzerger, J., & Lefkowitz, B. (1987). *Dropouts in America.* Washington, DC: Institute for Educational Leadership.

Holdzkom, D. (1987). Appraising teacher performance in North Carolina. *Educational Leadership, 44* (7), 40–44.

Killian, J. E., & McIntyre, D. J. (1988). Grade level as a factor in participation during early field experiences. *Journal of Teacher Education, 39* (2), 36–41.

Koretz, D. (1987). *Educational achievement: Explanation and implications of recent trends.* Washington, DC: Congressional Budget Office.

Lanier, J. E., & Featherstone, J. (1988). A new commitment to teacher education, *Educational Leadership, 46* (3), 18–22.

Levine, D. U., & Havighurst, R. J. (1988). *Society and education.* (7th ed.). Needham Heights, MA: Allyn and Bacon.

Lynd, R. S., & Lynd, H. M. (1929). *Middletown: A study in American culture.* New York: Harcourt, Brace.

Maeroff, G. I. (1988). Withered hopes, stillborn dreams: The dismal panorama of urban schools. *Phi Delta Kappan, 69,* 632–638.

McLaughlin, M. W (1986). Why teachers won't teach. *Phi Delta Kappan, 67,* 420–426.

National Assessment of Educational Progress. (1985). *The reading report card.* Princeton, NJ: Educational Testing Service.

National Assessment of Educational Progress. (1988). *Who reads best.* Princeton, NJ: Educational Testing Service.

National Education Association. (1987). *Status of the American public school teacher 1985–86.* Washington, DC: Author.

Ornstein, A. C. (1982). The education of the disadvantaged: A 20 year review. *Educational Research, 24* (3), 197–211.

Ornstein, A. C. (1984). Urban demographics for the 1980s. *Education and Urban Society, 16* (4), 463–477.

Ornstein, A. C. (1987). Emphasis on student outcomes focuses attention on quality of instruction. *National Association of Secondary School Principals, 71* (495), 88–95.

Ornstein, A. C. (1988). The changing status of the teaching profession. *Urban Education, 23* (3), 261–279.

Ornstein, A. C. (1989a). For teachers, about teachers. *Peabody Journal of Education,* in press.

Ornstein, A. C. (1989b). Private and public school comparisons: Size, organization, and effectiveness. *Education and Urban Society, 21* (2), 192–206.

Ornstein, A. C., & Levine, D. U. (1989). *Foundations of education* (4th ed.). Boston: Houghton Mifflin.

Rosenshine, B. (1987). Explicit teaching and teacher training. *Journal of Teacher Education, 38* (3), 34–36.

Rothman, R. (1988, May 4). Black achievement in science and math up during 80s: Board finds. *Education Week.* p. 5.

Slavin, R. E. (1988). Cooperative learning and student achievement. *Educational Leadership, 46* (2), 31–34.

Unks, G. (1986). Product oriented teaching: A reappraisal. *Education and Urban Society, 18* (2), 242–254.

U.S. Government Printing Office. (1980). *High school and beyond study.* Washington, DC: Author.

U.S. Government Printing Office. (1985). *The condition of education 1985.* Washington, DC: Author.

U.S. Government Printing Office. (1986). *The condition of education 1986.* Washington, DC: Author.

U.S. Government Printing Office. (1987). *The condition of education 1987.* Washington, DC: Author.

Vroman, W (1988). Relative earnings of black and white men: What will close the gap? *Urban Institute Policy and Research Report, 18* (2), 9–10.

Watkins, B. T. (1988, November 2). Educational Testing Service to replace National Teacher Examination by 1992. *Chronicle of Higher Education,* p. A32.

Yao, E. L. (1987). Asian immigrant students: Unique problems that hamper learning. *National Association of Secondary School Principals, 71* (503), 82–88.

Reading and Writing Activities

PRELIMINARY RESPONSE

Notes.   As you read, record your reactions (questions or comments) to "Social Class, Race, and School Achievement" in your reading journal.

You may react to one or more of a number of factors in the reading. You might, for example, consider the ten "realities" that Allan Ornstein and David Levine analyze—whether some are more important than others, whether some equally important "realities" have been overlooked.

Discussion.   In class, compare your reactions in reading groups of five or six. Appoint a recorder to keep track of similarities and differences, consensus or disagreement, arising from the discussion. The recorder may summarize your group discussion for the rest of the class later.

Freewriting.   In a 10- to 15-minute freewrite, consider possible causes for the relatively poor academic performance of disadvantaged and minority children. Distinguish between those causes that might be blamed on individuals (teachers, parents, children) or the educational system (administrators, textbooks, teacher training) and those that might not be. Read your freewriting in groups of two to four. As others are reading, take written note of areas of agreement or disagreement, questions that arise in your mind, and ideas that might be qualified or extended. After everyone has read, appoint a recorder to keep track of similarities or differences, consensus or disagreement, that arises in the ensuing discussion. The recorder may summarize your group discussion for the rest of the class later.

SUMMARIZING

1. Make a scratchline, cluster representation, or notes indicating the progression of ideas in "Social Class, Race, and School Achievement"—one that reflects your consideration of the freewriting and discussion of group members. Note in particular the distinction between "realties" that can be blamed on individuals or the educational system and those that cannot be.
2. Write a summary paragraph or two, using your scratchline, cluster representation, or notes.
3. Read summaries in groups. Compare the focus of each summary. How do the summaries differ? How are they the same? Again, check to see if you are *reacting and responding* to the reading selection instead of summarizing the central topics.

FOCUSED CRITICAL READING

1. In paragraph 28, Ornstein and Levine say that schools should hire more minority applicants, regardless of whether they have passed

proficiency tests. What are the strongest arguments in favor of that assertion?

2. In presenting "Reality 1" in paragraph 15, the authors say that teachers may occasionally "reject the . . . lifestyle and culture" of some students. How might that happen?

3. In paragraph 20, the authors refer to such figures of speech as "battle fatigue" and "blackboard jungle" by which teachers express and reinforce despair. What similar figures of speech do students use?

4. Does "Reality 6," presented paragraph 21, constitute a persuasive argument for corporal punishment?

5. In paragraph 36, the authors say that "teaching is part science and part art. " What kinds of abilities could be placed under each of those headings? Which do you consider more important?

Benjamin P. Bowser and Herbert Perkins

Success Against the Odds: Young Black Men Tell What It Takes

◆

The relatively poor academic performance of many ethnic minorities has been documented in a number of studies, some of which are cited by Allan Ornstein and Daniel Levine in "Social Class, Race, and School Achievement." Although many scholars and journalists have attempted to account for this phenomenon, the authors of the following article have taken a more direct approach, interviewing Hispanic and African-American students who succeed academically. Benjamin Bowser is a professor of sociology at California State University, Hayward; Herbert Perkins is a professor of anthropology at Lawrence University, in Wisconsin.

While there are many aspects of a young person's life which can be judged as a success or failure, their educational achievement is decisive. Success in school is a prerequisite for maximizing life chances and for taking advantage of new opportunities. Ironically, the single most difficult piece of information to find is what goes on in the lives of academically successful Black and Hispanic adolescents? How do they beat the odds? The importance of this information is obvious. If we can find out what successful Black and Hispanic students do and have in common, then we have some idea of what can be done to intervene into the circumstances of the majority who are not succeeding.

The Interviews

There is research underway that looks directly at the lives of successful Black students. The primary focus is on the role that parents play in their academic success. At different times since 1960 the schools, community, peers and parents have been identified as primary factors in academic success and failure. Researchers have more often found the family to be the most important factor. Because of this history, the authors developed a series of questions to be used by focus

389

group leaders to probe student relations with parents, relatives, teachers, peers, other people and organizations within their community.

3   The students who participated in our focus groups consisted of forty Black and Hispanic high school sophomores through seniors. Roughly half of the students were males and most of the males were Black. The students were evenly divided across the three academic years. They had 3.0 plus grade point averages in college preparatory tracks and were the top minority academic achievers in three integrated suburban high schools in California. What made this group of students interesting to us is that it cut across virtually all categories. Most had attended segregated junior high schools. They were doing well in integrated suburban high schools where the academic programs were very competitive and demanding. Virtually all of these students came from working-class households and half had single parents. Their parents worked, for example, as nurses, bus drivers, mechanics, stock clerks, physical education instructors, part-time ministers and hospital attendants. Only three students had parents who were professionals—a lawyer, teacher and engineer. Also their community reflected what will be the more common circumstance for Blacks and Hispanics in the next century. They are mostly from working-class households living in suburban racial ghettos.

4   Several years ago their high school district realized that they had very few academically successful minority students. The district principals decided that the first step was to identify the few who were doing well and encourage their efforts. They developed a district program where any minority student in their schools who achieved a 3.0 plus grade point average (GPA) was to be rewarded and encouraged with field trips, recognition and opportunities to meet, interact and encourage one another. These students represented a unique opportunity to derive insight on what makes for academic success for working-class minority students in suburban integrated schools. These students were brought to the California State University at Hayward campus and spent an afternoon divided into six focus groups, led by student service staff and faculty. We asked the students to tell us in taped discussions: What did they do to perform well in school; who in their family, school, community and peer groups played important roles; what were the barriers; was race a factor; and how would they account for their peers' lack of success?

5   The students were assured that their individual identities would be kept confidential. With the formalities over, they lit up and had a lot to say. No one had asked them these questions before, so they were eager to respond. In no session did the focus group leader dominate the discussion. The students responded to the questions with amazing candor and detail. While we had a special interest in what the young Black men had to say, it was very clear right from the beginning of the ses-

sions that the students' experiences and insights cut across gender and ethnicity. The following is what they told us, based on a review of the tape recordings of each session.

Students' Reflections on Academic Success

Relations with Family

Past and current research suggests that there is a very close relation   6
between student academic success and parents. Early in each focus group a number of students said that their parents were important as sources of encouragement. These students reported that their parents always had time for them, would help them with their homework, clearly rewarded success, punished failure and were generally "on their case." One student had a mother who corrected her papers and a father who tutored her in mathematics. But when we probed this response and got all of the students in the discussion, a far more complex picture of relations with parents emerged. Most of the students had a different situation. After the groups became more comfortable, several "acknowledgers" as well as most who had remained quiet said that their immediate parents were really not their main source of support. The key persons, who they named as their main sources of family support for high academic achievement, consisted of grandparents or, more often, older brothers or sisters. While parents may or may not have been "on their case" and were pleased that the student was doing well, it was actually some other member of the family who helped the student to define his long-term career goals and who turned him on to high academic achievement.

> My older sister really got me going. She is in the Navy, is doing well and has told me many times what I need to do to be successful. I have admired her and have always listened to her.

Ironically, most of the people who were reported as the main source   7
of family motivation were not successful in school. Many of our high achievers as elementary and junior high school students had watched their parents struggle with older siblings. These older brothers and sisters had made all sorts of mistakes, primary of which was failure in school. The outcomes in troubled lives, purposelessness, underemployment and unemployment are now very apparent within each family. It turns out that the experiences of these older brothers and sisters serve as a powerful source of motivation to take some other route. The students said repeatedly that they would do anything not to end up like their older siblings who were models of the consequences of underachievement. In many cases, these older sibling became directly involved in

making certain that their younger brother or sister did not end up as they did. One student who was the sixth and youngest boy in his family reported:

> All five of my older brothers did not do well in school and have been in some form of trouble at one time or another. One day they got together and sat me down in the middle of them and told me that they wanted me to do better and that I had to get A's and B's in school. No matter what they're doing, they all check my report card. If it's good, they really make me feel great. If it's bad, they'll kick my ass.

8   Another student said, "All I have to do is look at how my parents ended up unhappy and fighting all the time and I know I have to do well in school—I work harder and harder." Other students reported that what got them achieving was an older sister's struggle to graduate from high school as a single parent, defiance aided by an older brother against parents who don't believe "I can do it," and a brother's trouble in college because he was not well prepared. What all of these high achieving students had in common is that there was somebody outside of school in their immediate or extended family who was "on their case" and who more often served as a direct example of what happens to those who do not achieve.

Relations with School

9   It is overly simplistic to assume that home motivation, regardless of its source, translates directly into high academic achievement. Work which focuses exclusively on family and academic achievement makes such an assumption by default. In reality, schools can either take advantage of or frustrate homebased motivation to achieve. It is also necessary to look at the related influence of schools on individual academic achievement. Otherwise, schools appear to be culturally neutral and totally objective entities—an impossibility. Our high achievers come to school with very strong motivation from home to do well. But it is also clear from the focus groups that family motivation is not all that it takes to maintain a 3.0 plus grade point average in college preparatory courses.

10   What was said in all of the focus groups was that someone at school took a personal interest in each student's work. There was at least one teacher who held each student in high regard and who told them repeatedly that they could do well. The students reported that these "mentor" teachers then worked with them.

11   The "mentor" teachers were important to the initial translation of personal and home derived motivation into actual high grades. Several students reported having a series of supportive teachers who showed them that they could do good work—repeatedly. Others had only one

teacher now and then who took a special interest in them. In addition to a "mentor" teacher all of the high achievers had counselors. The fewer supportive teachers they had, the more important were these counselors. Even with a series of supportive teachers, caring counselors were essential to monitoring, encouraging and getting students into good classroom experiences.

Active counselors were also reported to be essential in their role as in-school advocates and for coaching students through classes with unsupportive teachers who could have easily broken their motivation and early successes. 12

Several focus group leaders explored with their students the nature of the relation the students reported having with "mentor" teachers and counselors. Amazingly the responses were consistent across each focus groups. The students reported that the people in school who were supportive treated them more like friends or close relatives than like students. It was very important that the formal student-teacher and student-counselor relation be reduced to a more personal one-on-one relation. 13

> Mrs. X treats us like her son. She is excited about me, shares with me her feelings, makes me feel special and a part of her life. I even have her home telephone number.

The students reported that it was easier and even fun to study with a teacher who really cared and "did not talk down to you." Teachers who would stop them in the hall while they were with other students and ask how they were and how were things going were well regarded. One student said that he really did not believe that he could do superior work until he realized that two of his teachers were willing to stay after school to work with him on science and math problems. But besides being personal and supportive, these significant school persons held high expectations and did not hesitate to monitor each student's progress, in which case, the students' relations with their "mentor" teachers and counselors became additional motivation to do well. Poor grades and lack of effort would have violated these positive personal relations and would have hurt and disappointed their mentors. 14

In contrast, teachers who insisted on being impersonal, who showed no signs of caring and had no time or interest in the student, drew angry, hurt comments. "Mr. Y would see me on the street and wouldn't even say 'hello' and, if you ask him a question in class, he would tell you 'go look it up—I already talked about that in class.'" Especially hurtful were teachers who were clearly very positive toward their White students, but were very impersonal with minority students in the same class. 15

16   One of the more fascinating elements in the students' discussion about school was when they began to realize that they really could be high achievers. The first time they attained their 3.0 plus in high school was not the point at which they realized that their achievement was special. The seniors had had at least two years of high grades and had no doubts about accepting and identifying with their achievement. The seniors told us that their earlier confidence was closer to what the sophomores reported. The less experienced achievers said that, while they knew that they were doing well, they still did not think that what they had done was exceptional or important—even after making the dean's list several times and being part of a program for high achieving minority students! One student had a 3.9 GPA at the end of his freshman year and seriously considered dropping out for a temporary labor job. He knew that a 3.9 was a high average, but he had no sense of its meaning in his own life or what he could attain by maintaining that average. Another student had so thoroughly identified with the stereotype that minority students do poorly in school that she assumed that her 3.6 was simply not good enough.

17   High initial attainment in itself was not sufficient to be a source of motivation for continued effort nor did it mark special status. One of the Black males with high grades was also a top athlete. Like the others, he did not think of his academic achievements as important. At first, his only concern about his grades was that they be high enough for him to continue playing ball. The turning point for him and the others came with some public declaration that their academic achievement was "special." The athlete did not fully realize that he was also an exceptional student until the city newspaper sent a reporter and photographer to his home. They took pictures and did a story with a focus on him as an athlete who was also a top student. Another student was called to the principal's office. He thought that he was in some sort of trouble. Instead, the principal gave him an award for his academic achievement.

18   The other students indicated that the minority scholar's annual awards and recognition banquet was the turning point for them. At this banquet each student received an academic award with their peers and parents present. A number of students had part-time jobs after school—they were assisted in placement by their school counselors. People on their jobs were aware of their academic achievements and also encouraged them. The students were asked by the people they worked with if they ever considered going to particular colleges and universities. The students had always assumed that these schools were beyond their means and abilities. They were asked if they knew about various fields of study in college. Again they either had no knowledge or simply never associated themselves with the fields. On some of these jobs there were college students who offered to help them with their homework and told them to consider going to their university— they could get in. These events impressed on them that what they were

doing was important and was not to be taken for granted. But it was equally important that the point be made to their parents, friends and peers. After public acknowledgment, each student had a new identity to live up to and a sense that the opportunities before them were real.

Finally, if you ever thought that high academic performance was largely due to proper study skills, what these young people reported was shocking. They violated every rule for efficient and effective study. They studied with their radios on. They studied lying down. They studied in between classes and on the run. They studied when they were tired. They studied for examinations the night before or just an hour before. Occasionally, they did not study at all! Only a couple of students reported studying consistently several hours per night. Out of the entire group only two students studied together and at the library. Ironically, they all knew how they were supposed to study, but the proper way was simply not how they did it. With regard to study habits, they seemed to have only two points in common: They all did some sort of studying and they were all diligent about completing homework assignments on time. But they may have had an additional and very subtle point in common. Several students mentioned that they paid very close attention to what went on in each class and practiced recalling what they learned right after classes. I suspect that there is a close relation between their relations with teachers and how well they retained information. Being personally close to teachers makes recall easier, while the formal social distance common to the teacher-student relation makes retention and recall more difficult.

Relations with Community

Virtually all of these high achievers lived in low income, working-class suburban communities which are segregated by race and by economic class. The students were asked if there were other nonfamily members in their community who contributed to their academic achievement. The most common response was emphatically "none." In exploring their community experiences we found a rough and tragic terrain. The students saw academic achievement as a way out of depressed and dangerous environments. One student said, "You do whatever you can to get out of X."

Others commented that their community was varied by income and people and was not all negative. Everyone's concern was that others, especially their White peers at school, held consistently negative stereotypes about their communities and all of the people who lived there. People who lived in X community were considered to be "stupid, lazy and criminal." This stereotype was a formidable barrier to how others treated the students. Only one student said that his community motivated him. He wanted to get an education so that he could return to help turn it around. Another student realized that education was the only way out after having worked during a summer on a survey project. The households he interviewed that had the least education were the poorest and the most troubled.

22   Virtually all of these high achievers conveyed a sense of walking a fine line in their community lives. The subject that got them all especially animated was drug trafficking in their communities. This was the most threatening aspect of their community life. They could live with poverty and the stereotyping, but drug trafficking was another matter. They had family members involved as sellers and users. Neighbors and friends also used and sold "crack." This is what the "crowd" did and there was considerable peer pressure on them to also get involved. One student said "you can't act like they [drug sellers and users] don't exist. They are family, neighbors and friends. You got to live with them." But the fine line is that "you have to not be a part of them while they are all around you." Another student said "I stay by myself away from the crowd and spend as much time as possible outside of the community." The consensus was that you either do well in school or you do drugs. There was literally no other option. Focusing on school was banking on the future because in the present those who sold drugs clearly had the money, cars, clothes and high regard of the "crowd."

23   We asked about church and other institutions in their community. Were community institutions viewed as supportive of their high achievement? The responses were mostly negative. One church was mentioned where the pastor acknowledged student academic achievement in the congregation. He always asked, "How are you doing in school?" and never forgot to tell them "to keep up the good work." But most of the other churches the students attended only gave lip service to the need for students to do well in school. Individual student achievements were not recognized or acknowledged. There is no place in the format or tradition of the Catholic masses for this sort of acknowledgment. And as one student put it, his church was so down on young people that they wouldn't know how to recognize him even if they knew of his work. Two female students, whose families were Pentecostal and Jehovah's Witnesses respectively, told stories of how their churches actually opposed their focus on school. The time they spend at school would be better spent at church and it was not good to become too much a part of "the world." Only three students talked of being a part of youth groups in their communities. A number of organizations for young people existed some years ago, but not any more— "there is no money for them and people are now scared of the dope."

Relations with Peers

24   "It helps to have someone to talk to and work with." But more typically these students did not have peers whom they were really close

to. They had many acquaintances but few close friends. Even participation in the three schools' minority scholars program did not change
their relative isolation. There were enough differences among these
students that they rarely got together outside of program activities.
They were also spread across three high schools and several communities. The lack of close friends highlighted the need for open and warm
friendships with teachers and counselors. The students gave a variety
of explanations for their situation. One of the Black males said "When
the kids I used to hang with found out that I was doing well [in
school], they didn't want to hang with me no more." Most of the students reported that very few of the young people they spent their time
with were doing well in school. When the achievers were together with
their friends, they simply did not talk about school. In some cases,
friends who were doing poorly were pleased to have a partner who
was "smart" and encouraged their achieving friend to continue doing
well.

Friends were mostly of the same sex and race. But occasionally   25
support and motivation came from unanticipated places. Several
female students spoke of their boyfriends as being very supportive of
their achievement—especially friends in colleges who were a year or
two older. One male student said, "I wanted to be friends with a girl
who was a good student. But she don't want to be bothered with me
when my grades were bad. When your grades are good, you can go out
with a lot more girls." Most White students expected the minority students to do poorly and were often openly hostile to those who managed to be exceptions. Several of our achievers had experiences similar
to a student who said, "When the White students in my classes found
out that I was getting As, they stopped talking to me. At first they
thought I was there for their entertainment—to talk about sports. Several said to me that Blacks aren't suppose to get As—especially those
from my community." Another student said, "When I answer questions correctly in class, the White students turn and look at me in
amazement."

Not all of the White students constantly mirrored prejudice. One   26
student told of an incident in one of his classes when an examination
was being returned. A White student asked, what grade did he get?
Before he could answer another White student said laughingly, "He
probably got a D." The comment hurt and the Black student resented it,
but he and the White student who made the comment are now good
friends. Another student told the group that, if it had not been for a
White friend from junior high school, he would not have enrolled in
college preparatory courses.

His White friend kept after him to get into the right classes—he had   27
no idea that a decision in the eighth grade would make a difference.

28   As part of the focus group questions, each facilitator asked the students to tell us why they felt other "bright" Blacks and Hispanics did poorly in school. The achievers began discussing other students who were smart and did better work than they did in junior high school. Their explanations ranged across school, peers, family and community. They pointed out that if there was no one in the family who actively cared, the young person was finished. A student not on the college track by the ninth grade was also finished—"Nobody is going to go back to take the right courses." They called for more guidance counselors and wondered why, the very year their district high schools were integrated, the guidance departments were cut out? They also pointed out that the low achievers were unwilling to give up their friends for school. Other comments were that their peers did not believe in themselves—just as our scholars had not. The low achievers thought that they could not do any better because deep down they really believed that Blacks and Hispanics are dumb—precisely what many White teachers and students believe. So there was no point in committing themselves to studies. The worst part of what they reported was that alienation from school fed directly into alienation in the community. There were no opportunities for a young person to simply make mistakes, sort out their lives and mature. The drug scene was there waiting with open arms.

The Significance of Race

29   We asked the students, had they experienced racism and, if so, did it have any effect on their academic performance? Most replied that they had no direct experience with racism. What they meant was that they had not experienced blatant and obvious discrimination like that which existed in the South during Jim Crow segregation. Instead, what they experienced were actions directed at them personally that kept them guessing whether it was or was not racist. Not really knowing was worse than the acts. There were key teachers in the college preparatory track who seemed friendly toward their White students, but were cold and matter-of-fact with Black and Hispanic students. One student with a B average in the class got a D as a final grade. The teacher said it was because he did poorly on the final examination. When the student's counselor and father demanded to see the examination, the teacher claimed that it was lost. The grade was changed. Another "unfriendly" teacher wanted to give the student a failing grade for one unexcused absence. The student knew of White students in his class with unexcused absences who were not failed. It turned out that the teacher could not fail this minority student after all, because he had really not been absent. Another student remarked, "It seems like they [unsupportive teachers] are just laying for you and looking for an excuse to mark you down. It is hard to go all semester and make no mistakes."

In listening to the focus group tapes it was interesting to note that   30
only males reported that teachers were "laying for them." The female
students also experienced covert mistreatment, but there appeared to
be greater tolerance among unsupportive teachers for Black and Hispanic females being exceptional students. White students exhibited
covert racism by assuming that all Black and Hispanic students were
dumb and by wanting to maintain this belief even when they encountered exceptions. Sometimes underlying racial hostility would be manifested in actions. Students reported occasionally opening their lockers
and finding notes stuffed in through the air holes. The contents of these
anonymous notes were personally insulting, racist and derogatory.
These covert acts of racism took a much greater toll in anger and personal hurt than the overt acts. "It is hard to get your mind off of it [an
anonymous act of racism] and study, especially when it came from a
teacher." In addition, those who held jobs pointed out that they saw
racist behavior on the job. It was usually directed at Blacks and Hispanics in lower-level roles. In these cases, racism was an incentive to study
in order to be better employed.

Conclusion

What we have uncovered from these interviews are insights from   31
the lives of a group of Black and Hispanic students as to why they are
successful in school. They have also given us a glimpse of the price
they are paying for choosing to focus on school.

What these students provided in one intense afternoon is by no   32
means the whole story. Black and Hispanic students from other social
class and community circumstances could undoubtedly give us additional insight on what it takes to be academically successful. This small
group of students went quickly beyond the demographic and statistical
picture of success and got into the factors and processes that account
for their achievement. Others may wish to use this information to
design surveys to see just how representative the experiences are of the
students who participated in our focus groups. If we learned anything
from these group discussions, it was the value of involving teens in an
inquiry about their lives and experiences.

There are a number of specific points which the students raised   33
that are well worth testing and considering:

1. Both family and school involvement and encouragement are essential to student motivation to succeed. Also both sources of
   motivation have to be complementary.
2. A student's family should be defined more broadly so that it includes extended relations. We should note that there is a bias to-

ward crediting parent(s) with influence even when the primary motivation comes from some other, non-parent family member.

3. Students can be motivated to succeed by family and friends who are not themselves "successful" role models.

4. An effective and motivating relation between students and their teachers and counselors begins when teachers and counselors take a personal interest in the students and work with them. Willingness to drop the formal teacher-student or counselor-student role is important.

5. Public acknowledgment and identification of an achieving student are essential to those students' realization that they are indeed doing exceptional work and can qualify for opportunities in the larger society outside of their community. Acknowledgment is also very important for encouraging continued support from a high achiever's peers and family.

6. The specific study strategies that lead to high academic achievement are primarily to study consistently, to pay close attention in class and to be diligent in turning in assignments. Specific study techniques or number of hours per day of study are of secondary importance.

34   The Black and Hispanic students we interviewed are paying a very high price in being shunned and isolated from their peers and community. They have to literally disassociate themselves from their communities and normal friendships in order to maintain their motivation to academically succeed. Also they cannot afford to make mistakes in walking the fine lines in their communities between drug trafficking and resentment over their choice or at school between racist teachers "laying for them" and White students who do not accept their competitiveness. The personal price these students are paying for their academic achievement is remarkable and ironic. It is remarkable because they have to pay such a price at all. It is ironic because all well-meaning individuals and institutions in American life profess to support and would applaud their achievement. Yet they are isolated, shunned and could not achieve without a system of special support. The problem is that for these students professions willing to have them as important players in the larger society are too far away from their day-to-day reality.

The Community Factor

35   The students we interviewed are doing well academically because of extraordinary efforts from their schools which have made it possible for individual teachers and counselors to take interest in each student and to work with them. Their achievement also required someone at

home to convince each student to forgo the immediate world around them and to count on school and the future for a better life—another extraordinary effort. Why are these extraordinary efforts necessary in order to produce high achievers? It is very clear that if motivators at home or at school had not taken special interest and given attention to these students, we would not have had any Black and Hispanic high achievers to interview. These young people would be indistinguishable from their peers—many of whom are just as talented. The answer can be found by looking at the factor the students found least supportive and hoped to escape from: the community.

Researchers may be able to conceptually separate families from communities and then research the relation between families and academic achievement as if the community were not a factor. But the family lives of the young people we interviewed would suggest that to separate family from community is to ignore very important factors in student motivation. The community more than any other factor is a reflection of the morale, expectations and life conditions of its residents. It is also the community that serves as the immediate environment for family life. If we focus on what the students told us about their parents and older brothers and sisters, we get a glimpse of a real struggle. That struggle is not simply between family members; it is about the family living in its environment. It was through the community that older brothers and sisters got into their troubles. It was peers in the community that parents competed against in shaping their children's lives and in controlling them amidst fast money and other potentially destructive distractions.

Current research suggests that Black student academic achievement is largely due to family influences, in which case declining achievement is due to declining family support. What researchers might be really looking at is declining community morale and declining social resources mediated through the family. By overlooking community influence, one can focus on the extraordinary uphill struggles of those few families who do produce a high achiever and overcome their communities. But this is to ignore the obvious. The obvious is that if the majority are failing because of community influences, the majority can also succeed if community becomes positive and supportive. Our students' older brothers and sisters and friends are a testimony to this fact. The interviewers asked each group of students to name the one thing which could be done to produce more academically successful students like themselves. We fully expected them to focus on improvements within their schools such as expanding special programs. To our surprise the most common answer had to do with community improvement—get rid of drugs and get more jobs.

Reading and Writing Activities

PRELIMINARY RESPONSE

Notes.   As you read, record your reactions (questions or comments) to "Success Against the Odds" in your reading journal.

You may react to one or more of a number of factors in the reading. You might, for example, compare and contrast the interviewees' comments about family, community, teachers, and peers with your own experiences.

Discussion.   In class, compare your reactions in reading groups of five or six. Appoint a recorder to keep track of similarities and differences, consensus or disagreement, arising from the discussion. The recorder may summarize your group discussion for the rest of the class later.

Freewriting.   In a 10-minute freewrite, assess the relative importance of factors contributing to the success of students interviewed by Benjamin Bowser and Herbert Perkins. Then, in another 10-minute freewrite, assess the relative importance of factors that impede their success. Read your freewriting in groups of two to four. As others are reading, take written note of areas of agreement or disagreement, questions that arise in your mind, and ideas that might be qualified or extended. After everyone has read, appoint a recorder to keep track of similarities or differences, consensus or disagreement, that arise in the ensuing discussion. The recorder may summarize your group discussion for the rest of the class later.

SUMMARIZING

1. Make a scratchline, cluster representation, or notes indicating the progression of ideas in "Success Against the Odds"—one that reflects your consideration of the freewriting and discussion of group members. Note in particular the tension between individual achievement and community values.
2. Write a summary paragraph or two, using your scratchline, cluster representation, or notes.
3. Read summaries in groups. Compare the focus of each summary. How do the summaries differ? How are they the same? Again, check to see if you are *reacting and responding* to the reading selection instead of summarizing the central topics.

FOCUSED CRITICAL READING

1. Would most (or all) students, minority or otherwise, benefit from having a mentor? Is it reasonable to expect public schools to provide mentors?
2. Many of the students interviewed by Bowser and Perkins were influenced by negative role models—family members who did not do well in school. Do you think theirs is a typical or common response to negative role models?
3. In paragraph 34, Bowser and Perkins conclude that the students they interviewed "have to literally dissociate themselves from their communities" to succeed academically. Is it reasonable to ask these students to retain any ties to that community in the future?

Ann H. Beuf

The World of the Native American Child: Education

———————◆———————

The following selection, which describes the educational experience of many Native Americans, makes extensive reference to the Coleman Report, a document discussed in the introduction to this chapter. The author, Ann Beuf, has taught sociology and women's studies at the University of Pennsylvania and at Cedar Crest College. Her interests as a writer include health care and the welfare of children.

1   Education presents a dismal picture . . . with dropout rates fifty percent higher than the rest of the population. Fewer than eighteen percent of students in federally run Native American schools go on to college. Results of tests indicate that while Native American children perform almost as well as white children on achievement tests that are nonverbal, their verbal work is affected by their lack of English language skills and knowledge of white culture.

2   The same inconsistency that prevailed in territorial and economic matters has been the rule in education. At first a few schools teaching technical skills were established on or near reservations. Two eastern boarding schools, the Haskell Institute and the Carlisle Indian School, in the latter half of the nineteenth century took Native American children away from home, until outcries against the uprooting of children and separation of families brought about the establishment of schools nearer home. However, because of the distance involved, many of these are also boarding schools. These schools, unfortunately, did not seem to train children for economically successful life, nor did they really prepare the Native American child for higher education by teaching the academic subjects that would permit him or her to go on to college. In all instances, an effort was made to de-Indianize the Native American. Children were sometimes kidnapped from their homes by BIA employees and forced to attend BIA schools. Physical punishment, unheard of in most Native American cultures, was and sometimes still is cruelly applied.

3   Both Parmee, who studied the Apache, and the Waxes, who studied education at Pine Ridge, noted that reservation parents do not take an active interest in their children's education, and they stress the need to make education relevant to the parents as well as to the children.

404

Often, because the values of home and school are so different, the child must choose between being a good Native American and being a good student. The Wax study places more importance on the effect on Native American children of interaction between the two cultures, stressing as they do two different sets of values. In addition, white teachers are considered in their roles as socializers, not as beings who come into the child's life after his personality is completely formed. The parents' exclusion from active involvement with the schools (an example of institutional racism) is presented as a wedge driven between the two worlds in which the child lives. The Waxes urge those coming in contact with Native American children and their families to become sensitized to Native American values and to attempt to make educational programs responsive to the needs of the entire community. Parmee's study of Apache education also points to the incompatibility of school and reservation life, but he bluntly includes the anti-Native American attitudes of white educators in his explanation of the Native American child's passive failure in school.

The Coleman report found that the deficiencies of Native American children in school work were most strongly related to language problems, "cultural deprivation," and negative self-concept. Those factors frequently cited as reasons for poor performance—facilities, curriculum, and quality of teachers—were not strongly correlated with the performance of Native American youngsters. This finding is particularly significant if we consider it in the light of a theory of institutional racism. All three of the major variables are related to each other and attributable to institutional racism.   4

The "language problem," as it is called, reflects the cultural white supremacy and ethnocentric Anglo bias of the educational system: the language problem would not be a problem at all if children were taught in their own language. Language is obviously a major problem for children who, at home, speak something other than standard middle-class English. Native American children who have, until first grade, spoken a tribal language or even "reservation English," find themselves in a classroom where the most basic skills are being conveyed in a language they do not comprehend. Some children literally have no idea what the teacher is saying. To compound the problem, the children are tested on these skills and their performance judged in terms of a national "norm." Small wonder that by such measures they appear to be behind majority-group children.   5

Incidentally, such tests are very good examples of institutional racism in action. A "correct" answer for test items is based on Anglo culture and the norms that flow from it. Especially on verbal tests, there may be no *intrinsic* correctness to a response but only a correctness as the majority culture defines it. In other words, the performance of white middle-class children establishes the norm for these tests, and   6 the performance of other children is deemed "good" or "bad" depending on the degree to which it conforms to that norm. Thus we can see the arbitrary establishment of an ethnocentric cultural system within the educational institution.

7   Children who speak a language other than English are not alone in suffering from these arrangements. Children who speak an English that is not middle-class suffer as well. The black ghetto child, the reservation Native American, and the working-class white (who says "he don't" or "they was") all may do poorly on verbal tests. The unfortunate aspect of this situation, of course, is that those in the field of education (and many others) do not view correct English simply as conformity to middle-class verbal norms, but tend to equate it with intelligence. Thus children who speak some variant of the language emerge from the testing situation and from interaction with their teachers labeled stupid, not just speakers of another kind of English. This link between the speaking of standard English and concepts of intelligence affects both teacher expectations for students and students' feelings about themselves.

8   Teachers have been observed by many social scientists to be very much attuned to language differences and to show more positive behavior toward students who use standard English. More attention is given to the intellectual and emotional growth of these middle-class children when, for example, compositions are discussed in class. The working-class child's work in this situation is discussed in terms of what grammatical corrections are needed.

9   Certainly those students who are treated seriously and with respect by their teachers are likely to perform better and to enjoy school more than children who are constantly treated with disapproval. Such children may lose self-esteem and come to view school as an unfriendly place. This is reflected in the high dropout rate among groups of nonstandard English speakers. As long as racial and social class speech patterns influence the expectations and attitudes of teachers, we can safely say that language and the schools will serve to perpetuate the existing class system of the society. Higher education is an important pathway to upward mobility, and the lack of it confines these children to the same occupational options which were available to their parents, maintaining the status quo for another generation. Thus language may function to lower self-esteem and future expectations on an intraracial level, as well as for minority racial groups, with poor whites being victimized by sanctions against their own "non-normative" speech patterns.

10   In the case of Native Americans, language has always been recognized by white educators as being of key importance, although, as we have seen, not always for the right reasons. Physical punishment for the speaking of tribal languages characterized almost all of the early

schools and is still employed in some schools. There are two reasons for this. The first is the educators' fear of children who could have secrets from them by speaking in a "foreign" tongue. The second reason was the desire to use the schools as deculturating institutions, turning little Native Americans into English-speaking, Christian, Anglo-like citizens, much as the children of the immigrants were being deculturated by the schools in the East.

The introduction of Native American teachers and teacher's aides,   11
and growing community participation in educational matters on the part of many Native American parents, as well as the enlightened establishment of bilingual programs on reservations, have eased the situation somewhat. However, there is a need for more Native American teachers. In the absence of these, some tribal groups are requesting that white teachers be required to demonstrate a knowledge of tribal language and culture before being permitted to teach on the reservation.

The Coleman report cites cultural deprivation as a second major   12
factor in determining the academic achievement of Native American children. "Cultural deprivation," as Chadwick has pointed out in his paper, "The Inedible Feast," would be better phrased as cultural differences. Wax has called the entire notion of cultural deprivation "vacuum" ideology, implying as it does that there is no culture in Native American homes. Here we have a perfect example of the Western assessment of those who spring from other cultural backgrounds: they are not different but deprived; their culture is not unusual or interesting, it does not exist. The Coleman report may have told us more about the schools than about the children, for if cultural deprivation, which is really cultural difference, is strongly associated with poor school performance, may it not be precisely because our educational system is predicated upon a familiarity with white culture, that it is mysterious and to an extent irrelevant to those who do not share that familiarity? The Eskimo child confronted by a test in which cows, picket fences, and the ubiquitous Spot figure prominently is being confronted by a series of symbols which are utterly void of meaning for him.

Considering all of this, it is hardly surprising that poor self-concept   13
figures as the third important variable in the Coleman data. But rather than see these as three separate variables relating to the degree of accomplishment in the school, they would be better viewed as a feedback system.

Most Native American children attend one of three types of   14
schools: BIA-run boarding schools, BIA day schools or public schools which are predominantly white, and religious boarding or day schools.

A great deal has been written about the poor conditions that exist   15
at many BIA boarding schools. Among these conditions are physical punishment, poor housing, inadequate staff-pupil ratios, the ethnocentrism of teachers, the cruelties of half-blood against full-blooded chil-

dren, and the use of such powerful tranquilizing drugs as thorazine for disciplinary purposes. Christianity has historically and in the present era been stressed over indigenous religion. In short, efforts to destroy Native American culture and make the Native American pupil ashamed of his or her identity have characterized this system of education. While Havighurst and Fuchs, in their recent comprehensive study of Native American education, dispute the inadequacies of these schools and cast doubt upon some of the horror stories, testimony from adult Native Americans makes it clear that attendance at such schools was very often an unhappy and frightening experience for children. This is especially true when very small children are removed from their families and transported such distances to school that it is impossible for their parents to visit them.

16   The BIA day schools are also staffed by BIA personnel and thus fall prey to many of the same problems as the boarding schools, ethnocentrism and shaming in particular. Burnett states that teachers in the Navajo schools have been observed using the children's own culture as a disciplinary threat: for example, "All right, go ahead and talk while we're working, if you want to spend the rest of your life living in some old hogan!" Although the BIA offers an optional course on Native American cultures for its teachers, few avail themselves of the opportunity to learn about the societies in which their students spend their daily lives. Also, since having textbooks like the rest of the society is regarded as a step forward (better than out-of-date texts), these children are being exposed to the same colorful but unfair image of their own people as white children. History as it is taught in these schools is history from the white perspective. Custer is a national hero, his opponents are "savages." It is difficult to involve parents in the activities of the schools: their own experiences with white education have been either minimal or of the boarding-school variety, and they are alienated from the schools.

17   Native American children who attend the white day schools have become political pawns. Under the Johnson-O'Malley Act, public schools in which Native American children are enrolled may receive payments from the BIA for every Native American child in the school. Thus even very racist schools attempt to raise their Native American enrollment, because these pupils bring in more money. While the Johnson-O'Malley Act was intended to improve the quality of Native American education through the application of these funds to remedial language programs and others of special help to Native American youngsters, there has been flagrant violation of this intent. Schools use Johnson-O'Malley funds for many purposes: new football fields or pianos, for example, which Native American children never use. Only recently has legislation been proposed which would give tribal groups control over their own Johnson-O'Malley funds. If the funds were

being ill used, under this new act the tribe could refuse to continue funding and could remove its youngsters from the school.

Getting an education is difficult for the Native American youngster. He or she must contend with the conditions described above or more. Merely getting to school may be difficult. Some Native American children must rise at five o'clock in the morning, walk several miles to the schoolbus stop, then ride for fifty miles over unpaved and bumpy roads to get to school. In the evening they must repeat this process in reverse. Many are ashamed of their inadequate or "un-cool" clothing. This poverty-related problem is compounded by the difficulties of keeping neat and clean in a situation where there is no water except what is brought from miles away in buckets every day. Poor health may raise the rate of absenteeism, and a child who is already having academic problems because of the language difference may fall even further behind because of illness.   18

Given all the cultural and social-structural obstacles to getting an education, the amazing aspect of Native American life may not be that the dropout rate is so high, but that not everyone drops out. Those who push on to high school, despite all the hurdles, meet with more problems at that level. Dating begins then, and for Native Americans in white schools many racial slurs may occur in this context. Also these students may be labeled "disciplinary problems" if they try to stand up for their rights or refuse to "play the Indian role"—quiet and stoic. At this level of the educational system, the Native American student begins to meet persons who have accepted the cultural stereotype of the nonscholastic Native American. These people refuse to believe that he or she is capable of good work, even when presented with evidence to the contrary. Prejudice emerges as the embarrassed white flounders about for an explanation of the behavior which contradicts his image of what Native American students are like. Thus, one highly intelligent woman who was, when I knew her, a promising prelaw student at an Ivy League university, recalled that during her high-school years, she was accused of cheating every time she did well on a test or homework assignment.   19

This tendency also emerges in the advice guidance counselors give Native American youngsters. One prominent Native American leader recalls that when he asked about college, his high-school advisor laughed at him. The idea of a Native American wishing to go to college struck him as singularly amusing.   20

Thus, few do go on. Many who do become overwhelmed or angered by university life and return home, but increasing numbers are going through college, and some go on to graduate and professional schools. Interestingly, because so many Native American problems are rooted in law and in treaties, a large number of Native Americans who have gone on to graduate work have elected to study law.   21

Reading and Writing Activities

PRELIMINARY RESPONSE

Notes.   As you read, record your reactions (questions or comments) to "The World of the Native American Child" in your reading journal.

You may react to one or more of a number of factors in the reading. You might, for example, compare and contrast the schooling of Native Americans with your own educational experiences.

Discussion.   In class, compare your reactions in reading groups of five or six. Appoint a recorder to keep track of similarities and differences, consensus or disagreement, arising from the discussion. The recorder may summarize your group discussion for the rest of the class later.

Freewriting.   In a 10- to 15-minute freewrite, try to distinguish among the effects that ignorance, insensitivity, and deliberate cruelty have on the school experiences of Native American children; identify examples of each and try to determine which is most pervasive. Read your freewriting in groups of two to four. As others are reading, take written note of areas of agreement or disagreement, questions that arise in your mind, and ideas that might be qualified or extended. After everyone has read, appoint a recorder to keep track of similarities or differences, consensus or disagreement, that arise in the ensuing discussion. The recorder may summarize your group discussion for the rest of the class later.

SUMMARIZING

1. Make a scratchline, cluster representation, or notes indicating the progression of ideas in "The World of the Native American Child"— one that reflects your consideration of the freewriting and discussion of group members. Note in particular the effects of ethnocentrism on the educational experiences of Native American children.
2. Write a summary paragraph or two, using your scratchline, cluster representation, or notes.
3. Read summaries in groups. Compare the focus of each summary. How do the summaries differ? How are they the same? Again, check to see if you are *reacting and responding* to the reading selection instead of summarizing the central topics.

FOCUSED CRITICAL READING

1. In paragraph 16, Ann Beuf cites an example of misguided motivation—denigrating a student's culture by saying "All right, go ahead and talk while we're working, if you want to spend the rest of your life living in some old hogan!" How does this differ from the presumably effective motivation described in paragraphs 7–8 of "Success Against the Odds"?

2. In paragraph 6, Beuf points to the cultural biases of intelligence, aptitude, and achievement tests. Do you think it is possible to construct tests without cultural bias? Would the absence of unbiased tests be an argument against testing?

3. In paragraph 12, Beuf points to the ethnocentrism inherent to a phrase like "cultural deprivation." Can a person ever be culturally deprived?

Mitsuye Yamada

Invisibility Is an Unnatural Disaster: Reflections of an Asian American Woman

◆

It is widely believed—and readings in previous chapters have suggested—that, as a group, Asian Americans do well in school, outperforming other ethnic groups, including white Anglo-Saxons. Therefore, many might be startled to discover an Asian American who holds grievances against the educational system. In the following selection, Mitsuye Yamada, an English instructor at a community college in California, responds to the surprise that many people express when made aware of her anger.

1   Last year for the Asian segment of the Ethnic American Literature course I was teaching, I selected a new anthology entitled *Aiiieeeee!* compiled by a group of outspoken Asian American writers. During the discussion of the long but thought-provoking introduction to anthology, one of my students blurted out that she was offended by its militant tone and that as a white person she was tired of always being blamed for the oppression of all the minorities. I noticed several of her classmates' eyes nodding in tacit agreement. A discussion of the "militant" voices in some of the other writings we had read in the course ensued. Surely, I pointed out, some of these other writings have been just as, if not more, militant as the words in this introduction? Had they been offended by those also but failed to express their feelings about them? To my surprise, they said they were not offended by any of the Black American, Chicano or Native American writings, but were hard-pressed to explain why when I asked for an explanation. A little further discussion revealed that they "understood" the anger expressed by the Black and Chicanos and they "empathized" with the frustrations and sorrow expressed by the Native American. But the Asian Americans??

2   Then finally, one student said it for all of them; "It made me angry. *Their* anger made *me* angry, because I didn't even know the Asian Americans felt oppressed. I didn't expect their anger."

3   At this time I was involved in an academic due process procedure begun as a result of a grievance I had filed the previous semester against the administrators at my college. I had filed a grievance for vio-

lation of my rights as a teacher who had worked in the district for almost eleven years. My students remark "Their anger made me angry...I didn't expect their anger," explained for me the reactions of some of my own colleagues as well as the reaction of the administrators during those previous months. The grievance procedure was a time-consuming and emotionally draining process, but the basic principle was too important for me to ignore. That basic principle was that I, an individual teacher, do have certain rights which are given and my superiors cannot, should not, violate them with impunity. When this was pointed out to them, however, they responded with shocked surprise that I, of all people, would take them to task for violation of what was clearly written policy in our college district. They all seemed to exclaim, "We don't understand this; this is so uncharacteristic of her; she seemed such a nice person, so polite, so obedient, so non-trouble-making." What was even more surprising was once they were forced to acknowledge that I was determined to start the due process action they assumed I was not doing it on my own. One of the administrators suggested someone must have pushed me into this, undoubtedly some of "those feminists" on our campus, he said wryly.

In this age when women are clearly making themselves visible on all fronts, I, an Asian American woman, am still functioning as a "front for those feminists" and therefore invisible. The realization of this sinks in slowly. Asian Americans as a whole are finally coming to claim their own, demanding that they be included in the multicultural history of our country. I like to think, in spite of my administrator's myopia, that the most stereotyped minority of them all, the Asian American woman, is just now emerging to become part of that group. It took forever. Perhaps it is important to ask ourselves why it took so long. We should ask ourselves this question just when we think we are emerging as a viable minority in the fabric of our society. I should add to my student's words, "because I didn't even know they felt oppressed," that it took this long because we Asian American women have not admitted to ourselves that we *were* oppressed. We, the visible minority that is invisible.

I say this because until a few years ago I have been an Asian American woman working among non-Asians in an educational institution where most of the decision-makers were men; an Asian American woman thriving under the smug illusion that I was *not* the stereotypic image of the Asian woman because I had a career teaching English in a community college. I did not think anything assertive was necessary to make my point. People who know me, I reasoned, the ones who count, know who I am and what I think. Thus, even when what I considered a veiled racist remark was made in a casual social setting, I would "let it go" because it was pointless to argue with people who didn't even know their remark was racist. I had supposed that I was practicing passive resistance while being stereotyped, but it was so passive no one noticed I was resisting; it was so much my expected role that it ultimately rendered me invisible.

6   My experience leads me to believe that contrary to what I thought, I had actually been contributing to my own stereotyping. Like the hero in Ralph Ellison's novel *The Invisible Man*, I had become invisible to white Americans, and it clung to me like a bad habit. Like most bad habits, this one crept up on me because I took it in minute doses like Mithradates' poison and my mind and body adapted so well to it I hardly noticed it was there.

7   For the past eleven years I have busied myself with the usual chores of an English teacher, a wife of a research chemist, and a mother of four rapidly growing children. I hadn't even done much to shatter this particular stereotype: the middle class woman happy to be bringing home the extra income and quietly fitting into the man's world of work. When the Asian American woman is lulled into believing that people perceive her as being different from other Asian women (the submissive, subservient, ready-to-please, easy-to-get-along-with Asian woman), she is kept comfortably content with the state of things. She becomes ineffectual in the milieu in which she moves. The seemingly apolitical middle class woman and the apolitical Asian woman constituted a double invisibility.

8   I had created an underground culture of survival for myself and had become in the eyes of others the person I was trying not to be. Because I was permitted to go to college, permitted to take a stab at a career or two along the way, given "free choice" to marry and have a family, given a "choice" to eventually do both, I had assumed I was more or less free, not realizing that those who are free make and take choices; they do not choose from options proffered by "those out there."

9   I, personally, had not "emerged" until I was almost fifty years old. Apparently through a long conditioning process, I had learned how *not* to be seen for what I am. A long history of ineffectual activities had been, I realize now, initiation rites toward my eventual invisibility. The training begins in childhood; and for women and minorities, whatever is started in childhood is continued throughout their adult lives. I first recognized just how invisible I was in my first real confrontation with my parents a few years after the outbreak of World War II.

10   During the early years of the war, my older brother, Mike, and I left the concentration camp in Idaho to work and study at the University of Cincinnati. My parents came to Cincinnati soon after my father's release from Internment Camp (these were POW camps to which many of the Issei* men, leaders in their communities, were sent by the FBI), and worked as domestics in the suburbs. I did not see them too often

*Issei—Immigrant Japanese, living in the U.S.

because by this time I had met and was much influenced by a pacifist who was out on a "furlough" from a conscientious objectors' camp in Trenton, North Dakota. When my parents learned about my "boy friend" they were appalled and frightened. After all, this was the period when everyone in the country was expected to be one-hundred percent behind the war effort, and the Nisei[*] boys who had volunteered for the Armed Forces were out there fighting and dying to prove how American we really were. However, during interminable arguments with my father and overheard arguments between my parents, I was devastated to learn they were not so much concerned about my having become a pacifist, but they were more concerned about the possibility of my marrying one. They were understandably frightened (my father's prison years of course were still fresh on his mind) about repercussions on the rest of the family. In an attempt to make my father understand me, I argued that even if I didn't marry him, I'd still be a pacifist; but my father reassured me that it was "all right" for me to be a pacifist because as a Japanese national and a "girl" *it didn't make any difference to anyone.* In frustration I remember shouting, "But can't you see, *I'm* philosophically committed to the pacifist cause," but he dismissed this with "In my college days we used to call philosophy, foolosophy," and that was the end of that. When they were finally convinced I was not going to marry "my pacifist," the subject was dropped and we never discussed it again.

As if to confirm my father's assessment of the harmlessness of my opinions, my brother Mike, an American citizen, was suddenly expelled from the University of Cincinnati while I, "an enemy alien," was permitted to stay. We assumed that his stand as a pacifist, although he was classified a 4-F because of his health, contributed to his expulsion. We were told the Air Force was conducting sensitive wartime research on campus and requested his removal, but they apparently felt my presence on campus was not as threatening.   11

I left Cincinnati in 1945, hoping to leave behind this and other unpleasant memories gathered there during the war years, and plunged right into the politically active atmosphere at New York University where students, many of them returning veterans, were continuously promoting one cause or other by making speeches in Washington Square, passing out petitions, or staging demonstrations. On one occasion, I tagged along with a group of students who took a train to Albany to demonstrate on the steps of the State Capitol. I think I was the only Asian in this group of predominantly Jewish students from NYU. People who passed us were amused and shouted "Go home and grow up." I suppose Governor Dewey, who refused to see us, assumed we were a group of adolescents without a cause as most   12

[*]Nisei—Second generation Japanese, born in the U.S.

college students were considered to be during those days. It appears they weren't expecting any results from our demonstration. There were no newspersons, no security persons, no police. No one tried to stop us from doing what we were doing. We simply did "our thing" and went back to our studies until next time, and my father's words were again confirmed: it made no difference to anyone, being a young student demonstrator in peacetime, 1947.

13   Not only the young, but those who feel powerless over their own lives know what it is like not to make a difference on anyone or anything. The poor know it only too well, and we women have known it since we were little girls. The most insidious part of this conditioning process, I realize now, was that we have been trained not to expect a response in ways that mattered. We may be listened to and responded to with placating words and gestures, but our psychological mind set has already told us time and again that we were born into a ready-made world into which we must fit ourselves, and that many of us do it very well.

14   This mind set is the result of not believing that the political and social forces affecting our lives are determined by some person, or a group of persons, probably sitting behind a desk or around a conference table.

15   Just recently I read an article about "the remarkable track record of success" of the Nisei in the United States. One Nisei was quoted as saying he attributed our stamina and endurance to our ancestors whose characters had been shaped, he said, by their living in a country which has been constantly besieged by all manner of natural disasters, such as earthquakes and hurricanes. He said the Nisei has inherited a steely will, a will to endure and hence, to survive.

16   This evolutionary explanation disturbs me, because it equates the "act of God" (i.e. natural disasters) to the "act of man" (i.e., the war, the evacuation). The former is not within our power to alter, but the latter, I should think, is. By putting the "acts of God" on par with the acts of man, we shrug off personal responsibilities.

17   I have, for too long a period of time accepted the opinion of others (even though they were directly affecting my life) as if they were objective events totally out of my control. Because I separated such opinions from the persons who were making them, I accepted them the way I accepted natural disasters; and I endured them as inevitable. I have tried to cope with people whose points of view alarmed me in the same way that I had adjusted to natural phenomena, such as hurricanes, which plowed into my life from time to time. I would readjust my dismantled feelings in the same way that we repaired the broken shutters after the storm. The Japanese have an all-purpose expression in their language for this attitude of resigned acceptance: "Shikataganai." "It can't be helped." "There's nothing I can do about it." It is said with the shrug of the shoulders and tone of finality, perhaps not unlike the

"those-were-my-orders" tone that was used at the Nuremberg trials. With all the sociological studies that have been made about the causes of the evacuations of the Japanese Americans during World War II, we should know by now that "they" knew that the West Coast Japanese Americans would go without too much protest, and of course, "they" were right, for most of us (with the exception of those notable few), resigned ourselves to our fate, albeit bewildered and not willingly. We were not perceived by our government as responsive Americans; we were objects that happened to be standing in the path of the storm.

Perhaps this kind of acceptance is a way of coping with the "real" world. One stands against the wind for a time, and then succumbs eventually because there is no point to being stubborn against all odds. The wind will not respond to entreaties anyway, one reasons; one should have sense enough to know that. I'm not ready to accept this evolutionary reasoning. It is too rigid for me; I would like to think that my new awareness is going to make me more visible than ever, and to allow me to make some changes in the "man made disaster" I live in at the present time. Part of being visible is refusing to separate the actors from their actions, and demanding that they be responsible for them. 18

By now, riding along with the minorities' and women's movements, I think we are making a wedge into the main body of American life, but people are still looking right through and around us, assuming we are simply tagging along. Asian American women still remain in the background and we are heard but not really listened to. Like Musak, they think we are piped into the airwaves by someone else. We must remember that one of the most insidious ways of keeping women and minorities powerless is to let them only talk about harmless and inconsequential subjects, or let them speak freely and not listen to them with serious intent. 19

We need to raise our voices a little more, even as they say to us "This is so uncharacteristic of you." To finally recognize our own invisibility is to finally be on the path toward visibility. Invisibility is not a natural state for anyone. 20

Reading and Writing Activities

PRELIMINARY RESPONSE

Notes.   As you read, record your reactions (questions or comments) to "Invisibility Is an Unnatural Disaster" in your reading journal.

You may react to one or more of a number of factors in the reading. You might, for example, note the causes of Mitsuye Yamada's invisibility and the effects of her struggles against it.

Discussion.   In class, compare your reactions in reading groups of five or six. Appoint a recorder to keep track of similarities and differences, consensus or disagreement, arising from the discussion. The recorder may summarize your group discussion for the rest of the class later.

Freewriting.   In a 10- to 15-minute freewrite, respond to the ways in which other people's expectations and notions of what is "natural" have affected Yamada over the years. Read your freewriting in groups of two to four. As others are reading, take written note of areas of agreement or disagreement, questions that arise in your mind, and ideas that might be qualified or extended. After everyone has read, appoint a recorder to keep track of similarities or differences, consensus or disagreement, that arise in the ensuing discussion. The recorder may summarize your group discussion for the rest of the class later.

SUMMARIZING

1. Make a scratchline, cluster representation, or notes indicating the progression of ideas in "Invisibility Is an Unnatural Disaster"—one that reflects your consideration of the freewriting and discussion of group members. Note in particular the distinction that Yamada makes between what is viewed as "natural" and what is caused by human agency.
2. Write a summary paragraph or two, using your scratchline, cluster representation, or notes.
3. Read summaries in groups. Compare the focus of each summary. How do the summaries differ? How are they the same? Again, check to see if you are *reacting and responding* to the reading selection instead of summarizing the central topics.

FOCUSED CRITICAL READING

1. In paragraphs 1–3, Yamada talks about how many people react to unexpected anger. What do you suppose accounts for their reaction?
2. Does Yamada overstate the case when she describes Asian American women as the "most stereotyped minority of all"?
3. When Yamada speaks in paragraph 18 of contributing to "changes in the 'man made' disaster I live in at the present time," do you get the impression that she is talking about more than just the effects of racism and sexism? What might she be talking about, and how does it relate to the topic of her essay?

Marcus Mabry

The Ghetto Preppies: Giving Kids "A Better Chance" Is Not So Easy

◆

The following article, originally published in Newsweek *in 1991, describes the efforts of A Better Chance, an organization that supports the efforts of a few academically gifted African American children to avoid negative peer pressure by enrolling in elite, predominantly white private schools.*

Growing up on the South Side of Chicago, Walter Clair had to duck bullets and gangs to get to school. He was one of eight children and his mother was on welfare. But he was intelligent—and lucky. A relative heard about a program called A Better Chance, Inc., that sent smart inner-city kids to private schools, and submitted Walter's application. In short order, the exclusive St. Mark's School, in Southborough, Mass., accepted him for the fall of 1969. After four years, he moved on to Harvard, earning three degrees including his M.D. Today, he is a cardiologist at Duke University Medical Center. He says he could not have done it without A Better Chance: "It's one of those quiet programs that makes a difference. It ranks right up there with Head Start." 1

Not all ABC stories have such happy endings. In 1976, Tony Ashby left the South Bronx for the Groton School in Massachusetts. He did well there, and he, too, went on to Harvard. But, along the way, things fell apart: Ashby lost his drive to "get out" of the ghetto. Since he finished Harvard in 1986 he has bounced from job to job. He lived in a cramped tenement in Harlem until his landlord recently kicked him out. 2

Founded in 1963 by a group of Ivy League administrators and prep-school headmasters, ABC epitomized the idealism of the times: by sending poor kids to elite private schools, they would adopt the mannerisms and mind-sets of their white preppie peers and thus be lifted from poverty. It hasn't always worked out that way. Making the transition from one world to the other was difficult for most students, impossible for some. The most famous failure was Edmund Perry, the Exeter alumnus who was killed in 1985 while allegedly mugging an undercover New York City policeman. 3

4   The program has prospered—growing and spawning imitators. Wealthy benefactors from Manhattan's Perfumed Stockade to the Hollywood Hills have embraced whole classrooms of inner-city kids, guaranteeing them college educations if only they'll finish high school. But like ABC before them, they've found that helping kids to succeed is more complicated than giving well-intentioned grants. Poor kids—like rich kids—need guidance; they need adults who can muffle their culture shocks and hear their frustrations. The help can take many forms —counselors, summer-long retreats, an autumn walk in the woods— but it's as essential as the tuition check itself. Poor kids—like privileged kids—need a chance to fall, a break from being the best little person their neighborhood ever produced. Poor kids—like rich kids—need space to be themselves; the process of absorbing the refined values of elite prep schools and colleges must not come at the cost of feverish self-hatred. And rich benefactors must understand that some kids are still going to fail.

Reaching Out

5   To its enduring credit, ABC made mistakes and learned from them. By the mid-'70s, the program was reaching out to find kids from ever more abject circumstances. Those youngsters needed the most support, but as funding dried up ABC had to abandon its summer-long residential pre-prep program. As a result, admittees lacked mentors like Clair's, and more kids had trouble in school. Unable to reinstitute the summer orientation, ABC adjusted its recruiting, shifting toward kids from lower-middle-class and poor but stable families.

6   Despite the changes, ABC administrators insist that the program's goal remains the same. "Sometimes people come to us who can afford to send their children to school," says Judith Griffin, president of ABC. "But we look in the Bronx and on the South Side of Chicago. We look for these kids and there they are and they are poor." Griffin says that a third of ABC children still come from welfare families. This year about 1,100 students are scattered among 160 schools. More than two thirds are African American; most of the rest are Latino.

7   Over the years, more than 7,000 students have graduated from ABC. *Newsweek* has chosen three—Clair ('74), Ashby ('81) and Lisa Partin ('89)—to illustrate ABC's slow and sometimes painful evolution and the inevitable collision of idealism with the realities of race and class:

The Winner

8   During his first year at St. Mark's, Clair received some rude lessons in the peculiar code of the prep school. He was relieved to hear that at some meals he could ditch his coat and tie for "casual" clothes. He

made the mistake of wearing his crisp new blue jeans, freshly pressed white T shirt and gleaming white Converse All-Stars sneakers to his first casual meal; he was turned away by a teacher. No jeans, even fresh ones, in the dining hall. Meanwhile, he recalls, his shabby genteel classmates were free to wear "Topsiders so ragged that they had to be held together by hockey tape, tennis shirts with holes and corduroy pants so worn that the seat was smooth."

Clair may have been unprepared for the cultural niceties of prep life, but he learned more important lessons at ABC's summer-orientation program before he was sent off to St. Mark's. For six weeks at beautiful Williams College, ABC admittees got a dose of discipline; they ate, slept, studied and played sports on a strict schedule. The ABC mentors instilled a sense of pride in Clair. "They reminded us that we were special kids and that any individual failure was a failure of the program," he says. "That was the feeling that kept me going at St. Mark's."   9

His first year was harrowing academically. He almost failed English. And even in classes where he did well, he encountered prejudice. Once, he yawned in Latin class without covering his mouth: "The teacher slapped me. He said, 'That's why we bring you kids here, to teach you some manners.'" Still, Clair says the experience was positive. Despite low faculty expectations of African American kids, his grades improved. And, through sports and extracurricular activities he formed strong friendships. He says, "As I adjusted to St. Mark's socially and did well academically, people viewed me as another Anglo-American who just had black skin."   10

That is, until it came time to apply to college. A classmate dubbed senior year "the year of the nigger," for the preference the black kids would get in college admissions. Most of his St. Mark's classmates assumed that "their social standing meant they would never have to compete with [blacks]," says Clair. "It was only when our blackness became an advantage that it was a problem. Even living as intimately as one could, as the stakes got higher, people's intolerance and their own feelings of being threatened got harder to hide. I saw it in college and again in medical school."   11

Clair is grateful for his St. Mark's education, and he says he might even send his own sons, ages 4 and 8, there someday. But he's a realist. Whatever advantages their school ties give them, the disadvantage of having two black parents in America "will have a larger influence on their lives."   12

The Drifter

The first thing Tony Ashby noticed when he stepped onto the Groton campus was the sprawling playing fields. The campus was awash   13 in deep greens late that New England summer; the concrete of the South Bronx was far away. The fields were the focal point of Ashby's years at Groton; he played football, lacrosse and basketball. The plaques in the field house that list team captains for football and lacrosse will "forever bear my name," he says proudly. "[Groton] challenged me to be my best." Unfortunately, for Ashby, prep school turned out to be preparation for nothing so much as prep school. The larger world, as he would find, did not play by the rules he learned at Groton.

14   Ashby and other ABC students of his time weren't sure if they were storming the barricades of the privileged or were being co-opted by the white establishment. ABC itself did little to help Ashby sort through his conflicts; during his five years at Groton, he says he never met an ABC representative. "ABC just puts you there and forgets you," he said.

15   But if ABC stumbled—grants were disappearing even as kids admitted into the program came from ever more difficult backgrounds—Groton became a haven. If anything, the school was perhaps too protective, too paternalistic, too good at making Ashby feel at home. "At Groton we were taught fair play," he says. When he got to Harvard "it was kill the next guy at any cost." To make things worse, Harvard was racially divided as well: blacks and whites usually did not mix. Ashby felt a tension between his allegiance to African-American peers and his comfort with his largely white group of friends. That tension finally drove him from many of his white friends after graduation. "Living with white people got to be too much after 10 years," he says. Ashby drifted between New York and Boston and worked as, among other things, a teacher, a paralegal and a youth counselor.

16   In his last interview, he sat in his cramped Harlem apartment and spoke with some defiance and some self-pity. "The one thing that no one can take away from me is my years at Groton," he said. "Groton gave me a lot of cultural refinement." When his landlord kicked him out, he left no forwarding address.

The New Ideal

17   Beginning in 1983, Lisa Partin commuted daily from Harlem to The Spence School on Manhattan's Upper East Side. She was from a stable, two-parent, working-class household. "There was always an emphasis on education in my house," she says. "My experience is very different from most kids' in Harlem because of my parents." For ABC, Partin was an ideal candidate.

18   Not only had ABC changed by the 1980s, but attitudes at prep school had changed as well. "My best friends were white and we're still in touch," she says. By the '80s blacks were a part of most prep schools. Few people questioned their qualifications to be there; most

teachers searched for ways to make the curriculum and the faculty more inclusive. In fact, class, not race, was the most important difference for Partin. After vacation "girls came back from Europe and I had only gone to Florida," she says. The irony, she says, is that "a lot of them envied me. They were raised by nannies and they envied me for my parents."

19   After Spence, Partin went to Harvard. "My close friends were almost all black. We had a lot more in common, the parties we went to, the music we liked. We all went to the same place to get our hair done," she says. Still, she got along better with whites than some other blacks did, thanks to her prep-school experience. "I couldn't imagine going in as a (black) freshman and having to adapt." She earned her bachelor's degree in three years and then joined the Bank of Boston as a management trainee. Along the way, she has run into the other "smart girls" from her Harlem junior-high-school class. "During an internship at an investment bank in New York I ran into a girlfriend who competed with me for grades; she was a secretary there. Another is a cashier and another one has a baby. The only difference is that I was given a chance."

Reading and Writing Activities

PRELIMINARY RESPONSE

Notes.   As you read, record your reactions (questions or comments) to "The Ghetto Preppies" in your reading journal.

You may react to one or more of a number of factors in the reading. You might, for example, respond to the inconsistent success of A Better Chance.

Discussion.   In class, compare your reactions in reading groups of five or six. Appoint a recorder to keep track of similarities and differences, consensus or disagreement, arising from the discussion. The recorder may summarize your group discussion for the rest of the class later.

Freewriting.   In a 10- to 15-minute freewrite, respond to the methods and results of A Better Chance. If you have read "Success Against the Odds," you might consider whether Benjamin Bowser and Herbert Perkins would have any reservations about A Better Chance. Read your freewriting in groups of two to four. As others are reading, take written note of areas of agreement or disagreement, questions that arise in your mind, and ideas that might be qualified or extended. After everyone has read, appoint a recorder to keep track of similarities or differences, consensus or disagreement, that arise in the ensuing discussion. The recorder may summarize your group discussion for the rest of the class later.

SUMMARIZING

1. Make a scratchline, cluster representation, or notes indicating the progression of ideas in "The Ghetto Preppies"—one that reflects your consideration of the freewriting and discussion of group members. Note in particular the tension between school success and alienation from one's native culture.
2. Write a summary paragraph or two, using your scratchline, cluster representation, or notes.
3. Read summaries in groups. Compare the focus of each summary. How do the summaries differ? How are they the same? Again, check to see if you are *reacting and responding* to the reading selection instead of summarizing the central topics.

FOCUSED CRITICAL READING

1. Students chosen by A Better Chance are described as "smart inner-city kids." How do you suppose such children are identified? How might the selection process reflect cultural bias? How might it try to avoid such bias?
2. Do you suppose that Walter Clair is pleased or disturbed by the perceptions of his classmates at St. Mark's School, who viewed him "as another Anglo-American kid who just had black skin"?
3. Marcus Mabry emphasizes the benefits of A Better Chance for the persons to whom it awards scholarships. What are the benefits for elite prep schools that accept ABC students? Should Mabry have mentioned those benefits? How might that have influenced a reader's response to his article?
4. Suppose that the last sentence of Mabry's article had read: "The only difference is that I *took* a chance." How might that have affected your view of Lisa Partin and, perhaps, of the entire article?

Christopher Jencks
(with Henry Acland, Mary Jo Bane, David Cohen, Henry Gintis, Barbara Heyns, Stephan Michelson, and Marshall Smith)

Conclusions about Inequality in the Schools

◆

In 1972, Christopher Jencks and his associates at Harvard University's Center for Educational Policy Research completed a study of schooling and social mobility in the United States. The publication of that study, ti-tled Inequality: A Reassessment of the Effect of Family and School-ing in America, *coincided with growing disillusionment about government programs aimed at liberal reform. Although Jencks and his colleagues disputed the notion that these programs ought to bring imme-diate, quantifiable results, they advanced other, equally controversial claims—that education cannot be expected to bring about social equality and that good schooling may contribute little to academic achievement or future success.*

The authors of Inequality *certainly did not view their conclusions as a warrant for abandoning liberal reform, let alone the ideal of social equal-ity. Instead, they disputed the belief that prolonged school attendance is always and necessarily a desirable end, arguing that this belief reflects a white middle-class bias. And, because it provides the rationale for public funding of higher education, Jencks and his colleagues reasoned that the tendency to equate school attendance with virtue serves the interests of a dominant elite whose children are more likely to attend college. Further-more, since there is no fair and democratic way to enforce school atten-dance after a certain age, the authors concluded that*

> *what America needs is a system of finance which provides alternative services to those who get relatively few benefits from the educational sys-tem. If people do not want to attend school or college, an egalitarian soci-ety ought to accept this as a legitimate decision and give these people*

subsidized job training, subsidized housing, or perhaps simply a lower tax rate.

In the following excerpt from Inequality, *the authors list the conclusions of their study.*

1   The evidence...suggests that educational opportunities are far from equal. This inequality takes several forms. First, resources are unequally distributed. Second, some people have more chance than others to attend school with the kind of schoolmates they prefer. Third, some people are denied access to the curriculums of their choice. None of these inequalities appears to us either necessary or just. What, then, might be done to remedy these problems?

2   Let us begin with the problem of equalizing different students' claims on the nation's educational resources. First, we need to make annual expenditures per pupil more equal. In order to equalize expenditures in different states, we would need to expand federal aid and drastically revise existing formulas for distributing such aid, so as to concentrate it on poor states. If we want perfect equality between districts in the same state, we must end the schools' dependence on local taxes and raise all school revenue from statewide taxes or federal aid.... Finally, if we want to eliminate disparities between schools in the same district, we must persuade school boards to provide extra resources to those schools that now spend relatively little. If, for example, schools in poor areas have high teacher turnover and hence have low average salaries, these schools must be given extra staff or other resources.

3   All these changes are easy to imagine, though not to implement. They grow naturally out of values that are already widely accepted in American society. But even if we were to succeed in equalizing annual expenditures per pupil, we would still be left with inequities that derive from the fact that some students get more education than others. Unlike differences in annual expenditure, differences in lifetime expenditure strike most people as entirely reasonable. Even those who have a generally egalitarian outlook usually assume that the ideal educational system would provide everyone with as much education as he wanted, and that we would finance this from a progressive income tax. They see no injustice in taxing high school dropouts to finance higher education, so long as the dropout is free to attend college if he wants to.

4   This attitude seems to us to derive from a mistaken analogy between education and other public services. In general, public services are free either because it is difficult to determine who benefits from them or because the beneficiaries are more needy than the average taxpayer. Public parks fall into the first category, while public hospitals fall into the second. Advanced education falls into neither

category. It is easy to identify the primary beneficiaries of subsidies for higher education, namely the students. It is also easy to predict that on the average these beneficiaries will be better able to pay for their education than is the average taxpayer.

It can be argued, of course, that higher education provides benefits   5
for those who do not attend college as well as those who do. Even the poor, for example, need lawyers. The mere fact of a public benefit is not, however, sufficient justification for a public subsidy. Hot dog vendors, for example, also render a public service, but they do not need a public subsidy. A public subsidy only makes sense if some necessary service will dry up in its absence. If, for example, lawyers earned so little that nobody was willing to pay for his own legal training, legal education might require subsidy. In fact, however, there are plenty of law school applicants, and there would be plenty even if would-be lawyers had to borrow against future income to finance the full cost of their training.

Public discussion of these issues is complicated by widespread   6
acceptance of a false dichotomy. Many assume that there are only two alternatives: a system in which access to education depends on parents' ability and willingness to pay, and a system in which costs are shared by everyone. There is, however, a third alternative. We can create a system in which access to education depends on the *student's* willingness to pay—not at the time he gets his education, but later, when he is presumably enjoying its benefits. Ideally, funds for advanced education probably ought to come from a surcharge on the income tax of those who have had education beyond, say, the age of 16. Failing that, it would still be fairer to finance advanced education through long-term loans to those who attend college and graduate school than through taxes on those who do not attend.

The primary objection to such a system of educational finance is   7
not that it would be inequitable, but that it would probably reduce the overall demand for education. We do not know how many students would drop out of school or college if they knew they would eventually have to pay for it, but some doubtless would. Despite widespread hostility to students as a class, most Americans feel that schooling is a good thing. They are reluctant to impose what looks like a tax on virtue (i.e. staying in school) in order to reduce the cost of vice (i.e. dropping out). If we accepted this basic moral equation, we too would favor a system in which higher education was financed from general taxation. Since we reject the equation of schooling with virtue, we prefer a system in which higher education is financed by taxing those who have benefited from it directly.

Equalizing access to privileged schoolmates is even more contro-   8
versial than equalizing claims on resources. Busing arouses more passion than state aid formulas. In principle, we believe that an ideal pupil

assignment system should give every student an opportunity to attend any public school he (or his parents) finds appealing. Indeed, we would go so far as to *define* a "public" school as one that is open to any student who wants to attend. All other schools, regardless of formal control or financing, are to some degree "private."

9   If we want to give everyone equal access to every school, certain reforms seem necessary. First, school districts ought to admit any student in the district to any school he wants to attend, regardless of whether he lives near the school or far from it. Second, they ought to pay the cost of transporting any pupil to any school in his district. Thus a student from a poor neighborhood who wants to attend a school in a rich neighborhood ought to have precisely the same opportunity to do so as a student who lives in the rich neighborhood. This might, of course, mean that some schools in rich neighborhoods became overcrowded. If this happened, demand might slack off. If it did not, the district could expand the school, using portable classrooms or whatever other expedients seemed feasible. If expansion were really impossible—which it rarely is—applicants could be admitted by lot. If popular schools got too large, they could simply be divided in half. Applicants could then be assigned randomly to one of the two new adjoining schools.

10   Those who believe in neighborhood schools object to this approach on the grounds that "outsiders will take over our schools." These are likely to be the same people who resist outsiders (i.e. blacks) moving into "their" neighborhood. Committed integrationists also object to such a system, on the grounds that it is simply a warmed-over version of what the North calls "open enrollment" and the South calls "freedom of choice." Such a system does not ensure that every black child will attend school with whites or vice versa. Blacks will only attend school with whites if they apply to schools where whites are enrolled. Whites can escape attending school with blacks if they can find schools that have no black applicants. In a community where blacks are expected to stay in their place, and are subject to all sorts of sanctions if they apply to an all-white school, a system of this kind will achieve almost nothing. In a community where the school administration believes in desegregated schooling and encourages black parents to attend desegregated schools, such a system could produce dramatic changes in attendance patterns. The "liberal" alternative, which is widely viewed as the road to racial equality, seems to be compulsory busing of blacks to white neighborhoods, and vice versa. This implies that black parents cannot send their children to all-black schools, even if they want to, because all-black schools are by *definition* inferior. This position strikes us as both racist and politically unworkable over the long haul.

11   When we turn from school assignment to curriculum assignment, we again lean to "freedom of choice" solutions. This means we think

schools should avoid classifying students whenever possible. At the elementary level, students should be assigned to classes randomly, and teachers should try to respond to students' individual interests, rather than expecting all students to learn the same thing. At the secondary level, students should not be segregated into "college preparatory" and "noncollege" curriculums that determine what they must study, but should be free to design their own curriculums from whatever courses the school offers. Students who hope to attend college must be told what academic courses they need to take, and encouraged to take them. But if they also want to take vocational courses, that too should be possible. Students who want some kind of job training should be given it, assuming the school can devise training programs of practical value. But if these students also want to take academic courses, they should also be encouraged to do so on the same basis as anyone else.

These reforms are not likely to make students appreciably more equal after they finish school. They would, however, give every student an equal claim on educational resources, desirable classmates, and interesting subject matter while he was in school. By recognizing that every child's needs are equally legitimate, they would not only make educational arrangements more egalitarian, but might spark similar reforms in institutions that serve adults.

Reading and Writing Activities

PRELIMINARY RESPONSE

Notes. As you read, record your reactions (questions or comments) to "Conclusions about Inequality in the Schools" in your reading journal.

You may react to one or more of a number of factors in the reading. You might, for example, consider whether, twenty years after their original publication, the proposals put forth by Christopher Jencks and his associates seem workable or naive.

Discussion. In class, compare your reactions in reading groups of five or six. Appoint a recorder to keep track of similarities and differences, consensus or disagreement, arising from the discussion. The recorder may summarize your group discussion for the rest of the class later.

Freewriting. In a 10- to 15-minute freewrite, make a deliberate effort to view the proposals put forth by Jencks et al. from two very different perspectives. First, try to see them as measures that would contribute to equality; then try to see them as ideas likely to perpetuate inequality. Read your freewriting in groups of two to four. As others are reading, take written note of areas of agreement or disagreement, questions that arise in your mind, and ideas that might be qualified or extended. After everyone has read, appoint a recorder to keep track of similarities or differences, consensus or disagreement, that arise in the ensuing discussion. The recorder may summarize your group discussion for the rest of the class later.

SUMMARIZING

1. Make a scratchline, cluster representation, or notes indicating the progression of ideas in "Conclusions about Inequality in the Schools"—one that reflects your consideration of the freewriting and discussion of group members. Note in particular any hidden cultural biases that might underlie ostensibly fair and equal educational policy.
2. Write a summary paragraph or two, using your scratchline, cluster representation, or notes.
3. Read summaries in groups. Compare the focus of each summary. How do the summaries differ? How are they the same? Again, check to see if you are *reacting and responding* to the reading selection instead of summarizing the central topics.

FOCUSED CRITICAL READING

1. Do you agree that equating school attendance with virtue and dropping out with vice is a class-based cultural norm? How do you think Benjamin Bowser and Herbert Perkins, authors of "Success Against the Odds," would respond to that idea?
2. Jencks and his colleagues seem to assume that most children from poor neighborhoods would prefer attending schools in more affluent neighborhoods. Can you point to any contradictory evidence in other reading selections from this chapter? If so, with whom are you more inclined to agree?
3. What do you suppose the authors mean by their reference to "desirable classmates" in paragraph 12?
4. In a quotation cited in the headnote to this reading, the authors refer to school dropouts as "these people." Consider the effect of changing that phrase to "such citizens." Do you think that the actual phrasing might serve to reinforce the view that dropping out of school is a vice?

WRITING SUGGESTIONS

1. Using the first three readings in this chapter as sources, write an essay that demonstrates the effects of teacher expectations on student performance.

2. In paragraph 3 of "The World of the Native American Child," Ann Beuf says that often "the child must choose between being a good Native American and being a good student." Using "Success Against the Odds" and "The World of the Native American Child" as sources, write an essay that demonstrates how school success can alienate a child from her native culture.

3. Compose a dialogue between E. D. Hirsch, Jr., author of "Literacy and Cultural Literacy" in Chapter 1 (pages 8–23), and Mitsuye Yamada, author of "Invisibility Is an Unnatural Disaster."

4. Traditional education has produced a number of hierarchies: the grading system, tracking, and standardized test scores, to name three. Write an essay that addresses one or more of the following topics related to educational hierarchies.

   a. Try to measure the extent to which hierarchies in education innocently reflect preexisting inequalities, perhaps even helping to prepare children for survival in a world full of injustice, and the extent to which they actually serve to perpetuate inequality.
   b. Try to distinguish between educational hierarchies that are unavoidable and those that are arbitrary.
   c. Speculate on the features of an educational system without hierarchies. What would it look like? How would it operate? What would be its likely results? You might start by envisioning a school in which everyone (teachers, administrators, custodial staff, cafeteria workers, secretaries, and students) were referred to as "educational workers."

Whichever topic(s) you choose, try to support your views with details from reading as well as personal experience and observation.

5. Evaluate the argument that children from minority cultures need to be schooled in mainstream culture to succeed as adults. Support your views with details from reading as well as personal experience and observation.

6. Argue for the precedence of freedom over equality or vice versa in the formulation of educational policy. Support your views with details from reading as well as personal experience and observation.

8

Identity and Polarization

———————◆———————

Nikki Giovanni suggests, in the first selection in this chapter, that groups who pioneered this country, despite differences in origin and purpose, have at least one commonality: they mostly came without choice. Nonetheless, differences—of race, gender, and age to name a few—shape the identity of groups and individuals in the U.S. and elsewhere in the world.

Today, race still shapes group identities in polarized neighborhoods. Howard Blum's report on "Bias Incident at Staten Island's Miller Field" describes two such neighborhoods. Gender also polarizes. Deborah Tannen, in "Asymmetries: Women and Men in Conversation," suggests that men and women operate from completely different systems of communication.

The next selections focus on degrees of differences that contribute to individual identity within ethnic groups. Mary Mebane, in "Shades of Black," describes the connection between color and status that contributed to the shaping of ethnic identity in the public schools and college community she remembers. David Updike, in "The Colorings of Childhood," shows that mixed marriages also complicate attempts to simplify ethnic identity.

Politics contribute to polarization, as illustrated in Toni Cade Bambara's "My Man Bovanne." And sometimes merely the passing of time does the same thing, for generational changes are at work also in the family Bambara depicts.

The final reading is about one of the most recent immigrant groups—the Haitian boat people. In Emile Ollivier's fictionalized account of a sea crossing from Haiti, the narrator describes a passage that ends in shipwreck. The survivors are taken into custody by the police on alien soil after "long days of terror, suffocation, and the uncertainty of the crossing."

Reading Complicated Texts

We have asked you throughout this book to think of the reading process as James Boyd White does. To read a text, he says, "as a composition made by one mind speaking to another, constructed out of innumerable choices of word and phrase—as a text whose author decides what belongs within it, and what shall be left out, and how its elements shall be characterized and related—is to read not merely as a reader, but as a writer or composer."[1] Of course, not all readers will compose the same reading of a text, especially complicated texts.

We can account for differences in readings by referring again to the idea (stated first in Chapter 2, page 78) that some readers may read too much into a text and others may read too little—some readings will be "exuberant," some "deficient." Louise Rosenblatt says: "We may not be able to arrive at a unanimous agreement concerning the best interpretation, say, of *Hamlet* or of 'The Second Coming,' but we can arrive at some consensus about interpretations that are to be rejected as ignoring large elements in the work, or as introducing irrelevant or exaggerated responses."[2]

To help you avoid problems of exuberancies and deficiencies in your readings, we have directed you, in the reading and writing activities following each reading selection, to use extensive writing and discussion to arrive at what David Bartholomae and Anthony Petrosky in *Ways of Reading* call "strong readings."[3]

The following questions may help you construct strong readings:

1. Have you read and reread the text?
2. Have you written and rewritten in response to the text—freewrites, scratchline (or clustering or other forms of notes), summary?
3. In writing a summary, did you work from a *heuristic,* that is a set of questions to help you establish the progression of ideas in the text (see Chapter 4 for an example)?
4. Have you paid attention to transition points and clues in the structuring of the text that help you understand it?
5. Have you asked what the writer is doing as he or she develops the text?

[1]James Boyd White, *Heracles' Bow: Essays on the Rhetoric and Poetics of the Law* (Madison, WI: University of Wisconsin Press, 1985), p. 123.

[2]Louise Rosenblatt, *Literature as Exploration* (New York: MLA, 1983), p. 281.

[3]David Bartholomae and Anthony Petrosky, *Ways of Reading,* 4th ed. (Boston: Bedford Books of St. Martin's Press, 1996), p. 8.

Nikki Giovanni

Pioneers: A View of Home

———————◆———————

Nikki Giovanni was born in Knoxville, Tennessee in 1943. She attended Fisk University, the University of Pennsylvania, and the School of the Arts at Columbia University. Giovanni has received honorary doctoral degrees from several universities, and other awards and grants throughout her distinguished career as a writer and has a number of books to her credit. The following selection is from her latest work, Sacred Cows ... and Other Edibles, *published in 1988.*

1   I don't own a class ring. Actually, I didn't graduate from high school, but that's not the reason I don't own a class ring. I was an "early entrant" to Fisk University but I am sure that, had I asked, Austin High in Knoxville would have let me purchase a high school class ring. It wasn't the lack of money, either. My grandmother, who simply adored any kind of ceremony, would have been as happy as a pig in you know what if I had wanted to come back to Knoxville to receive some sort of something with my class ... and purchase a class ring in the process. Nor did I forget. Proms and class rings aren't the sort of things you forget when you're sixteen or seventeen years old. No. It just seemed foolish. What do you do with a class ring after you are graduated? Give it to a girl if you are a boy, but if you are a girl ... maybe pass it along to your daughter? I know one mother who did that. Put it in your jewelry box? I know lots of people who did that. Lose it? Certainly. God knows it's a sign of a really sick mind to see grown people, adults with responsibilities, wearing class rings. I go so far as to submit you know a person is having a severe personality crisis if you see a high school class ring on a finger beyond the first semester in college. Male or female. It's a big sign saying NOTHING HAS MATTERED TO MY LIFE SINCE SENIOR YEAR.

2   I don't own a yearbook from college, either. I did pay my fees and really could have sworn that a yearbook was included but none ever arrived. A friend of mine recently went to live in Indonesia and left a copy of her yearbook with me. She thought, quite correctly, that I would want the book with the photo of me sleeping in the Honors Lounge. No one can tell it's me, though I happen to recognize the desert boots, but aside from those and a beige skirt that I actually hated, no one would know it's me. Still and all I admit pride that I made the yearbook one year. Maybe another year, too, but no one has

stepped forward with another copy. I'm not against pride. Not at all.
I'm just a little picky about what I take pride in.

There are actually people who take pride in their race. This is actu-   3
ally stupid. You would think, the way some people act, that there is a
Babyland somewhere in which babies could select their parents: "I'll
take the rich, white ones." "Well, I want the Black ones." "WHO'LL
TAKE THE POOR? WE NEED MORE POOR HERE." "Oh, hell. I'll take
them. You been yelling for that poor family for over a week!" "WHAT
ABOUT AMERICANS? WHO WANTS TO BE AN AMERICAN?" "I
want to live in Nepal. Got any Nepalese who want children soon?" No.
I rather doubt that it happens that way. More likely two people happened to meet, mated, and you were born. Not that anyone should be
ashamed of his race, it's just that when you think about it you had
nothing to do with it. Not your race, nor your age, nor your nationality.
Not even your name, though some of us sneak and vary our names
more to our liking somewhere between the fifth grade and college—
with which I sympathize. No one wants to be called "Snookums" or
"Boo-bee" through eternity. It's a question of style.

I was watching *Family Feud* recently on our rerun station. Some of   4
you remember *Family Feud*: Two families squared off with really silly
questions answered by the strangest one hundred people in the world
("We asked one hundred people to name a friendly neighborhood
bird") and the families had to guess what these fabled one hundred
had said ("Buzzards"), and whichever reached 350 points first ("The
number one answer—27 points") then got the chance to name national
products for $10,000. A Black family consisting of, if memory serves me
correctly, a father, mother, two daughters and a son-in-law was playing
a white family consisting of a father, mother and three sons in uniforms. As luck would have it, on the third round, where all values are
tripled, the Black family answered and got to play for the big money.
Richard Dawson went over to shake the hands of the white folks and
thank them for coming. You remember that you win the money in front
of you (*Family Feud* wasn't a cheap show like *Jeopardy*, where only the
winners get to keep the money), and Dawson pointed that out and said
he was sorry they didn't do any better. You understand, Dawson
wasn't expressing regret, just being polite, when one of the sons piped
up with, "Well, we still can fly." I guess they were in the Air Force, but
mostly that was such a racist remark. You Blacks may know what one
hundred people think but hey, we whites can fly. Totally unnecessary.
And tacky. I don't object to the boys being proud of flying; hey, if I
could fly I'd be proud too. As a matter of fact I'm proud of myself when
I *board* a flight! I'd be snuff in a pitcher's jaw if I could actually make
that thing leave the ground. No. It was the context in which the remark
was made. As if, "Well, hell, after all we're still white" could make up

for the fact that they lost. That's as bad as if the Black family had whipped out the old Red, Black and Green nationalist flag and proclaimed superiority for Blacks based on...*Family Feud?* In the words of Joan Rivers: "Oh, puhleeeaase."

5   It's so clear, now that we have photographs from the moon, and man-made satellites even farther away, that earth resembles nothing so much as a single cell in the human body. That's not my observation; it belongs to the biologist Lewis Thomas. I was never good at biology. You stood around in a room with lots of little dead animals in jars and you were expected to cut them up and discover things. Or you started with live worms or frogs and you killed them to discover twitching muscles and stuff. I don't deny the importance of Life under the microscope or scalpel...I just don't do it. But what a concept. That the planet upon which we live is no more than a specimen on a slide. We, who think humans are nature's greatest invention, may well turn out to be no more than the life we see swimming in an ordinary drop of water. What then is important? When Paul Tsongas, the former senator from Massachussetts, was told he had some form of cancer, he decided to quit the Senate. "No one ever died saying,'I should have spent more time at the office,'" he pointed out. No one ever died saying I should have hated more; I should have had more guilt or envy in my heart; I should have beaten my wife; I should have been less educated; I should have stifled my personal urge to explore my world and my life more. No. Most of us face our fading years wishing we had been more open, more loving, more capable.

6   They say Home...is where when you go...they have to take you in. I rather prefer Home...when you could go anywhere...is the place you prefer to be. I don't think of a home as a house, which is another thing I don't own. Certainly, though, I do live in a house that I have made my home. I won't even pretend living on the streets, sleeping in public parks, washing up at the bus or train station, eating out of garbage cans is a valid alternative to bedrooms, bathrooms and kitchens whiffing good smells every time the furnace blows. But I also readily concede if there is no love a building will not compensate. The true joy, perhaps, of being a Black American is that we really have no home. Europeans bought us; but the Africans sold. If we are to be human we must forgive both...or neither. It has become acceptable, in the last decade or so, for intellectuals to concede Black Americans did not come here of our own volition; yet, I submit that just as slavery took away our choice so also did the overcrowded, disease-ridden cities of Europe; so also did religious persecution; so also did the abject and all but unspeakable Inquisition of the Spanish; so also did starvation in Italy; so also did the black, rotten potatoes lying in the fields of Ireland. No one came to the New World in a cruise ship. They all came because they had to. They were poor, hungry, criminal, persecuted individuals

who would rather chance dropping off the ends of the earth than stay inert knowing both their body and spirit were slowly having the life squeezed from them. Whether it was a European booking passage on a boat, a slave chained to a ship, a wagon covered with sailcloth, they all headed toward the unknown with all nonessentials stripped away.

A pioneer has only two things: a deep desire to survive and an   7 equally strong will to live. Home is not the place where our possessions and accomplishments are deposited and displayed. It is this earth that we have explored, the heavens we view with awe, these humans who, despite the flaws, we try to love and those who try to love us. It is the willingness to pioneer the one trek we all can make . . . no matter what our station or location in life . . . the existential reality that wherever there is life . . . we are at home.

Reading and Writing Activities

PRELIMINARY RESPONSE

Notes.   As you read, record your reactions (questions or comments) to Nikki Giovanni's "Pioneers: A View of Home." Giovanni examines the things that are not important to her cultural identity.

You may react to a number of factors in the reading: the ideas, the language (especially vocabulary choice), the rhetorical structure, the unstated assumptions, or the relationship between writer and reader (audience, purpose, organization, development). You need not, however, attempt to react to all of these factors in the essay, at this time.

Discussion.   In class, compare your reactions in reading groups of five or six. Appoint a recorder to keep track of similarities or differences, consensus or disagreement, arising from the discussion. The recorder may summarize your group discussion for the rest of the class later.

SUMMARIZING

1. Create a scratchline of the ideas that Giovanni introduces to develop her essay. Focus on what she does at transition points. For example, what is she doing when she introduces the section about the TV program, *Family Feud?* Identify key words that mark topic shifts. At what point does the word *pioneer* begin to organize the meaning? What are the key words that organize each section of her text? Your scratchline should reflect the topic shift when Giovanni moves from talking about all the things that are not important to talking about things we can hardly take pride in, such as race.

Or you may prefer another approach to analyzing the parts of Giovanni's essay such as clustering.

2. Write a summary paragraph or two, from your scratchline or other preliminary work, of the topics that Giovanni introduces to develop her point of view on identity.

3. Read the summaries in your groups. Compare the focus of each summary. How do the summaries differ? How are they the same?

Howard Blum

"Bias Incident" at Staten Island's Miller Field: A Tale of Two Neighborhoods

◆

Howard Blum has written a number of books, including The Search for Nazis in America *(1978) and* I Pledge Allegiance: The True Story of the Walkers: An American Spy Family *(1987). His latest book, published in 1990, is* Out There: The Government's Secret Quest for Extraterrestrials. *The following reading selection appeared in* The New York Times *in 1987 and was later reprinted in* Racism and Sexism: An Integrated Study.

Gregory Cotton had adjusted the tan leather cap on his head to a   1
jaunty angle and was returning to the punchball game when he found
his path blocked by two husky teenagers.

"This field is for white people only," Gregory, a sixth grader,   2
remembers one of the youths calling to him. The other motioned with a
can of beer as if to underline the threat.

Some of Gregory's classmates saw the confrontation by the water   3
fountain and walked across Staten Island's Miller Field to intervene.

There were more threats. A punch was thrown. And then another.   4
And suddenly the Public School 139 graduation picnic had turned into
what the New York City police would later call "a confirmed bias incident."

All this happened on June 17, but weeks later it still affects the lives   5
of those involved, young and old. The children from Flatbush certainly
remember it. So do the teenagers from Staten Island. One of them was
sentenced on July 19 to perform 70 hours of community service for his
actions that afternoon on Miller Field.

"Our reports show there was a racial incident that afternoon," said   6
Lieut. James I. Radney of the Federal park police, which patrols the
field, part of the Federal Gateway National Recreation Area.

It was only one racial incident in a city where, according to the   7
Police Department, there were 71 "confirmed bias incidents" in the first
six months of this year.

But what happened that afternoon remains a jumble of frightening   8
images to the 12-year-olds from the Brooklyn school: a group of perhaps

439

15 white teenagers throwing rocks and shouting racial epithets as they chased them across the field; cries of "Go back to where you belong"; a teacher swinging a bat frantically as he tried to defend his pupils, and rocks and bottles flying through the air, hitting children, crashing through school bus windows.

9   The sixth grade of P.S. 139 left the picnic on Staten Island under a police escort. The pupils made the trip back to Brooklyn in different buses from those in which they had arrived; the original school buses, their windows shattered, were littered with shards of glass. Six of the pupils—one Hispanic youth and five blacks—were treated in the emergency room of Staten Island Hospital for minor cuts and bruises.

10   Their class picnic had become a racial incident. And it had become the story of two divergent communities and a generation coming of age on the issue of race.

"A Neighborhood to Protect"

11   The bungalows at New Dorp Beach on Staten Island were built after World War II as summer getaway homes. As the completion of the Verrazano-Narrows Bridge made Staten Island more accessible to the rest of the city and the economy made second homes less accessible to many, these bungalows, with some insulation, gradually became year-round residences.

12   It was not long before developers moved in to plow dusty roads through the woods and erect rows of adjoining red-brick town houses and clapboard houses with neat front lawns. A community, just a stone's throw from the Atlantic Ocean, evolved.

13   Many of the second generation of New Dorp Beach residents—the teenage children of Civil Service and other middle-class workers—hang out on summer nights at the General Store on Topping Street, across from a strip of dunes leading to a rocky beach. Seated on a low fence near the store is a row of teenagers, boys and girls, in an orderly line like birds perched on a wire.

14   Two antiquated gas pumps stand in front and the inside is crowded with a haphazard assortment of food and soda. A video game across from the front door is surrounded by youngsters; the machine fills the store with a steady background of shrill, high-pitched noises. About a block away is Miller Field.

15   "We got a neighborhood to protect," explains Ralph Fellini, 31, the owner of the General Store and the only one in the crowd outside willing to answer questions. "That's really what the whole thing on Miller Field was about."

16   "Hey, you guys know what went down at the field that day," he says to a group of uncommunicative youths. "You got nothing to be ashamed of. Tell the man."

"Well, if Ralphie says it's all right," decides a youth who had moments before denied even knowing the location of Miller Field.   17

"This is our neighborhood," says Darren Scaffidi, 15. "You let in one colored, you gotta let in a thousand."   18

"They don't have to come to Staten Island," says Petey Smith, 14. "Couldn't they go to Prospect Park in Brooklyn or some place like that?"   19

"I mean what would happen if we went up to Harlem?" asks Mike Cumminsky, 17.   20

"Look," says Charles Trainer, 17, "sure black people got a right to come to the field. It's public property. But they should know they don't belong here. The teachers who took them here are to blame."   21

The specifics of the incident have also taken on a reality unique to the logic of the neighborhood: A half-dozen voices insist that it could not have been a sixth-grade class that was attacked.   22

"They were really big dudes—huge," John Coe argues.   23

"Oh, maybe there were some little kids," Kevin McCarthy Jr., 15, finally agrees. "But they were day-care center kids. They should know better than to bus day-care center kids out here.   24

Mr. Fellini, a parent himself, sums it up: "These are good kids. They're not troublemakers. They're like I was when I was growing up in this neighborhood. They're just trying to make sure New Dorp Beach stays the kind of place where they'll want to raise their kids someday."   25

"The Racial Mix of the Real World"

P.S. 139 on Cortelyou Road in the Flatbush section of Brooklyn is on the fringe of a neighborhood of grand Victorian homes that seem out of place in Brooklyn. Tiled fireplaces, paneled rooms, wainscoting, parquet floors—all are common amenities surviving from a more comfortable era. Even the street names—Buckingham, Marlborough, Rugby—suggest the sort of gracious and static vision of Britannia that fuels romantic imaginations.   26

Yet Flatbush is a neighborhood hectic with modern-day problems and transition. Signs on the streets announce the private security police patrol the neighborhood. It is not an unrealistic precaution: in the 70th Precinct, which includes P.S. 139, the police report there were 3,534 burglaries in 1982.   27

And although the people whose children were attacked on Staten Island talk as though it could not happen here, there were also, police records show, four "confirmed bias incidents" in the precinct during that year. The incidents involved anti-Semitic actions and resulted in the arrests of youths aged 10 to 17.   28

29   From a population that was heavily Jewish and white in 1970, the 1980 census found Flatbush 30 percent white, 50 percent black, 13 percent Hispanic and 7 percent Asian.

30   P.S. 139 also reflects the changing character of the neighborhood. According to Lawrence Levy, the school's principal, 70 percent of the school's 1,500 pupils are black, Hispanic or Asian.

31   It was this racial cross-section of students that the principal addressed at a special assembly two days after the events in Staten Island.

32   "I simply told the children," Mr. Levy recalled, "that there are some people in this world who are determined to hate other people because of their race or religion. This is not the way things are at P.S. 139, but we can't ignore that such hatred exists elsewhere. "

33   "Part of the strength of P.S. 139 is that it reflects the racial mix of the real world," said Jackie Lieberman, whose sixth-grade child had been at the picnic. "And it would be wrong for our children simply to forget what happened that day. They should remember so that they can someday do something about the hatred which exists in this very imperfect but very real world."

34   So one day, a group of sixth graders gathered in a shady corner planted with day lilies across from the school's playground to discuss how they felt about what happened at Miller Field.

35   "They think we're still going to be slaves," says Bruce Johnston, 11. "I was scared, but I'd rather be scared than a racist."

36   "I was angry," says Charlene Ohayon, 11. "This is a free country, and we got a right to play anywhere."

37   "They could come here if they want," says Stephen Delabstide, 12. "Maybe they should. Those kids from Staten Island in their punk rock T-shirts should see that all kinds of kids can get along out here."

38   "Yeah," says Tricia Moretti, 11. "They grow up in that neighborhood hating people who are strange to them. It's their parents who teach them that. Their parents taught them to hate people who are different, and now it's too late. Their parents are to blame."

"We Don't Want All This Destroyed"

39   Rose Lanza's 16-year-old son, Nicholas, was arrested and charged with six counts of second-degree assault, reckless endangerment, criminal mischief and resisting arrest for his purported role in the incident on Miller Field. On July 19, after plea bargaining, Nicholas was sentenced to perform 70 hours of community service.

40   The boy's lawyer, Dennis M. Karsch, contends that his client is not guilty. "Nicholas Lanza did nothing wrong," says Mr. Karsch. "He was just walking up the street when he was arrested. He didn't call any names or throw any rocks. He didn't do anything."

"What really bothers me," Mr. Karsch continues as he sits in his Staten Island office, "is the way some people have thrown racism into this. There's no proof. Some people are just trying to fire things up by calling this a racial issue. I think it was just a group of kids who had an argument that led to a fight with another group of kids."   41

Mrs. Lanza, a school crossing guard, breaks into tears when she discusses her son. In the living room of her brick town house, there are plastic seat covers on the blue couch and a wedding picture of her and her husband on a wooden coffee table.   42

"I'm a widow," she manages to say through her tears, "and I have to raise Nick all by myself. Now look what they done to him. They kept him in jail overnight. Jail in Brooklyn. They made him drink coffee. I never let my son drink coffee. He's just a boy. A good boy. How could they do that to him?   43

"And now what's going to happen to us? If our name is in the paper, they'll come back here and rob us. Those kids from Brooklyn have relatives. Uncles, Brothers. What if those people from Brooklyn come after us? I was robbed last winter. I couldn't live through another robbery. Why did they have to pick on my son?"   44

Esther Scaffidi's son Kevin, 15, was also arrested by the park police after the incident at Miller Field. Kevin was arrested in front of the General Store while he was trying to prevent the park police from arresting a friend who he said was innocent.   45

The authorities agreed that Kevin had not been at Miller Field that afternoon, and he was released after his mother paid a $25 fine and he promised to buy a new pair of sunglasses for a park police officer who had his broken in the scuffle.   46

Mrs. Scaffidi is disabled. She sits in the living room of her bungalow in New Dorp Beach while her son and Ralph Fellini listen.   47

"I don't know the Lanza boy," she says, "but I'm sure he's a good kid like all the other kids in the neighborhood. It isn't that we're prejudiced. People out here just work hard. We don't want all this destroyed. It's wrong for black people to yell prejudice. We're not racists."   48

Reading and Writing Activities

PRELIMINARY RESPONSE

Notes.   As you read, record your reactions in your reading journal (questions or comments) to Howard Blum's description of the "bias incident" involving groups of teenagers from two different ethnic groups.

Note the rhetorical structure of this report, the unstated assumptions, the relationship between teenagers and adults in the community where the incident occurred.

Discussion.   In class, compare your reactions in groups of five or six. Appoint a recorder to keep track of similarities or differences, consensus or disagreement, arising from the discussion. The recorder may summarize your group discussion for the rest of the class later.

Freewriting.   After the class discussion, freewrite for 5 to 10 minutes about Blum's point of view. Read your freewriting in groups of two to four.

SUMMARIZING

1. Create a scratchline of the ideas that Blum introduces to develop his essay about racial incidents in New York. Focus on key words that mark topic shifts. For example, note the topic shift when Blum moves from one group to another for the story of what really happened.
2. Write a summary paragraph or two, from your scratchline or other preliminary work, of the topics that Blum introduces to develop his point of view on bias incidents.
3. Read the summaries in your groups. Compare the focus of each summary. How do the summaries differ? How are they the same? Are there significant portions left out of any of the summaries? Are any "exuberant"?

FOCUSED CRITICAL READING

1. What rhetorical structure does Howard Blum use to tell the story of the racial incident?
2. What does he leave unsaid in his interviews with the two ethnic groups involved in the racial incident?
3. Blum states that the specifics of the incident "have also taken on a reality unique to the logic of the neighborhood." What does he mean by the phrase "reality unique to the logic of the neighborhoods"?
4. What does this report of a "bias incident" tell you about ethnic identity in these two neighborhoods, Flatbush and New Dorp Beach?

Deborah Tannen

Asymmetries: Women and Men Talking at Cross Purposes

◆

Deborah Tannen is a professor of linguistics at Georgetown University. The focus of her work is the analysis of cultural and gender differences in conversations. In addition to her bestselling book You Just Don't Understand: Women and Men in Conversation *(1990), she has also published* That's Not What I Meant! How Conversational Style Makes or Breaks Your Relations with Others *(1986). She argues that women and men do not only have different language patterns in conversation but that their identities are shaped by different systems of communication. The following selection is from her book on conversation and gender. Her latest book is* Talking from 9 to 5: How Women's and Men's Conversational Styles Affect Who Gets Heard, Who Gets Credit, and What Gets Done at Work *(1994).*

Eve had a lump removed from her breast. Shortly after the operation, talking to her sister, she said that she found it upsetting to have been cut into, and that looking at the stitches was distressing because they left a seam that had changed the contour of her breast. Her sister said, "I know. When I had my operation I felt the same way." Eve made the same observation to her friend Karen, who said, "I know. It's like your body has been violated." But when she told her husband, Mark, how she felt, he said, "You can have plastic surgery to cover up the scar and restore the shape of your breast."

Eve had been comforted by her sister and her friend, but she was not comforted by Mark's comment. Quite the contrary, it upset her more. Not only didn't she hear what she wanted, that he understood her feelings, but, far worse, she felt he was asking her to undergo more surgery just when she was telling him how much this operation had upset her. "I'm not having any more surgery!" she protested. "I'm sorry you don't like the way it looks." Mark was hurt and puzzled. "I don't care," he protested. "It doesn't bother me at all." She asked, "Then why are you telling me to have plastic surgery?" He answered, "Because you were saying *you* were upset about the way it looked."

3   Eve felt like a heel: Mark had been wonderfully supportive and concerned throughout her surgery. How could she snap at him because of what he said—"just words"—when what he had done was unassailable? And yet she had perceived in his words metamessages that cut to the core of their relationship. It was self-evident to him that his comment was a reaction to her complaint, but she heard it as an independent complaint of his. He thought he was reassuring her that she needn't feel bad about her scar because there was something she could *do* about it. She heard his suggestion that she do something about the scar as evidence that *he* was bothered by it. Furthermore, whereas she wanted reassurance that it was normal to feel bad in her situation, his telling her that the problem could easily be fixed implied she had no right to feel bad about it.

4   Eve wanted the gift of understanding, but Mark gave her the gift of advice. He was taking the role of problem solver, whereas she simply wanted confirmation for her feelings.

5   A similar misunderstanding arose between a husband and wife following a car accident in which she had been seriously injured. Because she hated being in the hospital, the wife asked to come home early. But once home, she suffered pain from having to move around more. Her husband said, "Why didn't you stay in the hospital where you would have been more comfortable?" This hurt her because it seemed to imply that he did not want her home. She didn't think of his suggestion that she should have stayed in the hospital as a response to her complaints about the pain she was suffering; she thought of it as an independent expression of his preference not to have her at home.

"They're My Troubles—Not Yours"

6   If women are often frustrated because men do not respond to their troubles by offering matching troubles, men are often frustrated because women do. Some men not only take no comfort in such a response, they take offense. For example, a woman told me that when her companion talks about a personal concern—for example, his feelings about growing older—she responds, "I know how you feel; I feel the same way." To her surprise and chagrin, he gets annoyed; he feels she is trying to take something away from him by denying the uniqueness of his experience.

7   A similar miscommunication was responsible for the following interchange, which began as a conversation and ended as an argument:

> *He:* I'm really tired. I didn't sleep well last night.
> *She:* I didn't sleep well either. I never do.
> *He:* Why are you trying to belittle me?
> *She:* I'm not! I'm just trying to show that I understand!

This woman was not only hurt by her husband's reaction; she was mystified by it. How could he think she was belittling him? By "belittle me," he meant "belittle my experience." He was filtering her attempts to establish connection through his concern with preserving independence and avoiding being put down.

"I'll Fix It For You"

Women and men are both often frustrated by the other's way of responding to their expression of troubles. And they are further hurt by the other's frustration. If women resent men's tendency to offer solutions to problems, men complain about women's refusal to take action to solve the problems they complain about. Since many men see themselves as problem solvers, a complaint or a trouble is a challenge to their ability to think of a solution, just as a woman presenting a broken bicycle or stalling car poses a challenge to their ingenuity in fixing it. But whereas many women appreciate help in fixing mechanical equipment, few are inclined to appreciate help in "fixing" emotional troubles.

8

The idea that men are problem solvers was reinforced by the contrasting responses of a husband and wife to the same question on a radio talk show. The couple, Barbara and William Christopher, were discussing their life with an autistic child. The host asked if there weren't times when they felt sorry for themselves and wondered, "Why me?" Both said no, but they said it in different ways. The wife deflected attention from herself: She said that the real sufferer was her child. The husband said, "Life is problem solving. This is just one more problem to solve."

9

This explains why men are frustrated when their sincere attempts to help a woman solve her problems are met not with gratitude but with disapproval. One man reported being ready to tear his hair out over a girlfriend who continually told him about problems she was having at work but refused to take any of the advice he offered. Another man defended himself against his girlfriend's objection that he changed the subject as soon as she recounted something that was bothering her: "What's the point of talking about it any more?" he said. "You can't do anything about it." Yet another man commented that women seem to wallow in their problems, wanting to talk about them forever, whereas he and other men want to get them out and be done with them, either by finding a solution or by laughing them off.

10

Trying to solve a problem or fix a trouble focuses on the message level of talk. But for most women who habitually report problems at work or in friendships, the message is not the main point of complaining. It's the metamessage that counts: Telling about a problem is a bid for an expression of understanding ("I know how you feel") or a similar complaint ("I felt the same way when something similar happened

11

to me"). In other words, troubles talk is intended to reinforce rapport by sending the metamessage "We're the same; you're not alone." Women are frustrated when they not only don't get this reinforcement but, quite the opposite, feel distanced by the advice, which seems to send the metamessage "We're not the same. You have the problems; I have the solutions."

12   Furthermore, mutual understanding is symmetrical, and this symmetry contributes to a sense of community. But giving advice is asymmetrical. It frames the advice giver as more knowledgeable, more reasonable, more in control—in a word, one-up. And this contributes to the distancing effect.

13   The assumption that giving advice can be oneupmanship underlies an observation that appeared in a book review. In commenting on Alice Adams's *After You've Gone,* reviewer Ron Carlson explained that the title story is a letter from a woman to a man who has left her for a younger woman. According to Carlson, the woman informs her former lover about her life "and then steps up and clobbers him with sage advice. Here is clearly a superior woman...." Although we do not know the intention of the woman who wrote the story, we see clearly that the man who reviewed it regards giving advice as a form of attack and sees one who gives advice as taking a superior position.

Parallel Tracks

14   These differences seem to go far back in our growing up. A sixteen-year-old girl told me she tends to hang around with boys rather than girls. To test my ideas, I asked her whether boys and girls both talk about problems. Yes, she assured me, they both do. Do they do it the same way? I asked. Oh, no, she said. The girls go on and on. The boys raise the issue, one of them comes up with a solution, and then they close the discussion.

15   Women's and men's frustrations with each other's ways of dealing with troubles talk amount to applying interpretations based on one system to talk that is produced according to a different system. Boys and men do not respond to each other the way women respond to each other in troubles talk. The roots of the very different way that men respond to talk about troubles became clear to me when I compared the transcript of a pair of tenth-grade boys talking to each other to the transcripts of girls' conversations from videotapes of best friends talking, recorded as part of a research project by psychologist Bruce Dorval.

16   Examining the videotaped conversations, I found that the boys and girls, who expressed deep concerns to each other, did it in different ways—ways that explain the differences that come up in daily conversations between women and men. The pairs of girls at both the sixth grade and tenth grade talked at length about one girl's problems. The

other girl pressed her to elaborate, said, "I know," and gave supporting evidence. The following brief excerpts from the transcripts show the dramatic difference between the girls and boys.

The tenth-grade girls are talking about Nancy's problems with her 17 boyfriend and her mother. It emerges that Nancy and Sally were both part of a group excursion to another state. Nancy suddenly left the group and returned home early at her mother's insistence. Nancy was upset about having to leave early. Sally reinforces Nancy's feelings by letting her know that her sudden departure was also upsetting to her friends:

> *Nancy:* God, it was *bad*. I couldn't believe she made me go home.
> *Sally:* I thought it was kind of weird though, I mean, one minute we were going out and the next minute Nancy's going, "Excuse me, gotta be going." [Both laugh] I didn't know what was going *on,* and Judy comes up to me and she whispers (the whole place knows), "Do you know that Nancy's going home?" And I go, "What?" [Both laugh] "Nancy's going home." I go, *"Why?"* She goes, "Her mom's making her." I go [makes a face], "Ah." She comes back and goes, "Nancy's left." Well, I said, "WELL, that was a fine thing TO DO, she didn't even come and say goodbye." And she starts boiling all over me. I go [mimicking yelling], *"All right!!"* She was upset, Judy. I was like "God"—

Sally's way of responding to her friend's troubles is to confirm Nancy's feelings of distress that her mother made her leave the trip early, by letting her know that her leaving upset her friends. In contrast, examining the transcript of a conversation between boys of the same age shows how differently they respond to each other's expressions of troubles.

The tenth-grade boys also express deep feelings. Theirs too is trou- 18 bles talk, but it is troubles talk with a difference. They don't concentrate on the troubles of one, pursuing, exploring, and elaborating. Instead, each one talks about his own troubles and dismisses the other's as insignificant.

In the first excerpt from these boys' conversation, Richard says he 19 feels bad because his friend Mary has no date for an upcoming dance, and Todd dismisses his concern:

> *Richard:* God, I'm going to feel so bad for her if she stays home.
> *Todd:* She's not going to stay home, it's ridiculous. Why doesn't she just ask somebody?

Yet Todd himself is upset because he has no date for the same dance. He explains that he doesn't want to ask Anita, and Richard, in turn, scoffs at his distress:

> *Todd:* I felt so bad when she came over and started talking to me
> last night.
> *Richard:* Why?
> *Todd:* I don't know. I felt uncomfortable, I guess.
> *Richard:* **I'll never understand that.** [Laugh]

Far from trying to show that he understands, Richard states flatly that
he doesn't, as shown in boldface type.

20   Richard then tells Todd that he is afraid he has a drinking problem.
Todd responds by changing the subject to something that is bothering
him, his feelings of alienation:

> *Richard:* When I took Anne home last night she told me off.
> *Todd:* Really?"
>   . . .
> *Richard:* You see when she found out what happened last Thurs-
> day night between Sam and me?
> *Todd:* Mhm.
> *Richard:* She knew about that. And she just said—and then she
> started talking about drinking. You know?.... And then she
> said, you know, "You, how you hurt everybody when you do
> it. You're always cranky." And she just said, "I don't like it. You
> hurt Sam. You hurt Todd. You hurt Mary. You hurt Lois."
>   . . .
> I mean, when she told me, you know I guess I was kind of
> stunned. [Pause] I didn't really drink that much.
> *Todd:* **Are you still talking to Mary, a lot, I mean?**
> *Richard:* Am I still talking to Mary?
> *Todd:* Yeah, 'cause that's why—that's why I was mad Friday.
> *Richard:* Why?
> *Todd:* Because.
> *Richard:* 'Cause why?
> *Todd:* 'Cause I didn't know why you all just wa- I mean I just went
> back upstairs for things, then y'all never came back. I was go-
> ing, "Fine. I don't care." I said, "He's going to start this again."

As the lines printed in boldface show, when Richard says that he is
upset because Anne told him he behaved badly when he was drunk,
Todd responds by bringing up his own concern: He feels left out, and
he was hurt when Richard disappeared from a party with his friend
Mary.

21   Throughout the conversation, Todd expresses distress over feeling
alienated and left out. Richard responds by trying to argue Todd out of

the way he feels. When Todd says he felt out of place at a party the night before, Richard argues:

> *Richard:* **How could you feel out of place? You knew Lois, and you knew Sam.**
> *Todd:* I don't know. I just felt really out of place and then last night again at the party, I mean, Sam was just running around, he knew everyone from the sorority. There was about five.
> *Richard:* **Oh, no, he didn't.**
> *Todd:* He knew a lot of people. He was— I don't know.
> *Richard:* **Just Lois. He didn't know everybody.**
> *Todd:* I just felt really out of place that day, all over the place. I used to feel, I mean—
> *Richard:* **Why?**
> *Todd:* I don't know. I don't even feel right in school anymore.
> *Richard:* I don't know, last night, I mean—
> *Todd:* I think I know what Ron Cameron and them feels like now. [Laugh]
> *Richard:* [Laugh] **No, I don't think you feel as bad as Ron Cameron feels.**
> *Todd:* I'm kidding.
> *Richard:* Mm-mm. **Why should you? You know more people—**
> *Todd:* I can't talk to anyone anymore.
> *Richard:* **You know more people than me.**

By telling Todd that his feelings are unjustified and incomprehensible, Richard is not implying that he doesn't care. He clearly means to comfort his friend, to make him feel better. He's implying, "You shouldn't feel bad because your problems aren't so bad."

Matching Troubles

The very different way that women respond to the telling of troubles is dramatized in a short story, "New Haven," by Alice Mattison. Eleanor tells Patsy that she has fallen in love with a married man. Patsy responds by first displaying understanding and then offering a matching revelation about a similar experience:

> "Well," says Patsy. "I know how you feel."
> "You do?"
> "In a way, I do. Well, I should tell you. I've been sleeping with a married man for two years."

Patsy then tells Eleanor about her affair and how she feels about it. After they discuss Patsy's affair, however, Patsy says:

"But you were telling me about this man and I cut you off. I'm sorry. See? I'm getting self-centered."

"It's OK." But she is pleased again.

The conversation then returns to Eleanor's incipient affair. Thus Patsy responds first by confirming Eleanor's feelings and matching her experience, reinforcing their similarity, and then by encouraging Eleanor to tell more. Within the frame of Patsy's similar predicament, the potential asymmetry inherent in revealing personal problems is avoided, and the friendship is brought into balance.

23   What made Eleanor's conversation with Patsy so pleasing to Eleanor was that they shared a sense of how to talk about troubles, and this reinforced their friendship. Though Eleanor raised the matter of her affair, she did not elaborate on it until Patsy pressed her to do so. In another story by the same author, "The Knitting," a woman named Beth is staying with her sister in order to visit her sister's daughter Stephanie in a psychiatric hospital. While there, Beth receives a disturbing telephone call from her boyfriend, Alec. Having been thus reminded of her troubles, she wants to talk about them, but she refrains, because her sister doesn't ask. She feels required, instead, to focus on her sister's problem, the reason for her visit:

> She'd like to talk about her muted half-quarrels with Alec of the last weeks, but her sister does not ask about the phone call. Then Beth thinks they should talk about Stephanie.

The women in these stories are balancing a delicate system by which troubles talk is used to confirm their feelings and create a sense of community.

24   When women confront men's ways of talking to them, they judge them by the standards of women's conversational styles. Women show concern by following up someone else's statement of trouble by questioning her about it. When men change the subject, women think they are showing a lack of sympathy—a failure of intimacy. But the failure to ask probing questions could just as well be a way of respecting the other's need for independence. When Eleanor tells Patsy that she is in love with Peter, Patsy asks, "Are you sleeping with him?" This exploration of Eleanor's topic could well strike many men—and some women—as intrusive, though Eleanor takes it as a show of interest that nourishes their friendship.

25   Women tend to show understanding of another woman's feelings. When men try to reassure women by telling them that their situation is not so bleak, the women hear their feelings being belittled or discounted. Again, they encounter a failure of intimacy just when they were bidding to reinforce it. Trying to trigger a symmetrical communication, they end up in an asymmetrical one.

A Different Symmetry

The conversation between Richard and Todd shows that although   26
the boys' responses are asymmetrical if looked at separately—each dismisses the other's concerns—they are symmetrical when looked at
together: Todd responds to Richard's concern about his drinking in
exactly the same way that Richard responds to Todd's feeling of alienation, by denying it is a problem:

> *Richard:* Hey, man, I just don't feel—I mean, after what Anne said
> last night, I just don't feel like doing that.
> *Todd:* **I don't think it was that way. You yourself knew it was no**
> **big problem.**
> *Richard:* Oh, Anne—Sam told Anne that I fell down the levee.
> *Todd:* **It's a lie.**
> *Richard:* I didn't fall. I slipped, slid. I caught myself.
> *Todd:* **Don't worry about it.**
> *Richard:* But I do, kind of. I feel funny in front of Sam. I don't want
> to do it in front of you.
> *Todd:* **It doesn't matter 'cause sometimes you're funny when**
> **you're off your butt.**

Todd denies that Richard was so drunk he was staggering ("It's a lie")
and then says that even if he was out of control, it wasn't bad; it was
funny.

In interpreting this conversation between tenth-grade boys, I ini-   27
tially saw their mutual reassurances and dismissals, and their mutual
revelations of troubles, in terms of connection and sameness. But
another perspective is possible. Their conversation may be touching
precisely because it was based on asymmetries of status—or, more precisely, a deflecting of such asymmetries. When Todd tells his troubles,
he puts himself in a potentially one-down position and invites Richard
to take a one-up position by disclaiming troubles and asymmetrically
offering advice or sympathy. By offering troubles of his own, Richard
declines to take the superior position and restores their symmetrical
footing, sending the metamessage "We're just a couple of guys trying
to make it in a world that's tough on both of us, and both of us are
about equally competent to deal with it."

From this perspective, responding as a woman might—for exam-   28
ple by saying, "I can see how you feel; you must feel awful; so would I
if it happened to me"—would have a totally different meaning for
boys, since they would be inclined to interpret it through the lens of
status. Such a response would send a metamessage like "Yes, I know,
you incompetent jerk, I know how awful you must feel. If I were as
incompetent as you, I'd feel the same way. But, lucky for you, I'm not,
and I can help you out here, because I'm far too talented to be upset by

a problem like that." In other words, refraining from expressing sympathy is generous, insofar as sympathy potentially condescends.

29   Women are often unhappy with the reactions they get from men when they try to start troubles talk, and men are often unhappy because they are accused of responding in the wrong way when they are trying to be helpful. But Richard and Todd seem satisfied with each other's ways of reacting to their troubles. And their ways make sense. When men and women talk to each other, the problem is that each expects a different kind of response. The men's approach seeks to assuage feelings indirectly by attacking their cause. Since women expect to have their feelings supported, the men's approach makes them feel that they themselves are being attacked.

"Don't Ask"

30   Talking about troubles is just one of many conversational tasks that women and men view differently, and that consequently cause trouble in talk between them. Another is asking for information. And this difference too is traceable to the asymmetries of status and connection.

31   A man and a woman were standing beside the information booth at the Washington Folk Life Festival, a sprawling complex of booths and displays. "You ask," the man was saying to the woman. "I don't ask."

32   Sitting in the front seat of the car beside Harold, Sybil is fuming. They have been driving around for half an hour looking for a street he is sure is close by. Sybil is angry not because Harold does not know the way, but because he insists on trying to find it himself rather than stopping and asking someone. Her anger stems from viewing his behavior through the lens of her own: If she were driving, she would have asked directions as soon as she realized she didn't know which way to go, and they'd now be comfortably ensconced in their friends' living room instead of driving in circles, as the hour gets later and later. Since asking directions does not make Sybil uncomfortable, refusing to ask makes no sense to her. But in Harold's world, driving around until he finds his way is the reasonable thing to do, since asking for help makes him uncomfortable. He's avoiding that discomfort and trying to maintain his sense of himself as a self-sufficient person.

33   Why do many men resist asking for directions and other kinds of information? And, it is just as reasonable to ask, why is it that many women don't? By the paradox of independence and intimacy, there are two simultaneous and different metamessages implied in asking for and giving information. Many men tend to focus on one, many women on the other.

34   When you offer information, the information itself is the message. But the fact that you have the information, and the person you are

speaking to doesn't, also sends a metamessage of superiority. If relations are inherently hierarchical, then the one who has more information is framed as higher up on the ladder, by virtue of being more knowledgeable and competent. From this perspective, finding one's own way is an essential part of the independence that men perceive to be a prerequisite for self-respect. If self-respect is bought at the cost of a few extra minutes of travel time, it is well worth the price.

Because they are implicit, metamessages are hard to talk about. 35 When Sybil begs to know why Harold won't just ask someone for directions, he answers in terms of the message, the information: He says there's no point in asking, because anyone he asks may not know and may give him wrong directions. This is theoretically reasonable. There are many countries, such as, for example, Mexico, where it is standard procedure for people to make up directions rather than refuse to give requested information. But this explanation frustrates Sybil, because it doesn't make sense to her. Although she realizes that someone might give faulty directions, she believes this is relatively unlikely, and surely it cannot happen every time. Even if it did happen, they would be in no worse shape than they are in now anyway.

Part of the reason for their different approaches is that Sybil 36 believes that a person who doesn't know the answer will say so, because it is easy to say, "I don't know." But Harold believes that saying "I don't know" is humiliating, so people might well take a wild guess. Because of their different assumptions, and the invisibility of framing, Harold and Sybil can never get to the bottom of this difference; they can only get more frustrated with each other. Keeping talk on the message level is common, because it is the level we are most clearly aware of. But it is unlikely to resolve confusion since our true motivations lie elsewhere.

To the extent that giving information, directions, or help is of use to 37 another, it reinforces bonds between people. But to the extent that it is asymmetrical, it creates hierarchy: Insofar as giving information frames one as the expert, superior in knowledge, and the other as uninformed, inferior in knowledge, it is a move in the negotiation of status.

It is easy to see that there are many situations where those who 38 give information are higher in status. For example, parents explain things to children and answer their questions, just as teachers give information to students. An awareness of this dynamic underlies one requirement for proper behavior at Japanese dinner entertainment, according to anthropologist Harumi Befu. In order to help the highest-status member of the party to dominate the conversation, others at the dinner are expected to ask him questions that they know he can answer with authority.

Because of this potential for asymmetry, some men resist receiving 39 information from others, especially women, and some women are cautious about stating information that they know, especially to men. For example, a man with whom I discussed these dynamics later told me that my perspective clarified a comment made by his wife. They had gotten into their car and were about to go to a destination that she knew well but he did not know at all. Consciously resisting an impulse to just drive off and find his own way, he began by asking his wife if she had any advice about the best way to get there. She told him the way, then added, "But I don't know. That's how I would go, but there might be a better way." Her comment was a move to redress the imbalance of power created by her knowing something he didn't know. She was also saving face in advance, in case he decided not to take her advice. Furthermore, she was reframing her directions as "just a suggestion" rather than "giving instructions."

"I'll Fix It If It Kills Me"

40   The asymmetry implied in having and giving information is also found in having and demonstrating the skill to fix things—an orientation that we saw in men's approaches to troubles talk. To further explore the framing involved in fixing things, I will present a small encounter of my own.

41   Unable to remove the tiny lid that covers the battery compartment for the light meter on my camera, I took the camera to a photography store and asked for help. The camera salesman tried to unscrew the lid, first with a dime and then with a special instrument. When this failed, he declared the lid hopelessly stuck. He explained the reason (it was screwed in with the threads out of alignment) and then explained in detail how I could take pictures without a light meter by matching the light conditions to shutter settings in accordance with the chart included in rolls of film. Even though I knew there wasn't a chance in the world I would adopt his system, I listened politely, feigning interest, and assiduously wrote down his examples, based on an ASA of 100, since he got confused trying to give examples based on an ASA of 64. He further explained that this method was actually superior to using a light meter. In this way, he minimized the significance of not being able to help by freeing the battery lid; he framed himself as possessing useful knowledge and having solved my problem even though he couldn't fix my camera. This man wanted to help me—which I sincerely appreciated—but he also wanted to demonstrate that he had the information and skill required to help, even though he didn't.

42   There is a kind of social contract operating here. Many women not only feel comfortable seeking help, but feel honor-bound to seek it, accept it, and display gratitude in exchange. For their part, many men feel honor-bound to fulfill the request for help whether or not it is convenient for them to do so. A man told me about a time when a neighbor

asked him if he could fix her car, which was intermittently stalling out. He spent more time than he could spare looking at her car, and concluded that he did not have the equipment needed to do the repair. He felt bad about not having succeeded in solving her problem. As if sensing this, she told him the next day, and the next, that her car was much better now, even though he knew he had done nothing to improve its performance. There is a balance between seeking help and showing appreciation. Women and men seem equally bound by the requirements of this arrangement: She was bound to show appreciation even though he hadn't helped, and he was bound to invest time and effort that he really couldn't spare, in trying to help.

Another example of the social contract of asking for help and showing appreciation occurred on a street corner in New York City. A woman emerged from the subway at Twenty-third Street and Park Avenue South, and was temporarily confused about which direction to walk in to reach Madison Avenue. She knew that Madison was west of Park, so with a little effort she could have figured out which way to go. But without planning or thinking, she asked the first person to appear before her. He replied that Madison did not come down that far south. Now, she knew this to be false. Furthermore, by this time she had oriented herself. But instead of saying, "Yes, it does," or "Never mind, I don't need your help," she found a way to play out the scene as one in which he helped her. She asked, "Which way is west?" and, on being told, replied, "Thank you. I'll just walk west." 43

From the point of view of getting directions, this encounter was absurd from start to finish. The woman didn't really need help, and the man wasn't in a position to give it. But getting directions really wasn't the main point. She had used the commonplace ritual of asking directions of a stranger not only—and not mostly—to find her way on emerging from the subway, but to reinforce her connection to the mass of people in the big city by making fleeting contact with one of them. Asking for help was simply an automatic way for her to do this. 44

"I'll Help You If It Kills You"

Martha bought a computer and needed to learn to use it. After studying the manual and making some progress, she still had many questions, so she went to the store where she had bought it and asked for help. The man assigned to help her made her feel like the stupidest person in the world. He used technical language in explaining things, and each time she had to ask what a word meant she felt more incompetent, an impression reinforced by the tone of voice he used in his answer, a tone that sent the metamessage "This is obvious; everyone knows this." He explained things so quickly, she couldn't possibly remember them. When she went home, she discovered she couldn't 45 recall what he had demonstrated, even in cases where she had followed his explanation at the time.

46   Still confused, and dreading the interaction, Martha returned to the store a week later, determined to stay until she got the information she needed. But this time a woman was assigned to help her. And the experience of getting help was utterly transformed. The woman avoided using technical terms for the most part, and if she did use one, she asked whether Martha knew what it meant and explained simply and clearly if she didn't. When the woman answered questions, her tone never implied that everyone should know this. And when showing how to do something, she had Martha do it, rather than demonstrating while Martha watched. The different style of this "teacher" made Martha feel like a different "student": a competent rather than stupid one, not humiliated by her ignorance.

47   Surely not all men give information in a way that confuses and humiliates their students. There are many gifted teachers who also happen to be men. And not all women give information in a way that makes it easy for students to understand. But many women report experiences similar to Martha's, especially in dealing with computers, automobiles, and other mechanical equipment; they claim that they feel more comfortable having women explain things to them. The different meanings that giving help entails may explain why. If women are focusing on connections, they will be motivated to minimize the difference in expertise and to be as comprehensible as possible. Since their goal is to maintain the appearance of similarity and equal status, sharing knowledge helps even the score. Their tone of voice sends metamessages of support rather than disdain, although "support" itself can be experienced as condescension.

48   If a man focuses on the negotiation of status and feels someone must have the upper hand, he may feel more comfortable when he has it. His attunement to the fact that having more information, knowledge, or skill puts him in a one-up position comes through in his way of talking. And if sometimes men seem intentionally to explain in a way that makes what they are explaining difficult to understand, it may be because their pleasant feeling of knowing more is reinforced when the student does not understand. The comfortable margin of superiority diminishes with every bit of knowledge the student gains. Or it may simply be that they are more concerned with displaying their superior knowledge and skill than with making sure that the knowledge is shared.

49   A colleague familiar with my ideas remarked that he'd seen evidence of this difference at an academic conference. A woman delivering a paper kept stopping and asking the audience, "Are you with me so far?" My colleague surmised that her main concern seemed to be that the audience understand what she was saying. When he gave his

paper, his main concern was that he not be put down by members of the audience—and as far as he could tell, a similar preoccupation was motivating the other men presenting papers as well. From this point of view, if covering one's tracks to avoid attack entails obscuring one's point, it is a price worth paying.

This is not to say that women have no desire to feel knowledgeable or powerful. Indeed, the act of asking others whether they are able to follow your argument can be seen to frame you as superior. But it seems that having information, expertise, or skill at manipulating objects is not the primary measure of power for most women. Rather, they feel their power enhanced if they can be of help. Even more, if they are focusing on connection rather than independence and self-reliance, they feel stronger when the community is strong.

50

"Trust Me"

A woman told me that she was incredulous when her husband dredged up an offense from years before. She had been unable to get their VCR to record movies aired on HBO. Her husband had looked at the VCR and declared it incapable of performing this function. Rather than accepting his judgment, she asked their neighbor, Harry, to take a look at it, since he had once fixed her VCR in the past. Harry's conclusion was the same as that of her husband, who was, however, incensed that his wife had not trusted his expertise. When he brought it up years later, the wife exclaimed in disbelief, "You still remember that? Harry is dead!" The incident, though insignificant to the wife, cut to the core of the husband's self-respect, because it called into question his knowledge and skill at managing the mechanical world.

51

Trust in a man's skill is also at issue between Felicia and Stan, another couple. Stan is angered when Felicia gasps in fear while he is driving. "I've never had an accident!" he protests. "Why can't you trust my driving?" Felicia cannot get him to see her point of view—that she does not distrust *his* driving in particular but is frightened of driving in general. Most of all, she cannot understand why the small matter of involuntarily sucking in her breath should spark such a strong reaction.

52

"Be Nice"

Having expertise and skill can reinforce both women's and men's sense of themselves. But the stance of expert is more fundamental to our notion of masculinity than to our concept of femininity. Women, according to convention, are more inclined to be givers of praise than givers of information. That women are expected to praise is reflected in a poster that was displayed in every United States post office branch

53

inviting customers to send criticism, suggestions, questions, and compliments. Three of these four linguistic acts were represented by sketches of men; only compliments were represented by a sketch of a woman with a big smile on her face, a gesture of approval on her fingers, and a halo around her head. The halo is especially interesting. It shows that the act of complimenting frames the speaker as "nice."

54   Giving praise, like giving information, is also inherently asymmetrical. It too frames the speaker as one-up, in a position to judge someone else's performance. Women can also be framed as one-up by their classic helping activities as mothers, social workers, nurses, counselors, and psychologists. But in many of these role—especially mothers and nurses—they may also be seen as doing others' bidding.

Overlapping Motivations

55   When acting as helpers, women and men typically perform different kinds of tasks. But even the same task can be approached with eyes on different goals, and this difference is likely to result in misjudgments of others' intentions. The end of my camera story underlines this. At a family gathering, I brought the camera to my brother-in-law, who has a reputation in the family for mechanical ability. He took it to his workshop and returned an hour and a half later, having fixed it. Delighted and grateful, I commented to his daughter, "I knew he would enjoy the challenge." "Especially," she pointed out, "when it involves helping someone." I felt then that I had mistaken his displayed concern with the mechanics of the recalcitrant battery cover as reflecting his ultimate concern. But fixing the camera was a way of showing concern for me, of helping me with his effort. If women directly offer help, my brother-in-law was indirectly offering help, through the mediation of my camera.

56   A colleague who heard my analysis of this experience thought I had missed an aspect of my broken-camera episode. He pointed out that many men get a sense of pleasure from fixing things because it reinforces their feeling of being in control, self-sufficient, and able to dominate the world of objects. (This is the essence of Evelyn Fox Keller's thesis that the conception of science as dominating and controlling nature is essentially masculine in spirit.) He told me of an incident in which a toy plastic merry-go-round, ordered for his little boy, arrived in pieces, having come apart during shipping. His wife gave the toy to her uncle, renowned in the family as a fixer and helper. Her uncle worked for several hours and repaired the toy—even though it was probably not worth more than a few dollars. The uncle brought this up again the next time he saw them, and said he would have stayed up all night rather than admit he couldn't put it together. My colleague was convinced that the motivation to gain dominion over the

plastic object had been stronger than the motivation to help his sister and nephew, though both had been present.

Furthermore, this man pointed out that he, and many other men, 57 take special pleasure in showing their strength over the world of objects for the benefit of attractive women, because the thanks and admiration they receive is an added source of pleasure and satisfaction. His interpretation of my revised analysis was that my niece and I, both women, would be inclined to see the helping aspect of an act as the "real" or main motive, whereas he still was inclined to see the pleasure of demonstrating skill, succeeding where the camera expert had failed, and whacking the recalcitrant battery lid into line as the main ones.

The element of negotiating status that characterizes many men's 58 desire to show they are knowledgeable and skillful does not negate the connection implied in helping. These elements coexist and feed each other. But women's and men's tendencies to place different relative weights on status versus connection result in asymmetrical roles. Attuned to the metamessage of connection, many women are comfortable both receiving help and giving it, though surely there are many women who are comfortable only in the role of giver of help and support. Many men, sensitive to the dynamic of status, the need to help women, and the need to be self-reliant, are comfortable in the role of giving information and help but not in receiving it.

The View From A Different Mountain

In a story by Alice Mattison, "The Colorful Alphabet," a man 59 named Joseph invites another man, Gordon, to visit his family in the country, because Gordon's wife has just left him. During the visit, they all climb a mountain. On the way down, they stop to rest, and Gordon realizes that he left his beloved old knapsack on the mountaintop. Joseph volunteers to climb back up to get it, because Gordon is not used to climbing and his feet are sore. Joseph's wife goes with him, but she is too tired to climb all the way to the top, and he leaves her on the path to complete the mission himself. When he finds her again, he is empty-handed: The bag wasn't there. He says then that he knew it wouldn't be, because he had seen a man carrying the bag pass them when they all stopped to rest. He explains why he didn't just say that he had seen someone go by with the bag: "I couldn't tell him I'd seen it and hadn't been smart enough to get it back for him." Instead, he says, "I had to *do* something."

Exhausted and frustrated, the wife is not so much angry as incred- 60 ulous. She can't understand how he could have preferred reclimbing the mountain (and making her reclimb it too) to admitting that he had seen someone carrying Gordon's bag. "I would never have done that," she says, but she speaks "more in wonder than anger." She explains,

"I'd have just blurted it out. I'd have been upset about making the mistake—but not about people *knowing*. That part's not a big deal to me." Her husband says, "Oh, is it ever a big deal to me."

61   This story supports the view of men's style that I have been proposing. Joseph wanted to help Gordon, and he did not want to let it be known that he had done something he thought stupid. His impulse to do something to solve the problem was stronger than his impulse not to climb a mountain twice. But what struck me most strongly about the story was the wife's reflections on the experience. She thinks:

> It was one of the occasional moments when I'm certain I haven't imagined him: I would never have done what he'd done, wouldn't have dreamt it or invented it—Joseph was, simply, *not me.*

62   This excerpt reflects what may be the subtlest yet deepest source of frustration and puzzlement arising from the different ways that women and men approach the world. We feel we know how the world is, and we look to others to reinforce that conviction. When we see others acting as if the world were an entirely different place from the one we inhabit, we are shaken.

63   We look to our closest relationships as a source of confirmation and reassurance. When those closest to us respond to events differently than we do, when they seem to see the same scene as part of a different play, when they say things that we could not imagine saying in the same circumstances, the ground on which we stand seems to tremble and our footing is suddenly unsure. Being able to understand why this happens—*why* and *how* our partners and friends, though like us in many ways, are *not* us, and different in other ways—is a crucial step toward feeling that our feet are planted on firm ground.

Reading and Writing Activities

PRELIMINARY RESPONSE

Notes.   As you read, record your reactions (questions or comments) to Deborah Tannen's "Asymmetries."

You may react to a number of factors in the reading: the ideas, the language (especially vocabulary choice), the rhetorical structure, the unstated assumptions, or the relationship between writer and reader (audience, purpose, organization, development). You need not, however, attempt to react to all of these factors in the essay at this time.

Discussion.   In class, compare your reactions in reading groups of five or six. Appoint a recorder to keep track of similarities or differences, consensus or disagreement, arising from the discussion. The recorder may summarize your group discussion for the rest of the class later.

SUMMARIZING

1. Create a preliminary analysis of central ideas within each section of Tannen's essay.
2. Write a summary paragraph or two, from your work, of the topics that Tannen introduces within each titled section of her text.
3. Read the summaries in your groups. Compare the focus of each summary. How do the summaries differ? How are they the same?

Mary Mebane

Shades of Black

◆

Mary Mebane was born in Durham, North Carolina and received her undergraduate degree from North Carolina Central University. She has also earned an M.A. and a Ph.D. from the University of North Carolina at Chapel Hill. The following selection is taken from the first volume of her autobiography, Mary, *published in 1981.*

1   During my first week of classes as a freshman, I was stopped one day in the hall by the chairman's wife, who was indistinguishable in color from a white woman. She wanted to see me, she said.

2   This woman had no official position on the faculty, except that she was an instructor in English; nevertheless, her summons had to be obeyed. In the segregated world there were (and remain) gross abuses of authority because those at the pinnacle, and even their spouses, felt that the people "under" them had no recourse except to submit—and they were right, except that sometimes a black who got sick and tired of it would go to the whites and complain. This course of action was severely condemned by the blacks, but an interesting thing happened—such action always got positive results. Power was thought of in negative terms: I can deny someone something, I can strike at someone who can't strike back, I can ride someone down; that proves I am powerful. The concept of power as a force for good, for affirmative response to people or situations, was not in evidence.

3   When I went to her office, she greeted me with a big smile. "You know," she said, "you made the highest mark on the verbal part of the examination." She was referring to the examination that the entire freshman class took upon entering the college. I looked at her but I didn't feel warmth, for in spite of her smile her eyes and tone of voice were saying, "How could this black-skinned girl score higher on the verbal than some of the students who've had more advantages than she? It must be some sort of fluke. Let me talk to her." I felt it, but I managed to smile my thanks and back off. For here at North Carolina College at Durham, as it had been since the beginning, social class and color were the primary criteria used in determining status on the campus.

4   First came the children of doctors, lawyers, and college teachers. Next came the children of public-school teachers, businessmen, and anybody else who had access to more money than the poor black working class. After that came the bulk of the student population, the children of

the working class, most of whom were the first in their families to go beyond high school. The attitude toward them was: You're here because we need the numbers, but in all other things defer to your betters.

The faculty assumed that light-skinned students were more intelligent, and they were always a bit nonplussed when a dark-skinned student did well, especially if she was a girl. They had reason to be appalled when they discovered that I planned to do not only well but better than my light-skinned peers.

I don't know whether African men recently transported to the New World considered themselves handsome or, more important, whether they considered African women beautiful in comparison with Native American Indian women or immigrant European women. It is a question that I have never heard raised or seen research on. If African men considered African women beautiful, just when their shift in interest away from black black women occurred might prove to be an interesting topic for researchers. But one thing I know for sure: by the twentieth century, really black skin on a woman was considered ugly in this country. This was particularly true among those who were exposed to college.

Hazel, who was light brown, used to say to me, "You are *dark*, but not *too* dark." The saved commiserating with the damned. I had the feeling that if nature had painted one more brushstroke on me, I'd have had to kill myself.

Black skin was to be disguised at all costs. Since a black face is rather hard to disguise, many women took refuge in ludicrous make-up. Mrs. Burry, one of my teachers in elementary school, used white face powder. But she neglected to powder her neck and arms, and even the black on her face gleamed through the white, giving her an eerie appearance. But she did the best she could.

I observed all through elementary and high school that for various entertainments the girls were placed on the stage in order of color. And very black ones didn't get into the front row. If they were past caramel-brown, to the back row they would go. And nobody questioned the justice of these decisions—neither the students nor the teachers.

One of the teachers at Wildwood School, who was from the Deep South and was just as black as she could be, had been a strict enforcer of these standards. That was another irony—that someone who had been judged outside the realm of beauty herself because of her skin tones should have adopted them so wholeheartedly and applied them herself without question.

One girl stymied that teacher, though. Ruby, a black cherry of a girl, not only got off the back row but off the front row as well, to stand alone at stage center. She could outsing, outdance, and outdeclaim everyone else, and talent proved triumphant over pigmentation. But the May Queen and her Court (and in high school, Miss Wildwood) were always chosen from among the lighter ones.

12   When I was a freshman in high school, it became clear that a light-skinned sophomore girl named Rose was going to get the "best girl scholar" prize for the next three years, and there was nothing I could do about it, even though I knew I was the better. Rose was caramel-colored and had shoulder-length hair. She was highly favored by the science and math teacher, who figured the averages. I wasn't. There was only one prize. Therefore, Rose would get it until she graduated. I was one year behind her, and I would not get it until after she graduated.

13   To be held in such low esteem was painful. It was difficult not to feel that I had been cheated out of the medal, which I felt that, in a fair competition, I perhaps would have won. Being unable to protest or do anything about it was a traumatic experience for me. From then on I instinctively tended to avoid the college-exposed dark-skinned male, knowing that when he looked at me he saw himself and, most of the time, his mother and sister as well, and since he had rejected his blackness, he had rejected theirs and mine.

14   Oddly enough, the lighter-skinned black male did not seem to feel so much prejudice toward the black black woman. It was no accident, I felt, that Mr. Harrison, the eighth-grade teacher, who was reddish-yellow himself, once protested to the science and math teacher about the fact that he always assigned sweeping duties to Doris and Ruby Lee, two black black girls. Mr. Harrison said to them one day, right in the other teacher's presence, "You must be some bad girls. Every day I come down here ya'll are sweeping." The science and math teacher got the point and didn't ask them to sweep anymore.

15   Uneducated black males, too, sometimes related very well to the black black woman. They had been less firmly indoctrinated by the white society around them and were more securely rooted in their own culture.

16   Because of the stigma attached to having dark skin, a black black woman had to do many things to find a place for herself. One possibility was to attach herself to a light-skinned woman, hoping that some of the magic would rub off on her. A second was to make herself sexually available, hoping to attract a mate. Third, she could resign herself to a more chaste life-style—either (for the professional woman) teaching and work in established churches or (for the uneducated woman) domestic work and zealous service in the Holy and Sanctified churches.

17   Even as a young girl, Lucy had chosen the first route. Lucy was short, skinny, short-haired, and black black, and thus unacceptable. So she made her choice. She selected Patricia, the lightest-skinned girl in the school, as her friend, and followed her around. Patricia and her friends barely tolerated Lucy, but Lucy smiled and doggedly hung on, hoping that some who noticed Patricia might notice her, too. Though I felt shame for her behavior, even then I understood.

18   As is often the case of the victim agreeing with and adopting the attitudes of the oppressor, so I have seen it with black black women. I

have seen them adopt the oppressor's attitude that they are nothing but "sex machines," and their supposedly superior sexual performance becomes their sole reason for being and for esteeming themselves. Such women learn early that in order to make themselves attractive to men they have somehow to shift the emphasis from physical beauty to some other area—usually sexual performance. Their constant talk is of their desirability and their ability to gratify a man sexually.

I knew two such women well—both of them black black. To hear 19 their endless talk of sexual conquests was very sad. I have never seen the category that these women fall into described anywhere. It is not that of promiscuity or nymphomania. It is the category of total self-rejection: "Since I am black, I am ugly, I am nobody. I will perform on the level that they have assigned to me." Such women are the pitiful results of what not only white America but also, and more important, black America has done to them.

Some, not taking the sexuality route but still accepting black soci- 20 ety's view of their worthlessness, swing all the way across to intense religiosity. Some are staunch, fervent workers in the more traditional Southern churches—Baptist and Methodist—and others are leaders and ministers in the lower status, more evangelical Holiness sects.

Another avenue open to the black black woman is excellence in a 21 career. Since in the South the field most accessible to such women is education, a great many of them prepared to become teachers. But here, too, the black black woman had problems. Grades weren't given to her lightly in school, nor were promotions on the job. Consequently, she had to prepare especially well. She had to pass examinations with flying colors or be left behind; she knew that she would receive no special consideration. She had to be overqualified for a job because otherwise she didn't stand a chance of getting it—and she was competing only with other blacks. She had to have something to back her up: not charm, not personality—but training.

The black black woman's training would pay off in the 1970s. With 22 the arrival of integration the black black woman would find, paradoxically enough, that her skin color in an integrated situation was not the handicap it had been in an all-black situation. But it wasn't until the middle and late 1960s, when the post-1945 generation of black males arrived on college campuses, that I noticed any change in the situation at all. *He* wore an afro and *she* wore an afro, and sometimes the only way you could tell them apart was when his afro was taller than hers. Black had become beautiful, and the really black girl was often selected as queen of various campus activities. It was then that the dread I felt at dealing with the college-educated black male began to ease. Even now, though, when I have occasion to engage in any type of transaction with a college-educated black man, I gauge his age. If I guess he was born after 1945, I feel confident that the transaction will turn out all right. If he probably was born before 1945, my stomach tightens, I find myself taking shallow breaths, and I try to state my business and escape as soon as possible.

Reading and Writing Activities

PRELIMINARY RESPONSE

Notes.   As you read, record your reactions in your reading journal (questions or comments) to "Shades of Black" and Mary Mebane's discussion of discrimination against what she refers to as "black black" skin in African-American communities.

You may react to a number of factors in the reading: the ideas, the language (especially vocabulary choice), the rhetorical structure, the unspoken assumptions, or the relationship between writer and reader (audience, purpose, organization, development). Your prior experience of the situation Mary Mebane discusses will be a factor in the way you respond to the essay. You need not, of course, attempt to react to all of these factors in the essay at this time.

Discussion.   In class, compare your reactions in reading groups of five or six. Appoint a recorder to keep track of similarities or differences, consensus or disagreement, arising from the discussion. The recorder may summarize your group discussion for the rest of the class later.

Freewriting.   After the class discussion, freewrite for 5 to 10 minutes about Mebane's point of view. Read your freewriting in groups of two to four.

SUMMARIZING

1. Create a scratchline of the ideas that Mebane introduces to develop her essay about shades of color. Focus on key words that mark topic shifts. For example, note the topic shift when Mebane moves from describing status and color in college to reporting that by the twentieth century "really black skin was considered ugly in this country."

   Or you may prefer another approach to analyzing the parts of Mebane's essay such as clustering.
2. Write a summary paragraph or two, from your scratchline or other preliminary work, of the topics that Mebane introduces to develop her point of view.

3. Read the summaries in your reading groups. Compare the focus of each summary. How do the summaries differ? How are they the same? Do any omit reference to large portions of Mebane's essay?

FOCUSED CRITICAL READING

1. Mebane writes about "fitting in" as it relates to black communities in schools and colleges in the mid-'50s to mid-'60s. How were students accepted or rejected in these communities as she describes them?
2. As they came of age, what did women in the communities that Mebane describes need to know about shades of black and success?
3. Mebane claims that some "black black" women, because they accepted the community standards of attractiveness and believed that their shades of color were unattractive, shifted attention from physical attractiveness to sexual availability thus compensating for lack of attractiveness. Do you know of women who are not African American adopting the same strategy?
4. What other responses (other than making themselves sexually available) were available to "black black" women, according to Mebane?

David Updike

The Colorings of Childhood: On the Burdens, and Privileges, Facing My Multi-Racial Son

——————————◆——————————

Born in New York in 1957, David Updike holds degrees from Harvard and Columbia Universities. He has published a collection of short fiction as well as several works for young adults. The following selection appeared in the January 1992 issue of Harper's.

1　　Five or six years ago, when my older sister revealed to the rest of our family her intention of marrying her boyfriend, from Ghana, I remember that my reaction, as a nervous and somewhat protective younger brother, was something like "Well, that's fine for them—I just wonder about the children." I'm not sure what I was wondering, exactly, but it no doubt had to do with the thorny questions of race and identity, of having parents of different complexions, and a child, presumably, of some intermediate shade, and what that would mean for a child growing up here, in the United States of America.

2　　I had no idea, at the time, that I, too, would one day marry an African, or that soon thereafter we would have a child, or that I would hear my own apprehensions of several years before echoed in the words of one of my wife's friends. She was a white American of a classic liberal mold—wearer of Guatemalan shawls, befriender of Africans, espouser of worthy causes—but she was made uneasy by the thought of Njoki, her friend from Kenya, marrying me, a white person. She first asked Njoki what my "politics" were and, having been assured that they were okay, went on to say, "Well, I'm sure he's a very nice person, but before you get married I just hope you'll think about the children."

3　　I recognized in her remarks the shadow of my own, but when it is one's own marriage that is being worried about, one's children, not yet conceived, one tends to ponder such comments more closely. By this time, too, I was the uncle of two handsome, happy boys, Ghanian-American, who, as far as I could tell, were suffering no side effects for having parents of different colors. Njoki, too, was displeased.

"What is she trying to say, exactly—that *my* child will be disad- 4
vantaged because he looks like me?" my wife asked. "So what does
she think about me? Does she think I'm disadvantaged because I'm
African?"

I responded that our liberal friend was trying to get at the compli- 5
cated question of identity, knowing, as she did, that the child, in a
country that simplifies complicated, racial equations to either "black"
or "white," wouldn't know to which group he "belonged."

"To both of them," Njoki answered, "or to neither. He will be Kenyan- 6
American. The ridiculous part is that if I was marrying an African she
wouldn't mind at all—she wouldn't say, "Think of the children," because
the child would just be black, like me, and it wouldn't be her problem.
She wouldn't have to worry about it. Honestly," she finally said, her head
bowed into her hand in resignation, "this country is so complicated."

But her friend's reaction is not, I suspect, an uncommon one, even 7
among those who think of themselves as progressive and ideologically
unfettered: They don't mind, in principle, the idea of interracial unions,
but the prospect of children clouds the issue, so to speak, and raises the
identity issue—if not for the child, the *beheld,* then for us, the beholders.
For as I slowly pondered the woman's remarks, it occurred to me that
she was not saying, "He won't know who he is" but something closer
to, "*I* won't know who he is—I won't know to which group this child
belongs, the black people or the white." Added to this is the suppressed, looming understanding that, however the child sees himself,
however we see the child, the country at large will perceive the child as
"black," and, consequently, this son or daughter of a friend, this child
to whom we might actually be an aunt or uncle, parent or grandparent,
cousin or friend, this person whom we love and wish the best for in
life, will grow up on the opposite side of the color line from us and, as
such, will be privy to a whole new realm of the American Experience,
which we, by virtue of our skin color, have previously avoided; and
this—for the vast majority of white Americans—is a new and not altogether comforting experience.

Harlem, Anacostia, Roxbury, Watts: In every major city in America, 8
and most minor ones, there is a neighborhood that most whites have
never been to, will never go to, and regard, from a distance, with an
almost primordial fear, akin to the child's apprehension of the bogey-
man. They have read about this place in the paper and heard on the
nightly news of the crime and violence there, but the thought of actually going there for a visit is almost unthinkable; if they ever found
themselves there, they imagine—got off at the wrong subway stop or
took an ill-fated wrong turn—they would be set upon by hordes of
angry, dark people with nothing better to do than sit around waiting

for hapless white people to amble into their lair. Most white Americans, I suspect, would be more comfortable walking through the streets of Lagos, or Nairobi, or Kingston, than they would be walking through any predominantly black neighborhood in America.

9   For a couple of years Njoki lived in Harlem, on Riverside Drive and 145th Street, and was visited there one evening by a couple of our friends and their one-year-old child. When it came time to leave, after dark, the woman asked Njoki if she would walk them to the corner, to hail a cab—as if the presence of a black person would grant them free passage and protect them from the perils of the neighborhood. Njoki explained that it was okay, that the neighborhood was quite safe and they wouldn't be singled out for special attention because they were white.

10   "It's okay for us," the friend explained. "I just wouldn't want anything to happen to the baby."

11   Njoki relented and walked them over to Broadway, but as they went she wondered what made her friends think the residents of Harlem wanted to attack a couple with a baby, or why she, an African and a stranger to this country, was called upon to somehow protect her American friends from their own countrymen. At the corner they hailed a cab, and they were whisked off to some safer corner of the city, leaving Njoki to walk back alone to her apartment, at far greater risk, as a single woman, than any group of people, white or black, would ever be.

12   Which is not to say that I myself felt at perfect ease walking through the streets of Harlem, but simply that the more time I spent there the more I realized that no one was particularly interested, or concerned, that a pale man in collegiate tweeds was walking through the neighborhood. During the two years that my wife lived there, I walked often from her apartment, down to City College, where I taught, and from there to Columbia University, and I was never bothered or heckled by anyone. As a friend of mine, a resident of Harlem, said to me once, "Black people are around white people all the time."

13   But as a child growing up, in a small New England town, I was almost never around black people. My impressions of the world beyond, or of African-Americans, were mostly gleaned from television and magazines and movies, from which, it seems to me, it is nearly impossible not to acquire certain racist assumptions about people, however slight and subtle; and even when one has become aware of them they are nearly impossible to shed entirely. Like astronomers who can hear the "background radiation" that marks the beginning of the universe, so can one hear, in the background of one's own thoughts, the persistent, static hiss of American history.

14   By the time my second nephew was born I had written two children's books, both about a boy and his dog and their various adventures in the small New England town where they lived. As I began to

think about a third book in this series it occurred to me that the boy could now have a friend, and if he was to have a friend it might be nice if his complexion was somewhat closer to that of my two nephews, so that when they read the book they would find a character who, in this regard, looked somewhat like themselves. I wrote such a book and sent in the manuscript with a letter explaining that, although there was no reference to race in the book, I would like the second boy to appear darker than his friend in the illustrations.

A few weeks later I received the editor's response: He liked the plot and story line, he said, but was confused by this new character, which seemed underdeveloped and vague. The editor didn't understand what this character was doing in a small New England town. I ran the risk, too, of being accused of "tokenism" by some of the members of the library association—black women especially, he pointed out—who were on the lookout for such things.   15

I wrote back and, among other things, suggested that children are less encumbered by problems of race and ethnicity than their parents or teachers, and I thought it unlikely they would worry what he was doing in a small New England town. I was willing to run the risk of being accused of tokenism either by reviewers or watchdogs of the children's-book world. In the end, we agreed on a few small editorial changes, and when the book came out the character in question was indeed of brown skin, and I never heard another word about it either from teachers or reviewers or disgruntled children. But this editorial skirmish gave me a taste of the children's-book world I had not quite imagined, and I've since had dealings with several other publishers, most of whom, it seemed to me, exhibited a kind of heightened vigilance when it came to books about "children of color," so wrought were editors with anxieties about tokenism and marketing and whatever other obstacles lie between them and a slightly broader vision of what constitutes suitable subject matter for children.   16

Njoki is often asked what my family thinks of my being married to an African woman, a black woman, but she is almost never asked what her family thinks of her being married to a "mzungu"—a white person. Her interviewers are surprised to learn that my parents don't mind and that hers don't either, and that her parents regret much more that neither she nor I is a practicing Catholic. They are also surprised to learn that there would be much more apprehension and mutual suspicion had she married a Kenyan of another ethnic group, or an African of another country. And I am married to an African, not an African-American, and in my case, too, the suspicions and animosities of history are diffused by the absence of a common and adversarial past. And, similarly, for Njoki, the thought of her being married to a white Kenyan—the descendants of Karen Blixen (more commonly known as Isak Dinesen) and her ilk—is almost laughable.   17

18   Several summers ago we spent six weeks in Kenya and passed much of our time there in a middle-class suburb of Nairobi called "Karen," named after this same Karen Blixen, who once lived here in the shadow of the Ngong Hills. One night we were invited to dinner at the house of a neighbor—a couple in the tourist industry who had invited a group of traveling Americans over to their house for dinner. Their home was in the typically grand style of the Kenyan middle class, the "grounds" surrounded by a tall barbed-wire and electrified fence, and further protected by an all-night watchman and several roaming dogs. But inside the floors were polished wood parquet, the furniture was tasteful, and, aside from a few African prints, we could have been in an upper-middle-class dwelling in Los Angeles, or Buenos Aires, or Rome. The other guests had already arrived, and sat on couches eating and drinking and talking with their hosts. As it turned out, all of the guests were African-American, mostly from New Jersey and New York; we were introduced, and joined them, but it became clear that some were not very happy to find me, a white American, here in the home of an African, 8,000 miles from the country they and I so uneasily shared. When I tried to speak to one of the African-American women she would answer in clipped monosyllables and stare into distant corners of the room; another woman had brought a tape recorder, with which to record some of the conversations, but whenever I spoke, it was observed, she would turn off the machine and wait for my polluting commentary to pass. I did find one woman who was not, outwardly, troubled by my presence, and spent much of the evening talking with her, but my otherwise chilly reception had not been lost on Njoki's sister and brother-in-law and niece, who were both mystified and amused. On the car ride home we tried to explain—about the history of the United States, and slavery, and about African-Americans' identification with Africa as the place from which their ancestors were taken, stolen, for hundreds of years. Njoki tried to explain how their visit here was a kind of homecoming, a return to the continent they probably would have never left, were it not for the unpleasant fact of slavery.

19   "Yes, but that was West Africa—it has nothing to do with here. And besides, they're Americans now—and you're American, too."

20   "Yes, but...."

21   "And you're a guest. You have as much right to be here as they do."

22   "Yes, but...."

23   It is difficult to accurately convey the complexities of race in America to someone who has never been here, and they remained unconvinced. Our American dinner companions, I suspect, would have been saddened, if not maddened, by our sour postmortem of the evening,

and I was sorry to have been, as far as they were concerned, in the wrong place at the wrong time, was sorry to have diminished their enjoyment of their visit. But I still felt that I had more in common with my fellow African-American guests than either of us did with our Kenyan hosts—an idea to which they might have heartily objected. They shared with our hosts a genetic and, to some extent, cultural "Africanness," and the experience of being mistreated by peoples of European ancestry; I shared with my hosts the experience of growing up in a place where people of one's own ethnicity, or color, were in the majority; but with my fellow guests I shared the more immediate experience of having grown up in America, where our experiences have been rather different, where we also live, as uneasy acquaintances, on opposing sides of the same, American coin.

I am asked, sometimes, either directly or by implication, how it is   24
that both my sister and I—New Englanders of northern European extraction—came to marry Africans, people of another culture and color and continent. I have never had much of an answer for these people, except to say that both my sister and I are compatible with our respective spouses in ways neither of us had been with previous companions, all of whom were far closer to our own complexions. When I was five or so, and my sister seven, my family lived for two months on a small island in the Caribbean, and it is my mother's rather whimsical theory that it was from impressions gleaned during this trip—for my sister from the somewhat older boys she played with in an old, rusty model T that sat beside our house, and for me from the long-limbed, beautiful baby-sitters who used to take care of us—that led us both, thirty years later, to marry Africans. Nor do I think that it was any strain of "jungle fever" that caused us to marry who we did. More likely, my sister and I both married Africans because, as children, we were not conditioned not to, were not told that this was not one of life's options, and so, when the opportunity arose, there were no barriers—neither our own nor our parents'. And in the "white liberal" world in which I grew up, it would have been uncouth to make any outward show of disapproval—though I suspect some amused speculation went on behind closed doors about my sister's and my choice of mates, and I believe some of my parent's friends expressed quiet concern, but I have never personally received any negative commentary, neither from friends nor passersby. It had been more of an issue for Njoki, who has some friends who believe marrying a white man is a "sellout" of some kind, a "betrayal" of the race, and that with it comes the loss of some strain of political correctness. But such friends either tend to adjust or to fade away into a world more cleanly divided between black and white, where they will be irritated and confused no more.

25   By some unexpected confluence of genes our son Wesley's hair is, to our surprise, relatively straight—long, looping curls that tighten slightly when it rains—and this, too, will mean something in America, means something already to the elderly neighborhood women who tell us, with a smile, that he has "good" hair, and to other people, friends and strangers both, who tell us he looks like he is from Central America, or India, or the Middle East, implicitly meaning *rather than black.* Children, however, are less circumspect in their observations, and I have no doubt my son will be called a few names while growing up, both by white children and by brown; he may be told that he is really "black," and he may be told that he thinks he's "white"; in Kenya, I have been assured, he will be considered "half-caste"—an unpleasant linguistic relic from colonial days. He may also be treated badly by teachers prone to impatience, or a lack of empathy, with students of lighter, or darker, complexions than their own. He may be embarrassed by the sound of his mother's language; he may be embarrassed by my whiteness. He may go through a time when he is, indeed, confused about his "identity," but in this respect I don't think he will be much different from other children, or teenagers, or adults. There is no way of my knowing, really, what his experience as a multi-racial child will be, or, for that matter, how helpful I or his mother will be to him along the way. We can only tell him what we think and know, and hope, as all parents do, that our words will be of some use.

26   We are not bothered by mothers in the park who seem to get a little nervous, overly vigilant, when their children begin to commiserate with other, darker children, as if their children are in some sort of subtle, ineffable danger—too close for comfort. Their fears seem laughable, absurd, and one comes to almost pity the children who will grow up in the shadow of such fearful, narrow people, from whom they will inherit the same nervous bundle of apprehensions and pathologies. Many of them will be sent to private schools, not because the public schools in our city are not very good but because of the subconscious assumption that schools with so many children of other races can't be that good: Such schools and students will hold their own children back somehow. But in the end, these people tend to recede, not disappear, exactly, but shrink before the simple, overwhelming presence of your child, who shrieks with joy at something as simple as the sound of your key turning in the door.

27   Wesley will visit Africa and live there for a time, and will know the Kenyan half of his family there and the American half here, and into the bargain will know his Ghanian uncle and his Ghanian-American cousins and a whole West African branch of his extended family. And it may just be that, contrary to the assumptions of concerned friends, this child of a "mixed" marriage will suffer no great disadvantages at all, but rather will enjoy advantages denied the rest of us; for as the child of

two cultures he will "belong" to neither of them exclusively but both of them collectively, will be a part of my Americanness and Njoki's Africanness, and will be something neither she nor I ever will be—African-American—and as such will be a part of a rich and varied culture that will always hold me at arm's length. And in these layers of identity lies an opportunity for a kind of expansion of the world, a dissolution of the boundaries and obstacles that hold us all in a kind of skittish, social obeisance, and he thus may be spared the suspicions and apprehensions that plague those of us who have grown up with an exclusive, clearly defined sense of belonging. In the end, my son will be, simply, an American child, an American adult. His will be a wider, more complicated world than mine was, and to him will fall the privilege and burden, as it falls to us all, of making of it what he will.

Reading and Writing Activities

PRELIMINARY RESPONSE

Notes.   As you read, record your reactions in your reading journal (questions or comments) to "The Colorings of Childhood," David Updike's examination of the "thorny questions of race and identity, of having parents of different complexions."

You may react to a number of factors in the reading: the ideas, the use of language (especially vocabulary choice), the rhetorical structure, the unstated assumptions, or the relationship between writer and reader (audience, purpose, organization, development). Your prior knowledge and experience with the problems Updike describes will also be a factor in your reaction. You need not, of course, attempt to react to all of these factors in the essay at this time.

Discussion.   In class, compare your reactions in reading groups of five or six. Appoint a recorder to keep track of similarities or differences, consensus or disagreement, arising from the discussion. The recorder may summarize your group discussion for the rest of the class later.

Freewriting.   After the class discussion, freewrite for 10 to 15 minutes about Updike's point of view. Read your freewriting in groups of two to four.

SUMMARIZING

1. Create a scratchline of the ideas that Updike introduces to develop his essay about his son's mixed parentage. Identify key words that

mark topic shifts. For example, your scratchline will note the topic shift when Updike moves from describing his wife's friend's reaction to their marriage to describing the reactions in general from a "progressive" group of people.

   Or you may prefer another approach to analyzing the parts of Updike's essay such as clustering.

2. Write a summary paragraph or two, from your scratchline or other preliminary work, of the topics that Updike introduces to develop his point of view on the way American culture views mixed marriages.

3. Read the summaries in your groups. Compare the focus of each summary. How do the summaries differ? How are they the same? Does anyone read too much into the Updike reading (is the summary "exuberant," or a somewhat exaggerated response) or ignore large portions of the essay?

FOCUSED CRITICAL READINGS

1. How does David Updike describe the relationship that existed between his wife and her white friends?

2. How does he describe his relationship with his wife's Kenyan family and friends?

3. How does he describe his relationship with the editor of the children's books he wrote?

4. What is suggested by his description of the way African Americans relate to his appearance at a neighbor's dinner party in Kenya?

Toni Cade Bambara

My Man Bovanne

♦

Toni Cade Bambara was born in 1939 and educated at Queens College and the City College of New York. She has published The Salt Eaters, *for which she won an American Book Award in 1981, and* Gorilla, My Love, *(1972), a collection of short stories from which the following selection has been taken.*

Blind People got a hummin jones if you notice, Which is under- 1
standable completely once you been around one and notice what no eyes will force you into to see people, and you get past the first time, which seems to come out of nowhere, and it's like you in church again with fat-chest ladies and old gents gruntin a hum low in the throat to whatever the preacher be saying. Shakey Bee bottom lip all swole up with Sweet Peach and me explainin how come the sweet-potato bread was a dollar-quarter this time stead of dollar regular and he say uh hunh he understand, then he break into this *thizzin* kind of hum which is quiet, but fiercesome just the same, if you ain't ready for it. Which I wasn't. But I got used to it and the onliest time I had to say somethin bout it was when he was playin checkers on the stoop one time and he commenst to hummin quite churchy seem to me. So I says, "Look here Shakey Bee, I can't beat you and Jesus too." He stop.

So that's how come I asked My Man Bovanne to dance. He ain't my 2
man mind you, just a nice ole gent from the block that we all know cause he fixes things and the kids like him. Or used to fore Black Power got hold their minds and mess em around till they can't be civil to ole folks. So we at this benefit for my niece's cousin who's runnin for somethin with this Black party somethin or other behind her. And I press up close to dance with Bovanne who blind and I'm hummin and he hummin, chest to chest like talkin. Not jammin my breasts into the man. Wasn't bout tits. Was bout vibrations. And he dug it and asked me what color dress I had on and how my hair was fixed and how I was doin without a man, not nosy but nice-like, and who was at this affair and was the canapés dainty-stingy or healthy enough to get hold of proper. Comfy and cheery is what I'm tryin to get across. Touch talkin like the heel of the hand on the tambourine or on a drum.

But right away Joe Lee come up on us and frown for dancin so 3
close to the man. My own son who knows what kind of warm I am

479

about; and don't grown men call me long distance and in the middle of the night for a little Mama comfort? But he frown. Which ain't right since Bovanne can't see and defend himself. Just a nice old man who fixes toasters and busted irons and bicycles and things and changes the lock on my door when my men friends get messy. Nice man. Which is not why they invited him. Grass roots you see. Me and Sister Taylor and the woman who does heads at Mamies and the man from the barber shop, we all there on account of we grass roots. And I ain't never been souther than Brooklyn Battery and no more country than the window box on my fire escape. And just yesterday my kids tellin me to take them countrified rags off my head and be cool. And now can't get Black enough to suit em. So everybody passin sayin My Man Bovanne. Big deal, keep steppin and don't even stop a minute to get the man a drink or one of them cute sandwiches or tell him what's goin on. And him standin there with a smile ready case someone do speak he want to be ready. So that's how come I pull him on the dance floor and we dance squeezin past the tables and chairs and all them coats and people standin round up in each other face talkin bout this and that but got no use for this blind man who mostly fixed skates and skooters for all these folks when they was just kids. So I'm pressed up close and we touch talkin with the hum. And here come my daughter cuttin her eye at me like she do when she tell me about my "apolitical" self like I got hoof and mouf disease and there ain't no hope at all. And I don't pay her no mind and just look up in Bovanne shadow face and tell him his stomach like a drum and he laugh. Laugh real loud. And here come my youngest, Task, with a tap on my elbow like he the third grade monitor and I'm cuttin up on the line to assembly.

4   "I was just talkin on the drums," I explained when they hauled me into the kitchen. I figured drums was my best defense. They can get ready for drums what with all this heritage business. And Bovanne stomach just like that drum Task give me when he come back from Africa. You just touch it and it hum thizzm, thizzm. So I stuck to the drum story. "Just drummin that's all."

5   "Mama, what are you talkin about?"

6   "She had too much to drink," say Elo to Task cause she don't hardly say nuthin to me direct no more since that ugly argument about my wigs.

7   "Look here Mama," say Task, the gentle one. "We just tryin to pull your coat. You were makin a spectacle of yourself out there dancing like that."

8   "Dancin like what?"

9   Task run a hand over his left ear like his father for the world and his father before that.

10   "Like a bitch in heat," say Elo.

"Well uhh, I was goin to say like one of them sex-starved ladies gettin on in years and not too discriminating. Know what I mean?"

I don't answer cause I'll cry. Terrible thing when your own children talk to you like that. Pullin me out the party and hustlin me into some stranger's kitchen in the back of a bar just like the damn police. And ain't like I'm old old. I can still wear me some sleeveless dresses without the meat bangin off my arm. And I keep up with some thangs through my kids. Who ain't kids no more. To hear them tell it. So I don't say nuthin.

"Dancin with that tom," say Elo to Joe Lee, who leanin on the folks' freezer. "His feet can smell a cracker a mile away and go into their shuffle number post haste. And them eyes. He could be a little considerate and put on some shades. Who wants to look into them blown-out fuses that—"

"Is this what they call the generation gap?" I say.

"Generation gap," spits Elo, like I suggested castor oil and fricassee possum in the milk-shakes or somethin. "That's a white concept for a white phenomenon. There's no generation gap among Black people. We are a col—"

"Yeh, well never mind," says Joe Lee. "The point is Mama . . . well, it's pride. You embarrass yourself and us too dancin like that."

"I wasn't shame." Then nobody say nuthin. Them standin there in they pretty clothes with drinks in they hands and gangin up on me, and me in the third-degree chair and nary a olive to my name. Felt just like the police got hold to me.

"First of all," Task say, holdin up his hand and tickin off the offenses, "the dress. Now that dress is too short, Mama, and too low-cut for a woman your age. And Tamu's going to make a speech tonight to kick off the campaign and will be introducin you and expecting you to organize the council of elders—"

"Me? Didn nobody ask me nuthin. You mean Nisi? She change her name?"

"Well, Norton was supposed to tell you about it. Nisi wants to introduce you and then encourage the older folks to form a Council of the Elders to act as an advisory—"

"And you going to be standing there with your boobs out and that wig on your head and that hem up to your ass. And people'll say,'Ain't that the horny bitch that was grindin with the blind dude?"

"Elo, be cool a minute," say Task, gettin to the next finger. "And then there's the drinkin. Mama, you know you can't drink cause next thing you know you be laughin loud and carryin on," and he grab another finger for the loudness. "And then there's the dancin. You been tattooed on the man for four records straight and slow draggin even on the fast numbers. How you think that look for a woman your age?"

23   "What's my age?"

24   "What?"

25   "I'm axin you all a simple question. You keep talkin bout what's proper for a woman my age. How old am I anyhow?" And Joe Lee slams his eyes shut and squinches up his face to figure. And Task run a hand over his ear and stare into his glass like the ice cubes goin calculate for him. And Elo just starin at the top of my head like she goin rip the wig off any minute now.

26   "Is your hair braided up under that thing? If so, why don't you take it off? You always did do a neat cornroll."

27   "Uh huh," cause I'm thinkin how she couldn't undo her hair fast enough talking bout cornroll so countrified. None of which was the subject. "How old, I say?"

28   "Sixtee-one or—"

29   "You a damn lie Joe Lee Peoples."

30   "And that's another thing," say Task on the fingers.

31   "You know what you all can kiss," I say, gettin up and brushin the wrinkles out my lap.

32   "Oh, Mama," Elo say, puttin a hand on my shoulder like she hasn't done since she left home and the hand landin light and not sure it supposed to be there. Which hurt me to my heart. Cause this was the child in our happiness fore Mr. Peoples die. And I carried that child strapped to my chest till she was nearly two. We was close is what I'm tryin to tell you. Cause it was more me in the child than the others. And even after Task it was the girlchild I covered in the night and wept over for no reason at all less it was she was a chub-chub like me and not very pretty, but a warm child. And how did things get to this, that she can't put a sure hand on me and say Mama we love you and care about you and you entitled to enjoy yourself cause you a good woman?

33   "And then there's Reverend Trent," say Task, glancin from left to right like they hatchin a plot and just now lettin me in on it. "You were suppose to be talking with him tonight, Mama, about giving us his basement for campaign headquarters and—"

34   "Didn nobody tell me nuthin. If grass roots mean you kept in the dark I can't use it. I really can't. And Reven Trent a fool anyway the way he tore into the widow man up there on Edgecomb cause he wouldn't take in three of them foster children and the woman not even comfy in the ground yet and the man's mind messed up and—"

35   "Look here," say Task. "What we need is a family conference so we can get all this stuff cleared up and laid out on the table. In the meantime I think we better get back into the other room and tend to business. And in the meantime, Mama, see if you can't get to Reverend Trent and—"

36   "You want me to belly rub with the Reven, that it?"

37   "Oh damn," Elo say and go through the swingin door.

"We'll talk about all this at dinner. How's tomorrow night, Joe Lee?" While Joe Lee being self-important I'm wonderin who's doin the cookin and how come no body ax me if I'm free and do I get a corsage and things like that. Then Joe nod that it's O.K. and he go through the swingin door and just a little hubbub come through from the other room. Then Task smile his smile, lookin just like his daddy and he leave. And it just me in this stranger's kitchen, which was a mess I wouldn't never let my kitchen look like. Poison you just to look at the pots. Then the door swing the other way and it's My Man Bovanne standin there sayin Miss Hazel but lookin at the deep fry and then at the steam table, and most surprised when I come up on him from the other direction and take him on out of there. Pass the folks pushin up towards the stage where Nisi and some other people settin and ready to talk, and folks gettin to the last of the sandwiches and the booze fore they settle down in one spot and listen serious. And I'm thinkin bout tellin Bovanne what a lovely long dress Nisi got on and the earrings and her hair piled up in a cone and the people bout to hear how we all gettin screwed and gotta form our own party and everybody there listenin and lookin. But instead I just haul the man on out of there, and Joe Lee and his wife look at me like I'm terrible, but they ain't said boo to the man yet. Cause he blind and old and don't nobody there need him since they grown up and don't need they skates fixed no more.

"Where we goin, Miss Hazel?" Him knowin all the time.

"First we gonna buy you some dark sunglasses. Then you comin with me to the supermarket so I can pick up tomorrow's dinner, which is goin to be a grand thing proper and you invited. Then we goin to my house."

"That be fine. I surely would like to rest my feet." Bein cute, but you got to let men play out they little show, blind or not. So he chat on bout how tired he is and how he appreciate me takin him in hand this way. And I'm thinkin I'll have him change the lock on my door first thing. Then I'll give the man a nice warm bath with jasmine leaves in the water and a little Epsom salt on the sponge to do his back. And then a good rubdown with rose water and olive oil. Then a cup of lemon tea with a taste in it. And a little talcum, some of that fancy stuff Nisi mother sent over last Christmas. And then a massage, a good face massage round the forehead which is the worryin part. Cause you gots to take care of the older folks. And let them know they still needed to run the mimeo machine and keep the spark plugs clean and fix the mailboxes for folks who might help us get the breakfast program goin, and the school for the little kids and the campaign and all. Cause old folks is the nation. That what Nisi was sayin and I mean to do my part.

"I imagine you are a very pretty woman, Miss Hazel."

"I surely am," I say just like the hussy my daughter always say I was.

Reading and Writing Activities

PRELIMINARY RESPONSE

Notes. As you read, record your reactions in your reading journal (questions or comments) to Toni Cade Bambara's short story "My Man Bovanne."

You may react to a number of factors in the reading: the characters, the language (especially features of the black dialect), the rhetorical structure, the unspoken assumptions, or the relationships, between the characters (especially between those of different generations). Your prior knowledge and experience with dialects and the kind of community that is the setting for Bambara's story will be a factor in your reactions.

Discussion. In class, compare your reactions in groups of five or six. Appoint a recorder to keep track of similarities or differences, consensus or disagreement, arising from the discussion. The recorder may summarize your group discussion for the rest of the class later.

Freewriting. After discussion, freewrite for 5 to 10 minutes about Bambara's story.

SUMMARIZING

1. Create a scratchline of the characters and events that Bambara introduces to develop her story. For example, note the topic shifts when Bambara moves from one character to another, from one event or situation to another. Or you may prefer another approach to analyzing the parts of Bambara's story, such as clustering or taking notes after highlighting parts of the essay.)
2. Write a summary paragraph or two, from your scratchline or other preliminary work, about the characters and events in Bambara's story.
3. Read the summaries in your reading groups. Compare the focus of each summary. How do the summaries differ? How are they the same?

FOCUSED CRITICAL READING

1. There are differences between the narrator's language and her children's language. How does Bambara use language to develop her characters?
2. This mother and her children have different values about public dress and behavior. What is surprising about which generation is having difficulty with these different value systems?
3. What can we infer about the mother of this family from what Bambara leaves unsaid?
4. Is the mother powerless in this generational struggle?

Emile Ollivier

The Shipwreck of "La Caminante"

———————◆———————

Emile Ollivier was born in 1940 in Haiti. He studied at the Sorbonne before earning a master's degree from the University of Ottawa and a Ph.D. from the University of Montreal. Both a writer and an educator, Ollivier has published several novels: Mere-Solitude *in 1983,* La Discorde aux Cent Voix *in 1986, and* Passages *in 1991. The following selection, from* Passages, *appeared in 1992 in the literary journal* Callaloo, *in a special issue devoted to the literature and culture of Haiti.*

1   When we were even with the Windy Channel, a strong swell shook the hull of "La Caminante,"* waking us up. Rushing over to the tiller, Amédée ordered the mainsail lowered. Above us, threatening clouds swept across the sky. Before the men had time to begin lowering the mainsail, long sustained gusts had brought down the aftermast that we had taken such pains to shore up. The stem, planking, and rigging were constantly groaning. "Don't let the sails flap," Amédée kept yelling.

2   Dazed by blasts of salt spray, the men on the bridge were struggling with the ballooning sails. They were carrying on a real battle against the furious gusts of wind. It was all they could do to stay on their feet, grabbing anything that seemed at all secure to keep from being swept overboard. It was painful to keep their eyes open. The salt spray stung. The heavy, gray waves kept breaking on the bridge. The wind kept gaining in intensity. The oarsmen kept stroking with all their might, struggling against the furious sea. Time after time, "La Caminante" would rise on the crests, then fall back into the troughs between waves. The hull resounded and made cracking noises. Amédée's voice sounded above the tumult: "Look out! Look out! Good God, help her!" Dropping the tiller, he leapt forward as he yelled.

3   What I saw next paralyzed me with fear. With a sail wrapped around her, Noelzina, with her feet braced, was holding to the railing. She turned toward the ocean. Was she calculating the frightening depth? A lurch of the boat, struck by the great waves, slowed down the movement of everyone trying to reach her. Then, everything happened

*"The Voyager" (Spanish).

all of a sudden. Noelzina's feet rose from the deck. Draped in the white sail, with the corners flapping about her, she flew over the railing and remained suspended for an instant, her body stretched out, in mid-air. Like a weightless monarch, she glided with an imperceptible flapping of wings until a wave engulfed her. She reappeared twice in the middle of foaming whirlpools. The third time she went under, she did not come back up. We were all yelling, "Noelzina! Noelzina. . . .! Noelzina!"

It would be useless for me to try to hide my grief as I remember this   4
event. In spite of all of our precautions, we had never thought about providing our ship with life boats, poles, life buoys—instruments that might have let us come to Noelzina's aid. The fury of the waves prevented any maneuver to come around to the trough where she went down. Maybe she was carried away to the dwelling of the master of the great depths. Noelzina, you will long shine in our memory, a secret star!

Noelzina's disappearance left us exhausted and depressed. "La   5
Caminante" sailed on all night under the assault of the waves. Regardless of our prayers and supplications, the sea did not calm down. The winds kept their bad temper. We felt that we were lost. We had gone down into the hold, dazed with horror and fatigue, with our faces swollen, our eyes stung with salt, numb in our wet clothes. Crumpled in a corner, Philéus Corvolan was reciting a rosary of Psalms. Odanis Jean-Louis promised the Virgin Altagrâce that he would walk to Sault d'Eau* if he came out of this adventure alive.

Amédée was talking to himself as he sat erect, legs crossed, head   6
bowed, with closed eyes and furrowed brow. His words, which I could not make out at first, gradually became comprehensible and pushed the catastrophe of the moment from my consciousness. In Amédée's calm voice, I could detect terrible suffering. He was talking about Noelzina, her passion for life, the ardor with which she threw herself into everything that she undertook. Once more, I saw the scene just before the storm. I could see this man, more than sixty years old, and that woman, barely thirty, dancing. Amédée was still a striking man, in spite of his white hair. With a sturdy build, the rigors of age seemed to have brushed over him without any trace. I had the impression of sliding over a precipice without being able to stop. A great void filled me and I did not have the will to struggle against it. An atrocious, awful suspicion flooded into my mind. The idea that Amédée had carried on some lasting relationship with Noelzina welled up and burned through all the fibers of my being.

As I have already said, sir, I knew Amédée and I knew that he pos-   7
sessed the secret of attracting women. When I questioned him about

---

*·A waterfall, east and north of Port-au-Prince; place of pilgrimage.

the women he had seduced, his answers were always couched in humorously discreet terms. As long as I lived with him, I had always fought my instinct of jealousy, knowing intuitively that, if he shared any other beds than mine, it was not a very serious matter. I was certain that Amédée loved me.

8   I looked at Amédée sitting in front of me, motionless, not even recognizing me. I had the impression that he would never again move, as if he were petrified. If we had not made this voyage, I could have continued to believe in my happiness. I could have remained wrapped in my love like a caterpillar in its cocoon. I do not regret undertaking the trip: it has shattered appearances. Now I am disillusioned.

9   I do not know how long Amédée continued his monologue. I was overwhelmed by an emotion that I had never known up to that moment. When I glanced at him again, his head was swaying loosely and his shoulders were rising and falling with his heavy breathing. His body shook with irregular spasms. I thought that he had gone to sleep.

10   A child complained about being wet. Nobody had noticed that the hold was filling with water. Hiladieu checked the hull. At one of the seams, there was a gaping hole. In spite of all efforts, the men were not able to fill the breach. I will spare you the details of the dance of pots, goblets, and bowls that went into the fight against the rising water. With this load of water, "La Caminante" was wallowing around with its masts half torn off and its sails in shreds. Although the wind had gone down, the high waves were still pushing the boat around in an aimless trajectory. The men decided to row. They were exhausted and shivering and had no dry clothes. Hunger pangs were beginning to gnaw at their bellies. "May God please to bring us into sight of land quickly!"

11   The sun, which had been invisible during the entire storm, made a brief appearance as it was going down. Something surprising happened: one of the boys had brought a disgusting collection of little creatures on the boat. Among them, there was a cricket whose silence since the beginning of the trip had saddened the boy, who liked the grating song of the insect. Unexpectedly, that evening, in the midst of general despondency, the cricket began its strident music. Everyone sat up. "Land is close," Amédée muttered, breaking his silence for the first time since he had begun grieving.

12   Shading our eyes with our hands and with our hearts pounding, we scanned the horizon. We could not see any land. Was that a false move by the rowers who had turned around at the announcement? "La Caminante" was shaken by a violent shock and before we could wonder about the cause, we were thrown into the sea. Like a dead star, "La Caminante" sank into the ocean, leaving a few fragments of its hull floating around. We grabbed onto pieces of the wreckage as well as we could. Swept around by the still stormy sea, we drifted a good part of the night. At dawn, a launch picked us up. Its skipper spoke no language that we knew. He gave us some water and a little food. Of the

sixty-seven persons who had set sail from Port-à-l'Ecu, only twenty-two were left. Dead from horror and fear, we did not dare talk to each other about the fate of our other shipmates.

With a lot of gesticulation, our benefactor explained that he could not take us to the city where we could see the neon lights. The shore still seemed quite distant to me and I was surprised to feel the sand moving under the soles of my feet when he lowered me over the side. At one moment, I began looking at the little troop of men and women with the sense of not being part of it. An inexperienced onlooker would not have been able to tell them from people who had simply gone into the sea for a refreshing dip. I saw that they were thinner than when we left, even emaciated, with eyelids swollen from the salt water, eyeballs protruding, looking older after having survived unthinkable experiences. They walked on leaning on one another, closer through friendship and the fraternity of common misfortune. Amédée, with his clothes in shreds, was among them, trying to walk straight in spite of his exhaustion.

We had gotten there alive, after long days of terror, suffocation, and the uncertainty of the crossing. There we were on the beach—crabs regurgitated by the breakers. I was walking in a cloud of indecision on unknown soil. I turned around and enviously watched the white gulls as they rose back up over the sea, masters of their own fate. I saw Amédée glued to the spot as the others walked away from the sea, which had become a shroud. I went back to him. Although I was exhausted, I managed to take him on my back. His feet swept the wet sand. The incongruity of our situation made me think of the song we used to sing in good times in Port-à-l'Ecu, "In Bruno's house, the women carry their men on their back." Burdened down by my heavy load, I managed, long after the others, to get to the top of the little hill from which we could see some cute little white houses nested in a grove of trees on the other side of the road. Out of breath, I stopped. I had the impression that I recognized this place, which I had never seen. Were these images from a distant time that my mother, Hilda, had recounted to me, about the marvels she had seen during underwater voyages?

Some adolescents, children—first two, then three, then a whole swarm of them—greeted us in some incomprehensible jargon. I tried to get away. My fatigue and the weight of Amédée on my back made me trip and roll down the slope. Great peals of laughter from the children. With the indifference of their age, they quickly tired of the sad spectacle that we made and they disappeared in the direction of the beach, jabbering and shoving each other. I got back up painfully and readjusted Amédée—I had not let go of him during the fall.

In front of me, there was a great black river of asphalt of impressive breadth. In comparison, the main road going through Port-à-l'Ecu was nothing but a goat path. A bleating herd of vehicles of all colors and shapes was flying by at dizzying speed. How could I manage to cross without getting crushed? A few meters farther on, our companions in misfortune were contemplating in the same panic that teeming, busy road, the emblem of an America of which compatriots had told us.

17   I began walking again, limping as well as I could on the cracked soles of my feet. There was the surface of a low wall. I leaned against it. Sirens sounded. I gave a start. Amédée's body slipped and fell onto the road, a limp marionette.

18   A troop of vehicles waltzed around us with green and red lights flashing, tires screeching, uniforms jumping out, and boots clacking on the pavement. I sensed rather than saw them, armed with clubs and revolvers. They were yelling, but the awful noises from their radios drowned their voices. Two of them bent over Amédée's body and stuffed it onto the back seat of a car. They hoisted me beside him. "What a fine outing we've had, Amédée! What a fine tour, my captain!"

Reading and Writing Activities

PRELIMINARY RESPONSE

Notes.   As you read, record your reactions (questions or comments) to "The Shipwreck of 'La Caminante'" in your reading journal. A great deal is unsaid in this story, so you may want to mark places that leave you with questions about what the writer does not say.

You may react to a number of factors in the reading: the ideas, the language (especially vocabulary choice), the rhetorical structure, the unstated assumptions, or the relationship between writer and reader (audience, purpose, organization, development). Your prior knowledge of new immigrants and boating will also be factors in your reaction to Ollivier's story. You need not, however, attempt to react to all of these factors in the essay at this time.

Discussion.   In class, compare your reactions in reading groups of five or six. Appoint a recorder to keep track of similarities or differences, consensus or disagreement, arising from the discussion. The recorder may summarize your group discussion for the rest of the class later.

Freewriting.   After the class discussion, freewrite for 10 to 15 minutes about Ollivier's story. Read your freewriting in groups of two to four.

SUMMARIZING

1. Create a scratchline of the events that Ollivier introduces to develop his story about the shipwreck and the men and women who attempt-

ed to make the crossing from their homeland to a foreign country. Focus on key words that mark new characters or new situations.

Or you may prefer another approach to analyzing the parts of Ollivier's story, such as clustering.

2. Write a summary paragraph or two, from your scratchline or other preliminary work, of the events and people that Ollivier introduces to develop his short story.

3. Read the summaries in your groups. Compare the focus of each summary. How do you agree? How do you differ? Why do you think you differ? Are the differences significant? Has anyone left out large portions of Ollivier's story? Does anyone have an "exuberant" response to the story?

FOCUSED CRITICAL READING

1. What important points about the conditions during the crossing must you, the reader, infer from what the writer leaves unsaid?

2. What important points must you infer about the nature of the ship and crew that rescued the survivors. What type of ship, for example, picked them up? What was the business of that ship? Why did the captain of the ship put the survivors down on the beach?

3. What can you infer from Ollivier's description of the place of their arrival on shore?

WRITING SUGGESTIONS

1. Write a short essay (2–3 pages) on conflicting values between generations in the same family or within the same community. Use your summary of "My Man Bovanne" to introduce the topic and issue for this essay.

2. Research changing roles for men and women in a particular community. What problems arise in times of fundamental change? How does change in the community you are researching compare to change in mainstream American communities? Present your findings in four or five pages; include a "Works Cited" page and parenthetical citations of sources within the text. Check Chapter 4, page 179 for examples of analysis and synthesis in a documented essay.

3. Ask several people what it means to them to be American. Record their responses (on audiotape, perhaps) and compare their responses to your response to the same question. Present your results and conclusions in a short essay (2–3 pages). Or videotape the responses and present the videotape in class.

4. Write a critical review (2–3 pages) of the content and rhetorical structure of the Howard Blum "bias incident" essay. How much must you infer from what Blum does not report? What questions do you have for the adults in the New Dorp Beach neighborhood? For the teenagers? How is it possible for these participants from New Dorp Beach to reconcile the police reports and smashed school buses with their rhetoric, with their view of what happened?

5. Write a journal entry (about 250 words) about what you know of your own ethnic identity and the identity of the men and women in the community you consider home. What role models helped or hindered your development of a sense of personal identity? How easy or difficult is it for you to identify with your ancestors? Is their ethnic identity lost in the past or very much a part of your community and family?

6. Write a journal entry (about 150 words) on the topic of "Shades of Black." What did you already know about color and identity within the community Mebane describes? What did you learn from discussing, reading, and writing about this subject? What would you like to know about the issue of community standards of attractiveness that Mebane's essay did not provide?

Keep in mind that these short writings in your journal can be the starting point for extended essays.

7. Write a response to the issue of identity and ethnicity using two or three (or more if you wish) selections in this chapter which suggest to you similar or contrasting ideas. Use your summary writing and reading journal entries to develop your response.

8. If the subject interests you, research information on those refugees from Haiti who tried to reach the United States in the early 1990s, mostly by boat. This flood of refugees presented quite a dilemma for the U.S. government at the time; newspapers and magazines carried extensive reports of the refugees and the problems they left behind in Haiti. Compare the life the refugees left behind to the life they found in the United States. See also Joel Dreyfuss's article, "The Invisible Immigrants," in Chapter 5, page 282, for information on the history of immigrants from Haiti.

9

Telling Stories, Revealing Cultures

◆

Our stories are always written against two possible evils: that they will make no sense at all, or that they will make sense but of an unendurable kind.

James Boyd White, *Heracles' Bow*

William Carlos Williams once said to Robert Coles (in a conversation about telling stories) that, "their story, yours, mine—it's what we all carry with us on this trip we take, and we owe it to each other to respect our stories and learn from them."[1] Coles, who, like Williams, used doctors' narratives to help medical students learn about medical ethics and patients' needs, agreed. Of the power of stories, he says: "A compelling narrative, offering a storyteller's moral imagination vigorously at work, can enable any of us to learn by example, to take to heart what is, really, a gift of grace."[2] The "gift of grace" Coles refers to is the recognition of oppression as a result of connecting with a storyteller's moral imagination. He illustrates what he means by telling a story, describing a group of rather cynical young adults who, despite their cynicism, were "powerfully affected by [Tillie] Olsen's capacity to give her readers pause." Her stories, he reports, "worked their way into the everyday reality of their young lives: Watching their mothers iron, and thinking of a story; watching a certain heavy-drinking friend, relative, neighbor, and thinking of a story; watching children in church, and themselves in school, and thinking of a story."[3]

James Boyd White claims further that telling stories is a "fundamental characteristic of human life" and that the need to tell stories

---

[1] Quoted in Robert Coles, *The Call of Stories: Teaching and the Moral Imagination* (Boston: Houghton Mufflin, 1989), p. 30.

[2] Ibid, p. 191.

[3] Ibid, p. 57.

may be "the deepest need of that part of our nature that marks us as human beings, as the kind of animal that seeks for meaning."[4] This human need to tell our stories, we believe, is not confined to particular ethnic groups. Whatever the ethnic group, whatever the gender, whatever the class, people tell stories. They make up stories, they report stories, they communicate their innermost feelings in stories. They pass on traditions, they report the news or research findings. They teach by telling stories and reveal something about their communities to others.

As Robert Coles suggests, *reading* stories, whether about us or others, often helps us connect to something previously unrealized about ourselves, something we may not even dream of otherwise. So, as we have done throughout this book, in this final chapter we offer stories about critical issues in contemporary culture—through a mix of voices telling specific stories in a variety of forms (short story, news story, news interview, essay).

The first two stories are about people who "came out" in different ways. First, David Broder tells a story of being in New York attending a play. The audience at the play that night was made up of mostly gay men and women, in town to attend the "Gay Games," an international athletic competition for gay men and women. This audience raucously celebrated their "outing" (release) from the closet, cheering and applauding the actors and action as the play unfolded. Next, Carolyn Pittman describes her struggle to reveal her sexual orientation while still in college.

Valerie Matsumoto and Jamaica Kincaid both tell us stories about gardens. Matsumoto's narrator tells a story of sexual oppression that is difficult to confront because the oppressor is a friend's husband. But she does confront him, finally, by showing him what happens to predators in her garden (scorpions)—and, by analogy, what might happen to him. Jamaica Kincaid raises the question of another kind of oppression, of one class by another. She tells us about Antigua, her native country, about Antiguans, about gardens and the British slave owners' cultivation of lawns, plants, and trees. Kincaid has no love of gardens and manicured lawns and does not cultivate lawns around her present home in Vermont. At issue here is the caretaking of lawns, gardens, and crops by working-class men and women for the benefit of a much more leisured class of people.

The next narratives concern African-American communities. Louis Farrakhan tells his story—in a news interview with Sylvester Monroe—in response to an outcry against the Nation of Islam because of public statements about Jews by representatives of that religious

---

[4]James Boyd White, "Telling Stories in the Law and in Ordinary Life," *Heracles' Bow: Essays on the Rhetoric and Poetics of the Law* (Madison, WI: University of Wisconsin Press, 1985) p. 169.

group. These statements resulted in strained relations between leaders in both communities. Leading writers and scholars then respond to Farrakhan's remarks.

The final story of this chapter and the book is about mother and daughter relationships. In Tillie Olsen's "I Stand Here Ironing," a mother looks back on all the things that went wrong as she raised her first child. She reviews what she might have done better to shape the character and personality of her daughter Emily. She understands, but still regrets, that not everything was in her power to change; she did the best she could as a single mother who received very little help from the community.

Review of Reading and Writing Activities

Before responding to the reading selections in this chapter, we recommend that you review the reading strategies presented in Chapters 2 through 8 and note strategies that seem useful. You might note, in particular, sets of questions that help you analyze what you are reading (see Chapter 4, page 179) or sets of questions that help you think about what the writer is doing (rhetorically) in the text you are reading, especially before or after transition points (see Chapter 5, page 231). Think about yourself as composer as you read (see Chapter 8, page 433, for a discussion of readers as composers). We also recommend that you review the directions for reading and writing activities following each chapter, if you happen to be *beginning* the book with this final chapter. Following each reading in this chapter, we only list the activities (spelled out in earlier chapters) for integrating reading and writing. Although these activities are presented here in a numbered list, critical questions can be asked at any time during reading, free writing can occur early or late in a reader's process, discussion can also occur early or late, and revision is ongoing as you read and write your way to what may not be the end of your response to a given issue—it's only an end for now.

David Broder

Gay Pride Claims a Place in U.S. Politics

———————◆———————

David Broder is a syndicated columnist for the Washington Post. *The following selection appeared after the "Gay Games" took place in New York, in June 1994. This sports event gave gay men and lesbian women an opportunity to gather in a massive public display of support for one another.*

1   To be a heterosexual male in parts of New York last weekend was to find yourself, maybe for the first time, part of a minority. It was not an unpleasant experience, but it certainly was different.

2   My visit was scheduled around a performance by an actor-director son at an Off-Broadway playhouse. It was only in the last few days beforehand that I realized that the city was playing host to the Gay Games, an international athletic competition that attracted more than 20,000 participants, and a march by 100,000 people to Central Park, marking "Gay Pride Day."

3   The weekend celebrated the 25th anniversary of "the Stonewall Rebellion," an incident in a Greenwich Village bar, where homosexuals fought back against police harassment, giving a symbolic start to the gay liberation movement.

4   New York is big enough that all this could have been going on out of my sight—except for one thing. Our plans for the weekend included joining my son and his wife at the Saturday evening performance of *Angels in America—Perestroika*, the second part of Tony Kushner's award-winning drama.

5   The first part, which we had seen together last year, had been one of the great theater experiences of a lifetime, and the sense of anticipation about the evening was very high.

6   The Walter Kerr theater was largely filled when we walked over from our dinner restaurant, and it was instantly evident that Mr. Kushner's "gay fantasia on national themes," as he describes his play, was a hot-ticket item for the Stonewall anniversary visitors.

7   The audience was at least 90 percent male and the two generations of Broders were perhaps 10 percent of the heterosexual couples in the theater.

An important, and amusing, side-effect: At the end of the very long 8
opening act, the line to the men's room was endless, while the women
came and went with great dispatch—exactly the opposite of the usual
pattern.

But that was the least of the role-reversals. 9

In covering politics, you become accustomed to being the outsider, 10
set aside by race, religion, regional origin or motivation from the vast
majority of others in the room, whether it be at a Jesse Jackson rally, a
George Wallace campaign event or a Moral Majority meeting. You learn
to shed—or disguise—any self-consciousness and do your best to listen
and note clearly what the others are saying.

What was instantly remarkable about this theater audience was 11
that its reaction to the play and the actors was as profoundly political
as that of the Jackson or Wallace or Falwell crowds.

Like them, these men thought of themselves as an oppressed 12
minority, and their anger needed expression. Any speech, any line, that
contained a putdown of "straight" conventions or attitudes or asser-
tions of authority—and there are a lot of them in the script—was
greeted with hoots of delight and raucous cheers.

Some of these jokes were good, and I wanted to laugh. But in the 13
face of this reaction, anything as mild as a laugh seemed out-of-place.

At the matinee performance at which we'd seen the first half of the 14
play, called *Millennium Approaches,* my impression was that same-sex
and mixed-sex couples were both well-represented and the humor
seemed to be going over equally well with both.

This Saturday night, the audience's intensity—its urge to react as 15
if the play were a polemic—changed the tone, threw off the actors'
timing (or so it seemed to me) and broke the rhythm of Mr. Kushner's
dialogue.

But nothing can overcome genius, and *Angels in America* is so over- 16
whelmingly a work of genius that it leaves you breathless with wonder.
Every one of the characters Tony Kushner has created is utterly convincing, from the three young gay men at the center of the story to the
marvelous woman one of them introduces as "my former lover's
lover's Mormon mother."

Beyond these brave, funny and addled people, Mr. Kushner's 17
extraordinary imagination has incorporated a kaleidoscope of cultural
and historical references—from Jacob wrestling with the Angel, to Roy
Cohn and the Rosenberg case, to the final scene of the Wizard of Oz—
all familiar parts of our national experience, but marvelously transformed by his antic gay perspective.

The dark undercurrent of the drama is, of course, the AIDS epi- 18
demic, and in the final scene, when Stephen Spinella as the stricken
Prior vows that he and his friends will no longer go silently to their

fate, shut away or scorned, everyone in the theater—straight, gay, whatever—was breathless with poignancy and the courage of his thin voice.

19   Then the place exploded, and the curtain calls kept coming, one after another, with the actors responding to the cheers by applauding those who would be marching the next day, and signaling with clenched fists their solidarity.

20   And you knew, at that moment, how lucky you had been to be there that night, on the 25th anniversary of Stonewall—an evening when another group of Americans were claiming their place in our culture and politics.

Carolyn S. Pittman

Do They Hear Our Voices?

◆

Carolyn S. Pittman is a graduate student in the M.A. program at the University of North Carolina at Wilmington. She returned to school after serving in the military and working at a variety of jobs in the public sector. Pittman presented the following selection at the College Composition and Communication Conference *in San Diego in April 1993.*

As a recent college graduate, I guess it is typical to spend some 1 time reflecting over past undergraduate classes. What isn't typical, perhaps, is that I'm a lesbian. Upon first returning for my degree after twenty years of working various jobs, I thought I had to shield my sexual identity from the heterosexual mainstream of the university just as I had to shield it in the working world. However, professors called for me to write from my experiences—to develop the material in a manner in which I could give it meaning. Recognizing that I could express my thoughts and opinions without "shading" my experiences as a lesbian did not come easily. I can still remember how difficult it was for me as a student of a small Southern college to write freely in the beginning. Let me illustrate what I mean by drawing from my experiences in two classes. In the first class, a freshman composition course taken in my first semester, I did not reveal my sexual identity. In the second class, a linguistics course that examined language and gender, I felt sufficiently confident of my identity to come out—at least in that particular class.

In the freshman English class, when I wrote an essay, "The Beauty 2 Myth: Reflections in a Distorted Mirror," I thought that to include my sexual orientation as part of the beauty dilemma would distract from the issue by placing me in a subcategory of women. Further, I felt that my personal conflict in trying to obtain either a sense of self or femininity would be dismissed altogether because of misconceptions about lesbians. Therefore, I believed I had to write a paper that would read realistically to the heterosexual without disclosing the underlying feelings of the homosexual. But once I began writing, I realized that this need to disguise my identity was making it difficult to develop my essay. This need was affecting both the content and style, for I found myself coming back to weigh words, meanings, and ideas.

Consequently, I developed my essay in what I thought were general 3 and rather awkward terms. I wrote, "The pressure to conform to the traditional woman's role was constantly upon me. However, I still rejected

499

the lifestyle of my mother and of other women I knew. I believed that as a woman I could be self-sustaining. My identity was independence." At least these statements appeared general to me because I couldn't give specifics. When I wrote about being self-sustaining, I really meant sustaining a gay lifestyle and that my identity is that of a lesbian.

4   Consider the wording in what follows: ". . . Place me in a room with any number of women, their femininity emanating from their presence, and I am immediately insecure, self-conscious, and inadequate. Demeaning myself through comparisons, I leave the room with all aspects of my identity depleted." I had a terrible time committing myself to this.

5   What I wanted to say was that I become insecure and self-conscious among women because I have been conditioned to see femininity as an ingrained characteristic of heterosexuality and the lack of it as a stereotypical trait of lesbians. I am resistant to the stereotypes of femininity, but to be unfeminine accentuates my difference from other women.

6   Similarly, in showing the social pressures on women to be feminine, I wrote: "Because I could not fit the feminine role, I was tagged a tomboy by the first and subsequent boys I chose to have a crush on." Now in my mind, we don't choose our crushes—we either have one or we don't. But I couldn't make myself rewrite the text as "the boys I *had* a crush on." Instead, I thought the heterosexual reader would take 'chose' to imply 'picked', as girls do tend to pick out potential boyfriends, and if so, all would be well since my sexual identity was not disclosed.

7   I may not have contemplated this dilemma further were it not for taking an upper-level class the following semester. In this course, I studied semantic concepts which prompted me to reflect upon my freshman composition paper. And as I connected these concepts with "The Beauty Myth," I realized the dilemma had been more than one of disguising parts of my identity.

8   Consequently, for semantics, I wrote a paper titled "Heterosexual Maps/Homosexual Territories" that examines from my lesbian viewpoint the relationship of rhetoric and reality. Alfred Korzybski claims that most of our knowledge is received verbally, whether from parents, friends, literature, television, etc.—and constitutes our verbal world. Yet the knowledge that comes to us through our own experiences constitutes the actual world. Therefore, he stresses the importance of having these two worlds match—just as a map should represent the territory, rhetoric should represent the reality. In addition, Korzybski states that "by means of imaginary or false reports or by false inferences from good reports or by mere rhetorical exercises, [we] can manufacture at will, with language 'maps' that have no reference to the [actual] world."

9   Now these principles can create difficulty even in a heterosexual world, but I stepped out into a homosexual territory carrying an inher-

ited heterosexual map, and I am still wandering around in circles trying to figure out my identity within the confusion of crossed maps and territories. For example, let me tell you about a lie-detector test. Homosexual marriages were not accepted by society in the early seventies, and it happened that during this time I was asked to take a lie-detector test for a job I held. One of the questions on the test was, "Have you ever been married?"

Twice I answered, "No." But both times the machine registered that 10 I was lying. Now, I was in a relationship at the time, but I was not legally married—nor had I ever been married. And as far as I was concerned, marriage was a word without meaning in a homosexual world. But the concept of marriage apparently had affective connotations where I was concerned. Associating my relationship with the same feelings of commitment and sharing a life as I attribute to a legalized, heterosexual marriage, my feeling about the response to the question, "Have you ever been married?," in reality, was "yes." Therefore, when I answered "no" to what I saw as a legal reality the machine recorded my response as a lie. Luckily, the test administrator chose not to delve farther into my apparent deception in this case but, considering the cultural climate of the time, the conflict that appeared between the map and its territory—the word 'marriage' and my experiences—could easily have jeopardized my position within the firm.

Earlier, perhaps my struggle over the use of the word 'chose' in the 11 freshman essay seemed exaggerated. But, as shown in the lie-detector example, my quandary was logical because I tried to match the verbal world to my lesbian experiences even though I was writing for a heterosexual audience. Even prior to understanding my sexuality, I never had a crush on a boy. Yet, if I wanted to fit in with my girlfriends, it seemed important that I have one. So I would decide on a boy who appeared to be the most disinterested in me and profess to my friends that I had a crush on him. I carefully and deliberately 'chose' my boyfriends. Consequently, if I had written the "boys I *had* a crush on," the rhetoric and the reality would not have matched.

And there were other conflicts that arose in trying to write the 12 freshman essay. A central source for this essay, Naomi Wolf's view of the beauty myth, is based on a heterosexual concept of women's societal roles, which, from a lesbian perspective, becomes yet another map that does not match the territory. I'm certainly not oblivious to Wolf's point that women are pressured to conform to a beauty ideal which is oriented towards males. But nevertheless, since I don't relate to men with the same emotional focus as I perceive in heterosexual women, I'm not sure that my experiences are comparable with theirs. I do have a conflict with femininity and I, too, feel a social pressure to be more feminine. However, the truth is that this pressure derives from my concern with being accepted by other women and not feeling isolated due to a lesbian stereotype. Therefore, as I constructed the freshman essay, I shuffled the two realities.

13   Similarly, trying to illustrate the beauty dilemma, I wrote the following: "The psychological pressures within society to conform to the beauty role leaves few women unaffected. Even women trying to develop a self-image outside of the beauty myth are unable to evade its overwhelming presence. Women who cannot or choose not to identify with the myth, have their lack of an identity peering back at them in every other woman they encounter." Perhaps this statement does serve well to exemplify the feelings of women in general, but I felt very constricted as I worked it out because I knew my thoughts stemmed primarily from my lesbian experiences. And because of this awareness, I was constantly concerned with what identity was coming through.

14   In contrast, even though the linguistics essay deals with the subject of homosexuality which I felt I could not disclose in "The Beauty Myth," I found the paper much easier to write. Since my audience was examining the same information and my data seemed relevant to the issue, the content allowed for more openness on my part. Not having to deal with a conflict between my words and my experiences, I decided to reflect on the difficulty I had in composing my freshman essay. Focusing on how "The Beauty Myth" was the first paper that I inwardly struggled with because of confusion between the heterosexual and homosexual connotations of certain words, I wrote:

15   "So I sit for hours with my pen in hand and debate how a heterosexual person will interpret the sentence, "I was labeled 'different' by my girlfriends," in comparison to, "I was labeled 'queer' (or gay) by my girlfriends." As Robin Lakoff would say, "It's just semantics!" But is it not heterosexual semantics trying to be understood from a homosexual rationale? And if it is—I am no longer sure that I'm not just playing connotational games with myself."

16   Finally, in composing these essays, I realize that I am very conscious of the word choices and the images that I work to develop within my papers. The awareness of who and what I am, and how I present that, and how it is accepted is an integral part of where I am in my own development of a sense of self. Further, I believe that it is somehow related to the woman's voice and the desire for bonding through language, in that I have always considered writing to be my one recourse to honest communication between myself and others. It is how I present myself, in the past, in the present, and hopefully in the future.

Reading and Writing Activities

1. Note your reactions during your first reading(s) to Carolyn Pittman's "Do They Hear Our Voices?"

2. Discuss these reactions in groups, if possible.
3. Freewrite after reconsidering the reading.
4. Write a preliminary analysis of the reading—note the parts that relate to the whole, transition points, clues to topic shifts, and details of audience, purpose, structure and development of meaning. You may want to review, at this point, sets of analytic questions and questions about what the writer is doing (rhetorically) in Chapters 4–7.
5. From preliminary analytic work, write a summary analysis.
6. Compare summaries in discussion groups, if possible.
7. Reconsider and revise summaries.
8. Think of three or four central questions you have about this reading.
9. Write the questions and present them in your reading groups. Compare your questions; answer as many from each group member as appropriate.

Valerie Matsumoto

Two Deserts

———————◆———————

Like Hispanic Americans, Asian Americans represent a number of separate cultures—Chinese, Japanese, Korean, Filipino, South Asian, and Southeast Asian. The following story describes the experience of a Japanese American, formerly a victim of the American internment during World War II. The author, Valerie Matsumoto, holds a doctorate in American history and teaches at UCLA. "Two Deserts" appeared originally in Making Waves: An Anthology of Writings by and About Asian American Women, *published in 1989.*

1   Emiko Oyama thought the Imperial Valley of California was the loneliest place she had ever seen. It was just like the Topaz Relocation Camp, she told her husband, Kiyo, but without the barbed wire fence and crowded barracks. Miles of bleached desert, punctuated sparsely by creosote bush and debris, faced her from almost every window in their small house. Only the living room had a view of the dirt road which ended in front of their home, and across it, a row of squat, faded houses where other farmers' families lived. They waved to her and Kiyo in passing, and Jenny played with the Garcia children, but Emiko's Spanish and their English were too limited for more than casual greetings.

2   Emiko felt a tug of anticipation on the day the moving van pulled up to the Ishikawa's place across the road—the house which in her mind had become inextricably linked with friendship. She had felt its emptiness as her own when Sats, Yuki, and their three children gave up farming and departed for a life which later came to her in delicious fragments in Yuki's hastily scrawled letters. Yuki made the best sushi rice in the world and had given her the recipe. She could draw shy Kiyo into happy banter. And her loud warm laugh made the desert seem less drab, less engulfing.

3   The morning of moving day Emiko had been thinking about Yuki as she weeded the yard and vegetable plot in preparation for planting. Sats and Yuki had advised her to plant marigolds around the vegetables to keep away nematodes, and she liked the idea of a bold orange border. Emiko liked bright colors, especially the flaming scarlet of the bougainvillea which rose above the front door, where Kiki their cat lay sunning himself. There was a proud look in those amber eyes, for Kiki the hunter had slain three scorpions and laid them in a row on the

porch, their backs crushed and deadly stingers limp, winning extravagant praise from Jenny and Emiko. The scorpions still lay there, at Jenny's insistence, awaiting Kiyo's return that evening. Emiko shuddered every time she entered the house, glancing at the curved stingers and thinking of Jenny's sandaled feet.

Emiko had finished weeding the front border and was about to go inside to escape the heat, when she saw the new neighbor woman plodding across the sand toward her. A cotton shift could not conceal her thinness, nor a straw hat her tousled gray curls. Her eyes were fragile lilac glass above a wide smile.

"Hello, I'm Mattie Barnes. I just thought I'd come over and introduce myself while Roy is finishing up with the movers. Your bougainvillea caught my eye first thing, and I thought, 'Those are some folks who know what will grow in the desert.' I hope you'll give me some advice about what to plant in my yard once we get settled in."

They talked about adjusting to desert life and Emiko learned that Mattie's husband Roy had recently retired. "We decided to move here because the doctor said it would be better for my lungs," Mattie explained, wiping her brow.

"Would you like a glass of lemonade?" Emiko offered. "Or maybe later, after you've finished moving."

"Oh, I'd love something cold," Mattie said, adding vaguely, "Roy will take care of everything—he's more particular about those things then I am."

Emiko led Mattie into the house, hoping that Jenny was not lying on the cool linoleum, stripped to her underwear. As she crossed the threshold, Mattie gave a shriek and stopped abruptly, eyeing the scorpions lined up neatly on the porch.

"What on earth are these things doing here?"

"Our cat killed them," Emiko said, feeling too foolish to admit her pride in Kiki's prowess. "Jenny wants me to leave them to show her father when he comes home from the field."

"Awful creatures," Mattie shuddered. "Roy can't stand them, but then he can't abide insects. He said to me this morning, 'Of all the places we could have moved to, we had to choose the buggiest.'"

There was no buggier place than the Imperial Valley, Emiko agreed, especially in the summer when the evening air was thick with mosquitoes, gnats, and moths, and cicadas buzzed in deafening chorus from every tree. They danced in frenzied legions around the porch light and did kamikaze dives into the bath water, and all of them came in dusty gray hordes, as though the desert had sapped their color, but not their energy. And late at night, long after Kiyo had fallen into exhausted sleep, Emiko would lie awake, perspiring, listening to the tinny scrabble of insects trapped between the window glass and screen.

14 "...but I like the desert," Mattie was saying, dreamily clinking the ice cubes in her glass. "It's so open and peaceful. As long as I can have a garden, I'll be happy."

15 Within a few weeks after their arrival, the Barneses had settled into a routine: Roy made daily trips to the local store and the Roadside Cafe; Mattie tended her garden and walked to church once a week with Emiko and Jenny. By the end of June, Mattie had been enlisted with Emiko to make crepe paper flowers for the church bazaar.

16 "My, your flowers turned out beautifully," Mattie exclaimed one morning, looking wistfully at the cardboard box filled with pink, yellow, scarlet, and lavender blossoms set on wire stems. "They'll make lovely corsages." She sighed. "I seem to be all thumbs—my flowers hardly look like flowers. I don't know how you do it. You Japanese are just very artistic people."

17 Emiko smiled and shook her head making a polite disclaimer. But the bright blur of flowers suddenly dissolved into another mass of paper blooms, carrying her more than a decade into the past. She was a teenager in a flannel shirt and denim pants with rolled cuffs, seated on a cot in a cramped barrack room, helping her mother fashion flowers from paper. Her own hands had been clumsy at first, though she strived to imitate her mother's precise fingers which gave each fragile petal lifelike curves, the look of artless grace. The only flowers for elderly Mr. Wasaka, shot by a guard in Topaz, were those which bloomed from the fingertips of issei and nisei women, working late into the night to complete the exquisite wreaths for his funeral. Each flower was a silent voice crying with color, each flower a tear.

18 "I did a little flower making as a teenager," Emiko said.

19 "Will you come over and show me how?" Mattie asked. "I'm too embarrassed to take these awful things, and I've still got lots of crepe paper spread all over the kitchen."

20 "Sure," Emiko nodded. "I'll help you get started and you'll be a whiz in no time. It isn't too hard; it just takes patience."

21 Mattie smiled, a slight wheeze in her voice when she said, "I've got plenty of that, too."

22 They were seated at the Barnes's small table, surrounded by bright masses of petals like fallen butterflies, their fingers sticky from the florist tape, when Roy returned from shopping. When he saw Emiko, he straightened and pulled his belt up over his paunch.

23 "A sight for sore eyes!" he boomed, giving her a broad wink. "What mischief are you ladies up to?"

24 "Emi's teaching me how to make flowers," Mattie explained, holding up a wobbly rose.

25 "Always flowers! I tell you," he leaned over Emiko's chair and said in a mock conspiratorial voice, "all my wife thinks about is flowers. I keep telling her there are other things in life. Gardening is for old folks."

"And what's wrong with that?" Mattie protested, waving her   26
flower at him. "We *are* old folks."

"Speak for yourself," he winked at Emiko again. "What's so great   27
about gardens, anyway?"

"I hold with the poem that says you're closest to God's heart in a   28
garden," said Mattie.

"Well, I'm not ready to get that close to God's heart, yet." There   29
was defiance in Roy's voice. "What do you think about that, Emi?"

"I like working in the yard before it gets too hot," she said carefully.   30
Her words felt tight and deliberate, like the unfurled petals on the yellow rose in her hands. "I don't have Mattie's talent with real flowers,
though—aside from the bougainvillea and Jenny's petunias, nothing
ever seems to bloom. The soil is too dry and saline for the things I used
to grow. Now I've got my hopes pinned on the vegetable garden."

"Vegetables—hmph!" Roy snorted, stomping off to read the paper.   31

"Oh, that Roy is just like a boy sometimes," Mattie said. "I tell you,   32
don't ever let your husband retire or you'll find him underfoot all day
long."

"Doesn't Roy have any hobbies?" Emiko thought of her father and   33
his books, his Japanese brush painting, his meetings.

"He used to play golf," Mattie said, "but there's no golf course   34
here. He says this town is one giant sand trap."

"There have been times when I felt that way, too," Emiko admitted   35
lightly.

"Well, don't let Roy hear you say that or you'll never get him off   36
the topic," Mattie chuckled. "The fact is, Roy doesn't much know how
to be by himself. I've had forty years to learn, and I've gotten to like it.
And I suppose maybe he will, too."

Her voice trailed off, and Emiko suddenly realized that Mattie   37
didn't much care whether he did or not.

One day while Emiko was engrossed in pinning a dress pattern   38
for Jenny, she suddenly heard a tapping on the screen, like the scrab-
bling of a large beetle. She half turned and felt a jolt of alarm at the
sight of a grinning gargoyle hunched before the window. It was Roy,
his nose pushed up against the glass, hands splayed open on either
side of his face, the caricature of a boy peering covetously into a toy-
store.

"Hey there! I caught you daydreaming!" he chortled. "Looks to me   39
like you need some company to wake you up."

"I'm not daydreaming; I'm trying to figure out how to make a two-   40
and-a-half yard dress out of two yards," she said. "Jenny is growing so
fast, I can hardly keep up with her."

Roy walked into the house unbidden, confident of a welcome, and   41
drew a chair up to the table. He fingered the bright cotton print spread
over the table and gazed at Emiko, his head cocked to one side.

42   "You must get pretty lonesome here by yourself all day. No wonder you're sitting here dreaming."

43   "No," she said, her fingers moving the pattern pieces. "There's so much to do, I don't have time to be lonesome. Besides, Jenny is here, and Kiyo comes home for lunch."

44   "But still—cooped up with a kiddie all day." Roy shook his head. He chose to disregard Kiyo, who had no place in his imagined scenarios, and was hard at work miles away.

45   Emiko delicately edged the cotton fabric away from Roy's damp, restless fingers. "I'll be darned if I offer him something to drink," she thought, as he mopped his brow and cast an impatient glance at the kitchen. "I haven't seen Mattie outside this week. How is she feeling?"

46   "Oh, 'bout the same, 'bout the same," he said, his irritation subsiding into resignation. "She has her good days and her bad days. The doctor told her to stay in bed for awhile and take it easy."

47   "It must be hard on Mattie, having to stay indoors," Emiko said, thinking of her peering out through the pale curtains at the wilting zinnias and the new weeds in the backyard.

48   "I suppose so—usually you can't tear Mattie away from her garden." Roy shook his head. "Mattie and me are real different. Now, I like people—I've always been the sociable type—but Mattie! All she cares about are plants."

49   "Well, Kiyo and I have different interests," Emiko said, "but it works out well that way. Maybe you could learn a few things from Mattie about plants."

50   Even as the suggestion passed her lips, she regretted saying it. Roy viewed the garden as the site of onerous labor. To Mattie, it was the true world of the heart, with no room for ungentle or impatient hands. It was a place of deeply sown hopes, lovingly nurtured, and its colors were the colors of unspoken dreams.

51   "Plants!" Roy threw up his hands. "Give me people any time. I always liked people and had a knack for working with them—that's how I moved up in the business."

52   "Why don't you look into some of the clubs here?" Emiko tried again. "The Elks always need people with experience and time."

53   "Sweetheart, I'm going to spend my time the way I want. I'm finished with work—it's time to enjoy life! Besides, how much fun can I have with a bunch of old geezers? That's not for me, Emily, my dear." She stiffened as he repeated the name, savoring the syllables. "Emily... Emily... Yes, I like the sound of that—Emily."

54   "My name is Emiko," she said quietly, her eyes as hard as agate. "I was named after my grandmother." That unfaltering voice had spoken the same words in first, second, third, fourth, fifth, and sixth grades. All the grammar school teachers had sought to change her name, to make her into an Emily: "Emily is so much easier to pronounce, dear, and it's a nice American name." She was such a well-mannered child,

the teachers were always amazed at her stubbornness on this one point. Sometimes she was tempted to relent, to give in, but something inside her resisted. "My name is Emiko," she would insist politely. I am an American named Emiko. I was named for my grandmother who was beautiful and loved to swim. When she emerged from the sea, her long black hair would glitter white with salt. I never met her, but she was beautiful and she would laugh when she rose from the waves. "My name is Emiko; Emi for short."

"But Emily is such a pretty name," Roy protested. "It fits you." 55

"It's not my name," she said, swallowing a hard knot of anger. "I 56 don't like to be called Emily!"

"Temper, temper!" He shook his finger at her, gleeful at having pro- 57 voked her.

"Well, I guess I'll be in a better temper when I can get some work 58 done," she said, folding up the cloth with tense, deliberate hands. She raised her voice. "Jenny! Let's go out and water the vegetable garden now."

If Jenny thought this a strange task in the heat of the afternoon, it 59 did not show in her face when she skipped out of her room, swinging her straw hat. It still sported a flimsy, rainbow-hued scarf which had been the subject of much pleading in an El Centro dime store. At that moment, Emiko found it an oddly reassuring sight. She smiled and felt her composure return.

"Tell Mattie to let me know if there's anything I can do to help," she 60 told Roy, as he unwillingly followed them out of the house and trudged away across the sand. After they went back inside, Emiko, for the first time, locked the door behind them. When Kiyo returned home, his face taut with fatigue, she told him it was because of the hoboes who came around.

Emiko went to see Mattie less and less frequently, preferring 61 instead to call her on the phone, even though they lived so close. Roy, however, continued to drop by, despite Emiko's aloofness. His un-seemly yearning tugged at her with undignified hands, but what he craved most was beyond her power to give. She took to darning and mending in the bedroom with the curtains drawn, ignoring his insis-tent knock; she tried to do her gardening in the evening after dinner when her husband was home, but it was hard to weed in the dusk. She was beginning to feel caged, pent up, restless. Jenny and Kiyo trod qui-etly, puzzled by her edginess, but their solicitude only made her feel worse.

Finally one morning Emiko decided to weed the vegetables, 62 sprouting new and tender. Surely the midmorning heat would discour-age any interference. Although perspiration soon trickled down her face, she began to enjoy the satisfying rhythm of the work. She was so engrossed she did not notice when Roy Barnes unlatched the gate and stepped into the yard, a determined twinkle in his faded eye.

63   "Howdy, Emi! I saw you working away out here by your lonesome and thought maybe you could use some help."

64   "Thanks, but I'm doing all right," she said, wrenching a clump of puncture vine from the soil and laying it in the weed box careful to avoid scattering the sharp stickers. Jenny was close by, digging at her petunias and marigolds, ignoring Mr. Barnes, who had no place in the colorful jungle she was imagining.

65   "If I had a pretty little wife, I sure wouldn't let her burn up out here, no sir." His voice nudged at her as she squatted on the border of the vegetable plot. If Mattie looked out of the window, she would see only a pleasant tableau: Roy nodding in neighborly fashion as Emiko pointed out young rows of zucchini and yellow squash, watermelon, cantaloupe, eggplant, and tomatoes. Mattie would not see the strain on Emiko's face, which she turned away when Roy leaned over and mumbled, "Say, you know what I like best in this garden?"

66   Emiko grabbed the handle of the shovel and stood up before he could tell her, moving away from him to pluck a weed. "I know Mattie likes cantaloupe," she said. "So do I. Kiyo prefers Crenshaws, but I couldn't find any seeds this year. What do you and Mattie have in your garden?"

67   "Just grass," he said, undeterred. "Mattie's always fussing over her flowers—you know what she's like," he chuckled indulgently. "But I'd rather spend my time doing other things than slaving in the yard."

68   Emiko hacked away at the stubborn clumps of grass roots and the persistent runners with myriad finer roots, thread-thin, but tough as wire. She worked with desperate energy, flustered, her gloved hands sweating on the shovel handle, forehead damp. She was groping for the language to make him understand, to make him leave her in peace, but he was bent on not understanding, not seeing, not leaving until he got what he wanted.

69   "You know what, Emi?" He moistened his dry lips, beginning to grin reminiscently. "You remind me of somebody I met in Tokyo. Have you ever been to Tokyo?"

70   "No," she said, digging hard. "Never."

71   "You'd like it; it's a wonderful place, so clean and neat, and the people so friendly. When I was in Tokyo, I met up with the cutest geisha girl you ever saw—just like a little doll. She'd never seen anybody with blue eyes before, and couldn't get over it." He chuckled. "I couldn't think who you reminded me of at first, and then it just hit me that you are the spitting image of her."

72   "Did Mattie like Tokyo, too?" Emiko said, continuing to spade vigorously, as his eyes slid over her, imagining a doll in exotic robes.

73   "She didn't go—it was a business trip," he said impatiently. Then his voice relaxed into a drawl, heavy with insinuation. "After all, I like to do some things on my own." He was moving closer again.

74   Then she saw it. Emiko had just turned over a rock, and as she raised the shovel, it darted from its refuge, pincers up, the deadly tail curved menacingly over the carapaced back. It moved a little to the left and then the right, beginning the poison dance. Emiko glanced to see where Jenny was and saw Roy jump back hastily; the scorpion, startled by his movement, scuttled sideways toward Jenny, who lay on her stomach, still dreaming of her jungle.

75   The blood pounded in Emiko's head. She brought down the shovel hard with one quick breath, all her rage shooting down the thick handle into the heavy crushing iron. She wielded the shovel like a samurai in battle, swinging it down with all her force, battering her enemy to dust. Once had been enough, but she struck again and again, until her anger was spent, and she leaned on the rough handle, breathing hard.

76   "Mommy! What did you do?" Jenny had scrambled to Emiko's side. There was fear in her eyes as she gazed at the unrecognizable fragments in the dirt.

77   "I killed a scorpion," Emiko said. She scornfully tossed the remains into the weed box, and wiped her brow on her arm, like a farmer, or a warrior. "I don't like to kill anything," she said aloud, "but sometimes you have to."

78   Roy Barnes recoiled from the pitiless knowledge in her eyes. He saw her clearly now, but it was too late. His mouth opened and closed, but the gush of words had gone dry. He seemed to age before her eyes, like Urashima-taro who opened the precious box of youth and was instantly wrinkled and broken by the unleashed tide of years.

79   "You'll have to leave now, Mr. Barnes. I'm going in to fix lunch." Emiko's smile was quiet as unsheathed steel. "Tell Mattie I hope she's feeling better."

80   She watched him pick his way across the dirt, avoiding the puncture vine and rusted tin cans, and looking as gray as the rags that bleached beneath the fierce sun. Jenny stared past him and the small houses of their neighborhood, to the desert sand beyond, glittering like an ocean with shards of mica.

81   "Do you think we might ever find gold?" she asked.

82   They gazed together over the desert, full of unknown perils and ancient secrets, the dust of dreams and battles.

83   "Maybe." Emiko stood tall, shading her eyes from the deceptive shimmer. "Maybe."

Reading and Writing Activities

1. Note your reactions during your first reading(s) to Valerie Matsumoto's "Two Deserts."
2. Discuss these reactions in groups, if possible.

3. Freewrite after reconsidering the reading.
4. Write a preliminary analysis of the reading—note the parts that relate to the whole, transition points, clues to topic shifts, and details of audience, purpose, structure and development of meaning. You may want to review, at this point, sets of analytic questions and questions about what the writer is doing (rhetorically) in Chapters 4–7.
5. From preliminary analytic work, write a summary analysis.
6. Compare summaries in discussion groups, if possible.
7. Reconsider and revise summaries.
8. Think of three or four central questions you have about this reading.
9. Write the questions and present them in your reading groups. Compare your questions; answer as many from each group member as appropriate.

Jamaica Kincaid

Alien Soil

◆

Jamaica Kincaid was born in St. John's, Antigua, in 1949. She now lives in Vermont and is a staff writer for The New Yorker *magazine. Her stories have also appeared in* Rolling Stone. *She has published a book of short stories,* At the Bottom of the River *(1984), and also a novel,* Annie John *(1985). The following selection appeared in* The New Yorker *in June, 1993.*

Whatever it is in the character of the English people that leads them to obsessively order and shape their landscape to such a degree that it looks like a painting (tamed, framed, captured, kind, decent, good, pretty), while a painting never looks like the English landscape, unless it is a bad painting—this quality of character is blissfully lacking in the Antiguan people. I make this unfair comparison (unfair to the Antiguan people? unfair to the English people? I cannot tell, but there is an unfairness here somewhere) only because so much of the character of the Antiguan people is influenced by and inherited, through conquest, from the English people. The tendency to shower pity and cruelty on the weak is among the traits the Antiguans inherited, and so is a love of gossip. (The latter, I think is responsible for the fact that England has produced such great novelists, but it has not yet worked to the literary advantage of the Antiguan people.) When the English were a presence in Antigua—they first came to the island as slaveowners, when a man named Thomas Warner established a settlement there in 1632—the places where they lived were surrounded by severely trimmed hedges of plumbago, topiaries of willow (casuarina), and frangipani and hibiscus; their grass was green (odd, because water was scarce; the proper word for the climate is not "sunny" but "drought-ridden") and freshly cut; they kept trellises covered with roses, and beds of marigolds and cannas and chrysanthemums.

Ordinary Antiguans (and by "ordinary Antiguans" I mean the Antiguan people, who are descended from the African slaves brought to this island by Europeans; this turns out to be a not uncommon way to become ordinary), the ones who had some money and could live in houses of more than one room, had gardens in which only flowers were grown. This made it even more apparent that they had some money, in that all their outside space was devoted not to feeding their

1

2

families but to the sheer beauty of things. I can remember in particular one such family, who lived in a house with many rooms (four, to be exact). They had an indoor kitchen and a place for bathing (no indoor toilet, though); they had a lawn, always neatly cut, and they had beds of flowers, but I can now remember only roses and marigolds. I can remember those because once I was sent there to get a bouquet of roses for my godmother on her birthday. The family also had, in the middle of their small lawn, a willow tree, pruned so that it had the shape of a pine tree—a conical shape—and at Christmastime this tree was decorated with colored lights (which was so unusual and seemed so luxurious to me that when I passed by this house I would beg to be allowed to stop and stare at it for a while). At Christmas, all willow trees would suddenly be called Christmas trees, and for a time, when my family must have had a small amount of money, I, too, had a Christmas tree—a lonely, spindly branch of willow sitting in a bucket of water in our very small house. No one in my family and, I am almost certain, no one in the family of the people with the lighted-up willow tree had any idea of the origins of the Christmas tree and the traditions associated with it. When these people (the Antiguans) lived under the influence of these other people (the English), there was naturally an attempt among some of them to imitate their rulers in this particular way—by rearranging the landscape—and they did it without question. They can't be faulted for not asking what it was they were doing; that is the way these things work. The English left, and most of their landscaping influence went with them. The Americans came, but Americans (I am one now) are not interested in influencing people directly, we instinctively understand the childish principle of monkey see, monkey do. And at the same time we are divided about how we ought to behave in the world. Half of us believe in and support strongly a bad thing our government is doing, while the other half do not believe in and protest strongly against the bad thing. The bad thing succeeds, and everyone, protester and supporter alike, enjoys immensely the results of the bad thing. This ambiguous approach in the many is always startling to observe in the individual. Just look at Thomas Jefferson, a great American gardener and our country's third President, who owned slaves, and strongly supported the idea of an expanded American border, which meant the extinction of the people who already lived on the land to be taken, while at the same time he was passionately devoted to ideas about freedom—ideas that the descendants of the slaves and the people who were defeated and robbed of their land would have to use in defense of themselves. Jefferson, as President, commissioned the formidable trek his former secretary, the adventurer and botany thief Meriwether Lewis, made through the West, sending plant specimens back to the President along the way. The *Lewisia rediviva,* state flower of Montana, which Lewis found in the Bitterroot River valley, is named after him;

the clarkia, not a flower of any state as far as I can tell, is named for his co-adventurer and botany thief, William Clark.

What did the botanical life of Antigua consist of at the time another   3 famous adventurer—Christopher Columbus—first saw it? To see a garden in Antigua now will not supply a clue. I made a visit to Antigua this spring, and most of the plants I saw there came from somewhere else. The bougainvillea (named for another restless European, the sea adventurer Louis-Antoine de Bougainville, first Frenchman to cross the Pacific) is native to tropical South America; the plumbago is from Southern Africa; the croton (genus *Codiaeum*) is from Malay Peninsula; the *Hibiscus rosa-sinensis* is from Asia and the *Hibiscus schizopetalus* is from East Africa; the allamanda is from Brazil; the poinsettia (named for an American ambassador, Joel Poinsett) is from Mexico; the bird of paradise flower is from Southern Africa; the Bermuda lily is from Japan; the flamboyant tree is from Madagascar; the casuarina is from Australia; the Norfolk pine is from Norfolk Island; the tamarind tree is from Africa; the mango is from Asia. The breadfruit, that most Antiguan (to me) and starchy food, the bane of every Antiguan child's palate, is from the East Indies. This food has been the cause of more disagreement between parents and their children than anything else I can think of. No child has ever liked it. It was sent to the West Indies by Joseph Banks, the English naturalist and world traveller, and the head of Kew Gardens, which was then a clearing house for all the plants stolen from the various parts of the world where the English had been. (One of the climbing roses, *Rosa banksiae,* from China, was named for Banks' wife.) Banks sent tea to India; to the West Indies he sent the breadfruit. It was meant to be a cheap food for feeding slaves. It was the cargo that Captain Bligh was carrying to the West Indies on the ship Bounty when his crew so rightly mutinied. It's as though the Antiguan child senses intuitively the part this food has played in the history of injustice and so will not eat it. But, unfortunately for her, it grows readily, bears fruit abundantly, and is impervious to drought. Soon after the English settled in Antigua, they cleared the land of its hardwood forests to make room for the growing of tobacco, sugar, and cotton, and it is this that makes the island drought-ridden to this day. Antigua is also empty of much wildlife natural to it. When snakes proved a problem for the planters, they imported the mongoose from India. As a result there are no snakes at all on the island—nor other reptiles, other than lizards—though I don't know what damage the absence of snakes causes, if any.

What herb of beauty grew in this place then? What tree? And did   4 the people who lived there grow anything beautiful for its own sake? I do not know; I can only make a straightforward deduction: the frangipani, the mahogany tree, and the cedar tree are all native to the West Indies, so these trees are probably indigenous. And some of the botany of Antigua can be learned from medicinal folklore. My mother and I were sitting on the steps in front of her house one day during my recent visit, and I suddenly focussed on a beautiful bush (beautiful to me now, when I was a child I thought it ugly) whose fruit I remembered playing with when I was little. It is an herbaceous plant that has a red stem covered with red thorns, and emerald-green, simple leaves, with the same red thorns running down the leaf from the leafstalk. I cannot remember what its flowers looked like, and it was not in flower when I saw it while I was there with my mother, but its fruit is a small, almost transparent red berry, and it is this I used to play with. We children sometimes called it "china berry," because of its transparent, glassy look—it reminded us of china dinnerware, though we were only vaguely familiar with such a thing as china, having seen it no more than once or twice—sometimes "baby tomato," because of its size, and to signify that it was not real; a baby thing was not a real thing. When I pointed the bush out to my mother, she called it something else; she called it cancanberry bush, and said that in the old days, when people could not afford to see doctors, if a child had thrush they would make a paste of this fruit and rub it inside the child's mouth, and this would make the thrush go away. But, she said, people rarely bother with this remedy anymore. The day before, a friend of hers had come to pay a visit, and when my mother offered her something to eat and drink the friend declined, because, she said, she had some six-sixty-six and maiden-blush tea waiting at home for her. This tea is taken on an empty stomach, and it is used for all sorts of ailments, including to help bring on abortions. I have never seen six-sixty-six in flower, but its leaves are a beautiful ovoid shape and a deep green—qualities that are of value in a garden devoted to shape and color of leaf.

5   People who do not like the idea that there is a relationship between gardening and wealth are quick to remind me of the cottage gardener, that grim-faced English person. Living on land that is not his own, he has put bits and pieces of things together, things from here and there, and it is a beautiful jumble—but just try duplicating it; it isn't cheap to do. And I have never read a book praising the cottage garden written by a cottage gardener. This person—the cottage gardener—does not exist in a place like Antigua. Nor do casual botanical conversation, knowledge of the Latin names for plants, and discussions of the binomial system. If an atmosphere where these things could flourish exists in this place I am not aware of it. I can remember very well the cruel Englishwoman who was my botany teacher, and that, in spite of her cruelty, botany was one of my two favorite subjects in school. (History was the other.) With this in mind I visited a bookstore (the only bookstore I know of in Antigua) to see what texts are now being used in the schools and to see how their content compares with what was taught to me back then; the botany I had studied was a catalogue of the plants of

the British Empire, the very same plants that are now widely cultivated in Antigua and are probably assumed by ordinary Antiguans to be native to their landscape—the mango, for example. But it turns out that botany as a subject is no longer taught in Antiguan schools; the study of plants is now called agriculture. Perhaps that is more realistic, since the awe and poetry of botany cannot be eaten, and the mystery and pleasure in the knowledge of botany cannot be taken to market and sold.

And yet the people of Antigua have a relationship to agriculture that does not please them at all. Their very arrival on this island had to do with the forces of agriculture. When they (we) were brought to this island from Africa a few hundred years ago, it was not for their pottery-making skills or for their way with a loom; it was for the free labor they could provide in the fields. Mary Prince, a nineteenth-century African woman, who was born in Bermuda and spent part of her life as a slave in Antigua, writes about this in an autobiographical account, which I found in "The Classic Slave Narratives," edited by Henry Louis Gates, Jr. She says:

> My master and mistress went on one occasion into the country, to Date Hill, for change of air, and carried me with them to take charge of the children, and to do the work of the house. While I was in the country, I saw how the field negroes are worked in Antigua. They are worked very hard and fed but scantily. They are called out to work before daybreak, and come home after dark; and then each has to heave his bundle of grass for the cattle in the pen. Then, on Sunday morning, each slave has to go out and gather a large bundle of grass; and, when they bring it home, they have all to sit at the manager's door and wait till he comes out: often they have to wait there till past eleven o'clock, without any breakfast. After that, those that have yams or potatoes, or firewood to sell, hasten to market to buy...salt fish, or pork, which is a great treat for them.

Perhaps it makes sense that a group of people with such a wretched historical relationship to growing things would need to describe their current relationship to it as dignified and masterly (agriculture), and would not find it poetic (botany) or pleasurable (gardening).

In a book I am looking at (to read it is to look at it: the type is as tall as a doll's teacup), "The Tropical Garden," by William Warren, with photographs by Luca Invernizzi Tettoni, I find statements like "the concept of a private garden planted purely for aesthetic purposes was generally alien to tropical countries" and "there was no such tradition of ornamental horticulture among the inhabitants of most hot-weather places. Around the average home there might be a few specimens chosen especially because of their scented flowers or because they were believed to bring good fortune.... Nor would much, if any, attention be

6

7

paid to attractive landscape design in such gardens: early accounts by travellers in the tropics abound in enthusiastic descriptions of jungle scenery, but a reader will search in vain for one praising the tasteful arrangement of massed ornamental beds and contrasting lawns of well-trimmed grass around the homes of natives." What can I say to that? No doubt it is true. And no doubt contrasting lawns and massed ornamental beds are a sign of something, and that is that someone— someone other than the owner of the lawns—has been humbled. To give just one example: on page 62 of this book is a photograph of eight men, natives of India, pulling a heavy piece of machinery used in the upkeep of lawns. They are without shoes. They are wearing the clothing of schoolboys—khaki shorts and khaki short-sleeved shirts. There is no look of bliss on their faces. The caption for the photograph reads, "Shortage of labour was never a problem in the maintenance of European features in large colonial gardens; here a team of workers is shown rolling a lawn at the Gymkhana Club in Bombay."

8   And here are a few questions that occur to me: what if the people living in the tropics, the ones whose history isn't tied up with and contaminated by slavery and indenturedness, are contented with their surroundings, are happy to observe an invisible hand at work and from time to time laugh at some of the ugly choices this hand makes; what if they have more important things to do than make a small tree large, a large tree small, or a tree whose blooms are usually yellow bear black blooms; what if these people are not spiritually feverish, restless, and full of envy?

9   When I was looking at the book of tropical gardens, I realized that the flowers and the trees so familiar to me from my childhood do not now have a hold on me. I do not long to plant and be surrounded by the bougainvillea; I do not like the tropical hibiscus; the corallita (from Mexico), so beautiful when tended, so ugly when left to itself, which makes everything around it look rusty and shabby, is not a plant I like at all. I returned from my visit to Antigua, the place where I was born, to a small village in Vermont, the place where I choose to live. Spring had arrived. The tulips I had planted last autumn were in bloom, and I liked to sit and caress their petals, which felt disgustingly delicious, like scraps of peau de soie. The dizzy-making yellow of dandelions and cowslips was in the fields and riverbanks and marshes. I like these things. (I do not like daffodils, but that's a legacy of the English approach: I was forced to memorize the poem by William Wordsworth when I was a child.) I transplanted to the edge of a grove of pine trees some foxgloves that I grew from seed in late winter. I found some Virginia bluebells in a spot in the woods where I had not expected to find them, and some larches growing grouped together, also in a place I had not expected. On my calendar I marked the day I would go and dig up all the mulleins I could find and re-plant them in a very sunny spot

across from the grove of pine trees. This is to be my forest of mulleins, though in truth it will appear a forest only to an ant. I marked the day I would plant the nasturtiums under the fruit trees. I discovered a clump of Dutchman's-breeches in the wildflower bed that I inherited from the man who built and used to own the house in which I now live, Robert Woodworth, the botanist who invented time-lapse photography. I waited for the things I had ordered in the deep cold of winter to come. They started to come. Mr. Pembroke, who represents our village in the Vermont legislature, came and helped me dig some of the holes where some of the things I wanted to put in were to be planted. Mr. Pembroke is a very nice man. He is never dressed in the clothing of schoolboys. There is not a look of misery on his face; on his face is the complicated look of an ordinary human being. When he works in my garden, we agree on a price; he sends me a bill, and I pay it. The days are growing longer and longer, and then they'll get shorter again. I am now used to that ordered progression, and I love it. But there is no order in my garden. I live in America now. Americans are impatient with memory, which is one of the things order thrives on.

Reading and Writing Activities

1. Note your reactions during your first reading(s) to Jamaica Kincaid's essay, "Alien Soil."
2. Discuss these reactions in groups, if possible.
3. Freewrite after reconsidering the reading.
4. Write a preliminary analysis of the reading—note the parts that relate to the whole, transition points, clues to topic shifts, and details of audience, purpose, structure and development of meaning. You may want to review, at this point, sets of analytic questions and questions about what the writer is doing (rhetorically) in Chapters 4–7.
5. From preliminary analytic work, write a summary analysis.
6. Compare summaries in discussion groups, if possible.
7. Reconsider and revise summaries.
8. Think of three or four central questions you have about this reading.
9. Write the questions and present them in your reading groups. Compare your questions; answer as many from each group member as appropriate.

Sylvester Monroe

Louis Farrakhan Interview: They Suck the Life from You

————————◆————————

Louis Farrakhan was born in 1933. Raised in Boston, he later attended college in North Carolina at Winston-Salem Teachers College. Farrakhan joined the Nation of Islam after hearing Elijah Muhammad speak in 1955. He now lives in Chicago.

Time correspondent Sylvester Monroe interviewed Farrakhan following the public outcry over a November 1993 speech by his aide, Khallid Abdul Muhammad. In this speech, Khallid attacked Jews for "sucking our blood in the black community." Following are excerpts from the two-and-a half hour interview published in Time *in February 1994.*

1   *Time:* What it the message that the Nation of Islam is imparting to African-Americans?

2   *Farrakhan:* That God is interested in us, that God has heard our moaning and our groaning under the whip and the lash of our oppressors and has now come to see about us. That's the appeal.

3   *Time:* How does the Nation of Islam take a person who has hit bottom with drugs or alcohol or crime and remake that person?

4   *Farrakhan:* Well, we can't do it without the help of God, and we can't do it until we can reconnect that person to the source of truth and goodness that is Allah.

5   So once we can reconnect him to God and show him his relationship to God, then you give him that knowledge of himself, his history. So by teaching us our history beyond the cotton fields, beyond our slave history in America, and teaching us our connection to the great rulers of ancient civilizations, the great builders of the pyramids and the great architects of civilization, and teaching us our relationship to the father of medicine, the father of law, the father of mathematics and science and religion, this makes us desire now to come up out of our ignorance and achieve the best that we possibly can achieve. And this is what begins to transform the person's life.

6   *Time:* It has sometimes appeared that you were building this sense of self-esteem by putting down another people.

Farrakhan: Now the truth of the matter is that white supremacists built a world on that ideology. If that system of white supremacy is based on falsehood, then the truth will attack that system at its foundation and it will begin to tumble down.   7

Now the truth of the matter is, whites are superior. They are not superior because they are born superior. They are superior because they have been the ruling power, that God has permitted them to rule. They have had the wisdom and the guidance to rule while most of the dark world or the darker people of the world have been, as they have called it, asleep.   8

Now it's the awakening of all the darker people of the world, and we are awakening at the level that the white world is now beginning to decline. And this is what Brother Khallid was talking about in his speech; I could not say he's a liar, [that] he's wrong. But this should never be taught out of the spirit of mockery.   9

And so to tear down another people to lift yourself up is not proper. But to tell the truth, to tear down the mind built on a false premise of white supremacy, that is nothing but proper because that will allow whites to relate to themselves as well as to other human beings as human beings.   10

Time: So what Khallid did, was that wrong?   11

Farrakhan: To me, it is highly improper in that you make a mockery over people. So why should we mock them? Why should we goad them into a behavior that is so easy for them to do harm to black people? And that's why I rebuked him.   12

Time: Have Khallid's remarks damaged your relationship with the mainstream black civil rights leadership?   13

Farrakhan: I don't feel that we can go down the road to liberation without a John Jacob, without a Jesse Jackson, without a Dorothy Height, without a Coretta Scott King or a Congressional Black Caucus or an N.A.A.C.P.   14

I mean, I have grown to the point, by God's grace, that I see the value of each and every one of these persons to the overall struggle of our people.   15

I feel that not only do they have something to offer me, but I have something to offer them. I'm not trying to be mainstream. I don't even know what that is. I don't know whether any black has ever achieved mainstream. But I do know this. I want the unity of black organizations and black leaders that we might form a united front and seriously discuss what we can do to better the condition of our people.   16

Time: Has there been any discussion about just that?   17

Farrakhan: We have never got to the point where we would sit down to open up these kinds of discussions. Unfortunately, there are those   18 who saw in me a poison that would infect that group. And so they used their influence to push that group away from me. Even if they liked me, they could not associate with me for fear of what it would do to them professionally and economically.

19   So now we have to get to this talk of anti-Semitism. Am I really anti-Semitic? Do I really want extermination of Jewish people? Of course, the answer is no. Now here's where the problem is. When I am accused of being a Hilter, a black Hitler, because of my oratorical ability and my ability to move people, there is fear that I'm not under control. By the grace of God, I shall never be under the control of those who do not want the liberation of our people. I cannot do that.

20   The idea is to isolate me, and hopefully, through the media and everybody calling me a hater, a racist, and anti-Semite, that I would just dry up and go away.

21   Now they have done this for 10 years, and I have not gone away. Now fortunately or unfortunately, they have forced other black leaders into silence on the basic issues of race and color and economics, and Farrakhan now has emerged as the voice that speaks to the hurt of our people.

22   Now I'm going to come to something that may get me in a lot of trouble. But I've got to speak the truth. What is a bloodsucker? When they land on your skin, they suck the the life from you to sustain their life.

23   In the '20s and '30s and '40s, up into the '50s, the Jews were the primary merchants in the black community. Wherever we were, they were. What was their role? We bought food from them; we bought clothing from them; we bought furniture from them; we rented from them. So if they made profit from us, then from our life they drew life and came to strength. They turned it over to the Arabs, the Koreans and others, who are there now doing what? Sucking the lifeblood of our own community.

24   Every black artist, or most of them who came to prominence, who are their managers, who are their agents? Does the agent have the talent or the artist? But who reaps the benefits? Come on. We die penniless and broke, but somebody else is sucking from us. Who surrounds Michael Jackson? Is it us?

25   See brother, we've got to look at what truth is. You throw it out there as if to say this is some of the same old garbage that was said in Europe. I don't know about no garbage said in Europe.

26   But I know what I'm seeing in America. And because I see that black people, Sylvester, in the intellectual fields and professional fields are not going to be free until there is a new relationship with the Jewish community, then I feel that what I'm saying has to ultimately break that relationship.

Just like they felt it necessary to break my relationship with the   27
Black Caucus, I feel it absolutely necessary to break the old relationship of the black intellectual and professional with the Jewish
community and restructure it along lines of reciprocity, along lines
of fairness and equity.

Time: How much does this black/Jewish controversy actually wind up   28
hurting black people?

Farrakhan: I did not recognize the degree to which Jews held control   29
over black professionals, black intellectuals, black entertainers,
black sports figures; Khallid did not lie when he said that.

My ultimate aim is the liberation of our people. So if we are to   30
be liberated, it's good to see the hands that are holding us. And we
need to sever those hands from holding us that we may be a free
people, that we may enter into a better relationship with them than
we presently have.

So yes, in one sense it's a loss, but in the ultimate sense it's a   31
gain. Because when I saw that, I recognized that the black man will
never be free until we address the problem of the relationship between blacks and Jews.

Time: If you could tell the readers of *Time* magazine anything you want   32
to tell them about Farrakhan or the Nation of Islam, what would
you say to them, or do you even care?

Farrakhan: Of course I care.   33

I would hope that the American people and black people
would give us a chance to speak to them not on a 30-second sound
bite or not even through *Time* magazine or any other white-man-
aged magazine or newspaper but allow us to come to the American people to state our case.

I would hope that before the House of Representatives or the   34
Senate will follow the advice of others to do things to hurt the Nation of Islam and our efforts in America at reforming our people,
that you would invite us before the Senate or before members of
the House of Representatives to question me and us on anything
that I have ever said in the past.

And if they can show me that I'm a racist or an anti-Semite   35
with all the legal brilliance that's in the government, and I, from
that lofty place, will apologize to the world for misrepresenting
what I believed to be the truth.

Responses to
They Suck the Life from You

◆

Time *asked leading writers and scholars to respond to Louis Farrakhan's remarks amid a growing tension between African-American and Jewish leaders. The following writers and scholars accepted the invitation from* Time. *Midge Decter, fellow at the Institute on Religion and Public Life; Cornel West, professor of religion at Princeton University and author of* Race Matters; *Michael Lerner, editor of the journal* Tikkun: A Bimonthly Jewish Critique of Politics, Culture and Society; *Randall Kennedy, professor of law at Harvard University and editor of* Reconstruction.

Midge Decter

Why Did Blacks
Turn on Jews?

◆

1   Anti-Semitic gutter talk of the sort favored in the precincts of the Nation of Islam has by now become routine in many places: from certain pulpits, for example; in mosques, to be sure; during prayer meetings in jails and prisons; and perhaps most significantly, in not a few black-studies classrooms on not a few college campuses across the land.

2   Nor is black anti-Semitism anything new. On the contrary, it has for at least a quarter-century been hanging like a lengthening shadow over black intellectual and political life—not quite so unabashedly ugly as now, perhaps, or so crudely inventive in its brutality, but nonetheless, a visible, and politically consequential, presence.

3   American Jews tended to ignore, or even alibi, black anti-Semitism because they had long been conditioned to hearing violent and plain-spoken hate talk about themselves from the extremist right, and for years had trouble discerning the very same noises coming from those whom they took, mistakenly, to be liberals like themselves. Members of the organized Jewish community also have an enormous investment in their relations with the black community, having for so long a time

been the most visible and generous nonblack allies of the civil rights movement.

Such an investment is, emotionally speaking, not so easily liqui- 4
dated; among those demanding special preferences for blacks, say, or advocating special leniency for black violence, Jews have customarily been the first to be heard from; and at least until a moment ago, every anti-Jewish incident in the black community, including the 1991 minipogrom in Crown Heights, has led to an invitation from Jews to the offending blacks to meet and repair relations. (The demand by some Jewish leaders that Jesse Jackson and others must once and for all repudiate Farrakhan, so unperceptively seen by some as an unfair application of a special standard to the black community, is in fact no more than an expression of the longing to be able to continue support-ing them without shame.)

What is most important about black anti-Semitism, however, is not 5
how or why the Jews respond to it as they do. Nor, while important enough, is it the degree to which most of the major organs of white opinion, in their coverage of even the most odious kind of trashing of the Jews by blacks, take a putatively "neutral" position—suggesting, for instance, that there might after all have been some wrong on both sides, or inappropriately invoking the principle of freedom of speech.

No, the truly interesting issue surrounding black anti-Semitism has 6
to do with the blacks. For one thing, why, of all people, the Jews? What is to be gained by blacks—what in the way of genuine strength, energy, sense of possibility, self-respect—in taking up so old and rusty a cud-gel? Very little, one might suppose, if what they were actually pursuing were such necessities as energy, possibility, and self-respect. Anti-Semitism does, however, provide the blacks with a simulacrum of toughness—of all the people they might hit, the Jews are least likely to exact equal retribution—and as evidenced on every street corner and schoolyard in the inner city, where real strength feels out of reach, toughness will have to do.

Minister Farrakhan and his imitators claim to be offering a new 7
kind of strength and discipline to their flocks, but they are in fact merely rearranging the terms of servitude: Get off drugs, and get your-self a substitute dependency on hatred—it's a whole lot quicker as a therapy than learning how truly to stand on your own two feet. In other words, the Jews as methadone.

The really loving advice to Farrakhan's minions would be, throw 8
away that Jewish crutch, which only weakens your muscles. You can very well make it on your own. Just try it and you'll see.

Cornel West

How Do We Fight Xenophobia?

◆

1 The fundamental issue regarding the unadulterated bigotry of Khallid Abdul Muhammad, the anti-Semitic claims of Minister Louis Farrakhan and the vicious demonization of both black Islamic fellow citizens by the mainstream media is—how do we talk about and fight all forms of xenophobia in American life? So far, we have failed miserably. Instead we have become even more polarized, owing to our distrust of one another and our flagrant disregard for the transformative possibilities of high-quality public conversation.

2 Let us go back to the beginning of this sad episode, namely, Minister Louis Farrakhan's remarks about Hitler, Judaism and the link of Jewish power to black social misery. Most Americans believe Minister Farrakhan praised Adolf Hitler and, by implication, condoned the evils done to the Jewish people. Yet this is simply wrong. As Minister Farrakhan has noted on many occasions, his statement that Hitler was "wickedly great"—like Alexander, Caesar, Napoleon and Stalin—meant that Hitler was famous for his pernicious ability to conquer, destroy and dominate others. Furthermore, Hitler hated black people with great passion. And given Minister Farrakhan's devotion to the cause of black freedom, he would not claim that Hitler was *morally* great. Nevertheless, the mainstream press portrayed Minister Farrakhan as a Nazi—that is, a devil in our midst. Surely, if we believe Minister Farrakhan was *morally* wrong to have once held that whites were devils, it is wrong of us to believe he is a devil.

3 His obsession with connecting black social misery to Jewish power, including his ugly characterization of Judaism as a "gutter religion" used to legitimate the state of Israel at the expense of Palestinians, is vintage anti-Semitic ideology. Judaism—like any religion—can be used for good or bad. His claim that Jews owned 75% of enslaved Africans in this country at a time when there were about 4 million black slaves and 5,000 Jewish slaveholders reveals this obsession. In fact, in 1861, Jews constituted roughly 0.2% of Southerners (20,000 out of 9 million) and 0.3% of slaveholders (5,000 out of 1,937,625).

4 Minister Farrakhan may be rightly upset that antislavery activism was not predominant among the 150,000 Jews then in America, or that there is no record of any Southern rabbi who publicly criticized sla-

very—but there were militant Jewish abolitionists (including Northern rabbis) such as Isidor Busch, Michael Helprin, Rabbi David Einhorn and August Bondi (who fought with John Brown). The expulsion of Jews from Tennessee by Ulysses S. Grant's Order No. 11 in 1862 and new waves of poor East European Jews would yield a more antiracist activism among American Jewry. But even though Minister Farrakhan's anti-Semitic claims are false and hurtful, this does not mean that he is a Nazi or that he has a monopoly on anti-Semitism in America.

If we are to engage in a serious dialogue about blacks and Jews, and how best to fight xenophobia, we must not cast all anti-Semitic statements as pro-Nazi ones, vilify black anti-Semites and soft-pedal white anti-Semites (or Jewish antiblack or anti-Arab racists) or overlook the role of some Jewish conservatives as defenders of policies that contribute to black social misery. We cannot proceed if we assume the worst of each other—that the majority of black people are unreconstructed anti-Semites or that the majority of Jews are plotting conspiracies to destroy black people. I have great faith and confidence in the moral wisdom of most blacks and Jews in regard to vulgar racist bigotry—yet our communities are shot through with more subtle forms. This is why it is incumbent upon blacks and Jews to fight *all* forms of xenophobia even as we try to alleviate the poverty and paranoia that feed so much despair and distrust in our time. 5

As for my brothers, Khallid Abdul Muhammad and Minister Louis Farrakhan, I beseech you in the precious name of the black freedom struggle and in the compassionate spirit of Islam to channel your efforts of black self-help in ways that do not mirror the worst of what American civilization has done to black people. 6

We rightly will not permit a double-standard treatment that casts you less than human, but we also must not allow your—or anyone else's—utterance to tar the black freedom struggle with the brush of immorality. For the sake of Fannie Lou Hamer, Abraham Joshua Heschel and El-Hajj Malik el-Shabazz—and those many thousands gone—we can do no other. 7

Michael Lerner

The Real Crisis Is Selfishness

◆

1   I don't get so upset by Farrakhan and the other punks who run around the country getting famous by stirring up black anti-Semitism, even though I detest them, think their movements should be ostracized by the black community, and find obnoxious the lies they spew out.

2   It's not that I think Jews are so secure that we could never be endangered by this kind of thing. Anti-Semitism in America has never been publicly confronted or its underlying assumptions challenged. The average educated person knows much more about the fallacies in standard racist fantasies about blacks than about notions that Jews control the wealth and the media, that Zionism is colonialism, or that Jews aren't "really" an oppressed group because they are financially secure in the U.S. Because most Americans identify as Christians, and Christianity has been the major perpetrator of anti-Semitism over the past 2,000 years, this culture has never been willing to examine the fallacies of anti-Semitism, because too many people still hold on to them.

3   Nor is it that I think black anti-Semitism is inconsequential. Not only should blacks be publicly denouncing Farrakhan's anti-Semitism and homophobia, they ought to be mobilizing every black church, radio station, newspaper, politician, businessman, entertainer, sports hero and media star to confront and ostracize anti-Semitism and homophobia in the African-American community.

4   So why don't I get more worked up about Farrakhan? Three reasons:

5   First, I can't stand the hypocrisy from a white media and white establishment that does everything it can to exploit and degrade blacks, then looks on in pretended horror when pathologies start to develop in the black community.

6   Second, I can't stand the hypocrisy coming from some in the Jewish world who for decades have used the Holocaust and the history of our very real oppression as an excuse to deny our own racism toward blacks or Palestinians. In our frantic attempts to make it in America, we not only fixed our noses and straightened our hair and learned to talk more softly and genteelly to be acceptable to Wasp culture, but we also began to buy the racist assumptions of this society and to forget our

Reprinted from Tikkun Magazine, a bi-monthly Jewish Critique of Politics, culture, and society. Subscriptions are $31.00 per year from Tikkun, 251 West 100th Street, 5th floor, New York, NY 10025.

own history of oppression. Jewish neoconservatives at *Commentary* magazine and Jewish neoliberals at the *New Republic* have led the assault on affirmative action (despite the fact that one of its greatest beneficiaries has been Jewish women); have blamed the persistence of racism on the victims' culture of poverty; and have delighted in the prospect of throwing black women and children off welfare as soon as possible.

But the third and most important reason I can't get exercised about 7 Farrakhan is because to do so distracts us from the deep underlying crisis of meaning in American society that is central to *why* people are in so much pain that they are willing to seek any kind of anesthetic, from drugs and alcohol to communities based on fascism and racism.

Reacting against the selfishness and materialism that are sanctified 8 by the competitive market—and that undermine our ability to sustain loving relationships—people hunger for communities of meaning that provide ethical and spiritual purpose. They are offered instead a myriad of nationalistic, religious or racial pseudocommunities that never challenge the "look out for No. 1" mentality of the market. So people soon find that their daily lives at work or in family life are just as empty as ever.

To explain why their lives don't feel better, these communities pick 9 a demonized Other who is supposedly responsible. Typically, Christian-based societies have chosen the Jews, though in the U.S. it has been African Americans and, more recently, homosexuals and feminists, who become the demonized Other.

Anti-Semitism and racism can only be undermined when we 10 develop a politics of meaning that speaks to this alienation and provides a direction for healing the wounds generated by a society based on selfishness and materialism. One tragic irony of black anti-Semitism is how easily it becomes yet another justification for some Americans to declare themselves "disillusioned" with the oppressed. So they succumb to the allures of American selfishness, lower their taxes by cutting social programs for the poor, and shut their eyes to the suffering of others.

Randall Kennedy

Some Good May Yet Come of This

━━━━━━━━━◆━━━━━━━━━

1   Considerable good is likely to flow from the outpouring of attention on the Nation of Islam and its relationship to the black political establishment. First, Khallid Abdul Muhammad's notorious, hateful speech at Kean College and Louis Farrakhan's affirmation of its substance (though not its style) demonstrated anew that racism resides at the core of the Nation of Islam. Bigotry is not one of its peripheral features but is instead a central element of its identity and appeal. Second, an issue of fundamental importance has been raised: Should racism expressed by African Americans be openly repudiated by other African Americans?

2   Some argue that at least with respect to whites, African Americans cannot be racist because, as a group, they lack the power to subordinate whites. Among other failings, this theory ignores nitty-gritty realities. Regardless of the relative strength of African-American and Jewish communities in New York City, the African Americans who beat Jews in Crown Heights for racially motivated reasons were, at that moment, sufficiently powerful to subordinate their victims. This theory, moreover, wrongly ignores the plain fact that African Americans—as judges, teachers, mayors, police officers, members of Congress and army officers—increasingly occupy positions of power and influence from which they could, if so minded, tremendously damage clients, co-workers, dependents and, beyond, the society as a whole.

3   Others deny the need for African Americans to repudiate openly other African Americans who express antiwhite or anti-Semitic sentiments. They maintain that public repudiations of this sort undermine African-American unity, sap the group's morale and consequently weaken it before a hostile society. They are mistaken. At the moment, an excess of conformity is far more dangerous than an excess of dissension to the well-being of the African-American community. A paucity of searching, highly public scrutiny of African-American leadership has had a disastrous effect on the tone of African-American political culture, rendering it vulnerable to the moral slackness that often develops when people feel free of accountability.

4   At the same time, there are others for whom the latest controversy has provided an opportunity for distancing themselves from Farra-

khan and reaffirming publicly their allegiance to humane values. Reacting thus is not only morally correct; it also makes good, practical political sense. African-American leaders suffer enough without compounding the difficulties they face by besmirching—as some seem intent upon doing—one of their diminishing but still important assets: a widespread sense that they continue to occupy the moral high ground as custodians of the civil rights revolution.

Many have noted that while writers and political leaders resolutely 5 denounced Muhammad's ravings, few initially paid any serious attention to Senator Ernest F. Hollings' demeaning slur against African diplomats in December when he alluded to them as cannibals. The Senate unanimously condemned Muhammad, who is highly unlikely ever to exercise any appreciable amount of governmental power. Yet, when called upon to react to the nasty aspersions of one of their colleagues, many Senators sought refuge in all manner of evasion. The exposure of this double standard will, unfortunately, be used by some as an excuse to avoid confronting Farrakhanian bigotry. But for others, the exposure will spur them to be more demanding and even-handed in their response to unjustified prejudices of all sorts.

Reading and Writing Activities

1. Note your reactions during your first reading(s) to Louis Farrakhan's interview and the following responses. You could divide the six responses to Farrakhan and assign readings to pairs of readers.
2. Compare reactions of each pair in whole group discussion.
3. Freewrite individually after reconsidering the readings.
4. Write a preliminary analysis of your reading in pairs—note the parts that relate to the whole, transition points, clues to topic shifts, and details of audience, purpose, structure and development of meaning. You may want to review, at this point, sets of analytic questions and questions about what the writer is doing rhetorically in Chapters 4–7.
5. Still in pairs, from preliminary analytic work, write a summary.
6. Read and compare summaries in whole-group discussion.
7. Reconsider and revise summaries.
8. In pairs, think of three or four central questions you each have about your assigned readings.
9. Write the questions and present them to your reading partner. Compare your questions; answer as many from each of you as is appropriate.

Tillie Olsen

I Stand Here Ironing

◆

Tillie Olsen was born in Nebraska in 1912. Among her publications are
Tell Me a Riddle *(1962),* Silences *(1978),* The Word Made Flesh
(1984), and Mother to Daughter, Daughter to Mother *(1984). Her*
short stories have been published in over one hundred anthologies, and her
books have been translated into eleven languages. The following selection
is from her 1962 novella Tell Me a Riddle.

1   I stand here ironing, and what you asked me moves tormented
back and forth with the iron.

2   "I wish you would manage the time to come in and talk with me
about your daughter. I'm sure you can help me understand her. She's a
youngster who needs help and whom I'm deeply interested in helping."

3   "Who needs help." Even if I came, what good would it do? You
think because I am her mother I have a key, or that in some way you
could use me as a key? She has lived for nineteen years. There is all that
life that has happened outside of me, beyond me.

4   And when is there time to remember, to sift, to weigh, to estimate,
to total? I will start and there will be an interruption and I will have to
gather it all together again. Or I will become engulfed with all I did or
did not do, with what should have been and what cannot be helped.

5   She was a beautiful baby. The first and only one of our five that was
beautiful at birth. You do not guess how new and uneasy her tenancy
in her now-loveliness. You did not know her all those years she was
thought homely, or see her poring over her baby pictures, making me
tell her over and over how beautiful she had been—and would be, I
would tell her—and was now, to the seeing eye. But the seeing eyes
were few or nonexistent. Including mine.

6   I nursed her. They feel that's important nowadays. I nursed all the
children, but with her, with all the fierce rigidity of first motherhood, I
did like the books then said. Though her cries battered me to trembling
and my breasts ached with swollenness, I waited till the clock decreed.

7   Why do I put that first? I do not even know if it matters, or if it
explains anything.

8   She was a beautiful baby. She blew shining bubbles of sound. She
loved motion, loved light, loved color and music and textures. She
would lie on the floor in her blue overalls patting the surface so hard in

ecstasy her hands and feet would blur. She was a miracle to me, but when she was eight months old I had to leave her daytimes with the woman downstairs to whom she was no miracle at all, for I worked or looked for work and for Emily's father, who "could no longer endure" (he wrote in his good-bye note) "sharing want with us."

I was nineteen. It was the pre-relief, pre-WPA world of the depression. I would start running as soon as I got off the streetcar, running up the stairs, the place smelling sour, and awake or asleep to startle awake, when she saw me she would break into a clogged weeping that could not be comforted, a weeping I can hear yet.

After a while I found a job hashing at night so I could be with her days, and it was better. But it came to where I had to bring her to his family and leave her.

It took a long time to raise the money for her fare back. Then she got chicken pox and I had to wait longer. When she finally came, I hardly knew her, walking quick and nervous like her father, looking like her father, thin, and dressed in a shoddy red that yellowed her skin and glared at the pockmarks. All the baby loveliness gone.

She was two. Old enough for nursery school they said, and I did not know then what I know now—the fatigue of the long day, and the lacerations of group life in the kinds of nurseries that are only parking places for children.

Except that it would have made no difference if I had known. It was the only place there was. It was the only way we could be together, the only way I could hold a job.

And even without knowing, I knew. I knew the teacher that was evil because all these years it has curdled into my memory, the little boy hunched in the corner, her rasp, "why aren't you outside, because Alvin hits you? that's no reason, go out, scaredy." I knew Emily hated it even if she did not clutch and implore "don't go Mommy" like the other children, mornings.

She always had a reason why we should stay home. Momma, you look sick. Momma, I feel sick. Momma, the teachers aren't there today, they're sick. Momma, we can't go, there was a fire there last night. Momma, it's a holiday today, no school, they told me.

But never a direct protest, never rebellion. I think of our others in their three-, four-year-oldness—the explosions, the tempers, the denunciations, the demands—and I feel suddenly ill. I put the iron down. What in me demanded that goodness in her? And what was the cost, the cost to her of such goodness?

The old man living in the back once said in his gentle way: "You should smile at Emily more when you look at her." What *was* in my face when I looked at her? I loved her. There were all the acts of love.

It was only with the others I remembered what he said, and it was the face of joy, and not of care or tightness or worry I turned to them—

too late for Emily. She does not smile easily, let alone almost always as her brothers and sisters do. Her face is closed and sombre, but when she wants, how fluid. You must have seen it in her pantomimes, you spoke of her rare gift for comedy on the stage that rouses a laughter out of the audience so dear they applaud and applaud and do not want to let her go.

19   Where does it come from, that comedy? There was none of it in her when she came back to me that second time, after I had had to send her away again. She had a new daddy now to learn to love, and I think perhaps it was a better time.

20   Except when we left her alone nights, telling ourselves she was old enough.

21   "Can't you go some other time, Mommy, like tomorrow?" she would ask. "Will it be just a little while you'll be gone? Do you promise?"

22   The time we came back, the front door open, the clock on the floor in the hall. She rigid awake. "It wasn't just a little while. I didn't cry. Three times I called you, just three times, and then I ran downstairs to open the door so you could come faster. The clock talked loud. I threw it away, it scared me what it talked."

23   She said the clock talked loud again that night I went to the hospital to have Susan. She was delirious with the fever that comes before red measles, but she was fully conscious all the week I was gone and the week after we were home when she could not come near the new baby or me.

24   She did not get well. She stayed skeleton thin, not wanting to eat, and night after night she had nightmares. She would call for me, and I would rouse from exhaustion to sleepily call back: "You're all right, darling, go to sleep, it's just a dream," and if she still called, in a sterner voice, "now go to sleep, Emily, there's nothing to hurt you." Twice, only twice, when I had to get up for Susan anyhow, I went in to sit with her.

25   Now when it is too late (as if she would let me hold and comfort her like I do the others) I get up and go to her at once at her moan or restless stirring. "Are you awake, Emily? Can I get you something?" And the answer is always the same: "No, I'm all right, go back to sleep, Mother."

26   They persuaded me at the clinic to send her away to a convalescent home in the country where "she can have the kind of food and care you can't manage for her, and you'll be free to concentrate on the new baby." They still send children to that place. I see pictures on the society page of sleek young women planning affairs to raise money for it, or dancing at the affairs, or decorating Easter eggs or filling Christmas stockings for the children.

27   They never have a picture of the children so I do not know if the girls still wear those gigantic red bows and the ravaged looks on the

every other Sunday when parents can come to visit "unless otherwise notified"—as we were notified the first six weeks.

Oh it is a handsome place, green lawns and tall trees and fluted flower beds. High up on the balconies of each cottage the children stand, the girls in their red bows and white dresses, the boys in white suits and giant red ties. The parents stand below shrieking up to be heard and the children shriek down to be heard, and between them the invisible wall "Not To Be Contaminated by Parental Germs or Physical Affection." 28

There was a tiny girl who always stood hand in hand with Emily. Her parents never came. One visit she was gone. "They moved her to Rose Cottage" Emily shouted in explanation. "They don't like you to love anybody here." 29

She wrote once a week, the labored writing of a seven-year-old. "I am fine. How is the baby. If I write my letter nicly I will have a star. Love." There never was a star. We wrote every other day, letters she could never hold or keep but only hear read—once. "We simply do not have room for children to keep any personal possessions," they patiently explained when we pieced one Sunday's shrieking together to plead how much it would mean to Emily, who loved so to keep things, to be allowed to keep her letters and cards. 30

Each visit she looked frailer. "She isn't eating," they told us. 31

(They had runny eggs for breakfast or mush with lumps, Emily said later, I'd hold it in my mouth and not swallow. Nothing ever tasted good, just when they had chicken.) 32

It took us eight months to get her released home, and only the fact that she gained back so little of her seven lost pounds convinced the social worker. 33

I used to try to hold and love her after she came back, but her body would stay stiff, and after a while she'd push away. She ate little. Food sickened her, and I think much of life too. Oh she had physical lightness and brightness, twinkling by on skates, bouncing like a ball up and down up and down over the jump rope, skimming over the hill; but these were momentary. 34

She fretted about her appearance, thin and dark and foreign-looking at a time when every little girl was supposed to look or thought she should look a chubby blonde replica of Shirley Temple. The doorbell sometimes rang for her, but no one seemed to come and play in the house or be a best friend. Maybe because we moved so much. 35

There was a boy she loved painfully through two school semesters. Months later she told me how she had taken pennies from my purse to buy him candy. "Licorice was his favorite and I brought him some every day, but he still liked Jennifer better'n me. Why, Mommy?" The kind of question for which there is no answer. 36

37   School was a worry to her. She was not glib or quick in a world where glibness and quickness were easily confused with ability to learn. To her overworked and exasperated teachers she was an over-conscientious "slow learner" who kept trying to catch up and was absent entirely too often.

38   I let her be absent, though sometimes the illness was imaginary. How different from my now-strictness about attendance with the others. I wasn't working. We had a new baby, I was home anyhow. Sometimes, after Susan grew old enough, I would keep her home from school, too, to have them all together.

39   Mostly Emily had asthma, and her breathing, harsh and labored, would fill the house with a curiously tranquil sound. I would bring the two old dresser mirrors and her boxes of collections to her bed. She would select beads and single earrings, bottle tops and shells, dried flowers and pebbles, old postcards and scraps, all sorts of oddments; then she and Susan would play Kingdom, setting up landscapes and furniture, peopling them with action.

40   Those were the only times of peaceful companionship between her and Susan. I have edged away from it, that poisonous feeling between them, that terrible balancing of hurts and needs I had to do between the two, and did so badly, those earlier years.

41   Oh there are conflicts between the others too, each one human, needing, demanding, hurting, taking—but only between Emily and Susan, no, Emily toward Susan that corroding resentment. It seems so obvious on the surface, yet it is not obvious. Susan, the second child, Susan, golden- and curly-haired and chubby, quick and articulate and assured, everything in appearance and manner Emily was not; Susan, not able to resist Emily's precious things, losing or sometimes clumsily breaking them; Susan telling jokes and riddles to company for applause while Emily sat silent (to say to me later: that was *my* riddle, Mother, I told it to Susan); Susan, who for all the five years' difference in age was just a year behind Emily in developing physically.

42   I am glad for that slow physical development that widened the difference between her and her contemporaries, though she suffered over it. She was too vulnerable for that terrible world of youthful competition, of preening and parading, of constant measuring of yourself against every other, of envy, "If I had that copper hair," "If I had that skin. . . ." She tormented herself enough about not looking like the others, there was enough of the unsureness, the having to be conscious of words before you speak, the constant caring—what are they thinking of me? without having it all magnified by the merciless physical drives.

43   Ronnie is calling. He is wet and I change him. It is rare there is such a cry now. That time of motherhood is almost behind me when the ear is not one's own but must always be racked and listening for the child cry, the child call. We sit for a while and I hold him, looking out over

the city spread in charcoal with its soft aisles of light. *"Shoogily,"* he breathes and curls closer. I carry him back to bed, asleep. *Shoogily.* A funny word, a family word, inherited from Emily, invented by her to say: *comfort.*

In this and other ways she leaves her seal, I say aloud. And startle at my saying it. What do I mean? What did I start to gather together, to try and make coherent? I was at the terrible, growing years. War years. I do not remember them well. I was working, there were four smaller ones now, there was not time for her. She had to help be a mother, and housekeeper, and shopper. She had to set her seal. Mornings of crisis and near hysteria trying to get lunches packed, hair combed, coats and shoes found, everyone to school or Child Care on time, the baby ready for transportation. And always the paper scribbled on by a smaller one, the book looked at by Susan then mislaid, the homework not done. Running out to that huge school where she was one, she was lost, she was a drop; suffering over the unpreparedness, stammering and unsure in her classes. 44

There was so little time left at night after the kids were bedded down. She would struggle over books, always eating (it was in those years she developed her enormous appetite that is legendary in our family) and I would be ironing, or preparing food for the next day, or writing V-mail to Bill, or tending the baby. Sometimes, to make me laugh, or out of her despair, she would imitate happenings or types at school. 45

I think I said once: "Why don't you do something like this in the school amateur show?" One morning she phoned me at work, hardly understandable through the weeping: "Mother, I did it. I won, I won; they gave me first prize; they clapped and clapped and wouldn't let me go." 46

Now suddenly she was Somebody, and as imprisoned in her difference as she had been in anonymity. 47

She began to be asked to perform at other high schools, even in colleges, then at city and statewide affairs. The first one we went to, I only recognized her that first moment when thin, shy, she almost drowned herself into the curtains. Then: Was this Emily? The control, the command, the convulsing and deadly clowning, the spell, then the roaring, stamping audience, unwilling to let this rare and precious laughter out of their lives. 48

Afterwards: You ought to do something about her with a gift like that—but without money or knowing how, what does one do? We have left it all to her, and the gift has as often eddied inside, clogged and clotted, as been used and growing. 49

She is coming. She runs up the stairs two at a time with her light graceful step, and I know she is happy tonight. Whatever it was that occasioned your call did not happen today. 50

51   "Aren't you ever going to finish the ironing, Mother? Whistler painted his mother in a rocker. I'd have to paint mine standing over an ironing board." This is one of her communicative nights and she tells me everything and nothing as she fixes herself a plate of food out of the icebox.

52   She is so lovely. Why did you want me to come in at all? Why were you concerned? She will find her way.

53   She starts up the stairs to bed. "Don't get me up with the rest in the morning." "But I thought you were having midterms." "Oh, those," she comes back in, kisses me, and says quite lightly, "in a couple of years when we'll all be atom-dead they won't matter a bit."

54   She has said it before. She *believes* it. But because I have been dredging the past, and all that compounds a human being is so heavy and meaningful in me, I cannot endure it tonight.

55   I will never total it all. I will never come in to say: She was a child seldom smiled at. Her father left me before she was a year old. I had to work her first six years when there was work, or I sent her home and to his relatives. There were years she had care she hated. She was dark and thin and foreign-looking in a world where the prestige went to blondeness and curly hair and dimples, she was slow where glibness was prized. She was a child of anxious, not proud, love. We were poor and could not afford for her the soil of easy growth. I was a young mother, I was a distracted mother. There were the other children pushing up, demanding. Her younger sister seemed all that she was not. There were years she did not want me to touch her. She kept too much in herself, her life was such she had to keep too much in herself. My wisdom came too late. She has much to her and probably nothing will come of it. She is a child of her age, of depression, of war, of fear.

56   Let her be. So all that is in her will not bloom—but in how many does it? There is still enough left to live by. Only help her to know—help make it so there is cause for her to know—that she is more than this dress on the ironing board, helpless before the iron.

1953–1954

Reading and Writing Activities

1. Note your reactions during your first reading(s) of Tillie Olsen's "I Stand Here Ironing."
2. Discuss these readings in groups, if possible.
3. Freewrite after reconsidering the reading.
4. Write a preliminary analysis of the reading—note the parts that relate to the whole, transition points, clues to topic shifts, and details of audience, purpose, structure and development of meaning. You may want to review, at this point, sets of analytic questions and

questions about what the writer is doing (rhetorically) in Chapters 4–7.

5. From preliminary analytic work, write a summary analysis.
6. Compare summaries in discussion groups, if possible.
7. Reconsider and revise summaries.
8. Think of three or four central questions you have about this reading.
9. Write the questions and present them in your reading groups. Compare your questions; answer as many from each group member as appropriate.

WRITING SUGGESTIONS

1. If the topic interests you, read more about issues involving Native American families in short stories and novels. Read some of the stories from Louise Erdrich's *Love Medicine*, for example. (The reading selection "Scales" in Chapter 5 is from that book.) Or read Barbara Kingsolver's *Pigs in Heaven*, or Michael Dorris's *Yellow Raft in Blue Water*. Then write a documented essay using your sources as a means of developing your response to, or understanding of, an issue on family values and traditions in Native American communities. (For a discussion about writing documented essays, see Chapter 4, page 179.)

2. Read some of the selections from other chapters in this book about issues of class and silent voices. Read the Joyce Carol Oates short story, "Is Laughter Contagious?" in Chapter 5, for example, for portraits of working-class people whose voices are not heard in that community. (There are many other selections throughout the book that address these issues.) Then write a documented essay.

3. Read more about issues involving gay men and women. Read David Broder's essay in this chapter and research, from newspaper and magazine reports, the "Gay Games," held in New York City in June 1994. Examine Carolyn Pittman's essay for a college student's experience with gender and language. Then write a documented essay using your sources as a means of developing a response to your reading.

4. Read more about issues involving sexual harassment of minority women. Research the sexual harassment case involving Anita Hill and Clarence Thomas in 1991. Compare sexual harassment at work and in social situations. Then write a documented essay using your sources as a means of developing your response to your reading.

5. From the data you have examined on the issue of relations between the Nation of Islam and the Jewish community (Farrakhan's interview, the responses to the problem from the writers and scholars,

and your group's collective responses that you have examined and written about in pairs and in the larger group), write, individually or in pairs, a documented essay that presents the issues involved in this clash between some in the African-American community and the Jewish community.

6. Read more about issues involving mother and daughter relationships in short stories and essays. Connect some of the selections from this chapter, such as Valerie Matsumoto and Tillie Olsen, or those from earlier chapters. Or read Isabel Allende's novel *The House of Spirits*. Once you have collected enough data, write a documented essay using your sources as a means of developing your response to your reading about mothers and daughters.

Readings*

---◆---

Adams, Lavonne. "The Holly Pageant." Unpublished manuscript. 1992.

Akinnaso, F. Nyi. "Literacy and Individual Consciousness." *Literate Systems and Individual Lives: Perspectives on Literacy and Schooling.* Ed. Edward M. Jennings and Alan C. Purves. Albany: State U of New York P, 1991. 75–93.

Bambara, Toni Cade. "My Man Bovanne." From *Gorilla, My Love.* New York: Random, 1972. 3–10. Copyright © 1971 by Toni Cada Bambara. Reprinted by permission of Random House, Inc.

Beuf, Ann H. "The World of the Native American Child." *Red Children in White America.* Philadelphia: U of Pennsylvania P, 1977. 15–57.

Birmingham, Stephen. "Telling Them Apart." From *America's Secret Aristocracy.* Boston: Little, Brown, 1987. 3–16. Copyright © 1987 by Stephen Birmingham. By permission of Little, Brown and Company.

Blum, Howard. "'Bias Incident' at Staten Island's Miller Field: A Tale of Two Neighborhoods." *New York Times.* Aug. 3 1983. Reprinted in *Racism and Sexism: An Integrated Study.* Ed. Paula S. Rothenberg. New York: St. Martin's, 1987. 31–5. Copyright © 1983 by The New York Times Company. Reprinted by permission.

Bowser, Benjamin P., and Herbert Perkins. "Success Against the Odds: Young Black Men Tell What It Takes." *Black Male Adolescents: Parenting and Education in Community Context.* Ed. Benjamin P. Bowser. Lanham, MD: UP of America, 1991. 183–200. Copyright 1991 by University Press of America. Reprinted by permission of the publisher.

Broder, David. "Gay Pride Claims a Place in U.S. Politics." [Wilmington, NC] *Morning Star* 29 June, 1994: 6A.

Campbell, Joseph. From *An Open Life: Joseph Campbell in Conversation with Michael Toms* by John M. Maher and Dennie Briggs. New York: Harper and Row, 1989. 119–129. Copyright © 1989 by the New Dimensions Foundation. Reprinted by permission of HarperCollins Publishers, Inc.

---

*You may note that the titles of some works have been altered for use in this text. The titles cited in this alphabetized list of the readings, however, are those used in the original place of publication.

Carcaterra, Lorenzo. "Loving Your Enemy." *New York Times Magazine* 28 March 1993: 16. Copyright © 1993 by the New York Times Company. Reprinted by permission.

Dannen, Fredric. "Annals of Crime: Revenge of the Green Dragons." Copyright © 1992 by Fredric Dannen. Originally published in *The New Yorker,* Volume 69, Issue No. 39. Reprinted by permission of McIntosh and Otis, Inc.

Decter, Midge. "Why Did Blacks Turn on Jews?" *Time* 28 Feb. 1994. 30.

"Doll of Easy Inches Is More Realistic Model." [Wilmington, NC] *Morning Star* 16 Aug. 1991: C6. Copyright © 1991 by The New York Times Company. Reprinted by permission.

Dreyfuss, Joel. "The Invisible Immigrants." *The New York Times Magazine* 23 May 1992: 20. Copyright © 1993 by The New York Times Company. Reprinted by permission.

Edwards, Margaret. "But Does the New Woman Really Want the New Man?" *Working Women.* May 1985: 54.

Eighner, Lars. "On Dumpster Diving." *Threepenny Review* Fall 1991: 6–8. Copyright © 1993 by Lars Eighner. From the book *Travels with Lizbeth* and reprinted with permission from St. Martin's Press, Inc., New York, NY. This essay first appeared in "The Threepenny Review" in Fall 1991.

Erdrich, Louise. "Scales." From *Love Medicine,* new and expanded version. New York: Bantam, 1984. 155–71. Copyright © 1984, 1993 by Louise Erdrich. Reprinted by permission of Henry Holt and Co., Inc.

Farrell, Warren. "Why Men Are the Way They Are." This article first appeared in the *Family Therapy Networker,* (Nov./Dec. 1988) and is copied here with permission.

Futrelle, David and Leora Tanenbaum. "Bootstrap Feminism." *In These Times* 8 August 1994: 33–36.

Gans, Herbert. "A Comparative Analysis of High and Popular Culture." Excerpt of three pages from *Popular Culture and High Culture: An Analysis and Evaluation of Taste.* New York: Basic, 1974. 65–118. Copyright © 1974 by Basic Books, Inc. Reprinted by permission of Basic Books, a division of HarperCollins Publishers, Inc.

Gatewood, Willard B. *Aristocrats of Color: The Black Elite, 1880–1920.* Bloomington, Indiana: University of Indiana Press, 1990. 141–48.

Giovanni, Nikki. "Pioneers: A View of Home." *Sacred Cows . . . and Other Edibles.* New York: Morrow, 1988. 163–67. Copyright © 1988 by Nikki Giovanni. By permission of William Morrow & Company, Inc.

Gray, Paul. "What Is Love?" *Time* 15 Feb. 1993: 47–49. © 1993 Time Inc. Reprinted by permission.

Hirsch, E. D., Jr. Excerpts from *Cultural Literacy: What Every American Needs to Know.* Boston: Houghton, 1987. 5–21, 194–195. Copyright © Houghton Mifflin Co. Reprinted by permission of Houghton Mifflin Co. All rights reserved.

Jencks, Christopher, and Henry Acland, Mary Jo Bane, David Cohen, Henry Gintis, Barbara Heyns, Stephen Michelson, and Marshall Smith. "Conclusions about Inequality in the Schools." Excerpt of four page from *Inequality: A Reassessment of the Effect of Family and Schooling in America*. New York: Basic, 1972. 37–41. Copyright © 1972 by Basic Books, Inc. Reprinted by permission of Basic Books, a division of Harper-Collins Publishers, Inc.

Kantrowitz, Barbara, and Amy Miller, Karen Springen, and Rita Phyllis. "Young, Gifted and Jobless: For a Rising Number of Professionals, the Dream of Financial Security Is Gone."From *Newsweek* 5 Nov. 1990: 48. © 1990, Newsweek, Inc. All rights reserved. Reprinted by permission.

Karenga, Maulana. "Black Male/Female Relations." *Introduction to Black Studies.* 2nd ed. Los Angeles: U of Sankore P, 1993. 285–97.

Kaufman, Margo. "Sitting Pretty." *New York Times Magazine* 18 April 1993: 16.

Kennedy, Randall. "Some Good May Yet Come of This." *Time* 28 Feb. 1994. 34.

Kincaid, Jamaica. "Alien Soil." *New Yorker* 21 June 1993. 47–51.

King, Ynestra. "The Other Body: Reflections on Difference, Disability and Identity." *Ms. Magazine* March/April 1993: 72–75.

Lemann, Nicholas. "Curse of the Merit Class: America's New Ruling Caste Is Bad News for the Country." *Washington Post* 9 Feb. 1992: C1.

Lerner, Michael. "The Real Crisis Is Selfishness." *Time.* 28 Feb. 1994. 31–34.

Lerner, Michael. *Surplus Powerlessness: The Psychodynamics of Everyday Life.* Oakland, CA: Inst. for Labor and Mental Health, 1986.

Ling, Amy. "Creating One's Self: The Eaton Sisters." *Reading the Literatures of Asian America.* Ed. Shirley Geok-lin Lim and Amy Ling. Philadelphia: Temple UP, 1992. 305–18.

Lowe, Felicia. "Asian American Women in Broadcasting." From *Making Waves: An Anthology of Writings by and about Asian American Women* by Asian Women United. Boston: Beacon, 1989. 176–84. Reprinted by permission of Beacon Press.

Mabry, Marcus. "The Ghetto Preppies: "Giving Kids 'A Better Chance' Is Not So Easy." *Newsweek* 4 Nov. 1991: 44. © 1991 Newsweek, Inc. All rights reserved. Reprinted by permission.

Manning, Richard, and John McCormick. "The Blue-Collar Blues: Hundreds of Thousands of Former Factory Workers Suddenly Constitute a Downwardly Mobile Class." From *Newsweek* 4 June 1984: 52. © 1984, Newsweek, Inc. All rights reserved. Reprinted by permission.

Matsumoto, Valerie. "Two Deserts." From *Making Waves: An Anthology of Writings by and about Asian American Women* by Asian Women United. Boston: Beacon, 1989. 299–308. Copyright © 1989 by Asian Women United. Reprinted by permission of Beacon Press.

Mebane, Mary E. "Shades of Black." From *Mary.* New York: Viking, 1981. 208–12. Copyright © 1981 by Mary Elizabeth Mebane. Used by permission of Viking Penguin, a division of Penguin Books USA Inc.

Monroe, Sylvester. "They Suck the Life Right from You." *Time* 28 Feb. 1994. 24–25. © 1994 Time Inc. Reprinted by permission.

Moore, Deborah Dash. "New York Jews." *A Home in America.* New York: Columbia University Press, 1981. 4–9. Copyright © 1981 by Columbia University Press. Reprinted with permission of the publisher.

Morales, Rosario. "The Day it Happened." *Callaloo* 15.4 (1992): 970–72. Reprinted with permission of Johns Hopkins University Press.

Oates, Joyce Carol. "Is Laughter Contagious?" *Harper's,* September 1991: 72. Copyright © 1991 by Joyce Carol Oates. Reprinted by permission of John Hawkins & Associates, Inc.

Oates, Joyce Carol. "Rape and the Boxing Ring." *Newsweek* 24 Feb. 1992: 60–61. Reprinted by permission of the author and Blanche C. Gregory, Inc. Copyright © 1992 by *The Ontario Review, Inc.*

Ogbu, John U. "Minority Status and Literacy in Comparative Perspective." *Literacy: An Overview by Fourteen Experts.* Ed. Stephen R. Graubard. New York: Hill, 1991. 161–68. Originally published in and reprinted by permission of *Daedalus,* Journal of the American Academy of Arts and Sciences, from the issue entitled, "Literacy in America," Spring 1990, Volume 119, Number 2.

Ollivier, Emile. "The Shipwreck of 'La Caminante.'" *Callaloo* 15.3 (1992): 568–71.

Olsen, Tillie. "I Stand Here Ironing," Copyright © 1956, 1957, 1960, 1961 by Tillie Olsen. From *Tell Me A Riddle* by Tillie Olsen. Introduction by John Leonard. New York: Dell, 1971. 1–12. Used by permission of Delacorte Press/Seymore Lawrence, a division of Bantam Doubleday Dell Publishing Group, Inc.

Ornstein, Allan C., and Daniel U. Levine. "Social Class, Race, and School Achievement: Problems and Prospects." *Journal of Teacher Education* 40.5 Sept./Oct. 1989: 17–23. Reprinted with permission. Copyright by the American Association of Colleges for Teacher Education.

Piercy, Marge. "Barbie Doll." From *Circles on the Water.* New York: Knopf, 1973. 47. Copyright © 1982 by Marge Piercy. Reprinted by permission of Alfred A. Knopf Inc.

Pittman Carolyn S. "Do They Hear Our Voices?" Paper presented at the College Composition and Communication Conference, San Diego, 2 April, 1993.

Pittman, Frank. "Beyond the BS & Drumbeating: Staggering Through Life As a Man." *Psychology Today* Jan.-Feb. 1992: 78–83. Reprinted with permission from *Psychology Today* magazine, copyright © 1992 (Sussex Publishers, Inc.).

Purves, Alan C. "General Education and the Search for a Common Culture." *Cultural Literacy and the Idea of General Education.* Ed. Ian Westbury and Alan C. Purves. 87th Yearbook of the Natl. Soc. for the Study of Educ. Chicago: NSSE, 1988. 1–7.

Raspberry, William. "What You See..." [Wilmington, NC] *Morning Star* 7 June 1994: A8. © 1994, Washington Post Writers Group. Reprinted with permission.

Richards, Eugene. "Long Island Shelter, Boston, Massachusetts." *Below the Line: Living Poor in America.* Mount Vernon, NY: Consumers. 1987. 142–52. Copyright 1987 by Consumers Union of U.S., Inc., Yonkers, NY 10703–1057. Reprinted by permission from Consumers Reports Books, June 1987.

Sanders, Scott Russell. "The Men We Carry in Our Minds." *The Milkweed Chronicle* Spring Summer 1984: 76–78. Copyright © 1984 by Scott Russell Sanders; first appeared in *Milkweed Chronicle;* reprinted by permission of the author and Virginia Kidd, Literary Agent.

Selzer, Richard. "Fetishes." *Taking the World In For Repairs.* New York: Morrow, 1986. 80–91. Copyright © 1986 by Richard Selzer. Reprinted by permission of Georges Borchardt, Inc. for the author.

Shimatsu, Yoichi, and Patricia Lee. "Dust and Dishes: Organizing Workers." From *Making Waves: An Anthology of Writings by and about Asian American Women* by Asian Women United. Boston: Beacon, 1989. 386–95. Reprinted by permission of Beacon Press.

Stengel, Richard. "No More MoonJune: Love's Out." *New York Times* 5 Aug. 1979.

Stone, Lawrence. "A Short History of Love." As reprinted in *Harper's* Feb. 1988: 26. Reprinted with the permission of The Free Press, an imprint of Simon & Schuster Inc. from *Passionate Attachments: Thinking About Love* by Willard Gaylin, M.D. and Ethel Person, M.D. Copyright © 1988 by Friends of Columbia Psychoanalytic Center, Inc.

Tannen, Deborah. "Asymmetries: Women and Men Talking at Cross Purposes" *You Just Don't Understand: Women and Men in Conversation.* New York: Ballantine Books. 1990. 49–73. Copyright © 1990 by Deborah Tannen, Ph.D. By permission of William Morrow & Company, Inc.

Torruellas, Rosa M., et al. "Affirming Cultural Citizenship in the Puerto Rican Community: Critical Literacy and the El Barrio Popular Education Program." *Literacy as Praxis: Culture, Language, and Pedagogy.* Ed. Catherine E. Walsh. Norwood, NJ: Ablex, 1991. 183–217.

Toufexis, Anastasia. "The Right Chemistry." *Time* 15 Feb. 1993: 49–51.

Updike, David. "The Colorings of Childhood." *Harper's* January 1992: 63–67. Copyright © 1992 by David Updike, first printed in *Harper's,* reprinted with the permission of Wylie, Aitken & Stone, Inc.

Villapando, Venny. "The Business of Selling Mail-Order Brides." From *Making Waves: An Anthology of Writings by and about Asian American Women* by Asian Women United. Boston: Beacon, 1989. 318–26. Reprinted by permission of Beacon Press.

Walker, Alice. "Beauty: When the Other Dancer Is the Self." From *In Search of Our Mother's Gardens.: Womanist Prose.* New York: Harcourt, 1983. 384–93. Copyright © 1983 by Alice Walker, reprinted by permission of Harcourt Brace & Company.

West, Cornel. "How Do We Fight Xenophobia?" *Time.* 28 Feb. 1994. 30–31. Reprinted by permission of the author and the Watkins/Loomis Agency.

Yamada, Mitsuye. "Invisibility Is an Unnatural Disaster: Reflections of an Asian American Woman." *This Bridge Called My Back: Writings by Radical Women of Color.* Ed. Cherrir Moraga and Gloria Anzaldúa. Latham, NY: Kitchen Table: Women of Color Press, 1988. Used by permission of the author and of Kitchen Table: Women of Color Press, P.O. Box 908, Latham, NY 12110.

Author Index

───────◆───────